WORLDCHANGING

A USER'S GUIDE FOR THE 21ST CENTURY

REVISED & UPDATED

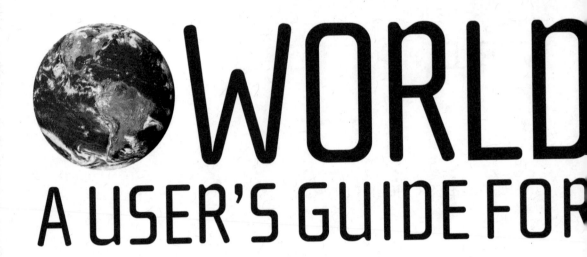

WORLD

A USER'S GUIDE FOR

CHANGING
THE 21ST CENTURY

REVISED & UPDATED

EDITED BY ALEX STEFFEN
WITH CARISSA BLUESTONE
INTRODUCTION BY BILL McKIBBEN
DESIGN BY SAGMEISTER INC.

Abrams, New York

POLITICS

PLANET

Foreword

Van Jones

You are no ordinary person. These are no ordinary times. And this is no ordinary book.

In fact, I don't think the item you are holding in your hands should be thought of as a book at all, really. In truth, it is a guide to the next phase of your life's epic adventure, cleverly disguised as a book.

I am glad you found it. Given the many contributions you desire to make in this world—and given the many obstacles and challenges that life is going to keep throwing your way—don't you *need* some kind of guide?

I am not trying to be presumptuous. But you probably wouldn't have bothered to even look at a tome entitled *Worldchanging* unless you already felt a profound yearning to make a huge difference with your life. I bet you have always felt this calling—even as a small child.

I am sure you already have been making various worldchanging efforts—staying abreast of issues, speaking up for your values, and seeking out ecofriendly products and companies. Maybe you have voted for candidates who reflected your ideals—or volunteered for causes dear to your heart. Perhaps you have even chosen a profession, taken a job, or even launched an enterprise—all based on your desire to make the world a better place.

But you know it is not enough. If our children are going to live in a world that is not being ripped apart by catastrophe and suffering, you know we need to dream bigger, think bolder, and take smarter actions. You are not alone. Even in these days of hope and heartbreak, millions of others still desperately long to bend history in a new direction—just like you.

That said, a burning desire for change ain't enough nowadays. Saving planets is a tough business. To survive and succeed, you need many things. Chief among them is *Worldchanging*, which takes the essence of humanity's very best ideas and solutions, concentrates them, and puts them where they can do the most good: in your hands.

Here are the very best solutions to humanity's toughest problems, chosen by people who've made finding solutions their life's work. We've never needed them more. A nightmare scenario is beginning to unfold, which threatens to cripple our ability to resolve the global crisis we face. Western nations are getting more and more ethnically diverse, but less and less economically prosperous. That combination is dangerous. It is not a recipe for the harmonious "common ground" we need to solve tough problems; instead, it is a recipe for a battleground. On cue, demagogues of all stripes are responding by trying to roll back diversity. They claim to be arguing for realism, but their arguments are an old fantasy of intolerance, exclusion, and separation through hatred. They are scapegoating immigrants, demonizing Muslims, and stoking racial paranoia. They are sowing seeds of division both at home and around the world.

Instead of hateful (and ultimately futile) efforts to limit diversity, we need redoubled efforts to expand prosperity—a prosperity that reconciles the needs of people today and people tomorrow. The answer is not building walls to keep people out; it's building bridges to connect our genius and talents, floors to support the most vulnerable among us, and roofs to keep all of us dry in an increasingly stormy time. With Big Media's strobe lights flashing in your eyes, it's easy to forget how simple the most fundamental assumption of this book really is, and how essential: we are one people, living on a single planet. We have just a few years to learn how to live together if we want our children to have a future worth living in. That's realism in the twenty-first century.

Perhaps it is best to imagine yourself as a space traveler, sent from beyond the cosmos to spend a few years rescuing and reviving a dying world (this one). You have been fortunate to discover this guidebook, full of deep insight and smart pathways to wise action. By picking it up, you have been entrusted to safeguard its wisdom and share its secrets with the planet's divided inhabitants. It only looks like a book. In reality, it's a planetary rescue plan.

Not only is the book cleverly disguised—so are you, when you pretend to be helpless. You are not. In fact, equipped with the knowledge in this book, you are a potential powerhouse of change.

You need this book. And this planet needs you.

Introduction

Bill McKibben

████ I can remember what it was like to give an Earth Day talk twenty years ago—you needed to keep your fingers firmly crossed, and hope. You could conjure up a rough image of, say, a solar-powered world, but a rough image was all it was. Actual solar power was still something for a few ex-hippies who were handy with a wrench and content to spend hours in the basement playing with their battery array. It wasn't anywhere near ready for prime time. Describing a bright green future took a strong imagination.

That's changed, and changed fast. I'm typing these words on my laptop, and the cord runs pretty much straight to the photovoltaic panels on my roof. They're also tied into the grid; on a sunny day my home is a little power plant, firing electrons to my neighbors. And of course—and perhaps most decisively of all—that computer is tied to a grid too, so that a whole new world of ideas and images and possibilities can be quickly and powerfully shared.

Worldchanging is a kind of distillate of that new world. It takes an old technology—print on paper—and produces a volume that captures at this particular moment the most exciting possibilities on the planet. To read *Worldchanging* is to understand the range of solutions from which we can draw to build a workable future, and to glimpse a vision of what that future might look like.

As a reporter and activist, I've had the chance to see that future in its early stages: for instance, I spent months in Curitiba, Brazil, where the modern idea of people-moving that we now call bus rapid transit (BRT) was born. I've wandered the urban farms of Havana, and seen big cities in China where virtually every home draws its hot water from solar arrays on the roof. Pieces of the bright green future envisioned in this book are facts on the ground in various spots around the world; they're just isolated and scattered.

That makes me even more grateful for the work of selection, insight, and synthesis on display in this volume, because we need to take our best solutions viral. When Jaime Lerner, architect-mayor of Curitiba, sketched his first plan for a bus that worked like a subway, it was easier to see the idea's problems than its potential to spread—but groups like Worldchanging have shown people around the planet the charming cities we can build if we take transit seriously, and BRT has taken off. Earlier this year I rode a BRT bus down an express lane in Beijing, and felt thankful for the networks of solutions-focused people who helped the idea jump from Brazil to Beijing and a thousand other cities.

If you look closely through this book, you'll see a spectrum of solutions emerging. At one end of the scale, many sensible designs for the future are likely to be relatively cheap and easy to execute. In a poor world facing deep physical limits, the future won't be mostly pushbuttons and jetpacks the way we once imagined: it will be built from bicycle drive trains that can power small grain mills, from biomethane digesters that turn one cow's manure into a steady stream of cooking gas for a family, from the sweaty miracles of double-dug vegetable beds. These are the kind of projects that can be microfinanced, drawing on the lessons that Grameen and other organizations have taught us about making capitalism work for people instead of against them.

On the other end of the spectrum, we need to rebuild systems themselves. In doing that job, new designs, innovative engineering, and community technologies—the bevy of smart phones and tablets that increasingly serve as extensions of our brains—are clearly accelerants of the rush toward sustainability. From wind farms to supergreen apartment retrofits, high-speed rail to New York's High Line linear park, the future demands that we not only improve the new, but restore and reimagine what we already have. This book will give you as fine an overview of sustainable designs and technologies as you can find between two covers anywhere.

At the heart of it all is community. The intrinsic efficiencies and pleasures of going beyond the American obsession with hyperindividuality are on display on almost every page. The future isn't one person in one electric car, or a solitary shopper in a giant Walmart buying a marginally greener product. The future is car-sharing clubs. The future is the farmers' market, the fastest-growing part of the U.S. food economy. On a rapidly urbanizing planet, community is key. As we're reminded in these pages, we can't build what we can't imagine.

This book is substantially different from the edition published five years ago. The world is different, too. The world today is comparatively buzzing with talk about sustainability solutions. Many are of limited value at best. We need to be able to judge for ourselves what's a real solution and what's just greenwashing. That means broad overviews of critical concepts are more important, and occupy a more important place in these pages. This book is an instruction manual for thinking for yourself and acting at the right scale to solve a given problem.

There's been another change, however, in the last five years, a grim one: it's hotter outside. Globally averaged, the planet's about one degree warmer than it ought to be. The fear of climate change, still theoretical a generation ago, is now a rapidly growing reality in our everyday life. The summer of 2010 was the most brutal people have ever witnessed across the Northern Hemisphere: wild Arctic melt, epic Russian drought and fire, biblical flood across Pakistan. And climatologists insist that one degree is set to become four or five degrees before the century is out, unless we make an extremely quick and dramatic transition away from fossil fuel.

If we fail to rapidly arrest global warming—and the other big environmental perils we face—then the innovations discussed in these pages will never have the time they need to flourish. If one disaster follows another in rapid train, as becomes statistically more likely on a hotter planet, we'll soon be spending all our energy (and money) on sheer survival, on disaster response and refugee aid.

So our job is to speed the transition to the other world these innovations promise—to make them not wonderful exceptions, but the rule. And doing that will be difficult, because the old world doesn't die away easily. At the moment, the most profitable businesses on earth involve discovering, refining, and burning fossil fuel. In 2009, Exxon Mobil made $45.2 billion, an all-time record for that company. And that money has brought them and their ilk enough power to stall and delay the transition everyone knows we need to make.

If there was a single action that would make a worldchanging game plan go to scale quickly, it's this: fossil fuel, the fuel of the past, should pay the price for the damage it does to the planet. There should be a stiff fee attached to coal and gas and oil—fossil-fuel companies should not be allowed to use the atmosphere as a free open sewer for their waste. If we demanded that fossil-fuel users pay their true costs, then the innovations in these pages would suddenly make sense in every way: not just human sense and ecological sense, but immediate economic sense as well. Ask yourself why so many of our greenest cities have emerged in western Europe: above all because the price of gasoline has always been $7 or $8 a gallon, and hence sprawl never made sense and trains and bikes always seemed like more obvious choices.

Winning that change is a political task—the political task of our time. So far we've failed: the power of the fossil-fuel industry collapsed the 2009 Copenhagen talks, and so far has wrecked any real legislation in Washington. But the very same tools that produced so many of the small miracles chronicled in these pages also give us at least a chance at winning that political fight.

A few years ago, I helped found 350.org, which took its name from a wonky concept: the amount of carbon dioxide, measured in parts per million, that scientists now think is the safe upper limit for the planet. It's a tough number—we're already well past it, at 390 ppm, which explains why the Arctic is melting and unprecedented wildfires are burning around the planet. Yet we've managed to build a huge international movement; in fact, CNN said our first global day of action in 2009 was "the most widespread day of political action in the planet's history," with 5,200 demonstrations in 181 countries. In the fall of 2010 we pulled off an even bigger event—and one very close to the spirit of this book. We called it a Global Work Party. In more than 7,000 places around the globe, people put up solar panels, or dug community gardens, or planted mangrove swamps, or repaired bikes by the thousand to get communities cycling. We did, in other words, all the things that communities can do now.

Getting to 350, though, will take more than community action, and it will take more than the largest political movement the world's ever seen. It will take making real the vision of a world where communities everywhere prosper within the limits of the planet's natural systems. That, in turn, will take new ideas: clever ideas, powerful ideas, brilliant ideas—worldchanging ideas.

Editor's Introduction

Alex Steffen

Five years ago, when I edited the first edition of this book, the future looked different. Mostly, it looked a lot farther away.

In the last five years, the scope, scale, and speed of the planetary challenges we face seem to have grown and accelerated. The ecological news has gone from bad and distant to terrible and immediate. We now realize that we are in the midst of a crisis that worsens with every passing day, and that things are worse than we thought.

That crisis can be measured. In 2009, a group of scientists led by the Stockholm Resilience Centre determined "planetary boundaries" for nine major natural systems that represent the earth's ability to sustain life, its "biocapacity": greenhouse-gas concentrations in the atmosphere, ozone depletion, ocean acidity, freshwater consumption, deforestation, the global nitrogen cycle, terrestrial biodiversity, chemicals dispersion, and marine ecosystems. They assigned a number for the safe upper limit of human impact on that system, such as the amount of the ozone layer that has been compromised. What they found was that humanity is close to straying beyond every one of these boundaries.

Though the boundaries are the subject of a global debate involving hosts of scientists and advocates, each is a massive issue in its own right, acknowledged to be a serious crisis by the experts involved. Put them together—as we must, since, as part of a single, living planet, they are all interconnected and affect one another—and we begin to see how massive the current ecological crisis is. It's crystal clear that humanity has pushed nature beyond its biocapacity and has overshot the planet's limits.

Signs of overshoot are erupting all around us: melting polar ice caps, freak weather, massive storms, ocean dead zones, wildfires, food shortages, heat waves, extinctions of species, rising seas, desertification, the spread of invasive plants and animals. The fabric of the biosphere is coming unraveled, and we're tugging on the loose threads.

Our unsustainably intensive uses of the earth have brought the increased risk of passing catastrophic tipping points; indeed, many eminent scientists warn that those tipping points now look less like distant threats than imminent dangers. Ecological damage and the resulting dangers are largely cumulative: add enough together, and the consequences grow far larger than the sum of the individual acts of destruction. We don't know when another day of environmental irresponsibility will set in motion not just a little more ecological destruction but a slide into a profoundly larger and more comprehensive catastrophe. We don't know which snowflake will tip us into an avalanche, but we know that the risk of avalanche is high.

With all of this in mind, it ought to be our goal to have no impact—to bring our ecological footprint below biocapacity, perhaps even to start reweaving the living fabric of the planet before the whole tapestry rips apart. We need to get back within planetary boundaries, and fast.

The concept of planetary boundaries helps us grasp our ecological peril, but it leaves out humanity. People's actions—how we live, how we treat each other, how we build our societies—are the other half of our planetary equation. We can't understand how much is changing without grappling with human aspirations and abilities and the very real generational thresholds looming in front of us.

The global population has mushroomed from 2.5 billion to over 7 billion in just the last sixty years. And we live on a planet where almost half of the population in the least developed countries consists of teenagers and children. There are a lot of young women about to enter their childbearing years (mostly in poor countries), and that means the number of humans is almost certain to grow.

Huge strides are being made toward slowing the population explosion—by educating young women, providing them with economic opportunities, and making sure they have access to family-planning information: the three best means of slowing population growth. But the odds are good that most young women will still want to have families, as we nearly all do. Even in the best-case scenarios we are headed toward a peak population of at least 9 billion people shortly after mid-century, before population growth levels off and population slowly begins to decline.

Almost all of those 9 billion people will aspire to greater prosperity, reaching for what they see as the good life. The Global North and the Global South—the "developed" and "developing" worlds—now live around the corner from each other and are mutually dependent. Everywhere in the world, the poor see how the rich live, if not out their windows, then on TV. People who live in shanties can compare the material quality of their own lives with that of people who fly over them in jets.

Kids from Cape Town to Caracas to Novosibirsk—and everywhere in between—want globally middle-class lives. They want refrigerators, scooters, smart phones, and the latest fashions. They want education, health care, good jobs, and governments that help them solve their problems. We can be sure that every one of the billions of kids now growing up wants a better life and has his or her own dreams.

Unfortunately, the model that people in the Global North used to get rich is no longer replicable. As a famous 2002 report, the *Jo'burg Memo*, put it, "There is no escape from the conclusion that the world's growing population cannot attain a Western standard of living by following conventional paths to development. The resources required are too vast, too expensive, and too damaging to local and global ecosystems."

There's no way the whole world could get rich the way Americans and Europeans did, even if we didn't care about the consequences. We're already beyond the planetary boundaries, and business as usual now has prohibitive environmental effects. We're running out of places to dump and spew waste without dire human cost. We've also used up a tremendous share of the planet's easy bounty—from old trees to cheap oil to big fish to virgin metals—meaning that conventional resource and energy use will largely depend on supplies that are increasingly difficult to obtain (and often more and more ecologically costly).

The combination of declining stocks (less good stuff to use) and shrinking sinks (fewer places to safely put the bad stuff) will make development as usual far more difficult for the world's poor. The "Western model" of development is bankrupt.

We need to replace that model of development with a new one. For a new model to work in the real world, it must be rugged and shockproof—because the world's a rough place these days:

More than 2 billion people have no access to electricity. About the same number have no safe means of disposing of their sewage. More than 1 billion drink fetid water. Over 1.2 billion don't always have enough to eat, and at least 840 million are suffering from chronic hunger and are only one bad harvest away from mass starvation. Hungry people don't have the energy to work as hard—economists estimate that somewhere between $64 billion and $128 billion is lost annually from developing-world economies because of malnutrition. Hungry people are sick people, and sick people, in turn, slide further into poverty.

Common, preventable diseases like childhood diarrhea kill millions of people every year, and other diseases are growing epidemic in a world where hundreds of millions have no medical care at all. AIDS alone is expected to kill 68 million people by the year 2020, leaving at least 20 million children orphaned. Some countries, like Botswana and Zimbabwe, will have lost half their adult population to the disease by the end of the decade.

Amid these sorts of societal holocausts, all other services decline, especially education: more than 800 million people worldwide are illiterate, 60 percent of them women. And uneducated people are, in turn, less likely to understand good hygiene, to be able to master new farming techniques, or to participate in democracy in any meaningful way (where it exists at all). For the poorest 1 billion people, life has become a series of vicious deteriorations and inescapable traps. For 2 billion of their neighbors, who are doing slightly better, this poverty creates instability and a nasty backdraft, making it harder to effect any progress at all. This is part of the context in which the environment is unraveling.

And with increasing regularity, ecological instability flares into outright chaos. James Gasana, Rwanda's minister of agriculture and environment in the early 1990s, told a lesser-known side of that country's tragic past in an article in *World Watch* magazine. We tell ourselves that Rwanda's genocide, in which at least 800,000 people were murdered, was the fruit of ancient and unsolvable ethnic hatred. But the reality is that such hatred was fanned into flame by a sharp wind: hunger. With a mostly mountainous terrain and a population that had grown from 1.9 million to nearly 8 million in just four decades, the tiny country simply couldn't feed itself. The genocide may have been driven by hatred, but it was set into motion by hunger, and the killing was worst in communities with the least to eat. Similar dynamics can be seen in Sudan, where decades of drought have exacerbated long-standing tribal and religious conflicts in regions like Darfur.

But dramatic ecological instability certainly can't account for all outbreaks of violence. The last decade has shown that even in countries that seem reasonably stable, chaos can spread quickly when pushed by power-mad men. Sarajevo was one of the most enlightened, multiethnic cities in the world . . . and a few years later it lay in ruins, under siege, surrounded by a land of mass graves and rape camps. Liberia was Africa's great success story . . . and a few years later an army of drugged teenagers with automatic weapons was wandering the streets of its capital in wedding dresses and fright wigs, shooting anything that moved.

In fact, thugs, gangsters, dictators, and tribal warlords run much of the world, often at a substantial profit. As Bruce Sterling writes in *Tomorrow Now*, "Outside (and sometimes within) the prosperous bounds of the New World Order is a large and miserable New World Disorder. It includes not only the smoking ground of the Balkans, but the Caucasus, South Central Asia, and vast, astonishing swaths of Africa . . . For the typical New World Disorder soldier, ethnicity and religion are not something you die for—they are stalking horses; useful pretexts for breaking down states and subverting police and governments. The resulting chaos can be structured, made to pay. Revolutionary idealists sometimes begin this process, but once the disorder fully flowers, their doctrines just get in the way. They will generally be rubbed out by greedier, more practical subordinates" (2002).

A far larger chunk of the world is more peaceful, but still rotting with corruption. The debt that chokes many developing countries is largely a legacy of that corruption, willingly abetted by developed-world banks. Academics studying development believe that one in every three dollars made in development loans from 1970 to 1990 ended up stolen, often winding up in secret private bank accounts in places such as Switzerland and the Caymans. Some argue that the figure is much higher, that when you count in kickbacks to bankers, sweetheart deals with multinational corporations, and a long train of local officials and businesspeople siphoning off their cuts, it may be that only one dollar in four was actually used to build anything. The problem seems to be even worse now. Global anti-corruption groups such as Transparency International have documented an alarming trend over the last decade: while some countries emerged into democracy and transparency, a far larger number of countries have a facade of democracy masking a level of corruption and influence peddling that approaches open kleptocracy.

Already, we see a huge gap between the laws and practices the nations of the world profess to embrace and the reality on the ground, where laws go unenforced and people are powerless to challenge the business interests that are destroying the systems upon which they must depend to live. Often those destructive projects are funded and advised by banks and development agencies in the Global North, in the name of fighting poverty. But poor people living in toxic landscapes of industrial waste or amid the burnt stumps of what were once forests can see in concrete terms the meaning of Paul Hawken's condemnation that we have an economy where we "steal the future, sell it in the present, and call it G.D.P."

Exploitation and corruption make the challenge more difficult—so much so that any new model of sustainable prosperity needs not only to take them into account, but to work to mitigate them. If the answer to our ecological crisis doesn't also lead to greater security for everyone and help spread democracy, rule of law, and open government and business practices, it is, in fact, no answer at all.

The other side of the corruption and exploitation coin is the ongoing waste of human potential and the growing cost of lost opportunities to engage the world's poor and young in transforming their own situations. A planet full of young people means a world of fresh starts, but a child today must be helped today: twenty years from now may be too late.

Another two decades of the status quo will make many of our goals nearly impossible. Needless deaths, injuries, sicknesses, and malnutrition today will impose astronomical costs on us over the coming decades. Missed opportunities to educate children (especially girls) leave lifetimes of limited options. The traumas of conflict and collapse, of natural disasters and family tragedies, combine with the strains of living in extreme poverty to leave hundreds of millions with lifelong difficulties with coping.

The disillusionment of a generation of young people, who find themselves trapped in corrupt or failing states, or simply shut out of opportunities for dignity and work in the global economy, can turn them away from productive engagement with the problems around them and lead some of them toward extremism and terror. As much as we want to believe in an endless potential for human transformation, the reality is that people's energy, spirit, and capacity for growth are themselves limited resources.

Right now, we're squandering their hopes in mind-boggling proportions. Every passing year makes it more difficult to raise billions of people out of poverty to become parts of stable, democratic states with functioning economic, legal, and health systems. Meanwhile, climate vulnerabilities, food shortages, and rising energy costs begin to undermine even the progress much of the developing world has managed so far. There are generational thresholds for change, and we may not be acting boldly enough to move through them.

The brutal reality is that failure is possible in human societies as well as in ecological systems. There are points beyond which
societal problems start to become impossible to solve. And when
you combine the two—an ongoing societal meltdown with massive
ecological degradation—the result can be real, catastrophic failure
that lasts for generations, perhaps effectively forever.

But failure is not the only option.

If we can tap into the best that people have to offer, we have
the capacity to transform both our social and our ecological problems at once. If we spend the next two decades in action, we may be
surprised at how much different life will be in forty years.

We may be on the verge of creating a bright green model of
development that not only reduces the ecological impact of prosperity, but is available to billions more people in ways that increase their
resilience to disaster and help make their social and political systems
more rugged. Just how dramatically different that model is, though,
is indicated by how strange its essential characteristics may seem to
us today. And its first characteristic is that people living in a bright
green world cause essentially no ecological harm.

It is simple common sense that practices that are unsustainable cannot continue, and we know that propping up unsustainable
practices with nonrenewable resources has even more dramatic
consequences. And yet we are currently growing rapidly less sustainable, and using more and more nonrenewable resources to keep the
ecological consequences at bay. This must stop. All of this is just
plain speaking, and ought to be obvious to any informed observer.

To say, however, that the standard of zero impact is not
widely understood and endorsed would be a whopping understatement. Most people rarely see the things they do, buy, and
use as being directly part of the living systems of the planet. Few
of those people who do think of their connection to nature have
ever thought through what their lives would feel and look like if
they were designed to have no impact at all. For most people, a
10- or 20-percent improvement sounds like a big deal—in large part
because the improvements they're most familiar with involve giving
things up. When they do encounter it, the idea of "zero" looms like a
giant wall of deprivation.

But zero-impact living, done right, is the good life. It
doesn't have to be a sacrifice; it may, in fact, make us wealthier,
healthier, and more satisfied. (It will certainly make our children and
grandchildren happier than they'd be on a ruined planet.)

Some of the changes a zero-impact future will demand are
solutions we've only just recently come to accept but that are main-
streaming fast, like converting from fossil fuels to wind and solar
energy. Some of them are innovations that are only now unfolding
around us, like radical energy efficiency and completely recyclable
products. Some of them are healthy lifestyle choices, like eating less
meat and becoming more strategic about how and why we shop,
buying less stuff at a better quality.

Already, many of these types of clean technologies and sustainable designs pay for themselves in cost savings and in better health. But this first generation of green solutions is just the beginning of the story. The main plot of that story is how we build the places where we live.

Because cities are the funnels through which raw materials and energy flow to create prosperity (and generate waste), environmental problems increasingly boil down to the structure of cities and the way urban dwellers' needs are met. Cities define the global economy as well, and for most of humanity, living in an innovative, dynamic, well-governed city means the difference between the most marginal existence and poverty alleviation, greater access to education and health services, and a better life for their children. From population growth to climate emissions, human security to public health, the driving forces of the twenty-first century will be defined on the streets of the world's cities and made manifest in their communities, infrastructures, and buildings.

How we build those communities and engineer the infrastructure systems that support them is going through extreme changes. The idea that contemporary suburban American lifestyles—with their McMansions, SUVs, and big-box stores—somehow represent the best form of prosperity we could possibly invent has become obviously ludicrous. But many of us are completely unprepared for the transformation that lies ahead in the next four decades.

To understand that transformation, we need to remember that more than half of humanity already lives in cities, with 200,000 new urban dwellers being added every day. This equates to roughly an urban area the population of Seattle every three days. By 2050, 70 percent of all humans, or 6 billion people, will live in cities. That means building roughly four thousand Seattles in the next forty years.

Even that shocking figure understates the reality that nearly all of humanity will live less than a day's travel from a midsize city. "Rural" life—as the opposite of urban life, disconnected from the global flow of information and trade—will simply cease to exist in all but the most remote corners of the earth. Whether this is a good or a bad thing is open to debate; whether it will happen is not.

Humanity will be an overwhelmingly urban species, and the making of the cities we call home will propel the global economy for the next forty years, transforming existing cities and driving the creation of new ones. By 2030, for example, China is expected to have more than 220 cities with populations larger than 1 million people. Asia as a whole may have more than four hundred. By comparison, all of Europe today has only thirty-five.

City-building at that scale will, of necessity, trigger a massive outburst of urban innovation. There will be no alternative to bright green designs and technologies to meet the consumption demands of 6 billion urbanites for everything from food to housing to transportation. And since most of the systems serving these new cities will themselves be new creations, we have the opportunity to deploy the smartest, most sustainable available technologies and designs. The emerging cities of the Global South could be far more sustainable than the cities of the Global North today, precisely because they are new and poor, and can't afford to use anything but the best possible solutions.

Cities offer us the chance to reinvent prosperity. We know that cities are the best leverage point we have for transforming the impacts of prosperity. At the city level, systems are big enough to make a difference on big problems like climate change and materials depletion, yet small enough to grasp. We can build zero-impact cities, and we need to. If carbon-neutrality and zero-waste systems are going to develop, they'll be led by cities.

We've never had more tools at hand for changing how cities are built. From Copenhagen to Curitiba, Melbourne to Vancouver, urban leaders are showing that both new developments and city centers can be rebuilt to promote compact urbanism, vibrant main streets, welcoming public places, a high quality of life, even car-free communities. Whether the task is retrofitting a historic building, building bike lanes, designing a solar-powered apartment block, or creating infill on a residential street with a cozy home on a small lot, a wealth of innovations have already been proven in the world's leading cities, and thousands more are on the way.

With radical new architectural designs, we're capable of making structures that use 90 percent less energy than the ones the last generation built. With approaches like green infrastructure and district energy, we can use water and power in far more sustainable ways. With new communications technologies suffusing our streets, we're able to forge entirely new relationships with our neighborhoods and redefine how and why we move around them.

And with new cultures of urban living, we're seeing the growth of innovative arrangements for providing for our needs, from car sharing to co-owning household products to providing community support for area farmers in exchange for fresh veggies on a weekly basis. We're even beginning to understand how to remake fraying suburbs into walkable towns, proving that even the most unsustainable places offer opportunities to create thriving metropolitan regions.

For those of us in the Global North, these new tools also highlight the fact that we have a job to do. We bear responsibility for most of the planetary harm humanity has so far caused (Americans alone, for instance, have contributed almost one third of all the greenhouse gases now heating up our planet). We're also much wealthier, with an inheritance of universities and intellectual institutions that gives us a much greater capacity for innovation than the rest of the world.

These realities—our responsibility and our capability—combine to make urban reinvention our duty. We need to lead the way in redefining what urban life can mean. We need to expand the tool set, invent new models, increase our technological abilities, provide case studies and proofs-of-concept, and, ultimately, show positive evidence that bright green urbanism works so that these emerging cities can adopt it as they grow. The urban future demands trailblazers.

The kicker is that all of these changes offer unexpected upsides. Bright green cities are not just more responsible to our obligations to the future: piles of research show that they also are more economically competitive, generate more innovation, are healthier and safer for their citizens, are better braced to withstand climate chaos, and are easier to make resilient in a turbulent world. We won't just live more virtuously in a bright green city, we'll live better.

That presents us with an amazing opportunity. If we think big, we have a chance, now, to improve our own lives, do the right thing, and help ensure that the future our kids inherit is one we'll want them to live in.

If we squander that opportunity, no amount of virtuous living, not even a tidal wave of small steps, will make up for it. Without action that responds to the scope, scale, and speed of the challenges we face, nothing else much matters. In that light, our personal behavior is essentially meaningless, especially if it isn't part of a larger effort to identify ways of changing our cities, transportation, agriculture, and energy systems to function much more sustainably. If we want to change our impacts, we need to change our systems, and on a scope we almost never talk about—stretching through essentially every aspect of our society.

We're not alone in that work. We may be facing an unprecedented planetary crisis, but we're also in a moment of innovation unlike any that has come before. We find ourselves in a time when all over the world, millions of people are working to invent, use, and share worldchanging tools, models, and ideas. We live in an era when the number of people working to make the world better is exploding. Humanity's fate rests on the outcome of the race between problem solvers and the problems themselves. The world is getting better—we just have to make sure it gets better faster than it gets worse.

We don't need a miracle to win this race; we need a movement. We need millions more people who are committed to doing their part to embrace good ideas, find new solutions in their own work, and live and share what they learn.

Each of us has a role to play, and each of us can be part of that movement to change the world. What's needed is not unflinching loyalty to some supreme leader or mystical adherence to some cult's belief system, but millions of us doing our best to think for ourselves and share what we know.

This book is meant to help you think through what part you might play in that movement. It's not a blueprint, or a manifesto, or a political platform. It's not here to tell you what to do. Instead, *Worldchanging* collects the most interesting and useful ideas we've found in seven years of exploration to give you a survey of the kinds of solutions humanity has to work with . . . and a sense of all the work that remains to be done. We try to provide a variety of jumping-off points in each section: books, Web sites, reports, worthy groups, and other resources for conducting your own explorations into the future ahead of us.

Few of the ideas discussed in this edition of *Worldchanging* are things you can do in an afternoon. They're systems and designs, policies and plans, movement-building tools and business models. If that's discouraging, we apologize. But the fact is that the work we need to do now is all about engagement. It's no longer enough to talk about simple steps or gestures of support. We need actual change. This book is meant for people who want to be changemakers, whatever their situation or walk of life.

If you're ready to change the world, the planet needs you and there's no time to lose. The crucial first step is to begin to imagine the future you'd like to see, because you can't build what you can't imagine. Flip through these pages. Find ideas that speak to you. Wonder about the possibilities ahead of us. Think about what life could be like in a bright green future—what *your* life could be like, in the city where you live, in a world improved by better ideas and new solutions.

Why is thinking about solutions important? Because we're starving for better thinking. The media bombards us with pessimism about the world's problems, portrays the world as a hostile place, urges us to define ourselves as consumers, and lauds political cynicism and mistrust of academia, science, and government. The average newscast is a lesson in isolated despair.

Pessimism and cynicism sap our willingness to confront the wrongs in the world. They make us fearful. They make us small. Optimism, on the other hand, makes us bigger. It helps us envision a better future, connects us to new friends and allies, turns our hopes into strengths: optimism makes us worldchanging. Intelligent discussion of solutions not only informs us, it feeds our optimism. We hope you'll find this book a feast.

STUFF

Our things define us.

What we buy, what we use, what we keep and throw away, what we waste and what we save: the stuff that surrounds us and flows through our lives is a key indicator of the kinds of lives we're living. To be an affluent twenty-first-century person is to float on a sea of material objects—each with its own history and future.

They may be hidden from our eyes, but in practical global terms, those histories and futures tend to be the most important aspects of the stuff we own. The moment we tear the wrapper from a new toy, that toy is already at the end of a sweeping story involving the mining of metals, the pumping of oil, the operation of huge factories, the shipping of cargo containers, the printing of packaging materials, the purchase of advertising, the careful arranging of store shelves, and the final drive home. Simply buying, say, a new laptop connects us with a web of activity that spans the planet.

Another story begins when we throw away our old laptop. It may find itself on a quick trip to the local dump, where it will lie, buried beneath a mountain of garbage, corroding and slowly leaking toxic chemicals for hundreds of years. It might, on the other hand, be shipped off to China, where its circuit boards will be stripped out and where poorly paid workers will extract by hand the valuable metals they contain. Parts of the laptop's titanium body may be sold as scrap and melted down for other purposes. Much of the rest will wind up in an open dump, where children will pick through the dissected electronic remains.

What's true for our new laptop is true for every product we buy: what we purchase from the store, as sustainable-design expert William McDonough [see Producer Responsibility, p. 118] points out in his iconic book *Cradle to Cradle*, is just the tip of a vast material iceberg, a gigantic pyramid of extracted resources and burnt fuel, toxic waste, and sweatshop labor. Similarly, our use of a product only marks the start of a new cycle—the product will spend most of its existence decaying in a dump somewhere. A Styrofoam carton may only spend fifteen minutes holding the Chinese food we have for lunch, but it could easily spend a hundred years decomposing in some trash heap.

The first problem with the secret life of our stuff is that it hides from us the consequences of our actions.

The second problem is that, most of the time, those consequences are not pretty.

The mountains of waste that telescope out from us before we buy something and after we throw it away choke the planet with deadly poisons, endanger our health, wreck natural systems, and force our fellow human beings to work in conditions many of us would never accept for ourselves. The system today obliges us to take part in creating a mountain of troubles for the world every time we plunk down our credit cards.

However, changes are happening; the things we live with every day are evolving, becoming lighter on the planet, fairer to people everywhere, safer for our health.

We know more than ever about how to see the hidden lives of things. We now have access to all sorts of information about products' lifecycles—information that gives us the ability to make better choices. More importantly, as the once arcane information about everything from materials' toxicity to engines' efficiency comes out into the open, a new wave of empowered designers is emerging; they are bent on shrinking our mountainous impacts into ecological molehills.

The changes rippling through the fields of art, design, engineering, material science, and biology are nothing short of revolutionary. Design tools, especially

software, are getting cheaper, more powerful, and easier to use; collaborative models and new thinking are bringing people together in new ways, enabling them to solve problems using approaches undreamed of a decade ago. Science is unlocking nature's secrets, allowing us to mimic nature's grace, strength, and ecological integrity in everything from product design to industrial systems. Art and technology now inform each other in ways previously unseen, revealing new vistas of possibility. In every field that touches on the conceptualization, manufacturing, and use of stuff, powerful combinations of transparent information, ecological understanding, and advancing technology are unleashing forces for change.

Because of these forces, a more radical evolution in design is under way, and a new generation of stuff is emerging. Imagine things that use minimal energy, that are made with no toxic chemicals, that are completely recyclable, that hurt no one—not even nature—but that perform better and last longer than what we have today.

These products still live mostly on the computer screens of cutting-edge designers, but that's changing quickly. And we have the power to make it change more quickly still. We may not all be designers, but we are all design consumers. By showing that we demand smarter stuff, we can help spur this transformation.

We have the power to choose the world we will live in, and through the stuff we choose to live with, we reveal that world every day. AS

Questioning Consumption

It's a small world, and it's getting smaller. Some aspects of this shrinking are heartening—it's easier to unite social networks, conduct business, and learn about places and people outside our immediate surroundings.

But the planet is shrinking for another, less auspicious reason: we're using it up. Every year we cut more forests, graze more cows, drive more cars, dump more trash. And since we're already taking more than the planet can give, every year nature has less to offer. To make matters worse, this spiral seems to be accelerating, and the gap between sustainability and everyday practice is widening.

For two hundred years we've defined prosperity very simply—as having more stuff. But we have to ask ourselves the fundamental question, how much stuff do we need? The relationship between material wealth and well-being would seem to be a proportional one: when one increases, so does the other. But as it turns out, measures of wealth and health rise together only to a point, and then the pattern shifts. In fact, research tells us that, assuming a basic level of comfort, happiness across most cultures is largely unrelated to material luxury.

Reducing our own levels of consumption saves us money and eliminates unnecessary clutter from our lives. In an era of big-box superstores and viral marketing, most of us go for quantity over quality, lured by the ease of getting more stuff cheaper. When we become conscious about what we buy, we end up with more space for appreciating the objects that surround us, and what we have actually can make us happier. AS

Preceding pages: 1000 *Trash People*, Lake Stelli, Switzerland, 2003.

Ecological Footprints

Exactly how much does our overconsumption impact the planet? To tally up the full cost of our "prosperity" would require more than some simple math, but we do have ways of guesstimating such numbers. In the past ten years, the "ecological footprint," a tool developed by Mathis Wackernagel to measure our personal impact based on representative consumer and lifestyle choices, has become an important coming-to-terms calculation.

Ecological footprints, which we can measure using simple online quizzes, provide us with a metaphor for understanding our impact on the planet and the meaning of sustainability: they boil down that impact to a single number that corresponds to the amount of land we require to sustain our lifestyle, often expressed in terms of global hectares. We can then compare that metaphorical land area to what constitutes a globally fair share of the planet. For example, according to the Global Footprint Network, the average ecological footprint is 6.4 acres (2.6 hectares) per person. But some of us have much bigger feet than others. The average American, for example, uses approximately 22.3 acres (9 hectares), while the average Chinese uses only about 4.6 acres (1.8 hectares), and the average Pakistani just 1.8 acres (about 7/10 of a hectare).

Today there are several different types of footprint systems—ecological footprints, carbon footprints, citywide footprints, industrywide footprints, and so on. Ecogeeks seem to argue a lot about whose footprint measurements offer the most accuracy. Their questions, though valid, are sometimes difficult to parse—for instance, does the formula incorporate public-sector activity undertaken on our behalf, or the ecological impact of our nation's military or university systems? A thousand considerations bubble up.

While none of these footprints is precise, and they may not help us decide whether or not to buy a new flat-screen TV, knowing our footprint before and after we make lifestyle choices can help us understand the scale of our overconsumption, thereby steering our decisions. In addition, most footprint systems clearly show the tremendous impacts of our homes and our car-based infrastructures, demonstrating the immediate benefit of choosing dense, urban areas with public transit over McMansion-filled, outer-ring sprawl.

Finally, you just can't beat the metaphorical power of some of these estimates. Take, for example, the "one-planet living" meme: If everyone lived like the average European, we would need three planets' worth of resources to survive; if everyone lived like the average North American, we would need five planets. Of course, we've only got the one. AS & SR

Choice Fatigue

According to happiness researchers (yes, there are experts who measure happiness), we are less happy than we used to be. There are a number of well-studied and well-documented reasons for this, and a few obvious ones (famine, poverty, disease, and war), but surprisingly, a leading cause of unhappiness, at least in developed nations, appears to be our overabundance of choice. In the last few decades, rates of depression have dramatically increased worldwide, a curve that corresponds with the upsurge in choice, indicating perhaps that having too many options fosters stress, anxiety, and uncertainty.

"Choice fatigue" seems counterintuitive, because choice is good, right? Well, not so fast. Our consumer culture is relentless, and the more choices we have—the more information we're bombarded with—the more effort we invest in evaluating our options, and the more likely we are to be dissatisfied with the outcome.

The more options we're given, the poorer our decision-making abilities become. Most of us hate making trade-offs and will avoid making decisions until we absolutely have to; the decision-making process is fraught with bad feelings from the start. At the same time, most of us are bad at dealing with uncertainty and at estimating odds, especially since we often don't possess enough information to properly calculate probabilities. After spending so much time weighing trade-offs and trying to sift through a deluge of information, our expectations rise so high that we often end up disappointed when the outcome is not as perfect as we had hoped. Consumer satisfaction is nothing more than the miracle of reality matching our expectations.

What's worse, we often adapt to our over-abundance of choices by picking things haphazardly and acquiring more than we need. The more we own, the more we get used to all of the stuff surrounding us, and the less special it feels. That's not to say that the only remedy for choice fatigue is getting rid of choice altogether. Rather, we need to find ways to maintain a level head when making choices, and to keep a healthy distance between the destabilizing allure of advertising and ourselves. NAB

The Aspirational Gap

We have switched from a model of "keeping up with the Joneses" to one of "keeping up with the Gateses" (Bill and Melinda, that is).

Juliet Schor, sociology professor

Our dreams used to be "horizontal" in nature. We'd glance over our picket fence to the left and right, and base our models of success and prosperity on what we saw in our neighbors' driveways and backyards. Although "keeping up with the Joneses" has always been an exhausting game in its own right, at least we were taking our social cues from folks whose lives somewhat resembled ours.

Today, thanks to increasing isolation from our neighbors, unmitigated media hype for luxury goods and brands, and easy credit, our aspirations have become decidedly "vertical." We no longer judge what we have in relationship to what we used to have or what our parents had; instead, we look to what the richest people on earth have. We've redefined middle-class comfort to reflect a lifestyle obtainable only by the very wealthy. As Juliet Schor, a professor of sociology at Boston College and an expert on the phenomenon of "vertical emulation," has noted, the dominant emulative target in the United States is a lifestyle that requires an annual income of at least $100,000. According to the U.S. Census Bureau, the average American makes about $28,000 per year.

Clearly, there's a huge gap between what we aspire to have and what we're able to afford. (Schor has a term for this as well: the "aspirational gap.") This gap provokes us to go on buying binges, rely too heavily on credit cards, and buy bigger houses than we need or can afford. Often, we buy things that feel like affordable approximations of richer people's toys. We build McMansions because we think they look like homes of the wealthy, even though they are actually pale (and poorly constructed) imitations of real mansions. We buy "luxury" items that cost a lot more than functional items (but far less than actual luxury goods) because we think they send a signal that we can afford more than we actually can.

Says Schor, "The amount of money we aspire to has increased; views of what is necessary have shifted to include former luxuries; the non-material components of what is considered 'the good life'—things like a meaningful job, children, and a happy marriage—have declined; and the material components—having a job that pays a lot more than the average job, having a really nice wardrobe, a second home, a second car, and owning other consumer products—have all increased substantially."

In the United States, the aspirational gap is evident in the troubling increase in consumer credit card debt (especially in households in the $50,000-to-$100,000 range) and the steady rise in personal bankruptcies (according to Schor, from about 200,000 per year in 1980 to about 1.4 million currently). But Schor believes the phenomenon has even larger implications, positing that the "cycle of work and spend" destroys social connections, which require time and care to foster. The "durable sources of well-being" such as healthy relationships with our family, friends, and communities suffer from our neglect while we devote ever more attention to maintaining fleeting comforts.

If the alternative to overconsumption is strategic consumption, what's the answer to the aspirational gap? Downshifting slightly to horizontal emulation, though it would help people live more within their means, hardly seems revolutionary. Schor feels that we should aim a few gears lower, by reemphasizing (or putting an entirely new emphasis on) nonstatus consumption. This would involve mainly an investment in public

Opposite, left: Many Americans carry credit card debt totaling an entire year's salary.
Opposite, right: A foreclosure sale sign in front of Los Angeles townhouses.

goods and services, ranging from education to parks, plus a greater investment in our own leisure time—all of the things that get crowded out while we're attending to status-oriented consumption.

The challenge is that to live in the modern world is to constantly sort through a lot of noise about which aspirations are reasonable and fit your true identity. And the choices we make in the face of all of these messages are emotional and hard to address rationally. We may know it's silly to want a Ferrari, but that doesn't necessarily stop us from thinking it would be nice or impressive to have one or from falling into the trap of leasing one.

To make this more complex, the phenomenon of vertical emulation is spreading across the globe; almost everyone in the world has a very specific view—designer names included—of what the good life looks like. So, every year there are more people wanting to buy and have more things. One of the conditions necessary for sustainability is a collective response to the aspirational gap: a more widespread understanding (and discussion) of what actually makes us happy, how we're affected by what we buy, and what messages we're sending to our neighbors when we buy the things we do. AS & CB

The Costs of Consumption

Overconsumption has huge environmental effects, but it also has huge economic effects. People who buy beyond their means and pay with credit often end up experiencing a lifelong financial impact from those choices. In 2007 Americans owed $850 billion in credit card debt,

with the average U.S. household carrying $9,659 in such debt. A 2009 Forbes.com report noted that in order to pay off credit card debt, Miami-area residents would have to earmark 22.61 percent of their income for repayment. Miamians aren't alone; Los Angeles residents, for example, would have to pony up 16.81 percent of their income. Nationwide, nearly one-third of U.S. bankruptcy filers owe an entire year's salary on their credit cards.

Many financial experts claim that the 2009 recession and real estate crash have served as a much-needed wake-up call for people who have long been living beyond their means. According to several Brookings Institute studies, the savings rate, which plummeted from nearly 10 percent of disposable personal income between 1965 and 1985 to below 0 percent in 2005 and 2006, is again slowly on the rise, up to 4.3 percent in the first half of 2009. But Americans are still spending too much and saving too little. People elsewhere do a little better, but savings rates are down almost everywhere.

There are two paths to financial stability and, eventually, independence: one is earning more money, which may or may not be possible, and the other is spending less money, which almost all of us can do. To look at a bold vision of how this could transform your life, see *Your Money or Your Life* by Vicki Robin and Joe Dominguez. This 1999 classic is one self-help book worth its salt: it focuses on simplifying your life by changing your relationship to money and building financial independence by needing less and investing more.

Robin and Dominguez write: "Most people in North America engage in the dominant myth of 'more is better' without questions, and

even good, caring people rationalize excess as necessity. Because of this, so many people, with a helpless shrug, say they need ever more money to meet the demands of 'modern life,' citing a vague boogey-person called 'cost of living.' 'More is better' now means 'more money is better.' This acquiescence to excess then requires putting up thicker and thicker walls between our consciences and the billions of people who live in poverty. If we were selling our time—and perhaps our souls— to a system that truly fed us, that would be one thing. But the economy is not designed for people; rather, people are trained to serve the economy."

Knowing what we really need and which things are beyond our needs will actually make us happy: sensible frugality is a tool for reducing impact and ensuring long-term financial health. CB

Strategic Consumption

████████   "Buy a better future." In the past decade, as businesses with dubious credentials have collectively pounced on the "conscious consumer"—the demographic identified by the standard marketing term of LOHAS (Lifestyles of Health and Sustainability)—buying our way into a better future has become the single-minded directive from green-lifestyle gurus.

But we cannot buy a better future, at least not the sort of bright green future we talk about at Worldchanging. That sort of future—a sustainable one, a future that itself has a future—is not available for purchase: it doesn't yet exist. We can't find it on shelves, and we can't even order it up custom, no matter how much money we're willing to spend.

At the moment, no matter how heroic our efforts, it's essentially impossible to live a North American consumer lifestyle and do no harm. We can buy only organic food, recycled products, and natural fibers, and we won't get there. We can even trade our cars for hybrids, harvest our rainwater, and only run our CFLs off backyard wind turbines, and we still won't get there. This is because the waste associated with consumerism is so massive and because the systems outside our direct control upon which we depend—from local roads to our nation's army to the design of the assembly lines used to build

our cars, rain barrels, and windmills—are still profoundly unsustainable. We cannot shop our way to a one-planet footprint; the best we can do is nudge the market in that direction.

The reality is that only massive systemic changes offer us the chance to avoid the catastrophes looming ahead. Stuffed animals with recycled filler are not leveraging much change in the system. Indeed, the vast majority of the green products around us are, at best, a form of advertisement for the idea that we should live sustainably, a sort of shopping therapy for the ecologically guilty.

There was a time when that was great— back in the early days when we were out to prove that green and stylish could be synonymous. But that was a decade ago, when we knew less and could do less. Now the point's been made. Even worse, the glut of green shopping opportunities is overshadowing the most basic message of all, which is that the most sustainable product is the one you never bought in the first place.

So, should we give up on trying to spend our money in ways that could do some good? Absolutely not. But we need to get better at buying in ways that make an impact. We need to begin to practice strategic consumption.

What makes consumption strategic? Multiplied leverage.

The ideal is to buy products that not only do their jobs more sustainably but send market signals back through the economy that are likely to result in more meaningful systemic changes.

If we want to see these changes, we should pursue five strategies, listed in order of increasing importance:

Defaulting to green: When relatively equal alternatives exist, routinely choose the greener one, even if its impact is only minimally better (for instance, choose recycled toilet paper whenever possible). This may not produce massive change, but it helps solidify the gains of greener products. We ought to work to put obviously dumb products—like bleached, pulped-forest toilet paper or toxic chemical household-cleaning solutions—out of business. That would be a pretty clear market signal.

Lengthening our time horizons: A great number of costlier green products are smart investments when viewed from the perspective of long-term cost. This is true of everything from more efficient home appliances (which can pay for themselves through energy savings) to low-flow showerheads. Some of these improvements are big-ticket items, requiring substantial industrial investment to manufacture. Buying them represents a wise investment and speeds up the process of higher standards being more widely adopted, but it also requires spending more up front—sometimes a lot more. (It would be easier if we all adopted the Japanese approach [see Using Energy Efficiently, p. 139] of requiring today's best performance levels to be the minimum allowable a few years hence.)

Greening our geeks: One of the best ways to pursue sustainable innovation is to have millions of people working to make their special areas of expertise and passion as green and socially responsible as possible. Gardeners, for instance, can plant native species, harvest rainwater, build rain gardens, and create backyard habitat, transforming what once was lawn into a thriving ecosystem. The same thing is true for home-improvement buffs, amateur chefs, travel hounds, and all sorts of other enthusiasts: we can take the activity we love and make it better, something that's not only satisfying to do, but satisfying in its consequences. As Bruce Sterling says: "I don't believe in 'average people' doing anything. People ought to support mitigation and adaptation within their own line of work, no matter how un-average that is. I mean: if you're a butcher, baker, ballerina, banker, or a plumber, envision yourself as the post-fossil-fuel version of yourself, and get right after it."

Being truly strategic in our consumption: A whole different level of committed consumption comes into play when consumers send major market signals by choosing to make big purchases that may not, strictly speaking, be rational, because we are confident that it will help shift an industry's practices. Hybrids, organic foods, green power, and ecotourism are all prominent examples, but let's push even further. Electronics are a gigantic social and environmental problem: e-waste creates horrific social and environmental problems all around the world. Better standards are starting to emerge, including the EPEAT (Electronic Product Environmental Assessment Tool) standard

here in the United States, which aims to be the LEED of electronics. At least one MacBook model has achieved a Gold rating. In this case, a good strategic-consumption move would be to make sure that such a laptop (assuming it works well) is a commercial success, by buying it ourselves, talking it up online, at work, and in our community, and generally doing everything we can to ensure that laptop manufacturers everywhere see it as a profitable trendsetter, not a failed experiment.

Tilting the playing field: If we really want to make big change happen, we've got to engage with movements designed to shift institutional behavior. We've got to lobby for better regulatory policies, invest in responsible companies, boycott bad players, destroy or reinforce companies' brands, and influence the media. We can't achieve these results single-handedly, but we can work together with others who share our values to exert enormous leverage on the marketplace. And, paradoxically, that may end up being the most surprising result of strategic consumption: shopping may actually lead us to civic reengagement. AS

███████ RESOURCES

Voluntary Simplicity by Duane Elgin (Harper Paperbacks, 1998)
The notion of voluntary simplicity hinges on the idea that knowing when you've had enough is the key to financial independence and to enjoying your stuff more. It's not about renunciation of wealth or social engagement: it's about focus. If you want to be able to work less, or retire early, the trick is to weigh out what you buy, what you need, and what you'll want in the future: "To live more voluntarily is to live more deliberately, intentionally and purposefully—in short, it is to live more consciously. We cannot be deliberate when we are distracted from life. We cannot be intentional when we are not paying attention. We cannot be purposeful when we are not being present. Therefore, to act in a voluntary manner is to be aware of ourselves as we move through life."

Running the Numbers

http://www.chrisjordan.com

Photographer Chris Jordan's jarring, perspective-changing images of consumer waste include the series "Running the Numbers," which uses manipulated digital pictures to illustrate some incomprehensible statistics. In one photo, a seemingly endless field of 100 million toothpicks represents the number of trees cut down each year in the United States just to make junk mail. In another, a re-creation of Georges Seurat's pointillist masterpiece, *A Sunday Afternoon on the Island of La Grande Jatte,* is revealed in close-up to be composed of 106,000 aluminum cans, the number used in the United States every thirty seconds. Jordan presents the whole series in print in *Running the Numbers: An American Portrait* (Prestel Publishing, 2009), but his Web site includes quite a few of the most arresting images. CB

Above: In *Cans Seurat* Chris Jordan re-creates George Seurat's *A Sunday Afternoon on the Island of La Grande Jatte* with 106,000 aluminum cans to illustrate consumer waste.

Opposite: A close-up of *Cans Seurat.*

Shopping Our Way to Safety: How We Changed from Protecting the Environment to Protecting Ourselves by Andrew Szasz (University of Minnesota Press, 2007)

Afraid to drink from public water fountains, we buy bottled water instead. By examining this type of phenomenon, sociologist Andrew Szasz lays out in clear language the ways in which Americans, especially wealthy ones, have retreated from the goal of solving problems like pollution and tried to weave around themselves a protective cocoon of lifestyle products and choices—what Szasz calls "inverted quarantines" (because instead of separating and containing contagious sick people to protect a healthy public, we try to isolate ourselves by purchasing things that will shield us from the harm everyone else is suffering). The result, of course, has been both a more dangerous world and more anxious consumers. It's an obvious point, but one you'll almost never hear made in debates about sustainable living.

"Environmental inverted quarantine products are often ineffective, but because people believe—falsely—that they are protected, they are less likely to feel an urge to voice support for the kind of regulatory controls that would be needed to really address the hazard . . . If a substance is circulating in the environment, inverted quarantine measures might or might not—often not, as we have seen—keep that substance from entering the body. If that substance is not in the environment in the first place, what or how one breathes, drinks, or eats is irrelevant." A5

The Freedom Manifesto by Tom Hodgkinson (Harper Perennial, 2007)
Hodgkinson, the iconoclastic editor of Britain's wonderful *Idler* magazine, seems to have an answer for everything that ails us: the book's subtitle is "How to Free Yourself from Anxiety, Fear, Mortgages, Money, Guilt, Debt, Government, Boredom, Supermarkets, Bills, Melancholy, Pain, Depression, Work, and Waste." Incorporating quotes from historic observers of the human condition (from Aristotle to Oscar Wilde), Hodgkinson offers simple advice on how to live a life free from self-destructive consumer urges. A5

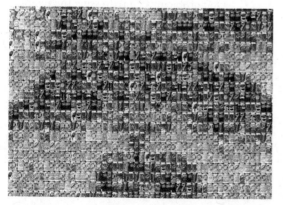

Knowing the Backstory

The things we own have mysterious pasts. To trace the backstories of most goods and services, we have to explore complicated relationships and patterns of cause and effect. But this detective work is essential, since by solving these mysteries we might prevent a massive intergenerational crime: the destruction of the planet's climate, ecosystems, and communities.

As the public gains interest and personal investment in living more sustainably, knowing the backstory becomes increasingly important. Whether we're talking about food, lifestyle products, or building materials, a big part of making good choices involves knowing where things come from, what's inside them, and how they wound up in our hands. If we know the backstory as consumers, we can make good choices; and if businesses and designers know they'll have to tell the story of their product, they'll make sure it's a story someone would want to hear.

What's a backstory? Well, in literature, the backstory is everything that led up to the situation in which the characters find themselves at the beginning of the narrative. In *Hamlet*, for instance, the backstory is that Hamlet's beloved father, the king, has been secretly murdered by his uncle while Hamlet was away at university. All of the action in the play unfolds from those essential events, which we never actually see.

Here, the backstory is what happened to our stuff before we bought it. Who made it? Where was it grown or mined or manufactured? Did the farmer use fertilizers and pesticides, or integrated pest management? Antibiotics or free-range grazing?

How did it reach us, and how was the money we spent on it distributed?

Already in foodie circles it is a mark of high distinction to know the provenance of one's food. Many of us like to eat local food. More of us demand to know that the seafood we eat was caught in sustainable ways, and often that means knowing where it came from. People are joining community-supported agricultural programs [see Buying Better Food, p. 53] and even signing up for "cow shares." Many consumers seem ready to hear the backstory.

The benefits of the backstory are clear. In fact, you could almost make a rule: the more transparent your stuff's journey from field to table, from factory to store, the better it is for everyone involved. For example, connecting directly to farmers means they, and not some middleman, get the revenues.

A focus on the backstory takes us to the "cradle" stage of a product's life-cycle, where the entire rest of its life is determined. This is the stage where change toward sustainable practices must start, and the most powerful place from which to begin a redesign of the material world. A5

Backstories and Bar Codes

One of the reasons backstories are becoming such potent tools for change is that technology is making it easier and easier to discover the real stories behind the stuff we buy and use. If we have a smart phone, we can increasingly coax products on the shelf to tell us their secrets.

An increasing number of sites offer insight into the backstories of products based on a simple scan of their bar code. Some, like Wattson [see Using Energy Efficiently, p. 140], help us figure out the energy and climate impacts; others measure against sets of preestablished criteria, like nontoxicity. Some are open and collaborative; others are paid services. The Web site Sourcemap offers backstories (or, as they call them, "open supply chains") for products based on information gleaned from a variety of sources and submitted by users around the world.

We're almost to the point where we can track the actual, specific object we're thinking about buying, at least when the producers are willing to cooperate. As more and more great companies see the benefit in touting their squeaky clean backstories, and offer the chance to look into the making of the very item we want to purchase, they drag behind them less virtuous companies, who are learning that they need to clean up their act or have the ugly history of their products revealed. A5

Backstory and Workers' Rights

Migrant workers, who harvest the bulk of the crops produced in the United States, are among the most abused and most poorly remunerated workers in the country. On average, they make around $10,000 a year—less than half the amount defined as the U.S. poverty line for a family of four. And even that number is probably high, including, as it does, the salaries of supervisors and other managerial staff. Tomato pickers in Florida, for example, receive between forty and forty-five cents for every thirty-two-pound bucket they collect. Although a 2007 agreement between farm workers and McDonald's ensured workers that they would earn a penny a pound more for tomatoes picked for the burger behemoth (similar to a 2005 agreement with fast-food giant Taco Bell), that agreement never went into effect; pressure from the Florida Tomato Growers Exchange, an industry group, prompted Burger King to refuse to implement a penny-per-pound increase of its own, and Taco Bell and McDonald's followed suit, leaving wages stagnant at levels that have scarcely budged in the last three decades.

One problem with redressing the plight of farmworkers is the issue of transparency. Increasingly, it's possible to know, in great detail, the origin story of the things you buy—whether the produce was treated with pesticides or grown with chemical fertilizer; whether the meat comes from animals fed on corn or grass; what kind of life the animals you consume lived, and how they were killed (kosher? cruelty-free? at a feedlot?); and where the food itself originated. But this transparency generally does not apply to the workers who helped to get those foods to market. Although the campaigns of advocacy groups like the Coalition

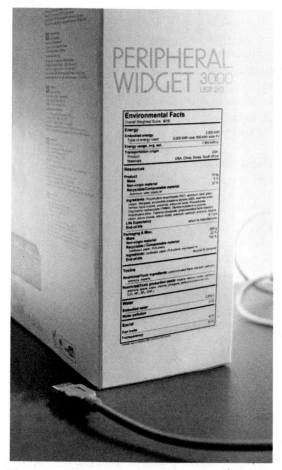

PERIPHERAL
WIDGET 3000 USB 2.0

Environmental Facts

Clothing with Nothing to Hide

Icebreaker, an outdoor clothing company based in Wellington, New Zealand—and the largest manufacturer of merino wool clothing in the world—tells its backstories with its adorably named Baacode program. Each of the garments Icebreaker makes is tagged with a code, which the consumer can enter on the Icebreaker Web site to check out the product's origins. Along with getting specific information on the high-country farmers who run Icebreaker's sheep stations, consumers can check on the living conditions of the animal that produced their wool and trace their garments through each stage of the production process.

MADE-BY, an Amsterdam-based organization that promotes social and environmental sustainability across the consumer fashion industry, launched a similar system for checking the backstory behind your clothing. The program is called Track&Trace, and it currently allows consumers to track the backstory of products they purchase from a short list of Netherlands-based fashion brands. Visit the MADE-BY site and enter a code printed on the garment's label to pull up a history of the product that describes the places it's been and the people who've played a role in its creation. The Track&Trace backstories take you step by step from the clothing-brand company to the actual garment manufacturer, the workers who spun the yarn, the farmers who grew the cotton. Each step along that journey is illustrated with a photograph of a real person, and a snippet of an interview talking about the labor conditions at that level. JVL

of Immokalee Workers, based in Immokalee, Florida, have gone a long way toward increasing awareness of the harsh working conditions and sorry pay that face migrant workers in Florida, the real potential for improving conditions for migrant workers in the U.S. and elsewhere has not yet been tapped.

What's needed is a backstory, an easily accessible resource detailing where the tomato on your McDonald's burger or your Taco Bell burrito came from, accompanied by a certification system to reassure consumers that the products they're consuming helped provide a living wage to the individual farmworkers who played such an integral role in bringing them to the table.

If consumers took the plight of farmworkers as seriously as they did, say, the presence of cancer-causing chemicals on their apples, such a certification system might not be far off on the horizon. ECB

■■■■■ RESOURCES

The Fair Tracing Project
http://www.fairtracing.org
The Fair Tracing project was created by a group of computer scientists and economic geographers in the United Kingdom. As they see it, the fair-trade

---

"Eco-nutrition labels," still largely theoretical, are important backstory tools, displaying the ecological costs of a product's manufacture as clearly and scientifically as nutrition information on a snack box.

movement faces obstacles to widespread adoption due to an ongoing divide between Northern consumers and Southern producers, as well as a lack of direct, specific information for customers about particular products. The Fair Tracing project proposes to enhance the growth of equitable global trade systems by adding digital tracing technology to individual items so that they can be tracked, and their stories recorded, as they move from farm to table.

"The Fair Tracing project believes that attaching tracing technology to Fair Trade products sourced in developing countries will enhance the value of such goods to consumers in the developed world seeking to make ethical purchasing choices. In turn, this may strengthen the commitment of existing customers to Fair Trade products as well as increase the marketability and thus sales of Fair Trade products."

It's a smart reversal of an existing application, using things like RFID (radio-frequency identification) not for corporations to survey consumer habits, but for consumers to monitor their providers' behavior. SR

Sourcemap

http://stage.sourcemap.org
Created by a team of designers and software developers based at MIT's Media Lab, Sourcemap is an open-source, volunteer-driven application that tracks supply chains of common consumer goods. Using Google Earth as a platform, Sourcemap tracks the journeys of all components of an item to help determine the product's true carbon footprint. A map of a typical laptop, for example, resembles the route map of a major international airline: dozens of lines connect cities all over the world, as metals are mined and transported, assembly is completed in China, and the finished product is shipped to us. Sourcemap is an ambitious project and was just getting off the ground at this writing. Although they're still working out the kinks in data collection and manipulation, the maps are stunning visual representations of the backstory.

Enough Project

http://www.enoughproject.org
The Enough Project focuses on the human angle of the backstory. For instance, the project's Come Clean 4 Congo campaign showed us the Congolese miners who are instrumental in the construction of our laptops and cell phones. Making the connections between our everyday items and the war and inequality that may be supported by the manufacture of these items is as important as calculating carbon footprints. The site has tools for putting pressure on companies to ensure their products are conflict-free.

The Footprint Chronicles

http://www.patagonia.com/usa/footprint/index.jsp
Outdoor gear purveyor Patagonia is one company that works hard to figure out how to change. Take the Footprint Chronicles, an exploration of the backstories of five representative Patagonia products. It's a really well done site, with compelling graphics, thoughtful explanations, even a blog, which appears to be pretty open and transparent in its discussion.

One of the products profiled is a wool sweater. The Footprint Chronicles traces the origin of the wool back to New Zealand, then shows it being woven in Japan, sewn into a sweater in California, and eventually departing for retail outlets from a distribution center in Nevada. Patagonia takes at least a brief look along the way at the materials involved, the energy used, and the labor standards practiced. It's nowhere near as detailed as some might like: the site would be more useful if you could really drill down into their data about

An ad for Icebreaker's Baacode program, which allows buyers to find out more about the sheep that produced the wool for the garments they purchase.

these processes. Still, Patagonia's is one of the best efforts at this sort of thing we've yet seen. A5

PIG 05049 by Christien Meindertsma
(Flocks, 2008)
Backstories are often complex. Designer Christien Meindertsma traced the fate of the parts of one slaughtered hog (the titular Pig 05049), following the meat, skin, bones, blood, hoofs, hair, and tail along industrial supply chains and into 185 different products. Some of the products whose backstories include parts of the pig were surprising; others were downright bizarre: not just food but matches, shampoo, paint, auto parts, medicines, and bubblegum. It's a fascinating, if disturbing, exploration of the intricate and interwoven stories that lie behind many aspects of modern life. A5

Branded! How the 'Certification Revolution' is Transforming Global Corporations by Michael E. Conroy (New Society Publishers, 2007)
Michael Conroy shows how a whole array of industries are now coming into compliance with third-party accountability systems that certify whether or not that company's actions meet basic environmental and social standards. It's not just coffee and chocolate anymore, but also mining, banking, apparel, chemicals, and so on. If you're in business, you can be sure that someone, somewhere has a certification system with your name on it. In this new phase, it is not enough simply to stop being evil. As Marks & Spencer executive Ed Williams said, "Consumers increasingly want to be sure that the companies they deal with reflect their values, can be trusted to behave responsibly, are who they say they are and are the kind of organization they like to be associated with." In simpler terms, companies are finding themselves held responsible for the whole backstory of their products. A5

Local vs. Global

When it comes to choosing what to buy, we all like simple rules. They clarify decision-making in what can be a bewilderingly interconnected world. We need to make sure, though, that those rules actually work, and most of the time, the very complexity that makes us crave simple rules demands that the rules themselves are nuanced and exploratory.

Food offers us a great window into that need for nuance. Most of us have been told to "eat local," and an increasing number of us make an effort to buy more locally produced food. But is local food actually always better?

It's not. Understanding why reveals how dealing with a global economy in the midst of a transition to sustainability demands the mental agility to think in terms of systems but to be open to the idea that simple rules don't always ring true.

Food Miles

If you've ever had a discussion with a locavore, or local-food enthusiast, you've probably encountered the idea of "food miles." Food miles are a rough measurement of the distance between the place the food was originally grown, raised, caught, or foraged and our plate.

Shipping food has ecological costs, certainly, but they're not always as meaningful as we've been led to believe. In 2008, in a comprehensive audit of climate emissions generated by food consumed by Americans, Carnegie Mellon University found that food miles counted for only 11 percent of the climate impacts of most vegetables, and only around 1 percent of the climate impacts of beef.

If we're concerned about climate change, how far food has traveled is much less important than how it was grown in the first place. That includes the farming practices involved, but also the effectiveness of producing certain foods in specific places.

The next time you buy lamb, for instance, you might want to look for a Made in New Zealand label. New Zealand has a strong commitment to energy efficiency in agriculture and some of the most productive livestock grazing land in the world. A recent study by Lincoln University in Christchurch, New Zealand, makes a strong case that, because of this built-in efficiency, shipping New Zealand lamb to Europe is actually less energy-intensive than raising European lamb, even after the transportation impact is included: when shipped to England, New Zealand lamb generated a mere quarter of the carbon emissions produced by lamb raised in England's less nutrient-rich pastures. The authors of that study conclude, "It is not the distance that should be assessed but the total energy used, production to plate, including transport."

Then, too, there is a social-justice element involved in measuring the ecological costs of food trade. Many farmers in the Global South depend on agricultural exports in order to generate the cash they need to live. By categorically avoiding foods raised elsewhere, we may be contributing to their ongoing impoverishment; food sold in a fair-trade arrangement may be more ecologically sound and offer a pathway out of poverty for the farm families involved. AS

When Local Makes Sense

While we need to acknowledge that the world is more complex than a simple "buy local" rule allows, there are still, in fact, many good reasons to buy local.

Locally grown produce is fresher, which makes it taste better and ensures that we're getting maximum nutrition for our buck. We can also get satisfaction from having a direct relationship with the farmers who grew our food, and feel more connected to our region and its seasons because of it.

Local food also has one giant benefit imported food can never offer: it helps preserve the local "foodshed." Foodsheds are the farmbelts around our cities that once provided most urban food. Many of these nearby small farms have suffered terribly from commodity food prices, lack of capital, and loss of farmland to sprawl. By supporting local food, we help our foodsheds grow strong again, and preserve agricultural land, traditions, and local varietal crops. This makes us more resilient in the face of global climate chaos, but it also has a direct restorative benefit to the rural land closest to where we live, and a healthy fabric of small towns and family farms improves the quality of life in the cities surrounded by that fabric. In addition, food that's both grown and sold locally skips many steps of processing, packaging, and transporting, sparing the environment and helping to keep more food dollars in the local economy.

Local food doesn't always make sense, but when it does, buying local means getting better food and a more secure future. AS

Combining Local and Global

Perhaps the best answer to the question of whether to buy globally or locally is to do both.

Certain kinds of crops—ones that grow well in our region, that make economic sense for our farmers to grow, and that can be produced with a competitive climate footprint—we should buy locally. For other kinds of food, we should seek more distant and efficient sources of supply, but we should also seek to reconnect directly to those suppliers. Through transnational CSAs [see Buying Better Food, p. 53], fair-trade agreements, and transparent grocery store supply chains, we can make sure that the food we're importing is as green as it can get, and that the money we spend on it is actually helping the farmers who grew it. We still want to buy food grown in our own backyards, but now we need to see those backyards as spanning the planet. AS

Preceding pages: Chinese workers processing chickens, Jilin Province, China, 2005.

Left: Container ship, Halifax, Canada, 2001.

Just Food: Where Locavores Get It Wrong and How We Can Truly Eat Responsibly by James E. McWilliams (Little, Brown & Company, 2009) McWilliams says that our worries about food miles, organic foods, and biotech concerns are misplaced: what we need to do is support good farms and aquaculture at the right scales, and eat a lot less meat.

"The decisions to create transparency, internalize environmental costs, and undermine perverse subsidies would together . . . replace the tragedy of the commons with the triumph of collective environmental stewardship. The ideal, anyway, is that we must demand more from those who produce our food, even as we strive to eat less meat, buy more of the right kind of fish, eat more vegetables and fruit, and work to learn about farms with healthy [backstories]." AS

Empires of Food: Feast, Famine, and the Rise and Fall of Civilizations by Evan D.G. Fraser and Andrew Rimas (Free Press, 2010) Fraser and Rimas use the history of premodern agriculture-based civilizations—medieval Europe, for example—to explore how the very techniques that helped these civilizations feed their swelling populations also led to collapse, including widespread famine. Ultimately, the book asks if our dependence on complex, global food systems sets us up for the same results. Although, as we've discussed in this chapter, global systems at times allow for gains in efficiency and global prosperity, *Empires of Food* offers a compelling narrative in favor of the "local" side of the debate.

Doing the Right Thing Can Be Delicious

▬▬▬   We've come a long way from a diet that is sustainable and healthy for our bodies, our communities, and our planet. Although the industrial food revolution of the last century promised abundance and an end to hunger, in many ways it has delivered the opposite. The United States produces more than twice the required daily caloric intake for every man, woman, and child, yet as many people in the United States go hungry as populate the entire country of Canada. According to the UN, worldwide 1 billion people go hungry every year, and 18,000 children die every day from needless hunger.

The industrial farming revolution of the last century—particularly the introduction of chemical pesticides, monocultural production, and confined animal feedlots—has made farming one of the world's worst polluters. In the United States alone, we blanket the country with billions of pounds of pesticides.

Industrial farming also has the dubious distinction of being one of the world's biggest contributors to greenhouse-gas emissions. Our petroleum-dependent farms eat up oil faster than you can say "Gulf War," using ten calories of fossil fuel for every one calorie they produce. According to journalist Richard Manning, author of *Against the Grain: How Agriculture Has Hijacked Civilization*, the production of just one two-pound bag of breakfast cereal burns the energy of half a gallon of gasoline.

Even worse, as industrial farming pollutes our environment, it also pollutes our bodies. Research from the Centers for Disease Control and Prevention on exposure to environmental chemicals indicates that most of us walk around with a significant "body burden" of chemical residues, many from farm chemicals.

Devouring the fast food, junk food, and fake food that saturates our supermarkets and restaurants has led to a host of health problems as well, from obesity-related diseases that lead to premature death, to certain cancers and neurological and hormonal problems that are associated with the chemicals used in our fields. Our fake-food culture is also largely to blame for the nearly 76 million annual cases of foodborne illness in the United States, which lead to more than five thousand deaths every year.

Yes, the twentieth century may have seen the fastest revolution in our dietary and agricultural practices in human history, but around the world, citizens (eaters, farmers, policy makers, researchers, and health advocates) have also fostered a different sort of revolution in food and farming, one that holds real hope. Indeed, this new century may see a revolution in food equally startling to the twentieth century's—only this one will be much better for us. Oh, and it will taste much better, too. AL

Slow Food

What ever happened to going to the market for fresh food, cooking at home, sitting down, and eating slowly enough to taste our meal? What happened to gathering together with family and friends to share conversation, trade recipes, and try something new in the kitchen? What happened is fast food. Hardly anyone has remained immune to the instant-gratification food culture we live in, or the breakneck pace of a regular day.

But one person did decide that this grave problem warranted a backlash, and in 1986, in response to an outrageous plan to build a McDonald's on the Spanish Steps of his native Rome, Carlo Petrini issued a rallying cry to citizens worldwide to drag their feet and slow down the acceleration of modern cuisine. Thus began the Slow Food Movement.

The movement encourages us to rediscover and rededicate ourselves to the pursuit of pleasure through food. But it's not just about delighting in all things edible. Slow Food is fundamentally about supporting local farmers, preserving cultural customs, promoting organic agriculture, and teaching people to rely on themselves—not on franchised eateries—for their sustenance. The Ark of Taste project seeks to catalog and preserve "forgotten tastes"—traditional foods that have become endangered by our modern food system (raw milk, which is not legal to sell in many places because of hygiene laws set by industrial agriculture, is a good example).

The Slow Food Movement's snail mascot has made its way speedily around the globe, leaving a trail of motivated slow foodies in forty countries. You can easily join your local association or start one in your hometown and be a participant in the Slow Food Movement's restoration of food culture. SR

The Climate-Friendly Diet

The simple act of feeding ourselves is one of the largest drivers of planetary destruction. By adopting better diets we can encourage more sustainable agricultural systems. But which diet to follow? Just looking at one aspect of food consumption—eating meat—reveals how thorny this issue can get.

Free-range eggs and organic asparagus, and a quiche made from the bounty.

Organic vegetable farmer and son, Washington.

Meat is bad, right? After all, livestock is responsible for 18 percent of greenhouse-gas emissions. Much of those emissions come from feedlots and factory farms where animals are fed grain or corn, crops that require the unsustainable farming of thousands of acres of arable land, including, in South America, some land that used to be rain forest. And even when we put cattle out on the range, on land that would never be cropland, we can't stop them from emitting large amounts of methane. So, it would seem that a salad is always a better choice than a meat dish. However, we may find that a modest portion of range-fed beef from a nearby sustainable farm tallies up reasonably well against a bagged salad from a Big Ag "organic" line that's been overly processed and packaged, and shipped across the country. Moreover, of the two protein sources most often touted to be replacements for meat—fish and soy—increasing the large-scale consumption of either carries its own environmental toll. Lastly, if we're concerned about food security or looking for ways to fix urban food deserts, we're likely to be proponents of adding backyard livestock like chickens and goats to urban farming, which we'll need a lot more of in order to feed growing city populations. So, meat is . . . not all that bad?

The waters are already muddy and we haven't even gotten to workers' rights, equitable trade, or the exclusivity of organic certification processes.

So what does a truly climate-friendly diet look like? Here are a few ground rules:

Stay away from factory farms and feedlots. There are no ifs, ands, or buts about this one. Along with the amount of cropland required to keep factory farms going, industrial livestock practices treat animals terribly and often pollute local water supplies. On the other end of the spectrum, a backyard chicken, when fed table scraps, is almost carbon neutral.

Eat local as much as possible, but don't obsess over food miles. In some cases, buying local has a greater impact than buying global [see Local vs. Global, p. 43 and Fish for the Future, p. 516].

Eat real food. By now, we've all heard the rule of shopping only in the outer ring of major supermarkets, as the middle aisles are packed with processed "foods" laden with high-fructose corn syrup, dyes, and preservatives. We can supplement smart supermarket shopping with farmers' markets, CSAs, and our own gardens.

Reduce consumption of red meat. Even if you're eating range-fed beef, cutting down on the amount of red meat you consume will greatly reduce your carbon footprint. Become a flexitarian [see Vegcurious, below].

Cut down on waste. The virtues of a good meal diminish if everything in that meal is individually packaged—or if most of the food ends up in the trash. Americans waste on average 27 percent of food available for consumption. A 2010 study by the Center for International Energy and Environmental Policy at the University of Texas at Austin concluded that this food waste is equivalent in energy waste to 350 million barrels of oil per year. In the United States, Waste-Free Lunches is just one movement that urges people to pack meals, whether for school or work, in which nothing ends up in the landfill. A few reusable containers aren't going to save the planet, but focusing on foods that are not prepackaged can encourage better meal planning and more home cooking. Concurrently, wasting food has links to larger behavioral trends. A recent study conducted in U.S. schools has shown that simply sending kids out to play before sitting them down to eat lunch (most U.S. schools do the opposite) significantly cuts down on food waste in cafeterias and encourages better eating habits among students—they tend to eat more slowly, drink more water, and complain less about feeling either sick or hungry after lunch. CB

Vegcurious

Although more and more people are aware of the impacts of a meat-intensive diet, making the switch to a more climate-friendly plan takes time. To test the waters, some people are trying out the advice of a nonprofit initiative called Meatless Mondays, which urges people to cut out meat completely one day a week (and, eventually, further decrease the number of meat-based meals per week). Others eat meat only at dinner or avoid specific types of meat, especially beef, altogether.

As the number of people who choose to eat mostly plants increases, so do the number of labels that describe what they eat. "Vegcurious" refers to those who do not identify themselves as vegan or vegetarian but are curious about reducing the amount of meat and dairy in their diet.

Some people also call this "flexitarian," describing people who occasionally eat meat, fish, and dairy products, but stick to a mostly vegetarian diet.

In addition to the traditionally strict vegetarian (no meat) and vegan diets (no animal products), there are also pescetarians, who will eat fish or seafood, and "freegans," who eat only free food (especially if it has been or is about to be tossed out) in order to make a political statement about food waste. SK

▬▬▬▬ RESOURCES

Fresh Food Fast: Delicious, Seasonal Vegetarian Meals in Under an Hour by Peter Berley (Regan Books, 2006)
Written by the former chef at New York City's vegan restaurant Angelica Kitchen, *Fresh Food Fast* makes good on its title with delicious menus, handy tip lists, and time-saving tricks. AL

Local Flavors: Cooking and Eating from America's Farmers' Markets by Deborah Madison (Broadway Books, 2002)
Fresh-foods maven Madison takes you on a trip through her favorite farmers' markets with recipes that celebrate the delicious fare she discovers. AL

The Organic Foods Sourcebook by Elaine Lipson (McGraw-Hill, 2001)
Lipson's book is sure to become a classic, if it isn't already, among organic-food advocates. Easy to read, clearly articulated, and compelling, *The Organic Foods Sourcebook* drives home the point that organic food doesn't just taste better or look better: it *is* better. With chapters on genetic modification, organic dairy, and everything in between, Lipson goes beyond simply explaining the benefits of organic food, to provide a plethora of resources for further reading on the organic-food movement. In her words: "If there is one thing the reader should take away, it is that we all have the power to create change that is felt at the highest levels. We do it with our choices every day and by sticking with those choices over the long haul. The details of the organic portrait will change with time, but we all must remain dedicated to the vision of a better, healthier way to feed ourselves and live on this planet."

Buying Better Food

We all value the modern convenience of one-stop-shopping. But when did it become normal to buy food at office-supply or home-decor stores? No matter what we go into a store for, we can almost always walk out the door with a snack in hand. And that's a problem because we are losing our connection to the source of our food; when we can buy it anywhere, it seems to come from nowhere.

By understanding a few basic things about how our food is grown and processed, how far it travels to get to us, and what happens to it on the way, we can make better choices about what we eat. We'll get fresher, better-tasting food, and in the process spare the environment and support the farmers who work every day to produce the food that sustains us. SR

Farmers' Markets

A few decades ago, farmers' markets were scarce in this country. Today, there are thousands of markets scattered from coast to coast. Depending on what we buy, we may pay a slightly higher price when shopping at the farmers' market, but there are two significant reasons to shell out a few more cents: first, we know exactly where that money goes—straight into a farmer's pocket; and second, that farmer's produce is certain to taste better than the grocery store variety.

If we can't find a farmers' market nearby, it's not very hard to start one for our community. It may take a while to find and secure an appropriate site and coordinate local vendors, but once it takes off we—and our community—will have an invaluable resource for better food, not to mention a great central meeting place that feels like a weekly neighborhood festival. SR

Buy Together

For the sake of convenience, many people now buy their food in big-box stores like Costco, or superstores like Walmart, where bulk quantities ensure less frequent shopping trips. These big chains make it very hard for small farmers to break into the bigger markets, and their use of central distribution hubs means that most of the food they sell has taken a world tour before it reaches your pantry. An alternative to the big boxes comes in the form of food co-ops.

Food co-ops are community groceries, often structured as worker-owned or member-owned businesses, meaning that the employees and customers have a say in what's on the shelves and where it comes from. The foodstuffs at the co-op usually don't incur a huge markup, because the workers and members have a personal investment in the quality and price of the inventory, meaning it's worthwhile to seek out items that offer optimal value—both economically and nutritionally. Where possible, the best way to do this is to source products from local farmers and vendors, a strategy that guarantees that our dollars support the local economy while buying us the freshest food possible. SR

Organic dairy farmer, Farmington Township, Minnesota, 2005.

Buy Direct

The ultimate local food is what you grow in your own garden. But not everyone has a green thumb, much less the time to cultivate tomatoes and eggplants at home. For the next best thing, you can participate in community-supported agriculture (CSA).

Farms that offer CSA programs sell you food directly, delivering a weekly box to your door or to a central location in your neighborhood. All you have to do is sign up, and you can be a part of their regular weekly rotation. With CSA, everyone wins: your local farmers get much better prices for their produce than they would if they sold to a corporate middleman, and you get fresh, wholesome (often organic) fruits and veggies that you can enjoy in the warm glow of having done the right thing. Plus, those boxes of food are usually a great value.

The only problem is that word *boxes.* Often, getting a share in a CSA means getting boxes and boxes of food—mounds of zucchini, mountains of kale—which is great if you're feeding a large household, but not so great for a single person or a couple. Most small households could never eat their way through such a pile of produce.

Many CSA initiatives are starting to respond to the demand for more manageable portions by offering more flexible memberships. For example, Full Circle Farm, outside of Seattle, allows members to sign up by the week rather than by the season, meaning you only have to budget by the week. This is a much more attractive option for those of us on a tight budget. Businesses like Seattle's New Roots Organics act as mobile farmers' markets, making weekly deliveries of small boxes (in portions small enough for one or two people) of organic, seasonal produce sourced from a small collective of organic and (mostly) local farms.

Community-supported agriculture programs allow farmers to keep land under cultivation rather than selling to developers, who are likely to turn the farms into more profitable residential developments. And CSA farms located close to cities allow urban dwellers access to fresh or organic produce, as well as the invaluable opportunity to see and understand where their food actually comes from.

Local farms easily fit this model, but Ecotrust, based in Portland, Oregon, is applying the thinking behind CSAs to try to create community-supported fisheries [see Fish for the Future, p. 517] that will allow residents of coastal areas, like the Bay Area around San Francisco, to support sustainable fishing practices in the bioregion that stretches from Baja to the Pacific Northwest. The CSA model itself can go beyond its local borders. When a crop makes sense climatically, when its transport is carbon-efficient, when growing that crop supports local farmers both at home and abroad, and when the trade arrangements are fair, getting certain products from global distributors is a good idea [see Local vs Global, p. 43]. In this case, the real task is inventing a model that combines community-supported agriculture and fair-trade models. What if we could create fair-trade arrangements directly with local farmers or farming communities from distant places with different crops and climates? What if we got our bananas directly from a transnational CSA in Guatemala, rather than a banana cartel? What if we could utilize transparent practices and global communications to be more sure that our food dollars were going to farmers, directly supporting the sort of world we want to see? Imagine, then, a network of such transnational CSAs, delivering great food from those places where export crops actually make ecological sense, so we get free-range lamb from New Zealand, organic plantains from the Caribbean, coffee from a co-op in Ethiopia, and even fresh flowers from a worker-run greenhouse in Peru. AS & SR

Farmers' market, Brooklyn, New York.

Buy Fair

Unfortunately, not everything you need grows on your local farm, or even within your state or country. You don't have to give up imported goods to be a responsible eater, but when you do buy them, be sure they are marked Fair Trade.

The fair-trade movement, initiated in the 1980s through collaboration between farmers in developing countries and farmers' rights advocates in Europe, has set the stage for fair-trade-labeling initiatives in twenty countries. Crops such as coffee, chocolate, and bananas traditionally come to us through supply lines riddled with injustice toward workers, contributing to the oppression and poverty of many people in the developing world.

For farmers in developing countries, fair trade addresses one of the barriers to a better life: the unpredictable whims of world-commodity market prices that their livelihoods are often subject to. Sometimes farmers get so little for their wares—and pay so much for supplies and equipment—they end up empty-handed at the end of the year, despite grueling work. Fair trade changes the dynamic of buying and selling in the world market by guaranteeing a fair price to hundreds of thousands of farmers in more than fifty countries.

Fair-trade-certified labels can now be found in dozens of countries. Since 1999, Trans-Fair USA has been certifying fair-trade products in the United States, and the distinctive logo can be found stamped on everything from bags of tea to bunches of bananas. Most coffee shops that purchase fair-trade beans advertise their responsible practices, so be on the lookout for java and other products with a clean history. AL

Greenwashed Food

As a result of the establishment of organic-certification programs in dozens of countries, food packages are now covered in labels to help consumers choose organic provisions. Along with these label initiatives, however, comes the inevitable misappropriation of language by large corporate food companies, which have adopted the word *organic* for marketing leverage and customer manipulation. This is the face of greenwashing in the food industry.

In 2002, the United States Department of Agriculture (USDA) implemented the first uniform national standard to regulate the labeling of foods as organic. Under the standard, in order to use the USDA's organic seal, a company must comply with all the following criteria: no use of irradiation, genetically modified (GM) substances, sewer-sludge fertilizers, or synthetic pesticides or fertilizers, and no antibiotics or hormones in meat.

While the regulations represented progress in terms of unifying the organic requirements and bringing organics closer to the forefront of consumers' minds, they also had negative implications for small farmers and food producers. The standards essentially boiled organics down to the lowest common denominator, making it difficult for farmers who already went above and beyond that level to demonstrate the superiority of their product. Even worse, the prohibitive costs associated with obtaining USDA certification made it impossible for many small organic farmers to label their goods "organic."

Large corporate food manufacturers were in some ways granted a free pass, with the ability to dole out funds to create adjunct organic brand names without having to dramatically change their practices. Companies created organic lines that had the illusory appearance of products from small family-operated farms; these include Seeds of Change (M&M/Mars), Boca Foods (Philip Morris/Kraft), and Sunrise Organic (Kellogg). The label designs, the names, even the Web sites give no indication of an affiliation with the umbrella company that manufactures the products. It is a deceptive and worrisome situation for conscientious consumers who want to support organics and not corporations.

How can you be sure your organic food is really organic? And how do you know whose pocket your money ultimately ends up in? The Organic Consumer Association and the Organic Trade Association both have abundant resources that help you learn some simple facts for better

Women pick tea leaves on a fair-trade farm.

navigation of your grocery aisle. Here are a few tips to start you off: Be sure to read the ingredients list and not just the brightly colored ad box on the front of the package to learn which and how many of the ingredients are really organic.

At the farmers' market, talk to the farmers and ask questions. Some farmers advertise their products as "transitional" instead of "organic," which means that they are in the process of eliminating pesticides and fertilizers. They may even be producing 100 percent organic goods, but without the stamp of government approval. It's worth it to be curious and to inquire about your food. After all, you are what you eat. SR

Dine Well

For some people, part of the joy of going out to dinner is not having to do any work until a plate of food arrives under your nose. What that also means is that generally, you don't have to put a single thought toward where that food came from. A variety of shocking and horrifying fast-food practices have inspired growing awareness in most people's minds. But all told, there's still a lot we don't know about the food we're being served in restaurants.

Fortunately, some savvy restaurateurs have realized that informing their customers about the food they're eating adds value to every plate. At a handful of fast-food chains and high-end eateries alike, organic vegetables, free-range meats, and local dairy foods are appearing on menus that aren't just the result of chef-inspired top-down food evangelism: it's a shift in what diners want.

One of the great pioneers in linking the urban restaurant world to rural agriculture is Blue Hill, an award-winning restaurant in New York City's Greenwich Village. When you scan the menu at Blue Hill, you'll find that the dishes center on ingredients that are available from farms in the Hudson Valley and the Berkshire Mountains of western Massachusetts—including owner Dan Barber's own Blue Hill Farm in Great Barrington.

In order to offer the "eat-local" experience to diners outside of the city, Blue Hill at Stone Barns opened in suburban Westchester County, New York. At this Blue Hill, you get more than just a phenomenal meal—you also get to see the local food economy in action. The restaurant includes a working farm that supplies produce and meat to the restaurants, and a classroom where cooking and farming demonstrations give visitors a better sense of their food's origins.

Even restaurateurs who don't have a family farm to harvest are finding ways to buy more of their ingredients from local farms using the CSA model. Through RSA (restaurant-supported agriculture) programs like Milwaukee's Braise RSA, farmers can sell thousands of pounds of their products to restaurants. Braise brokers the agreements between farms and eateries, ensures that farmers get paid on time with a portion paid in advance (very important to small farms), and helps educate local businesses on how to best use the seasonal produce they may not be used to working with. Braise's program seems to benefit everyone: restaurant owners have steady, reliable sources of fresh local ingredients, a particular concern in some areas of the Midwest; farmers can more easily keep regular CSA programs afloat because the farm overall is pulling in more profit; and restaurants save money through bulk-buying arrangements, which in turn motivates them to invest more in local ingredients. EG & CB

■■■■   RESOURCES

Fields of Plenty: A Farmer's Journey in Search of Real Food and the People Who Grow It by Michael Ableman (Chronicle Books, 2005)
This exquisite book, part travelogue, part cookbook, and part witness to the crossroads that agriculture and food face today, opens with a series of questions that writer-farmer-photographer Ableman poses while beginning a 12,000-mile (19,312-kilometer) tour of America's farms: "How do we make sure that pure food is available to all, not just those that can afford it?" Ableman beautifully recounts his quest, which takes him from rooftop greenhouses in Manhattan to the chili-producing deserts of New Mexico.

The Omnivore's Dilemma by Michael Pollan (Penguin Press, 2006)
Michael Pollan is the best American writer on the subject of food. He has an ability to see the food systems in which we are enmeshed in a clear and critical, yet fair, light. He won a James Beard Award for *In Defense of Food: An Eater's Manifesto*, and *The Omnivore's Dilemma* made him a trusted voice even among sustainable food skeptics.

"'Eating is an agricultural act,' as Wendell Berry famously said. It is also an ecological act, and a political act, too. Though much has been done to obscure this simple fact, how and what we eat determines to a great extent the use we make of the world—and what is to become of it. To eat with a fuller consciousness of all that is at stake might sound like a burden, but in practice few things in life afford quite as much satisfaction."

Civil Eats and ***The Ethicurean***
http://civileats.com
http://www.ethicurean.com
Follow these two blogs and you'll know everything there is to know about food systems and sustainable agriculture. From interviews with chefs who promote local sourcing to technical overviews of food-policy issues, both sites have tons of links to resources on food justice, urban farming, and responsible shopping—along with the occasional recipe.

Food, Inc. directed by Robert Kenner (2009)
Eric Schlosser (*Fast Food Nation*) and Michael Pollan, among others, weigh in on the corporate control of U.S. food supplies. This thoughtful documentary both condemns the corrupt practices of Big Ag and explores the challenges of expanding organic lines for sale at major retailers like Walmart. The companion book (PublicAffairs, 2009) has essays from Marion Nestle, Anna Lappe, and Muhammad Yunus.

Travel and Tourism

People love to travel. And whenever we enjoy leisure travel, we are consumers of one of the world's largest industries: tourism. In 2008 alone, there were 922 million international tourism arrivals, according to the World Tourism Organization, a specialized agency of the United Nations. At its current rate of growth, this number will reach 1.6 billion by 2020.

According to a recent World Travel and Tourism report, more than 9 percent of all jobs are linked, directly or indirectly, to travel and tourism. According to the UN, tourism generated $944 billion in 2008—meaning that a massive number of people the world over count on tourism revenues for their survival. In fact, for many countries, tourism is among the top three sources of foreign exchange.

As tourists, we may visit a certain community only once in our lifetime. But our experiences and memories stay with us forever. The impacts of our trips may linger just as long, which is why it's important for us to travel conscientiously. A certain amount of this involves voting with our wallets. When we go on vacation, we spend a lot of money—on transportation, lodging, food, entertainment, and souvenirs, for starters. And although we'd like to think that the bulk of our hard-earned money is going to support our destination's local economy, the reality is that much of it never reaches the community we are visiting. Some of our dollars go to an airline company headquartered in the United States or Europe, and the rest to a hotel owned by a multinational chain. This effect is exacerbated if we purchase an all-inclusive resort package, where food and excursions are often arranged through the hotel as well. Applying "buy local" principles to dining, lodging, and touring choices, as well as to souvenir selection, is a good first step.

But the challenges of creating green travel are myriad, and even altruistic solutions like carbon-neutral ecoresorts and voluntourism (see page 59) are laden with contradictions and trade-offs. In fact, despite all the fanfare about going green, the travel industry is seriously lagging behind other behemoth industries in committing to creating lasting change. (When one of the world's leading resort chains gets excited about replacing all of its existing golf tees with bamboo ones, you know the industry, as a whole, has lost sight of the goal.) This is partly because the "travel industry" is a mishmash of smaller industries—publishing, hotels, rental cars, airlines, governmental agencies.

But it's also partly because a lot of environmentalists have given up on including travel in the global prosperity equation, regardless of how much travel and its transformative nature have influenced their work. This has to do largely with airplane emissions—the travel industry's biggest quandary—but it is distressing how few environmentalists are willing to include in their global endgame fantasies a scenario in which we figure out how to help *more* people travel. This batten-down-the-hatches mentality is at odds with the

Our travels may take us to fragile places, where responsible tourism is imperative.

other messages we receive daily—that we should all work together and that global change requires an instant understanding of places we've never seen. If achieving and maintaining large-scale sustainability requires most, if not all, of us to think globally, then we must figure out how to protect the mechanisms that get us out into the world. CB & ZC

The Joyful Community

At a 2009 travel symposium in Seattle, Cecile Andrews, author of *Slow is Beautiful*, had some simple advice for anyone trying to green the travel industry: take a page from the Slow Food Movement [see Doing the Right Thing Can Be Delicious, p. 49]. According to Andrews, a lot of Slow Food's success had to do with how the movement focused first on experience—a vision of the "joyful community," as Andrews puts it—and let that vision spread before it became linked to the environment, or health, or any other issue. She suggests that the way to reframe travel, including the need for more vacation time, is to first emphasize the role leisure (and, by extension, vacations that are not only fun but also emotionally rewarding) plays in creating this joyful community. Certainly this would be a different message, and a more complete vision, than the one the travel industry currently spins—basically binging on relaxation. CB

Learning Journeys

Travel as education is a time-honored tradition. While it might seem that today we travel more than ever, in many ways our stamina for travel has decreased. We no longer imagine spending decades on the road, as many medieval travelers did. We travel less to learn than we do to get from point A to point B.

The need for travel as learning, however, has not gone away. As John le Carré writes, "The desk is a dangerous place from which to view the world." Since the rise of the "knowledge economy," many of us work in offices, behind desks, and deal with issues with which we have very

little direct, face-to-face experience. This creates a disconnect between our actions and their implications. It makes it difficult for us to understand the true significance and impact of what we do, what our politicians do, and who it all affects. It also means that we have a relatively limited understanding of our planet.

The point of learning journeys is to get out from behind our desks and into the world, to learn about the things that we wish to understand, change, or somehow influence. Regardless of how far we physically travel, the journeys are inevitably about cross-cultural communication. A learning journey is about creating the conditions for honest conversation across barriers.

Mbonise Cultural Concepts

Many tour operators offer visits to "authentic" villages, which turn out to be nothing more than pit stops in rural towns that have been entirely transformed into souvenir shops. Is it possible for us to truly engage in village and rural life in the Global South?

Mbonise Cultural Concepts, based in rural KwaZulu-Natal, South Africa, operates under the principle that we can. *Mbonise* is Zulu for "to show someone." The project's founders, Siphile Mdaka and Roland Vorwerk, shared a desire to offer visitors to KwaZulu-Natal deeper insight into real life in a rural Zulu community. Siphile explains, "This is a homestead, not a lodge or hostel." Visitors stay with families in the community and are guided through nature tours and community dialogues by specially trained hosts, themselves members of the community. The intention is not to simply create another cultural village conforming to tourists' expectations of cultural encounters, but to promote meaningful exchanges that really help us understand the current socioeconomic and cultural reality of a rural community. ZH

Sizing Up Sustainable Tourism

As more and more people take an interest in responsible travel, more and more businesses seem to be throwing around the term *ecotourism*. But many travelers have discovered that companies advertising ecotourism may actually know very little about the concept, other than that it attracts business. What do the terms *ecotourism*, *responsible tourism*, and *sustainable tourism* mean? And how can we find tour operators or hotels that are practicing the real thing?

The International Ecotourism Society states that ecotourism aims to conserve the environment and to improve the well-being of communities, by sponsoring responsible travel to natural areas. We can be responsible travelers by minimizing our impact on a community's environment, building environmental and cultural awareness and respect, contributing financially to conservation and to local people, and supporting human rights and labor agreements.

Whereas ecotourism is restricted to travel to natural areas, sustainable tourism applies these social, environmental, and economic considerations to all destinations. Sustainable tourism could mean reducing water usage at a large hotel. It could be initiating a guide-training program for residents who live near a sightseeing destination. It could inspire tour operators to collect funds for environmental education materials. Sustainable tourism is an approach to tourism, rather than a one-size-fits-all solution.

In trying to distinguish between sustainable tourism and false advertising, especially when we are booking hotels and tours ahead of time, we can become mired in confusion. But there are a variety of certification programs that can help us make wise decisions. Some programs, such as Costa Rica's Certification for Sustainable Tourism, focus on environmental standards. Others, such as Fair Trade in Tourism South Africa, monitor social and economic aspects like wages and working conditions. How do we know which standards a particular program gives priority to? Right now, that's still difficult, but the proposed Sustainable Tourism Stewardship Council would accredit the certification programs, enabling us to expect the same standards from participating certification programs around the world. The most important thing we can do at this point is to ask questions: ask about a hotel's environmental policies; ask tour operators about their involvement with the local community. By being active tourists, we can make businesses understand that we want to be responsible tourists. ZC

Creating Responsible Voluntourism

In 2006, when David Clemmons added a 150-word blurb on voluntourism to the first edition of this book, it was a concept that had yet to take off, even in sustainability circles. We couldn't have guessed that a few years later, voluntourism—planning a vacation to include short-term charitable work—would be featured in luxury travel magazines, or have a buzz worthy of its own backlash. The biggest question is no longer, will anyone do this type of trip? Rather, it's now: Is all this voluntourism actually doing any good?

Voluntourism is like a festive paper umbrella, stuck in the swirling cocktail of the "small steps" debate. Will switching your lightbulbs substitute for large-scale energy-policy changes? No. Will playing with a child for a half-day change the fact that there are more than 500,000 orphans in Cambodia? No. Are both actions still better than nothing? Well, that depends on whom you ask. The "does voluntourism make a difference?" debate will go on in perpetuity—until the last ice cube melts, anyway.

As voluntourism has hit the mainstream, the motivations behind taking such trips have multiplied: the earnest but unfocused desire to "give back" is further complicated by the need to reconcile wanderlust with environmental concerns—or worse, the promise of securing bragging rights as the most sensitive "traveler" in your circle (*ego*-tourism?). Certainly the range of

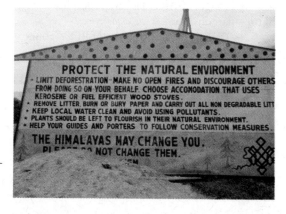

An ecotourism sign in the Himalayas outlines proper conduct for hikers and travelers.

emotions that prompt people to join more tradi-tional long-term volunteer projects like the Peace Corps is no less complex; however, voluntourists are creating a new industry (pushed now by the dollars of retired baby boomers) that, when done wrong, turns NGOs into vendors. What's more, because of this economic component, voluntour-ists' predilections—kids and animals get a lot of attention—can drive the market for certain types of programs to succeed at the expense of others, leaving the "sustainable" development of a region lopsided and completely dependent on a steady wave of foreigners. And that setup sounds a lot like regular tourism.

Daniela Papi, cofounder of PEPY Tours, a Cambodia-based company that is a model for responsible voluntourism, has a lot to say about volunteer-driven development. Her observation that voluntourists are first and foremost tour-ists is the kind of simple reality check that could help tour operators and travelers figure out the best path forward. Papi suggests that the most

Cambodia-based bike tour company PEPY Tours is a leader in responsible voluntourism.

successful programs—"successful" meaning of the greatest value to the communities they claim to serve—are the ones in which the volunteer under-stands, and is not offended by, his or her role as a tourist. A voluntourist is not there to save the world in three days.

"[PEPY Tours'] goal is that [tourists] walk away knowing that their funding helped sustain things which will last far longer than their short stay in Cambodia, and their new knowledge will help them be advocates for the causes they came in contact with, and will hopefully alter how they travel and give in the future." Although it seems pretty straightforward, this perspective is counter-intuitive to the way voluntourism is currently being marketed as shorthand for "cultural immer-sion" or "personal growth."

But by bringing the tourism aspect of voluntourism back into focus, not only is everyone operating on more honest assumptions, volun-tourism companies are free to compartmental-ize. PEPY Tours' pricing system is transparent: participants pay for the tour and also commit to a fundraising goal, the former paying the tour operator and sending money into the local economy, the latter going directly to the NGO. In this model, volunteer coordinators go back to primarily selling sustainable tourism—for example, a bike trip through Cambodia in which participants get a full picture of the country's socioeconomic challenges—and the volunteer part is left open-ended to meet the needs of the community, not the needs of the tourist.

This approach may take the pressure off companies to provide task-specific programs, which is generally where the efficacy of volun-tourism comes into question. Naturally, many travelers are more intrigued by programs that yield "tangible" results, i.e., something that can be photographed and easily explained upon returning home, like building a fence or painting a mural. But with the exception of wildlife conservation activities that are by their very nature task-specific and recurring (guarding nesting turtles from poachers, participating in bird counts), promising such events is a poor model for voluntourism.

Ultimately, PEPY Tours contends that good voluntourism organizations have the following characteristics: They put the wants and needs of their partner communities first by offering programs that support long-term sustainability goals. They turn down projects travelers are demanding if those projects do not have an obvious positive impact on the communities they support. In other words, they place travelers in an area where there is already a built-in need for volunteering—they don't create a new experience to cater to outside interests. CB

The Invitation

The invitation is probably the most indispensable tool we have when we visit nomadic and indigenous populations around the world; stumbling into a community is not a good way to arrive. When no invitation exists, most inter-cultural encounters serve only to deepen the gap between communities—or go horribly awry when ignorant travelers are unaware of or disrespect important customs.

The invitation is the first step toward ensuring a mutually beneficial and rewarding engagement. Many communities value their privacy and prefer not to engage with uninvited strangers, who, in the longer view, have included administrators, priests, soldiers, and smugglers—all with their own agendas for the community. If we are interested in a particular community, a first step might be to invite its members into our own community, into our own customs and rituals—even if this is an invitation to share a cup of coffee at a campsite. Suffice it to say, developing sensitivity toward the invitation is critical in building healthy relationships across traditional cultures. ZH

See It Before It Disappears

In recent years *vanishing* has been the watchword in mainstream travel media, with magazines and guidebook companies compiling must-see lists of disappearing landscapes. Most of the "vanishing places" roundups are vague when it comes to instructions on how to visit responsibly, a shortcoming that is less about the list-makers' understanding of sustainable travel and more about the system itself. Authors may do their best to explain why they recommend a certain tour operator, but case-by-case operator profiles aren't enough to guide all of the decision-making that goes into some of these trips. Therefore, third-party certification, although never enough on its own, is a must in these destinations.

Ecuador's Smart Voyager certification for Galapagos tour boats is a great example of a voluntary certification program, one that, according to adventure tour operator Troy Glennon, has succeeded in creating a ripple effect wherein tour companies view certification as part of staying competitive. This has prompted one-upmanship of the best kind—seeing who can go the farthest beyond the baseline criteria.

However, the Galapagos Islands are also a prime example of how a tourist destination can't rely completely on self-regulation by well-meaning operators. In 2009 the biggest news from the islands was the threat invasive mosquitoes pose to their fragile fauna; the mosquitoes hitched a ride on airplanes and tourist boats. Leeds University's Simon Goodman, one of the authors of a study on the subject, noted:

"The Ecuadorian government recently introduced a requirement for all aircraft flying to Galapagos to have insecticide treatment, but the effectiveness hasn't yet been evaluated, and similar measures still need to be introduced for ships. With tourism growing so rapidly, the future of Galapagos hangs on the ability of the Ecuadorian government to maintain stringent biosecurity protection for the islands."

With this in mind, some of the more promising initiatives have been intergovernmental in scale. More than forty organizations collaborated in 2008 to draft the Global Sustainable Tourism Criteria; in 2009, the World Tourism Organization, which has its own Global Code of Ethics for Tourism, became a member of UN-Water, "in order to stress the relevance of water for the tourism sector and to contribute to the common efforts of the UN." In addition, the Adventure Travel Trade Association is working on its own set of principles to help governments whose countries rank low on the Adventure Tourism Development Index expand tourism sustainably, instead of doing whatever will rapidly increase the volume of "heads and beds."

With the level of catastrophe facing some of these vanishing places, establishing a few sets of rules may seem like fighting off a cloud of invasive mosquitoes with a spritz of citronella—in other words, not a worthy alternative to completely curtailing travel. But because people will continue to visit vanishing places no matter how many "don't go"s are uttered and typed, and because some of these places now rely on tourism to survive, we have to forgo reconciliation to concentrate on regulation.

So how do travelers avoid contributing to the worst effects of "see it before it disappears" tourism? While there are no silver bullets, a few principles can help you make more responsible decisions:

Do some soul searching. Ask yourself why you're going. Many people visit vulnerable places out of sheer curiosity and wonder. The Great Barrier Reef, for example, has been on must-see lists for decades; its mystique predated its declining state, which has only served to increase its popularity. However, the "see it before it disappears" compulsion is also a branch of solastalgia, the pervasive sense of loss brought on by changes to our environment. And that's the main problem with these trips: they may tack on the "so you can save them"

clause, but they're ultimately focused on loss and resignation, not renewal or celebration. If you're looking for cocktail conversation fodder or want to luxuriate in loss, there are plenty of places to visit that are just as romantic but not quite as fragile. If you think your motivations are positive, read on.

Do some research. Although a few guidelines apply across the board, tourism is different in every place, even within the same country. Expeditions to remote places take months or years to plan, so it stands to reason that you should spend more than a week planning your vacation. Understanding the specific environmental and economic challenges of your destination is the only way to make good decisions on the ground.

Have a real conversation with your tour operator. Ask where every dollar goes. Get a full itinerary that includes as many details as possible regarding transportation, meals, and accommodations to fully assess the operator's sustainability claims. Ask if the trip has an educational component, both to explain the regulations travelers must obey and to provide context on the destination. Considering how expensive most of these tours are, and how much pride green outfitters take in their practices, your questions should be welcomed, not rebuffed.

Don't look for luxury in the middle of nowhere. Although it's not a hard-and-fast rule, the more "luxury" we expect, the more infrastructure operators have to build. By the time we're done having our gourmet picnic in the Arctic, zipping around our resort in a golf cart, or swimming in a pool mere miles from where animals and people alike scrounge for available water, our vacation's footprint is huge even if we're staying at an "ecoresort" or touring with a responsible operation.

Leave no trace—except contrails. If you're flying to your destination, you're leaving an impact. Until major innovations in jet fuel or intercontinental zeppelin flights become options, the closest thing we have to a solution actually involves

Puerto Egas, Galapagos Islands. The Galapagos need strict government oversight to survive the influx of tourists.

just doing some good to balance the harm we've brought: carbon offsets. Yes, any low-impact strategy you implement other than not flying will be a small step in comparison. But in fragile destinations, obsessing over proper trash disposal and water conservation is important. Similarly, a personal act like using biodegradable sunscreen, which may seem like green consumer misdirection, becomes a lot more noteworthy when you consider what chemical-laden sunscreens do to coral reefs.

Give back responsibly. The voluntourism industry has its own issues. However, voluntourism trips centered on wildlife viewing can be beneficial, as citizen science [see Citizen Science, p. 456] does have its place in monitoring threatened flora and fauna. Just make sure that the biggest contribution of your voluntourism trip is monetary—not only in support of wildlife conservation, but also in support of social programs that will help attendant communities become self-sustaining without tourism.

Create better top ten lists. We're living in a time of tremendous transition and uncertainty. Surely we can stand to refine our "must-sees"; we've already started with the idea of the staycation, which asks us to find the exotic in the next town over.

If we fixate on taking a last sorrowful look at the already doomed, we're not looking at the places that may well end up on next year's list, or at victories like UNESCO's expansion of its biosphere reserve network, which supports comprehensive environmental stewardship programs. Where's the "doing just fine" list? How about fifty places to see so they don't disappear? CB

Sustainable Travel and Vacation Laws

In one clip from *The Vacation Aversion*, a documentary by John de Graaf, the filmmakers interview visitors to Yosemite National Park. While we see crowds dashing from cars to designated viewpoints—including a shot of a man talking on his cell phone while distractedly snapping a photo of a jaw-dropping vista—a park ranger informs us that the average visit to Yosemite, a *1,200-square-mile* park and national treasure, lasts about five hours.

It's easy to scorn the hit-and-run tourists as unenlightened folks, but the lack of care we exercise when we travel isn't about decaying values or Web- and TV-induced disconnection from the actual stuff of life—it's about time. At this writing, the United States was the only nation other than the Guyanas, Nepal, and Myanmar without a paid-vacation law. Thirty percent of Americans don't get paid vacation; half get one week or less. It's no wonder Americans love environmentally unsound vacations—power-boating beerfests, three-day Cancun bacchanalias, check-your-mind-at-the-door packaged tours and cruises. The cultural psychosis that prompts Americans to travel this way is multilayered to say the least; however, a major factor is the devaluation of vacation time. With fewer days of vacation to look forward to, Americans face New Year's Eve–level pressure every time we plan a weekend trip. Just as we binge on food, on consumer goods, and on pop culture minutiae to anesthetize ourselves, we also binge on travel.

Protecting vacation time is the first step toward sustainable tourism; you can't have one without the other. Voluntourism programs and sustainably run soft-adventure trips both require time to plan and fully enjoy. Traveling in less destructive ways (trains vs. planes, for example) requires time. "Cultural immersion," the holy grail of adventure travelers and academics, requires time. Caring enough to make good decisions requires time. Continuing to preach sustainable tourism to folks without first securing their basic rights to time off is self-defeating.

Although the protection of vacation time seems a U.S.-centric problem, Global Northerners should pay attention, too. As de Graaf pointed out in a recent debate in *The Economist*, "a spectre is haunting Europe, the spectre of losing its healthy and happy leisure to the grindstone of American work demands." Indeed, some economists argue that Europeans take too much time off and would be better off working more and thereby increasing their take-home pay by a few thousand dollars than hanging on to those extra vacation days. But as we well know, there's more to life than GDP. CB

Staycations

For much of 2009, you couldn't talk about travel without hearing the word *staycation*. Although the definition varies—some people think it means not leaving the country, others think it means not traveling farther than "one tank of gas" (or low-impact public transit like trains) can take you, and still others interpret it as not leaving your town—the staycation is all the rage in sustainability circles. And with economic woes and fuel scarcities not abating anytime soon, it's probably here to stay.

It's hard not to get excited about the opportunities the staycation presents: saving money, exploring the region you live in, keeping your vacation footprint small, and practicing a "slow" form of travel unconcerned with airport delays and tightly packed schedules.

Beyond that, staycations can strengthen communities. First of all, they can keep money that would otherwise be spent in other destinations local. Second, they can reveal exactly what features a town does or doesn't have. As Jim Lewis of Western Michigan University, who with a colleague just started a study of staycations, noted, "your town now becomes an amenity, becomes a vacation spot . . . Community recreation programs now become part of tourism." Thinking like a tourist in your own town can allow you to see problems that you've just gotten used to, as well as the opportunities to fix them.

Most towns are not set up to be destinations unto themselves and would require significant boosts in cultural and recreational offerings to reap the economic rewards of the staycation trend. It sounds like a classic spend-money-to-make-money scenario, but community volunteering would go a long way toward offsetting some

of those costs. Gaylene Carpenter and Lori Hager of the University of Oregon have been researching ways to use staycations to bolster local arts scenes; they maintain that staycations could make community arts and cultural assets easier to create and maintain. Volunteer-minded staycationers could be a vital force in improving a community's "amenities," whether arts organizations or parks. CB

An Air Travel X Prize

Air travel presents one of the stickiest problems we face. On the one hand, in a rapidly globalizing world, we need to fly to do business, build networks, and see loved ones. Indeed, to many people, the ability to travel easily and keep a global community is one of the greatest accomplishments of our civilization.

On the other hand, air travel is frying the planet. While air travel contributes only 3 percent of humanity's total CO_2 emissions (making them a problem only a few times larger than, say, coal fires), it is growing at an astounding rate. And while engines are becoming more efficient, planes are also getting larger and flights more frequent, meaning that air travel may effectively undo many of the gains so far made in cutting CO_2.

Furthermore, for a variety of reasons having to do with chemical emissions and contrail formation (the white "tails" jets leave behind them), it turns out that airplanes have a climate impact that's actually two to four times greater than their CO_2 emissions alone would indicate. To make matters even worse, we seem unable to innovate our way out of this jam. Sure, there are plenty of ideas: We can run flights more efficiently, ensuring that more of them are full and their routes are as short as possible. We can outfit planes with electric motors for tarmac use, allowing them to run their jet engines less. We can replace the wiring with fiber optics, making the planes lighter. We can use biofuels to make the planes slightly more carbon neutral (at this writing, Dutch airline KLM was the most recent tester of biofuels, using a 50/50 blend of jet fuel and biofuel made from camelina, a low-impact feedstock).

But the brutal truth is that these are marginal improvements. And so far, we haven't done better than an average increase in efficiency of about 1 percent a year. At these rates, we won't get our technofix in time. If this is the case, it means that journeys around the world must be reserved for visiting the people you love, and that they will require both slow travel and the saving up of carbon rations. Many greens are just fine with this scenario, but here's the rub: we can't hold together a globalized society without frequent travel, and people are not going to stop traveling.

So, we need better jets. We need to crack a seemingly insolvable problem and design carbon-neutral, nontoxic air transportation. We have a pretty good mechanism for getting people to tackle dramatic challenges: prizes. Look, for instance, at the X Prize, which set a $10 million prize for the first group to fly a private craft into space twice.

What we need is a prize, a big prize, a prestigious prize, given to the first team that can, say, cut airplane emissions by three-quarters (got to start somewhere) in a commercially practical way. That's a goal vastly more meaningful and, in the long run, more vital than putting a colony on the moon.

The Federal Aviation Administration (FAA) seems to agree. In 2008 they started working with the X Prize Foundation to develop an "aviation alternative technologies and fuels prize" as a way to spur the innovation they need to make the airline industry more efficient and help offset the emissions that a projected doubling of air traffic by 2025 will produce. At this writing, the FAA was aiming to start the competition in 2011. AS

■■■ RESOURCES

Tourism 2023
www.forumforthefuture.org/projects/tourism-2023
This Forum for the Future report, created in conjunction with a UK-based panel of travel industry heavies (including British Airways and Thomas Cook), attempts to visualize what tourism in the 2020s will really look like, with the goal of creating a unifying vision for the travel industry that both preserves international travel and makes sustainable travel affordable.

The report ponders the challenges that external pressures like peak oil and carbon pricing will present. If the weekend trip to Ibiza is no longer feasible, how can companies adapt to accommodate vacationers who are taking longer trips while meeting their sustainability goals and staying in business? Lastly, as this is an industry report, along with the stats and carbon counting, it discusses another important issue—image. One of the questions posed is, what would it take to give overland travel, which is not currently very glamorous, a cachet strong enough to win over those people who could still afford to jet set?

The Practical Nomad: How to Travel around the World by Edward Hasbrouck (Avalon Travel Publishing, 2004)
One of the best ways to travel and learn about new places is to take a long-haul vacation, including but not limited to around-the-world trips. A veritable bible of world travel, *The Practical Nomad*, now in its third edition, contains invaluable resources on everything from air travel to rail passes to volunteering abroad. Says Hasbrouck, "the biggest mistake you could make, in my opinion, would be not to travel around the world, at least once in your life, if you have the chance." Even if we can't drop everything to troll the globe for six months, *The Practical Nomad* offers tips, resources, and advice sure to benefit the intrepid travelers among us.

Marco Polo Didn't Go There by Rolf Potts (Travelers' Tales, 2008)
There are plenty of great travelogues; writing about how a few weeks in the Italian countryside changed your life seems to be a cottage industry. But Rolf Potts's collection of travel essays gives us something the others don't: an explanation of how each piece was written, including revealing exactly where poetic license was the only thing holding the story together. Far from being an exposé of travel writing, however, *Marco Polo* ends up being a meditation on expectation, and the fulfillment we hope to find as soon as we land in a foreign place. Potts is an incredibly entertaining writer with a clear love of every bump in the road, and his candid analysis of the difference between what actually happens and what makes a great travel story is both poignant and humorous. CB

Giving Well

Charity is supposed to be the tidy opposite of consumption. Those of us lucky enough to have "disposable income" give it away without receiving anything in return—at least not anything material. Writing checks for worthy causes affords us a few moments of grace during which we see our money differently, not as a Technicolor security blanket but as a tool that can connect us to some intense and scary things outside our immediate frame of reference—and, ideally, help to jump-start change.

Charity, however, is a loaded concept. For too many donors, making a gift is the equivalent of swiping a credit card: your account gets debited, but you always get something in return, whether it's status points or guilty-conscience offsets. Most nonprofits now feel the need to incentivize donors, who now expect to receive a coffee cup or a tote bag for every good deed [see Effective Campaigning, p. 398]. In these ways, our patterns of giving are much more related to our patterns of consumption than we'd probably like to admit.

That doesn't mean you should never again click on a donation button. In many cases, parting with a few dollars is an easy way to bring relief to people thousands of miles away who are grappling with challenges you might never understand. But in the past decade, entrepreneurs have given us some exciting new philanthropic models. Microfinance [see Microfinance, p. 313], in particular, has been a revelation, both personalizing and streamlining standard donation procedures, and transforming "donors" and "victims" into business partners.

In addition, a number of organizations are playing with crowdsourcing and crowdfunding models, thereby helping us to expand our vision of giving: working the line at a soup kitchen is admirable, but so is tagging photos of earthquake victims to help their loved ones locate them. Whether we're giving time or money, we have a host of fresh approaches to provide thoughtful, effective aid. CB

New Rules for Global Giving: The Virtuous Circle

While there's no shortage of opportunities to support important causes, there's usually very little opportunity to see our money have measurable effects on the people we wish to help—especially when we only have a small amount to give. But there is a way for us to leverage the least amount of money into the largest measurable effect over time; there is a type of giving that multiplies itself.

Think of this approach as "enabling philanthropy": a virtuous action that enables someone else to take a virtuous action, like giving someone a microloan to start a small business that will eventually provide for all their needs. We don't have to give annual checks to umbrella organizations and hope that our money has actually done some good. We can take a relatively small amount of money and aim it at the precise point where it can do maximum good. We can give this money not as charity, but as an investment in the latent ambitions of poor people in villages and squatter cities, on the condition that the recipients magnify this seed by starting a small business or enlarging an existing one. In addition, we can strongly encourage them to take some small portion of their growing investment to help someone else as well.

This is a virtuous circle that keeps on giving, paying its benefits forward generation after generation. It's a beautiful thing, and it's the only type of love you can dispense with money. There is also an optimistic assumption in this scheme: the 2 billion poorest people in the world are really 2 billion entrepreneurs just waiting for their first seed money. If you give it, they will build upon it.

As you look for opportunities to start your own virtuous circles, keep in mind the following important guidelines:

- Aim your gift at those with the least means, to whom small amounts make a huge difference.
- Give at least two hundred dollars. Though it may seem like a small amount, it's enough to make a real impact on the poorest recipients and to allow them to address their dreams of tomorrow. If you give less than that, the money can only help with immediate needs.
- Ask yourself if the gift will be able to expand itself, gaining amplitude with each cycle.
- Focus your efforts on gifts that have a global range.
- Make sure that the agency that facilitates your donation sends the funds directly to individuals. The more steps between your donation and the recipient, the less impact it will have.

Erlinda Rubite received a microloan from Kiva to support her Chinese-style steamed-bun business in the Philippines.

The following three organizations are highly evolved programs that produce amazing results. Giving to these organizations will go far to make you optimistic about the world's future:

Heifer International: For fifty years, the Heifer Project has been providing families in developing countries (and in areas of the United States) with breeding pairs of animals: cows, goats, pigs, rabbits, water buffalo, ducks, and so on. In the world's poorest regions the cost of a cow or goat can exceed a year's income, preventing many families from acquiring animals. When a family receives a breeding pair, they get meat, milk, or eggs, but more important, they get a source of income: they can sell the offspring.

Each recipient must agree to give one breeding pair of offspring away to another family, thus paying the gift forward. So a small contribution can multiply as families gain food, a source of income, the means to help someone else—and pride. It's hard to imagine a better gift, or a more practical, proven lever for making a difference in communities of need.

Opportunity International: Microfinancing [see Microfinance, p. 313] is quite the rage in international circles for one truly amazing reason: the payback rate on tiny loans to workers in developing countries is greater than the payback rate on large loans to their home countries. In other words, from an outright profit perspective, you are better off loaning money to a Bolivian peasant than to the Bolivian government. Several nonprofits, starting with the Grameen Bank [see Social Entrepreneurship, p. 321] in Bangladesh, have pioneered microcredit loans on a large scale and for large investors. For a helpful citizen, though, it's easy to contribute funds to a wide variety of microloan programs through Opportunity International. This organization has been providing microloans for thirty years, since even before the term *microcredit* was coined. It works through Trust Banks, groups of twenty to thirty (mostly women) borrowers who meet weekly to cross-guarantee the loans.

Trickle Up: Rather than dispensing loans, Trickle Up issues outright grants (typically two hundred dollars) as seed capital for microenterprise hopefuls—with strings attached. What the recipients get is some start-up cash and a lot of training. Trickle Up makes grants to those looking to open small businesses like food stalls or repair shops, on the condition that grantees undergo basic business training, commit a minimum of 250 hours in the first three months to their venture, reinvest at least 20 percent back into it, and keep an account ledger. That means that when you contribute to Trickle Up, you are building up a social network of do-gooders to ensure good deeds persist. Each year roughly 10,000 businesses get started via

Trickle Up donations, and 30,000 budding entrepreneurs benefit from this global program; about 70 percent of grantees are women. Follow-up expansion grants are offered, too. KK

Smaller Circles, Enormous Impact

The virtues of helping a person in the Global South jump-start a small business are undeniable, but what do we do if we can't afford to make a two-hundred-dollar gift on our own? We can turn our twenty dollars into two hundred dollars by coordinating our donations through giving circles.

Giving circles are easy to set up and easy to manage: we donate a small amount of money and ask our friends and coworkers to match our donation. Pooling our resources and directing the combined donation to smaller, more specific causes can be much more effective than writing a small check to an organization that tackles "the environment" or "human rights abuses."

For example, One By One is building an online network to fight obstetric fistula, an injury to mothers during childbirth caused by long, obstructed labor—the kind that would be easily remedied in the Global North with a cesarean section. When left untreated, obstetric fistula can be devastating, often debilitating the mother and rendering her incontinent. This condition is relatively inexpensive to cure (it costs about three hundred dollars), but women in the developing world, particularly in Africa, rarely get the treatment they need.

One By One's network of fistula fighters come together to raise tax-exempt donations through the underfunded United Nations' Campaign to End Fistula. The donation of each giving circle goes directly toward buying one woman the surgery she needs. In other words, when ten people write checks for thirty dollars, one woman's life is drastically improved. AS

The Heifer Project is an established and well-regarded program aimed at lifting agricultural communities out of poverty through gifts of livestock.

Micropatronage

The Medici model of patronage may have worked for Michelangelo, but today, supporting innovation in journalism and the arts is largely up to the audience. Helping to feed a hungry child may seem more altruistic but investing in culture and innovative ideas can be a powerful way to help change the systems that produce hunger and poverty in the first place.

Currently, micropatronage is most closely associated with music: as secure-pay sites like PayPal became commonplace and MP3-sharing platforms evolved, independent musicians very quickly realized that they could bypass the music industry altogether to deliver uncompromised art directly to fans at maximum profit.

Musicians may own it right now, but the micropatronage model works for almost any endeavor. Spot.Us, an experiment by San Francisco's Center for Media Change, crowdfunds journalists, giving overlooked news stories a chance to see the light of day. Reporters set transparent fund-raising goals based on the expenses they're likely to incur while researching a piece. Although it began as a way to boost local Bay Area coverage, in 2009 Spot.Us proved that it could influence national news. Backed by a $6,000 grant from 116 Spot.Us donors, journalist Lindsey Hoshaw wrote a lengthy and important piece on the massive garbage patch swirling in the Pacific Ocean. The *New York Times*, which had originally declined Hoshaw's pitch because of what they considered to be prohibitive reporting expenses, ended up publishing the piece in its Science section. Hoshaw's article was the first extensive, multimedia story on the garbage patch to be published in the *Times*.

Slightly less earnest, but just as game-changing, are sites like Kickstarter.com. Kickstarter offers a stylish platform that allows patrons to help fund a film or album, pour some seed money into a worthy start-up, or simply encourage a random crowdsourcing experiment. Anyone can submit a project to Kickstarter; if a project doesn't make its fund-raising goal, it doesn't receive any of the pledge money. Unlike in microfinance schemes, funders don't technically get any return on their investments (beyond enjoying the art or service created), but Kickstarter projects can offer whatever incentives they like—anything from an advance copy of the completed work to a private screening of the documentary their donors helped to make.

Any crowdfunding free-for-all has some drawbacks—on Kickstarter, worldchanging inventors and humanitarian campaigns share space with a lot of "help me buy DJing equipment" requests. But the potential is great. Just like hundreds of Michelangelos shouldn't have to wait for their Medici to create great art, journalists, filmmakers, and social entrepreneurs shouldn't have to rely on elusive foundation grants to fund their projects. CB

Mash-up Tools for Volunteering

Our overall willingness to work on behalf of others is on the rise: approximately 109 million adults volunteer annually in the United States alone. However, finding the time to volunteer our time is often daunting; the greater the time commitment to get started, the more likely we are to put off action for another week, another month, another year.

We often assume that technology isolates us. Paradoxically, online tools are helping to get potential volunteers out of the house. VolunteerMatch is a leader in the nonprofit world dedicated to helping everyone find a great place to volunteer. Enter your zip code, your area of interest, and how far you're willing to travel, and VolunteerMatch will create an automated list of all the volunteer opportunities in your area that fit your criteria.

Some tools have eliminated even more of the preliminary steps to offer instant community-engagement gratification. Bored on the bus? Twiddling your fingers at the doctor's office? Why not use these micro–time slots to volunteer? The on-demand volunteerism organization The Extraordinaries, through its site BeExtra.org, allows volunteers to complete micro-tasks online or on their smart phones. You can help museums and educational institutions around the world tag photos for their digital archives or you can contribute to community mapping projects. Some "missions," like leaving voicemail messages for political leaders, even mimic analog activism. CB & SK

Philanthropic Footprints

When we have more to give, the challenge of good giving paradoxically gets tougher. Worldchanging philanthropy, both organizational and personal, requires a fine sense of the challenges facing the planet. We have to be aware of the law of unintended consequences and retain enough self-awareness to avoid the ethical pitfalls of power. This takes both a triage doctor's cold assessment of one's ability to affect a given situation and a good teacher's understanding of the fact that when brilliance emerges, it is not always subject to the normal rules.

We know now that efforts to fix a single problem with a single, simple solution rarely succeed. We are just beginning to see truly effective philanthropy that thinks about its grant-making in terms of systems, interconnections, leverage points, and payoffs that are slow but powerful. We can hope that this big-picture, long-term giving proves to be a growing trend.

Many philanthropists, however, currently run their foundations and trusts on exactly the opposite principle. Consider the Gates Foundation, the world's largest philanthropic outfit (and one whose giving, while certainly imperfect, has earned respect), and its counterproductive investment portfolio. In 2007 *LA Times* reporters discovered that the Gates Foundation was making massive investments not only in climate enemies like ExxonMobil but dozens of other companies that have been cited for consumer fraud, corruption, worker abuses, and ties to gambling, alcohol, tobacco, and child slavery. In other words, much of the billion-plus the Gates Foundation distributes each year to make the world better comes from tens of billions it invests in companies that are actively making the world worse.

This is the dirty secret of much philanthropy: often foundations and individual donors continue to directly invest in actions that undermine and contradict the change they are trying to bring into the world through their philanthropy.

To avoid such contradictions, we might suggest three new rules for larger philanthropic efforts:

Practice holistic assessment: This is in many ways the most difficult, and most needed, step. It's difficult because in the real world, everything's all stuck together: systems function with great complexity, causes and effects are linked indirectly, chaotic and emergent behaviors are everywhere, human beings do bizarre things, and it's hard to track the true consequences of our actions.

Today, we have an array of tools for judging the consequences—intended or not—of our organizational behaviors. There are guides to ethical corporate behavior for everything from investing to outsourcing, choosing materials to relating interpersonally. We are getting better and better at understanding systems, at modeling, at creating indicators [see Seeing the Big Picture, p. 366], at anticipating second-order effects, gaming change, and creating generative feedback.

But we can go farther than merely making sure our profits don't indirectly stem from genocide or child slavery; we can actively invest in the good. Right now, we lack effective mechanisms for finding and investing in socially transformative enterprises on a large scale. One thing that's holding us back is the idea that program officers are good at giving money, and fund managers are good at getting it, and things are smoothest when they stay the heck out of one another's way. That said, it's not at all difficult to imagine an organization where all financial transactions are seen as part of its program, and where those managing the money are seen as a special type of program officer, just as responsible for furthering the mission as those giving the money away. In a world full of such organizations, the trillions of dollars in the coffers of foundations, university portfolios, and public pension funds would become a gigantic lever for change, helping to create revenue for giving and to propel innovative, worldchanging enterprises at the same time.

Seek transformative impact: We must expect more than measurable temporary alleviation of suffering or partial mitigation of disaster: we must expect transformation, in all its slow and ungainly glory. We must aim to make big dents in problems (like ending poverty or redesigning our lives so they heal nature). We must also support new innovative initiatives that provide us with the ultimate proof of the possible: working models. In this context, pilot projects, trial efforts, beta tests, and model communities prove themselves to be far more than the fringe efforts they're usually dismissed as; offering the "threat of a good example" is never a waste. Bucky Fuller was quoted as saying, "You never change things by fighting the existing reality. To change something, build a new model that makes the existing model obsolete." You can't get people to defect from their current way of doing things unless you offer them a new model.

Offer utter transparency: Lots of people already espouse transparency in philanthropy. Funders increasingly demand transparency from grant recipients. The transparency and accountability demanded by large donors also facilitate small donors' effectiveness. Transparency and accountability help that process, as people want to know that the dollars they give away are properly spent: the Big Guys insisting on better practices makes the Little Guys more comfortable sending in a part of their paychecks.

But those of us managing fortunes on behalf of the public good can embrace a much more stringent form of transparency: open books and open impacts. Funders can reveal how they make their money, what is done to produce those profits, how much it costs them to earn that income, and what is spent on management. As we invest in change and embrace transparency, philanthropic organizations also ought to support open-source answers, facilitate the release of information in the public commons and offer incentives (instead of subtle barriers) to groups collaborating together.

Perhaps what's needed is some sort of philanthropic-footprint report—a process any philanthropic group could undertake to help it not only to see the direct and indirect effects of its practices but also to own up to them in public, spurring it on to better behavior where it has lagged and encouraging imitation where it has excelled.

Indeed, in an era when knowing the backstory [see Knowing the Backstory, p. 39] is fundamental to intelligent and ethical action, telling the story of our philanthropic footprint may become the new annual report, and the bottom line might just be truly transformative change. AS

■■■■■ RESOURCES

Council on Foundations
http://www.cof.org/
The Council on Foundations is a membership organization of more than two thousand grant-making foundations and giving programs. Its Web site is a wealth of information, with resources on everything from "Philanthropy in a Time of War" to a bibliography of Latino American giving patterns. Most important, the council provides training and education for everyone from newcomers to foundation chief officers—because shared innovation is the key to giving well.

The Center for Effective Philanthropy
http://www.effectivephilanthropy.com/
With a clear mission to "provide management and governance tools to define, assess, and improve overall foundation performance," the Center for Effective Philanthropy is one of the nation's leaders in providing assessment tools, data, and publications to foundations, in the hopes of improving overall performance on a variety of fronts. For the layman, the center's Web site offers some great tools for understanding and assessing foundations and their effectiveness.

Sarah McLachlan, pictured here performing at the G8 concert series, once donated the $150,000 allocated by her record company for a music video to purchase medicine and school supplies for kids in the Global South. She then made a video—for $15—that explained how easy it is to turn tremendous wealth into worldchanging actions.

Retail 2.0

We all shop, but more and more of us are questioning how much we shop and whether we need so much stuff in the first place. And in the last few years, a quiet revolution has been emerging in where and how we shop as well.

Right now, many of us in the developed world shop by driving to large chain stores. This is especially true in North America but has become common elsewhere too. The problem is, this way of shopping adds an enormous ecological burden to all the goods we buy: not only do we burn gas getting to the store and back, but the building and operation of that store and its parking lot have a huge impact. The supply chain that keeps huge stores stocked with masses of various kinds of goods adds more impact, while the packaging and sales presentation of these items tops it all off with more wasted energy and materials. From the lights to the loading docks, from the freezer cases to the shopping carts, conventional retail is unsustainable.

Retail today has other costs as well. Part of the savings we get by shopping in big chain stores—which are not generally known for good labor practices—comes from the mistreatment of the people who serve us while we're there. The volume of goods it takes to stock big-box chain stores dictates that they buy things only in huge orders, often from the lowest-cost big provider, which may mean supporting sweatshop work conditions, factory-farmed food, or toxic knockoff products. Furthermore, because the backstories [see Knowing the Backstory, p. 39] of the objects they sell can be so atrocious, big chain stores are often at the forefront of fighting transparency and labeling laws (Walmart's latest effort at eco-labeling may or may not be an exception to the trend).

Not all chains are bad, of course, and certain leaders, like Marks & Spencer, have shown that even giant retail corporations can take seriously their ethical obligations and offer better products, clearly labeled to indicate their ecological impacts, in more energy-efficient stores. But there are real limits to how much the model of big-box, auto-dependent chain stores can be improved.

A better model is emerging. Innovative companies are changing not only the stores themselves, but how the whole experience of shopping works and what it means. Think of it as bright green retail—Retail 2.0. AS

Microcommerce

Which came first, the rise of maker culture or the rise of microcommerce? Microcommerce—direct purchases from small producers (whether at a farmers' market or an online service like the craft site Etsy)—has allowed makers to become manufacturers. But where would microcommerce be without the hundreds of crafters, hobbyists, and amateur fashion designers who are answering the call for personal, handmade unique goods?

In the past decade, microcommerce went from a trend story to a serious moneymaker. Etsy, for example, has 2 million users, who spend almost $90 million annually. Sellers are already tweaking the simple business model: increasingly,

there are stores and markets designed to mix the webfront model [see The Future of Product Delivery, p. 74] with microcommerce, offering sample products from small-scale producers. São Paulo's Endossa, for example, provides a storefront for online sellers, who rent out a cubbyhole or two, giving potential customers more exposure to their products in a traditional shopping setting—in some cases, much more effective than waiting for shoppers to happen upon their Web site.

Other sellers are taking customization to new levels. Personalization is the cornerstone of many thriving online businesses, but shoppers are generally pretty limited in the choices they can make: do you want this design on a blue T-shirt or a gray T-shirt? But in another major step forward for maker culture and small-scale production, some businesses are giving customers the option of being full-fledged designers. Jewelry-makers Nervous System, based in Saugerties, New York, invite customers to create their own unique designs using applets on the company's Web site. Founders Jesse Louis-Rosenberg and Jessica Rosenkrantz draw on their backgrounds in science and architecture for inspiration in their designs, which reference the patterns in bacteria, coral reefs, skin cells, and other unlikely sources. Consumers can choose ready-made pieces or can click and drag one of the preset patterns to create their own works of art. Even larger sellers like Etsy are getting into this game: the "Alchemy" section of Etsy's site allows users to post requests for any item they may desire; sellers can see the request, and if one of them feels up to the challenge, he or she can negotiate price and terms with the user to create the custom item.

As Clive Thompson wrote in a *Wired* piece on Etsy: "[T]he physical world is going to be increasingly customized—built to your specs by craftspeople . . . The Age of Bespoke Everything, as it were." JVL & CB

Endossa, in São Paulo, allows online retailers to display select goods to brick-and-mortar shoppers—exposure without huge overhead costs.

Dual-use Packaging

Most of us are aware that product packaging is a largely unnecessary source of waste, but the scale of the problem may still come as a surprise. According to the United States Energy Information Administration, packaging is the greatest single source (32 percent) of all the waste generated in this country. In the EU, packaging waste accounts for about 20 percent of the weight and 40 percent of the volume of municipal waste. Not only does that packaging represent a significant volume of wasted material, but it's also money out of consumers' pockets—twice. We pay for excess packaging first as part of the sticker price of a given product, and again in disposal fees for getting rid of the empty boxes, Styrofoam, and plastic wrappers.

Packaging designed for multiple uses is a solution that can both add value to products and help reduce their environmental footprint. Fuseproject, a U.S.-based design firm founded by Yves Behar and responsible for the first design of Nicholas Negroponte's One Laptop Per Child, got a lot of attention in 2008 for its Y Water packaging. The organic children's beverage is packaged in four-lobed bottles that interlock with natural rubber connectors to become a building set when empty. And when no longer in use, the bottles can be recycled.

The most successful (and ultimately sustainable) types of dual-use packaging may not create auxiliary uses at all. Rather, the package is part of the product. In 2008, Hewlett Packard won a Walmart design challenge by creating a laptop computer that is sold inside a padded laptop bag—a companion product most buyers would have purchased anyway. By packaging the computer in this manner, HP reduced packaging waste by 97 percent, even before accounting for the fact that the bags themselves are made of 100 percent recycled material. In addition, since the laptop bags take up less space in transit, the manufacturer is able to save fuel and reduce CO_2 emissions associated with shipping. And the package-as-product concept can go even further: the shade of the lite2go lamp from the San Francisco firm knoend doubles as the packaging for the electrical cord, socket, and a CFL lightbulb. Plus it's made from recyclable plastic.

Eliminating packaging altogether is tough, because retailers and manufacturers still need to protect their products. But these innovative and fun designs for dual-use packaging are a step in the right direction—acknowledging that the lifecycle of a product begins with how it is packed and delivered to the consumer. GH

Packaging 2.0

Although designers are finding innovative ways to make individual product packaging more useful, there's another type of packaging waste that most of us never see: the materials that are stuffed between, wrapped around, and stacked beneath shipments of products on their way from factory to store. The endless disposable stream of wooden pallets, cardboard boxes, packing peanuts, plastic wrap, and more is not only a huge source of landfill waste; it's a large cost to manufacturers.

One option for reducing waste is simply using shipping materials that can be easily reused and recycled. Replacing wooden pallets and cardboard boxes with packaging made from sturdy plastic, for example, could offer significant environmental, economic, and social advantages. Plastic pallets and boxes can withstand heavy use to last much longer than conventional packaging; companies can recycle them into new containers again and again when they become damaged; and manufacturers can mold them ergonomically in standard sizes and shapes, which helps minimize injury to the employees who handle them.

Of course, in order to reap the benefits, companies must adjust their standard shipping procedures, since reusable containers must be reclaimed, shipped back to the company that owns them, washed, stacked, and transported back to the point where they will be refilled with goods. The Reusable Packaging Association, based in Arlington, Virginia, has conducted tests to see how RFID (radio-frequency identification) technologies could one day make it easy for companies to track and maintain their supply of reusable shipping materials. JVL

The Future of Product Delivery

Today's delivery system is subpar, at best. Products are shipped, flown, trucked, picked up, and driven home, wasting energy with every step. The answer is to move things, not people, and to move as few things as possible: deliver what we need, eliminate waste.

Some innovations for shipping products from maker to retailer and retailer to buyer have become increasingly popular in the last few years. Take the U.S.-based DVD-rental company Netflix. This product-home-delivery system saves time and money and reduces the number of times people get in their cars to drive back and forth to the video store. Home delivery has become quite popular, and if you live in a dense enough neighborhood, you can get just about anything delivered.

But even home delivery can be inefficient if the delivery company has to make multiple trips to deliver your package. One solution to this is Deutsche Post's Packstation, a personal product-delivery system. Think of packstations as neighborhood parcel ATMs: they hold packages that couldn't be delivered to you directly, and you

claim them with a swipe card and a PIN. These centrally located stations work best in urban neighborhoods, where you can use foot power to get to them.

That's not to say that the future of product delivery excludes brick-and-mortar shops. Some clothing retailers are exploring how to move online shopping back to the street. But to limit the amount of clothing they need to have in stock, retailers are investing in "webfronts." Shoppers test and try on clothes in the store, but when they're ready to check out, they order their purchases online at an automated kiosk, usually at a cheaper price than if they had purchased the same items in the store. Then the goods are delivered from a central warehouse directly to the shopper's home. One retailer that tried this model is the innovative clothing store Nau. Although they have moved mostly online, they were the first to experiment with webfronts. This still-developing model seems best suited to dense neighborhoods where you could walk to the storefront, thus eliminating many drives between home and store. 5K

Post-ownership

We already share many things. A library, for instance, is a system for sharing books. A gym is a system for sharing fitness equipment. New solutions, though, are greatly extending the idea that it's better to have access to something than to own it.

Take tools. Studies suggest that the average power drill is used for ten minutes in its entire lifetime (Thackara 2005) and yet almost half of all American households own one. If you think of all the energy and materials it takes to make, store, and then dispose of those drills—all the plastic and metal parts, all the trucks used to ship them and stores built to sell them, all the landfills they wind up in—the ecological cost of each minute of drilling can be seen as absurdly large. Each hole we put in the wall comes with a chunk of planetary destruction already attached.

What we want is the hole, not the drill. That is, most of us, most of the time, would be perfectly happy not owning the drill itself if we had the ability to make that hole in the wall in a reasonably convenient manner when the need arose.

Enter the tool library. Tool libraries are just what they sound like: places you can go to borrow tools. They're starting to appear all over the world, but Portland, Oregon, seems to have taken a special liking to them, with three already up and running, and talk of more. As the *Oregonian*'s Scott Learn reports, more than three thousand patrons use these libraries to share more than one thousand tools of all description

Opposite: Fuseproject's Y Water bottle, which holds a children's beverage, can be used as part of a building set when empty.

Left: DHL Packstations help delivery drivers make fewer trips.

(many of them donated). The service is free, as long as you can show you're a Portland resident. A patron who uses a wide variety of tools, say on a home-remodeling project, can find that he or she has saved thousands of dollars compared to the cost of buying new tools.

Because they save their patrons money, tool libraries also save their patrons another valuable commodity: time. We've all heard the phrase "time is money," but we rarely stop to think about how true the opposite is, too. Money takes time to earn; every dollar we spend demanded a certain amount of time at work. If we spend it, we'll have to work longer to reach our financial goals. If we avoid spending that dollar, we save ourselves time on the job in the future. So, while sharing systems may sometimes be less convenient in the short term, the money they save us can mean that we actually save serious amounts of time as well: seen as a whole, sharing can be time-saving.

Sharing is getting a lot easier, too. With technology permeating our lives, it's simpler than ever to know where things are, who plans to use them when, whether they're working properly, and how to get them most efficiently. Consider car-sharing. Already a host of car-sharing clubs and cars-on-demand businesses has begun proliferating around the world. With mobile phones, swipe cards, and walkshed technologies, it's now easy to find the nearest car in almost any major city in the world, quickly make a reservation, walk to its location, and swipe our way inside. Indeed, in sufficiently

dense neighborhoods, using a shared car is significantly less difficult than owning our own cars. It can also save you serious cash: not owning a car can save an American family almost $10,000 a year according to a 2010 report by the American Public Transportation Association.

Even better, car sharing offers major ecological benefits. Because much of the ecological impact of a car is incurred during its manufacture, maintenance, and disposal, sharing cars has an immediate and significant ecological benefit. If three people share one car to do the same amount of driving they used to do in three separate cars, they are already riding much lighter on the planet. And it turns out that a lot of people can use the same few cars. Zipcar founder Robin Chase told Worldchanging that they have found that every efficiently used shared car can replace as many as twenty private cars (that is, cars that users either sell or decide not to buy in the first place). That means that the backstory [see Knowing the Backstory, p. 39] impact of all those trips drops to as little as 5 percent of what it once was.

The benefits of car-sharing don't stop there, either. Because car-sharers' driving time is limited and measured (most pay by the hour), they tend to use it more efficiently, making fewer trips and planning routes more effectively, all of which means that they tend to use less fuel to accomplish the same tasks. Also, because the cars are being used more, they spend less time sitting in parking lots; as

car-sharing becomes more common, we will be able to slash the number of parking spaces in our cities, saving more land and energy.

Beyond all the benefits in time, money, and ecological impact, though, there's another nontrivial advantage to sharing systems: fewer hassles. Owning stuff is demanding. We have to select it, buy it, store it, maintain it, upgrade it, and dispose of it properly. One of the advantages of sharing is that someone else does all of that for us, meaning we just don't have to worry about it. We can focus on the satisfaction of using the things; indeed, since we often get to use better stuff than we could afford to buy (nicer tools, cars, work-out equipment), the actual experience of using that stuff can be more pleasant than if we owned it. A life based on access can end up meaning a more affluent existence.

Some sharing companies, in fact, are based on the idea that it's better to be able to use a top-of-the-line product once in a while than own it all the time. Luxury-car-sharing is becoming common in big cities. Seattle's Bag Borrow or Steal offers high-end jewelry, handbags, and accessories in an on-demand rental system, a model that's been called "Netflix for purses." New York's Rent the Runway takes the concept to fashion, allowing women to rent the latest couture for about a tenth of what it would cost to buy. This "borrowed luxury" changes the rules of consumerism, letting frugality and ecological awareness coexist on comfortable terms with a chic lifestyle.

Too often, we've been sold products we don't really need—or at the very least, rarely need—on the basis that these products will bring us closer to the experiences and relationships we crave. Consider the example of the power drill above. Tool-makers advertise power drills as tools for

providing for our loved ones' comfort, thus showing our love for them, winning their approval, or having the glow of a job well done (think of any number of ads showing a manly guy doing work around the house to the great satisfaction of his beaming wife). While we may well want to be handy around the house, the drill is just a means to the larger end. If we had easy access to a drill owned by someone else, we'd be just as happy.

But many of us guys have been taught (largely by advertising) that to be a man is to own tools, so there may be something a bit sissifying about belonging to a tool library. The London design firm Live/Work is trying to figure out ways of talking about, for example, sharing tools in such a way that it's obviously cooler and smarter to be a tool-sharer than a tool-owner, whether or not one cares about the environmental benefits. They call this idea "service envy": as sharing gets easier, sustainability gets more important, and luxury items become more affordable through product-service systems, expect to see people living lives that inspire plenty of it. AS

Reputation Systems

If you have a bad experience with an auto repair shop, the shop probably doesn't care too much—you're just one customer, after all. But if you happen to be a talk-show host or a newspaper writer, the repair shop treats you differently, since you could scare off other customers by spreading word of your bad experience far and wide. Reputation systems extend this power to all of us. By creating publicly available information via Web sites where anyone can share their service experiences, positive or negative, these systems help us to filter out the bad and highlight the good. Many of us, for instance, are familiar with "tagging" systems that let us vote for the things we like, and many of us use them almost every day to pick restaurants (Yelp), movies (Netflix), or books (Amazon).

Such opinion-sharing systems have great potential to increase trust among people who would otherwise be strangers. Those who rely on this kind of "social credit check" benefit from

---

Opposite, left: Zipcar, a successful U.S. car-sharing venture, helps eliminate the need for city dwellers to own cars.
Opposite, right: Atlanta's ToolBank has tools and wheelbarrows for borrowing.

judgments made collectively by groups of peers rather than by a few remote agencies. Reputation systems have been used by travelers sharing travel tips or simply endorsing or warning against places they visited, and by hosts offering lodging. Why shouldn't they be used for sharing rides, or tools, or civic contributions—in addition to information and knowledge? A successful reputation system must filter out ignoramuses and shills, survive legal challenges from parties who rate poorly, and account for reasonable differences of opinion. But when done right—with the interests of users in mind, with the goal of shining a spotlight on our better options—reputation systems foster good work and good deeds. HM

Creative Infill

In Jackson, Wyoming, the Everest Momo Shack is a family-owned café that in the evening serves the Nepalese dumplings that give the place its name. However, if you show up during the day you'll find a crew of bearded, suntanned, and decidedly American cooks serving up overstuffed breakfast burritos. By day, it's a burrito joint; four nights each week, it's the Momo Shack. Two businesses, each with unique menu and ambience, share one restaurant.

Much of the built (and furnished) environment stands empty and unused at any given time. Cafés in the financial district are closed at dinnertime; restaurants that specialize in dinner fare are silent until mid-afternoon; parking lots that fill during the workweek are largely vacant after 6:00 p.m. and on weekends. But imagine putting those darkened rooms, kitchens, galleries, and cafés—and those empty outdoor spaces—to use. What would you fill them with?

Taking advantage of these spaces requires letting go of (or at least becoming flexible about) the idea of permanence. Creating harmony, when both owner and sharer use the same space fluidly, requires a relaxation of control by both parties, and that can take some getting used to. How can we relinquish the idea that ownership equals success, that permanence means we've "made it"? Ownership has its benefits, but renters retain an enviable flexibility and a less tangible bonus from impermanence: the cachet of novelty. JVL

Third Place Studios

If expert artisans want to open a shop that's fully equipped to let them do their thing—carpentry, bike maintenance, sewing, etc.—it can be an expensive up-front investment. But by pairing their excess (in this case, the evening or weekend time that their studio sits idle) with a community need (hobbyists seeking limited access to equipment and resources), they can reach an elegant solution.

That solution might be thought of as a third place studio (referring to Ray Oldenburg's concept of third places—spaces that are neither strictly workplaces nor homes). The idea of the shared artisan studio is one of the concepts that appears in *Collaborative Services: Social Innovation and Design for Sustainability*, a two-hundred-page study on product-service systems and similar concepts produced by sustainable design visionaries François Jégou and Ezio Manzini. The report contains a wealth of great ideas for creating new shared services and making existing models more appealing and effective.

For example, the Wood Atelier would allow "gradual access to a professional carpentry workshop, meeting the personal needs and taking into account the skill level of each user and providing a space where people can benefit from the experience of the others."

According to this plan, members could access a fully equipped carpentry shop as needed to work on their own projects. An electronic key would let them enter the space and would give them access to certain pieces of equipment. Only the machines that a particular member was qualified to operate would be accessible through his or her specific key, so the key system doubles as a means of ensuring safe and responsible behavior.

Several versions of third place studios are already thriving. In 2005 Wendy Tremayne, an artist, teacher, event producer, and all-around innovator, launched Swap-O-Rama-Rama, a model for clothing swap-and-alter extravaganzas that help people make "street ready vintage" in cities around the world. Another model is being used by Seattle's Metrix Create:Space [see Engineer It Yourself, p. 89], a "hackerspace" where makers can come together to share ideas and clever inventions, and enjoy low-cost access to 3-D printers, laser cutters, and electronics tools. In combination, Metrix offers more tool capacity than a small electronics shop, without users having to own a single soldering iron—and both the coffee and the camaraderie are free. JVL

Designing a Sustainable World

▬▬▬▬   RESOURCES

Collaborative Services: Social Innovation and Design for Sustainability by François Jégou and Ezio Manzini
From shared carpentry studios to modern hitchhiking systems, this innovative study by sustainable design visionaries Jégou and Manzini demonstrates that owning less, sharing more, and utilizing systems that make cooperation easy could propel us toward a new future of sustainable communities that can maximize the potential of our space, time, and energy.

Shareable
http://shareable.net
Shareable is a fun and accessible online magazine dedicated to, well, sharing. From worker-owned cooperatives to bike-sharing ventures to hackers' tools—if it fosters collaboration, *Shareable* covers it. Many articles—such as "How to Turn an Old Payphone into a Library" and "How to Help Your Neighbors Go Solar"—are in tutorial form.

The critical issue—for people, organizations, and governments alike—is knowing where we want to be. The imaginary, an alternative cultural vision, is vital in shaping expectations and driving transformational change. Shared visions act as forces of innovation, and what designers can do—what we all can do—is imagine some situation or condition that does not yet exist but describe it in sufficient detail that it appears to be a desirable new version of the real world.
     John Thackara, *In the Bubble*

▬▬▬▬   For better or for worse, the material stuff that surrounds us shapes our lives. Products have brought what is arguably the zenith of human comfort to those who can afford them. We're knee-deep in useful things such as refrigerators and quality footwear, yet we're also laden with the detritus of the last generation of objects. The periphery of our comfort zone is lined with waste.

     The fact that all stuff—every ballpoint pen, every pair of flip-flops—was made with intention is almost as astounding as the sheer number of things around the world. Some designer ensured that it would take scarcely any thought to use our coffee percolator. While we weren't paying attention, the designer also made sure that it would look embarrassingly out-of-date as soon as possible. This habit of designing for obsolescence, using centuries-old

This David Hertz–designed coffee table is made using Syndecrete, a composite made from natural minerals and recycled materials.

manufacturing technologies, has created a huge set of challenges. We could resolve them by collectively renouncing all but the most basic of material comforts. Alternatively, we could accept the status quo. But while one approach seems retrograde, doomed to failure, the other is simply unthinkable. Perhaps our ticket to a better, more sustainable future is to do what human beings do best, given the chance—design our way out of the conundrum.

The inventor Edwin Land once referred to creative acts such as design as a "sudden cessation of stupidity." The twenty-first century has already seen a huge wave of such moments, and we have had the opportunity to make designed things more sustainable. We're not lacking in creative acts, ideas, or strategies: we have them in spades. Our greater challenge lies in knitting all of these together.

Product design isn't merely architecture for small things: it's a field in which a whole set of dynamic and unpredictable factors must be considered. We manufacture consumer objects by the thousands, and we release them into the world like flocks of birds. Today's product designer often has little control over where these objects go, how they are used, whether they get hacked, axed, or modified, and how they're disposed of when they break or wear out. Still, most of an object's ecological impact is determined at the design stage, so in this seeming chaos is a vast, often untapped opportunity for smarter, more effective design.

One thing that product designers have that architects lack is speed: things can be cranked out in a fraction of the time it takes for a building to be developed. The field of product design has also evolved quickly. In 2000, the well-known science-fiction author and renowned design visionary Bruce Sterling released his "Viridian Design Manifesto," in which he called for a completely new approach to industry, design, and "social engineering." The manifesto made an appeal for "intensely glamorous environmentally sound products," goods that would be irresistible to consumers for their sheer gorgeousness, that would establish a market in which buying unsustainable products would amount to fashion suicide. A decade later, Sterling's vision is coming to fruition.

Demand for truly ecofriendly products is now growing so fast designers can't keep up. Well into the 1990s, ecologically responsible furniture amounted to little more than globs of recycled plastic melted into the shape of chairs and sofas; today there's a good chance that a sleek, top-of-the-line office chair might be the most ecologically responsible choice.

Most of the green products on the shelf today are mere half-steps, metaphorical references to sustainability. A solar cell-phone charger should be more than a friendly, guilt-absolving talisman with an ecosensitive sheen. It should be made, used, and retired with biological cleverness and the lightest of impacts. Tiny, hesitant improvements are a terrific way

of perpetuating a broken system, but many of the components for fully overhauling this system are already here, waiting to be assembled. Sustainability can be applied to anything that's made.

We must bring about a full-scale convergence of sustainable approaches. Humans are relentless tinkerers; production and industry are central obsessions. Since the mid-1990s, crafty ecodesign has been seized upon, commodified, made bright and clean. We now know how to turn unneeded grass into cabinets, to weave flame-retardant cloth that will compost in a field, to send electronics back to their makers to be disassembled and made anew. We can power our toxin-free laptops by teasing energy out of the sun.

In trying to create this change, designers can spend a lot of time fussing about technical details that are often outside their purview, thereby failing to play to their greatest strengths. The liberation of sustainable design will mean changing the way we compose and conceive of our material world, piece by piece. Designers may be able to come up with great solutions for the complex challenges that humans create, yet they alone can't solve the ecological design problem. Businesspeople decide what gets made. Governments make rules. The global market rolls on. And at every moment we all make decisions to buy, to demand, to repair, or to opt out.

Design guru John Thackara writes: "We've built a technology-focused society that is remarkable on means, but hazy about ends. It's no longer clear to which question all this stuff—tech—is an answer, or what value it adds to our lives." If we step back from the surfeit of stuff, we can see the systems for change orbiting around us, but only if we get involved will they be able to maintain their momentum. We decide whether to share things with our neighbors or hoard them in the attic. We're the ones who can alter our clothing, customize our furniture, and choose to use things for years longer than is expected. Rather than waiting for green products to appear—stamped, sanctioned, and ready—we can demand them, or create them ourselves. □□

■■■■   RESOURCES

Autodesk Sustainability Workshop
http://students.autodesk.com/?nd=
sustainable_home
Worldchangers Dawn Danby and Jer Faludi have collaborated with Autodesk to create an excellent online workshop outlining the essential concepts of sustainable design. Tutorials cover such topics as "Whole Systems Design" and "Lightweighting." The workshop was created with mechanical engineers—specifically engineering students and their educators—in mind, and the language and tips provided are technical and actionable.

In the Bubble by John Thackara (MIT Press, 2005) John Thackara has been tracing the cutting edge of design and sustainability long enough to see how our cultivated obsessions with technology actually operate on a grand scale. Rather than microscopes, he contends, we need "macroscopes" to see the patterns and implications of all our small design decisions. Design exists, after all, to serve human

Opposite, left: These 100 percent recyclable Dalsouple rubber flooring tiles are produced in a system that recycles almost all of the waste generated during manufacture.
Opposite, right: These hay and resin garden chairs designed by Jurgen Bey for Droog Design can be composted at the end of their lifespan.
Left: TranSglass, designed by Emma Woofenden and Tord Boontje, is glassware made from recycled wine and beer bottles.

ends, and some of Thackara's most compelling and critical ideas focus on the concept of designing less for technology and more for people.

"Although many people perceive design to be all about appearances, design is not just about the way things look. Design is also about the way things are used; how they are communicated to the world; and the way they are produced. The dance of the big and the small entails a new kind of design. It involves a relationship between subject and object and a commitment to think about the consequences of design actions before we take them, in a state of mind—design mindfulness—that values place, time, and cultural difference."

Eternally Yours: Time in Design by Ed van Hinte (010 Publishers, 2005)
Durability and endurance create interesting enough challenges to have preoccupied the Eternally Yours Foundation for eight years. Their work is characterized by radically innovative engineering, as well as the sort of delicious Dutch product design that edges into conceptual art. They celebrate the objects we want to keep in our possession, and they wrestle with the paradoxes of longevity: long-lasting things can mean less consumption—or the preservation of mistakes.

This book is the result: a luxurious, distinctive little publication bound in embossed gold foil, with an exquisite binding that exudes care and preciousness. You'll want to keep it—which is exactly the point.

ecoDesign: The Sourcebook by Alastair Fuad-Luke (Chronicle Books, 2002)
Although as of yet there is no such thing as a truly sustainable product on the market, Alastair Fuad-Luke's *ecoDesign* (*The Eco-Design Handbook: A Complete Sourcebook for the Home and Office* in its second edition) is a pragmatic look at the current approaches, including everything from multifunctional furniture to innovative materials, solar gizmos, and energy-efficient refrigerators. His is the one and only sourcebook to catalog the various attempts at making sustainable products—as well as the materials, organizations, and designers responsible for the prototypes. Heavy on pictures and light on theory, *ecoDesign* celebrates any and every approach to sustainable product design,

even if the results are marginal. Though it clearly illustrates how much farther we have to go, the sourcebook is an important early indicator that there are hundreds of designers and engineers out there working hard to reimagine products, using an entirely new set of criteria.

The Total Beauty of Sustainable Products by Edwin Datschefski (Rotovision, 2001)
As Edwin Datschefski writes, "Only one in 10,000 products is designed with the environment in mind. Can a product really represent the pinnacle of mankind's genius if it is made using polluting methods?"

Datschefski is a real enthusiast for sustainable alternatives—as well as a passionate collector of examples. After years spent tracking products at the forefront of green design, he happily casts aside a minefield of jargon in discussing the way things are made. His simple rules—that things must be cyclic, solar, and safe; that an object's total beauty must not be undermined by hidden impacts—are a refreshing reminder that products need not be complicated to be effective.

Casting a wide net in his estimation— over objects as well as buildings and food— Datschefski contends that almost all environmental destruction is related in some way to unsustainable products. This doesn't stop him from uncovering a wealth of well-considered alternatives, each approaching sustainability from a slightly different angle. None are perfect, but they're all real, here, and pointing energetically toward the future.

Design Is the Problem: The Future of Design Must Be Sustainable by Nathan Shedroff (Rosenfeld Media, 2009)
The title says it all: Shedroff offers a clear and comprehensive overview of all the possible mistakes a designer could make while offering practical, real-world strategies for green design. He touches on all of the major approaches, from Cradle to Cradle thinking to biomimcry to lifecycle analysis, pointing out the gaps where they exist, and also delves into dematerialization, product-service systems, "informationalization" (switching from physical to digital), and design for durability.

Design for Development

While sitting with a group of students, Japanese designer Isao Hosoe pulls out a carefully folded map of Venice. The paper is precisely creased into a field of tiny hills, perfectly regular, which collapses into a pocket-size package. As he opens and closes it, the map folds with a single movement like an accordion. It has no moving parts, is made of common materials, and is embedded with no electronics. But this map, says Hosoe, is an ideal illustration of high technology: an object that is perfect for its context, as simple as it can possibly be. Those of us who want sustainable solutions for the world's poorest could learn a lot by taking this simple notion to heart. Combined with local knowledge and a willingness to listen, a sense of context is paramount if design is to succeed in the Global South.

Not all design for development incorporates the high technology of mobile phones, computers, or solar panels [see Green Power, p. 146]. In extremely rural areas, high tech may refer to deceptively simple but ingenious designs that don't require specialized materials or equipment to build or repair. For example, for a school on the Tibetan plateau, the international design and consultancy firm Arup created a latrine that uses the simplest of technologies to achieve a clean, low-odor washroom. The Ventilated Improved Pit (VIP) is a waterless toilet with a solar-operated flue that sucks fresh air through the latrine, down the pit, and out a vent. The mechanism is ideally matched to its environment, requiring no power or water infrastructure to be completely effective. It's a model of appropriate humanitarian design, influenced by the needs of the users, not solely by the ideas of foreign designers.

This kind of appropriate technology has been around for a long time. It's great when it works, but professional designers who don't live and work in, say, rural Kenya frequently lack the experience and insight to see where long-lasting solutions are hiding. Without knowing communities deeply, or getting local folks to participate, well-intentioned efforts risk becoming mere theoretical exercises.

Successful projects emerge when nonlocal designers take a hybrid approach: they may still bring in expertise from the outside, but they co-create solutions with the people in the communities they've come to serve. Even better, some of the field's best innovators are now focusing on developing the capacity for local people to become inventors, engineers, and designers themselves. ◻◻

Amy Smith: The Best Solutions Are Hiding in Plain Sight

In Africa, the women are the farmers. Women invented domesticated crops. If you're talking to the right people, they should be a group of elderly women with their hair in scarves.
      Amy Smith

Ever since she was a Peace Corps volunteer in Botswana in the 1980s, the Massachusetts Institute of Technology's Amy Smith wanted to work with people in the Global South to develop tools that would improve their lives. She's since brought engineering knowledge to communities that were formerly unable to test or purify drinking water or efficiently grind grain into flour. Whether they involved passively purifying water with the sun or fueling cooking with agricultural waste instead of trees, Smith's collaborative solutions have achieved high-tech brilliance with simple ingredients.

Take her Phase-change Incubator, for instance. In many Ugandan communities, lab workers can't access a reliable source of electricity.

But to test for bacteria (and therefore provide the correct medication), they must incubate samples at a precise temperature for twenty-four hours. Smith solved this problem by using direct heat instead of direct current, heating a chemical compound within the incubator to create a "phase-change" reaction that would maintain a steady temperature for long periods of time. For Honduras, D-Lab created a water-testing kit that costs twenty U.S. dollars, a fraction of the thousand U.S. dollars conventional apparatuses cost.

Smith and her D-Lab have overcome long-neglected fundamental challenges by taking engineers into the field and teaching them how to work with people in the developing world to overcome their obstacles. Together they have worked to uncover small solutions to big problems, solutions that are always elegant in their simplicity.

Many of the daily challenges faced by the developing world's communities are unknown to those outside. For instance, making just a few pounds of flour from grain takes about an hour of labor. A typical hammer mill, which cuts this time to just over a minute, employs a tiny replacement screen that commonly breaks down, rendering the machine useless. Smith created a screenless hammer mill that cleverly uses airflow to separate hulls from grain. Like many of the best designs for people living in the Global South, the hammer mill isn't patented, allowing wide access to the technology.

In the last few years, Smith's D-Lab has expanded well beyond just design and invention to include thirteen interdisciplinary classes, addressing topics such as dissemination, new ventures,

Above and opposite, left: People in Ghana making clean-burning charcoal briquettes to replace the need to burn firewood in deforested areas.
Opposite, right: Whirlwind's cheap, rugged wheelchairs are changing lives in the developing world.

health, and energy. Smith's philosophical emphasis has changed as well: D-Lab is working to go beyond participatory design and support Creative Capacity Building—with the notion that people can be the creators of their own technology solutions, not just the users or recipients.

Says Smith, "One of the things that we really want to do is turn the standard model of development upside down, and get away from the condescending giving away of technologies, and move to empowering people to create their own technologies.

"Creativity exists in these communities. And we strive to nurture that creativity and give people the confidence to believe that they can be making all sorts of things—that they can create technology, or work in partnership to create it.

"So we try to engage people throughout the entire design process, building on the Appropriate Technology and Participatory Development movements. The idea of Creative Capacity Building is that you engage with people to create innovative solutions to create technologies. That enables you to do co-creation, where designers and users work together to create solutions that evolve technologies. And that can't happen unless people feel comfortable about themselves as creators and designers." □□

Mobility: Ralf Hotchkiss and Whirlwind Wheelchair International

While *confined* is a word often heard in reference to wheelchairs, for persons with mobility disabilities a wheelchair is a liberating tool. Unfortunately, it's a tool unavailable to millions of poor people in need of one around the world. Engineer and long-time mobility advocate Ralf Hotchkiss has pointed out that of the 20 million people worldwide who need wheelchairs, 98 percent don't have one. For people injured by disease or war, a wheelchair can be a life-changing gift.

Hotchkiss has been working to bring mobility to such people in developing nations since 1980. He began building his own custom wheelchairs after a severe injury left him with paraplegia; at the time, American wheelchairs were prohibitively expensive, and it only made sense to him to build them from scratch. In his travels to Nicaragua, Hotchkiss discovered that wheelchairs were even more expensive there. However, the local people he met who used wheelchairs had insights that hadn't occurred to him. So Hotchkiss began working with people in the developing world to design wheelchairs appropriate to their location.

Of the organizations that are working for mobility, Hotchkiss's organization, Whirlwind Wheelchair International, is distinguished by its bottom-up approach; it focuses on designing and training over donation. Since each community comes with different terrain and with unique limitations, Whirlwind works on the ground, designing for a local context—and is committed to producing with local materials and skills; community building and local pride come with collaboration. Whirlwind compares its design development process to the open-source-software model; it promotes open access to knowledge about evolving wheelchair designs.

This kind of thinking is essential to sustaining a community. Having worked in more

than forty-five countries, Whirlwind has found that local differences—terrain, even the size of people in one community versus another—vary considerably. Whirlwind's rugged, innovative chairs are cheap, they work on unpaved roads, and they can be repaired with local materials. They're also lightweight, foldable, and able to navigate steep slopes without tipping—a problem with some conventional wheelchairs. Whirlwind has also created wheelchairs for very small children. Experience and support have allowed the initiative to help communities scale up their production so that they can produce chairs in larger volumes, to reach more users. Fundamentally, though, Whirlwind's work is about access. As Whirlwind designer Marc Krizack has written on the Whirlwind Wheelchair International Web site, "Providing wheelchairs is not about wheelchairs. It is about providing people with the one thing they need to move out into their own communities—to go where the action is. It is about integrating people with disabilities into their society." □□

Engineer It Yourself

The United States used to be a nation of tinkerers and inventors—what happened? Did they all go away when the megamarts moved in? Turns out, they're still out there, and they're closer than you think. Quietly, over the last few years, a small army of makers has been publishing discoveries, connecting with one another, and using the Internet to "make versus take." Some of us have been making things ourselves for years, but until now it was never possible to go so smoothly from idea to research to meeting other makers to producing a finished collaborative project that could be shared around the planet. The collection of tools, their ease of use, and the way they all work with one another is turning anyone with curiosity into an engineer. The physical objects around us are beginning to resemble computer code—they are describable and replicable. People are sharing, people are making things—and there's no stopping them. We can all vote with our ideas by bringing them into reality. On the Instructables Web site, anyone can share their creations with the world by posting how-tos, recipes, step-by-step guides, and annotated photos.

We're seconds away in Internet time from being able to literally fabricate our ideas almost immediately. Imagine designing a cell-phone cover and printing it out on a 3-D printer just as you would print a document on a paper printer. Already—from a company called eMachineShop—you can

The folks at Squid Labs deploy a candle-powered hot-air balloon. Directions for making the balloon are available on Instructables.com.

download free software, design an object, send off the file, and have the part sent to your door. For $1,000 you can put together your own "fab lab," a fabrication laboratory of open-source computer-controlled design and manufacturing equipment. Just a few years ago this would have required a multimillion-dollar investment; soon it will be cheaper than a high-end TV. The Center for Bits and Atoms at the Massachusetts Institute of Technology is dropping fab labs around the world, with the goal that they will become self-sustaining.

When anyone and everyone has the means to solve their own puzzles and problems, to share their ideas and works, and to invent new things, the creative human spirit will express itself in so many ways that it is impossible to predict just what we'll build together as citizen engineers. PT

Instructables

Instructables.com, the brainchild of half a dozen or so MIT PhDs, is an online collaborative repository of how-tos that anyone can access to learn how to make just about anything, and to share their own inventions. Instructions are linear, similar to recipes, and they're available for everything from a 3-D chocolate printer to home-canned applesauce to self-replicating robots. Makers join the site, upload photographs of their projects, tag photos with expanded information, then invite the world to comment or improve upon their designs. Take a look at the following Instructables' sample:

Make Your Own Pedal-powered Air Compressor: What can you do with an old electric motor and a bicycle? Make a pedal-powered air compressor to build other things, of course. Just grab an old motor mount and install an axle with one fixed cog and belt pulley. Welding the bike frame and handlebars and rigging a chair yield a Mad Max–like device that can reach up to fifty pounds per square inch in about fifteen minutes of pedaling. *Etch Your Own Circuit Boards:* If you have an itch to design your own electronics, you'll inevitably need a circuit board. Countries around the world

stamp these out by the hundred thousands, but you can make your own. Use a laser printer or copier to print out your electronic design on transparency paper, then transfer the toner from the paper onto a copper board by heating it with an iron. Next up, use some etching solution to remove the copper from the portions of the copper board not covered by the toner. After giving the board a quick scrub to remove the toner (your design will remain on the board in copper, which was protected from the etching solution by the toner), you're ready to drill some holes in the board for wiring. PT

Maker's Bill of Rights

Built-in hackability may seem like an oxymoron, but *Make* magazine has published a Maker's Bill of Rights to demand just that—hackability in products. Interestingly, the things that make a device hackable are the same things that make a device repairable and upgradeable, so design-for-hacking is also green design.

The Maker's Bill of Rights is as follows:

- Meaningful and specific parts lists shall be included.
- Cases shall be easy to open.
- Batteries shall be replaceable.
- Special tools are allowed only for darn good reasons.
- Profiting by selling expensive special tools is wrong, and not making special tools available is even worse.
- Torx is OK; tamperproof is rarely OK.
- Components, not entire subassemblies, shall be replaceable.
- Consumables, like fuses and filters, shall be easy to access.
- Circuit boards shall be commented.

Opposite, left: Makers discuss a project at Seattle's Metrix Create:Space.

Opposite, right: These fab lab students in Ghana are working on a vortex refrigeration system, which could, inexpensively, keep everything from food to vaccines cold, 2005.

- Power from USB is good; power from proprietary power adapters is bad.
- Standard connecters shall have pinouts defined.
- If it snaps shut, it shall snap open.
- Screws better than glues.
- Docs and drivers shall have permalinks and shall reside for all perpetuity at archive.org.
- Ease of repair shall be a design ideal, not an afterthought.
- Metric or standard, not both.
- Schematics shall be included.

Why is design for hackability the same as design for long lifetime? Because the things a hacker wants to do to a device today (for instance, to add memory, storage, faster processing, or peripheral extensions) are the same things required to keep a device from becoming obsolete years from now (when it will have to be faster/have more storage/connect to peripheral X, just to stay usable). Many devices have proven useful long past their original lifetimes—the Beowulf project has used old 486 and Pentium I computers (junk to any modern computer user; obsolete nearly ten years ago) to create "a computer which can operate in the gigaflop range" (better than all but the highest-end personal computers available today).

Design for hackability is also green design because when a device dies, it's usually just one part dying before the rest. How many times have you had nonreplaceable batteries die in a device? Or had your cell phone's screen break while the phone itself still functions? If every product came with schematics and manuals archived in perpetuity, as Make's list suggests, home users could get this knowledge and potentially save their device from the grave—if they're geek enough.

So let's hear it for the Maker's Bill of Rights, and hope more companies open their products up to hackability and life extension. JJF

The Neighborhood Fab Lab

Where do you go when you need to solder, make 3-D plastic printouts, and get a cup of coffee? Your friendly neighborhood hackerspace, of course.

Seattle's Metrix Create:Space is just one such spot for tinkering, etching, fabbing, and hanging out. A vending machine dispenses wires and solder (and candy); instructors teach open-to-the-public courses like Introduction to Electronics; and members pay monthly or hourly rates to use the laser cutter or MakerBot (a robotic fabbing machine).

Speaking of MakerBot, that company may well succeed in putting a fab lab in every apartment. Though incredibly cool in theory, fab labs are generally way too pricey for the average DIYer. But MakerBot's mini fab labs sell for under $1,000. And in true maker spirit, "the kits are modular, modifiable, and built to be hacked." CB

RESOURCES

Make Magazine
http://www.makezine.com
Make is what you'd get if your school's science fair was run by hackers, home energy nuts, and mad inventors in Day-Glo lab coats. Every issue bends

your mind. Even for those of us who couldn't solder a circuit if the fate of the world hung in the balance, it's great fun. AS

ReadyMade: How to Make (Almost) Everything by Shoshana Berger and Grace Hawthorne (Clarkson Potter, 2005)
This "do-it-yourself primer" by the cofounders of *ReadyMade* magazine includes projects that range from creating an Eames-style bookshelf out of discarded dresser drawers to fashioning a messenger bag from those wasteful wrappers that newspapers come sealed in when they land on our doorsteps. Informative sections detail the history and environmental legacy of our most commonly used materials—paper, plastic, wood, metal, glass, and fabric.

The book is written in *ReadyMade's* signature casual, humorous style. Die-hard DIYers might find it a bit too jokey at times—features like "How to Avoid Plastic Surgery" and "Iron Man: A Look Back at the Origins of Heavy Metal" are a questionable use of the (recycled) paper they're printed on. But the projects presented here are clearly illustrated and well explained, and will provide plenty of fodder for first-timers and reuse veterans alike. As the authors put it, "Perhaps you will try making a thing or two. Perhaps you only imagine the day when you will make something. Either way, we hope that the projects you see here have a catalytic effect, inspiring you to rethink the purpose of an old telephone book or bicycle wheel." CB

Bre Pettis: I Make Things
http://www.brepettis.com/blog/
Hyperactive inventor Bre Pettis is the cofounder of MakerBot Industries (of $1,000 fab lab fame), Thingiverse.com, and the Brooklyn hacker collective NYCResistor. His blog is a wealth of maker wisdom, fabbing breakthroughs, and video tutorials.

Art Meets Technology

We live in a world where mobile technologies, genetically modified organisms, and virtual realities are commonplace, and increasingly define our lives. People from a vast range of disciplines now use their skills to create objects that not only push the edge of innovative technology, but invite us to question our relationship to it, to comment on it, to use it for something other than its expected purpose, or to hack it ourselves.

The way artists use and misuse emerging technologies in their work can prompt deeper reflection about our society and its relationship to technology than a two-hundred-page report written by eminent sociologists can. But what really sets such work apart is its frequent exploration of issues that are immediately and achingly relevant. Scientific advancements, technological change, or notions about the environment fall into sharp relief when artists use familiar electronic detritus as raw material. Traditionally, there has been a divide between the mastery of hard technologies and their use as a medium for commentary, but that's changing fast.

Imagine a cell phone that monitored your location using networked surveillance sensors within the phone, and sent text messages to help you keep track of others. This is the premise behind LOCA: Location Oriented Critical Arts, a Finnish project that explores the use of consumer gadgets as nodes for monitoring networks. The idea could be both sinister and constructive; LOCA's projects test both sides of the fence.

If the idea of being tracked stirs uneasiness, there are other great

applications for sensing technologies. Myriel Milicevic's Neighbourhood Satellites allow users to playfully monitor the conditions of their environment through a handheld gadget that measures air quality, light, and cell-phone reception.

On another plane altogether, micro-Revolt's knitPro is a Web application for generating knitting patterns as protests against sweatshops. You can upload digital images of your choosing, and the application will generate a pattern, on a scalable graph, for knit, crochet, needlepoint, or cross-stitch projects.

Cultural artifacts such as these use technology to throw light on themselves. Their authors, however, often don't regard themselves as media artists but as engineers, architects, designers, or hackers. Those who do define themselves as artists usually operate outside contemporary art circles; you won't find their work in mainstream art exhibitions, magazines, or galleries.

Regardless of context, these works accomplish what art should accomplish: they trigger new experiences that transform our perceptions of what is and what could be. It's a whole new realm where art meets technology. DD & RO

Graphic novel–style panels explain a "mission" in Jane McGonigal's interactive game EVOKE.

Hug Shirt

The Hug Shirt, developed by Cute Circuits, allows you to feel the physical closeness of a distant loved one by generating the sensation of being hugged. How is this possible?

Embedded sensors and electronics in the shirts are able to pick up signals such as a heartbeat and body temperature from a loved one at the other end of a mobile phone. When the sensors process the signal, embedded mechanisms in the shirt re-create the physical pressure and warmth of a real hug. RD

EVOKE

Celebrated designer Jane McGonigal hopes to someday see a game developer win the Nobel Peace Prize. McGonigal has created several ambitious alternate-reality games that tackle real-world issues ranging from energy shortages to health pandemics.

A recent project, EVOKE, which she developed for the World Bank Institute, is a massive multiplayer game that follows fictional social innovators as they travel the world to solve crises. The game's narration is beautifully illustrated, written up in the style of a graphic novel. Players take on missions in which they try to figure out how to scale up small local solutions to fix big problems. One scenario exploring food security, for example, places the user in Tokyo in the future, after a famine has struck. Each mission has three components: learn, act, and imagine. In the Tokyo scenario, players learn by reading about food security, act by increasing the food security of one person in real life (for example, starting or volunteering at a community garden), and imagine what a meal of the future would look like. They share their ideas with other players via blog posts and video.

EVOKE was designed to run in seasons; the initial phase of the project included ten different episodes over several weeks. Players received feedback on their plans from social-innovation and World Bank Institute experts. After the season ended, the players with the best solutions were given year-long online mentorships and seed money to help develop their ideas for use in the real world.

As McGonigal told Worldchanging in an interview by Susie Boss, "When people think of computer or video games, they often think of playing in a virtual world that doesn't exist in reality. But alternate reality game designers are trying to get people to play in the real world. We want people to bring the same curiosity, wonder, and optimism that you feel when playing your favorite video games into your real lives and real problems." CB

Carbon-sniffing Robots

We live in a world of flows and systems that remain largely opaque to us. Making invisible things visible opens a window onto how our world actually functions—and sometimes suggests tactics for improving the world. We can't see the air, but that doesn't mean we're breathing free and clear. From off-gassing paints to factory emissions, potential health hazards hang thick in our air.

In response to this silent threat, artist Sabrina Raaf has created a carbon-sniffing robot.

This squat automated vehicle patrols the periphery of a room armed with a green crayon. Every few inches, the robot takes a reading of the carbon dioxide level in that particular spot and makes a vertical mark—corresponding with the CO_2 concentration—on the wall. The accumulation of green lines begins to resemble grass, its growth visible to—and entirely determined by—gallery visitors. The end result is a chart of the air quality in the space throughout the installation, and a reminder that, although we can't always see it, our lives are changing the air itself. RD

■■■■■   RESOURCES

Telepresence and Bio Art: Networking Humans, Rabbits, and Robots by Eduardo Kac (The University of Michigan Press, 2005)
Recognized worldwide for his interactive Internet installations, bio-art pioneer Eduardo Kac documents in this landmark book the evolution of his field—art that bridges the divide between biology, technology, and innovation. Using examples from his own cadre of worldchanging "events," Kac argues, "telepresence works have the power to contribute to a relativistic view of contemporary experience and at the same time create a new domain of action, perception, and interaction."

Creative Capital Foundation
http://www.creative-capital.org
Creative Capital is a different kind of arts funder: the foundation provides rigorously screened artists not only with sizable grants, but with professional development opportunities and critical connections. It supports both artists' projects and the artists themselves over an extended period of time, picking artists whose work has the potential for real impact in the world—artists like Sabrina Raaf, Red-Dive, and Critical Art Ensemble. If you want to know where to look for the next generation of worldchanging artists, keep an eye out for who Creative Capital is funding.

Ars Electronica
http://www.aec.net
The Ars Electronica annual festival (and the companion organization the Ars Electronica Center) consistently presents the most cutting-edge examples of work springing from the intersection of art and technology, to the extent that attending their annual show has become something of a pilgrimage among certain crowds. There are many people exploring the fringes of media arts and digital culture, and to some very real degree, they all orbit around Ars Electronica.

Opposite, left: KnitPro is a free Web application that helps users create their own subversive needlework patterns.
Opposite, right: The Hug Shirt delivers virtual hugs long-distance.
Above: Sabrina Raaf's *Grower* exhibit includes a carbon-sniffing robot that draws a green line on the wall every few seconds to represent the shifting CO_2 levels in the air.

Collaborative Design

Most of the newer objects in our lives started out as pure data. The curves on a Prius automobile share a digital hand-print with eyeglasses and ballpoint pens. While still in its virtual, 3-D form, digitized design is just information: a designer can e-mail a half-formed 3-D object to Singapore, and have a colleague manipulate it and pass it back. It can then be tested and even prototyped on demand. This is remarkable: it wasn't long ago that a standing army of machinists and draftspeople was needed to crank out detailed, hand-machined proto-types in model shops. Designers now have the freedom to refine and discard quickly and digitally.

Your toothbrush, your mobile phone: in every case, a designer used complex, powerful 3-D design software to make it, fitting pieces together and spin-ning them around in virtual space. There's nothing inherently green about this process, with the small exception of all the prototypes that didn't need to be machined by hand. Software files, however, are light-weight: easy to share and distribute. Soft-ware can transform data into real objects through quick fabbing technology, which is getting cheaper by the minute. Access to a team of skilled model makers used to be a huge barrier to making complex things, and now that barrier is gone. Product designer Ronen Kadushin makes his work available online as "Open Design," an extension of the open-source-software model.

Design is, and always has been, a collaborative field. Green design—which involves even more people, including recy-clers, disassemblers, and chemists—is even more so. But if one of the barriers to sus-tainable design has been that we, as users, haven't been able to make the rules, the democratization of design tools means that more people can enter the game.

Portable Light

For nearly as long as it's been available, electric light has relied upon heavy infrastructure. To light our homes, we must link into a network of wiring that brings electricity and provides a physical connection to power plants far away. On or off the grid, access to electricity requires serious investment. On top of that, most lighting systems are fragile, and most solar photovoltaic systems cumbersome. Until very recently, both were best suited to static use in buildings.

In Mexico's Sierra Madre mountains, the seminomadic Huichol (or Wirrarika) travel four hundred miles through rugged terrain during their annual pilgrimage, often on foot. During the wet and dry seasons, they return to the Sierra Madre to farm. Yet without electricity, the Huichol have limited access to education and employment. After sundown they can't see to read, work, or study, and many of them end up leaving for the cities to join the industrialized economy. Paradoxically, it's not electricity, but the lack of it, that poses a threat to Huichol culture. There are no grid connections in the mountains, and the means of delivering electricity are too impractical and expensive to serve the needs of the Huichol.

So it goes with older technologies. But the last few years have seen new developments in both light-emitting diode (LED) [see Light-ing, p. 132] technology and flexible, lightweight photovoltaics. Both are light and durable, and when combined, they're essentially self-powering. The use of high-brightness light-emitting diodes (HBLEDs) means that extremely bright, efficient light can be produced by a single miniature diode powered by small solar panels. When architect and interdisciplinary designer Sheila Kennedy and her colleagues traveled into the Sierra Madre, they unexpectedly saw the potential to apply these

The Portable Light demonstrates how high technology and collaborative approaches can improve the lives of people in remote communities.

new, transformative technologies to mobile light sources. Kennedy, who has embedded LEDs into fabric, conceived of a way to allow the Huichol distributed, decentralized access to light, enabling children to read and adults to work while still preserving their nomadic culture.

The resulting project, Portable Light, separated lighting and solar technology from permanent structures to create something entirely new. Kennedy's materials-research firm MATx first consulted and collaborated with Huichol community leaders to discern their needs. University of Michigan students then devised a whole series of self-powering prototypes based on a flexible skeleton of lights, batteries, and photovoltaics; the units are easy to wear or carry, and provide a range of power capacity. After five hours in the sun, the modular candles on the portable light unit, the Community Bag, can provide bright light to several people; the illumination can be extended by exchanging used lights with charged ones. Huichol are well known for their beading and sewing, so the team also created a Portable Workshop to allow artisans to work on craftwork in the evenings. Portable Light Reading Mats are covered with fabric that illuminates a school desktop, and are integrated into a larger Reading Stool, which folds into a backpack. Students can group their stools together to form a learning station. The stool itself is a traditional Huichol design, and therein lies an essential ingredient in the project: the technology is brought into a new context and modified, customized, and embedded into the local aesthetic. Kennedy's objective is to create Portable Light "light kits" so that textile artists can weave flexible solar panels and lighting directly into fabric.

The prototypes that the Portable Light team brought to the Huichol were not fixed; like the technology itself, they weren't static. Much of the project's strength actually lies in its lack of a single, finished design. Besides being stunningly simple, the Portable Light system is reconfigurable: with enough units, a community's systems can be aggregated, knitting a network of lights into a larger power array for community activities, or even minor surgeries. In the Sierra Madre, the Portable Light project is carving out a space where new technology is used to preserve indigenous culture. There is a growing need worldwide for tough, self-powering, portable sources of light. Untethered to the electricity grid, portable lighting could have huge potential beyond the realm of the Huichol. □□

■■■■ RESOURCES

Design for the Real World: Human Ecology and Social Change by Victor Papanek (Academy Chicago Publishers, 1985) and ***The Green Imperative: Natural Design for the Real World*** by Victor Papanek (Thames and Hudson, 1995) Victor Papanek was a UNESCO designer who, throughout the 1970s, made high-performing, inexpensive devices—such as a transistor radio fashioned from a used can—for the developing world. He refused to patent any of his works, being far more interested in creating a public domain of form and function. To Papanek, a design was most successful when it cost only pennies. He was uncommonly gifted in his ability to see simple, hybrid high-tech/low-tech solutions to tough problems.

Papanek was industrial design's original critic, famously calling his profession one of the most harmful in existence. But he was also a brilliant advocate for design in the interest of human need, and brought an unusual reverence and weight of responsibility to the field. In language suffused with the history of design, he describes the Inuit of Greenland and northern Canada, whom he lived with for a time, as the best designers in the world—all of their decisions, he suggests, are perfectly in balance with their environment. We rarely talk about design in these terms.

The Green Imperative follows up the classic *Design for the Real World*, and includes more than enough cautionary tales, but its ultimate focus is on solutions. Papanek isn't nearly as interested in clever technologies as he is in appropriateness—and merit: "The exploitation of cuteness, convenience or fashion manipulates people's reactions and emotions unscrupulously; it represents the engineering of desire. To put it differently: convenience is the enemy of excellence; fashion is the enemy of integrity; cuteness is the enemy of beauty."

Designing Durability

Durability is perhaps one of the oldest tenets of sustainability. If a product has staying power, it means that a replacement product doesn't need to be manufactured and transported to the consumer, and the original product stays out of the landfill.

It's worth noting, though, that durability isn't the best solution for every product. In some cases, it might make sense to design something to adapt to a radically shorter lifespan, like packaging that very quickly biodegrades. But when it comes to the everyday items we know we want to hold on to, and the materials in our buildings and infrastructure that are costly to constantly replace or repair, durability should still be square one for designers.

Durability is both functional and aesthetic. Designing an item to be beautiful is as important as constructing it to be rugged and easily repaired. More importantly, durability does not exclude other design strategies. This classic concept is well meaning on its own, but it's game-changing when combined with green materials, design for disassembly, and Cradle to Cradle planning. AP & CB

Heirloom Design

Durability alone doesn't ensure that something won't be thrown away. Heirloom design banks on something more: our desire as consumers to keep an object because it holds some meaning or is too beautiful or classic in its appeal to give away.

Saul Griffith, an inventor, mechanical engineer, and cofounder of Squid Labs and Instructables, proposed the concept of heirloom

design at the 2009 Compostmodern conference; he described it as design that is intended to last for generations.

"It sounds like I'm a pretentious wanker when I say 'green' is a Rolex and a Mont Blanc pen, but what I really mean is, you have to design things and experiences that will last a very long time, that have been thoughtfully designed and are very beautiful," Griffith explained.

Of course, "heirloom" is often synonymous with "expensive." But the point is not to limit heirloom-quality goods to certain people, but rather to recover an ideal of making things for everyone that will last for generations. In her book *Antiques of the Future*, product designer Lisa Roberts curated a collection of mass-produced objects that she believes will be valuable in the future, once they are no longer in production. Many of the items are relatively inexpensive, but are well made and attractive: one of her primary criteria in selection was just that the objects have "a strong and immediate visual appeal." Among her selections were Michael Graves's Alessi tea kettle and Karim Rashid's Garbino trash can.

Usefulness is a good general criterion for heirloom design. A classic multifunctional tool like the Swiss Army knife is likely to be handed from one generation to the next. Sentimental appeal is another reason something may become an heirloom, and designers can aim to create products that inspire emotional responses.

Though Roberts's book demonstrates that heirloom design doesn't have to be expensive, her work doesn't focus specifically on design that promotes sustainability. Griffith's strategy of choosing investment pieces isn't necessarily foolproof in this regard, either: a report by the World Wildlife Fund gave the world's largest luxury companies abysmal sustainability ratings. Even if an item is durable and provides heirloom appeal, limited raw resources and a growing awareness of the impact of waste means that manufacturers will need to consider lifecycle sustainability from the beginning. A few designers, however, are already using the concept of heirloom design as a way to consciously improve the sustainability of their products. Entermodal, an accessories design shop in Portland, Oregon, uses a Cradle to Cradle approach, modern ergonomics, and pre–Industrial Revolution construction techniques to create hip yet classic functional bags, luggage, and wallets that are designed to last decades—after which they can be easily disassembled.

In some types of products, like rapidly changing technology, the idea of heirloom design can be taken to new creative heights. It could take the form of long-lasting hardware that accepts software upgrades: perhaps, for example, a permanent computer or cell-phone case, with replaceable insides. Overall, the idea that products should last—and that consumers should want to keep them—is an important part of designing a sustainable future. AP

Self-Healing Materials

A rhino's horn contains no living cells, yet it quickly patches itself when a crack appears. Surrounding material disassembles, fills the crack, then somehow reassembles. It's a mystery of nature that may hold the key to designing products that almost never need repairs.

So-called self-healing materials are already in the works. Self-healing concrete is one

The simple, functional beauty displayed in Michael Graves's Whistling Bird teakettle can make ordinary objects heirloom pieces.

of Janine Benyus's favorite examples of biomimcry [see Biomimicry, right] in action. It's a "crude approximation" of the rhino's horn, in which capsules of epoxy break when concrete flexes, spilling their material into the crack and thereby fixing it.

Researchers are just beginning to envision the potential of self-healing materials. As Benyus told Worldchanging in May 2009, "One of my favorite ideas is embedding our materials with sensors so they can sense when they are damaged, and perhaps can heal themselves. It's a new way toward durability, which, when appropriate, is sustainability." NASA scientists have similar dreams: they are working on flexible materials embedded with nanosensors that would monitor a spaceship's exterior the way the human body keeps track of its own skin; self-healing components would quickly close up the holes created by fast-moving debris. CB

but at the right speed. It's about concentrating on quality instead of quantity. Slower life is also ecologically stronger life." And the slow way of doing things can be applied to almost anything—even design.

Made to Break by Giles Slade (Harvard University Press, 2006)
Slade provides an important guide to understanding the history and practice of planned obsolescence. Designing things not to last but to be used and thrown away is, Slade says, both an outdated business model and a cultural legacy of a certain time in American history: "During the next few years, the overwhelming problem of waste of all kinds will, I believe, compel American manufacturers to modify industrial practices that feed upon a throwaway ethic. The golden age of obsolescence—the heyday of nylons, tailfins, and transistor radios—will go the way of the buffalo." AS

■■■■■   RESOURCES

Antiques of the Future by Lisa Roberts (Stewart, Tabori & Chang, 2006)
Product designer Lisa Roberts showcases seventy mass-produced objects she believes will be valuable in the future, once their production is discontinued. Her idea that products should last—and that consumers should want to keep them—is an invaluable part of designing a sustainable future. As this collection of everyday items shows, anything can be made an heirloom—a salt shaker, a paperweight—if it is beautiful and durable. AP

In Praise of Slow by Carl Honoré (Orion, 2005)
Required reading for anyone interested in the philosophy of the slow life, *In Praise of Slow* is Canadian journalist Carl Honoré's chronicle of how he stopped being a speedaholic.

"My rhythm of life had gotten so fast that I was constantly trying to save a minute here, another there. My wake-up call came when I caught myself thinking of buying a collection of one-minute bedtime stories. At that point I realised that my speedaholism had gotten so bad that I was even willing to speed up the most intimate moment between me and my son."
As Honoré explains, "The idea behind slow life is not really about doing things at a snail's pace,

The unique surface structure of a lotus leaf is revealed under a microscope (left). Lotusan paint uses the structural properties found in lotus leaves to shed water and dirt (right).

Biomimicry

Biomimicry—usually called bionetics in Europe—is design inspired by nature. Velcro, for example, was inspired by the way burrs stick to fur—the scratchy side of Velcro acts like burrs, the soft side acts like fur. When well done, biomimicry is not blind imitation, but inspiration for transforming the principles of nature into successful design strategies. Although much of the work in biomimicry is still theoretical or exploratory, a few cutting-edge designs have proven that the science can be applied at any scale, from tape that imitates a gecko's skin to achieve super-adhesion; to paint that replicates the watertight properties of a lotus flower to make it resistant to mold, dirt, and water damage; to a high-rise that imitates a termite mound to achieve passive air-conditioning.

We humans have gotten ideas from nature for as long as we've been around. But our application of those concepts has often been haphazard and imprecise. Buckminster Fuller was the first to bring the idea to the world at large. Now designers are learning how to make biomimicry an actual methodology, rather than just occasional serendipity.

Nature is inspiring not because it's perfect, but because it's prolific. There are some drawbacks to nature's design: natural products need continual maintenance and/or rebuilding (though this can be an advantage in products meant to biodegrade or become obsolete), and organisms can't borrow designs from one another; they have to evolve from their existing designs. Evolution requires each solution to be better than the last; it's not a testing ground for new strategies that might get worse for a few generations before getting better. However, everything we see in nature has been field-tested for thousands or millions of years, and the earth has come up with countless clever solutions we might never have dreamed of. JJF

Biomimicry in Action

Biomimicry's core idea is, as Janine Benyus (the founder and president of the Biomimicry Institute and an internationally recognized authority on biomimicry) says, treating nature as model, measure, and mentor. Using nature as model, we can get ideas from organisms to solve our problems. Whatever we are trying to do, there are usually several organisms that have evolved successful strategies (like burrs sticking to fur) to do it. Applying nature as measure, we can look to the natural world to see what is possible. Spider silk, for instance, is stronger than steel and tougher than Kevlar (which itself is purported to be five times stronger than steel), but the "factory" that

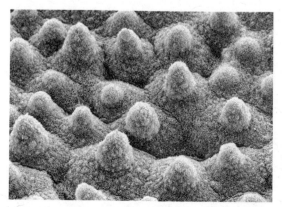

produces it—the spider—is smaller than your little finger, and employs no boiling sulfuric acid or high-pressure extruders. Taking nature as mentor, we are able to recognize that we are part of a larger system, and that we should treat nature as a partner and teacher rather than as a resource to be exploited.

Biomimicry can be achieved on different levels: the *form and function* level, the *process* level, and the *system* level, according to Benyus. Biomimetic *forms and functions*, such as Velcro, are the most common manifestations of biomimicry. Biomimetic *processes* manufacture products as nature would. The self-assembling coatings developed at the Department of Energy's Sandia National Laboratories are an example of biometric process—they grow from a solution the way seashells grow in seawater. These incredibly strong, transparent coatings, which could be quickly grown in laboratories, could revolutionize all kinds of finishes for everything from cars to contact lenses. Biomimetic *systems* feature closed-loop lifecycles [see Neobiological Industry, p. 108] that recycle the outputs and by-products of one process as inputs for another. As William McDonough and Michael Braungart note in *Cradle to Cradle* [see Producer Responsibility, p. 118), "waste equals food" in a biomimetic system. And today we can also add a fourth level: the *design* level. Biomimetic design processes—in forms such as genetic algorithms and iterative design—can produce cheap, green results never seen in nature. Nature's students are learning quickly. JJF

Leaflike Solar Cells

Solar power is supposed to be one of our renewable power saviors, but current photovoltaics have severe limits in functionality: most panels, in order to work optimally and gather enough energy to cover the needs of large buildings, must be mounted horizontally (requiring a certain amount of flat space on a building) and be exposed to direct sunlight. In addition, the manufacturing process of standard PV is anything but green, relying heavily on toxic metals like cadmium or telluride.

But there are natural solar collectors all around us, shading us in summer and crunching underfoot in fall, and several companies, including G24i in Wales and DyeSol in Australia, are working to perfect dye-sensitized solar cells that mimic the photosynthesis process in leaves. In DyeSol's design, a titanium dioxide paste creates a porous coating on glass panes that are then dipped in ruthenium, a metal whose light-gathering ability mimics that of chlorophyll. When these panes are fused to a second electrolyte-coated pane, the ruthenium is able to absorb available light and transfer it to the energy-conducting titanium dioxide.

Although leaflike solar cells lack the efficiency of standard PV cells, they have many other benefits: they work in shade or even indoors (no intermittency issues); they are cheap and easy to make (DyeSol's cells are simple enough to be assembled by kids); and builders can incorporate them into almost any part of a building, including on windows and steel cladding.

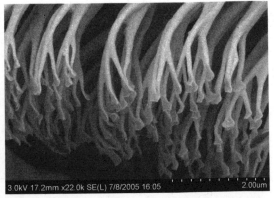

3.0kV 17.2mm x22.0k SE(L) 7/8/2005 16:05   2.00um

Janine Benyus, in a May 2009 interview with Worldchanging's Sarah Kuck, noted the potential of using these leaflike solar cells in promoting solar-energy collection in the Global South. Benyus and her colleague Paul Hawken are aiming with their Biomimicry Ventures Group to deliver twenty-five-cents-a-watt, nontoxic-dye solar cells that work on any substrate; because the dye would need recharging about every five years, these cells would have clean-energy jobs built into them. Benyus explained: "Everybody in other solar endeavors is very hung up on efficiency—getting that last little bit of efficiency. But our feeling is that that business model is wrong there. A five-year recharge allows you to upgrade. So the idea is to make the manufacture inexpensive and nontoxic enough that it can happen anywhere. It doesn't have to be behind razor wire in a centralized manufacturing plant somewhere." CB

Mining in a Box

What if the earth's richest mines were above ground? Currently, we have only the clumsiest version of this in current e-waste recycling, where we comb through tons of waste by hand in the hopes of extracting a few bits of metal for reuse. But biomimetic technologies could, in the words of Janine Benyus, help us to "think of remediation as the new mining."

It is only humans who have to bore so deep into the lithosphere to extract metals. Other organisms have much more graceful systems in place, allowing them to pick up metals, even in very small quantities, from varied sources—for example, from streams affected by industry where certain metals don't belong anyway. Benyus sees tremendous potential in thin-film chemistry that can mimic chelating molecules (those molecules present in bacteria that are able to scavenge metals). Humans know how to filter substances, but

biomimetic mining goes beyond filtering. What chelating molecules do so well is gather disparate elements and concentrate them. "You can imagine taking, for instance, e-waste," says Benyus, "grinding it up and making it into a slurry, and using this thin film to selectively pull out metals from that mixed waste stream to recover that metal. Basically, it's mining in a box." CB

Biomorphism: Designing with Nature

The designs nature creates are an unlimited source of stylistic inspiration; civilization will come to an end before we run out of brilliant ideas drawn from observing nature. Because design nearly always involves decisions about form, learning to follow the forms found in nature is, in itself, a powerful design strategy. That strategy is biomorphism—think of it as biomimicry's artsy sibling. Biomimicry endeavors to improve an object's performance or efficiency by modeling its functional design on natural principles; biomorphism simply seeks to improve that object's form. (However, improving an object's form becomes a type of efficiency when the results are so beautiful or unique that the object becomes an heirloom [see Designing Durability, p. 96].) Designers are employing biomorphism to create cutting-edge electronics, textiles, housewares, furnishings, and even entire buildings based on patterns that originated millennia ago.

Front, a Swedish design firm, practices biomorphism in some odd ways, and is bright as a flash-bang grenade. At Front, rats, snakes, and flies are part of the team. Many of the firm's products and experiments are dictated by letting critters do some artistic alteration of their own—rats gnaw on wallpaper until a pattern of holes and tears emerges that allows the old wallpaper to show through in a unique way; a motion-capture camera records a fly's seemingly random flight around a lightbulb, and then that flight pattern is molded into a beautiful lampshade.

Front also uses the greater forces of nature to create household items. By setting off a few sticks of dynamite in the snow, the design firm created a mold for a lounge chair. By examining the way different qualities of light transform

Insight into the gecko's ability to cling to nearly any surface has inspired a new kind of adhesive tape. Seen here are a laser-illuminated microsphere footprint (left) and an electron micrograph (right) of the spatular tips on a single gecko seta.

a room every day, the team came up with UV-sensitive wallpaper whose pattern waxes and wanes with the sunlight, changing a living room's decor continuously. SR

RESOURCES

Biomimicry: Innovation Inspired by Nature by Janine Benyus (Harper Perennial, 2002)
What is ecologically sustainable design but design in accordance with the natural world? As Janine Benyus puts it, "The core idea [is] that nature, imaginative by necessity, has already solved many of the problems we are grappling with. Animals, plants, and microbes are the consummate engineers. They have found what works, what is appropriate, and most important, what lasts here on Earth. This is the real news of biomimicry: After 3.8 billion years of research and development, failures are fossils, and what surrounds us is the secret to survival."

Cats' Paws and Catapults: Mechanical Worlds by Steven Vogel (W. W. Norton & Co, 2002)
What do spiders' legs and cherry pickers have in common? Ever thought of shells as the technical basis for corrugated cardboard? Nature and man use the same cadre of building materials, yet their designs diverge. In *Cats' Paws and Catapults*, Steven Vogel compares these two mechanical worlds and introduces the reader to the field of biomechanics, a fascinating exploration of humankind's improvements on nature's genius. Writing without jargon or pretense, Vogel hits the nail on the head when he argues that "perhaps the best encapsulation, if a trifle trite, is that nature shows what's possible . . . Sure, nature is wonderful. But bear in mind that we do what she doesn't."

The Biomimicry Institute
http://www.biomimicryinstitute.org
Founded by Janine Benyus, the Biomimicry Institute aims to educate the public and science communities on the potential of biomimicry as a conservation tool, and to support projects and research that further the field. Its affiliated site, AskNature.org, gives a great crash course on biomimicry, and includes an illustrated database of biomimetic products.

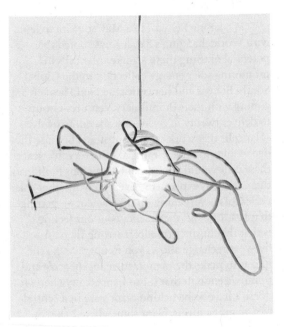

This Front Design lamp traces the path of a fly circling a light.

Nanotech

There are many definitions for nanotechnology (or nanotech), but the one we like the best is simply this: engineering functional technologies at the molecular scale. If we think about nanotech at all, we tend to associate it with science-fictional possibilities: self-organizing swarms of self-replicating nanobots, moving through the world reorganizing matter at will, perhaps getting loose and turning the planet into "gray goo," a term coined by nanotech pioneer Eric Drexler in *Engines of Creation*. These images have about as much to do with the nature of nanotech as artificial skin grafts on burn patients have to do with the bioengineered replicants in the movie *Blade Runner.*

Nanotech as it's actually emerging is prosaic, practical, and profound. With serious adoption of nanotechnology, we will begin moving from a "heat, beat, and treat" industrial era—jokingly summarized in the motto "If brute force doesn't work, you're not using enough of it"—to an age where nano-engineers talk about "nudging molecules into place" and "enticing" carbon atoms to "bond cleanly." The mindsets are as similar as those of a pile driver and a watchmaker.

Ultrafine manufacturing means that we're getting closer and closer to building machines designed to near-zero tolerances (making practically friction-less engine designs possible), producing raw materials with near-complete purity, even creating new materials that can be put together into stronger, lighter, and more flexible parts. Since it is theoretically possible to eliminate all but the most benign waste, manufacturing could be made almost completely nontoxic, and resources could be extracted from stockpiles that are inexpensive and widely available.

Advances in nanotechnology and other micromanufacturing don't just apply to one industry: they apply to everything that can be rendered in bits, including living molecules. Our ability to work at finer and finer scales applies to DNA as well as to digitized plastic prototypes. Some researchers, for instance, think that the ability of strands of DNA to "compute," to link up in specific combinations under specific circumstances, may one day give us the ability to build living computers, which would use biology instead of electricity to drive computation. AS

Nanotubes: Wonders and Risks

Nanotubes, one form of a particular type of carbon molecule called a fullerene, may well end up being one of the most important materials used in twenty-first-century manufacturing and design. They are nanotechnology's ultimate multitaskers, acting as conductors, semiconductors, or insulators, depending upon how they're shaped. They're also amazingly strong: by weight, they have fifty times the tensile strength of steel, and in theory could be up to a thousand times stronger; at the same time, nanotubes can be very flexible ("deformable") without losing resiliency. When used in a composite material, they can increase its toughness, change its electrical behavior, and allow it to store energy. Nanotubes can be used to make sensors, light-emitting diodes, even computers.

The main drawback of employing nanotubes has been the expense and difficulty of their production. In mid-2005, however, researchers at the University of Texas, Dallas, and the Commonwealth Scientific and Industrial Research Organization in Australia came up with a way to make strong, stable macroscale sheets and ribbons of multiwall nanotubes at a rate of 7 meters (23 feet) per minute. The team described potential applications of the process as including transparent antennae, high-quality electronic sensors, supercapacitors and batteries, light sources and displays, solar cells, artificial muscles, tissue-growth scaffolding, and much more.

As exciting as carbon nanotubes may be, it's important to remember that tiny particles can be highly toxic, even when made of otherwise innocuous materials. Some research has shown that nanotubes can irritate and cause inflammation of the skin and, when inhaled, particles the size of nanotubes appear to make asthma worse. Does this mean that carbon nanotubes are too dangerous to use? Maybe not. As it turns out, under real-world conditions, normal handling of carbon nanotube–based materials doesn't result in dangerous levels of nanoparticles. And researchers are finding ways to reduce the toxicity of the most dangerous nanotubes dramatically: a recent minor modification reduced the cytotoxicity (the dose at which 50 percent of affected cells die within forty-eight hours) by more than 10,000 times, making the modified nanotube essentially nontoxic. JC

Regulating Nanotechnology

We are, at most, decades from the emergence of powerful molecular manufacturing capabilities. Bottled genies deserve caution, and we can no longer let nanotechnology go unregulated. If, in fact, full-blown nanotechnology erupts into our lives in twenty years, the results are likely to be as disruptive as the first century of the Industrial Revolution, but compressed into a much shorter time. Therefore, it is the duty of those of us who would prefer an unimaginable future to an unthinkable one to take seriously the responsibility of handling nanotechnology carefully.

How might we go about that? The first step must be more research—on that, nearly all the thinkers worth hearing agree. We need to better understand the possible paths by which molecular manufacturing and other nanotech applications might develop. The Center for Responsible Nanotechnology, for example, has proposed "Thirty Essential Studies" that it believes will illuminate the way forward.

We also must start taking seriously the idea of national regulations and international agreements on the use of nanotechnology. If nanotechnology in fact bears both the importance and the dangers many claim, we will need effective, enforceable treaties and laws to stave off disaster.

We should start asking ourselves what sorts of institutions might respond effectively to these dangers: What sorts of labeling and consumer information ought to be mandated? How will products be tested? What sorts of trade rules ought to apply? There are many unanswered questions, and it is not too soon to start posing them in the public debate.

Lastly, we need a new generation of emerging technology activists: not just NGOs and networks of citizens concerned about nanotech, but also advocates for better biotech, robotics, ubiquitous computing, space programs, deep ocean exploration, climate interventions, and human-life-span extension techniques. We need heroic geek NGOs that can wrestle with issues we're only beginning to understand, and can use both strategic anticipation to change the debate and strategic communication to help the rest of us understand what's at stake. We, in turn, should all learn more about these technologies, so that we can discuss them intelligently and sway those working in the field to become partners in unleashing nanotech revolution the right way. AS

The Precautionary Principle

Writers of bad science fiction and easily startled doomsayers seem to fixate on the idea of out-of-control nanomachines—machines that self-replicate and devour everything in their path, leaving behind nothing but "gray goo."

Though that scenario has been largely refuted, it is still very plausible that nanotech and other new sciences could produce unforeseen and detrimental results; therefore, nanotechnologists need a managing principle akin to the Hippocratic oath. A reinterpretation of the Precautionary Principle—the idea that any actions whose outcomes are unknown or potentially negative should be avoided—is probably the best tool to keep those nanomachines in check.

A paper-thin, flexible, biodegradable battery designed by the Rensselaer Polytechnic Institute.

Rather than asking—like traditional risk-assessment methods—"how much harm is acceptable?" the Precautionary Principle should ask, "how much harm is avoidable?" Dale Carrico, who specializes in the history and philosophy of technological development, puts particular emphasis on the last part of the principle. He argues that the Precautionary Principle, when it is open to broad participation, has the best chance to both protect us from hazardous results and encourage innovation and experimentation. As he explained in a column on BetterHumans.com, "Even expert knowledge is most useful when it is answerable to multiple and contending stakeholders . . . rather than imposed unilaterally by an organized authority . . . When the Principle places a burden of justification on those who propose we undertake a risky development, this is not the creation of a new and arbitrary burden, but the fairer distribution of the burden of development onto all its stakeholders."

We have a need for rapid innovation, but we also have the right to demand that innovators behave responsibly. JC

Green Nanotechnology

One of the cool things about nanotechnology is that the more advanced it gets, the greener it gets. Nanoscale production techniques will let us dramatically reduce the amount of waste involved in manufacturing. As we get more adept at recycling and reusing materials, nanoscale production will let us do much more using less energy, less new material, and fewer scarce resources. Nanotech can also help us move toward a cleaner planet in the following ways:

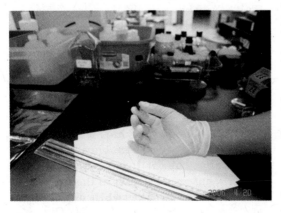

- Nanoscale materials are already being used as environmental sensors that are able to detect minute quantities of toxins and hazards. The same kinds of nanomaterials can also be used to filter contaminants such as metals, bacteria, and even viruses from water.
- Nanotubes can make the process of producing hydrogen from water twice as efficient, so they may play a big part in making hydrogen-powered cars possible.
- Photovoltaic cells made from nanotubes are more flexible, lighter in weight, and potentially less expensive than traditional silicon solar cells. In theory, we'll be able to do a lot more with them: embed them in fabrics, wrap them around curving structures, and paint them on walls and roofs.
- Paper-thin, flexible batteries can be made by impregnating cellulose with nanotubes, which act as electrodes. Small, light, powerful batteries are essential to pushing new technologies forward, especially those that may help a developing nation to leapfrog [see Leapfrogging, p. 248].
- The development of nanoscale wires able to turn heat into electricity and vice versa will mean refrigerators that can operate without pumps or chemicals, solar panels that are able to extract power from heat or light, and even vehicles that can draw power from the heat of engines. JC

Molecular Manufacturing

In the not-so-distant future, molecular manipulation and rapid prototyping will combine to produce a tabletop nanotech manufacturing system—a nanofactory. This sounds prosaic; it will be anything but. Molecular manufacturing has the power to transform the way we make things.

Consider the process of designing a butterfly-sized self-guided microairplane today. It would take many hours to find lightweight materials, and many more hours to construct the device by hand. The apparatus could carry only a tiny battery and a few bits of electronics. Building and testing each new design would probably require several weeks, and in the end, the microplane would not be able to do very much.

With a nanofactory, the picture would be very different. Building with molecules, nanofactories could develop supercomputers smaller than a grain of rice, motors smaller than a cell, batteries more efficient than the energy-storage mechanisms of real butterflies. Rather than spending days of labor building each new design, a nanofactory could produce it directly from blueprints in minutes. In fact, a tabletop nanofactory could build hundreds or thousands of butterfly microplanes in parallel. All the different material properties required could be obtained by rearranging molecules. All the nanoscale machine systems would have computer-controlled shapes, built directly by computer-controlled nanofactory machines. The nanoscale components could be assembled in a straightforward process into products the size of a butterfly, a car, or even a jumbo jet or spaceship.

Rather than taking several weeks to build and test one new design, a nanofactory could design and test several butterfly-sized self-guided microairplanes in one day. It would be more like software engineering than hardware research and development. Consider how fast the dot-com companies appeared, and how diverse they were, and you can imagine how rapidly new products could appear.

In fact, some designs could be developed even more rapidly by a semiautomated process. The designer would provide an outline for a design with a few parameters that could be tweaked. The nanofactory would build hundreds of variants of the design in parallel. The variants could then be tested in parallel, and those that worked best would be used as templates for the next round of variants—suffice it to say that designs could be optimized quite rapidly.

In a word, clamoring for better, greener, fairer designs, and for the ability to move quickly from idea to prototype to tested product, can help us build a better future. CP & MT

Neobiological Industry

▭ Two hundred years ago, as the Industrial Revolution gained momentum, it didn't much matter how we made things, because manufacturing was little and the earth was big. Today, however, we have a global population of more than 7 billion, and almost everything in our lives is a product of industrial manufacturing—now it matters a lot. The manufacturing process has fallen ill; escalating demand and hunger for profit have led to rapidly depleting resources and the degeneration of the environment. It can't go on, and it doesn't have to. We already have the tools to create healthier industry—we just need to use them.

Conventional industry is an ecological disaster because it makes things using a "heat, beat, and treat" [see Nanotech, p. 103] approach. Most of our materials don't come out of the ground ready for use; they have to be smelted, distilled, or reacted with toxic chemicals at high pressures, a wasteful process. The few materials that need no manipulation (and most of those that do) usually have to be cut into different sizes or shapes before becoming products, which creates even more waste.

Early on in the industrial age, nature's bounty was far more plentiful, and thus cheaper, than human labor. When it became clear just how many uses oil had, industry embraced the energy-dense resource and went into overdrive exploiting its tremendous range of applications—from fuel to plastics to pharmaceuticals. In a short time, our dependence on fossil fuels has become perilous to our existence on earth, not only because of the environmental damage wreaked while obtaining them, but because we simply don't have a lot left.

Today, to make the objects we use in daily life, we employ tens of thousands of chemicals—many known to cause cancer and mutations—and vast rivers of raw materials and energy. Extracting those natural resources has torn up the planet, and industrial waste has polluted our air, water, and soil and is changing our climate. This way of working is drawing to an end.

We can make some improvement by working *with* nature, but we can spark massive change by working *as* nature. This "neobiological industry" blurs the line between the born and the made—maybe to the point of meaninglessness. In addition to the revolutionary use of biomimicry and biomorphism [see Biomimicry, p. 99] in design, there is a growing role for what Janine Benyus labels "bio-utilization" and "bio-assistance."

Bio-utilization is the use of parts of organisms as raw materials—whether it be the use of wood for a house, or the use of horseshoe-crab blood for a cancer drug. Biological materials are being employed in many new ways. Plant oils are being used to form biodegradable plastics, and waste fibers from crops have been used to strengthen concrete. Even the art world is experimenting with bio-utilization— turning flowers into stereo speakers and grass into photo canvases.

Bio-assistance is the domestication and use of organisms—whether it be herding sheep for wool, or growing a virus for building a battery. This often involves biotechnology, which most of us think of in terms of either medical breakthroughs or genetically altered Frankenfoods. But there is a third kind of biotechnology that may play a much larger role in our future: industrial biotechnology. The term evokes images of ultra-high-tech gene tweaking and the creation of new kinds of organisms, but in what is probably its most useful environmental application, bioengineering will help us find more effective uses for naturally occurring organisms.

As we gain a better understanding of nature's systems, more and more of the work of our industrialized civilization looks like clumsy, even clownish, aping of work that nature does with precision, ecological health, and beauty. We're beginning to realize that our industrial technology is nothing next to the power living things have to digest, filter, grow, sense, and even compute—and that the true masters of manufacturing on this planet are microbes.

We can build industry that is far more sustainable using biotechnology to replicate nature's systems and designs. With the help of biotechnology, we can hack pools of common pond scum into nontoxic, highly efficient batteries, use tanks of tweaked fungus to convert garbage into methane, and train vats of tame microbes to design machines and structures with natural materials that resemble shells and spider silk.

Real concerns remain about the safety of bioengineered organisms, but the best way to realize the sustainability benefits of biotechnology while protecting the planet and ourselves is for all of us to understand the technology and to demand the best practices possible. As Stewart Brand of *Whole Earth Catalog* fame wrote in an article in *Technology Review*, "The best way for doubters to control a questionable new technology is to embrace it, lest it remain wholly in the hands of enthusiasts who think there is nothing questionable about it."

Tomorrow's industry will seek to produce objects that work as well as those in nature, through processes that run on sunlight and treat waste as energy. Tomorrow's industry will eat, digest, and secrete the things we need not just in imitation of living beings, but through the actual cells of living beings. Industry will not just be biomimetic, it will be neobiological. JJF & AS

Technical Nutrients

Sustainable architecture and design expert William McDonough [see Producer Responsibility, p. 118] maintains—and many agree—that recycling as we know it will never solve our massive waste problem. Running some glass and aluminum through another incarnation does divert it from the landfill, but ultimately does nothing to change the process by which these problematic items come to be floating around our commercial sphere. As one example of a deeper solution, McDonough's design firm, McDonough Braungart Design Chemistry (MBDC), designed an upholstery fabric from wool and cellulose that can be tossed into a compost pile at the end of its life to completely biodegrade. McDonough has dubbed the material a "biological nutrient"— when the "wasted" object is discarded it becomes food for cultivating more wool and cellulose, beginning the entire process again from its birth.

In contrast to the "biological nutrient," which has limited uses in the production of consumer items since it eventually loses its structural integrity on the way back to the earth, "technical nutrients" have a repeated lifecycle within industry. Well-designed synthetic materials can be reprocessed in their entirety, coming back to life as products of equal value or function. It's a process that improves upon standard recycling. In the new closed-loop system of material reuse, everything that reaches the end of its lifecycle gets reabsorbed, either harmlessly composting into soil or seamlessly finding another life in the industrial process. AS

Kalundborg and Industrial Ecology

"Closed-loop" thinking is already starting to spread. Industrial systems that employ the concept work like nature, according to MBDC: "Instead of designing cradle-to-grave products, dumped in landfills at the end of their 'life,' the new approach transforms industry by creating products for cradle-to-cradle cycles, whose materials are perpetually circulated in closed loops. Maintaining materials in closed loops maximizes material value without damaging ecosystems."

The best-proven example of this kind of industrial ecology is the Kalundborg industrial park in Denmark. At Kalundborg's center is a coal-burning power plant, which not only generates electricity but supplies waste steam to run a nearby pharmaceutical factory and oil refinery. Waste heat from those facilities is in turn used to heat 3,500 homes in the area. The refinery's waste water cycles back to the coal plant to provide more steam. Fly ash from the coal plant is turned into concrete at another factory, and so on. The whole industrial park is piped together into an "industrial ecology." Obviously, coal power plants and oil refineries are not sustainable businesses, but because it has been designed along industrial ecological lines, Kalundborg as a whole is more sustainable than it might otherwise be. Industrial ecology mitigates the bad effects of today's industry: it may well supercharge tomorrow's. AS

Green Chemistry

You can't do green design without green materials, and material innovations tend to come from chemists. Chemists also produce many products in their own right: paints, adhesives, cleaning products, whole industries. So what are chemists doing to save the world?

They're doing a lot of things, as it turns out. Some researchers are developing alternative plastics that don't use petrochemicals, some associations are prioritizing green initiatives within their membership, whole green-chem institutes are being founded, and groups are trying to teach chemists to green their processes. Sustainable chemistry is a baby, born thirty years ago but just now starting to crawl.

Currently there is little more than a trickle-down of green-chemistry knowledge among companies, governments, NGOs, and universities. Companies' chemical information is proprietary, and many environmental impacts have never been measured, much less publicized. Some universities and government agencies have data on a few specific chemicals, but lack a centralized clearinghouse of information. MBDC, cofounded by the world's most famous green chemist, Michael Braungart, may have the best database of chemical environmental data, but it is private and expensive information. Opening up the faucets of these knowledge flows, and

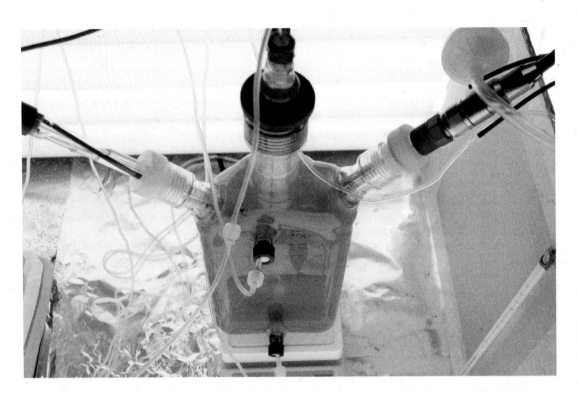

getting them all in one tub big enough to splash in, may be the most important step for the industry right now. Several groups are trying to crank the taps.

Britain's Chemistry Innovation Network has a roadmap for sustainable technologies, including trends and drivers, specific needs of the industry, a review of technologies, and case studies. These are aimed at everyone in the chemical industry. The Framework for California Leadership in Green Chemistry Policy of the University of California, Berkeley, recommends policy directions for lawmakers. Along with a Web page for their Twelve Principles of Green Chemistry, the EPA has another good tool in their downloadable Green Chemistry Expert System, a piece of software that "allows users to build a green chemical process, design a green chemical, or survey the field of green chemistry."

Will the chemical market start to go green by itself, as a few industries are starting to do? Not necessarily. In order for the field to advance, we need to close three fundamental gaps: 1) the data gap, by ensuring that chemical producers generate, distribute, and communicate information on chemical toxicity, ecotoxicity, uses, and other key data; 2) the safety gap, by strengthening government tools for identifying, prioritizing, and mitigating chemical hazards; and 3) the technology gap, by supporting research, development, technical assistance, entrepreneurial activity, and education in green chemistry science and technology. Michael Wilson, a researcher at UC Berkeley, said that "green chemistry entrepreneurs have a difficult time breaking into the market because there are fundamental data gaps in chemical toxicity that prevent buyers from choosing safer chemicals . . . [B]y requiring that producers generate and distribute standardized, robust information on chemical toxicity (for use by downstream industry, business, consumers, workers) we will open new markets for green chemistry entrepreneurs." JJF

Synthetic Biology

Engineering life is hard. It's made even harder by the law of unintended consequences: living beings are incredibly complicated, and they

Hydrogen may one day be produced by specially engineered algae, such as these at the National Renewable Energy Laboratory.

mutate quickly and in unexpected ways, and we simply don't yet understand them all that well.

Enter biological engineering, or synthetic biology. Biological engineering uses bits of DNA ("BioBricks") to build pseudo-organisms that can grow and act (even replicate) in precisely controlled ways. These "machines" are not quite like anything found in nature, and yet clearly, in most ways that matter, they are alive. Biological engineering is not ordinary biotechnology or genetic engineering. It is the application of engineering principles to the construction of novel genetic structures; in contrast, genetic engineering is often a trial-and-error process, with numerous unanticipated results. Many of the reasonable concerns about genetically modified foods and animals come from this hit-or-miss aspect of biotechnology. Biological engineers take a more systematic approach, using an increasingly deep understanding of how DNA works to make microorganisms perform narrowly specified tasks. (The Massachusetts Institute of Technology now has a major in biological engineering, the school's first new major in decades.)

Standardized, cheaper genetic engineering tools will lead to a better understanding of biological processes. This should allow scientists to avoid the unanticipated system interactions feared by knowledgeable opponents of biotech. Even if the technology is misused, the standardization of the process will make it easier to recognize and respond to accidents or malice.

As long as biological engineers approach their work with an appreciation for its ultimate effects, standardized components and rigorous design methodology could actually make the broader use of biotechnology a safer prospect. AS & JC

Viruses Making Batteries

What if we could grow rechargeable batteries in vats? Dr. Angela Belcher of the Massachusetts Institute of Technology (MIT) thinks she may have found a way to do just that. Along with her team at MIT, the 2004 MacArthur "Genius" established a technique that combines biomimicry and bio-assistance, using viruses to produce battery material based on the way the red abalone generates its shell—but much faster.

The viruses are not engineered, but are put into an environment they normally would never inhabit; their reaction to the surrounding materials turns them into a template that grows the desired material. Belcher and her team have also developed other viruses and yeasts that grow a variety of materials for engineering and medicine.

It is still just research, but it shows promise: a 2009 report by Belcher's team documents their success in creating a lithium-ion battery using a virus that incorporates carbon nanotubes, thereby increasing the conductivity of the battery's cathode (the more difficult part of the battery to build). The prototype looks and acts like a typical coin-cell battery, but the team expects to create flexible batteries that can mold to any container shape. Virus-produced batteries, which may be ready for commercial production after the phase of improvements is complete, will have the capacity to not only run our gadgets but to power plug-in hybrids.

This kind of engineering will increasingly dominate manufacturing, because of its inherent advantages. As Belcher told *Discover*, "An advantage over chemistry is that you have directed evolution on your side. So instead of being limited to a chemical that you pull off the shelf to build a material, you can evolve the bio-molecules to be better and better at doing what you want them to do." JJF

DNA Computers

Silicon Valley, the California epicenter of the dot-com boom, was named for the material that engineers use to create microprocessors, the mechanisms that made the boom possible. But just as the dot-com era saw an eventual decline, so silicon may approach its limits in satisfying the ever-increasing demand for speed in computer processing.

Can anything outrace silicon and endure rising expectations for performance? Believe it or not, our own DNA proves to be a more viable competitor than silicon. DNA molecules have the capacity to perform rapid simultaneous calculations—much faster than the fastest computer—and they clearly don't seem to be nearing an inevitable demise.

Scientists are now investigating ways to integrate the astounding abilities of life's genetic material into nanocomputers that will be able to perform much faster, and store vastly more data, than the machines we work with today. These DNA computers, embedded with "biochips," herald a future that used to seem like pure sci-fi, and that now appears to be around the next corner: the era of biological computation.

■■■■■ RESOURCES

Chasing Molecules: Poisonous Products, Human Health, and the Promise of Green Chemistry by
Elizabeth Grossman (Shearwater, 2009)
While writing her previous book on the afterlife of electronics, Grossman became increasingly disturbed by the amount of chemicals found in our air, water, and soil. Why were the Centers for Disease Control (CDC) finding the exact same chemicals in polar bears, newborn babies, and our food? She began wondering if it was possible to do better. Could products and the chemicals they are created from be made environmentally "benign by design"?

She decided to chase these dangerous molecules around the world, from the Arctic to the Great Lakes, to numerous waste sites and the Pearl River delta. Harmful chemicals were present at every site she visited. But Chasing Molecules is ultimately an optimistic book. Green chemists, writes Grossman, are redesigning the future and learning from nature to create new, nontoxic chemicals and products. And Grossman includes a couple of great examples of how companies are stepping up to do their part in the green-chemistry revolution.

For those who are new to the toxic-chemical debate, Chasing Molecules provides a strong argument for the implementation of green chemistry. For those who are aware and motivated, it provides a hopeful look at the benign design revolution already taking place.

Intervention: Confronting the Real Risks of Genetic Engineering and Life on a Biotech Planet
by Denise Caruso (Hybrid Vigor Institute, 2006)
Denise Caruso holds a somewhat legendary status among tech journalists. A columnist for the New York Times and founder of the Hybrid

Vigor Institute (an NGO dedicated to facilitating interdisciplinary and collaborative approaches to scientific problem solving), Caruso and her work have helped shape our society's thinking about the future of science.

In Intervention, Caruso lays out in chilling detail exactly why even (perhaps especially) those of us who are strong supporters of science and innovation ought to be extremely concerned about the unintended consequences of contemporary biotechnological industrial research.

"[W]hat we know from history is that every promise based on discovery or invention, no matter how positive, comes factory-equipped with its own unintended dark-side consequences . . . It is not especially difficult to come up with scenarios whereby mucking around in the genes of living organisms leads to serious biological, social and/or economic disruption."

Caruso then explores a number of cases in which scientists themselves have done a lousy job of risk assessment, and in which industrial regulatory capture has prevented further exploration of known risks, including the health effects of common plastics; the overuse of antibiotics; and the introduction of invasive species, either intentionally or through "escapes."

We can acknowledge that biotechnology has brought humanity incredible breakthroughs in pharmaceuticals and green chemistry and still demand that a reasonable precautionary principle be applied to actions. Caruso calls for an "analytic deliberative process," one that seeks out uncertainty, evokes foresight and speculation, and attempts to incorporate in its deliberations not just accuracy but wisdom. She thinks this can be achieved through a process of collaborative risk assessment, exercised with transparency. AS

Twelve Principles of Green Chemistry
Both the EPA (http://www.epa.gov/gcc/pubs/principles.html) and the Center for Green Chemistry and Green Engineering at Yale (http://greenchemistry.yale.edu/definitions) publish their own version of Twelve Principles of Green Chemistry. The principles range from the simple (practicing prevention and designing out waste) to the field-specific (avoiding "unnecessary derivatization"). This should make an excellent jumping-off point for further exploration.

Picking Green Materials

Materials are ingredients for human creativity. While one designer chooses shining plastics doomed for the landfill, another tries to figure out how to make cars from hemp and kenaf fibers.

What if we remade the world out of unbleached cotton and recycled bottles? Would it really emerge as something more reasonable and uncomplicated, smelling delightful, bathed in virtue? We're unlikely to see global material culture overcome by such restrictive aesthetic simplicity anytime soon, and besides, working from a tiny, spare palette of materials would be catastrophically impractical. Sure, we could make a mobile phone out of soy plastic, but when the ants start climbing into our pockets to eat our gadgets, we'll become all too aware of the drawbacks of narrow approaches to green design.

All good intentions become null and void when things cease to work. Objects like electronics need to be stable enough to function—to say nothing of surviving an onslaught of hungry insects. Crushed sunflower shells can make great coffee tables, but they make really terrible solar panels. Without plastics, we'd have neither pacemakers nor drip irrigation systems.

The truth is, material itself cannot make a product sustainable, because there's no such thing as a "sustainable material." Certainly, there are some materials that should not be used at all, particularly those that are toxic to life; but sustainability is a matter of what we do with the materials we choose. All materials are extracted, heated, and cooled; we pour still more energy into them every time we shuttle them about. Even recycled glass bottles eat up more energy than we care to admit. By using what we have, and wisely choreographing the flow of materials, we can start to eliminate the damage done along the way. ❍❍

Databases and Online Libraries

Sourcing materials involves so many tangled interdependent networks that it can be overwhelming to try to understand the behind-the-curtain elements of the goods we buy. Having more accessible information is key to understanding and gauging the impact of our products. There are a number of databases emerging that catalog the ingredients designers have available to them. When designers can look up materials and learn about their origins and applications, they gain a lot more power at their fingertips to make better decisions.

Matbase, an online project spun out of the Delft University of Technology, is one such resource. Targeted at engineers, it provides the

physical and mechanical properties of raw materials like metals and ceramics, along with information about, for example, the lifecycle impacts of stainless steel, as well as other environmental considerations like the availability of raw steel or scrap worldwide.

Among the best tools for exploring and uncovering new materials from suppliers are online resources such as Materia's Material Explorer and the international library at Material ConneXion. Both of these sites are curated and constantly updated to home in on the new and the strange. This saves hours of browsing aimlessly through search engines looking for, say, injection-moldable potato starch, or ultrathin recyclable packaging that mimics the chemistry of eggshells. Material ConneXion is the world's largest resource of information about new materials—from yarn made of seaweed and cellulose, to sheets of crushed almond shells—with libraries in major design centers like New York, Bangkok, and Cologne. Material Explorer's industrial curiosities aren't always space-age: elephant grass shares space with injection-molded wood, biocomposites, and acoustic panels made from sheep wool. Their information is also freely available.

We know that it takes a lot of energy to ship reclaimed lumber from Melbourne to Montreal, so one of the most useful things about any database is the localized, place-specific information we can find there. Material ConneXion and Materia connect us to suppliers of horsetail-hair fabric in Hong Kong, holographic tiles in the Czech Republic, and salago-shrub papers in the Philippines. The next logical steps are to create more transparent supply chains, connecting designers to local suppliers, and to foster better understanding of what goes into the materials they choose. ⊓⊓

▬ RESOURCES

Transmaterial by Blaine Brownell (Princeton Architectural Press, 2005)
Indoors, soft forms cover the walls to clarify voices in a room. Outdoors, Australian-engineered concrete quietly sucks carbon dioxide out of the air, and biomimetic [see Biomimicry, p. 99] paint—reverse engineered from lotus petals—repels rainwater on the building facades. Plants snake up recycled steel trusses, covering whole walls in greenery while keeping brick and mortar from being devoured by roots. When the sun goes down, photovoltaic windows stop collecting solar energy and start displaying graphics. Interior windows glow with curtains of electroluminescent vines embedded in silk.

Recombining matter in stranger and more varied ways than ever, materials science has been innovating like mad. *Transmaterial*, architect Blaine Brownell's collection of some of the best new ingredients for architecture, is a material enthusiast's dream. The picture catalog and guide to all things possible tidily classifies and lists materials, processes, and products by supplier. While combing the world for the most interesting substances, Brownell found such oddities as concretes that are translucent, aerated, recycled, and light reactive, neoprene for wrapping horses' joints, and discarded sorghum stalks that have been turned into smoothly finished cabinetry. Like wood that bends in several directions at once, the most exciting materials are unexpected, defying their natural properties.

Some of the most interesting applications featured in *Transmaterial* first saw the light of day in artists' installations. Sachiko Kodama

Opposite, left: Among the renewable materials catalogued on Material Explorer's searchable Web site are Lama Concept's Cell-carpets.
Opposite, right: Alulight energy absorbers, used to protect car passengers during impact, are made from lightweight metallic foam.
Right: The Tavern on Camac in Philadelphia uses rapidly renewable materials like bamboo, coconut husks, and pearlstone in its design.

and Minako Takeno created their Protrude, Flow sculptures with magnetic fluids that dynamically respond to temperature, sound, and light, changing shape as viewers move around them. Thom Faulders lined a listening room with NASA's memory foam, a material long neglected because it failed to withstand extreme temperatures in space thirty years ago. Down here on earth, our feet leave deep, clear footprints across Faulders's room.

Though *Transmaterial* focuses on small, improved material and energy efficiencies, it touches briefly on almost every entry's environmental qualities. Alulight, for example, is a strong and rigid foamed aluminum that's five times lighter than pure aluminum. Working on the same principle, Axel Thallemer's inflatable Airtecture structures replace matter with air. Airtecture supports whole rooflines and bears a building's load with air pressure, fabric, and various engineering heroics.

Since 2005, Brownell has published two more editions of the book, and each reflects the evolving interests of green designers. *Transmaterial 3*, for example, puts extra emphasis on biomaterials, biomimetics, and materials with low embodied energy. Transmaterial.net profiles dozens of these materials. ꝺꝺ

Design and Environment: A Global Guide to Designing Greener Goods by Helen Lewis, John Gertsakis, et al. (Greenleaf, 2001)
Designing for sustainability means building bridges between disciplines and presenting solutions in languages that are foreign to most designers. So there is a critical space for books on sustainable design that fill that realm: annotated, numbered, cross-linked, and brimming with frameworks. *Design and Environment* is, somewhat paradoxically, a deeply practical academic book, targeted at the businesspeople and managers who make so many of the decisions about our material culture.

"Designers are at the significant point of conjunction between technological and cultural worlds. They are therefore in a privileged position to capture and act on signals for change."

Producer Responsibility

Our everyday life is affected by our relationship to things. But if we limit our notion of this relationship to materials and energy choices alone, sustainable design will not take us as far as we need to go. The greatest promise for gains in sustainability lies not merely in designing things, but in designing the services and systems that take into account our interaction with our products and enable us to take responsibility for objects and waste.

We want to carry mobile phones in our pockets and make coffee at home; yet phones and coffeemakers are disposable. Expensive to repair and easy to throw away, their design quickly becomes obsolete, and their materials are rarely considered valuable enough to reclaim or remanufacture. As the sheer volume of waste that we produce becomes crushing, and new resources harder to capture, companies are trying to figure out how to redirect even the smallest extinguished products back to their manufacturers. ꝺꝺ

Extended Producer Responsibility and Product Takeback

Cars have always been disposable, peeled apart for scraps or left as dry husks on the landscape when they die. But scrap doesn't confer much worth—there's a downcycling that goes on, a loss of value. Steel gets weaker, colors duller. Other parts—seats and glove compartments and seas of tires—are politely ignored. In the early 1990s, Germany decided to change the rules, requiring automakers to take ultimate responsibility for the cars they sell. Aside from getting on car companies' nerves, the dictate meant that engineers and designers had to figure out a way to make those dead cars valuable and easy to take apart. As with any new development, the mandate initially cost companies time and gave them headaches—but then it started saving them money. It turns out that cars that are easier to disassemble are also easier to assemble.

The European Union adopted Germany's approach with their End-of-Life Vehicle Directive, a governmental regulation based on a simple concept: vehicle manufacturers are held responsible for the things they sell when they get old, broken, or obsolete. Taking stuff back as a matter of regulation is a different game. It's not purely for profit: it's an issue that's bigger than a single company.

Most electronic waste is sent to Asia to be disassembled by hand—the only available technique for recovering metals in products designed exclusively for their utility to the consumer, with no thought to products' "end of life." Regulations in Europe have required that manufacturers design for the electronic waste their products generate, and these guidelines have shaped similar regulations now being adopted by China. When refrigerators stop working in Europe, the company that produces them can no longer leave Europeans, their communities, or rural Asia buried under the weight of the defunct machines.

In some cases, companies have arranged their own take-back programs as part of their corporate sustainability efforts—before they've been mandated by regulations. For the Japanese company Toginon, UK-based Sprout Design developed a range of extremely high-quality knives, which come packaged with two blades. When one blade gets dull, which should take some time, the other blade can be used and the dull one sent back to Seki City—one of the last remaining sword-making towns in Japan—where Toginon's employees will sharpen it and return it to the consumer. Bosch, a major manufacturer, has been accepting expired power tools and appliances directly since 1994. Their tools are typically made of over two hundred components and contain valuable metals. Nokia's take-back initiative for mobile phones is similar, recognizing that such products can often be refurbished and reused before they're recycled. 5C

Design for Disassembly and Repair

We surround ourselves with useful things to open bottles, protect our feet, light the bathroom, keep our books off the floor. Yet even after breaking, they continue to take up space, as if waiting for another step that never comes. Ultimately, most objects break down, or unexpectedly drain themselves of their early seductive sheen. First the CD player became outdated, then it broke.

What's the best future that we can imagine for our disused stuff? What if products were designed to be fixed, upgraded, or eventually recycled? Designing for disassembly is common sense; making things in such a way that they can be easily repaired is even smarter.

Writer and "mediocre welder" Mister Jalopy posted a Maker's Bill of Rights [see Engineer it Yourself, p. 88] detailing a series of principles for repair-ready design, such as "Screws better than glues," "If it snaps shut, it shall snap open," and "Ease of repair shall be a design ideal, not an afterthought."

Steelcase's Think chair passes the test. It takes five minutes to take apart, even after it's spent a good fifteen years rolling around an office. Making something easy to take apart also makes it easy to repair, accounting not only for the time we spend using it, but also for the time we spend fixing it and making it last. DD

Pop-apart Cell Phones

Today most cell phones and other small electronics are shredded instead of being taken apart for recycling, because it costs more to pay someone to disassemble the phone than the phone's recyclable parts are worth. Well, what if the product disassembled itself?

Nokia has prototyped a cell phone that pops itself apart in two seconds, as opposed to the two minutes normally required for manual disassembly. The phone uses special alloys and polymers that change their shapes when heated with a laser—unthreading the screws, pushing apart the case, and popping off the circuit board (a technique called "active disassembly").

The temperature needed to disassemble the phone is 140–300 degrees Fahrenheit (60–150 degrees Celsius), cool enough to not melt the surrounding plastic, but hot enough to not be triggered accidentally.

In a world of pop-apart electronics, recycling becomes a snap. JJF & AS

Cradle to Cradle Protocol

Furniture that won't off-gas, toys that are nontoxic, cars that are completely remanufacturable—in most countries, including North America, no standards exist to ensure that we get these types of products from manufacturers. Companies are operating totally within their rights when they make appliances in toxic soup and sell them to us on the cheap. But while regulations set a low minimum threshold that products *have to* meet, certifications are the standards that products *get to* live up to. Instead of focusing only on preventing the very worst manufacturing practices, what if we reframe the problem by focusing on creating the very best things possible?

William McDonough is mainly known for shepherding green building into the American public mainstream, but his partnership with German chemist Michael Braungart has been helping to change the way small things are made. Their Cradle to Cradle (C2C) protocol, outlined in their book *Cradle to Cradle,* is the most thorough set of guidelines available for the voluntary certification of sustainable products, and among the best set of guidelines for making things that are high performing, efficient, and harmless to delicate ecologies in the air and the human body.

When you buy a toaster, you probably don't know or care precisely how much energy was used to make it. But it would be great to know that an honest, strict third party had stamped it as environmentally sensitive—neither carcinogenic, energy hogging, nor an offense to climate policy. Making a Cradle to Cradle product isn't easy, but it's based on a fairly simple notion: that everything we own should eventually be either recycled, remade, or buried in the ground to compost.

Like the label that guarantees that our carrots are organic and pesticide free, the Cradle to Cradle platinum rating cannot be applied to, say, an office chair unless the workers who made it are being treated and paid well, and the chair isn't full of poisons. Some chemicals are simply blacklisted for reasons of human and environmental health. Herman Miller, a company that helped pioneer ways to use Cradle to Cradle principles in design, applies this thinking to every product it makes. It simply won't do business with material suppliers who won't provide their recipes for proprietary chemicals.

The protocol is an unusual private certification, so C2C maintains control over its high standards. But it would take years or decades for most companies to duplicate McDonough and Braungart's research. What makes Cradle to Cradle protocol so compelling is that, for the first time, someone has set a remarkably high standard for genuinely sustainable design. DD

Zero Waste

Most of the stuff around us is waiting to become junk, designed to be short-lived. Most

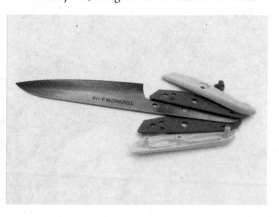

of it cannot be meaningfully recycled. Much of it is destined for landfills or incinerators. We live surrounded by a material culture that still assumes an endless supply of virgin materials and bottomless pits into which we can dump our refuse. Despite the fact that we live on a finite planet of dwindling raw materials and natural systems strained to the limits by pollution, we still live in a throw-away society.

That will change. On a finite planet, eventually our economy must become a set of circular material flows. Everything we're done with must become the raw material for something new. Already, recycling cans or paper and composting yard waste have become commonplace in many cities. But a much broader shift is under way: the shift to a zero-waste society.

Imagine life without a garbage can. Imagine a world where nothing you use is ever thrown away. Food and fiber are composted into soil. Every product is made to be broken apart and completely recycled. Every piece of packaging, every stick of furniture, every appliance, every gadget and gewgaw—everything we ever use—must be returned somewhere (be it a repair shop, a backyard compost heap, a curbside recycling bin, or the factory of the company that made it). In a zero-waste society, there are no garbage cans, because trashing anything is unacceptable.

That life is closer than most of us may think, and it may also be much better than we would imagine, improving the quality of the things we use, the food we eat, and the homes we live in. A zero-waste life can mean a life bursting with better design and more quality. AS

breaking them down, recycling and/or salvaging their parts, and getting them to the appropriate manufacturer for reuse—become necessary elements in the commercial system. As a result, companies that are brand-conscious may compete to offer the best return experience.

Returning used products may even become a major part of the shopping experience, with special stores emerging to facilitate consumer returns. We like to think of these reverse retailers as "drop shops." By offering amenities like café settings, public information on the company's products' backstories [see Knowing the Backstory, p. 39], and perhaps even repair services, drop shops may make the chore of recycling your goods more pleasurable while building brand loyalty in shoppers—who may enjoy returning a product almost as much as they enjoyed buying it. AS

Drop Shops and Reverse Supply Chains

As producer responsibility and zero-waste laws become more common, "reverse" supply chains—systems for taking back products,

---

Preceding pages: Workers recycle electric motors, Fengjiang, China, 2005.

Opposite: This Toginon knife is designed to be easily disassembled for repair, resharpening, and recycling.

SHELTER

We think of our homes mostly in terms of memory and emotion—a magnificent meal prepared in the kitchen, a child's first steps across the living room, a basement that always gives us the shivers. The longer we live in a home, the more the physical structure fades into the background. Our lives unfold within it, but we tend to forget about all the ways we continue to interact with and depend on the services our home provides.

At its most basic, a house is a tool for living, but most homes today are blunt, poorly designed tools. They waste energy and water, lack safety and comfort, and are often made from materials whose production has huge environmental and social consequences. According to the Worldwatch Institute, "People can live in a typical house for 10 years before the energy they use in it exceeds what went into its components— steel beams, cement foundation, window glass and frames, tile floors and carpeting, drywall, wood paneling or stairs—and its construction."

But better homes are on the way. A confluence of new technologies and approaches is beginning to allow us to create buildings of a whole new stamp: buildings that are light, airy, comfortable, and stylish; buildings that sip water and make all their own energy; buildings that are better for us and, over time, better for our pocketbooks.

These bright green homes are emerging from the same design explosion that is putting sustainable products on store shelves. Because building a home demands so much more of an investment than, say, making a toaster, the innovations are slower to arrive on your block. At the same time, because architects, designers, and engineers are learning so much so quickly, and increasingly sharing what they find, the year-to-year leaps in performance we're beginning to see in bright green buildings can be astounding. In addition, new building codes and standards are emerging that demonstrate that LEED criteria are merely a baseline. The best structures being built today would not have been possible ten years ago; the best structures we'll be able to build ten years from now may not even be imaginable today.

Homes are tools. We are building better ones. And when we build better homes, we build a better world. AS

Following pages: Blu Homes' mkBreezehouse, a prefab green home, features a solar-ready roof, eco-friendly materials, and energy-efficient mechanical systems.

Green Building

Our buildings don't last forever. They burn, they rot, they crumble, they are brought to the ground by earthquakes and reduced to dust by insects. Wars level them, fashions outdate them, newer buildings take their place. Some of our buildings last dozens of generations, but most do not. Even in cultures where continuity and tradition are prized, homes that last more than a few centuries are rare; many of the structures built today are meant to last only decades. Sooner or later, our buildings become rubble and waste.

But though our buildings don't last forever, their impacts can.

Once, these impacts were comparatively slight. In traditional societies, structures were mostly built with naturally occurring materials like wood, stone, clay, and thatch. When the building's life was over, these materials could generally be composted or recycled. Likewise, because energy was expensive in premodern times (and often came in the form of hardworking people and animals), traditional homes tended to be built with far less energy than modern ones. They were usually small, by today's standards, and built to last as long as possible. The ecological footprint of these buildings was fairly small and their useful lives were long, and because they were usually heated and lit by renewable fuels like wood and wax, the amount of ecological damage done by living and working in them each year was modest.

Today's buildings are different. They're enormous, by historic standards, and often made with huge volumes of non-renewable resources, from vinyl siding to tropical hardwood floors, sometimes shipped from thousands of miles away.

They're built quickly in energy-intensive ways, and often the developers who slap them together give very little thought to their long-term viability and usefulness. Once people are living and working in them, the buildings are energy sieves, using huge amounts of fossil-fuel energy to heat, cool, and light the spaces within. They suck up resources and energy and wear out quickly, meaning that each year spent living and working in them has a final ecological cost that is many times greater than that of homes built a few centuries ago. Indeed, the wasteful and slapdash character of the homes, stores, and offices we build these days is one of the main reasons why we in the Global North have such catastrophic ecological footprints; our buildings are environmental disasters.

And we're building many, many more of them than ever before. Swelling populations and rising standards of living have led us into a building boom greater than any humanity has ever seen before (or is likely to again), and we're not at the end of it yet. Hundreds of millions of structures will go up in the next few decades, and if they're all as wasteful and impermanent as the average building in North America today, it will be impossible to shrink humanity's ecological footprint to sustainable levels. In order to save the planet from permanent harm, we have to build better.

Luckily, we're starting to learn how to do that. AS

Right-Sizing and Design for Deconstruction

What would a truly sustainable modern building look like? No one's certain yet, but we have some pretty solid guidelines, and they all stem from two basic principles: balance and legacy.

The largest amount of damage done by a building is often the construction (and remodeling) of the building itself. We need to balance the impacts of buildings over the course of their lives, so that the harm caused by the materials inside them—and the energy that powers, heats, and cools them—fits within a sustainable and equitable ecological footprint for the people who live and work inside them. In addition, what remains behind after a building has completed its useful lifetime needs to be as safe and renewable as those wood and stone homes our ancestors built. A building's legacy needs to be healthy.

One way to improve this legacy is to design it with its end in mind. When we design things for disassembly [see Producer Responsibility, p. 115], materials get simpler and more recyclable. Certain elements (for instance, fine tiles) may take on an heirloom quality, and become incorporated into newer buildings when they've completed their initial lives. The construction techniques used to build the structure may change as well, to make it easier to take apart when the time comes.

Another way to improve buildings is to make sure they're the right size (and in the right place) to begin with. Small homes can promote more balanced living [see Small Green Spaces, p. 179], but they also can save enormous volumes of materials in their construction and huge amounts of energy in their operation. In addition, if they're sized correctly and oriented on their sites with the path of the sun and prevailing breezes in mind, it becomes much easier to heat and cool them (as we'll see below).

Today, when our buildings reach the end, they often become piles of semitoxic trash. In the future, every piece will find a useful end, either as a material for some other construction, or as compost or fuel. Thinking ahead and siting and sizing our buildings wisely are the first steps. AS

A Prefab Home

A prefab craze has captivated the international building market, inspiring ready-made solutions for livable spaces that are endlessly creative and customizable. The revival of this way of building has the potential to bring sustainability to the built environment on a massive scale. Prefabs, from mobile home double-wides to modular build-it-yourself kits, have been around for decades, but the boxy little houses were often associated with cheap materials and lowbrow design. Today's prefab home—a combination of cutting-edge modern design, simple efficiency, and ecological consciousness—has made the transition from stigma to style icon.

Off-site manufacturing does have some redeeming ecological qualities, such as the reduced impact on the housing site itself, the reduced transportation and energy required to build on-site, and the reduced waste due to mechanically precise measuring and cutting systems. A number of prefab-design pros, like Michelle Kaufmann of mkDesigns, have taken the innate ecological smarts of this approach much further by incorporating numerous additional green features such as photovoltaics, wind power, natural ventilation and shading, green roofs, FSC-certified lumber, recycled materials, efficient insulation, and replaceable modular components. Plus, most prefabs are relatively compact compared to standard homes, saving space and energy and permitting increased density.

Small entrepreneurial firms have led the way with modern, minimalist prefab, but larger companies are getting involved too. Modular furniture giant IKEA, for example, collaborated with the international development and construction firm Skanska to create a line of affordable, modern prototype homes currently available in Sweden, Denmark, Norway, Finland, and Great Britain. Prefabrication can also be a smart solution for communities in need. At MIT's Department of Architecture, experts and students in the Digital Design Fabrication Group are working on computer-generated architectural designs using friction-fit components with tabs and slots that join together so precisely they can be assembled using only a rubber mallet. This accessible method is a boon for disaster sites and communities in the developing world, where the demand for shelter is great but advanced machinery and skilled labor are in short supply.

Creativity runs wild in the prefab arena. In an eye-catching hybrid of prefab and reuse, for example, many designers have capitalized on the potential of steel cargo containers. The sturdy shipping modules are the ideal size and shape to take on new life as modern, minimalist minihomes, components in stacked-up office complexes, or even affordable dwellings for developing nations.

So what's in store for the future of prefab? Better business plans and marketing strategies are just beginning to catch up to the explosive creativity of prefab design, and new technologies like 3-D fabrication will no doubt have an impact on this form in years to come. Prefabrication also has the potential to piggyback on other product-lifecycle solutions: imagine structures designed for easier dismantling, reuse, and recycling, or even producer take-backs for mass-produced homes. With the right advances, prefab will move from a fashion obsession to a lasting strategy for more sustainable building. JVL & SR

Heating, Cooling, and Passive Design

Imagine a home lit and warmed by the sun, and cooled by natural shade and breezes. Many buildings today cut us off from the outside, with powerful heating and air-conditioning systems, dark interiors, even windows that don't open. But as more people recognize the energy costs of artificially producing a comfortable indoor environment, they're rediscovering the power of passive design.

At its roots, passive design is about creating buildings that are so well insulated that the energy required to heat or cool them is a fraction of what's needed to keep us comfortable in the leaky buildings most of us are used to. When the building itself is superinsulated, we can use the power of the sun to keep it a comfortable temperature by arranging the building properly on the site, orienting windows toward the south to optimize the benefits of sunlight, or installing a reflective or white roof to minimize unwanted solar gain.

Passive ventilation often goes hand-in-hand with solar orientation, since temperature, airflow, and comfort are closely linked. At a basic level, passive ventilation is about taking advantage of the physics of air movement—how air moves in response to being heated or cooled, or to changes in pressure—and enabling these natural systems to do their work. Making the best of the prevailing winds in the area can play a role, as can landscape elements like hedges and trees, which provide shade or shield a building from strong winter winds.

There are other promising strategies for regulating a building's temperature more efficiently. Geothermal heating and cooling, for example, is one of the fastest-growing technologies for controlling indoor temperatures around the world. Using a large heat pump that cycles water through loops of underground pipes, these systems can warm or cool a 2,000-square-foot home for as little as one dollar a day.

All these systems have been made user-friendly through new technologies. We no longer have to be engineers to keep our houses running efficiently with natural heating and cooling: the design does most of the work for us, and simple technologies like thermostats and automatic windows can do the rest. To help mitigate uncertainty, better digital modeling software now lets architects predict with more accuracy how, for example, air will flow throughout their finished structures. In many places, it's possible to get rid of furnaces and air conditioners altogether; that can drive down construction costs, save huge amounts of energy, and reduce the ecological footprint of the building dramatically.

Awareness and popularity of these systems is on the rise around the world, though up-front investment costs and shortages of both manufacturers and trained installation contractors still stand in the way of widespread adoption. Regulations and sometimes even green building codes can get in the way by specifying expensive heating and ventilation systems that make passive solutions less cost-effective. But perhaps the most difficult part of building passive buildings at a large scale is convincing lenders to invest in the still-experimental technologies.

The skepticism of lenders and bureaucrats makes Europe's PassivHaus movement a vital bright green solution. "PassivHaus" means, literally, "passive house," but don't mistake these buildings for low-tech. They are on the cutting-edge of design and technological innovation, taking natural heating and ventilation to new levels of sophistication.

The German PassivHaus Institut, founded in 1996, has led the way for better passive design with its PassivHaus certification, now in use across the EU and in the United States. Its standards guide the creation of buildings that stay comfortable year-round without boilers or air conditioning, even in variable climates like the American Midwest. PassivHaus structures easily outperform the energy-efficiency standards of most countries, and European research indicates that the standards produce more reliably energy-efficient buildings than the LEED rating system. Indeed, these buildings use up to 90 percent less energy to heat, cool, and light than conventional new buildings.

PassivHaus buildings must be airtight and insulated to the highest standards, permitting no air or moisture to leak in or out. This not only keeps the indoor environment comfortable, it also increases the building's life span by preventing common problems like mold and dry rot. In many climates, PassivHaus standards require triple-glazed windows and insulated doors. Inside, low-energy appliances and lighting produce less waste heat, reducing the need to cool the building during warm weather. Using PassivHaus modeling software, designers can modify building plans to meet the standards in a way that suits their region's climate.

Because they are so tightly sealed, PassivHaus-certified buildings utilize special fans that can recover heat from stale air as it flows out of the building, using that saved energy to heat up the air blowing in. This keeps the air inside fresh while losing a bare minimum of heat.

Although these top-quality components can incur significant up-front costs, residents who make the investment are rewarded not only with improved comfort but also drastically reduced energy and maintenance bills over the life of the home. According to Kym Mead, senior consultant for the UK-based Building Research Establishment, homes built to the PassivHaus standard require so little energy to operate that some owners are able to switch entirely to renewable power sources at a comparatively modest cost, because of the small systems these homes need. JVL

99K House

Can a new home be both green and affordable? Photo spreads featuring eco-mansions and luxe getaways have certainly made the two

seem mutually exclusive. But if we want green technologies to help transform the hundreds of millions of homes to be built in the coming decades, we need to make those technologies accessible to all.

In 2007, the Rice Design Alliance partnered with the Houston chapter of the American Institute of Architects to sponsor the 99K House competition, a challenge to envision a practical, low-impact home that could be built and sold for $99,000 or less. The contest's goal was to produce a prototype for a modestly priced, green single-family home that could be replicated throughout the Gulf Coast region.

The winning design, selected from among 182 entries, was submitted by architects from the Seattle firms HyBrid and Owen Richards Architects. It incorporates rainwater harvesting, recycled materials, and natural ventilation. The use of prefabricated components helps lower the cost of production. The standout feature, however, is the home's system of movable interior walls, which can be rearranged or removed altogether to change the space without a pricy remodel. A home office can become a child's bedroom, or the house's second story can become an independent apartment to generate additional income. In this way, the thoughtfully designed home becomes an enduring tool that supports a family's ongoing efforts to live more sustainably, comfortably, and affordably.

The 99K House was built in Houston's historic Fifth Ward, a residential downtown neighborhood, on a site donated by the city through the neighborhood-based Houston Hope affordable housing initiative, and was sold to a qualifying low-income family. JVL

The 99K House demonstrates that building green doesn't have to cost a fortune.

Zero-Energy Developments

One possibility opened up by passive designs and high-performance construction is zero-energy development. Also known as "net zero" development, these buildings use on-site systems (usually solar photovoltaics, but also sometimes wind turbines or even biomass systems [see Green Power, p. 146]) to generate the energy they need to operate. This means not only that the operations of the building itself have a tiny carbon footprint, but also that more energy is generated locally (which can be more efficient than sending electricity long distances over wires or pumping oil or gas through long-distance pipelines). This can help make clean district energy projects [see Green Power, p. 151] more practical.

In fact, if enough clean energy is generated, a zero-energy development can balance the ecological costs not only of manufacturing and installing the energy system itself, but of building the whole house. Architect Bill Dunster, whose Beddington Zero Energy Development (BedZED) is an iconic example, estimates that a building needs to generate only 15 percent more energy than it uses to balance out the energy used in its construction. "Take the average life of a building at about 100 years or so," Dunster told the *Times* [of London]. "The aim is to put back enough energy during its lifetime to compensate for the carbon used in its construction." A5

Living Building Challenge

When it comes to green buildings, is zero-energy development the highest goal we can strive for? Some predict the best buildings will one day go beyond zero: not only will they avoid any harmful impacts; they will actually contribute positively to the community and ecology around them. Like living things, these buildings will generate their own energy, process their own waste, and enhance the ecosystems in which they function.

Sustainable design innovator Jason McClennan has tried to tackle this ambitious goal with a certification program called the Living Building Challenge. This green building standard is different from many others because it is outcome-based. While other frameworks allow designers to pick and choose which "points" from a prescribed list they will earn to add up to certification, the Living Building Challenge simply looks at the finished building to determine whether or not it meets the objectives. Designers are free to achieve certification using the methods and technologies they deem appropriate, as long as their projects perform in the end. New buildings, renovations, infrastructure projects, landscapes, and even entire neighborhoods or community developments are eligible to apply.

The program measures achievements in seven areas: site, water, energy, health, materials, equity, and beauty. Projects must respond to local environmental conditions, generate all of their energy from renewable, noncombustion sources, and capture and treat 100 percent of the water used by occupants (if this is not legally possible, applicants must appeal to local government for policy exceptions). The standards encourage habitat preservation, urban agriculture, and dense, compact development that enables car-free living. The program was also designed to monitor actual—not predicted—performance, so each project must be monitored for at least twelve months of normal operation before it can be submitted for certification.

The nonprofit Cascadia Region Green Building Council (of which McClennan is CEO) first released the challenge in 2006 and continues to manage the program, now in its 2.0 version, under the recently founded International Living Building Institute (ILBI). At press time, more than sixty projects around the world were progressing toward the Living Building Challenge. Among the completed buildings in the assessment phase are the Tyson Living Learning Center in Eureka, Missouri; the Omega Center for Sustainable Living in Rhinebeck, New York; a private home in Victoria, British Columbia; and the Hawaii Preparatory Academy Energy Lab in Kamuela, Hawaii.

The major controversy facing the challenge has been the question of whether or not its standards for on-site energy production and on-site water systems work against the sort of dense development that low-carbon cities demand. Because any given piece of land can generate only so much clean energy (or capture so much rainwater), urban sites are paradoxically at a disadvantage in qualifying for the challenge, and might have to reduce their density in order to meet it. Some complain that this means sacrificing a necessity (dense development) for an arbitrary standard (net-zero energy, net-zero water). The Living Building Challenge, though, is itself an evolving entity, and recent revisions have already worked to resolve the conflict.

When an industry is evolving as quickly as green building, even the most cutting-edge standards risk becoming obsolete before the first buildings to bear their names are even built. By issuing a challenge to meet criteria rather than a prescribed checklist, the ILBI hopes to catalyze designers to continue innovating until they succeed in developing the highest-performance buildings possible. JVL

Opposite: A computer rendering of Zoka Zola's Zero Energy House, Chicago.
Right: BedZED, London's famous bright green housing development.

Cool Roofs/White Roofs

Dark surfaces coat our cities. Hot sunshine turns black rooftops into radiant heaters, which contribute to the urban-heat-island effect and bake the inside of buildings below.

The quickest and easiest solution? Turn hot, dark roofs into "cool roofs." Most homes have to be reroofed about every twenty years. Studies by several groups, including the Lawrence Berkeley National Laboratory, have shown that changing from a dark-colored shingle (once traditional because it was more "woodlike") to a light-colored shingle (titanium-based white or terra-cotta red) can shave air-conditioning costs by up to 40 percent.

Another solution is to create smart roof tiles that change color as the temperature shifts. A team of MIT grads has developed the "thermeleon" tile, which uses a polymer gel in a plastic case that is black on one side. When the gel "melts" at high temperatures, it becomes white, reflecting up to 80 percent of the sun's heat. When the mixture cools, the polymer redissolves into the gel, which becomes colorless, thereby revealing the black base of the tile. The tiles can then absorb up to 70 percent of the sun's heat to help warm buildings in winter. JC

Light-colored Concrete

Engineers refer to a surface's capacity to reflect light as albedo. The lower the albedo value, the more solar heat a surface absorbs, and the more it contributes to the urban-heat-island effect. We've all seen the heat shimmering off a stretch of black asphalt.

In New York City, the Design Trust for Public Space produced a comprehensive analysis of ways to increase the performance of the city's infrastructure. They found that if New York could raise its citywide albedo by just a fraction, it would make a dramatic positive impact on air quality, energy consumption, and the health of New Yorkers. As one major step, they recommended that the city replace much of its black asphalt with light-colored concrete.

Reducing the heat-island effect would decrease ground-level ozone, which causes eye and lung irritation, not to mention an increased demand for AC. According to a 2005 study by the Design Trust for Public Space, if New York City's temperatures came down by just 3 degrees Fahrenheit (or by just 1.7 degrees Celsius), urban air quality would improve as much as if an entire fleet of the city's gasoline-powered buses or service trucks were replaced with electric-powered vehicles. AS & SR

◼◼◼   RESOURCES

Green Building A to Z: Understanding the Language of Green Building by Jerry Yudelson (New Society Publishers, 2007)
A great primer on green building, this is the best simple resource for understanding the industry's terminology. Yudelson has the gift of not only writing clearly about complex topics, but also knowing what to leave out.

U.S. Green Building Council
http://www.usgbc.org
"Build green. Everyone profits." That's the motto of the USBGC, which works as the central hub to the entire American green-building industry, offering professional training and accreditation, sharing information about new green-building innovations, and overseeing the LEED rating system. Though they have limited information for the casual worldchanger, if you're even thinking about embracing green building in some way in your business, this should be your first stop.

And if you're new to the field, USGBC's Emerging Green Builders is a program you should know about. Emerging Green Builders links together young architects, designers, builders, and planners who have a passion for sustainability, through an e-mail listserv and through cool events in a number of cities.

A Place of My Own: The Education of an Amateur Builder by Michael Pollan (Delta Publishing, 1997)
Many of us cherish the dream of one day building our own dream homes. And the writers among us tend to obsess about a particular subset of dream home: the writing studio. Writer Michael Pollan went a bit further than dreaming,

though: he not only imagined a better place to write, but he set about building it, and then shared his experiences in this little gem of a book. And in every step of the process—from sketching out his writing cabin to doing the finish work—he found insight into the meaning of home and building history.

"The development of clear, leaded glass in 1674, followed a century later by sheet glass made with iron rollers, coincided with—and no doubt helped to promote—important changes in people's attitude towards the world beyond the window. Beginning with the Enlightenment, people were less inclined to regard the world outside as perilous or profane; indeed, nature itself now became the site of spiritual sanctity, the place one went to find oneself, as Rousseau would do on his solitary walks. Nature became the remedy for a great many ills, both physical and spiritual, and the walls that divided us from the salubrious effects came to be seen as unwelcome barriers."

A Good House: Building a Life on the Land by Richard Manning (Penguin Books, 1993)
We've been hoping to find places where we can live in some more balanced way with the land around us almost since the Industrial Revolution began. Richard Manning decided to spend a year building a green home on a rural lot in Montana, and chronicled not only the construction process itself but the ways in which the work and the thought he put in helped him rebuild his own life, after he lost his job as a muckraking environmental journalist. Technically, this book is a bit out-of-date, but the journey Manning takes us on couldn't be more timely:

"My environmental reporting, my investigations, the thing that had smashed my career, had taught me that there is enormous consequence to the way each of us lives our lives. Distilled to its simple forms this means a house takes forests from mountains. A house takes coal from the hills. A house takes life from the planet. Yet each of us must have a house. For those of us who value nature, this is the primary contradiction of our lives.

"It occurred to me that I was uniquely situated to investigate this matter from one end to the other, not by reading or interviewing or thinking but by asking the question in a more basic manner, by asking the questions of each board and wire in my house. Could I build a house in such a way as to ensure my happiness and still do minimum damage to the earth?"

Dwell
Rejecting the conventions of most home and architecture magazines, where design and interiors are portrayed devoid of a human element, *Dwell* set out to highlight the energy, diversity, and charming imperfection of well-lived-in spaces: "At *Dwell*, we're staging a minor revolution . . . We think that good design is an integral part of real life. And that real life has been conspicuous by its absence in most design and architecture magazines . . . We want to demonstrate that a modern house is a comfortable one."

Dwell has also been largely responsible for the renaissance of prefab home design, which has played a significant role in the modern perception of what makes a home green, emphasizing that compact spaces and off-site fabrication are key elements of sustainable living today.

Lighting

It's become a common slide at conferences: a map of the earth at night, with the wealthier and denser areas shining brightly and Africa largely dark. The point of the slide: look at how much energy some people have access to and how little others do, and, by inference, see what gaps in economic prosperity persist.

But these maps don't actually display prosperity, or even energy use: instead, maps of brightness illustrate light pollution and energy waste. The blazing light our satellites photograph while whizzing above us in their orbits, well, that's light that's serving no useful purpose (unless you imagine our glowing cities to be a form of art meant for distant eyes). Light seen from space is bouncing off illuminated surfaces or being shone directly from bulbs aimed up. Neither is helping us on the ground see our cities or our spaces better.

We could, we should, be treating light as precious, and getting clever about illuminating our lives with only the light we need. Using the minimum needed lumens would not only save a fair bit of energy, it would also bring the night sky back to our cities; it's the light bounced back by the atmosphere that hides the stars. Seen from above, a bright green city would be only a smudge of light. AS

Light-emitting-and-collecting Interiors

Everyone knows that natural light is good for us. Ideally every space would be designed for maximum natural light, but the fact is we have a lot of dismal existing space to deal with, from dreary cubicles and windowless offices to basement apartments.

Full-spectrum lightbulbs are the most common (and affordable) tool we have to mimic the benefits of natural sunlight. But some ingenious designers have taken a more direct approach, letting sunlight flow right into furniture and dark rooms through fiber-optic cables.

Sunlight-transport System
The Swedish company Parans developed a system that collects sunlight in outdoor panels, transmits it through fiber-optic cables, and reemits it indoors through a well-designed overhead fixture. A combination of different types of beams gives the impression of natural light filtered by trees. Placing the outdoor sun-collecting panels at varying angles allows the indoor fixture to maintain a high level of natural light throughout the day, as the sun moves across the sky. Lund University installed a Parans system to brighten a gloomy meeting room; and Södertälje Hospital has several systems in its radiology department, where workers and patients would otherwise never encounter natural light.

LiTraCon
Designed by Hungarian architect Aron Losonczi, LiTraCon (light-transmitting concrete) is a

Left: A photo of the earth at night, showing the intensity of light pollution in North America.
Opposite, left: LiTraCon is a light-permeable building material made from optical fibers and fine concrete.
Opposite, right: The Parans lighting system brings sunlight inside.

composite of fine concrete and glass fiber optics molded into blocks. LiTraCon blocks can be purely decorative: the fiber optics form eye-catching patterns, and a single panel of blocks can be placed in front of a window as a shade; the Hungarian Embassy in Paris built a chic reception desk out of the material. But the blocks can also be functional. Because they are 96 percent concrete, they are structurally sound, and designers have used them in rooms that need both natural light and a bit of privacy—building walls without blocking out the light.

"Sunlight Table"

The "Sunlight Table" concept by Random International emits natural light via a grid of fiber optics contained in the table's surface. An input device (which can be placed near any window) collects the sunlight, and a few cables carry the light to the table. Not only do we get the benefit of the light itself, but we also get to watch the light fluctuate as birds or falling leaves brush by, giving us the sense that we aren't quite so disconnected from the movement and the life right outside our windows. Although the table was developed as a concept project and is not available for purchase, it's a sure sign of bright and bold things to come. SR, JF & CB

Daylighting

Natural light is the human body's most important regulator; it contains blue spectrum light, which is what our Circadian rhythms respond best to—and what our artificial light almost completely lacks.

A seminal study on daylighting by Heschong Mahone Group of Sacramento, California, surveyed the performance of 20,000 students in California, Colorado, and Massachusetts; standardized test scores for students who attended classes in buildings with plentiful natural light were as much as 26 percent higher than the scores of students whose classrooms had no natural light. A similar study of daylighting in hospitals has noted that patients with access to natural light heal up to 11 percent faster.

Managing daylight better not only improves our health, it lowers energy costs and the carbon emissions related to energy use.

Heliostatic Lighting

Daylighting is not a new concept, and neither is one of its more common solutions: heliostatic lighting, which uses large sun-tracking mirrors to redirect daylight into interiors and shaded spaces. New York's Carpenter Norris Consulting specializes in heliostatic lighting. For one of their clients, Morgan Lewis Law Offices in Washington, DC, the company constructed the Solar Light Pipe, essentially a 120-foot-long cylinder installed in the atrium that passes through all fourteen floors, diffusing daylight from a rooftop heliostat into each floor's elevator lobby. The firm's recently completed heliostats at Tear Drop Park South in Manhattan's Battery Park City use three adjustable mirrors to direct sunlight into a two-acre park that, because it's surrounded on three sides by towers, would otherwise never receive direct sunlight.

Heliostatic systems come in all sizes. The SunTracker Two model from Ciralight, for example, is a hybrid of a standard skylight and a heliostat. The skylight has a heliostat in a glass

bubble that is hooked up to a solar-powered GPS tracking mechanism to ensure a consistent source of light all day. According to Ciralight, the Sun-Tracker produces the equivalent of 800 watts of fluorescent lighting but draws no power to do so. When the clothing company Patagonia installed SunTrackers at its distribution center in Reno, Nevada, the building's need for artificial lighting dropped by two-thirds, cutting operational costs by one-third.

Daylighting in Building Design

One of the great things about the renewed focus on daylighting is the creative new forms it has prompted in building design. The Philology Library in Berlin by Foster and Partners resembles Buckmister Fuller's geodesic dome with a twist—it has a curved translucent skin that diffuses daylight. Stefan Behling (an eco-expert with Foster and Part-ners), told *Metropolis* magazine that being in the

library was akin to "sitting with a white umbrella under a tree and watching leaves cast shadows to create a play of light and pattern: 'In the library, if you are reading and look up from your book, you actually notice how clouds move over the building because the light changes on that surface. It's like a natural light projection screen.' "

The Green Lighthouse, a CO_2-neutral building at the University of Copenhagen, was sited for maximum solar orientation employing a sundial shape with thoughtfully placed skylights to maximize daylighting. With rooftop solar panels soaking up the rays as they pour in through the skylights and windows, the Green Lighthouse is a building that gets all of its power from the sun.

Retrofits

It's easy to build daylighting into a new home or tower, but what do we do with all of our existing stock? Office buildings from the 1970s and '80s, of which North America has a lot, are particularly bad at harnessing this natural asset, with floor plans that keep most workers as far from windows as possible and old windows that may be good at blocking glare but are equally good at blocking light.

Heliostatic systems can solve problems in existing structures, but some architects are taking even more creative approaches. The 10 Hills Place building is a great example of how an old building can be retrofitted to deliver daylight. For one wall of the office building, located on a dark London corner, Amanda Levette Architects built a new skin—undulating aluminum cladding over a lightweight steel frame based on both the artwork of Lucio Fontana and high-tech ship-hull design. Several strategically placed large skylights in the facade do what the building's original windows couldn't: funnel in daylight that would normally get lost in the narrow divide between office towers. CB

Lighting Our Streets

Our interiors aren't the only spaces that need a lighting makeover. When we step outside our front door at night, we're either blinded by light pollution or, if we live in more residential areas, plunged into darkness, making evening walks a risky prospect. To preserve both our safety and our nightscapes, several designers are transforming the streetlight into something that's responsive and low-energy.

San Francisco–based design collective Civil Twilight received the grand prize in *Metropolis* magazine's 2007 Next Generation competition and made it to the finals of the 2009 Index Awards with a project called Lunar-Resonant Streetlights. In this project, LEDs are hooked up to a photosensor to gauge the brightness of ambient moonlight, and the streetlight emits only as much light as is needed. Not only does this save energy on cloudless nights, it also minimizes light pollution so people may actually see a few stars twinkling around that big old moon.

Similarly, Philips is developing the Light Blossom, which resembles, depending on your viewpoint, a lovely unfurling flower or a ceramic vase in your great aunt's living room. This LED lamp is solar- and wind-powered (the "petals" rotate as needed to catch the wind). At night the petals close up a bit to ensure precision lighting, which reduces light pollution. The streetlights also remain dim until they detect motion. CB

Energy

Energy is the lifeblood of advanced civilizations. Just a few centuries ago, our ancestors had only basic forms of energy— the muscle power of humans and animals, the heat and light of a burning fire, and a few simple machines like waterwheels and windmills—with which to work.

Today, in the Global North, cheap power courses through our lives. Flip a switch and electricity from a distant power plant lights up our rooms. Start the car and fossilized plants compressed over millions of years burn in our engines— and off we go to work. Turn the thermostat up and gas piped in from faraway places fires the furnace and makes our homes cozy.

But satisfying today's hunger for energy comes with enormous and severe environmental costs: climate change, air pollution, oil spills, river-killing dams, and nuclear waste. Our addiction to cheap energy is the driving cause behind not only the massive disasters we all fear, but also the longer, slower emergencies that threaten to undermine our entire society, from energy shocks to the climate crisis.

The social impacts of our dirty energy system are no better. Our addiction to cheap oil links us to dictators and repressive regimes, wars and terrorism. It enriches a few, at costs borne by many. And cheap, dirty energy allows us to make many questionable choices—like building sprawling suburbs that require long daily commutes and undermine other values we hold dear (like spending time with our families and friends, and feeling part of a close community of neighbors).

In the Global South, too, the situation demands change. Hundreds of millions of people still struggle to make a living with only the most basic forms of energy and sustenance (oxen, open fire, hand-pumped well water). They are quite understandably eager to use more energy—to work their fields more efficiently, to light their homes, to refrigerate their food. The kind of energy they adopt will not only determine their quality of life, but will have global impacts. A world of solar-powered villages is a world of less poverty and greater climatic stability.

We do have options—a clean energy future could be ours. AS

Using Energy Efficiently

The most direct path to a clean energy future starts with simply using less energy to get things done. Most of our homes leak heat; most of our appliances waste energy; and a lot of the power we use is spent doing things (like lighting and heating empty rooms) that we don't actually need to be doing. Green buildings and sustainable products can increasingly deliver us the good life without wrecking the planet, but we can all start being more energy-smart right now.

Sometimes little actions don't mean much. The opposite is true when it comes to powering our lives. Small adjustments, minor improvements, and simple steps can not only slash our electric and heating bills, but can let us take part in a global movement to do more with less. Imagine if this year we each cut the amount of energy we wasted by just 3 percent—say by changing all of our lightbulbs to compact fluorescents and turning off lights when we're not using them—and then, next year, we made the commitment to use 3 percent less again—say by installing a more efficient washing machine or reinsulating our attics. Imagine if we continued like that each year, gradually investing more in making our homes greener, using better technologies as they

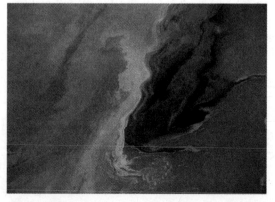

Left: In 2010, BP's Deepwater Horizon wellhead spilled more than 200 million gallons of oil into the Gulf of Mexico, contaminating more than six hundred miles of coastline.
Opposite: Replacing incandescent bulbs with compact fluorescents and installing insulation are two modest measures that can greatly reduce a home's energy needs.

became available, being more mindful of ways to cut useless power consumption—like the "vampire power" our televisions and cell-phone chargers keep sucking even when they're "off." Imagine if we continued to get smarter about how we use energy, aiming for a constant 3 percent improvement—the "clean three"—year after year. It would obviously grow more challenging as the easier things got checked off our lists, but we would also have more and better green technologies at our disposal as time went on.

What difference could the "clean three" make? A lot. If all we did was deliver our "clean three" each year, and we kept it up for the rest of the century, we could, by 2100, be using less total energy than we do now, even if we had a planet of 10 billion people all as wealthy as the average European. This is what energy experts call "the conservation bomb."

And, in fact, we may be able to do better than 3 percent a year without breaking the bank. Many efficiency measures save more money over time than they cost to undertake. McKinsey & Company estimates that the United States, for instance, could quite affordably cut its greenhouse-gas emissions as much as 28 percent by 2030, with 40 percent of those cuts having negative lifetime costs. In other words, 40 percent of the efficiency actions needed would already make us money; they would be investments. A bold national push for greater efficiency innovations could lead to even greater returns.

In the meantime, pushing the efficiency envelope in our own lives not only helps us save money but also changes the world around us. It primes the market for more efficient products. It builds the market for green-power utilities. It creates momentum behind innovations that can benefit the planet's poorest people. It even helps us prepare to disconnect from the grid altogether and start creating that bright green future. AS & JC

The 2,000-Watt Life and Carbon-neutral Communities

We're used to measuring our impact in terms of carbon, but we can also measure it in terms of watts. Worldwide energy use averages 17,500-kilowatt-hours per person per year (equaling roughly a continuous consumption of 2,000 watts per person). However, as with CO_2 emissions, these averages hide the lopsided distribution of such allotments between Western nations and the developing world. The average Western European person uses 6,000 watts; the average American 12,000. But the average person in the Global South uses a mere fraction of the 2,000 watts.

The "2,000-watt society," a Swiss vision of sustainability, is about both energy efficiency and climate fairness. By decreasing energy use through better materials, infrastructure changes, and personal choices, a 2,000-watt society dials down its energy use enough to allow for new clean-energy sources to meet power demand in climate-friendly ways. Ideally, adopting the 2,000-watt lifestyle would create balance while leaving no one in the

dark—quality of life may rise in the South, but it won't dip in the North.

According to studies by the Swiss Federal Institutes of Technology and other institutions, a 2,000-watt life is feasible for Switzerland. In 1960, before breakthroughs in clean tech and green materials, the country was a 2,000-watt society. "Smarter Living," an overview of 2,000-watt goals by Novatlantis, a joint research commission of the Swiss Federal Council of Education and the Federal Institutes of Technology, points out the opportunities for energy savings in our buildings alone: the average residential building requires 1,400 watts per person, whereas a similar home built to Minergie-P standards (the Swiss equivalent of PassivHaus design [see Green Building, p. 126]) requires only 350 to 550 watts per person.

Amory Lovins, a bright green visionary and head of the Rocky Mountain Institute, told Worldchanging in 2009 that the 2,000-watt society could work even in the United States. In fact, said Lovins, "I actually think that, with integrated design and even newer technologies, 1,000 watts is probably realistic—and it may even be cheaper [than 2,000 watts]."

Currently, there are only a few isolated examples of places where very low energy use and clean energy have combined to make a community carbon-neutral. The Danish island of Samsø is net-carbon-negative, thanks to many islandwide assets, such as a system of land-based and offshore wind turbines (in which hundreds of islanders own shares) and several biomass-burning district energy plants. It may be difficult to imagine the success of an island with fewer than five thousand residents scaling up to the size of our biggest cities, but one of Samsø's best lessons is how little the day-to-day business of life has changed.

This wouldn't surprise proponents of the 2,000-watt society, who are quick to explain that this is not a lifestyle of sacrifice. Said Lovins, "It can look like whatever you want. Because so much can be done with just technical efficiency, there's a great deal of flexibility—in how and where people live, what houses look like, how we get around,

what our settlement patterns are . . . You can mix technical and social change however you want." With larger cities from Copenhagen to Seattle making plans to go carbon-neutral [see The Bright Green City, p. 194], both ambitious goals and flexibility will be needed. CB

Japan's Top Runner Program

Making our homes more efficient can be as simple as eliminating obvious wastes of energy by insulating and weather-stripping, but making appliances more efficient demands hard-core engineering innovation. To make a refrigerator or stove or washing machine more efficient, companies must have an incentive to invest large amounts of money in research and development.

Japan has found one way to provide the incentive. Its Top Runner program sets the efficiency standards for a wide variety of products (from vending machines to air conditioners to TVs) sold in Japan. On a regular basis, officials test all the products currently available in a category, determine the most efficient model, and make that model's level of efficiency the new baseline. The best available becomes the new normal. This drives other companies to try to make even more efficient models to compete, which in turn means the next time officials set standards, the best available products will be even more efficient.

As a result, Japan not only has one of the most energy-efficient economies in the world, but is improving even more quickly, and by 2030 plans to be 30 percent more efficient than it is now (measured by energy use compared to economic growth). When standards are raised quickly, innovation can happen even faster. AS

Home Energy Meters

How much power do we use at home? Our monthly electric bill gives us the total, but how can we figure out which of our various toys and appliances need to be replaced with something greener?

Two devices, the Kill A Watt and the Wattson, help make the invisible visible. Plug any appliance into the front of the Kill A Watt, plug

Offshore wind projects, like this one at Kentish Flats, United Kingdom, can provide the clean energy sources needed for a region to aspire to a 2,000-watt life.

the Kill A Watt into a wall outlet, and the system will show you how much power you're using. The kilowatt-hour readout in combination with the time-used readout makes it easy to figure out which appliances should be at the top of the "must replace" list.

The Wattson is a next-generation Kill A Watt. A combination energy meter/portable display, the Wattson provides real-time information about household energy consumption, both as a text readout of current power demand and as an accumulated "burn rate" of cash. In addition, a colored LED screen indicates your home's overall energy health with an ambient red light that dims in accordance with how much power your electronics are consuming at any given moment. The Wattson can even be hooked up to home computers to archive information and to connect Wattson users to online information and idea exchange. JC

Vampire Power

Much like a leaky faucet—which slowly wastes a valuable resource—an appliance that is turned "off" but still plugged in consumes power through passive energy consumption, often referred to as vampire power. In fact, some devices use almost as much energy off as they do on—certain TVs and stereo systems expend up to 70–80 percent of their power when "off." According to the U.S. Department of Energy, 20 percent of Americans' monthly power bills goes toward vampire power. Many electronics manufacturers don't even use the word *off* anymore, substituting *standby*, which more accurately reflects the state of the appliance: perpetually at the ready.

The U.S. Department of Energy wants to instate manufacturing standards requiring products to be engineered so that they do not draw energy—or at least not as much—when they're not in use. In the private sector, a company called Power Integrations offers electronics manufacturers a technical quick fix in the form of a chip that can be built into products to reduce standby power drainage by 75–90 percent. For now, though, all we need to do to eliminate vampire power is to unplug appliances when we're not using them, or to plug them into power strips that we can switch off when we leave a room. JJF

Water Heaters

Water heaters may be the most forgotten mechanism in the home-energy puzzle—let's face it, they're just not as sexy as smart meters or solar panels. But according to the U.S. Department of Energy, water heaters can use as much as 25 percent of a home's energy—enough to prompt Energy Star to create criteria for certification. This has already sparked innovation from home-appliance leaders like GE, which unveiled a hybrid electric water heater that the company claims uses a whopping 62 percent less energy than standard water heaters. The heat-pump heater pulls in ambient heat to warm the water stored in the tank; the electric mode is standby.

Solar water heaters use the heat of the sun to deliver hot water. In most settings in the Global North, they're combined with conventional water heaters and are primarily an energy-saving tool (they heat the water up before it gets to the conventional water heater, meaning less energy is spent getting the water hot enough for our taps). They're about to get much more common: China in particular has charged forward to become the world leader of solar water heaters, and Chinese homeowners have installed tens of millions of systems in the last decade, helping to improve performance and lower costs. CB & AS

Mandatory Disclosure

In most places, homeowners and landlords conduct energy audits on a voluntary basis, usually if they are planning to remodel or to upgrade a facility's metering system. However, in a few places energy audits are mandatory, generally when the building is sold.

In 2010 Australia's federal government rolled out a two-phase program for mandatory disclosure of energy efficiency in commercial buildings. Immediately, owners of commercial office buildings were required to conduct audits (valid for twelve months) whenever selling or leasing space of more than two thousand square meters. The second phase of the program looks to extend mandatory disclosure to other commercial building types (hotels, stores, apartment complexes, schools, and hospitals). The city of Austin,

efficiency is boosted greatly by small measures like weatherization or installing a more efficient water heater—repairs that are affordable enough to be more than offset by higher asking prices.

Cutting energy use in our existing building stock is a big part of creating a sustainable world. Therefore, a building with a very low efficiency rating should be considered a fixer-upper, just as a building with a leaky roof or other structural integrity issues would be. Buyers should be aware of how much work it will take to fix the energy leaks in their new home. And if such disclosure simply becomes part of the selling process, building owners can start to work on efficiency measures well before they're ready to sell, and may actually see their repairs pay for themselves before the property changes hands. CB

Energy-efficient Mortgages

The rewards for having an energy-efficient home don't just show up on utility bills; they can also show up on your monthly mortgage statements. Homes that qualify for energy-efficient mortgages (EEM) receive lower interest rates on mortgages. EEMs are given for homes that already rate high, like Energy Star–certified homes. EIMs (energy-improvement mortgages) offer the same incentives to retrofitters. A homeowner aims to improve the efficiency of his or her building by a certain percentage above standards specified by the International Energy Conservation Code (IECC); the cost of the repairs is added into a new mortgage at a much lower interest rate so that when all is said and done monthly payments are actually less than they would be with a standard mortgage and no improvements.

Architecture 2030, a New Mexico–based nonprofit that has issued a challenge to the building industry to become carbon neutral by 2030, supports such incentives to help us boost energy efficiency while encouraging governments to invest in the private building sector, creating green jobs in retrofits and green construction. Founder Ed Mazria told Worldchanging in 2009,

Texas, requires private homeowners to conduct an energy audit when they put their home on the market. Homeowners are not required to make any improvements based on the energy audit, just to make the report readily available to buyers. Similar proposals in Canada, Germany, and the UK are moving forward as we write this.

Mandatory audits are controversial no matter where they're implemented because sellers are concerned that buyers will use a low energy rating to negotiate a lower asking price. It's a valid concern, though one that illustrates a major disconnect in the way homeowners view the systems that keep their homes running. Making sure a property you own—and intend to lease or sell one day—is well-insulated and uses up-to-date, energy-efficient equipment is no less a part of home ownership than keeping a building in general good repair or creating and maintaining an attractive facade and yard. And, in many cases, a home's

A hybrid electric water heater by GE.

when Architecture 2030 was pushing EEMs and EIMs as a component of a U.S. economic stimulus plan, "We think people will be lining up at the doors to take advantage of this . . . The one place we think people *will* invest is in their own house. The other thing we think is, by taking advantage of the lower rates, people would not only make the efficiency upgrades but they would probably spend some more to do some things that they had put off for a while because the rates are fairly lucrative. Our analysis just took into account the spending on efficiency, but we think there would be a lot more spending as we go along."

An even better model is pay-as-you-save (PAYS). Under a PAYS program, a local government funds efficiency or home-energy-system improvements, and the homeowner pays back the loan with the money they save on their energy bill. At this writing, PAYS pilot programs were under way in New Hampshire, Oregon, and Ohio. CB

Smart Grids

The "conservation bomb" [see Using Energy Efficiently, p. 137] can make our lives radically more efficient; carbon pricing and consumer demand for green energy can spur our power companies to invest in a new generation of renewable power technologies; and getting off the grid can turn our homes into little clean power plants. Individually, these are all great steps toward smarter energy use. But what if we put them all together? What if a new kind of power grid could weave together improvements in energy performance, a variety of big green-energy sources, and home-energy systems while maximizing the effectiveness of each?

Meet the smart grid.

The energy grid we grew up with is outdated. A map of the North American power grid shows hundreds of thousands of miles of power lines woven into one another, linking areas larger than most European countries. Power plants at one end produce huge amounts of energy (and greenhouse gases), which get sent down the pipeline to a comparatively small number of substations. These substations mete out this bulk energy to the lines that run into our homes. The slightest disruption in one substation can cause a domino effect that trips outages in multiple states. For instance, in August 2003, an overloaded transmission line in northwestern Ohio took down some power lines and started a cascade of outages that ultimately left 50 million people from Toronto to New York City without power, many for a full day.

Incidents like that blackout illustrate the limitations of a system that was developed before the age of the microprocessor, yet the power industry's response to such debacles is to call for more and bigger power lines. This approach is as impractical as it is unsustainable: not only would it fail to shore up the weak links, but it would lead to more greenhouse-gas emissions and the sacrifice of more wildlife habitats to new power-line corridors.

Until recently, the only alternative to supporting this system was to go off the grid, which meant building independent, expensive home-energy systems and dealing with their flaws and fluctuations. But avoiding the grid altogether is no longer necessary—the grid is about to evolve, and those of us who've stayed on it may still get to enjoy a sustainable, and high-tech, shared utility system.

Power poles, emissions-spewing plants, and miles of wires: out. Computers: in. An infusion of digital controls and sensors is making the grid "smart," able to identify surges, downed lines, and outages, and to implement damage control before engineers even realize there's a problem. Better yet, the new digital system is interactive: you can regulate your own utilities, feeding power back into the grid from home-energy systems, and maybe zeroing out your power bills.

Smart grids and distributed energy are central to a bright green future. By decentralizing power generation and adding digital intelligence to the power network, we can build an energy infrastructure that's more flexible, better able to take advantage of renewable energy technologies, and more resilient in times of crisis. PM & AS

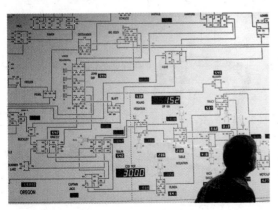

Smart Grids: More Reliable and More Sustainable

Our current grid is highly susceptible to natural and human-made disasters. What's more, this fragile grid is currently protected only by a small cadre of operators sitting in control rooms, who during crises can become overwhelmed by the grid's equivalent of the fog of war.

By contrast, a smart energy network is resilient in the face of troubles, capable of rapid recovery from disasters—its ability to adapt parallels nature's. Grid stability in a smart energy network is the task not of a few overworked humans, but of millions of distributed software agents located throughout the system. "Cops on the beat" in grid-watch posts will still monitor the overall system, but they will have the aid of "eyes-on-the-street" software agents on the lookout for trouble and ready to respond. Those agents will automatically check failures that otherwise might cascade through the system.

In Ashland, Oregon, the municipal utility controls power-demand peaks, thus eliminating need for overbuilt power infrastructure by sending signals to homes through the cable system. Energy-hungry appliances such as hot-water heaters and pool pumps automatically turn down to consume less power. If that proves inconvenient, users can jump online and override the low-power mode.

With a smart grid in place, distribution-level software agents can respond nimbly when a storm with high winds downs lines and blacks out power. The agents quickly detect the troubles and report the location of broken lines to repair crews, enabling line people to speedily restore service. As juice begins to flow again, smart appliances turn back on in a staggered fashion rather than all at once, avoiding demand surges that could shut down power all over again.

Smart energy will be cleaner energy. Think of smart grids as "energy webs." Less advanced systems can't handle multiple

At the California Independent System Operator, which manages the flow of electricity in that state, a map board shows a jump in electricity consumption due to a heat wave.

contributions from outside renewable-energy sources like home-solar outfits or small-scale wind farms, but smart grids can: the smarter our grids get, the greater the range of energy producers they can unite.

Smart grids also make it easier for consumers to buy green energy. With a smart grid in place, power companies could be required to report the emissions coming from each of their plants, as well as their asking price for the energy produced at those plants. Software could then sort and catalog the data and automatically hook consumers up to the cleanest source they can afford. Eventually, entire regions could be giant virtual energy markets, where we buy energy online, getting better prices and cleaner power. PM

Smart Appliances

In your home, you may already have several "smart" appliances—machines that automatically shut off or go into a sleep mode to conserve power. These appliances use built-in features that would react the same way whether they were plugged into the wall outlet or connected to some space-age power supply.

But a new generation of truly intelligent appliances is emerging. These machines actually interact with smart grids to help protect both your wallet and the grid itself.

For instance, the GridWise project, a collaboration between the U.S. Department of Energy's Pacific Northwest National Laboratory, Whirlpool, and IBM, has already developed machines that can detect drops in power from the grid and cycle down just enough to reduce power demands. The shift is virtually imperceptible to consumers using appliances at home, but it eases the burden on the grid enough to prevent a crash.

The GridWise project could be the first concrete sign that a power revolution is at hand. Eventually, interwoven networks of machines, grids, and power sources might pay constant attention to one another, keeping the grid working and safe. In a yearlong experiment in smart power distribution, GridWise connected hundreds of homes in the cities of Yakima, Washington, and Gresham, Oregon, to a new intelligent-power network, combining real-time monitoring of consumption and

pricing, Internet-based usage controls, and smart appliances.

GridWise households have access to their energy-use information through both software and Web sites. This kind of transparency is key to the project's success. The grid does a lot to cut energy consumption, but GridWise participants also have to change their energy habits to maximize the benefits of hooking up to an integrated grid. Consumers are most likely to make long-term changes when they can see the direct results of their choices—end-of-month summaries and community consumption averages are simply not enough. Researchers are confident that the success of GridWise will help make the project a standard part of the regional power grid. SR & JC

Bright Green Meters

Most meters in your home are only there to determine how much money you owe to some company or another. But a new breed of reversible meters could actually make you money. "Net metering" allows surplus energy from your solar-power system to flow back into the grid. You get credit for contributing to the grid, which can greatly offset your electric bill, depending on how much power your system is producing.

Net metering is cheap and simple, and it benefits both you and your utility company. You get maximum value from your system, especially during the day, when you're not likely to be around to use up all the power your system is cranking out. The utility company has to worry less about system overloads when its customers are feeding the grid, particularly during peak times.

Net metering is catching on—thirty-five U.S. states offer it, though their policies vary. Canada, Japan, Germany, and Switzerland also have net metering.

The technology has one drawback: if the power grid goes down in your area, you can't draw power from your home system, even if the afternoon sun is making your solar shingles output power like crazy. Fortunately, a company called GridPoint makes a device that serves as a combined "inverter" (for connecting your solar-power system to the grid) and battery backup. It draws enough power from your solar panels to keep a stash of batteries charged up, so when the grid goes down, you can still run your home. JC

The Prius Effect

When we measure things, we tend to use them differently. Bring energy meters inside the home, studies in the UK and Germany have shown, and we cut our power use by 7 to 10 percent. The constant reminder of the cost of energy serves as enough incentive to do the little things like switch off lights and turn off idling appliances. Put interactive mileage meters inside our cars, and we begin to drive differently in an attempt to improve our mileage. As we change our behaviors, our cars effectively teach us how to become more energy-efficient drivers (the so-called Prius effect).

We change our behaviors even more quickly when we can not only see our own usage, but compare our progress with that of others. Seattle Public Utilities, for instance, sends water bills that chart whether the user is saving water (and money) compared to previous months, show how the user's bill stacks up against that of an average Seattleite, and recommend specific next steps for water conservation. As smart systems become more common, we're likely to see this kind of comparative evaluation—How are we doing? How are others doing? What should we focus on doing better?—become more common wherever we're being asked to conserve. AS

Home-energy meters like the Onzo (available in the UK and Ireland) help homeowners keep tabs on their daily usage.

Decoupling Utilities

Right now, most energy utilities are in the business of selling power. The more of it they sell, the more profit they make. This gives them a strong incentive to oppose energy efficiency, smarter grids, and distributed-power systems, since all of these things can result in their selling less power.

"Decoupling" utilities—separating energy sales from utility-company profits—is one way to combat this. With this system, a regulator sets targets for energy services and uses a neutral auditor to determine whether consumers are getting more or less value for their dollar; if efficiency efforts and infrastructure improvements mean that customers are able to do more with less energy, the utility is allowed to charge more for the energy it sells (which means that people are paying roughly the same cost to maintain their lifestyle, on average, and the utility is making money even though it's selling less power). Decoupling can be a very effective catalyst for utilities to provide efficiency improvements whenever possible. It makes saving energy a business model. AS

Electric Cars and Smart Garages

We're all going to be driving less in the near future. Climate change and rising oil costs make that clear. Even in auto-dependent nations like the United States and Australia, many households will drop from owning two cars to one, or even give up cars entirely. Cars, however, probably won't be going away entirely anytime soon, so the more efficient our cars become, the better off we'll be.

Many design improvements can make our cars more efficient—they can be smaller, for instance, or manufactured from lighter but tougher materials—but the single best step in that direction is making them electric. While many design challenges remain for electric cars (we need long-lasting batteries, for instance), existing models are already as much as four times more energy-efficient than comparable gas-powered vehicles.

And when these electric cars are connected to smart grids, they really shine. Because electric cars are essentially batteries with wheels, if millions of them are connected to a smart grid, that grid will have enormous storage capacity. Utilizing that storage capacity during off hours could save us both money and energy.

The amount of energy we use peaks at certain times of day, especially in the hours after work. In order to keep power flowing during those times, we have to allow for much more generation potential than we use most of the time; whole coal-fired power plants sit idle, just waiting for that one hour a day when everyone wants to watch TV and run the washing machine at the same time. With the kind of storage potential that could come from connecting electric vehicles to a smart grid, existing power plants could run more constantly (and thus more efficiently), filling car batteries when demand is lowest, then drawing down that power when the demand spikes.

Better yet, these vehicle-to-grid connections could help green the power system more affordably. Currently, the biggest problem with clean energy is that it can be intermittently available—when, for instance, the wind isn't blowing and the sky is dark. Without a way to store large amounts of energy when it is being generated by clean sources, we need more constant energy sources like nuclear or coal to keep our lights on. Add a huge amount of storage in the form of electric cars, though, and those batteries can easily be filled with clean energy.

Though cars are humanity's biggest environmental challenge, electric cars may, paradoxically, prove to be a key transition technology to a cleaner, brighter future. AS

Green Power

If we want to combat climate change and reduce harmful air and water pollution (from smog to oil spills), we need to move away from fossil fuels, and quickly. With breakthroughs in wind, solar, and other clean-energy technologies, an oil- and coal-free future is increasingly possible.

Most citizens of the Global North rely on the power grid. That is, wires run from our homes to utility poles and power lines that bring us electricity from faraway power plants, which burn coal or oil or use nuclear radiation. We buy this power from a company or from our local government, and usually we don't think much about what kind of energy we're supporting or what alternatives we have.

But we do have options. Our power utilities can use green energy, and we can use our leverage as consumers to encourage them to do so. What's more, a number of new, innovative power sources are on the way, offering the possibility of clean, diverse, and abundant energy. AS

Buying Green Power

Energy is so ephemeral that it's hard to think of it as a consumer product. But it is, and not all energy products are created equal. Choosing to buy green power generated from renewable, low-impact sources such as solar panels or wind farms is as basic and important to energy conservation as turning off the lights when you leave the room.

You can do your part by buying energy from utilities that generate their power directly from renewable or zero-emissions sources. Bright green utilities are still few and far between, so it's likely that you'll have to choose the green-power

The Empire State Building as seen from New Jersey during the 2003 North American blackout.

option from your standard utility company—meaning you pay slightly higher rates to enable your utility to purchase a certain amount of their power from a renewable source. You don't directly receive that renewable energy, since it all goes into a kind of melting pot. But your utility will use your fees to build new wind farms, solar arrays, or other systems, which helps move the electricity infrastructure away from the oil economy.

If there are no renewable sources or green-power programs in your area, you can still do your part by purchasing renewable-energy certificates (RECs, also known as green tags). By doing so, you are funding the advancement of renewable power in other areas that are investing in clean energy. CB

The Cost of Green Power

A popular myth holds that renewable power is always more expensive than fossil-fuel power. Not so: under the right conditions, good wind farms and solar thermal facilities can already produce power at competitive rates.

This is doubly true if we count all the costs and subsidies. Some maintain that clean energy is already subsidized too much by governments, but the reality is the exact opposite: globally, direct fossil-fuel subsidies in 2008 alone amounted to $557 billion, according to the International Energy Agency. Add to that the indirect costs like maintaining highways used by fuel tankers and supporting military intervention in oil-producing regions, and the total subsidies for dirty fuels are almost certainly in the trillions of dollars per year.

That means fuels like oil are cheaper than they would be if consumers paid their full cost at the pump (instead of indirectly with their taxes)—so much cheaper that simply eliminating subsidies to dirty fuels could result in a 10 percent drop in global greenhouse-gas emissions by 2050, says the Organization of Economic Co-Operation and Development. Add a carbon tax or cap-and-trade system to the equation, and dirty fuels would be more expensive than clean energy in many settings. Solar photovoltaics are expensive compared to the grid, but in remote locations, installing solar panels is often cheaper than running power lines; they will be comparatively cheaper in more places when coal and oil cost more.

Another myth has to do with "intermittency," the idea that renewable energy sources cannot provide power reliably. It's true that photovoltaics are ineffective at night, and wind turbines are nonproductive in still air, but when used together and combined with smart grids and effective storage, alternative energy sources can deliver a steady flow of power when we need it most.

No one source of renewable, clean power is going to single-handedly replace our current energy infrastructure. Instead, we're going to see a mix of technologies, policies, and systems. This will make the resulting energy grid more flexible—but the political path to this future will be challenging. JJF & AS

Solar Power

The sun sends a tremendous amount of power to every square meter of the earth every day. Though clouds and shade can reduce the incoming energy, and though there's no incoming power at night, solar power is a great renewable resource. There are two types of solar-energy systems: solar-thermal systems collect radiant energy to produce heat; photovoltaic-cell systems (those large glossy roof panels) convert direct sunlight into a stream of electrons to produce electricity.

Photovoltaic (PV) systems have been around since the 1970s, but they're still fairly expensive, so they're mostly used in off-grid applications. However, as new materials come on line over the next ten to twenty years, prices should drop and make PV systems competitive in grid-connected applications. Flexible thin-film and organic-plastic solar panels are extremely rugged and adaptable to an enormous variety of applications, from building materials and gadget-holding cases to energy-producing backpacks and laptop bags. New technologies and designs could make solar power even cheaper and more versatile. For instance, researchers funded by the U.S. Department of Energy have discovered that by using nanotechnological "quantum dots," or nano-crystal semiconductors, they could capture more of the energy hitting a solar panel. If their work plays out, it could double the efficiency of solar photovoltaics. And other innovations are waiting in the wings.

Spurred by government incentives, German companies have invested heavily in solar power, putting up nearly half of the world's installed photovoltaic-energy systems, many in the nation's so-called Solar Valley near Freiburg. The result has been a region that's fast becoming one of the green power capitals of the world, a sort of Silicon Valley of clean energy. China, not to be left behind, has announced plans to build a Solar Valley of its own.

One of the world's largest solar-power facilities, however, won't use a single photovoltaic cell. Instead, the 4,500-acre (1,821-hectare) solar farm that Southern California Edison is building in the desert near Victorville, California, will use technology that's nearly two hundred years old: the Stirling engine.

Stirling engines are "external combustion engines" whose cranks are pushed not by explosions in their chambers, but by the expansion of a gas that's heated from the outside of the engine. The gas itself stays in a closed loop, continually being heated, expanding, using up its energy to push a piston, and condensing again. The external heat source can be anything; the Stirling Energy Systems' product Dish Stirling uses sunlight focused by a parabolic mirror array.

Many other solar-thermal projects are already under way around the world. Lacking deserts of their own, many European nations are looking to close deals with companies building solar-thermal plants in the Sahara. The German-led Desertec Industrial Initiative is a $400 billion plan to supply 15 percent of Europe's electricity by 2050 with Saharan solar power. JC, JJF & AS

Wind Power

Wind power is the cleanest alternative energy source; harvesting wind via windmills or turbines emits no air pollution. Large wind farms generate the most wind power, but small clusters of megawatt-range utility-scale turbines are popping up. This is especially true in the upper Midwest, where the turbines have received significant public policy support. In addition, farmers are starting to use smaller turbines to power their farms.

The wind's potential to generate electricity is like a free gift waiting to be unwrapped. Wind is plentiful all around the world. It's clean. It will never run out. So why aren't we letting the wind run our entire planet?

The answer is simple: price. Wind power has historically been more expensive than power from coal, oil, or natural gas. But wind power is growing (from 4,800 megawatts generated in 1995 to 158,000 megawatts in 2009, according to the Worldwatch Institute), and as more people build wind farms, the price of wind power drops. In fact, some recent wind projects are cranking out electricity that is priced competitively with coal and oil, and far cheaper than nuclear power, with none of the radioactivity or greenhouse-gas pollution.

The Battelle Pacific Northwest National Laboratory estimates that as wind power's price drops to a competitive level, wind could quickly supply 20 percent of the United States' electricity. Many other researchers think that, given consistent regulation, equal access to new transmission lines, and more modern power grids (which need to be built anyway), wind power could supply a third of the nation's electricity by 2020—and do so economically. The American Wind Energy Association goes even further, claiming, "North Dakota alone is theoretically capable (if there were enough transmission capacity) of producing enough wind-generated power to meet more than one-third of U.S. electricity demand."

The potential worldwide may be even more impressive. The U.S. Department of Energy has concluded that the world's wind could generate more than fifteen times as much energy as the world is currently using, while a 2002 Danish study sponsored by the European Wind Energy Association, "Wind Force 12," found that with even comparatively modest technological advances and policy support, wind could supply 12 percent of the world's electricity by 2020. In some places, wind power is so abundant that switching from fossil fuels is a no-brainer. Wind already completely powers the Danish island of Samsø. In fact, the community is a net-energy exporter.

The magnitude of wind power's potential can be seen in two recent projects in the United Kingdom, both of them offshore wind farms positioned in the Thames estuary (offshore wind farms generate more power than land-based ones). Kentish Flats, the largest UK wind farm thus far, began operating in December 2005. Its thirty wind turbines can generate enough power for 100,000 homes while reducing carbon dioxide emissions by 245,815 tons (223,000 metric tons) per year.

But London Array, which is still in the planning stages, will easily steal the spotlight. The project expects to use 341 turbines to power more than 750,000 homes. At 1,000 megawatts, London Array would prevent the release of more than 2 million tons (1.8 million metric tons) of carbon dioxide every year. London Array's first phase consists of 175 turbines, generating an expected 630 megawatts of power. It is scheduled to be operational for the London 2012 Olympics. JJF

Opposite: A worker inspects photovoltaic panels at a solar power plant in southern Germany.

Right: A wind farm in Kansas.

Tidal Power

Few people are familiar with "hydro-kinetic" energy, the use of water motion to generate power. The potential is great, but commercial systems are only now starting to be developed. Questions remain, too, as to the impact of hydrokinetic-power systems on ocean environments. However, these systems don't clutter scenic areas like wind-power systems, and they are far less intermittent than either wind- or solar-power systems.

The power of the ocean's constant movement can be harnessed by using the flow of water from tides or the kinetic energy of waves. Generating power from the flow of tides is simple, but less benign than other methods. The power facility involved resembles a hydroelectric dam, built across an estuary. At high tide, water flows freely into the estuary, but when the tide turns, the water can flow out only through a hydroelectric turbine.

In theory, it is also possible to generate power from the ocean's temperature fluctuations, but so far inventors have not figured out how to do it. Oceans absorb a vast amount of thermal energy from the sun—the approximate equivalent of 250 billion barrels of oil per day, according to the National Renewable Energy Laboratory. Only a small fraction of this could be extracted without having an impact on ecosystems, but with the right engineering, hydrothermal power could be a constant, reliable, minimal-impact power source. Though the idea has been around since the 1930s, ocean-thermal-energy conversion plants have yet to emerge from research labs. Many test projects have demonstrated the concept's effectiveness, but a financially viable system has yet to be produced. JC & JJF

Biofuels, Biomass, and Biochar

Biofuels, especially those made from agricultural crops like corn and soy, are a bad idea. They often generate more greenhouse gases than even their dirty alternatives. They tax soils and divert needed food from people's plates. Other biofuel approaches, including using algae to break down agricultural waste and human sewage,

may be more promising, but also face serious challenges.

Turning wood, agricultural waste, and other biomass into charcoal offers more benefits. The resulting "char" can be used to improve soils [see Soil and Sustainable Agriculture, p. 494], but agricultural char can also be burned or pyrolyzed to produce energy in a process called gasification: the chemical reactions that break down the long hydrocarbon chains in the biomass also give off hydrogen gas, methane, and various other burnable fuel gases (as well as tars and nonuseful gases like CO_2). The fuel gases can be burned for heat, or if they're pretty clean (that is, if the tar levels are low), they can be used to power an engine. Gasification is not a new concept; in fact, according to Professor Tom Jeffries at the University of Wisconsin, "Over a million wood gasifiers were used to power cars and trucks during World War II," when Europeans often lacked access to oil. JJF & AS

Geothermal

Most renewable energy comes from the sun (solar and wind) or the moon (tidal), but geothermal energy is earth energy. "Enhanced" geothermal plants pump water deep underground to be heated by rock made hot by pressure (like the molten core of the planet, but closer to the surface). The hot water is then used to turn turbines. Geothermal energy is not available everywhere, but it is nearly limitless where it is available and emits virtually no greenhouse gases. Improved technologies are rapidly driving down the cost. AS

Combined Heat and Power

Waste heat is one of the world's great untapped resources. Each year, we generate so much waste heat—heat that rises from engines, goes up power plant and factory chimneys, and leaks from household systems—that tapping the readily accessible supply would reduce CO_2 emissions in the United States by 20 percent. Systems already exist for generating or using power and capturing the resulting waste heat. These "combined heat and power" systems are widespread in

Finland, Denmark, and the Netherlands. Wider adoption in other countries may well be a major source of energy in coming decades. A5

Nuclear

▬▬▬ Nuclear power is one of the most divisive issues in energy politics. Supporters say that it is a proven energy technology with a low carbon footprint. Opponents point to an industry plagued by safety problems and cost overruns, and say that if you eliminate subsidies, wind and solar energy are cheaper options. At Worldchanging, we tend to think the opponents have the stronger argument, based primarily on the rapidly falling costs of wind and solar power, both of which are completely safe and have almost no direct environmental impacts when sited correctly. A5

District Energy

▬▬▬ The city of St. Paul actually learned something from the energy crisis of the late 1970s. In

A prototype of the Pelamis Wave Energy Converter in Orkney, Scotland. The Pelamis uses the motion of the waves to activate hydraulic motors, which in turn drive electrical generators.

1983 it started what has become North America's largest and most successful district energy project. The combined heat-and-power (CHP) biomass-burning plant heats more than 185 buildings and 300 single-family homes through Minnesota's brutal winters. At night the plant also chills 6.5 million gallons of water during off-peak electrical hours. What makes District Energy St. Paul such a success is that customers enjoy the same benefits as those at a standard utility, and in many cases better ones—rates are stable and intermittency is never a aproblem.

Portland's nonprofit Neighborhood Natural Energy (N2e) aims to create small district energy projects all over the city. Current projects in various stages of development range from Salmon Street Energy, a small solar thermal unit that will power fourteen surrounding homes, to Sunnyside Neighborhood Energy (SunNE), an ambitious plan to power more than fifty blocks—including the school, several hundred homes, and several commercial districts—by turning a local school's outdated boiler system into a state-of-the-art solar thermal storage and biofuel boiler system that will pipe hot and cold water through hydronic insulated pipes. SunNE will be a new member-owned utility separate from the city's other power providers.

SunNE takes its inspiration from district energy projects in Sweden, Denmark, and Canada, and there are many good examples of district energy throughout the world. The Danish island of Samsø, for example, is a 2,000-watt society [see Using Energy Efficiently, p. 137] thanks to many different district energy endeavors.

Naturally, the movement for creating district energy has a clever name: locavolt. The locavolt approach is as varied as the communities it serves, but the shared aim is freedom from the power company based on local generation points tailored to a community's needs and resources. An added bonus: once set up, district energy projects help their communities keep pace with technological advances. As better tech becomes available, entire neighborhoods can be upgraded simultaneously, which is much more efficient than waiting for each home or business owner to adopt the latest measures on his own. CB

RESOURCES

Because we use energy—directly or indirectly—to run nearly every system in our civilization, the move away from fossil fuels to clean energy will not be simple. There are myriad policies, technological pathways, planning barriers, subsidy, taxation, and financing questions to be dealt with. No one person could possibly grapple effectively with every discipline and issue area involved.

That's why these six resources, some of the best recent books and reports on clean energy, are so vital. Each is an effort to outline a path forward to a renewable-energy economy, and each is the result of a large team of researchers, scientists, and experts putting their heads together.

The differences between them are illuminating, but any one of them will provide a good overview of the issues involved. Al Gore's book (full disclosure: he wrote the foreword to the first edition of our own book) is the most readable and nicely designed; it's also the only one you can't download for free. *Our Choice, Plan B 4.0,* and *Renewable Revolution* are all global in scope, while *Climate 2030* and *Energy [R]evolution* focus on the United States and *Zero Carbon Britain 2030* examines the UK's energy future. Other, essentially comparable national reports can be found easily online for most northern European countries, often with an English translation.

If anyone ever tells you that getting to a green-power future is impossible, these resources will give you the facts to prove them wrong.

Our Choice: A Plan to Solve the Climate Crisis by Al Gore (Rodale Books, 2009)

Plan B 4.0: Mobilizing to Save Civilization by Lester R. Brown (W. W. Norton, 2009)

Energy [R]evolution 2010: A Blueprint for Revolutionizing a Broken Energy Economy (Greenpeace, 2010), available for download at http://www.greenpeace.org/usa/news/energy-revolution-2010

Climate 2030: A National Blueprint for a Clean Energy Economy by Rachel Cleetus, Steven Clemmer, and David Friedman (Union of Concerned Scientists, 2009), available for download at http://www.ucsusa.org/global_warming/solutions/big_picture_solutions/climate-2030-blueprint.html

Worldwatch Report: Renewable Revolution: Low-Carbon Energy by 2030 by Janet L. Sawin and William R. Moomaw (Worldwatch Institute, 2009), available for download at http://www.worldwatch.org/node/6340

Zero Carbon Britain 2030: A New Strategy (Zero Carbon Britain Project, 2010), available for download at http://www.zcb2030.org

This Dish Stirling solar-power system employs mirrors that focus sunlight onto a thermal receiver to drive an electric generator.

Water

No matter where we live, there is a water crisis unfolding around us.

For some, this crisis is a matter of life and death. Globally, one in five of us does not have access to clean drinking water. Two in five do not have adequate sanitation facilities—water to wash with and to clean with, or even a safe place to answer nature's call. Hundreds of millions of farmers lack adequate water and/or the proper tools for irrigating their fields. Many more are struggling with the effects of the mass privatization of water.

Those of us in the wealthier parts of the world have our own looming problems. Many aquifers—huge underground lakes, filled up in trickles over centuries or millennia—are being pumped dry so quickly that they will be completely emptied within our lifetimes.

Meanwhile, worldwide, too many people with too many needs using water too wastefully have pummeled natural systems that depend on a steady flow of water. Some of what were the largest lakes in the world, such as the Aral Sea and Lake Chad (once the fourth-largest lake in Africa), have almost completely dried up, and rivers around the world are shrinking as water is pumped from them (the Rio Grande, for example, now sometimes goes dry before reaching the Gulf of Mexico). Even in the rainy Pacific Northwest, once-abundant salmon runs have been brought to the edge of extinction as huge demand for water has lowered river levels. Add to these problems nearly ubiquitous water pollution from farms, factories, and cities, and nature is in for a hard slog.

Climate change already exacerbates these problems, yet even worse problems are still to come. Rainfall patterns that have held more or less constant for generations are shifting, making some areas drier and deluging others. Depending on where we live, we can expect more droughts, more heavy downpours, or both.

If we are to navigate this crisis, we must start looking at water in a whole new way. We have to save water every chance we get. Just as we need to find more efficient ways of using energy, we need to find more effective water technologies. Many already exist, and many more are on the way—but the speed with which we adopt them will have much to do with our success or failure in meeting this crisis.

We should see all the water coursing through and around our homes and businesses as a valuable resource worth conserving. The rainwater that falls on our roofs, the "gray water" from our showers and sinks, the water used by industry and farming: with the right tools, all this water can be cleaned and used again in a variety of ways. But beyond simply conserving and reusing water, we need to change our understanding of our place within the planet's water systems—to think of the places we live as part of the landscape of water itself. Our cities drink rivers and release floods of wastewater; our streets run with streams of storm water; our gardens, street trees, and cisterns drink up rainfall and release

Much of the world's population, like these children in Uganda, still lacks access to safe drinking and bathing water.

it over time—we live amidst water, and we need to learn to do so sustainably. AS

Thinking Differently About Water

Imagine if we woke up one morning to find out that we would be supplied that very day with the entire quantity of fresh water we'd ever be able to use. Given global inequity, our share might fill a wading pool, a swimming pool, or a supertanker, but whatever the amount, that would be it for the rest of our days—not a drop more. Knowing this, and seeing the entire bulk of our water supply in one place, chances are we'd do everything in our power to guard that water and make it last. We'd become compulsive about finding ways to conserve, to reuse, to purify and distill. Remaining aware of how much water we'd used—and how much was left—would constantly be at the forefront of our mind.

Of course, the beginning of this scenario is implausible. We'll never see our whole life's water supply in one place. But the need to measure and plan and remain constantly aware of our water use is real. Although we know that water is an extremely limited resource, most of us in the Global North don't experience a sense of responsibility as we watch it flow into the drain. Any awareness we have of the stream of water running through our lives is likely to be merely a hassle or, at best, just a number on our water bill. Rain falls from the sky, runs down our roofs, and washes into the sewer. We rinse a dusty glass and allow nearly clean water to be piped miles away to a sewage-treatment plant. Then we complain that water rates are too high.

But just as we needn't waste the water coming from our taps, we needn't ignore the water falling on our roofs or running down our drains. A whole slew of innovative tools can capture that rainwater (and recycle the slightly dusty tap water) to serve other needs. Some of these technologies make even more sense in the Global South, where there are often no pipes or sewers to begin with.

Most of us in the Global North could fairly easily go off the electrical grid if we wanted to; going "off the pipe" is quite a bit harder. But we can save both water and money by making the best use of the water we're given. AS

The Soft Path

The way we manage water is a paradox: we often can't seem to get enough of it, and yet nearly every time it storms, we have too much. We treat water that flows from the tap as a resource (largely because we pay for it), while treating as a nuisance that which falls from the sky and courses through our cities. We have come to rely upon a centralized system that imports water from vast distances and quickly exports that which falls on our cityscapes, overlooking ways to use or detain water locally and on-site.

Given the historical context, the centralized system makes sense. In the United States at least, centralized systems for supplying water were first built in response to the problems of urban living: in densely populated places, small, distributed, uncoordinated systems failed to prevent episodes of cholera (and other waterborne diseases) and were of little use in fighting devastating fires. Centralized water systems enable cities to prosper and grow, but they come with costs and weaknesses such as overbuilding the system to match peak demand. Extensive networks of pipes are expensive to maintain and replace, particularly in built-up areas. This centralized approach of traditional "hard-path" systems focuses on increasing supply and expediting drainage through pumps, pipes, and storage while discounting the use of behavioral modification and on-site, integrated techniques to manage demand. Perhaps it's time to prime the pump with some new models.

Over the past few decades, distributed "soft-path" approaches have emerged to complement and augment the hard path of centralized systems. Hard-path engineers think mostly in terms of laying pipes and pumps, but soft-path advocates think more broadly, looking to a variety of disciplines (demand management, social marketing, economics, even landscape architecture) to not only deliver the water we need, but to make the system more flexible and resilient, and even to make the places we live more beautiful and comfortable.

Taking the soft path requires thinking about water management in an integrated way: every kind of water—drinking water, rainwater, storm water, and wastewater—is a potentially useful resource. Incremental, distributed approaches to managing these various resources add capacity and flexibility to the system. The soft path handles water as a service rather than a commodity. Demand is driven not by a need for water itself but by a need for what water can do. We think of water in terms of what it gives us (clean dishes, fresh sheets, healthy houseplants)—not in terms of the number of gallons it takes to have these things. When we approach water as a service rather than a commodity, we can use pricing, marketing, land-use regulations, and tools from other disciplines to manage demand for water while securing the services we want. We get our dishes, sheets, and plants, but we also get a hardier water system and a healthier environment. PF

Rainwater Harvesting

The tools in the soft-path kit are numerous. Plumbing codes, incentives for highly efficient appliances, social marketing of conservation practices, green roofs, and permeable pavements are just a few examples. Another is rainwater harvesting, a tool that has been around for millennia. Rain that falls on the roofs of homes (and sometimes other structures) is directed through downspouts into cisterns that store it for use in a variety of applications. We can use the rainwater—instead of drinkable, or potable, water—to irrigate the garden and flush the toilet. This is one of rainwater harvesting's attractive elements: the quality of the water can be matched to the role it will serve. The most ambitious applications provide all of a home's water needs, including drinking water. If properly managed, cisterns are even capable of reducing flooding by capturing storm water and controlling its release. A network of cisterns could potentially serve as a mini–flood pocket, which could be emptied electronically by the local utility in order to distribute runoff slowly.

While simple in concept, rainwater harvesting can get complicated quickly. Rainwater's potential varies dramatically depending on an area's rainfall patterns, a given structure's roof size, and a cistern's capacity. In addition, when a homeowner starts altering plumbing, health officials and utility companies get nervous about the potential

cross-contamination of drinking water via rainwater flowing back into the pipelines.

From Germany and Australia to Texas and Seattle, engineers, architects, researchers, and government employees continue to develop rainwater-harvesting technology. Arguably even more work is being done in the developing world. Rainwater harvesting is becoming a legitimate, reliable element of the soft path, and the soft path is gaining support as a tool for a bright, greenish blue future. PF

Australian Regulations

Australia is largely a desert continent, albeit one with a highly variable climate. Because of the unpredictable and sometimes infrequent rainfall, and because of a desire to protect coastal waterways, Australians are especially interested in rainwater harvesting. The city of Adelaide recently announced that all homes constructed after July 2006 must have plumbed rainwater tanks. The city may also require that tanks be installed in existing homes when they are resold. What's exciting about this mandate is that developers will have to incorporate rainwater harvesting into their plans for new construction, thereby making it an embedded component of water use.

Meanwhile, Melbourne has combined water-sensitive urban design, constructed wetland systems, and water recycling (20 percent of the water used in the city is recycled for playfields, parks, and landscaping) with aggressive household conservation measures to become one of the most water-conscious cities in the world. The average person in Melbourne now uses just 154 liters (41 gallons) of water per day, according to the Victorian government (as opposed to, for instance, the average Canadian, who uses 778 liters [205 gallons] a day). PF & AS

Fog Catching

Fog collection is a beautifully low-tech way to supply fresh water in areas with negligible rainfall. Chile, Nepal, and southern Africa have successfully installed fog-catching arrays, fine nets that are stretched vertically between poles, with a gutter at the bottom. As fog droplets pass through the nets, they impact on the fibers and run down into the gutter; the water is then channeled into reservoirs. Depending on the amount of water collected, the reservoirs can supply homes, irrigation systems, or whole villages with water. The systems require minimal maintenance—they're inexpensive devices with no moving parts and no need for power. The water needs no treatment to be potable; in fact, it is usually much cleaner than all but the best well or river water.

FogQuest, a Canadian nonprofit, is the first organization to successfully deploy fog collectors. According to the organization, its first installation, in the Chilean village of Chungungo, accumulated an average of 3,963–26,417 gallons (15,000–100,000 liters) of water per day throughout ten years of operation. The village was able to stop importing water by truck, and to begin growing gardens and fruit trees; its population subsequently doubled, reversing the migration to cities that had kept it low.

A new and improved fog catcher from UK-based QinetiQ uses biomimicry [see Biomimicry, p. 99] to increase the effectiveness of the nets. A material that has a microtexture like that of a Namibian desert beetle's back composes QinetiQ's nets. The Namib Desert is an incredibly hot, dry environment where occasional morning fog is the only source of water. The beetles that live there have evolved a shell that has a combination of hydrophilic bumps on hydrophobic furrows, which strain moisture from the air and concentrate it. JJF & DD

Virtual Water

When we grow crops, we are in a sense embedding water within them. If it takes a thousand liters of water to grow a kilo of wheat from sowing to harvest, we can, in a way, think of that kilo as virtually containing that thousand liters.

When we consider how much water is embedded in the food we transport around the planet, not to mention in certain water-intensive manufactured products, it becomes clear that there is a massive trade in "virtual water." Though you might think that the wetter regions of the world would ship vast amounts of embedded water every year to the drier parts of the planet, in practice, water-stressed regions are sometimes in effect exporting water they need. This trend has gigantic ecological and geopolitical consequences and, as climate change intensifies, could produce great friction.

One helpful way to keep track of all the water we use—both in our homes and embedded in the things we buy—is to measure our water footprints (a number of online calculators can help us do this). Such measurements reveal the shocking fact that most of us in the Global North use several times as much water virtually as we do directly, at home. This has prompted some people to propose that we pay far more attention to reducing our virtual-water footprints and worry less about how long our showers are.

In an article for Worldchanging, Jeremy Faludi even proposed the idea of water offsets, pointing out that it might be cheaper and more effective for someone developing a new building to invest money in equipping a farmer with an efficient drip-irrigation system than it would be to install waterless urinals and green roofs. Because it takes enormous amounts of energy to pump water to distant farms, more efficient irrigation would also save energy and greenhouse-gas emissions.

Where should we save water? Obviously, the answer is, "everywhere." It's important to remember, though, that most of the water we want to save is water we'll never see being used. AS

Fog catchers strain moisture from the air for collection, Fralda Verde, Chile.

Water Purification

Silver Pot

In Latin America, the group Potters for Peace has designed a low-tech, low-cost water purifier that can be manufactured by local potters; it has been used by the Red Cross and Doctors Without Borders. The Filtrón is a pot made from clay infused with sawdust and colloidal silver. Water poured into the pot filters through its walls into a second, outside pot; in the process most bacteria get trapped, since they're too large to travel through the porous clay; the silver in the clay kills any bacteria that are small enough to pass through. The pots cost about nine dollars apiece and last for three years. Their manufacture also helps boost local economies; a Filtrón factory can be set up for just three thousand dollars.

Solar Watercones

The best-yet solar water purifier is the Watercone, a solar still that uses the sun's heat to evaporate water, which then condenses on the inside of its cone—flip the funnel-like cone over and you can pour the water right into a container. This cheap, rugged system can purify about 1.6 quarts (1.5 liters) of water per day, not only killing all waterborne pathogens but also removing particulates, many chemicals, and heavy metals. Better yet, it can also desalinate seawater—an important function for the world's sizable coastal populations. JJF

Q Drum

In Africa, a simple plastic cylinder has improved the lives of thousands of women and children. The Q-Drum greatly simplifies the task of fetching water—an activity that usually requires several trips, several hours, and a lot of back-breaking work carrying cumbersome containers. Rather than requiring heavy lifting, the Q-Drum rolls easily along the ground, and can hold up to 13 gallons (50 liters) of water (previous containers held 1.3 gallons [5 liters] of water at best). It's also durable: it's pulled along by a rope—instead of handles or other breakable parts—which can easily be replaced or repaired anywhere on the continent. A screw-on lid greatly improves sanitation by preventing contaminants from entering the water. A similar product is the Hippo Water Roller. Though less sturdy, it has a larger capacity, and comes with a kit for a drip-irrigation attachment. JJF

Worldchanging Water Pumps

It's one thing to improve water-carrying techniques, it's quite another to build water pumps that function without infrastructure—without being connected to a public water system or electricity, both of which are out of reach for many rural poor people. Two new devices do just that.

KickStart's MoneyMaker

KickStart is a nonprofit organization founded by American engineers to create a middle class in Africa. KickStart's Super-MoneyMaker has become their best-selling product; the device allows users to pump water for irrigation using their feet, which facilitates a higher yield for farmers, who can increase tillable area and sell surplus goods for a small profit. The pumps cost $90, which is a sizable investment, but the paybacks are huge. One woman was able to radically transform her horticulture business in one year—from a subsistence farm bringing in $93 a season to a five-person operation bringing in $3,200 a season. She was thus able to send her children to school, instead of into the fields.

Left: The Watercone uses sunshine to distill water, Aden, Yemen.

Opposite: The Q-Drum (left), a rollable water container, makes it easier to bring water home, while the Super-MoneyMaker Pump (right) makes it easier to irrigate the land at low cost.

PlayPump

South Africa's Roundabout PlayPump is powered by a very unusual source: a merry-go-round. As kids play on the merry-go-round, the rotation pushes a reciprocating pump that pulls water from a well up into a small water tower, for storage. Villagers can then get water at their convenience from a faucet. Billboards on the water towers providing public health messages and commercial advertisements pay for the system's maintenance and repair. In the field PlayPump has met with some challenges. However, it remains a great example of innovative thinking applied to a long-standing problem. JJF

■■■■■   RESOURCES

Blue Gold: The Fight to Stop the Corporate Theft of the World's Water by Maude Barlow and Tony Clarke (The New Press, 2002)

In *Blue Gold*, authors and activists Maude Barlow and Tony Clarke aim to document the rapid privatization and commodification of water. The book tells the story of how recent international trade agreements are enabling big business to buy up the world's water, making the global water-shortage crisis even worse. *Blue Gold* also provides information and strategies for taking action locally and globally to become responsible custodians of fresh water.

Who Owns the Water? by Klaus Lanz et al. (Lars Müller Publishers, 2006)

Who Owns the Water?, a stunning coffee table book, is a meditation on the fundamental importance of water to life on Earth, to human cultures, and to every aspect of our society. The accompanying text is at times difficult to read—the picture it paints of our water future is unrelentingly grim—but it's packed with valuable information. This ranges from useful new distinctions—like the difference between economic and physical water scarcity (not being able to afford water, as opposed to there not being enough water to go around)—to inspiring ideas fueling the Blue Revolution ("more crop per drop"). Most important, *Who Owns the Water?* provides a thorough illustration of how much we need to change the systems that support our lives, communities, and economies to better use the planet's most precious resource. AS

Rainwater Collection for the Mechanically Challenged by Suzie Banks and Richard Heinichen (Tank Town Publishing, 2004)

Don't be put off by the fact that this looks like a children's book—it's full of accessible, amusingly written instructions that will help you set up and troubleshoot your own rainwater-collection system, and enjoy the project, too.

The authors write from their own experience: "We guttered our house and bought our first tank, foolishly believing we were 'settling' for rainwater. Now, after years of living with 'the gold standard'—water with a hardness of zero, that tastes fresh and leaves our faucets and tiles sparkling—we realize no matter what conditions we had faced, choosing rainwater is not 'settling' for less in any sense. Rainwater is, simply, the best."

A word to the wise: the authors acknowledge up front that their experience is very region-specific (Austin, Texas), so you may have to take other factors into account before applying their methods to your home.

Landscaping

We may not realize it, but we're in dysfunctional relationships with our lawns. They take and take and never give back. Like big green sponges, our lawns suck up water, fertilizer, pesticides, and money, and if we leave them alone for too long, they start to look sad until we give them some more. According to NASA's Ames Research Center, lawns are the largest irrigated crop in the United States.

The typical American lawn has almost nothing to do with nature. A dense carpet of overbred alien grasses, usually coated with toxins, it keeps competitor plants (like villainous dandelions) withering before they sprout. Almost nothing "natural" can survive there. The average lawn makes an overgrown abandoned lot look like a rain forest.

Maybe we feel compelled to keep up appearances by tending to our needy lawns, keeping them as vibrant and immaculate as our neighbors'. But we will never get ahead of our lawns' constant needs, and they will exhaust not only us, but also the natural resources they require to stay alive.

There are better ways to relate to the spaces outside our houses. Landscaping our property intelligently can mean long-term savings—savings on water, with self-sufficient, climate-appropriate plants; on electricity, with shade trees that decrease the need for AC; and on sundries, with fewer treatment, tool, and nursery purchases. There are many resources available, both from city governments and private organizations, to help us develop relationships with yards that give a little bit back. SR

Kill Your Lawn

Putting a stop to the destructive cycle of all take and no give is as easy as giving the space around our homes some purpose. Lawns are passé. In some places, it's become trendy to pave over lawns, which seems ludicrous for all kinds of reasons (not least of which is that skinning a knee on cement feels a whole lot worse than falling on some nice, forgiving soil). But for all its softness, grass has plenty of drawbacks. If we want to get a little back, the best thing to do is the most obvious: Plant something productive. Create a garden. Fill it with food.

Radical designer Fritz Haeg created Edible Estates as an alternative to the water-guzzling, pesticide-drenched grasslands of American front yards. Edible Estates helps homeowners replace their grassy lawns with productive gardens. Besides the known pesticide-intensive lawn-care issues, the cultural barriers that lawns present are a topic Haeg stresses on Edible Estates' Web site: "The lawn divides and isolates us. It is the buffer of anti-social no-mans-land that we wrap ourselves with, reinforcing the suburban alienation of our

sprawling communities. The mono-culture of one plant species covering our neighborhoods from coast to coast celebrates puritanical homogeneity and mindless conformity."

The first Edible Estates lawn revival took place in Salina, Kansas, where a family offered up their conventional front yard for transformation (like a reality TV show for lawn makeovers), and vowed to maintain the garden as a living, thriving edible installation. Reclaiming front yards through this process not only furnishes families with a hearty supply of nourishing food, it also provides an education in seasonal cycles, organic gardening, and regional biodiversity.

Those of us who think a garden sounds too time intensive are not limited to having an emerald carpet. Even deserts and alpine areas have native grasses, shrubs, and flowers that will thrive on their own with a little water and sunlight. Eliminating the homogenous sod that covers most lawns can be as easy as getting down to the dirt and sprinkling some wild-grass seed. What sprouts will be a beautiful, diverse array of grasses and wildflowers—a little originality in the midst of a green sea of uniformity. SR

Backyard Biodiversity

Garden styles vary almost as much as clothing styles, with trends that change over time. The traditional English rose garden, for example, with pristinely manicured shrubs of identical flowers, contrasts with the complex and strategically chaotic gardens that fill so many beautiful yards today. Besides the aesthetic appeal, a diverse garden that integrates many plant varietals offers a number of ecological benefits. This variety—called biodiversity—actually fortifies gardens, making them more adaptable, more resistant to pests and disease, and more productive.

A growing, though still small, number of Americans have torn up their lawns and planted native ground cover, shrubs, and trees, which not only need far less water and fertilizer than lawns (and often no poisons at all), but also offer homes for passing songbirds, butterflies, even frogs. Add a backyard compost pile for your kitchen scraps, and harvest the rainwater that runs off your roof, and your house can soon be a wild oasis in a sea of clipped lawns and asphalt.

The real payoff, though, comes as those oases multiply, forming a mosaic of habitats dotting the city. Indeed, imagine more and more backyard wildlife sanctuaries, woven into a larger urban fabric of green roofs, street trees, and restored streams and wetlands—an urban landscape where nature is at home.

Tips for a Biodiverse Backyard

There are lots of ways to promote biodiversity in our own backyards. Creating curved and irregular perimeters, instead of planting square plots, allows for gradual transitions between various areas and plant varieties. Planting in tiers—or at least being conscious of the gradation in height and size of the shrubs and trees we choose—also works well in biodiverse gardens by mimicking the natural irregularities of plant habitats. To attract bird and insect life, as well as to nourish the members of our households, we can plant edible crops that reach maturity on a rotating cycle through the year, and fruit trees, which have beautiful blossoming cycles before the fruit ripens.

Lawn care can be easy: By avoiding invasive species and taking a step back from obsessive maintenance, we can allow naturally occurring plant life to spring up and become part of a pleasant, diverse garden. By planting native species, we can integrate our own yards into the larger ecosystem. Plants are better able to take care of themselves in their native habitat, which means we have less work to do.

To attract hummingbirds and butterflies to our backyards, we can plant vibrant-colored flowers and masses of plants rather than single flowers. Planting flowers in the sun, near a natural windbreak such as rocks or trees, and looking especially for tubular flowers with a high sugar content also works wonders.

Whether we plant a biodiverse garden for its ecological value or simply for the dramatic variety of shape, size, and color it offers, we will find that our yards come alive with fresh vegetables, vibrant flowers, and the constant dance of birds and bees. SR

A home before and after its transformation, effected with the help of Edible Estates, Salinas, Kansas.

The American Society of Landscape Architects
http://www.asla.org
While officially a professional organization with broad interests, the Amercian Society of Landscape Architecture (ASLA) has increasingly moved to the forefront of the discussion about the role of landscape design and construction in building more sustainable communities. Indeed, hitting the Web site or listening to some of the ASLA's leading members, you might imagine you're dealing with an environmental group. So if you're thinking about incorporating bright green landscaping into your professional life, you need to pay close attention to these folks. And even if your interest in landscaping stops at your back fence, you're sure to benefit from the Web site's valuable learning tools.

Space for Nature
http://wildlife-gardening.org.uk
This British group hosts an amazing Web site full of ideas both practical and inspirational for growing a garden that welcomes native birds, butterflies, and other forms of wildlife. While many of the suggestions are particularly relevant to the United Kingdom, there's plenty here for Brits and non-Brits alike—and lots of great leads that will set you on a path toward luring life into your backyard.

The Brooklyn Botanic Garden
http://bbg.org
Botanical gardens, arboretums, and conservatories are great old institutions we tend to overlook, rather like research libraries, but they often (and increasingly) have outstanding programs to inform, educate, and facilitate public action. When it comes to gardening with native plants, local botanists are often your best resource, and the ones who work at public gardens are often eager to help. The Brooklyn Botanic Garden is, of course, just one of many such places; it hosts a fine Web site and offers some great reading on the basics of responsible landscaping.

The Sustainable Sites Initiative
http://www.sustainablesites.org
A partnership of the American Society of Landscape Architects, the University of Texas at Austin, and the United States Botanic Garden, among others, the Sustainable Sites Initiative has created a voluntary certification system that's like LEED for landscaping. The rating system is based on four years of input from sustainability experts and case studies. Reports on the performance benchmarks, plus the full guidelines to certification, are available for downloading. A two-year pilot program was started in late 2010 to test the guidelines in the field. The United States Green Building Council has participated in the initiative and may incorporate some of its standards into future versions of LEED for Neighborhood Development (LEED-ND).

Pollinator Pathway
http://www.pollinatorpathway.com
This Seattle-based organization is turning standard planting strips—those long strips of tortured grass between the sidewalk and the street—into mini-gardens that contain the types of plants that pollinating insects need for food and habitat. Because many of these planting strips are the responsibility of home- and business-owners, Pollinator Pathway is a community engagement project: the organization provides the plants and coordinates volunteers to create the gardens, but the homeowners take over after receiving training on how to maintain them. Though the project is in its infancy, the organization's Web site provides great inspiration, as well as garden design templates and links to resources for understanding pollination and choosing native plants.

Lawn People: How Grasses, Weeds, and Chemicals Make Us Who We Are by Paul Robbins (Temple University Press, 2007)
A technical but accessible overview of why our lawns are harmful to the environment and our own health, *Lawn People* also delves into the cultural and psychological drivers behind Americans' obsession with having the perfect lawn.

Green Retrofits

Older buildings are vital to bright green cities. When we can reasonably make new use of an existing building, we often come out ahead, both financially and ecologically. This is especially true if the building we're retrofitting is part of an existing compact community or can become the cornerstone for a new one. Great historic buildings add texture to the fabric of our neighborhoods, but even a less-inspiring, unloved building can provide an opportunity for a small neighborhood transformation, where the renewal of a worn-out building makes not only a better structure but also a more welcoming place.

The rest of the world has much to learn from Europe when it comes to preserving, restoring, and retrofitting historic buildings, but increasingly the buildings that need attention are not from past centuries, but from the last generation: apartment towers, modern single-family homes, twentieth-century industrial buildings, and the like. The art of coaxing new life from these more modern buildings is still evolving, but as the demand intensifies for homes and workplaces in our cities in coming decades (and as resources get scarcer), it's an art form we should all encourage. AS

Toronto Tower Renewal Project

Could Toronto's aging concrete high-rises be North America's most promising frontier for sustainable suburban development? A new plan is banking on it. The mayor's Tower Renewal Project aims to tackle retrofitting at an incredibly large scale, by transforming 1960s apartment blocks—built to provide affordable housing, but now suffering, like so many similar social housing projects, from urban blight—into sustainable, walkable hubs of community and economic opportunity.

The project, which stemmed from research at the University of Toronto and the work of Graeme Stewart, an associate at ERA Architects, comprises a series of recommendations for reviving these concrete housing communities. "These buildings were built like tanks," says Stewart. "It would cost a lot more to tear them down, both economically and socially, than to reinvest and make them work." In January 2009, the city identified four pilot sites and launched a new corresponding civic department to oversee the program.

The residential density that these apartment towers brought to Toronto's first-ring suburbs kept sprawl in check, helping to make Toronto's metro area denser today than even Vancouver's (the city that is often held up as the shining example of Canadian urban sustainability). Post–World War II developers didn't

As part of Toronto's Tower Renewal Project, a new exterior insulation and finish system (EIFS) and solar thermal wall are added to the Green Phoenix apartment tower.

do density right, however, and the shortfalls are now becoming clear. With leaking windows and woeful insulation, the towers have become some of Toronto's biggest energy sieves. The neglected buildings now house the city's most impoverished residents, many of them new immigrants. Tenants here find themselves in a paradox of dense sprawl: apartment communities with as many as 30,000 residents are isolated from grocery stores, green space, and other basic amenities.

But the towers already have the foundations they need to become a model for bright green, compact development. The sturdy structures (usually in clusters of five or more) are surrounded by open space (as much as 80 percent of each property is devoted to open space, much of it surface parking), and arranged close enough to each other to provide ideal nodes for public transit and mixed-use development. The difference between failing and succeeding here is just a matter of recognizing opportunities.

The first step: bringing the buildings up to date. The city will achieve an enormous reduction in carbon by retrofitting the aging towers for energy efficiency—overcladding walls and balconies, installing new windows, updating HVAC and mechanical systems, and even possibly adding newer green building options like geothermal heating, solar water heating and photovoltaics, living roofs, rainwater retention, and graywater recycling. Revising outdated zoning laws would allow the towers' owners to use these large lots for innovative retrofits that are normally inhibited by space constraints, such as district energy projects or wastewater-management systems.

The second step: making these communities livable. At this scale, green retrofits can have social implications along with the standard energy savings. The renewal plan envisions replacing the developments' bland lawns with amenities like real parks. Some lawns could be turned into urban farms and native-plant gardens. With many of the towers on the path of Toronto's planned suburban light rail network, tower residents will automatically get better access to the city's amenities. But revising zoning laws would also allow the towers' owners to use some of the wasted open space in between buildings to create new mixed-use development—smart infill measures that would help landlords recoup the cost of retrofitting their towers and enable residents to attend to more of their daily needs, like grocery shopping, without having to commute to Toronto or to a nearby burb.

Toronto's program also stands out among social housing projects because most of the towers are privately owned. "The response we've been getting from building owners is that they think this is a great opportunity to reinvest in their properties, possibly develop new housing that they couldn't before, and improve their rate of return," says Stewart. "In return, they could have some obligations in terms of urban design or making sure the rents stay affordable. It's a new way for owners to create new wealth with their properties while cutting carbon and improving neighborhoods." JVL

Retrofitting Neighborhoods

Even one rehabbed home can lower a community's energy emissions, but it's like a single flower snaking out of the cracked concrete of an abandoned lot. When an entire neighborhood

is running at maximum efficiency, then we've got progress.

LEED's new Neighborhood Development standard [see Developing Green Housing, p. 186] is helping developers create smart infill and new neighborhoods, but so far there aren't nearly enough programs to bring existing neighborhoods up to the same standards. A few, however, are helping neighbors to implement basic upgrades together.

In British Gas's Green Streets program, groups of neighbors compete against one another to see which community can make the greatest reduction in its collective energy consumption. The first Green Streets challenge, in 2008, included eight streets in eight cities. British Gas performed an energy audit on each participating house and handed out £30,000 (about U.S.$45,000) per street for improvements; it was up to the residents to determine how to parcel out the money to maximize energy savings in each home. By the end of the competition the average street had reduced energy use by 25 percent and CO_2 emissions by 23 percent. The winning team, in Leeds, achieved a 35 percent reduction in energy use; British Gas awarded them £50,000 (about U.S.$77,000), which the community donated to a local charity. The next Green Streets challenge, under way at this writing, has upped the ante: fourteen communities are splitting £2 million (about U.S.$3 million) to attempt more ambitious microgeneration projects. The winners will receive an additional £100,000 (about U.S.$155,000) in funds to use for a future energy project.

A little friendly competition is a sure way to get people interested in energy efficiency. It's well documented by now that when people are able to compare their personal energy use to that of their neighbors, they work harder to reduce their consumption [see Smart Grids, p. 145].

But there are other reasons why homeowners choose to participate in group retrofitting schemes. A Washington State nonprofit, SustainableWorks, has created several pilot projects

in which signing up for a group retrofit is voluntary. Although federal subsidies reduce the cost of the initial energy audit, homeowners must still pay for it, and for any repairs they agree to make. Despite the decided lack of freebies or the thrill of competition, SustainableWorks has been able to get hundreds of houses in a neighborhood to sign up. Portland's Clean Energy Works operates on similar principles: the energy audit is free, an "energy advocate" explains to homeowners their options, the homeowners choose the measures that make sense for them, and retrofits are paid off in small amounts on monthly utility bills. Both programs appeal to homeowners not only because of the discounts offered (by pooling the retrofits, SustainableWorks gets better deals from contractors) and reasonable repayment terms, but also because of the green jobs created: both programs train technicians to conduct energy audits and make retrofits. Portland's program may create as many as 10,000 stable jobs over ten years. CB

Re-skinning

We're used to hearing about old buildings getting "face-lifts." But why make a few nips and tucks when you can get a whole new skin? Re-skinning, essentially putting an entirely new facade on a building, can save an older structure when standard retrofits like installing insulation fail to make it more energy-efficient.

There's no single approach to re-skinning. The winners of the ZEROPrize, a re-skinning award from ZeroFootprint (in conjunction with UNHabitat and others), worked on a variety of structures from a typical single-family house in Toronto to a large bank headquarters in Ludwigshafen, Germany. The former, a sixty-year-old bungalow called the Now House, achieved an energy savings of 70 percent after it was given a new envelope with high-quality insulation and a new roof with integrated solar panels, among other improvements.

The most beautiful project in the winners' circle was 355 Eleventh, a small industrial building in San Francisco. Aidlin Darling Architects replaced the original steel cladding with a new skin of perforated, corrugated metal laid over new walls that included operable windows (something

Designs by the Alley Flat Initiative in Austin, Texas, which aims to meet the demand for new housing on the city's East Side by creating accessory dwelling units (ADUs) that utilize green building principles.

the original building lacked). The result is a striking modern building full of light and natural ventilation that retains its historic character. The retrofit reduced energy consumption enough to earn the building a LEED Gold designation. CB

Accessory Dwelling Units

▨▨▨▨▨   You don't always need an entire city block or vacant lot to create impact with urban infill. In some residential urban neighborhoods, the collective potential of a hundred backyards adds up to prime retrofit real estate.

"Granny flats" or "mother-in-law apartments"—small dwellings built within or next to an existing home—have been common for decades in the form of garage conversions, basement apartments, and coach houses. But now prefab housing options for accessory dwelling units (ADUs) are making it possible in some cities to find a prototype, customize the details, and have a sleek, modern unit ready for renters within months.

Cities including Santa Cruz, Seattle, and Vancouver have passed new codes that allow these kinds of dwellings in single-family areas. Some local governments are even providing design and administrative support to boost production. Santa Cruz's award-winning Accessory Dwelling Unit Development Program, created in 2005, provides preapproved, architect-designed prototypes for compact living spaces, so homeowners don't need to start from scratch to create a well-designed small home for rental. The program also offers online tutorials on permits, building, and becoming a landlord.

The Alley Flat Initiative in Austin, Texas, envisions ADUs as a leading strategy for providing new housing in the city's East Side. Architecture students in the Sustainable Design and Development Workshop at the University of Texas have developed prototype ADU designs that incorporate cutting-edge green technologies like rooftop solar power, rainwater harvesting, daylighting, and passive ventilation.

Because no new land has to be purchased, ADUs cost less to build than new homes on undeveloped lots, and thus can be rented at an affordable price while still earning a profit for the homeowner. The result: affordable housing options that blend right into the surrounding neighborhood—and are built at virtually no cost to taxpayers. JVL

Historic Green

▨▨▨▨▨   Preserving high-quality historic buildings is a cultural and aesthetic investment: old buildings tell stories about the neighborhoods they anchor. They are landmarks that help us feel connected to our communities while making urban living more attractive. Historic preservation is also a strategy for deep green building. According to one UK study, it can take thirty to fifty years for a new energy-efficient home to conserve enough to offset the energy embodied in its construction. Reusing an existing structure, on the other hand, requires fewer materials and therefore uses less energy.

European cities have long had strict historic preservation standards, but within the United States leading organizations are finally recognizing the link between the reuse of existing buildings and sustainability. In 2009 the National Trust for Historic Preservation launched its Preservation Green Lab, which is partnering with cities and states to create and disseminate policies that support preservation and reuse of individual buildings, as well as retooling of existing neighborhoods, as part of their climate-change action plans. Currently, for example, the Green Lab is partnering with the city of Seattle to create a long-term framework for energy codes based on measured outcomes rather than prescriptive checklists, which can be ineffective for older buildings.

In New Orleans, an annual event called Historic Green brings together volunteer architects, planners, engineers, and other professionals for two weeks of intensive work in the Holy Cross neighborhood and the Lower Ninth Ward. Teams use their skills to help residents rebuild their historic homes, community centers, parks, and playgrounds. The group's educational and charitable activities integrate historic preservation with

Doorknobs and electrical outlets await reuse at the ReBuilding Center, Portland, Oregon.

sustainability strategies from weatherstripping to planting rain gardens.

Preservation can also be a competitive business strategy. The Jonathan Rose Companies, a green multidisciplinary real estate firm, purchases and renovates historic buildings in transit-oriented urban growth areas through its Rose Smart Growth Investment Fund. The firm identifies opportunities for green upgrades that will reduce operating costs and create a better experience for tenants. Its retrofit of the historic Joseph Vance Building in downtown Seattle (led by designers at Zimmer Gunsul Frasca Architects LLP and engineers at ARUP) earned a Regional Top 10 "What Makes It Green?" award from AIA Seattle in 2009. By capitalizing on the building's L-shaped design, which maximizes sunlight and ventilation, and incorporating modern green building techniques, the team created a healthier and more productive office space. JVL

Reuse Centers

Much of the material that gets thrown away during building renovations and demolitions could be reused instead. Most of it is still viable and functional, and there is no reason for it to go to a landfill. Why does it get thrown away? Because it's easy for contractors to fill up dumpsters, and it's hard for homeowners to find exactly what they want by picking through gutted interiors.

Reuse centers have alleviated the burden on both sides by collecting used building materials, organizing and storing them, and reselling them at a reasonable price. The service these

centers offer saves an enormous amount of solid waste from the landfill, and saves money for everyone during the remodeling process. On top of that, reuse centers are the best places to find unique decorative components to help create beautiful, personal homes.

The ReBuilding Center, in Portland, Oregon, is the largest not-for-profit reuse center in North America, containing 52,500 square feet (4,877 square meters) of ever-changing inventory. It also offers reuse workshops, hosted by offshoot ReFind Furniture, which designs and produces residential and office furniture made from reclaimed wood and materials dropped off at the center.

According to the center, in 2009 it diverted over 3,250 tons (2,948 metric tons) of reusable building materials from the landfill. Compared to the approximately 250,000 tons (226,796 metric tons) of construction and demolition debris generated annually in Oregon, this number is relatively small, but the combined savings from all reuse centers eliminates a thick layer of garbage and redistributes it as usable ingredients. SR & JF

RESOURCES

Superuse

http://www.superuse.org

We all know that green issues, sustainability, and reuse are often associated with dull, unstylish, or ugly objects and buildings that no one would lust after. But the authors of *Superuse* demonstrate that, in many places, "dull" is on its way to the dump as a descriptive term for reuse projects. The examples in their book make

reuse look original and fun. "You could recycle, discard or even burn them of course: cable reels, window frames, washing machines, diapers, crates, carpet tiles, double glazing panels or old buses. The other option is to put them to good use: Superuse." RD

Green Remodeling: Changing the World One Room at a Time by David Johnston and Kim Master (New Society Publishers, 2004)

If you want to bore down into the underlying principles of green building and really know that you're making the right choices in your remodel job, Johnston and Master's book is an essential resource. There are the normal to-do lists and tips here, but there is also a depth of carefully explained research into why certain decisions are greener than others. You don't need this book if all you're doing is replacing the flooring in your kitchen, but if you're trying to truly make a green home, you'll probably find yourself dog-earing pages and underlining passages … and learning a lot along the way.

As Johnston and Master explain, "The energy that buildings require starts accumulating long before the buildings and homes are even in existence. The energy required to extract, trans-port, manufacture, and then re-transport materials to the point of use required a substantial amount of energy at a significant cost to the environment.

The sum of all the energy required by all the materials and services (including the costs of upkeep and maintenance) to go into construct-ing a building is called the embodied energy … For example, stones excavated from a nearby hillside for a new patio have lower embodied energy than stones that must be transported from another state."

Green Home Remodel

http://www.ci.seattle.wa.us/sustainablebuilding/greenhome.htm
These online PDF guides are the best currently available free resource on sustainably remodeling your home—period. Covering painting, roofing, and landscaping, plus salvage and reuse and working with a contractor, these guides are simply indispensable; if you're thinking about making changes to your home, start here. You'll get more excellent advice like the following:

"Initial price gives only a peephole view of the true cost of a product or design over the lifetime of your home. A low purchase price may mean a good deal, or it may signify a lack of quality or durability. Or it may mean that some environmental, health, or social costs are not included in the price. A higher purchase price can mean a better deal in the long run: you can actually reduce the cost of living in your home by choosing resource-efficient fixtures (lowering monthly utility bills) and durable materials (requiring less frequent replacement). Lenders are beginning to recognize the value of ongoing savings to the homeowner. The savings from a more efficient home can cover and even exceed the incremental addition to your mortgage payment, meaning the improvements pay for themselves, and then some."

G/Rated

http://www.portlandonline.com/bps
Portland's G/Rated, a service of that Oregon city's Office of Sustainable Development, offers an excellent set of online guides to building with the planet in mind. Though some of the information applies only to the local area, much is solid and useful no matter where you live. Every city ought to have a service like this.

G/Rated Home Remodeling Guide: Designing and Building a More Sustainable Home

(G/Rated, 2005) http://www.ecotrust.org
If you're more of a paper person, you can get much of the best information from the G/Rated program distilled into a handy little book, avail-able for purchase online.

Greening Infrastructure

Living in dense urban neighborhoods gives us a big leg up on living in a more ecological way. When we live in compact communities, it's easier to drive less, share more, and tread lightly on the planet. If there's a single top priority for living sustainably in the Global North, it's to build compact communities.

But often our cities themselves are a bit of a mess. Although cities do help us reduce our environmental impact on distant areas (in that we don't have to slash into forests or blast hillsides to create homes), the natural systems closest to cities often degenerate into shattered remnants of what they once were.

This is tragic, because most cities have grown up where nature was particularly bountiful—where the farmland was rich, fishing was good, and water was abundant. So, as cities grow, the best land often ends up paved with asphalt or concrete, the best water polluted with sewage and runoff. The layers of separation that old methods of infrastructure place between urban dwellers and the natural world cloud our ability to make smart, long-term decisions with the interests of the earth in mind.

We need urban infrastructure that allows us to live in harmony with the natural systems that sustain us—we need to start thinking of the whole planet as home. After all, there's no such thing as an entirely human place. When you stand on the sixtieth floor of a Manhattan skyscraper, in one sense you stand as much in nature as if you were in the middle of the woods. The water coming out of the tap came from the hills of upstate New York, and then spiraled down the drain to a sewage-treatment plant on the East River. The walls around you are built of stones pulled from quarries, metals dug from deep mines. The climate that prevents the building from being buried under the snows of a new ice age remains in relative balance through the workings of forests and ocean plants the world over. Tug on any aspect of your life, and you will find it connects back to nature, if you follow the string far enough.

It is time, then, for change. It is time, to paraphrase writer Wallace Stegner, to live on this planet as if we planned to stay. To do that, to build a civilization that is broad in time, we need to begin building cities whose workings resemble as closely as possible the workings of the rest of nature.

That goal, of greening our cities until they are part of the working fabric of nature, seems impossibly far off, surrounded as we are by asphalt and concrete, cars and buildings, clanking machinery and suspended wires, in places where nature (think rats and pigeons) survives off our trash or is shoehorned into tiny parks and the edges of lawns. But the first strides toward greening our cities may be easier than we'd tend to imagine.

How much greener could cities get if we took nature as a model? Well, much of the infrastructure that makes urban life possible is overdue for green replacements. The price tag for rebuilding urban infrastructure is not small, but the cost of maintaining the systems we now use is pretty huge over the long haul. This makes the idea of gradual replacement of these systems entirely realistic, if we approach it as the work of decades. AS

Living Wall

What if instead of plugging in our air fresheners, we watered and weeded them? In Ontario's University of Guelph-Humber's main building, designers built an indoor wall of plants as a living air purifier.

The four-story biofilter holds a thick jungle of ferns, ivy, and other plants that work together to break down harmful airborne contaminants into water and carbon dioxide. Since the plants absorb pollutants and break them down naturally, the wall requires no cleaning. Additionally, the fresh air generated by the mass of greenery reduces the need for ventilation systems, promising big savings for the university.

The "living wall" gives a big boost to the aesthetics of the building, as well. Like a work of living art, the lush greenery towers high into the building's atrium. Scientists have been attempting to quantify the psychological benefits of the biofilter, predicting that the presence of so much greenery will improve attendance. For those of us accustomed to regurgitated oxygen from ventilation ducts, this kind of innovation is a breath of fresh air. SR

Trees for a Green LA

The way we build cities can actually make hot places hotter. Tar, asphalt, concrete, and stone all bake in the sun and radiate heat. The overall temperature in a city can rise by as much as ten degrees Fahrenheit (or by as much as six degrees Celsius) above temperatures in areas surrounding the city, in a phenomenon known as the urban-heat-island effect. The problem is particularly noticeable in Los Angeles, with its streets, parking lots, and freeways. Understandably, Angelenos remedy the situation by cranking their AC, but that costs them an arm and a leg, not to mention releasing copious amounts of greenhouse gas into the air.

Landscape architect Patrick Blanc is known for his ambitious vertical gardens and green walls, like this one at the Taipei Concert Hall.

A more economical remedy? We can plant more trees around our houses. Shade trees not only cool down our homes, but they also generate oxygen, limit soil erosion, and beautify our neighborhoods. Careful planting strategies, such as arranging the trees to provide maximum shade, can ensure we'll get the most out of a shade tree while putting in the least amount of maintenance. In Los Angeles, residents can even take lessons in tree care.

The Los Angeles Department of Water and Power (LADWP) established Trees for a Green LA to offer free trees and tree-care lessons to local homeowners. Participants need only complete one short workshop (twenty minutes online or one hour in person) on planting and caring for trees before the city will deliver shade trees that they can plant and care for around their homes.

The LA program offers thirty different species for residents to choose from, and each home is entitled to seven trees. This sounds like one of the best deals around: more greenery, fresh air, cool shade, and all for an attractive price: free! Programs like this have caught on in a number of other cities, and for obvious reasons. The benefits speak for themselves: decreased need for AC, decreased cost of electricity, decreased air pollution—not to mention increased property value and beautification of the urban landscape. SR

Green Roofs

As recently as 2005, green roofs were still typically boutique projects—and convincing city governments and building owners to invest in their widespread production seemed like a major challenge. But the game has truly changed. Cities including Los Angeles, Toronto, Berlin, and Tokyo now offer incentives for developers to add green roofs to their buildings. These rooftop gardens are terrific insulators that absorb UV rays, generate oxygen, soak up rainwater, and add beauty to dense urban landscapes. With so many benefits, it's hard to imagine wanting a plain, unusable black space over your head.

Designers of green roofs use different arrangements, soil depths, and mixes of plants to create specialized products. Rooftops can become meticulously landscaped gardens for people to enjoy, or plots for community agriculture. Thicker soil layers can support storm-water-guzzling rain gardens or even trees. Large green roofs that aren't visited often by people can even help revive urban biodiversity. The six-acre roof atop the Vancouver Convention Centre, for example, houses more than 400,000 native plants and grasses, as well as hives for 60,000 bees.

Turnkey options have made green roofs more accessible. Installation has become easier than ever with the development of mineral soil mats with implanted cuttings that are pregrown and roll out just like sod. Architects at Seattle-based GGLO are currently experimenting with a system of moss mats that will crown a school science building designed to meet the standards of the Living Building Challenge [see Green Building, p. 128]. The moss grows in a felt layer just two inches deep at its thickest points, making it a low-risk load on the building and very easy to install.

One unexpected indicator of the growing popularity of green roofs and other green building solutions is that they've started to bump up against one another: in the school project, for example, architects had to be extra creative to find enough space atop the small building for the project's green roof, solar panels, and rainwater-harvesting system. JVL

Bioswales

When rain falls in the city, it picks up pollutants from the impervious surfaces it falls on; the pollutants then travel along with the rain into storm drains. If that runoff, however, reaches exposed earth, which can absorb water, many of the toxins can be filtered or broken down by plants.

Bioswales, shallow dips or trenches that are planted with low-maintenance native vegetation, can absorb and filter rainwater and runoff, recharging groundwater. In Vancouver, a combination of bioswales and permeable pavement reduced water pollution from runoff in local creeks so much that local salmon populations that had all but disappeared started to return just a few months after the project's implementation. Seattle has also seen small-scale projects yield promising results—in one case, an existing storm-water ditch that was converted to a bioswale not only reduced runoff at the site by 97 percent but also reinvigorated the surrounding soil. The city is now gearing up to build a two-block-long biofiltration swale in the South Lake Union neighborhood. The swale, which will be completed in phases through 2012, will be the largest natural drainage system yet to be built in an urban streetscape, with the capacity to treat more than 188 million gallons of storm water every year. Its position at the foot of one of Seattle's many hills means that it will catch and filter the water flowing from the elevated neighborhood, which until now has flushed pollution and debris straight into Lake Union.

Rain gardens, which are essentially small bioswales, can be planted in any spot around the house that catches runoff from impermeable surfaces. Both rain gardens and bioswales are often features of good green alleys [see p. 175], and are part of many cities' sustainability plans. Melbourne, Australia, for instance, has been studying rain gardens for a decade as part of its comprehensive plan to retain precious water resources. AS & CB

Left: The green roof atop this garage in Seattle's Mt. Baker neighborhood was planted mostly with Eco-Turf (a mixture of turf grasses and perennials like clover) and drought-tolerant sedums. Harrison Architects says that the roof has needed much less maintenance than a traditional roof. **Opposite:** Living walls, like this one at the University of Guelph-Humber in Toronto, clean the air while providing a beautiful backdrop.

Permeable Pavement

When it rains in the city, impervious surfaces such as asphalt and concrete repel water and send it directly into storm drains. The flooding that occurs on curbs and corners comes from overloaded drains, and causes problems far more serious than the inadvertent splashing and hydroplaning of passing cars. Among other things, plants and trees in urban environments miss out on the rainwater that should be their most obvious source of moisture. Paving compromises the health of the botanical life that keeps our cities beautiful, shaded, and cool; it also contributes to the wasting of water, since the trees must be irrigated by other means.

Pavement does have its upsides, however: it's stable, even, and firm—ideal for cars, bikes, and pedestrians. A new material called permeable pavement preserves all the functionality of regular pavement but eliminates the downsides. Permeable pavement can be laid anywhere concrete and asphalt usually go; it creates the same hard surface but allows rainwater to filter through into the ground. This prevents street flooding and keeps urban greenery healthier, with less work and less water.

Permeable pavement hasn't found its way into many areas yet, but Vancouver embraced its benefits early. To test the effectiveness of new pavement technologies, the city incorporated the material into its Country Lanes project, a demonstration area in which the city redesigned a series of streets to be only partially asphalt—and partially covered by permeable surfaces, which provide a solid, durable surface, but allow grass and plants to grow through. The permeable surfaces reduced storm runoff and improved air and water quality; they also enhanced the appearance of the streets, adding greenery to stretches of formerly bare concrete. Pringle Creek, a thirty-acre development in Salem, Oregon, had, at this writing, the largest system of permeable-pavement streets in the United States. In November 2006, when the Salem area had a record-breaking fifteen inches of rain, Pringle Creek's roads didn't flood; the same couldn't be said for most other sidewalks and streets in the region.

One kind of permeable pavement used in parks and other urban public spaces is Biopaver, a

Green Facades

Green facades act like sunscreens for the sides of buildings. They cover outside walls in greenery, generally with climbing ivies that can be trained to grow vertically and create thorough coverage. In hot areas, green facades help to keep escalating temperatures at bay by shading absorbent surfaces from the sun's rays. Like many other strategies for natural temperature control, this one has the great advantage of making a building's exterior more attractive, and of being largely self-regulating, once a vine is trained in the right direction—and provided that the climate doesn't tend toward serious drought. (In older buildings, or those with painted facades, many people choose to use trellises or other structural devices that hold the vines at a few inches' distance from the building itself, to prevent structural and cosmetic damage.) Like most environmentally motivated design strategies, a green facade also saves a homeowner money on cooling bills. What's better than that? SR system of interlocking concrete blocks that have compost and seeds built into the middle. You can lay these blocks in your driveway or on a sidewalk in place of cement. Over time, the compost biodegrades and seeds sprout from within the concrete square; the structure remains intact, but becomes partially obscured by grass. The roots of the plants take in pollutants from the ground beneath the pavement and clean up the soil. Joe Hagerman, Biopaver's creator, is now looking into how his design could be used to simplify the installation of green roofs on existing buildings like schools. Permapave (also called Xeripave) is another paver that's suitable for light traffic areas. Made of attractive natural stone composite, each square foot can filter up to 1.5 gallons of water per second while removing most toxic chemicals from the water in the process.

Permeable pavement is finally getting some attention outside of green housing developments and city-sponsored pilot projects. In 2009 the EPA, as part of its Green Infrastructure Research Program, launched an official test of permeable pavement. The organization paved a 3,995-square-meter (43,000-square-foot) parking lot at its Edison, New Jersey, facility with three types of pervious materials (interlocking concrete, porous concrete, and porous asphalt). The EPA, already behind the curve, intends to study the results for a decade; however, the data they collect can only help to further legitimize the strategy for planners and developers. SR & CB

Beyond Living Machines

If we want to make a city run like nature, we need to create systems that can handle our waste in natural ways. Back in the 1960s, biologist John Todd began designing systems that used healthy, thriving ecosystems to clean sewage—gracefully coordinated tools he called Living Machines.

Living Machines are hothouses and artificial marshes in which sewage runs through a series of small faux ecosystems—tanks of bacteria, algae, plants, crustaceans, and fish. The plants and animals break down, filter out, or absorb some part of the sewage and turn it into living matter. What comes out the other end, after it is fed on by all these living components, is water (sometimes cleaner than the water in our taps) and biomass (living matter that can be composted for soil, fed to livestock, or otherwise returned to nature). And Living Machines themselves can be quite beautiful: the tanks often resemble well-groomed gardens of water plants.

Living Machines were a great—arguably revolutionary—invention in principle, but in practice they often proved too finicky to build and maintain on a scale that would make them practical for cities. Some of the flora and fauna in the Living Machines could not handle the toxic witches' brew that runs through sewers. As William McDonough and Michael Braungart put it in *Cradle to Cradle*, "In addition to biological wastes, people began to pour all kinds of things down the drain: cans of paint, harsh chemicals used to unclog pipes, bleach, paint thinners, nail-polish removers. And the waste itself now carried antibiotics and even estrogens from birth control pills. Add the various industrial wastes, cleaners, chemicals and other substances that will join household wastes, and you have highly complex mixtures of chemical and biological substances that still go by the name of sewage" (2002).

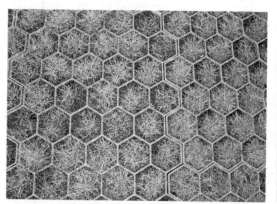

But some industrial microbes find sewage tasty. Researchers are trying to breed microbes and algae that eat sewage and secrete hydrogen [see Neobiological Industry, p. 109]. Other researchers have identified bacterial membranes that can filter most organic matter from inorganic matter. And certain scientists believe we may be able to tame particular kinds of fungi to extract heavy metals in concentrations sufficient to be reclaimed.

Living Machines and industrial microbes could, of course, work together, with microbes cooking off hydrogen in vats linked to tanks of marsh plants and hungry snails—producing energy and cleaning water at the same time. (For one vision of how such a system might work, check out Nicola Griffith's excellent science fiction novel *Slow River*, which centers on mysterious doings at a high-tech biomimetic sewage-treatment plant.)

As technology advances and Living-Machine designers gain experience, these kinds of systems are almost certain to become cheaper and more competitive with conventional sewage treatment. Within a few decades, living organisms might be recycling most of the nutrients in our sewage—if we can stop mixing that sewage with toxins. AS

The "Elevated Wetlands"

One of the best ways to clean large quantities of polluted water is also one of the most beautiful. Bioremediation—the process of restoring contaminated land and water using living organisms—introduces vibrant plant life to formerly lifeless landscapes. In Toronto, marshlands between the Don River and a wide stretch of highway received a revelatory work of ecological art that transformed the space around it. Noel

Harding's "Elevated Wetlands" made a noticeable impression far beyond its immediate surroundings, standing as a multilayered example of both bioremediation and transformative public art. Locals refer to the plastic sculptures that compose the piece as a parade of giant molars or as polar bears marching across a green marsh. All agree that even from a distance the "Elevated Wetlands" seems alive. Not long before the artwork was created, the site had been a salt desert: a desiccated piece of land wrecked by too many winters of roadside salt spray.

Although bioremediation can be an astonishingly complex technology, in this case its gesture on the landscape is simple and elegant. A remarkable marriage of functioning public art and scientific invention, the thriving site now attracts wildlife rather than repelling it. Inside the plastic forms lies a key innovation: layers of plastic from old bottles and nonmetal automobile waste form a hydroponic environment for the plants—a soil system made from recycled plastics, with pumps quietly powered by solar panels. As tainted upstream water is pumped through the wetland, the plants absorb polymers and heavy metals, aerating the water and sending it back out clean. "One of the great discoveries was the relationship of solar power and plant intake," says Harding. "Part of the lesson learned is that along all rivers and wetlands, plants take in water by sunlight; you can pump water by sunlight. It's not really quite a work until the water's flowing." DD

Green Alleys

In cities where cars dominate planning decisions, alleys have become breeding grounds for urban problems. It's no wonder these shadowy spaces, where pools of dirty rainwater collect amid dumpsters and idling trucks, are forgotten at best and shelters for criminal activities at worst. The biggest ecological problem that alleys create, however, is runoff. Their paved surfaces channel millions of gallons of water directly into overtaxed sewer systems every year.

It doesn't need to be that way. City governments have begun to realize that relatively simple solutions can transform alleys from nuisances into assets. In Chicago, for example—where

Opposite, left: Permeable pavement allows water to filter through the ground, preventing flooding and keeping urban greenery healthier, Vancouver.
Opposite, right: Living Machines could provide a sustainable alternative to treating wastewater with chemicals.
Following pages: Noel Harding's "Elevated Wetlands" at Taylor Creek has transformed its surroundings, Toronto.

more than 1,900 miles of alleyways make up the largest such system in the world—the Department of Transportation in 2006 began replacing conventional concrete and asphalt with permeable pavers made from recycled industrial materials. The new pavers reflect sunlight instead of absorbing it, reducing the urban-heat-island effect, while also absorbing runoff. All upgraded "green alleys" are also augmented with energy-efficient, dark-sky-compliant streetlights [see Lighting, p. 135]. The model has worked so well that the Chicago DOT has committed to making it the standard for every alley it refurbishes. And taxpayers needn't flinch: economies of scale have cut the price of permeable pavement by more than 60 percent, so that the watershed-friendly infrastructure costs roughly the same as conventional systems.

Alleys have social potential as well. In Baltimore, groups of neighbors can obtain city permits to install gates to separate their alleys from the street, improving safety and security and allowing them to redesign the space as a form of communal backyard. Even better, however, are public alley improvements that allow the entire neighborhood to blossom. By adding planters, trees, art, and benches, communities can turn their alleyways into parklike urban oases. Some neighborhoods even go as far as to rip up pavement and plant the areas with grass.

Helle Soholt of Copenhagen-based Gehl Architects points out that because cozy alleyway widths are often the perfect scale for pedestrians, alleys can become the "green lungs" of a city. It's easy to imagine how a citywide network of green alleys could provide invaluable neighborhood connectivity, offering safe spaces for children and adults to walk between schools, parks, shops, and one another's homes. By keeping these spaces clean, adding plants or outdoor art, and opening storefronts that face the alley, communities can activate these unused spaces as backgrounds for vibrant public life. JVL

The city invested heavily in diverting runoff by building rainwater reservoirs, which can hold the excess water until the sewage system empties enough to accommodate the load. Nowadays, it takes a particularly heavy rainfall for any wastewater to reach the harbor.

By 2002 the city was able to open its first public swimming area, near Islands Brygge. The Harbour Bath, a series of supersleek docks with a lifeguard station and a diving platform, has transformed how Copenhageners relate to the harbor: it's no longer just a place for industry but a free public amenity and a natural extension of the city's beach parks. Perfect for sunbathing and socializing, these swimming docks make the city that much more livable. A second series, playfully named Copencabana, is in Vesterbro, and more swimming clubs are in the works. The water that flows through the city has become part of public life. CB

Harbour Bath

Few European harbors are clean enough to swim in. The Copenhagen harbor is one that is, even though as recently as 1995 its waters were polluted by both sewage and industrial waste.

Andrea Zittel, *A-Z Management and Maintenance Unit: Model 003*, 1992. Steel, wood, carpet, plastic sink, glass, and mirror, 86 × 94 × 68".

Small Green Spaces

Urban living is better for the planet [see The Bright Green City, p. 194]. So why does living in a city so often evoke a sense of resignation?

Any good designer can tell you that limits and constraints often improve the design of things. The same can be true of compact spaces. Done right, small spaces can be some of the most pleasant living environments around. A compact living space is intrinsically less wasteful and less expensive than a sprawling space. Simplicity and efficiency in a living space are a statement of a truly empowered existence.

With this in mind, designers are turning our most sustainable dwellings into spaces we love to live in. In North America, this process started nearly a century ago with the invention of the Murphy bed; the only multipurpose, space-saving item that can compare is the futon. But we've come a long way since the Murphy bed; flexible systems like easily customized, modular shelving make apartments more livable and stylish, while new "microhomes" use prefab designs to give people the best of both worlds—compact spaces that are still stand-alone units. SR

Not So Big House

Are there rooms in your home that you almost never enter? In recent decades, the "bigger is better" mentality convinced many people to measure the value of their home by its square footage, the number of bedrooms and baths it contained, or the inclusion of separate rooms for formal entertaining. As a result, many homeowners found themselves with larger-than-necessary houses, overwhelmed by maintaining all that extra space and lacking a feeling of connection to their home.

In 1998, architect and author Sarah Susanka faced the problem head-on, by introducing the idea that living well is linked to the quality of the space, not the quantity. She coined the term "Not So Big House" to describe homes that are thoughtfully planned so that each space is inviting and appropriate for everyday use. Through her books, articles, and Web site, she explains how structural details rather than square footage can be used to create a comfortable home. Instead of correcting a house that feels cramped by tacking on a huge addition, for example, she suggests making the existing space more functional by adding windows or tearing down a wall between the kitchen and living room.

"It was the first time that an architect tried to explain to the general public something about how design wasn't just about decoration, but about more fundamental issues: rethinking the way a house actually works," says John Brown, an architect and the founder of the design site Slow Home.

Susanka's message struck a nerve with readers around the world who sought solutions for simplifying their homes and much more. Her 2007 book, *The Not So Big Life,* uses her approach to home design as a metaphor for creating a life that is fulfilling and fully inhabitable. JVL

Andrea Zittel's "A-Z Living Units"

In a small space, the more we can fold, tuck, and trundle away our things, the better. We may think our apartments look better after we've shoved the laundry under the bed, but imagine how streamlined our spaces would be if we

could tuck away our appliances, stovetops, and bathroom sinks.

Designer and artist Andrea Zittel makes this possible with "A-Z Living Units," freestanding compartments that contain everything from full minikitchens and lounge areas with bookshelves to utility rooms—all packed in a box.

The units, which can be custom-made, are not only brilliantly compact, but they're also great looking: modern, clean, and simple. They're perfect for renters who want to be able to move from place to place while keeping things consistent and efficient. Sharing a house with multiple room-mates gets a lot less stressful when every roommate essentially has a mini-apartment in their room.

In her more recent projects, Zittel contin-ues to find ways to help us simplify our lives and our spaces. Her Raugh (pronounced "raw") line of furniture is even more ambiguous than the Living Units. Based on shapes found in nature, Raugh pieces can morph to meet the user's needs: wooden slats, for instance, hang on the wall to make a shelv-ing unit or stack to become a desk or bench. SR

Reno's Rehabbed Microhomes

In recent years, the design world's fasci-nation with small spaces has inspired a new craze for doing more with much, much less. One prod-uct of the trend, the "microhome," combines high-quality finishes and uber-efficient design to pack all the appeal of a dream house into a space that's smaller than the average U.S. hotel room (about 325 square feet). While these miniature homes are often portrayed as the boutique, superfashion-able, and somewhat extremist end of sustainable housing, two entrepreneurial women in sprawling Reno, Nevada, thought the idea would be a hit with more typical homebuyers.

Pamela Haberman and Kelly Rae of HabeRae Investments Inc. purchase and retrofit unwanted buildings on existing city lots, then turn them around as beautifully designed and efficient minimalist living spaces. Since 1998, the group has created more than 34,000 square feet of new living space from unused land within city limits, mak-ing a point to locate these homes within walking distance of community amenities like parks, restaurants, and grocery stores. Among their latest projects: an update of a 192-square-foot, 105-year-old house, and a retrofit of an abandoned fire station into loft residences with organic garden plots where tenants can exercise their green thumbs.

Rae can whip up a sleek and perfectly serviceable kitchen in only eight feet of space that includes an eighteen-inch, Energy Star–rated dishwasher, a stainless steel sink, a twenty-inch stove, a twenty-three-inch refrigerator, and a twenty-five-inch stacked washer and dryer. In a tiny space, she says, a developer can afford upgrades like travertine tiles and beautiful modern faucets.

"You must make it so that when someone walks in, they say, 'Oh! It looks like a custom home!' even though it's only 200 square feet." JVL

RESOURCE

Space: Japanese Design Solutions for Compact Living by Michael Freeman (Universe, 2004) Combating the idea that small spaces impose limitations and curb possibilities for interior design, *Space* presents a compelling argument that, in fact, tiny living quarters invite tremendous creativity, largely through the use of flexible and multifunctional parts such as sliding doors and foldaway furniture. Through short profiles and mesmerizing photographs, Michael Freeman leads us through the various elements that comprise a well-conceived compact space.

"Material success allows bigger homes, and this expansion of personal, proprietary space is rarely questioned as a good thing," Freeman points out. However, with increasing urban density and rapidly depleting resources, massive, energy-intensive homes are not only becoming an unquestionably bad idea, but they are in many places simply not possible. These Japanese urban minihomes are a testament to "less is more" thinking—evidence that compact houses can feel airy and spacious with the right planning.

Big Green Buildings

When we were children, the tall buildings around us seemed wondrous. A city stroll was an adventure simply because of the sheer size and bustle of our public places. Where is that wonder now?

We don't expect much from big buildings anymore. Those of us who work in bland office towers trudge off to work each day knowing that at best the drab interiors will be a bit depressing; at worst, we suspect, the poor ventilation and artificial light will leave us feeling sick. But buildings can be better. We can revolutionize offices by bringing in more daylight, growing indoor plants, improving airflow, and providing access to outdoor space. Productivity in such an atmosphere usually skyrockets, and overhead costs drop. But well-designed buildings can have a positive impact far beyond their footprints.

Truly great buildings can change the entire urban experience, helping to lift depressed cities up to new levels of cultural vitality and transforming the skyline—a symbol of progress to the rest of the world. If we want to create bright green cities, we need buildings that illuminate our course, give us reason to raise our expectations for great architecture, and restore our long-lost sense of wonder.

The new breed of design in contemporary skyscrapers and public buildings aims to affect visitors with dramatic architecture and an unconventional use of space while promoting ecological integrity and a sense of well-being. SR

One of HabeRae Investments' rehabbed microhomes.

Pearl River Tower

The Pearl River Tower in Guangzhou, China, is a breakthrough in large-scale sustainable design: a zero-energy big building. The world's greenest skyscraper (at this writing, at least), it was, unfortunately, built for one of the world's least sustainable industries (CNTC Guangdong Tobacco Corporation), but the inspiration green builders can draw from it goes a long way toward mitigating that fact.

As with most cutting-edge green buildings, Pearl River Tower would gain attention for its looks alone. The seventy-one-story building has a much slimmer profile than most skyscrapers, with an undulating, rounded facade—it looks like a space-age blobject. This design is the product of the passive wind and solar technologies that make the tower zero-energy. The points where the facade dips in are wind funnels that power internal turbines. The facade itself is made up of triple-glazed windows and integrated solar panels; many of the panels are on the roof, to provide maximum direct exposure.

Everything about the building serves to boost its energy efficiency. Its slightly diagonal siting—the south-facing building doesn't sit quite square to the street corner—makes the most of sun and wind patterns. As the sun shifts, metal blinds open and close automatically to help keep temperatures stable. Solar heat gets trapped in an eight-inch gap between the building's two skins and is then pushed up to heat exchangers before it gets a chance to enter the building. This dramatically lowers the building's need for air conditioning, one of the worst energy drains in a big building, especially in a hot climate.

Inside, the building has all the bells and whistles: graywater recycling, ample daylighting, a chilled ceiling system, and under-floor ventilation. In fact, Pearl River is something of a best-practices case study—the first skyscraper to incorporate so many of the individual strategies that have been successful in buildings around the world. CB

The Reichstag, Berlin

Among all the factors that make a government trustworthy, transparency [see Demanding Transparency, p. 405] sits firmly at the top of the list. When we have access to the official processes that (generally) occur behind closed doors, we can feel at ease with the workings of our social and political systems. In Germany, a country whose history is a case study in the dangers of government secrecy, transparency takes on even greater importance. Nowhere is this clearer than at Germany's parliament building, the Reichstag.

The Reichstag has seen both extreme malfeasance and tremendous civil renewal. A devastating fire in the building in 1933 destabilized Germany and enabled the Nazi Party to take control. Later, after World War II, the Reichstag lay in ruins for decades. It was eventually reconstructed in the 1960s, and in 1990, Germany's reunification ceremony was held there.

At that point, Germany saw an opportunity to create an architectural symbol of their renewed state by rebuilding the Reichstag to reflect the values and vision of German democracy. In 1992, architect Sir Norman Foster was appointed to design a new incarnation of the German parliament building.

The Reichstag was already one of Berlin's most iconic buildings, and Foster's version is a remarkable example of the way cultural, social, and political conditions can be embodied in architecture. The building is full of light; interior meeting rooms are enclosed in glass, allowing

Left: The Swiss Re (Reinsurance) headquarters in London, known affectionately as the "Gherkin."
Opposite: The Reichstag in Berlin is a symbol not only of transparency in government, but of environmental responsibility.

visitors to witness parliamentary sessions. This complete visual transparency is a powerful symbol of the openness of German government today. The features that make the Reichstag transparent also make it green. The building uses a forward-thinking energy strategy, meeting its energy needs with biofuels (refined vegetable oil). According to a 2002 report by the Rocky Mountain Institute, this clean electricity means a 94 percent reduction in the building's carbon dioxide emissions.

The Reichstag's cupola, preserved from earlier generations, was restored, and is central to the lighting and ventilation strategies. A light sculpture in the middle reflects sunlight into the parliamentary chamber, with a movable sunshade to control glare. On the project's Web site, Foster calls the cupola "a beacon, signaling the strength and vigor of the German democratic process." SR

The Swiss Re Headquarters

The Swiss Re (Reinsurance) headquarters in London, designed by Ken Shuttleworth of Foster and Partners (Sir Norman Foster's firm),

has become an icon among modern skyscrapers modeled on biomorphic principles [see Biomimicry, p. 101] and incorporating ecologically sound construction and operations. The concept for the structure was inspired by Buckminster Fuller's theoretical work examining the relationship between nature's patterns and human work environments. Its shape has earned it the nickname the "Gherkin."

The building is encased in a structural skin of aluminum, steel, and glass, which blurs the boundaries between roof and wall and increases energy efficiency by eliminating wasted space. A unique diagonal structure allows interior spaces to be open, and interrupted only by support columns. Separating the offices are open social spaces, placed in different locations on each floor such that they spiral up the building. Ventilation passages in the facade of the building connect these social areas, creating uninterrupted vertical openings that permit light and air to travel through the entire structure. This design reduces the need for forced air and AC, saving energy, reducing operating costs, and contributing to the occupants' well-being. SR

██████ RESOURCES

Inhabitat

http://inhabitat.com

The blog Inhabitat offers "future-forward design for the world you inhabit," covering sustainable furniture, interior design, and architecture that's both really stylish and truly green. The blog also has the latest news on every big building hoping to land a LEED certification, and covers not only buildings that are under construction, but also the coolest conceptual designs that emerge from competitions.

BLDGBLOG

http://bldgblog.blogspot.com

Geoff Manaugh writes about architectural news and concepts. From skyscrapers covered in gardens to swimming pools turned into spare bedrooms, the real and imagined buildings featured on Manaugh's site often provoke thoughtful discussion and debate about the future of architecture and design. He compiled some of his best essays in *The BLDGBLOG Book* (Chronicle Books, 2009).

Architecture of Change: Sustainability and Humanity in the Built Environment edited by Kristin Feireiss and Lukas Feireiss (Die Gestalten Verlag, 2008)

This gorgeous book showcases buildings that are both beautiful and well-built. These projects show that passive solar design, green materials, rainwater harvesting, and daylighting don't have to mean any sacrifice in the quality of the spaces architects create; indeed, "the ecological performance of buildings is becoming the new architectural aesthetic." This is three hundred pages of beautiful green inspiration, full of insight into what bright green buildings might look like and feel like to live in. AS

Architecture 2030

http://www.architecture2030.org

Architecture 2030 has rallied key organizations in the U.S. building industry around the goal of making all new and renovated buildings carbon-neutral by 2030. Its leader, Ed Mazria, has developed guidelines for communities to modify their building codes to meet this goal, as well as dramatic visualizations of how much of the nation's coastal areas will be lost with the climate-related rise in sea level.

Metropolis

http://www.metropolismag.com

Metropolis is a gem among green-minded media. The magazine consistently uncovers and presents sustainable design innovation, yet its identity first and foremost is neither granola-flavored nor hemp-lined—just razor sharp and perched where the next brilliant inventions emerge. It runs an annual design competition called Next Generation, which pushes young designers to find the highest meeting point of good design and problem-solving for the particular challenges we face on a compromised planet.

Ten Shades of Green: Architecture and The Natural World by Peter Buchanan (The Architectural League of New York, 2005)

In *Ten Shades of Green* (based on the traveling exhibit of the same name) curator Peter Buchanan uses ten buildings that combine environmental responsibility and innovative design to argue that sustainability is not only good for the planet, but that it also offers architects new opportunities for creativity and innovation—that there is no such thing as the monolithic "green aesthetic."

Chock-full of photographs, diagrams, and sketches, the book truly proves that "the architecture of the emergent new long-term paradigm must be born from an evolutionary and ecological perspective, to be good for both planet and people and grounded in the complex and sensual realities of place and lived experience."

Big & Green: Toward Sustainable Architecture in the 21st Century edited by David Gissen (Princeton Architectural Press, 2002)

This architectural showcase book is the best single-volume guide to the movement of designing large buildings that protect the planet while improving

---

The Bank of America Tower, the second-tallest building in New York City, obtained LEED Platinum certification thanks to features like plentiful daylighting, rainwater harvesting, greywater recycling, and the use of recycled materials.

their communities. *Big & Green* reveals in beautiful illustrations and clear text that even the densest, highest, most modern parts of our city can herald the arrival of a bright green future.

As Gissen puts it, "Most conventional practitioners of modern design and construction find it easier to make buildings as if nature and place did not exist. In Rangoon or Racine, their work is the same. Fossil fuels make buildings in both locales inhabitable, lighting them, cooling them, heating them. An ecologically aware architect would design those buildings different. She would immerse herself in the life of each place, tapping into natural and cultural history, investigating local energy sources, the availability of sunlight, shade, and water, the vernacular architecture of the region, the lives of local birds, trees and grasses. Her intention would be to design a building that creates aesthetic, economic, social and ecological values for the surrounding human and natural communities— more positive effects, not fewer negative ones. This would represent an entirely new approach: Following nature's laws, one might discover that form follows celebration."

Developing Green Housing

If building green houses is good, then building green housing developments is even better. When you combine sustainable design with densely planned neighborhoods, you get future-friendly city living. Considering the breakneck speed of urban growth around the world, dense, green housing complexes may be the only way to shelter everyone without compromising the planet.

A handful of forward-thinking cities have been fervently installing solar panels and planting rooftop gardens in the last few years, but overall, developers have been slow to go green, assuming that the extra cost of sustainable building isn't worth the investment. The truth is, green building actually gets cheaper as builders scale up the size of their developments, and larger projects can more easily finance better designs.

In addition, green housing is much more marketable than conventional housing, and will only gain appeal as green features take on more importance to homeowners.

This idea is so simple to understand that you would think large-scale developers would embrace green building, recognizing the many benefits and appreciating the roughly equivalent costs. But despite the apparent gains, developers are slow to change their ways, and investment banks lag far behind them. Still, there is no doubt that the trend is approaching a tipping point, and those who still build conventionally may soon find themselves in the minority. In the meantime, developers who have pushed ahead with their green dream buildings despite the extra costs are proving that these complexes can not only meet a dizzying array of low-impact goals, but can also be exciting spaces to live in. SR

LEED-ND

Take the greenest new housing development you can think of. Add in all the bells and whistles: renewable energy, luxurious, sustainably built homes, ample parkland. Then plunk it in the middle of nowhere, disconnected from neighboring towns and cities (or even neighboring neighborhoods) and severed from employment, shopping, and entertainment opportunities. Not so green after all, huh?

The green building craze, which has made LEED certification shorthand for sustainable, has created a lot of these one-off developments where extensive car travel is still necessary to reach basic services or the nearest metropolitan area. So the U.S. Green Building Council responded by upping the ante on their own standards and creating LEED Neighborhood Development certification. Using the same points system and scale (all the way up to Platinum) as LEED for commercial buildings, LEED-ND rates a development, whether it's completely new or an example of creative infill, based on its context, connectivity, and self-sufficiency.

Points are awarded for things like siting the project near existing transit; ensuring that pedestrian- and bike-friendly streets connect the development itself and connect the development to other neighborhoods and transit hubs; building on brownfields or greyfields (rather than farmland or forest); retaining historic structures and other placemaking features when applicable; and including multiuse buildings that encourage residents to work, shop, and play in their neighborhood, thereby further reducing vehicle miles traveled. And, of course, you get points for building green, making as many individual structures LEED-certified as possible. CB

Dockside Green

In terms of North American development, Dockside Green is the current gold standard—in fact, the project aims to be the first carbon-neutral development on the continent. On fifteen acres of former industrial land in Victoria, British Columbia, Dockside Green will eventually include 1.3 million square feet of residential, office, retail, and light industrial space. Developers hope it will become a global showcase of new techniques for bright green development.

Not only do the builders say they hope to certify the entire project LEED-ND [see left] and all twenty-four buildings in it LEED Platinum (there are fewer than one hundred such buildings worldwide as of this writing), they're planning to exceed almost all the current environmental performance standards for green buildings in Canada. All the buildings will use 50 percent less energy than even the Canadian Model Building code suggests, primarily by bundling the buildings in R17 wall insulation and R22 roof insulation, installing low-e double-glazed windows, and using the heat in air exhaust from the buildings to warm fresh air being brought in through the ventilation system. LED lighting, energy-efficient appliances, motion sensors, and energy dashboards in all the homes will complete the package. Power will be created on-site by a waste-wood biomass gasification plant and district energy [see Green Power, p. 151] systems.

They've put a smilar amount of thought into the water systems: through cisterns, green roofs, swales, and a large central green space, the buildings will harvest rainwater and slow runoff. The project won't even be hooked up to the

The "Synergy" building at Dockside Green in Victoria, B.C.

municipal storm-water system. A suite of water-saving technologies will help residents use two-thirds less water than their average neighbors.

The homes are designed with flexible living spaces, allowing easy reconfiguration without remodeling and the heaps of waste it generates. Interior design follows suit, using renewable/low-impact materials like bamboo flooring, wool carpets, cork paneling, and wheat-board substrates in cabinets.

The project is off to a good start. The first two phases—"Synergy" and "Balance"—have already far exceeded the number of points needed for LEED Platinum certification. "Synergy" includes four residential buildings—three towers ranging from four to nine stories, with commercial units on the ground floors plus one two-story townhouse development—on a common parking garage. It was completed in March 2008 and grabbed a spot on the AIA Committee on the Environment's 2009 Top Ten Green Projects. AS

The Mountain

A LEED-Platinum high-rise in a bustling downtown is one thing; a daylit, passively heated home with a chicken coop in the countryside is another. In many rapidly developing places, however, spatial and social context requires a solution that balances a bit of one with a bit of the other. The Mountain proves that advanced green building techniques can work beautifully at a large scale, and can even make dense, green suburbia possible.

The Mountain is a landmark among many flashy modern buildings in Orestad, a district of Copenhagen that's growing up quickly around the city's new Metro line. The structure gets its name from its innovative sloping facade. Approached to build both a large parking garage and living spaces, the Bjarke Ingels Group (BIG) decided to combine the two, creating a ten-story sloped garage and placing eighty apartments above in stairstep fashion. Atop the customized hillside, each home enjoys a penthouse view, a private garden, and plenty of fresh air and sunlight. A bonus: this design also helps conceal the parking areas from the other residential buildings around The Mountain.

Architect Ingels calls the project "architectural alchemy" because it not only blends parking and housing, but also combines an essentially suburban form—the house with a garden—with a very contemporary, dense urban environment. Rather than clashing, the components form a symbiotic relationship. The two functions share one material-intensive foundation, and the dense housing lends a feeling of safety to the parking garage at all hours. In turn, the height of the garage allows each of the apartments, even those at ground level, to enjoy optimal conditions for light, views, and ventilation—a noteworthy achievement in flat Copenhagen. All apartments have large south-facing windows to maximize daylighting and passive solar energy.

Ingels chose exterior materials carefully to reflect the structure's hybrid nature. The parking side, which faces the public sidewalk, is sheathed in sheet metal that's embellished with multicolored lights and murals (one of Mt. Everest), and contains a few shops at the ground floor that engage passersby. The residential side features hardwoods, softened by cascading ivy. Outdoor planters, carefully positioned to maintain privacy between units, double as rainwater collectors, storing water to use for irrigation during the dry season.

The Mountain isn't perfect: public areas are pretty sterile and some are poorly planned (for example, an ornamental manmade canal lies directly underneath the elevated train tracks). And living in a green housing development in Orestad, which is in the middle of nowhere, still isn't as green as living closer to Copenhagen's core. But The Mountain is a great example of how to responsibly develop an area recently connected to a major city by public transit, one that begins to make cars a less visible part of urban life. Although it needs to grow into itself, The Mountain will ultimately be a model for future development in Orestad and in similar suburbs around the world. JVL

Treasure Island

Developments like Dockside Green and the Mountain Dwellings do a great job of hiding parking structures, making sure this inconvenient fact of life doesn't interfere with elegant design or maximization of living space. But Treasure Island, where it's proposed that 13,500 people will live in a self-contained sustainable community in the middle of the San Francisco Bay, goes one step further to push cultural boundaries about density and car ownership.

What distinguishes Treasure Island's plan from similar LEED-certified developments is the willingness of those involved to radically deemphasize car ownership on the island, while ensuring that housing is concentrated at seventy-five units per acre in order to create open space and make infrastructure efficient. Residents will commute into San Francisco by ferry from a new terminal on the island that will resemble the city's Embarcadero.

Treasure Island's dense pedestrian focus pales beside Helsinki's planned Jätkäsaari community, where cars will be banned outright from most city streets, and dense green housing for 15,000 people will be built along three tram lines. Garbage will even be removed underground, in order to keep trucks off the streets. AS

One of the units for The Mountain, a green housing development in a Copenhagen suburb by the Bjarke Ingels Group.

CITIES

We live on an urban planet. For the first time in history, a majority of us live in cities. How we grow those cities, how we build neighborhoods, how we provide housing, how we choose to get around, how well we incorporate nature into the places we live—these are the challenges that will largely determine our future.

The challenges are daunting. In the metropolises of the Global North, we face legacies of neglect and pollution, traffic jams, housing shortages, aging infrastructures, and suburban sprawl. Meanwhile, in the booming megacities of the Global South, the problems look massive and unsolvable: exploding populations, crippled local governments, poverty, need, and collapsing systems. And with millions and millions of people moving every year from the countryside to the city, all of these difficulties can seem even more insurmountable. The United Nations estimates that over 3 billion more people will live in the cities of the Global South by 2050. Seventy percent of humanity will be urban then, and almost everyone will live within a day's trip of a city.

Appearances, however, can be deceiving. For, along with the boom in urbanization, we're seeing a boom in urban innovation. Simply put, we're getting better at building cities.

But are we getting better fast enough? Are the problems getting worse quicker than we can imagine solutions? We're in a race between urban possibility and urban collapse. The hopes of humanity depend on the outcome. Cities are the key to a better future, and in order to ensure that future, we need to understand them, to consider why they matter, and to try to make them better.

In some ways, urban life feels timeless. In depictions of cities from a thousand years ago, we can recognize people practicing their trades, buying and selling at markets, building homes, and celebrating holidays. Human behavior does not change very quickly. In a number of different ways, though, the cities we live in today are entirely new creations. Their size, the speed at which they change, the disparity between their richest and poorest residents, the global interconnection they give rise to, and the varieties of cultures they host—these are all unique to the twenty-first century. The magnitude and velocity of change in the world's cities today dwarf anything we've ever known.

If we could deconstruct a city like we can strip an engine, and lay all the pieces out on a cloth on the lawn (a very big cloth, a very big lawn), we'd be stunned by how many moving parts a city has. Leaving aside the most interesting part of urban life—the people and their relationships to one another (for cities are, above all else, the original social software)—we'd find a mass of large systems: the power lines strung out in a patchwork (in some cities, crisscrossing the entirety; in others, reaching only the richest neighborhoods); the branching pipes that carry water (in some cities, delivering it to home taps; in others, to central pumps from which people carry their water home in buckets); the spun glass of telephone lines and radio waves and satellite signals (in some cities; in others, the weekly mail-delivery bicycle). Everywhere, we'd find the overlapping grids and weird rootlike structures of flight paths and train tracks and roads and sidewalks and trails. Cities are the most complicated machines we have ever built.

When we think of large cities, we're used to thinking of London, New York, Tokyo. But by 2015, there will be dozens of new megacities—many about which most of us in the developed world know little. What, for instance, do most of us know about Lagos, Nigeria, [see Lagos, p. 230] and the lives of its people? If we answer "nothing," we're hardly alone. And yet, the UN predicts that by the year 2015, the city will be home to more than 24 million people—making it the third-largest city in the world. As is true in much of the Global South, many of the people who live in Lagos live in slums. Unfortunately, this common occurrence contributes to why we're used to thinking of cities as problems.

But in reality, cities hold out tremendous promise as we try to steer a course toward sustainability. Urban living, especially in compact communities, is a powerful tool for reducing our ecological footprint. Growth that is concentrated rather than sprawling preserves farms and forests outside the city, and helps facilitate the adoption of new technologies and techniques for building green cities, which will have a great impact on the planet's future. If we are serious about sustainability, one of the most consequential things we can do is to vote with our address and live in a city where bright green solutions abound.

Cities also promote prosperity. They are the engines of our global economy, offering greater opportunities for finding a job, educating our kids, starting a better life. Urban theorist Richard Florida likes to point out that forty of the largest megacities in the world, home to 18 percent of the world's population, "produce two-thirds of global economic output and nearly nine in 10 new patented innovations." But well-designed cities don't just help us become prosperous; they meet our most basic needs—from clean water and adequate housing to education, health care, and other social services—better than spread-out suburbs do.

And no two cities are alike. Even present-day cities modeled on past ones (like Shanghai's Bund, built to resemble a European city) end up entirely unique as people live in them, use them, and change them.

A few people know almost everything about their city and can tell you its history, shed light on its character, and reveal its hidden corners. And though such people, with a lifetime of knowledge,

are extremely rare, they are the maps and encyclopedias that can help us figure out how to transform our cities. Before the breed vanishes, we need to learn its secrets. We have to know a place to make it better, because no single urban-planning tool will ever work for every city, and because the more we know and love a place, the more we want to participate in determining its evolution. Much of the power to direct our cities' futures rests in the hands of politicians, planners, and powerful interests (the wealthier the place, the truer this is), but it's increasingly the case that we citizens hold the tools, models, and ideas to demand better solutions, and even to begin implementing them ourselves. We are the collaborative architects of the cities we inhabit. AS

More than 3 million Greeks, one third of the country's population, now opt for an urban lifestyle in Athens.

The Bright Green City

███████ We need cities that are both prosperous and sustainable—bright *and* green—if we're going to tackle the planet's most pressing problems. But cities in the wealthy Global North today find themselves with housing, transportation, industries, and infrastructure that are often extremely unsustainable, and would be unaffordable in the Global South.

Redesigning those systems to create carbon-neutral, zero-waste, livable communities will not only slash the ecological impacts of growth in those cities, but will also help build models for urban development that are cheaper and more replicable in other cities across the planet. Inventing better urban systems in wealthy cities can provide a pool of technical and design innovation on which poorer cities can draw to solve their own problems.

This isn't a purely altruistic endeavor. Cities that are first movers in this arena—Vancouver, Melbourne, Copenhagen, and Portland, Oregon, among them—will find themselves with new, highly competitive industries. On an overwhelmingly urban planet facing severe ecological and social pressures, the economic future may well belong to those cities that change most quickly and learn to sell their accumulated expertise in urban change.

Especially in the United States, the city will become the natural leverage point for sustainable change. The city as a place for us to live new values. The city as a hotbed of innovation, an epicenter of cultural change, and a locus of democracy. The city as a fabric of infrastructures and a mosaic of neighborhoods. The city in collaboration with its region. The city in contest with conservative suburbs. The city as a national political force. The city as a tool for readying ourselves for the arrival of the future—in short, for crafting a new world.

What makes the city such a natural leverage point is that it encourages participation at the right scale. At the city level, systems are large enough to make a difference with big problems like climate change and materials depletion, yet small enough for individuals to feel involved. Transparency and accountability are easily engaged, and new efforts can find allies without needing to first find the funding to scale massively. Good cities promote all sorts of achievable innovations, and good citizens demand them. AS

Bright Green Cities Are More Competitive

███████ Cities drive the global economy. Bruce Katz of the Brookings Institution's Metropolitan Policy Program says that cities "are the unequivocal engines of national prosperity because they concentrate at an unprecedented level the assets that matter, assets like innovation, human capital, infrastructure, and quality places."

Metropolitan regions drive the global economy; central cities drive regional economies;

Dense, urban communities use less energy and far fewer resources than do sprawling suburbs.

and creative cores drive the economic success of cities. The spillover effect of people working on related projects in proximity to one another is profound: when enough creative people from overlapping fields are concentrated in a city, a critical mass of entrepreneurship and innovation can drive rapid economic progress. That's why there's fierce competition between cities to draw and retain creative workers.

Bright green cities draw these workers disproportionately, not least because fields like sustainable design and clean energy are magnets for talent these days. Places that are doing a good job addressing such issues will draw people interested in working in these fields; soon they will develop a bright green creative core that helps drive future growth and innovation. The bright green get brighter and greener as time goes on.

In a world undergoing rapid economic transformation, bright green action at the city level provides a distinct competitive advantage. By fostering innovative compact communities, making buildings greener, slashing emissions, developing clean energy, and embracing new models of prosperity, we meet our ethical obligation to protect the ecological foundations of civilization, and we also create the kind of economy that's going to lead the way in the twenty-first century.

By taking these actions, we save money directly: energy and materials are expensive, and (all other things being equal) using less of them to generate more economic activity is profitable. The money we spend making greener profits is not a cost, but an investment. And if we extend our horizon out even a few years, we can see that a large percentage of these changes will make us money. This is particularly true when we're dealing with shifts in big systems, like rebuilding auto-dependent communities and investing in clean energy. Many of the changes we're seeking already make more economic sense than maintaining the status quo, if all the costs are counted (and harmful subsidies eliminated) and we plan for a reasonable time frame.

But, in some ways, the innovations that aren't yet directly profitable are even more important. When we're pushing boundaries, our learning curve will always carry a cost. The knowledge we gain in the process, however, is worth

money—lots of money. Our expertise in transformational technologies, designs, and practices will be the economic reward for being a bold, aggressive first mover in bright green innovation. The speed with which cities move is almost certainly going to determine which regions are globally competitive in coming decades.

This reality is often obscured by the lobbying and public relations efforts of incumbent businesses. But regional governments free of old-industry influence can see the astonishing pace of transformation for what it is: the best economic development strategy. Raising building codes and design standards to the best known level (and then continuing to raise them, ensuring that local architects, builders, engineers, and designers are on the cutting edge of their fields); encouraging dense and walkable urbanism and the development of new walkshed technologies [see Density Done Right, p. 205] and product-service models (and working to actively revoke subsidies for auto-dependence, from parking to free roads to externalized costs for health and environmental damage); moving toward zero-waste policies with hefty penalties for products that can't be safely disassembled and recycled; investing in watershed and foodshed management and ecosystem preservation—the list goes on and on, but all of these actions have one thing in common: although they look radical and unrealistic when seen through the filter of the status quo, they will in fact create vibrant, competitive, prosperous places over the next decade.

There's no trade-off here. The old dirty industries offer no future and drain taxpayer money while harming people and the planet. Every dollar spent supporting them is a dollar burned. On the other hand, new, profitable industries that emerge from building bright green cities will offer prosperity and health while protecting the planet for future generations. For smart cities, there's only one sensible choice. A5

Vancouver's Bright Green Future

In 2009 Vancouver made waves with its new ten-year plan, entitled *Vancouver 2020: A Bright Green Future.* Inspired by the Swedish idea of sustainability within a generation, the plan is

an explicit bid to become a world leader in urban sustainability—what Vancouver calls "green urban strategies."

Vancouver 2020 has set bold targets for the next decade, including reducing greenhouse-gas emissions to 33 percent below 2007 levels; cutting water use by one-third; cutting the CO_2 footprint of the city's food supply by one-third; and creating 20,000 new green jobs.

The whole plan is based on the idea that sustainable prosperity is an advantage, not a burden: "Why green? Because in the highly competitive, highly mobile modern world, the elements that make a community healthy also make it wealthy. Functionally, a compact, efficient city with a well-organized transportation system and a light environmental footprint is cheaper to run and easier to maintain. The bright, creative people who are the key to conceiving and expanding a globally competitive economy also gravitate to the most desirable—most livable—cities."

Much of the plan involves improving infrastructure and economic systems (for instance,

increasing the supply of clean energy and making water systems more efficient), but it also builds on Vancouver's earlier success promoting "eco-density," a strategy for adding infill housing and offices to make areas dense enough to support transit and new infrastructure. Eco-density is working: though tens of thousands of people have moved downtown in the last twenty years, the number of cars on the road there has actually decreased, the quality of life has improved, and the city's retail districts have weathered the recession, even thrived. This phenomenon proves that when you design a city with pedestrians in mind,

Above: The massive green roof of the Vancouver Convention Centre symbolizes the city's commitment to sustainability.

Opposite: Vancouver is one of the most livable cities in the world, thanks to its compact communities, walkable streets, and green buildings.

the pedestrians will come, along with all of the attendant benefits.

A walk through the streets of the West End, one of the city's densest neighborhoods, reveals short blocks complemented by plenty of trees and grass. Everything is built on a human scale to make pedestrians and bicyclists feel welcome. Instead of resembling "projects," lower-income complexes are interspersed with luxury buildings and designed in architectural styles similar to those of the surrounding buildings, making them almost indistinguishable. Transit is ubiquitous, by North American standards, and green space is plentiful.

It's no coincidence that demand for housing in compact communities has grown faster than developers can build it, resulting in steeply rising housing costs: people want to live in places that deliver density with grace, and Vancouver has got the formula right. AS

Copenhagen: Beyond Bikes and Wind Power

Copenhagen may have already established itself as a green city by becoming a world leader in bicycling and hosting the 2009 COP15 climate summit, but it hasn't stopped there. Instead, the city has moved forward with aggressive plans to become the first CO$_2$-neutral capital in the world by 2025; and to prove that this is not just speculative talk, Copenhagen plans to reduce its already comparatively low greenhouse-gas emissions a further 20 percent by 2015.

If Copenhagen's plan has two obvious symbols, they are the bicycle and the wind turbine.

The Danes are famous for their embrace of both, and moving away from the car and toward clean energy are at the very core of their climate plans. But Copenhageners have also improved building standards, created district energy systems [see Green Power, p. 151], and are building several new sustainable neighborhoods.

And because the city's residents realize that urban sustainability is ultimately about people, they're making a big push to extend education and training in bright green business and environmental stewardship to the next generation. The effort includes training 1,500 "climate ambassadors," children capable of explaining energy conservation and climate-smart behaviors, as well as extending green skill sets into business and professional schools, cultural institutions, professional associations, and government ministries. One of their key goals is to have the world's best-educated workforce for the bright green economy by the time they become one of the first bright green cities. AS

Melbourne's Climate-ready Planning

Few cities in the world are experiencing climate change as directly as Melbourne. Australia has gone through a prolonged drought, severe dust storms, wildfires, and a series of other climate disruptions, which have made the need for both changed behaviors and more resilience readily apparent to all.

As a result, Melbourne has moved to become a leader in emission reductions, pushing for instance to have 90 percent of all trips be made on foot, by bike, or by public transit by 2030. Even more visibly, Melbourne has become a leader in building a climate-resilient city, specifically through its "city as a catchment" approach. Melbourne's water plan recognizes that climate change poses "a large threat to the water security of the city" and responds to its new position as a city in an arid region by treating every drop of water there as precious.

The core of Melbourne's approach is what the city calls "total watercycle management." The plan views the entire city in terms of the streams of water that flow through it: some in pipes from distant reservoirs, some down roofs and through gutters, some through drains and sewers. The plan will drastically reduce the amount of fresh water the city needs to draw down to survive (cutting per capita water use by 40 percent by 2020, compared to what was used in 2000). It will greatly increase the amount of rainwater and recycled water used in the city (about 10 percent of all water used by 2020, with 70 percent as the long-term goal). Finally, it will use storm water and treated wastewater to help maintain the health of the area's waterways [see Greening Infrastructure, p. 172]. Street trees, rain gardens, swales, rainwater tanks, and permeable pavement will allow water to seep into the earth instead of washing down streets and into sewers (and carrying pollution into the local waters as it does).

The plan is radical, yet radically practical: it will not only spur innovation to help reduce the fragility of Melbourne's water supply in the face of rapid climate change, but it will also help the city develop a wide expertise in new water-smart building and design techniques that will give its economy a competitive advantage in decades to come. AS

Sustainable South Bronx's Green Jobs

Hope for the future lies in learning how to build a better city. In the Global South, where urban growth is proceeding headlong, the challenge is to keep up, to invent new models that can be deployed rapidly enough to provide for the needs of the billions of people who are moving to the new megacities in search of better lives. In the Global North, though, the challenge is often quite different: here, one of the biggest urban challenges is our legacy of neglected neighborhoods, polluted land, and impoverished families.

For decades, New York City officials have tacitly regarded the South Bronx as a dumping ground. The neighborhood has been home not only to some of the largest dumps and waste-processing plants in the region (particularly Hunt's Point) but also to some of the poorest people in the New York City area.

Majora Carter is working to solve both problems at once. Her organization, Sustainable South Bronx (SSBx), tackles environmental, social, and urban-design problems simultaneously, so that the South Bronx can become not only healthier and greener, but more prosperous. We can, as she puts it, "green the ghetto."

To date, SSBx has provided ecological-restoration training for area youth, created a Hunt's Point farmers' market, fought against expansion of Hunt's Point solid-waste facilities and power plants, and spread awareness of green-building technology throughout the community. Now SSBx is getting even more ambitious: it is working to create a recycling/industrial park in the Bronx, which will be a manufacturing-based ecoindustrial park that will create three hundred to five hundred jobs and serve as a cutting-edge model for industrialization. The organization is also pushing for policy changes that would allow for the widespread adoption of green roofs and cool roofs throughout the neighborhood, and is designing a comprehensive rainwater-harvesting and energy-efficiency plan for the community. Working tirelessly to establish new urban-design standards for new development, SSBx is demanding that the city move away from big-box commercial development and toward community economic development, and from an emphasis on freight mobility and big trucks to an emphasis on bike paths and walkable streets.

Sustainable South Bronx's fab lab students designed benches as a place-making exercise.

One of Carter's most powerful levers for changing the minds of government officials and business leaders is illustrating the real costs of getting it wrong, through SSBx's cutting-edge research. As Carter said in an interview with Worldchanging, "having communities this poor actually costs the region more money. And rich communities have an incentive not to truck off their crap to some poor community, both because of the health of the people [there] and for the sustainability of those rich communities." The organization's research is showing that the health costs, lost productivity, and environmental damage caused by the dumping practices in the South Bronx outweigh the economic benefits of running those dumping facilities. That's a message few expected but more and more are ready to hear: "Folks are understanding that there's such a thing as an urban environment. What we need to do now is to educate people on the bigger picture: how sprawl creates social problems as well as ecological problems, and that what happens in our urban communities has a huge impact where they live. We need to start seeing regions as a whole."

This is not an easy message to get across, however. "The city seems completely incapable of engaging in comprehensive planning," Carter told Worldchanging in 2007, when SSBx's feasibility study on the recycling plant was being measured against the city's interest in building a jail on the site instead. (Could you ask for a more literal illustration of the "green jobs, not jails" challenge?) According to Carter, city leaders are obsessed with "high-profile, monumental projects" like big-box retail chains and sports stadiums. "That lack of comprehensive thinking gets in the way of everything we're trying to do to sustainably develop a neighborhood. New York may have its own particular issues in learning to become a sustainable city, but the sort of "silo vision" that SSBx is running up against is common everywhere. AS

Civic Activism for Bright Green Cities

Plans are like the DNA of a city: while a million small decisions ultimately go into creating a city's future, plans often determine how those decisions will work together. Today, city plans are very abstract, specialized documents; people pursue advanced degrees simply to learn to read and write them. Unfortunately, this inaccessibility deters inhabitants from getting involved in the planning of their cities, which in turn stifles innovation and prevents residents from acting on their own to improve their neighborhoods. Opaque plans can also promote a backlash against ideas that citizens don't fully understand and feel are imposed from above. When these problems with planning are expanded to a regional scale, you get a near-complete failure to design futures that people feel are their own.

Too often, plans are opaque because powerful political interests benefit from them in ways that would outrage the public if they knew the implications. In many North American metro regions, for instance, developers and construction industries have pushed hard to block growth management, because it is in their best interest to build more and more sprawl in the outer rings of suburbs, which then need to be served by more freeways and roads and new infrastructure, often paid for at public expense. Though such results are bad for almost everyone [see The Ruins of the Unsustainable, p. 218], their impact on the public is generally obscured by plans and studies that are hard to fully understand. They confuse and bore people into inaction. Environmental historian Richard White writes in *The Organic Machine: The Remaking of the Columbia River*, "Planning is an exercise of power, and in a modern state, much real power is suffused with boredom. The agents of planning are usually boring; the planning process is boring; the implementation of plans is always boring. In a democracy, boredom works for bureaucracies and corporations as smell works for a skunk. It keeps danger away" (1996). But plans can be clear as day: they can, in fact, help us grasp the vast, complex systems we depend on. Furthermore, once the layers of exclusionary expertise, regulation, and jargon are removed from the plans created by the powers that be, we are capable of not only understanding the systems around us, but of imagining and inventing their replacements, and mobilizing the constituencies to make it happen.

More people are realizing that the best plans are created in an open, transparent process by large numbers of people in the communities being planned. "Open future initiatives," where large-scale, long-term plans are developed in consultation with groups of citizens, already exist in places like New York and Melbourne, but even more specific nuts-and-bolts-type planning can be done collaboratively online. A pioneering effort in this realm is The Open Planning Project (TOPP), which uses online tools to involve more citizens in planning development and public spaces. Portland, Oregon, has used its OpenGeo suite of software to plan its bus routes.

And such initiatives are just the beginning. Citizens are beginning to come together to revitalize city and regional planning in all sorts of creative ways, and to ask the questions that will lead to new planning paradigms:

- Finding places where systems have been draped in complexity and revealing them in clear, beautiful, interesting ways. How can we reveal the workings of the systems around us in ways that help people see the usefulness of change?
- Making public life exciting where boredom has dampened people's enthusiasm, if not driven them completely away from civic involvement. Being part of democracy ought to feel exciting and invigorating. How can we simultaneously reject needless processes in favor of quick, transparent, and measured decisions and enliven participation?
- Reclaiming the media by supporting local journalism that reveals, informs, and educates. What means can we use to support reporting, writing, filmmaking, and public discussion that advances our understanding of planning, leaving behind the tired debates of the last generation?
- Reinventing or replacing the kinds of civic institutions—university departments, think tanks, research labs, planning agencies—that democracies need to make informed decisions. How can we foster institutions that are more effective in facing the challenges ahead of us?
- Diffusing innovation through our local businesses and industry groups. Unsustainable business is bad business, even in the short run; getting businesses involved in replacing broken systems is sound economic strategy.

How do we build local business cultures that support the opportunities inherent in transformation?

With this resurgence in urban citizenship, people are starting to grasp the power of planning in shaping our future. Using new tools and insights, citizens gain leverage for changing the codes that shape urban life. And allies can be found everywhere. Public life is full of people who want to see change, but who need more political cover or new inspiration to do so. Change agents in government agencies, businesses, schools, political parties, and media are ready to act. If we can engage the systems in which they've been quietly laboring *at the systems level* rather than the level of individual behavior, we will find unseen helpers in unexpected places. AS

■■■■■   RESOURCE

Century of the City: No Time To Lose (Rockefeller Foundation, 2009), available for download at http://www.rockefellerfoundation.org/news/ publications/century-city-no-time-lose This Rockefeller Foundation–led survey gives an excellent overview of the problems cities face, discussing topics like climate change resilience and transportation challenges in U.S. cities, and the need for sharing research and innovations between cities of the Global North and the Global South.

Density Done Right

What makes cities work? Density done right.

As more people gather together in a relatively compact neighborhood, the possibilities for that neighborhood change. More people means there are more shops and workplaces, which in turn means more of the necessities of daily life are within walking distance. With more people walking, providing more public transit becomes cost-effective. More transit reinforces people's ability to live without cars, which in turn decreases the amount of space they need to live comfortably. As density increases, options for work, commerce, and leisure multiply, even as driving decreases and more people right-size their homes.

As compact communities reach a critical mass of density, living in a sustainable way becomes easier. Living in close proximity to other people, for instance, makes it more practical to share or rent big items like cars and gym equipment than to own them. Because of limited storage space in dense neighborhoods, people begin to put a premium on quality over quantity, and tend to buy better stuff that will last longer. Smaller homes are easier to retrofit for efficiency, while multi-unit buildings can be made more efficient from the get-go. Living car-free gets more practical as transit and walkability improve. A virtuous spiral emerges, where our neighborhoods get better as they get denser.

This concept by MisoSoupDesign for New York City housing demonstrates the flexibility of urban infill designs.

Living in a compact community saves us money, too. Studies by Chicago's Center for Neighborhood Technology have shown that when you add transportation costs and housing costs together, denser, more central neighborhoods are almost always more affordable than car-oriented suburbs. Urbanites also tend to be healthier and thinner, and to see their family and friends more regularly, than their suburban counterparts, all of which improves their lives and helps them live longer.

The ecological benefits of compact neighborhoods, though, are even greater. Nearly every aspect of our lives is made more sustainable by density. Smaller homes require less energy to build and far less to heat and cool. People who live without cars (or who only drive occasionally) are responsible for a small fraction of the transportation emissions of suburbanites. Because they have less space to clutter up, urbanites tend to consume fewer disposable goods. Even the infrastructure in dense communities is more efficient: as the United Nations report *State of the World's Cities 2006/7* puts it, "The concentration of population and enterprises in urban areas greatly reduces the unit cost of piped water, sewers, drains, roads, electricity, garbage collection, transport, health care, and schools." The denser the place, generally, the lower the ecological impact to live there.

There doesn't actually appear to be any upper limit to the energy benefits of increased density. The most energy-efficient cities in the world are the densest ones, where people live in communities that are much denser than many North Americans or even Europeans would consider livable. The average citizen in Asian cities like Tokyo, Hong Kong, Shanghai, and Singapore uses a fraction of the energy that an average American of comparable wealth would. These extremely dense cities, however, are finding it hard to provide a high quality of life for their citizens: their air quality is often very poor, and they generally lack enough green space and other amenities.

In other words, the virtuous spiral works best when density grows hand in hand with quality-of-life measures like parks, bikeways, and boulevards. It's possible to build dense cities that demand driving, that funnel their commerce into urban malls, that separate homes and jobs and shopping far away from one another, or that simply ignore all needs other than development, encasing the city in cold concrete. In those cases, density may still be more ecologically sound, but it usually fails to lead to a bright green city.

Density and livability are best delivered together. AS

Cities Fix Transportation Problems

▬▬▬   Some people make the argument that the built environment changes too slowly for us to make transformative changes in the urban fabric, and that if we want to green our communities we should look not to buildings and streets, but to greener products, such as electric cars. This makes sense if we think of cars as things that are replaced often and buildings as things that rarely change. But that will not be the case over the next few decades in North America. Because of population growth, changing preferences for urban living, ongoing development churn in cities (as buildings are remodeled or replaced), and the need for large-scale new infrastructure projects, at least a third of our built environment in 2030 will have been built in this century. If done right, all that new construction could allow for a complete overhaul of the American city.

This is especially true since we don't need to change every home to transform a neighborhood. Many inner-ring suburban neighborhoods, for instance, could become terrific places simply by creating infill and converting strip-mall arterials to walkable mixed-use streets. Such a transition could happen in just a few years. In comparison, it takes at least sixteen years to replace 90 percent of our automotive fleet. And since it takes years to move a design from prototype to production, it seems likely that the cars most people in the United States will have available to them in 2030 will not be all that different from the more efficient electric cars today, which still bear a large ecological footprint [see Questioning Consumption, p. 33].

If we spend the next twenty years developing compact neighborhoods with green buildings and smart infrastructure, we can reduce the ecological impacts of American prosperity by jumps that are now somewhat hard to imagine. Whether or not car technology improves quickly, building bright green cities is a winning strategy: if cars don't evolve, we'll clearly need to make changes in our land-use strategies to save our planet; if they do evolve, they might well fit quite nicely into the new fabric of sustainable urban life, and we'll all be better off for it—the air will be that much cleaner, the grid that much smarter, our economic advantage in clean technology that much greater.

What's true for North American cities, meanwhile, is doubly true in the Global South. Two hundred thousand people a day are expected to swell urban areas, every day for the next forty years, and the vast majority of them will live in cities in South America, Africa, and Asia. If these cities can use their growth constructively (rather than being swamped by it), they may be able to make the transition into bright green cities far more rapidly than we now expect. AS

Deep Walkability

Walkability is critical to bright green cities. You can't advocate car-free or car-sharing lives if people need cars to get around. But being able to walk in our own neighborhoods does not necessarily make our neighborhoods walkable; the places where we live must be connected (by walking routes and easy transit) to other places worth walking to.

Unfortunately, in North America many great neighborhoods are pedestrian-friendly islands in a sea of pedestrian-hostile sprawl. They may offer a lot of services close by—we may be able to walk to buy a quart of milk or get a cup of coffee in the café—but going anywhere else involves a choice between a long walk through forbidding surroundings along dangerous streets or an unhappy wait for inconvenient and under-funded transit. This is unfortunately true even in some neighborhoods that pride themselves on their green buildings. But if you can't walk out of a neighborhood, it's not sustainable, no matter how many solar panels and green roofs it has.

To live in an isolated neighborhood is to understand the full impact of a half century of planning and public investment that treated a person walking as an afterthought at best, and often as an inconvenience to cars that ought to be discouraged. No matter how great the cafés, sidewalks, and street trees are, these neighborhoods

are not truly walkable: unless we want to feel like prisoners trapped within their boundaries, we still must own cars.

The true test of walkability is this: Can you spend a pleasant half hour walking or on transit and end up at a variety of great places? The quality of having a feast of options available when you walk out your front door is what we call "deep walkability," and this is what ought to be the top priority for urban design and development in our communities. We should be looking at how to knit our walkable communities together and how to make friendlier streets between them.

That would mean redevelopment and curative street design, such as slowing down car traffic, converting road lanes to train rails or bike trails, and discouraging parking and auto-oriented development in favor of sidewalk-focused density and transit-oriented development.

The idea that we can "balance" fast car traffic and pleasant sidewalk life is a dangerous illusion. The only way to make pedestrians and bikers safe and welcome is to slow cars down, to make drivers pay attention to the area they're passing through, and, whenever possible, to get cars off the streets and out of the way of trains, buses, bikes, and strollers.

Assert the primacy of people enjoying the act of walking, and eventually density becomes community, transit becomes an essential amenity, and life begins to orient around experiences and access rather than accumulation and convenience. The act of walking is at the very foundation of so many other bright green possibilities. In fact, a place that embraces deep walkability could almost be considered the very definition of a great city. AS

Farmers' markets add to the vitality of urban street life and help create opportunities for socializing locally.

Go Ahead, Play in the Street

▦ Any student of urban planning can tell us horror stories about the destruction of once-thriving urban neighborhoods diced up or isolated by new freeways. Paradoxically, totally eliminating cars from a neighborhood or shopping district isn't really healthy either. Pedestrian malls sound good in pitch sessions, and look good in the form of artists' conceptions, but many of these well-intentioned efforts to rebel against Autotopia have resulted in retail ghost towns. Is there a way to lay out a neighborhood or shopping district that is safe and fun to walk around, but that allows access to taxis, delivery trucks, and the occasional private car?

For decades, municipalities have been using "traffic calming" techniques—speed bumps, rotaries, and deliberately inconvenient traffic grids—to keep drivers from turning local streets into ersatz highways. The Dutch have taken this a step further with the *woonerf*. *Woonerf* means "street for living," and the concept includes totally integrating pedestrian and vehicular spaces, eliminating curbs and placing amenities normally associated with sidewalks—planters, benches, and streetlights—in what would normally be the middle of the street. Faced with these obstacles and with the people using them, drivers are forced to not only slow down, but to be aware that they are in a community. The theory is, if we feel like we are driving through someone's yard, where kids play and pedestrians stroll, we'll automatically slow down and widen our awareness, knowing that we have to be on the lookout for the unexpected.

There is also a more scientific theory behind *woonerf* zones: slowing cars saves lives. When drivers are moving at twenty miles per hour, only 5 percent of pedestrians they hit with their cars will die, according to the UK Department of Transportation; at thirty miles per hour, 37 percent will die; at forty miles per hour, 83 percent of the pedestrians will be killed. At the same time, a driver's ability to make and retain eye contact with things and understand what he or she is seeing

above twenty miles per hour is greatly diminished. So if we lower speeds, and add more elements for drivers to interact with, we will undoubtedly produce safer streets. More important, cities often experience less congestion when they lower speed limits; if people are driving more slowly, they don't need as many traffic lights and major intersections, which are the real culprits of congestion. Of course, only some streets can be treated in this manner; heavier, faster travel must be handled with ring roads, bus lanes, and other approaches.

But safety and congestion aren't the only reasons to adopt this course. *Woonerf* streets are more attractive. With the exception of a sign alerting motorists that they are entering a *woonerf* zone, there are no signs or traffic signals. The street is all on one grade, and there are no yellow or white lines painted on it. Plus, the elements that make motorists pay attention to their surroundings—small green spaces with benches; streetlights that are positioned to highlight houses and pedestrians instead of streets and cars; and a smattering of unobtrusive parking spaces—also make streets more pleasant overall. SJ

How to Make a Great Place

▦ The nature of a great place is that it's unique. There's a lot to be learned from going to other people's great neighborhoods, but ultimately the answers we need are going to spring from the particular genius of the places in which we live. If we want to make places that foster community, all we have to do is look around. All around us there are indicators of the potential our neighborhoods hold.

A *woonerf* in Asheville, North Carolina.

It's sort of like parenting: reading guides to child rearing may give us some good ideas and help us avoid some common problems, but ultimately everyone's parenting style is shaped by their children. Similarly, the right community spaces are the ones that reflect and respect their surroundings. Every good neighborhood is at its best when it is most like itself.

There are some general strategies that tend to work. Meet the neighbors. Promote good, compact development. People naturally gravitate toward certain locations and atmospheres, so allow established spaces to form around organic hubs.

Really good places make us want to hang out. The street, in essence, becomes an outdoor living room. Small parks, bike paths, historic buildings, sidewalk cafés, street trees, benches, and public art can all make being out in public a pleasure; a well-designed neighborhood keeps us from wanting to retreat to the safety of our isolated homes.

Socialize locally. Networks don't live by bits and bytes alone. Networks are made of people, and in order to do truly remarkable things, people need to get together, rub elbows, trade gossip, try out ideas, flirt, schmooze, encourage, and learn to trust, admire, and love one another. Conferences are great for this. Festivals can galvanize an entire zeitgeist. But movements really rise or fall on the strength of ongoing social events—salons, showcases, the right bar, the right café, the place it's happening. These "third places" are the epicenter of any movement [see Post-ownership, p. 78], whether the goal is overthrowing a dictator or getting a stop sign put in on the school's corner.

Want to make a difference? Find the epicenter in your town and look for allies. AS

Walkshed Technologies

There was a time when people thought the Internet would isolate us from one another, that we'd all end up spread out across the landscape in suburban enclaves, too absorbed with television and the Internet to want to actually meet anyone. A funny thing happened on the way to that asocial future, though: we discovered that the most important thing about the Internet is that it connects people, and that connected people tend to want to meet, socialize, and work together. Rather than separating us, the Internet has made us more social than ever, both online and in the "real" world. In fact, the more connected we are online, the more time we're likely to spend hanging out offline with friends, family, and neighbors.

As technology has suffused our cities— think not only smart phones and Google Maps, but community ratings of restaurants and shops, real-time traffic reports, smart electrical grids, even hyper-local news sites—it has magnified the feedback loop between online connection and in-person conversation. We're learning that public space and cyberspace are symbionts; physical community and technology fuel each other. And the trend is only accelerating. Technology has gotten smaller, and has spread out to become ubiquitous in urban space. We're surrounded by data points, sensors, and layered information about everything from transit delays to weather reports to the bar where our friends are meeting for happy hour.

As cities become smarter, urban living becomes much more efficient and, in many ways, more pleasurable. With the street as a platform for technology, it becomes much easier to find the things we want, who has them, and how they're being used. We're used to thinking of acquiring things in a twentieth-century way, where you get in your car and drive around until you find what you want; and convenience is defined by the easiest drive with the least traffic, or by owning an object (like a home gym, for instance) so you never have to worry about where to find it. Convenience in a smarter city is different: it's about

Turning urban streets into community spaces can make the difference between cities that survive and cities that thrive.

knowing where the stuff you want is so you don't need to own it or make long trips to get to it. Just as search engines like Google have allowed us to quickly find what we want, ubiquitous technology makes the city increasingly "searchable."

And, as Dan Hill notes in his seminal essay "The Street as Platform," we're only just beginning to realize how smart our cities can get:

"Facilitated by networks of sensors, the data emerging from the new nervous system appears limitless: near-imperceptible variations in air quality and water quality, innumerable patterns in public and private traffic, results of restaurant inspections, voting patterns in public referenda, triggers of motion sensors, the output of heating ventilation and air conditioning systems, patterns of water usage, levels of waste recycled, genres of books returned at local libraries, location of bicycles in the city's bike-sharing network, fluctuations in retail stock controls systems, engine data from cars and aeroplanes, collective listening habits of music fans, presence of mobile phones in vehicles enabling floating car data, digital photos and videos locked to spatial co-ordinates, live feeds from CCTV cameras, quantities of solar power generated and used by networks of lamp-posts, structural engineering data from the building information models of newly constructed architecture, complex groupings of friends perceptible in social software multiplied by location-based services, and so on. Myriad flows of data move in and around the built fabric. As many or most objects in the city become potential nodes in a wider network, enabled through the natural interoperability of systems influenced by the Internet and its open-source philosophies and standards-based protocols, this shimmering informational field provides a view of the entire city."

All this technology will change the way it feels to live in dense communities. Most of us feel comfortable walking only a certain distance from our homes—a range that urbanists call our "walkshed." But as we gain insight into the places around us and connection to the people nearby, our walksheds can unfold with possibilities. Sure, it gets easier to catch the right bus, reserve a car-share vehicle, or borrow a power drill from the tool library, but that's just the beginning. That church we always ignored, we find, hosts a book swap; the small corner store sells spices we've had a hard time finding; parents with young children are invited to matinee shows at the local movie theater; people meet to practice their French every Wednesday at the café around the corner. Our cities are bursting with opportunities we miss simply because they're not visible from the street. Walkshed technologies make visible the invisible neighborhoods we stroll through every day.

Of course, this new future will be full of perils as well as promise, with new threats to privacy from nosy or creepy people, concerns about corporate abuse of information gathered about us, and questions about the reliability of the information we're depending on. It might even be that we miss the randomness and serendipity of moving through blind spaces, of not knowing what we'll find. On the other hand, it may be that our cities become ever more interesting as their workings are made more accessible to us. AS

■■■■■■■   RESOURCE

The Great Neighborhood Book: A Do It Yourself Guide to Placemaking by Jay Walljasper (New Society Publishers, 2007)
Neighborhood-building is as much an art as a science. Jay Walljasper's *The Great Neighborhood Book* is a rough-hewn little gem, full of both specific examples and suggestions (many drawn from projects affiliated with Project for Public Spaces, for whom Walljasper wrote the book) and more gut-level observations about what makes places work. *The Great Neighborhood Book* feels, well, neighborly. We get the sense that Walljasper would be a great guy to have live down the block. He *gets* people, and likes them too—a trait rarer in urban theorists than we might wish. All of the suggestions he makes seem focused on making space not just livable, but lively. This is no manifesto, and it's not a masterpiece. But like a Wednesday barbecue in a friend's backyard, with homegrown produce on the table, chicken on the grill, and cold beer in the cooler, it doesn't have to be perfect to be well worth the walk. AS

Mobility

Mechanical transportation was one of the giant breakthroughs of the industrial era, starting with steam engines in nineteenth-century England and continuing all the way up through our current world of jets and bullet trains. The ability to not only go more places faster but also to transport things from far away cheaply and regularly is part of what has defined life in our modern cities.

Mechanical transportation is here to stay, but the role it plays in our cities has begun to change profoundly. Until recently urban planners treated mobility as the solution to myriad urban problems: if we needed more housing, we could build sprawl; if we had pollution, we could put the factories in one place and homes in another; if we wanted cheap consumer goods, we could move manufacturing plants to parts of the world with low wages, and then sell the products in huge, low-overhead stores on the suburban fringe.

All of these solutions required moving people and stuff faster and over longer distances, a strategy that has had horrific social and environmental consequences: a recent NASA study concluded that cars are the biggest net contributor to climate change, and according to the World Health Organization, auto accidents are the leading cause of death for Americans aged ten to twenty-four. Furthermore, our dependence on mechanical transportation blinds us to its real costs and to the opportunities inherent in new approaches.

Fundamental to these new approaches is the idea of access by proximity [see Density Done Right, p. 203]—which means, simply, putting more products and services within walking distance, so we don't have to drive as often. A critical insight here is that driving isn't free: building roads costs an enormous amount of money, as does building cars and fueling them (not to mention sitting in traffic, or lying in the hospital if we've been injured in a car accident). We can actually compare how cheap and convenient different ways of getting around are; when we compare living in the city to living in a suburb where driving is essential, what we find is that people in the walkable community actually save enormous amounts of money and time. It may seem like walking to the store is incredibly inconvenient, but the reality is that the amount of money you save and the health benefits you get from taking that walk actually mean that you are spending less of your life moving. Alan Durning of the Sightline Institute notes that the largest-ever study on walking found that due to improved health and increased life expectancy resulting from walking, we get three minutes back for every minute we spend strolling the sidewalks. That means walking can actually save you time, since the time you spend walking is time you would have spent dead.

What all of this means is that we're looking at how to move people through cities in new ways. We're starting to build cities that emphasize access over mobility, and that provide whatever mobility we do need in more sustainable ways. AS

My Other Car Is a Bright Green City

Today's cars are costly, dangerous, and an ecological nightmare. Transportation generates over a quarter of the greenhouse gases in the United States, according to the EPA. A portion of that comes from moving freight around, but more than 20 percent comes from personal transportation, the vast majority of which is auto-related.

Our tailpipe emissions are a major contributor to climate change, but the exhaust we're spewing is only the beginning of the story. We can't see most of the ecological and social impacts of auto-dependence in our daily lives—effects that are so massive that arguing about fuel-efficiency standards fails to acknowledge what we're up against with this crisis.

First, there are the non-exhaust-related impacts of the cars themselves. Studies show that between 15 and 22 percent of all the energy consumed by a vehicle is used in its manufacture. And though sources disagree, it appears that procuring the materials to make and maintain a car (and then dispose of it at the end of its life) may account for almost half of the direct climate impact of that car.

Second, it's worth considering all the car-related pollution that has little or nothing to do with the energy used to make or move that car. Road-building itself disrupts watershed hydrology. The crappy cars we drive today spew toxins in every direction—motor oil leaks, lubricants burn, brakes wear away, engines emit particulates, batteries erode. And keeping roads clear for our cars involves road salt and roadside herbicides. A leading study explains that the cost of water pollution caused by cars in the United States alone "totals $29 billion per year . . . Note that this estimate excludes costs of residual runoff, shoreline damage, leaking underground storage tanks, reduced groundwater recharge and increased flooding due to pavement, so it is considered a conservative value" (Entranco, 2002).

With a massive network of roads and an average of more than three parking spaces per car (less in dense cities, more in suburbs), auto-focused transportation infrastructure in North America contributes mightily to the heat-island effect, which worsens air quality and increases energy used for air conditioning. While asphalt that uses lighter-colored rocks can offer some relief, the basic problem is the amount of paved surface itself; cars demand the most pavement per person of any form of transportation.

And what about the climate impact of all that road-building? A study quoted in the September 2005 issue of the *Journal of Urban Planning and Development* estimates that the greenhouse gases emitted while building and maintaining roads add another 45 percent to the average car's annual climate footprint. We continue to build roads at a rapid rate all across North America; even many shrinking cities are seeing an increase in road-building on their suburban fringes.

All of that driving takes a pretty big social toll, too, of course. Car accidents are a leading cause of death and disabling injury in the United States. Auto-dependence is a major contributor to obesity and other chronic illnesses. The increase in obesity attributable to car-centered lives and fast-food diets accounts for 9.1 percent of all U.S. health-care costs.

In addition, more and more people are finding themselves with longer commutes in the car: more than 3.5 million Americans now drive more than three hours a day to get to and from work, spending a month of their life on the road every year, and long car commutes are spreading to China and Europe. Meanwhile, people who live in the newer fringe burbs are reportedly the least happy group among Americans, and the long commutes they endure are a major reason why.

This is what economists call "the commuting paradox." Most people travel long distances with the idea that they'll accept the burden as a trade-off for a bigger house, a higher salary, or a better school. But a commuter who travels one hour each way to work would have to make 40 percent more than his current salary to be as satisfied with his life as a noncommuter, say economists Bruno S. Frey and Alois Stutzer of the University of Zurich's Institute for Empirical Research in Economics. People usually overestimate the value of the things they'll obtain by

Traffic moves along LA's 405 Freeway, which is undergoing a $1 billion upgrade. Both car emissions and auto-related infrastructure have huge ecological impacts.

commuting—more money, more material goods, more prestige—and underestimate the benefit of what they'll lose: social connections, hobbies, and health.

So, even though the picture of a smart car hooked up a smart grid may be an attractive alternative to what we currently see in our garages, the solution to the problems our cars create has more to do with where we live than what we drive. AS

Housing and Transportation Affordability Index

How much does your house really cost? Though most of us may think we've paid for our homes once we've written our rent or mortgage checks, there's a lot more to the story. Green building has taken off so quickly in part because many of us have come to recognize that what we pay for power, water, gas, food, and garbage collection is determined (to greater and lesser degrees) by the design of our houses.

Now we're also starting to realize that what we pay for transportation is determined largely by the location of our homes, so much so that researchers at the Center for Neighborhood Technology and the Center for Transit Oriented Development have created the Housing and Transportation Affordability Index. The index reconciles housing costs with "location costs" so that potential homeowners can see the full impact of their housing decisions. According to the study, the average transportation costs for the median-income household in the United States in 2003 were 19.1 percent of total household expenditures—second only to the cost of housing.

Access by proximity—living in a place with a healthy walkshed [see Density Done Right, p. 203]—saves you money, and may be one of the most effective means we have for battling climate change. As we've said before, solutions to the problems created by cars will not all be found under the hood. AS

Making Cars Pay Their Way

The Institute of Transportation Studies recently asked a simple question: "Do motor-vehicle users in the U.S. pay their way?" Predictably, the answer was no.

The taxes paid by drivers fall far short of public spending on highway expenses, transportation bonds, police and ambulance services, legal and judicial costs related to driving, and the military costs associated with maintaining a steady supply of Middle Eastern oil. In the United States, federal, state, and local governments spend more than $100 billion a year to build and maintain roads and provide road-related services (such as highway patrols) for drivers. The difference between what they spend and what drivers contribute is made up by throwing all sorts of other taxes into the pot: income taxes, sales and use taxes, property taxes, and business taxes, to name a few. Even if you don't drive, in other words, you're still subsidizing someone else's driving.

A "fair" or equitable system would have drivers contributing most of the $100 billion to pay for roads and services, but obviously that's not going to happen. So what can be done? Looking at other countries, particularly in Europe, it's clear that the system in the United States isn't the only choice.

Unlike the United States, European countries charge drivers close to (or, in some cases, more than) the true cost of driving, according to the Sightline Institute, somewhere between 1 and 3.5 cents more per mile. European countries also have adopted very different pricing schemes, relying far more heavily on tolls, congestion zones, restrictive parking policies, and direct carbon pricing (charging more for larger trucks, for example) to make sure the economic burden doesn't fall disproportionately on those who use the roads the least. ECB

Free Parking Isn't Free
We don't give much thought to parking spaces, unless we're circling a building looking for one; most of the time we take free parking for granted, especially the kind that comes in great asphalt fields in front of big-box stores. And yet parking spaces have a powerful effect on our individual behavior, as well as our economy and land-use patterns.

In terms of determining our behavior, free parking encourages us to drive more. According to a study conducted by the New York City

Department of Transportation, 19,200 fewer vehicles would enter Manhattan every day if the city eliminated free parking. Car-owning urbanites often make housing decisions based on the availability of free (or cheap) parking. A city dweller who can afford the rent on an apartment in a dense, central neighborhood close to her job and social life may get priced out of the place when she factors in a steep monthly garage fee. She may choose to move farther afield, where free on-street parking is plentiful—and then drive more just to get back to the neighborhood she'd prefer to live in.

Many urban planners and economists contend that minimum parking requirements—the minimum number of spots a developer must include per unit or shop or occupant—are among the biggest contributors to suburban sprawl. These requirements encouraged large businesses to move farther out of urban cores and fostered the razing of multiuse buildings to make way for parking lots and garages. To make matters worse, parking minimums are rarely based on average needs; shopping malls, for example, generally provide enough parking to accommodate Christmas crowds (which explains why even a busy mall's lot is nearly empty on a Tuesday in May).

And free parking isn't literally free. Parking spaces for a development can cost between $10,000 and $50,000 a piece, which drives up the cost of everything associated with that development. As Donald Shoup, professor of urban planning at UCLA and author of *The High Cost of Free Parking*, calculates, with each space costing tens of thousands of dollars, almost none of which is directly paid for by the people who park there (even paid parking doesn't usually recoup the money spent on the space), the total subsidy for off-street parking in the United States was between $127 and $374 billion in 2002 alone. And developers aren't going to throw that kind of money in for free—they get their money back in higher rents and pricier homes and in steeper prices in the shops and businesses we visit.

So what's the solution? Policy changes like eliminating minimum off-street parking requirements would certainly help. Copenhagen is reducing parking spaces on its streets by up to 3 percent a year (Makousky, 2002); the slow attrition of parking encourages residents to leave

their cars at home. Other cities are experimenting with "dynamic metering" to get a better picture of the true demand for parking. San Francisco's SFpark is outfitting 6,000 curbside spaces and 11,500 garage spaces with sensors to gather real data on occupancy rates. The main goal of collecting real-time data is to adjust parking prices based on desirability and availability—instead of every meter charging twenty-five cents per hour, pricing will range up to six dollars per hour based on demand (or even twenty dollars for, say, a prime spot by a stadium on game day). SFpark believes that this will influence behavior enough that demand will even out—there will always be at least one open space on each of the pilot-program blocks, which will cut down on the circling and double-parking that slows down public transit. The hope is that dynamic metering will disincentivize driving while making parking more efficient for those who do need to drive. CB

Pay as You Drive

"Car insurance is currently sold like an all-you-can-eat meal plan," says the Sightline Institute. "Once you've made the purchase, you may as well gorge." And just as a person on a restricted diet wouldn't get his money's worth at an all-you-can-eat restaurant, a person who drives infrequently pays disproportionately for car ownership.

Pay as you drive (PAYD) insurance schemes, on the other hand, expect drivers to pay not for owning their cars, but for using them. At this writing, the largest trial of a PAYD system was about to start in the Netherlands. Over five years, the nation will switch all of its nearly 9 million motorists to pay-by-the-kilometer pricing. Every vehicle will be outfitted with a GPS system that records the number of kilometers traveled within the Netherlands, from highways and major roadways to residential areas. Per-kilometer fees will be based on the vehicle type and its level of fuel efficiency; surcharges will be added during rush hour in particularly congested regions.

The Netherlands is expecting, based on prior research supporting the project, that PAYD will reduce the number of kilometers driven by 15 percent and boost public transit rides by 6 percent, reducing CO_2 emissions by more than 10 percent. And although heavy drivers will see costs increase under the new system, in most cases motorists will save money: in conjunction with the program the Netherlands is abolishing its 25 percent tax on motor vehicles. People who drive infrequently will save a lot of money, and people who drive modest amounts will not spend more than they did under the old system. (There are other savings built into PAYD: lowering driving rates means less wear on roads, particularly important in nations where taxpayers bear the burden of roadwork projects.)

Smaller pilot programs are popping up in the United Kingdom, where Norwich Union offers PAYD insurance, and in the United States, where MileMeter and Progressive are trying it out. Progressive's plan includes a custom device that can track the car's speed, helping the company better assess driver behavior and, therefore, driver risk. CB

Charging for Congestion

The cores of many large cities have superb mass-transit systems. It is entirely possible for the residents of Manhattan, for example, to go their entire lives without owning a car—and many do. Tourists and commuters headed to New York are strongly encouraged to leave their cars at home. Still, the streets of New York and other cities are frequently clogged with private traffic, making life dangerous for pedestrians and cyclists, and getting in the way of efficient alternatives like buses and taxis. Some cities are fighting back, not by banning private cars, but by charging for the "privilege" of adding to congestion.

Congestion pricing involves charging drivers who wish to enter a city center or other congested area. London has had great success with its congestion-pricing scheme. Private automobiles (taxis, buses, motorcycles, and bicycles are exempt) entering the city's bustling central zone during its most congested hours are charged an £8 (U.S.$14) fee, payable online or at kiosks. A network of cameras around and in the zone feeds images to a central bureau, where an optical recognition system notes license plate numbers. Drivers who haven't paid in advance are "dinged" extra fees. Trying to beat the system altogether results in a fine of up to £150 (U.S.$267).

In the first year after it was implemented in 2003, congestion pricing reduced the number of vehicles entering London's central zone by 30 percent (60,000 vehicles). This success has been noted by other cities tired of congested streets. Stockholm and Milan have implemented similar systems: Stockholm city officials have reported a 22 percent decrease in traffic in the tolled zone, and Milan has reported a 12.3 percent decrease in the tolled zone and a 3.6 percent decrease outside this zone. Stockholm residents recently voted to make the congestion charge permanent. SJ

Car Shares and Ride Shares

Car-sharing companies are everywhere these days: Zipcar and I-GO in the United States, AutoShare in Toronto, Streetcar in London, and Sunfleet in Sweden's major cities are just a few. The car-sharing model has been around for decades, but not until recently did it become so easy to use (with efficient booking systems accessed primarily online or on smart phones), or profitable enough to sustain on a large scale—Zipcar and Sunfleet are just two that operate branches in major cities in their respective countries, giving customers access to car-sharing privileges while on vacation or business trips.

Now, some people are riffing on these models, tweaking the collaborative services and using them to play by their own rules. Innovative individuals are harnessing the power of information technology to set up personalized car-sharing groups and real-time ride-sharing.

Some solutions are designed for ready-made networks of people. In their report

London's congestion zone, with its pricing scheme, has proven effective in reducing traffic.

Collaborative Services: Social Innovation and Design for Sustainability, François Jégou and Ezio Manzini discuss how residents of multiunit buildings could create a group car-share account to ensure that they have access to a vehicle nearby or in their building's lot. The company can adjust how many vehicles it makes available to the building based on demand, and when the cars are not being used by residents, they are available to other members, thereby helping to keep the whole endeavor profitable.

A similar project called Zimride takes this idea from the condo complex to the campus dorm. The site combines the technology of Google Maps with the social networking power of Facebook to find rides for people at twenty-five public and private institutions across the United States.

In the United States car-sharing just got easier. In September 2010 California passed a law allowing car owners to "lend" their vehicles to car-sharing services without voiding their insurance. At this writing, San Francisco–based City CarShare was starting its Spride Share pilot program. Members can have car-sharing hardware installed in their vehicles and elect when to make their cars available to the network. Car owners receive payment when their cars are used (potentially thousands of dollars per year) and they help City CarShare expand its fleet.

Ride-sharing is a little different because it asks you to share something you might not be comfortable with: space. Although sharing rides is nothing new, the way we're arranging them is. Services like Avego now allow for instant ride-sharing by combining information technology and GPS-enabled cell phones to match up drivers and riders who are headed in the same direction. SK

The Copenhagen Wheel

▬▬▬▬ The Copenhagen Wheel, a project developed by MIT researchers, turns any bicycle into an Internet-ready hybrid electric. The Copenhagen Wheel isn't a bike itself but rather, well, a wheel built around a smooth disk of candy-red plastic containing a three-speed internal hub, a battery, a GPS receiver, and a variety of sensors to monitor ambient conditions such as temperature and pollution levels.

The key to the Wheel's design is that it requires no cabling, so it can easily be added to any conventional bike frame, instantly turning it into a hybrid electric. You may be wondering how you change gears on a wheel with no cables. That's where your iPhone comes in. Wheel owners mount their iPhone (or other smart phone) on the handlebars and use it as a controller via a Bluetooth connection to the hub.

At this writing, Ducati was planning to put the devices into production next year, and the city of Copenhagen may start buying them on a trial basis to retrofit bikes and make them a replacement for government cars. The bad news is that the Wheel will cost about as much as a standard electric bicycle. But innovations like this one may help to convince fair-weather cyclists—those who like their bikes but dread tackling long distances or large hills without a little assistance—to cycle more often. ARS

Bicing

▬▬▬▬ Becoming a bike commuter is a lot more involved than learning how to pedal. There's gear to buy and storage space to procure, and for many people, the maintenance involved in bike ownership makes it seem nearly as inconvenient as car ownership.

One way to make bike commuting more attractive is to remove the headaches of ownership. Bike-sharing programs integrate bike commuting with larger transportation networks—filling in the gaps where buses or trains may not run. Despite some over-reported bumps in the road for France's Vélib bike-sharing program (including reports of theft and vandalism in Paris), this uniquely urban mobility solution has proved to be phenomenally successful in Europe.

A bicycle equipped with the Copenhagen Wheel, which turns any standard bike into a hybrid electric.

To date the shining example is Barcelona's Bicing program. Bicing, like many bike-sharing programs, uses the same model as car-sharing services (minus the advance reservations). Members pay an annual fee of thirty euros and register their credit card information. Bicing issues swipe cards that unlock any of its available bikes. All a member has to do is walk up to a station, select a bike, swipe the card, and pedal away. The first thirty minutes of any trip are free; after that members pay thirty eurocents per half-hour (making it the city's cheapest public-transportation option). Bikes must be returned after two hours, but they may be returned to any Bicing stand in the city.

Less than a year after the service's start date in early 2007, Bicing expanded dramatically—from one hundred bicycles at 14 bike stations around the city to more than six thousand bikes at 375 stations. Stations are heavily clustered in the city's core to ensure they're close to other public transportation like metro and bus stops—and that you don't have to walk far to find one.

One of the interesting things about Bicing is that its proponents often downplay the direct environmental impact of having more people bike. To its advocates, bike sharing, which clearly contributes to Barcelona's already sizeable bike-commuting community (tens of thousands strong), is more about creating a different type of flow on city streets that calms traffic and changes the cityscape. In fact, according to the *Huffington Post*, the specific complaints made by motorists, pedestrians, and cyclists when the Bicing program was installed forced city officials to review the city's entire biking infrastructure. Among other measures, the city created eighty miles of new bike lanes and lowered speed limits in Barcelona's core. CB

Bike-frastructure

Creating bicycling infrastructure is one of the classiest moves a city can make. Adding bike lanes and bike parking, anticipating the needs of cyclists when they reach their destinations in the city's core—these things say, unequivocally, that cycling is a legitimate and important mode of transportation. As Elisabeth Rosenthal recently wrote in the *New York Times,* there will soon be only two kinds of city leaders: those who are implementing bike amenities and bike-sharing programs, and those who plan to do so soon.

Bike infrastructure isn't just about bicyclist safety. In order to encourage reticent cyclists to use their pedal power, a city must do more than install a few bike lanes—it must provide secure storage for bikes and adequate on-street parking, as well as facilities like changing rooms and showers for long-distance commuters. Some of us could even use a little help up the hill.

Bike Boxes and Bike Lanes

Otherwise known as "advanced stop lines," bike boxes work with a simple concept, providing a colored box at the front of intersections where cyclists can wait at a red light. Cars sit behind this line, and are often restricted by law from making a right turn on red. These brightly colored boxes succeed in raising awareness of cyclists, and also help to eliminate potential conflicts that may arise at intersections. In Portland, Oregon, bike lanes themselves are going green—literally. Whether an entire lane is painted or just those sections leading into intersections, a colored patch of "green-crete" serves as a reminder to automobile drivers that a cyclist may be right alongside them.

In Copenhagen, grade-separated bike paths make cycling even safer than standard lanes. In addition, the city, which has the world's most impressive bike culture, is now creating "conversation lanes" on some of its busiest thoroughfares. These extra-wide lanes are roomy enough for friends to ride side by side and chat (skinnier adjacent lanes are "fast lanes" for cyclists who can't linger). A truly brilliant innovation, conversation lanes acknowledge that a real biking infrastructure

must accommodate cyclists of all abilities, and must promote cycling as something that can be leisurely and fun. And did we mention that creating such lanes involves reclaiming even more of the road from cars?

Bike Highways

What's even more impressive than a bike lane? A bike superhighway. Copenhagen is developing thirteen of these to run right alongside major auto-packed roads, giving commuters (defined as anyone who travels more than ten kilometers [six miles] to work) a healthier, safer way to access the city from the suburbs. These superhighways provide direct routes with a "Green Wave" system—the timing of stoplights so that cyclists pedaling twenty kilometers (twelve miles) per hour don't ever hit red lights—at busy intersections, and even bicycle-repair stations along the way. Worldwide, cities such as Montreal, Bogotá, and London have embraced and provided these lanes.

Bike Storage and Parking

In 2009 the city of Portland announced that it would use $1 million of its federal stimulus money to add bike-parking structures along its TriMet transit system (trains and buses cannot accommodate many bikes). This follows the European model of providing ample bike parking at transit centers so that cyclists, like drivers, may park and ride.

In Tokyo, where finding extra space for anything is a challenge, underground may be the only place to go. Giken's ECO-Cycle is an automated underground parking kiosk that can hold up to 9,400 bikes. Cyclists purchase prepaid cards to use the kiosk. You swipe your card, load your bike (no extra locks necessary) onto a platform that whisks it to the underground storage facility via a tiny freight elevator. The structure itself is a spiral of single-track storage platforms that surround the lift, each holding one bike. Your bike is pushed (still upright) onto an empty rack. When you return, you swipe your card again and the system retrieves your bike in a matter of seconds. For

cities that don't need to cater to such high volume, there's a Spanish spin-off called Biceberg—an almost identical concept, except that the Biceberg holds less than one hundred bikes, making excavation a lot simpler.

Bike Facilities

From Penny Farthings, a design group in Brisbane, Australia, Green Pod is a great solution for building owners who want to help bikers commute to work. A single parking space can hold the pod, which contains a solar-powered shower, a changing room, lockers, and up to ten bike-storage spots.

Bikestation, which operates bike-transit centers in several U.S. cities, not only offers its members secure parking spots in central locations, but also lockers and changing rooms, as well as loaners and rental bikes. Some stations have showers and even cafés with Wi-Fi.

Hill-climbing Help

Another thing that unites Copenhagen and Portland? They're mostly flat. Cities like Seattle and San Francisco have some famously killer hills, and while the nimble and proud may make it to the top every day, a city's beloved topography can crush the spirits of a novice cyclist. In such cities, something like the Trampe, a bike-lift system in Trondheim, Norway, may be a desirable piece of bike infrastructure. Cyclists aren't required to dismount to use this escalator; they simply slide their wheels into the track and activate the lift using a keycard. This amenity emphasizes the pleasure of bike-riding while also giving tired cyclists more incentive to use their bikes for errands like grocery-shopping. CB, SDC & KP

Bus Rapid Transit

Passenger buses are one of the most cost-effective methods of mass transit, able to move large numbers of people along existing roads. Unfortunately, in the United States, buses are not used to their full potential. When most Americans think of municipal bus service, they picture lumbering diesel behemoths that get nowhere fast, tracing circuitous routes that emphasize coverage over speed. Given the choice between driving a car and taking a bus that might require long waits and

Bicyclists gather at a Critical Mass rally to demand their right to the road.

transfers between lines, most Americans opt to take the car.

Public buses may never offer every convenience that a private car does, but there are many ways to make them more efficient, more attractive, and faster. Pioneered in Curitiba, Brazil, bus rapid transit (BRT) uses special high-speed express buses in place of commuter rail lines. The buses run on high-occupancy vehicle (HOV) lanes or, ideally, their own dedicated roads, often paralleling existing freeways. Separated from the traffic grid, they are able to run between stops at high speeds, increasing capacity and making the service attractive to harried commuters. Before boarding, BRT passengers pay their fares on the platform (speeding up the process), then gain entry to special ramps that allow them to embark without climbing stairs.

Mexico City's recently introduced Metrobus replaced 350 microbuses and vanpools with ninety-eight low-pollution Volvo buses that move much faster than traffic thanks to a dedicated twenty-kilometer (twelve-mile) lane that runs down busy Insurgentes Avenue, stopping at thirty-six stations along the way. A journey that might take over two hours now takes less than one hour, and the city decreases greenhouse-gas emissions by an estimated 35,000 metric tons per year.

In 2009 Istanbul introduced the world's first intercontinental BRT line, with dedicated lanes on the Bosphorus Bridge, which connects Europe and Asia. The trip along the eleven-kilometer (seven-mile) route takes just thirty minutes—a big difference from the two to three hours it can take crossing the bridge by car. The route is an extension of the city's Metrobus corridor, which means travelers on the Istanbul side can make

quick and easy connections to public transportation immediately after crossing.

And there's still room for innovation on local bus routes. Small, agile vehicles designed to zip through residential neighborhoods could deliver riders to BRT stops or light-rail stations to maximize the system's potential. SJ

One Bus Away

Not knowing how long you'll have to wait for a bus or train is one of the things that make public transit irritating and inconvenient. Although digital displays at subway and train stops showing estimated times of arrival are becoming more common worldwide, they're not ubiquitous; many bus stops look much the way they did half a century ago.

Simple digital tools can take the guesswork out of commuting. One Bus Away is just one example. Seattleites can text the word onebus along with their bus stop number to 41411. The system responds by telling you which buses are about to arrive at that stop, and in how many minutes, based not on the posted schedule but on the location of the buses en route to where you stand. Smart phone users can access a more sophisticated version.

A similar app called NextBus uses Google Maps to give real-time arrival information for transit options in select U.S. and Canadian cities. Other services are launching in the United Kingdom and Scandinavia.

In a world of jam-packed schedules, a little information goes a long way toward making public transit easier and more pleasant. JVL

Community-specific Transportation Solutions

Light rail, bike infrastructure, BRT . . . all great solutions, seemingly one-size-fits-all. But sometimes communities best solve their transportation problems by thinking outside the bike box.

The efficient bus-rapid-transit system in Curitiba, Brazil, is being copied around the world.

Steve Dale's blog, the Gondola Project, sings the praises of the world's many urban cable-propelled transit systems. One of Dale's favorite CPTs is the Hungerburgbahn system in Innsbruck, Austria, which is a hybrid funicular—a cross between a cable car, a funicular, and a gondola. The system starts underground in the downtown core, surfaces to street level, ascends to a river crossing, and goes underground once more (this time below a highway) before surfacing to climb a mountainside. The Hungerburgbahn isn't without its drawbacks—it's not fully integrated into the city's public transit system, for one—but its pros are more compelling. Besides being able to traverse the Innsbruck area's varied topography, the system itself, including its stations, is very compact, blending well into the urban landscape and requiring stations that are far less intensive to build than those for standard aerial trams.

On the other end of the technology spectrum, UN-Habitat has praised the very local solution embraced by the Cuban city of Bayamo. The city was suffering from a dearth of public transit, especially in the Zona Norte section, which had not been urbanized enough to support many mechanized options. So the city introduced an organized system of horse-drawn carriages (which have always been a presence in the city), complete with a bit of quick infrastructure (a few designated coach stops and improved pedestrian routes leading to and from those stops). According to the Cities Alliance, this simple system has taken care of 40 percent of residents' transportation needs. Not only is this solution appropriate for the city, it is low impact and more sustainable for a place already dealing with fuel-scarcity issues. CB

content provides readers with unique stories of how not only bikes, but the people who ride them, can help us reimagine our city streets.

Copenhagenize: The Copenhagen Bike Culture Blog

http://www.copenhagenize.com

Arguably one of the best blogs out there on all things pedal-powered, Copenhagenize is jam-packed with bite-sized posts that may interest any cyclist. Whether you're curious about bicycle superhighways for commuting, finding the best bike for the little ones in your life, or using cargo bikes to launch your next business endeavor, look no further. With its awe-inspiring stories and examples of bike culture both in Copenhagen and abroad, Copenhagenize does its best to showcase how the bicycle can provide multiple solutions to many of the challenges facing urbanites.

■■■■■■ RESOURCES

Streetsblog

http://www.streetsblog.org

Streetsblog provides news and views on cities, bikes, and policies, and includes films and a wiki that helps foster future-forward thinking. Its daily

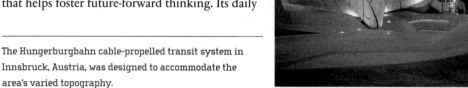

The Hungerburgbahn cable-propelled transit system in Innsbruck, Austria, was designed to accommodate the area's varied topography.

The Ruins of the Unsustainable

The ruins of the unsustainable are the 21st century's frontier.
        Bruce Sterling

In North America, several decades of bad development (and the government policies that enabled and encouraged it) have resulted in unchecked sprawl, which has played no small part in our global financial meltdown. Housing was built in places where no real demand existed, funded by loans that proved to be essentially scams, and now foreclosures and abandoned buildings outnumber occupied homes in many such neighborhoods. These far-flung exurban areas have swallowed up miles of open space, replacing farmland and woods and meadows with pavement and lawns. In the process, they've required taxpayers to invest a fortune in what is possibly the least efficient form of infrastructure: providing utilities and public services to a small number of people spread out over a large area. North Americans will be paying off the costs of the last wave of sprawl for decades to come.

The social costs of sprawl are just as harmful. Exurban areas are unhealthy for people who live in them. Lots of time spent in cars has been correlated in numerous studies with being overweight and having high blood pressure. While it's possible that fat, angry people like to move to the suburbs, it's more likely that the strains of driving are to blame. Worse yet, driving is one of the most directly dangerous activities North Americans participate in, with more than 42,000 Americans a year killed in collisions. Conversely, walkable communities are healthier: for instance, despite living in a city with poor air quality and a fast-paced way of life, New Yorkers have the highest life expectancy in the United States, mostly because they walk more than any other group of Americans, getting a lot of exercise on a daily basis.

Sprawl impoverishes many of its residents as well. As we know from the Housing and Transportation Affordability Index [see Mobility, p. 209], people who have to drive everywhere they go are at an economic disadvantage. The American Automobile Association, in its 2010 annual survey of car-ownership costs, found that the average household spends $8,487 a year for each car they own, without counting parking and tolls. The average family would save $9,242 a year for every car they gave up, even after factoring in the cost of taking public transit. Living in a community where every adult needs a car to get through the day can cost a family a significant portion of its after-tax income.

More and more people understand these dynamics. Consequently, the suburbs—once the heart of the American Dream—have fallen from grace. According to leading thinkers in urban planning like Arthur C. Nelson and Christopher B. Leinberger, a majority of Americans now find living in walkable urban communities desirable. Middle-class North Americans are already beginning to move in large numbers back into central cities, while property values on the suburban fringe have plummeted. A 2009 study by CEOs for Cities, a cross-sector network of urban leaders, found that a one-point increase in a house's Walk Score (which rates walkability on a scale of 1 to 100) correlated with a $500 to $3,000 increase in its value. People are willing to pay more to be able to walk, and decades of underinvesting in walkable communities have left us with more demand than supply. The result has been a boom in urban infill.

The approaching end of sprawl is a good thing, but it leaves the future of the suburbs uncertain. Foreclosures, unemployment, and retail losses have already been a disaster for many suburban towns, and experts warn that suburbs are fast becoming the next slums, as low-income families who have been priced out of the central cities replace the middle-class residents who head back to urban life. Already, poor suburban Americans outnumber poor urbanites.

Smart growth policies and long-term regional land-use plans can prevent more sprawl, concentrate growth in the urban core, and help restore vitality to existing communities. And we can also retrofit some of the ruins of the unsustainable damaged environments—the empty malls and superstores, vacant parking lots, six-lane roads, and McMansions that the collapse of the suburbs leaves behind. JVL & AS

Vauban: The Car-free Burb

It's difficult for many people—particularly North Americans—to envision car-free suburbs. But some existing communities can be transformed into mini-cities that function best without private vehicles. In Vauban, a suburb of Freiburg, Germany, nearly all streets are car-free and there are only two parking garages. The community's residents, 70 percent of whom don't own a private vehicle, report feeling safer and happier as a result of the suburb's smart planning.

Vauban is a former military base, which now has two thousand homes and more than five thousand residents. The town's narrow layout and the decentralization of amenities (like shopping) encourages residents to bike or walk instead of drive. A more direct incentive is the cost of a parking space: U.S.$23,000. An annual tram pass, on the other hand, is free. Car-sharing is available for times when residents do need cars, and some families own communal vehicles.

From its first stages of planning, in the early '90s after the army base closed, Vauban has

been a beacon of ecological living and a haven for younger generations in a country with an aging demographic. Vauban is the sort of nonurban development that even a green-shy househunter would want to live in, simply for its style, proximity to a major urban center, and livability. In a world where millions still treasure the space and pace associated with suburban life, car-free suburbs might be one solution for pleasing multiple factions. JVL & SR

Improving the Inner Ring

Many inner-ring suburbs already have both proximity to an urban center and a dense Main Street–type commercial area. Suburbs like these, ones that have good bones, are the easiest to improve. Creating regional transit plans that extend public transportation out to the inner ring and adding transit-oriented development around new and existing public transit are two ways to patch up an inner-ring burb—encouraging the development of neighborhoods where businesses can thrive and residents can escape auto-dependence.

Effective transit plans can be combined with other strategies for increasing density while enhancing character and livability. Incentives to create infill development are a good place to start. Some city governments, like Vancouver's, have realized that it's beneficial to encourage homeowners to contribute to density; they've eased zoning restrictions and updated housing codes to allow, for example, the building of accessory dwelling units (ADUs) [see Green Retrofits, p. 166]. Older strip-mall developments have

In Vauban, built on a former military base outside Freiburg, Germany, most of the suburb's five thousand residents don't own cars.

already been successfully converted into more pedestrian-oriented shopping areas in a number of places through strategies like filling in overly large parking lots with new buildings, outdoor cafés, and greenery. JVL & AS

Greyfield Redevelopment

North America is in the grip of a dead-mall epidemic. Suburbia is littered with abandoned malls, many of them built in the 1960s and nudged out of use by bigger, hotter malls in the '90s. These run-down strips, along with other greyfields, are some of the biggest eyesores and wastes of space in suburbia. Fortunately, developers and concerned communities are no longer ignoring them and are actually turning them back into viable, livable space.

Greyfield redevelopment varies based on its site and purpose. A mall, for example, might be demolished and cleared outright. Or the inward-facing stores might be turned outward, to develop a relationship with the street. Then it's a matter of varying the scale of the neighborhood, so that a monolithic, car-scale mall becomes a friendlier neighborhood to navigate.

Smaller streets encourage pedestrian traffic and discourage speeding cars. Public areas like parks, squares, and playgrounds offer places for people to stop as they move through the neighborhood. Mixed-use, multilevel buildings go up where the small cookie-cutter street-level storefronts were. Asphalt parking lots are filled in with buildings or green space—parking can be accommodated by garages that fit in with the street profile.

Greyfield redevelopments are often excellent examples of transit-oriented development. This transition is logical: these sites were chosen by developers years before because they were in central locations. Greyfield developers take advantage of the position of rail corridors, light-rail developments, or rapid buses to provide other options than private automobile use.

Denver, Colorado, is winning national acclaim for its sprawl-fighting greyfield redevelopments. The greyfields are a necessity, because Denver is a booming city: 3.8 million people are expected to live in the region by 2030. If Denver's footprint were to follow current development trends, according to the Denver Regional Council of Governments, its metro area would double in size by 2030. But planners from the city and surrounding areas are trying to keep the sprawl in check, containing it in and around a set of defined centers (many in suburban areas). Dealing with the local greyfields is an important part of the plan.

Stapleton was home to Denver's airport from 1929 to 1995; it's now the largest urban redevelopment in the country. In its new incarnation, it will ultimately house 30,000 people in a combination of single and multifamily homes for mixed incomes and age groups. Rather than just functioning as a bedroom community, Stapleton will offer employment for 35,000 workers. A third of its 4,700 acres (1,902 hectares) is green space, which is being allocated to open areas, a community farm, and parks and squares throughout the denser areas. The redevelopment's award list is long and includes recognition from the United Nations for its sustainable approach.

Belmar Urban Center, another acclaimed Denver-area greyfield redevelopment, is the

Right: Even big-box stores can find new lives: this medical center is housed in a former Walmart.
Opposite, left: Communities like the Crossings show that better suburban development—with higher density living and easier access to shopping and public transportation—is possible.
Opposite, right: Street life at Belmar, a Colorado shopping and residential district converted from a dying regional mall.

downtown that the suburban Colorado city of Lakewood never had. In 1966, Lakewood built a 1.4-million-square-foot (130,064-square-meter) mall on a 106-acre (43-hectare) site. When it opened, Villa Italia was the largest shopping mall west of Chicago, but by the early 1990s, it began to atrophy when its anchor tenants moved out and competing malls opened in the area. At the mall's lowest point, retail tenants occupied a mere 30 percent of its massive space.

The new plan for Belmar is multimodal—that is, it offers a number of sustainable transportation methods for its residents and visitors. It's positioned on local and express bus lines, with rail corridors only a few miles away. The new street grid creates a number of smaller blocks with public squares and plazas that lead to the larger streets. It aims to be a community with a heavy retail and office base: there will be almost a million square feet (92,903 square meters) of available retail space and 760,000 square feet (70,606 square meters) of office space.

On a related front, some communities are also practicing big-box reuse. Big-box stores go under all the time—even Walmart, which seems poised on the brink of global domination, has left behind a lot of ghost stores around the country. Like shopping malls, if big boxes are naked and unused, they end up just hulking wastes of space. When they're in an actual neighborhood (think large supermarkets), they tend to take the whole neighborhood down with them when they close. Once a big box pulls out, the small businesses around it quickly decline.

These massive and ugly buildings are even more difficult to redeem than dead malls are, but communities are finding clever ways

to reincorporate them into town life. The good thing about abandoned big boxes is that they're relatively easy and cost-efficient to move into and adapt. They already have parking lots, fairly new electrical systems, and structural elements that make them reliable and sturdy buildings. In addition, because they're usually at a crossroads of some sort, they are great places for businesses or institutions that need to serve several communities. This perhaps explains why big boxes in the United States have often notably been turned into community centers and churches. Some even become charter schools, like the Snowy Range Academy in Laramie, Wyoming, which is housed in a renovated Walmart. Perhaps the most wonderfully whimsical reuse of a big box yet is the Spam Museum in Austin, Minnesota—in a former Kmart.

Reusing big-box stores doesn't change the landscape as dramatically as greyfield development does; sometimes the facades change very little, save for a paint job and a new sign. But reuse, in any form, is never a bad thing. MWS & CB

Development for Disassembly

▬▬▬   Turning a dead mall or big-box store into a school (or a Spam Museum) is a good idea in theory, but one of the challenges of converting these commercial spaces is that they were always meant to be temporary. Big-box stores are generally designed to last only twenty to twenty-five years, which makes investing in a major retrofit, or installing a more permanent community like a church or community group, a bit risky. Plus, the cavernous shells of a Best Buy or a Sam's Club

are suited for very few purposes beyond storing massive quantities of consumer goods. Often, old big-box stores are just abandoned, left to become centers of blight.

Ultimately, most of these buildings will need to come down, and adopting a long view as early in the construction phase as possible will mean less material is wasted. Design for disassembly [see Producer Responsibility, p. 115] is hot in the world of consumer products—smart designs that allow product components to be dismantled easily, so that they can be sorted and reused as "nutrients" in the industrial life cycle. It seems like big-box stores would be an ideal starting point for city-mandated building codes that require adherence to best practices for materials reuse. After all, if it's likely that the store will be defunct in less than three decades, it would be a major benefit to be able to take it down and return the massive pile of components to the building nutrient stream. What if you could dismantle a shopping mall and build a school using the same materials? JVL

Innovation Zones

▬▬▬   Because the worst suburban ruins are worthless—or worth little—pioneering types with big, risky, and exciting ideas have a better shot at making their schemes work there than anywhere else in America. In many cases, it seems that these up-for-grabs properties are inspiring a kind of experimental "what-if" boldness that's less common in established urban neighborhoods, where cost, regulations, and NIMBY-ism can stand in the way. An abandoned home that's already been stripped of its conventional wiring and plumbing, after all, is an ideal frame on which to build a home-energy system entirely out of renewable sources—and the neighbors aren't likely to fuss about such modifications.

Creative reuse is a hot trend, with pioneers rapidly innovating ways to make dead-space liabilities into repurposed assets. Resourcefulness like this has gone on for a long time in neglected urban spaces, and continues to make headlines during this economic contraction—we've seen artists reclaiming abandoned or foreclosed homes in Detroit for neighborhood renewal and district energy projects, and hipsters in industrial areas of

New York turning unused dumpsters into swimming pools for a little summer fun. Sturdy urban relics have become famous sites for renaissance in cities around the world: iconic rehabbed warehouse districts include Portland's Pearl District, Brooklyn's Dumbo, and Amsterdam's Docklands. But will this trend spread to suburbia?

The problems inherent in the gutted outer-ring suburbs are hard to overstate. They're completely auto-dependent in a time of rising fuel prices; their infrastructures are too expensive for their tax bases to maintain; there are no industries, and hence no jobs, nearby; even the land itself has often been scraped clean of much of its topsoil and shaped in ways that make farming impossible. But all those challenges may just prove to be the spur for truly radical innovation. It's possible that one day, these sites will be the Kitty Hawks—the original testing grounds—of some of the most important innovations that future generations will take for granted.

We could easily imagine hard-hit exurbs boldly experimenting with dividing McMansions up into condos and adding lots of prefab infill housing and small shops, creating a more compact community on the cheap. District energy and green infrastructure like bioswales could replace bankrupt municipal systems. Woonerfs [see Density Done Right, p. 204] in the cul-de-sacs, and paths in between properties, connecting pocket to pocket, could weave a walkable fabric out of streets that previously demanded driving. A strong plan for transit-oriented redevelopment on the subdivision's arterial streets could create a town center out of dead strip malls and big-box stores. Such radical innovation might even turn the tide of suburban decline. JVL & AS

What's the Big Deal with Portland?

▬▬▬   If we hang out with planners, we hear a lot about Portland, Oregon. It's small—not a "global city." We might say, "What's the big deal?" The answer is this: Portland is the only U.S. city to have created a regional government with the power to control sprawl.

The Oregon system was created under the leadership of Republican governor Tom McCall, who lead the effort to pass state Senate Bill 100 in 1969. This bill, motivated largely by the desire to protect agriculture from encroaching urban sprawl, required every local jurisdiction to have a growth-management plan. The system did not emerge all at once but in steps: the Land Conservation and Development Commission formed, the state adopted planning priorities, a land-use board of appeals got to work. Over time, Oregon built a framework for true statewide planning. This system has been challenged in voter initiatives several times. But the basic idea is that state government enacts broad land-use planning goals and requires local governments to comply with state standards. The Land Conservation and Development Commission, which is responsible for overseeing all of this, says that state officials "acknowledge" rather than "approve" local plans, phrasing meant to assuage our very American distrust of centralized government.

In 1978, Portland—Oregon's largest metropolitan area—established a regional government. Metro, as it is called, replaced a conventional council of local governments, which most areas in the U.S. have. Metro was given the job of defining urban-growth boundaries for the region and ensuring that all of the twenty-four cities (and parts of three counties) it served in the Portland metropolitan area complied with the regional plan. If all of this sounds strangely European, it was also given a distinctly American twist: Metro is governed by a directly elected board. In 2009 the city's Bureau of Planning and its Office of Sustainable Development merged into the Bureau of Planning and Sustainability to ensure that all planning is done with sustainability in mind.

Why does any of this matter? Because planners face a profound problem almost everywhere: the scale of political institutions is smaller than the scale of the actual regions that need to be planned. A metropolitan area includes hundreds of distinct "governments"—cities, counties, transit districts, water districts, port authorities, school districts, and more. Metropolitan areas may include multiple state governments and, in some cases, multiple counties. It is common for metropolitan areas to have an association of local governments, a sort of United Nations for a region. There is almost never an actual regional government with powers that matter. Portland is the exception. Metro shows us that the choice to place wide-scale decisions within the jurisdiction of a centralized governing body can have positive effects, while preserving the voice and participation of small communities within the region. GM

The Coalition for a Livable Future

If there's one thing that community advocates and activists know, it's that progress happens through collaboration. Portland's Coalition for a Livable Future draws its strength from the numerous groups who come together to focus on single urban issues. The coalition pools multiple perspectives and voices to build a formidable force for change.

In 1994, Myron Orfield, a state legislator from Minnesota, arrived in Oregon with a warning for Portland residents. Having observed and analyzed patterns of social polarization in Minneapolis and St. Paul over the years, Orfield predicted that even with growth management, urban sprawl in Portland could undermine the social fabric of the city, not to mention the environment, with the added impact of congestion caused by commuting and insufficient public transit. Moved to action by Orfield's prediction, a diverse group of community organizations banded together into Coalition for a Livable Future, a citizen presence poised to help redirect Portland's course.

Out of all North American cities, Portland, Oregon, has done the best job of managing growth.

Cobbling together expertise in areas ranging from ecology to public transportation, social justice to affordable housing, the coalition created a unified agenda for preserving the integrity of Portland's infrastructure, open spaces, and communities. In 1995, a number of the coalition's member groups, including the organization 1,000 Friends of Oregon, formally presented the Metro 2040 Growth Concept, a fifty-year plan (antedated to 1990) for Portland that put equal emphasis on the protection of urban and rural ecology, support for the local economy, intelligent transportation systems and infrastructure, and accessible, socially just housing options. The 2040 plan, and the savvy way the coalition has subsequently built political support for its execution, serve as an example to cities everywhere that it's possible to accommodate a growing population while improving the urban experience and protecting natural habitats. GM

■■■■■■   RESOURCES

The Option of Urbanism: Investing in a New American Dream by Christopher B. Leinberger (Island Press, 2007)
Leinberger's excellent book outlines the supply-and-demand argument for creating more urban space: we've already entered an age when the market for walkable urbanism has grown larger than the market for drivable suburbanism, and the main challenge now is building enough compact communities, well enough, fast enough. Leinberger considers the desire to live in a pleasant walkable urban community as the new American Dream.

While he's making his case, Leinberger traces the history of sprawl in North America, explaining Wall Street's puzzling role in encouraging the development of cookie-cutter auto-dependent communities and big-box stores:

"Because low-density, drivable sub-urban products became the basis of what Wall Street could finance, and Wall Street was new to real estate finance, there has been great hesitancy to broaden the list of conforming products . . . It does seem strange the Wall Street investment bankers have a hard time financing walkable urbanism. At the end of the workday, most of them leave their office building in downtown or

midtown Manhattan, which is probably among the most expensive in the world, and walk home past shops that pay the most rent on the planet to their $1,000- to $2,500-per-square-foot loft, condominium, or townhouse, again some of the most pricey in the country. They are living, working, and shopping in some of the best and, not coincidentally, most expensive walkable urbanism in the country."

Big Box Reuse by Julia Christensen (MIT Press, 2008)
A great coffee table book for the planning geek, *Big Box Reuse* surveys 10 successful retrofits of defunct Wal-Mart and Kmart stores. The famous Spam Museum is included, of course, but most of the projects profiled are far less whimsical, consisting of schools, senior centers, and health centers. The photos, of things like school murals where stockrooms used to be, are inspirational.

Sustainable Urbanism: Urban Design with Nature by Douglas Farr (Wiley, 2007)
If you want a textbook approach to the fundamentals of good urban planning, suburban redevelopment, and sustainable approaches to infrastructure, Farr's book is the best single source. Though written before the housing crash (and thus more sanguine about the future of suburbia than it might be today), *Sustainable Urbanism* offers introductions to many best practices and most notable examples.

Retrofitting Suburbia: Urban Design Solutions for Redesigning Suburbs by Ellen Dunham-Jones and June Williamson (Wiley, 2008)
An overview of the best suburban redevelopment projects in North America, *Retrofitting Suburbia* is the first place to go if you want to know what solutions have already proven themselves in the real world. The authors explain, in clear if somewhat dry language, what has made each redesign project successful and what lessons have been learned. It's inspiring to see what we already know will work, and it allows us to ponder what might work with enough imagination.

Crabgrass Frontier: The Suburbanization of the United States by Kenneth T. Jackson (Oxford University Press, 1985)

Kenneth T. Jackson's 1985 classic of urban history was the first full-scale look at the development of the American suburb, and a prophetic view of the growth in American housing.

Tracing suburbanization from the nineteenth century onward, Jackson argues that the spaces around us condition our behavior, and that "history has a fundamental relevance to contemporary public policy." He goes on to comment, "I would hope that this book indicates that suburbanization has been as much a governmental as a natural process . . . For better or for worse, the American suburb is a remarkable and probably lasting achievement."

Once There Were Greenfields: How Urban Sprawl Is Undermining America's Environment, Economy and Social Fabric by F. Kaid Benfield, Matthew D. Raimi, and Donald D. T. Chen (National Resources Defense Council, 1999)
If you want the goods on why sprawl is bad, look no further: here are the numbers, the studies, the horror stories, the case made in full. The book's emphasis is not on providing tools for change, but as a resource on urban sprawl as it exists, *Once There Were Greenfields* is unmatched.

According to the authors, "The plight of so-called 'soccer moms,' for example, stems from the fact that many women not only hold full-time jobs but also perform more child care and household duties than their spouses. This requires women to make more automobile trips. Because fringe living forces most of these responsibilities to be met by driving automobiles longer and longer distances, the inevitable result is stress, fatigue, and less time with family."

Healing Polluted Land

Development on the rural fringes of cities is a problem. Development in the heart of cities is a solution. Because density is inherently more sustainable than sprawl, and because redeveloping land that has already been developed is more ecologically sound than cutting down forests and paving farms, our goal should be to use every urban acre as effectively as possible. Unfortunately, many of the places that have been used most intensely in the past have suffered for it and been left derelict, contaminated by the industries that first brought them to life. In every city there are vacant lots, polluted former factory sites, discarded buildings—places we refer to as *brownfields*. With new and better ways to clean up and restore these places, they are now hotbeds of opportunity for the new frontier of bright green urbanism.

Building on abandoned lots and polluted land, rehabbing forgotten buildings, creating great places from the most wounded spaces: these efforts are on the cutting edge of what it takes to make cities better. The architect Peter Calthorpe said

Formerly polluted or abandoned lands can be reclaimed, even turned into parks, like this site in Irvington, New York.

if we want to know how to make a neighborhood better, we should start with the worst places and put the best things we can possibly imagine there. By using discarded lots and brownfields, we not only foster compact development, we also heal the city.

One way to clean up a contaminated piece of land and make way for the regeneration of flora and fauna is to put plants into the polluted ground. Many types of living organisms act as filters for toxins and pollutants in soil and water. Known as bioremediation, this organic process involves the absorption of contaminants into the plants, where they either get broken down into nonhazardous components and rereleased, or extracted and concentrated in a way that makes disposal easy. There are many varieties of bioremediation, each involving a specific type of organism as the cleaning mechanism. Plants have incredibly powerful natural abilities to extract everything from heavy metals to crude oil and turn them into harmless elements.

Many brownfields are now undergoing bioremediation—it's an efficient cleaning method, in terms of both labor and cost. Some of these areas have been prepped for housing and commercial development; others have become spectacular parks. AS

Mycoremediation

Can mushrooms clean up our polluted world? Mycologist Paul Stamets says they can. He has coined the term *mycoremediation* to refer to a specific type of bioremediation that uses fungus to break down pollutants. Stamets, the king of this far-out science, has demonstrated that the magic worked by the spores of a few fungi can transform a heap of hazardous waste into a heap of lush greenery—that a vibrant ecosystem can be created anew by letting mushrooms eat up toxins and fertilize soil.

As biological filters, mushrooms work extremely effectively, because they are, by their very nature, decomposing agents. Mycelia—the parts of the mushroom that absorb nutrients and turn them into usable matter and waste matter—are able to eat up some environmental toxins and efficiently break them down into nontoxic components. Mushrooms can remediate soil and sediment contaminated by heavy oils, petroleum products, pesticides, alkaloids, polychlorinated biphenyls (PCBs), and even *E. coli*.

One of Stamets's best-known case studies involved cleaning up a diesel-oil spill using oyster mushrooms. The study demonstrated not only that mycelia were the best tools for the task, but that the mushrooms that flourished in the contaminated soil contained no harmful agents once the pollutants had been cleaned. Many environmental-protection groups are now considering mycoremediation as a viable solution for threats such as marine oil spills, mercury contamination, and mining residues. Stamets's water cleanup work in the Pacific Northwest, where he is based, may clear the way for restoring wild fish populations and protecting marine ecosystems. 5R

Duisburg-Nord, Germany

Just because we clean something up doesn't mean we must erase its past. We see the preservation of our cities' industrial histories everywhere now, in the conversion of old warehouses and factories into residential and office spaces, where the facade is preserved intact to evoke the building's gritty past. In the remediation of contaminated land, the relics of destructive forces on human and environmental health can be a profound example of how far we've come, and how far we have to go.

In Duisburg, Germany, the well-known landscape park Duisburg-Nord stands upon a former brownfield. The park was designed to embrace rather than eradicate the industrial history of the site by incorporating artifacts of its past, such as blast furnaces, gas tanks, and storage bunkers. In contrast to many urban parks, such as New York's Central Park or Paris's Parc André Citroën, Duisburg-Nord does not attempt to isolate itself from its city surroundings, nor does it attempt to conceal the remnants upon which it was built. "Landscape is not the opposite of the town," says Peter Latz, one of the park's designers. "Landscape is culture." Walkways weave through the site's blast-furnace buildings; lily pads float in old cooling tanks. A few areas of the site remain too toxic for human use, but most of the formerly unusable, unsightly land has been turned into a vibrant park that serves a city of nearly 100,000 people. 5R

Pearl District, Portland

In many urban centers around the world, run-down industrial neighborhoods have undergone face-lifts that both restored their vitality and boosted their economies. Among many, Portland's Pearl District stands out as a great success.

The Pearl District has come to life in stages. In the mid-1990s, an old rail yard was turned into a residential neighborhood by Hoyt Street Properties; it was an endeavor that required earnest convincing on the part of the developers to keep the city of Portland from building a highway off-ramp through the area's center. By preserving the cohesiveness of the district, the developers were able to create superior alternative- and public-transit options, including pedestrian and bike routes and free bus and light rail, within a designated zone. Today, mixed-use real estate

Opposite: Certain plants, fungi, and bacteria have extraordinary power to clean horribly polluted sites, like this former industrial waste facility in Houston.
Left: The landscape park Duisburg-Nord in Duisburg, Germany, incorporates blast furnaces and other remnants of the site's industrial past.

helps to preserve socioeconomic diversity in the area, offering options for people well below the city's median income level.

A subsequent redevelopment near the original Pearl project includes the Brewery Blocks, higher-end residences in converted breweries. The area now includes a number of LEED-certified buildings; the builders diverted some 96 percent of the construction waste away from landfills into recycling plants.

Chosen in 2005 by the Project for Public Spaces as one of the top sixty places in the world to live, the Pearl District stands as a shining example of how cities can invert sprawl and begin rebuilding from their urban heart. Industrial zones frequently offer sturdy old buildings with great structural potential, proximity to downtown, and even waterfront locations; they have also taken on distinctive aesthetic appeal.

This is where the next generation of homeowners wants to live. Easy transportation; lively, tight-knit communities; pedestrian-friendly paths and parks; and thriving commercial enterprises make inner-city redevelopment synonymous with a superior quality of life. SR

Minimart City Park

The Seattle artist collective SuttonBeres-Culler is know for being humorous and disruptive. There's the time they set float on one of their installations (a manmade island complete with palm tree) next to a major commuters' bridge and needed to be rescued when the wind picked up. Then there's the time they built a tiny park with a bench and a small fountain on a flatbed trailer, and towed it around Seattle.

One of their latest, and more permanent, experiments is just as outrageous, though it's as much about renewal as provocation. The trio wanted to turn an abandoned minimart into a temporary city park as an art installation, but after receiving a $50,000 Creative Capital grant, they sought out a site that they could make a permanent greenspace. They settled on a former gas station and minimart in the industrial Georgetown neighborhood.

The site, seated atop highly toxic soil (not only from diesel fuel and a former dry-cleaning business, but from surrounding industrial sites), had long been abandoned and become a place for shady dealings and prostitution. Georgetown is home to a growing residential and artist population, but the area, very close to Boeing Field airport, has a high percentage of brownfields and almost no park space. Certainly no developers were willing to touch the site, because of its location and toxicity.

SBC's plan includes keeping the basic structure of the gas station intact, though rotting wooden walls have to be replaced, and literally greening the space: the building will be partially buried under a grassy knoll, with a path leading up to a sitting area on the roof of the old building. The interior will function as an arts space staffed by volunteers.

Most model remediation projects are big in scale, but SBC's reimagining of the gas station minimart shows how a small group of people with a grant or two and a bit of moxie can heal a little piece of the city. CB

Retrofitting Urban Infrastructure

████ It's not unusual for structures to outlive the uses for which they were built. In the United States, for example, factories that opened with fanfare in the early 1900s have long since been shuttered as manufacturing jobs moved overseas. Yet these buildings remain, often rotting on land polluted with industrial waste.

The Olympic Sculpture Park in downtown Seattle came into being when the Seattle Art Museum partnered with the Trust for Public Land to transform a contaminated industrial site into a recreational space with thriving ecosystems. Landscape designers re-created the site's original topography to encourage native species to return, and laid a specially engineered layer of soil to filter rainwater, reduce runoff, and support plant regrowth. They restored the shoreline to both provide habitat for salmon and strengthen the seawall. Now the park, free to the public year-round, showcases contemporary art as well as gorgeous views of Elliott Bay, the working waterfront, and the Olympic mountains.

Aging and outmoded infrastructure can also be a canvas for creative reuse. New York City's High Line park, which opened in June 2009, was constructed on an elevated steel structure that carried freight trains through an industrial district in Manhattan from the 1930s to 1980. The High Line now provides a very different type of infrastructure: a public place where New Yorkers can get above the city bustle and walk along the promenade, enjoying views of the Hudson River and the city skyline. JVL

potentially worldchanging of his pursuits is mycoremediation—the use of mushrooms to clean up toxic sludge. He's done it a number of times, turning heaps of contaminated waste into verdant hills full of insects and birds. As he puts it: "I see mycelium as the Earth's natural Internet, a consciousness with which we might be able to communicate . . . With mycoremediation, brownfields can be reborn as greenfields, turning valueless or even liability-laden wastelands into valuable real estate." Stamets has also been at the forefront of some groundbreaking research into the use of fungus for treating epidemic diseases such as cancer and HIV.

████ RESOURCE

Mycelium Running: How Mushrooms Can Help Save the World by Paul Stamets (Ten Speed Press, 2005)
Paul Stamets is the indisputable king of mushrooms. Among the more fascinating and

The Seattle artists' collective SuttonBeresCuller plans to turn a former gas station and minimart in an industrial neighborhood into a park and arts space.

Lagos

▬▬▬ What do you know about Lagos?

Most of us in the Global North know very little. We may not even be able to find it on a map. And yet this Nigerian megacity is well on its way to becoming one of the planet's biggest: if it continues growing at its current rate, the UN says, by 2015 only Tokyo and Mumbai will be larger, and more than 24 million people will call Lagos home.

Life is not easy in Lagos. Most residents live in informal slums that are growing at astounding rates. Indeed, so much of the city has emerged in ad hoc neighborhoods that there is no way to even be certain of exactly how many people live there. Roads and houses spring up that have never seen a government official; maps are out-of-date before they're even printed. Poverty is endemic (most residents live on less than one dollar a day) and infrastructure is a relative term—only a tiny fraction of homes are connected to sewers; raw waste runs down the middle of the streets; and entire parts of the city are submerged in the rainy season. Traffic is so bad that Lagos's residents have invented their own term for mega—traffic jams: the *go-slow*. A blanket of smog hangs perpetually in the

skies. By some estimates, half the population is infected with malaria.

"For the politicians, administrators and community leaders who have to manage this complex, heaving mass of urban humanity," writes Nigerian journalist Paul Okunlola in a paper for the United Nations Human Settlements Programme (UN-HABITAT), "the quantum of decaying infrastructure, widespread urban poverty, massive unemployment, pervasive security inadequacies, emerging slums and overwhelming environmental decay have become the major characteristics that progressively define the city's fortunes."

Most outside observers find Lagos all but incomprehensible; almost all find it terrifying. It is reputedly the most dangerous city in the world, a place where rent-a-cops have submachine guns and half-wild dogs, and where there is less than one official police officer per thousand residents. But more than anything, it is the chaos of the place that puts fear into visitors used to a different kind of city. "Lagos seemed to be a city of burning edges," writes architect Rem Koolhaas of the time he spent studying the city's future prospects. "Hills, entire roads were paralleled with burning embankments. At first sight, the city had an aura of apocalyptic violence; entire sections of it seemed to be smoldering, as if it were one gigantic rubbish heap."

Lagos's residents watch their backs, but say they find their city an exciting place to live. Lagos drives the entire West African regional economy. More than 250

languages are spoken in its streets. Even after the oil boom that started its explosive growth sputtered out, people have continued to pour in, seeking a better life.

"The streets aren't all paved with concrete, let alone gold," writes UNESCO journalist Amy Otchet, "but Lagos appears as an El Dorado in the poverty-stricken countryside, where work can be found and dreams come true." Lagos has a dearth of formal jobs but a thriving underground economy, where at least half of all city residents make their living bartering, hustling, doing odd jobs, and trading on their skills and energy to get by while they keep an eye out for opportunity. In Lagos, being business-savvy isn't a career choice: it's a survival skill.

Even Rem Koolhaas came to admire the spirit of improvisation and enterprise he met there: "Dangerous breakdowns of order and infrastructure in Nigeria are often transformed," he writes, "into productive urban forms: stalled traffic turns into an open-air market, defunct railroad bridges become pedestrian walkways." Lagos, Koolhaas came to believe, is the future—and he means that in a good way.

Megacity Opportunities

The problems Lagos faces are uniquely severe, but they are not unique—neither is the energy of its people. Indeed, all across the Global South, emerging megacities like Mumbai, Delhi, Kolkata (Calcutta), Dhaka, Karachi, Jakarta, São

Paulo, and Mexico City are poised to become the largest human settlements in history. By 2015, only two of the ten largest cities in the world—Tokyo and New York—will be in what we now consider the developed world.

So many people are moving into cities that we are building an urban area the size of Seattle every four to seven days. By some estimates, two-thirds of the urban areas that will cover the planet in 2030 don't even exist yet; put another way, two-thirds of the planet's future cities have not yet been built.

As Lagos illustrates, poor cities that grow rapidly face potentially disastrous problems. But urbanization is by no means all bad. In some ways, the rise of megacities offers us incredible opportunities to address challenges that might seem otherwise insurmountable.

Take jobs. Most people leave their farms and villages for the exact same reason that Europeans and Americans did generations ago: because that's where the work isn't. Villages have local economies, but they often burn slowly, like small hearth fires; cities—especially those most connected to the global economy—are, by comparison, blast furnaces. Rural economies may grow slowly, if at all, but some of the fastest growth in the world is in the emerging megacities, as whole new economies sprout up—formal and informal, woven by hand or pulsing with the latest technologies.

On this young planet, more than half the people are under the age of thirty and roughly one-third are under the age of fifteen. Far too many people are unemployed, undereducated, and lacking avenues for working constructively to make their lives better. Frustrated and resentful young men are a breeding ground for radical violence, from gang warfare and terrorism to political paramilitary repression and genocide. Creating better opportunities for young men is one of our best strategies for building a better world, and urbanization can be a tool for doing just that.

Opposite: Lagos, Nigeria—fast becoming one of the world's largest megacities—serves as an example of how pressing the need is for better urban solutions.

Left: Young women, like this one working in a call center in Nairobi, are more likely to find work in expanding cities than in rural economies.

São Paulo, Brazil, is an emerging megacity poised to be among the largest on the planet.

But young women can gain even more from city life. While the perils they face, from sweatshop conditions to forced sex work, increase when they arrive in the city, their freedoms and opportunities increase far more. Young women in cities are much more likely to have jobs, to be educated, to avoid childhood marriages, and, ultimately, to control their own destinies and family-planning choices. These ingredients for young women's success have planetary implications as well. Again, because a majority of people on the planet are young, the choices young women make about childbirth have global implications. If the women of the global "youth bulge," as some name it, have many children of their own, we will wind up on an even more crowded planet. If they have fewer, we will find all the problems we face substantially easier to solve. And in general, one rule has held true: urban women have more control over their lives. They marry later, they have children later, and they ultimately choose to have fewer kids. In the long term, this is a very good thing.

Finally, life in megacities offers at least a chance to address many of the social needs that so press us. While local governments often find themselves essentially powerless to channel, much less direct, their cities' growth today, that doesn't mean that innovation is impossible, or that social services and health care can't be provided. Indeed, in many ways it is easier to provide for the public needs of people who live close together—even when they live in a squatter camp—than it is to provide for equally poor people living scattered in the hinterlands.

The very energy and ambition that is driving people to pick up and move to megacities is also fueling an explosion in homegrown urban innovation. Local solutions deriving from ad hoc responses to local problems combine with new models of assistance (like microcredit [see Microfinance, p. 313]) to yield dramatic, rapid improvement in people's lives.

Megacities may still prove to be one of the best levers we have for changing the world. AS

Chinese Cities of the Future

If we want to see the future of cities, we must look to China, a country that is urbanizing at an unprecedented rate. Between now and 2030, according to the McKinsey Global Institute, Chinese cities are expected to add more than 350 million people, swelling to a total urban population of more than 1 billion. By then, China will have more than 220 cities with populations of more than 1 million (Europe today has only thirty-five such cities), and twenty-four emerging megacities with more than 5 million inhabitants.

Building that many cities is an almost incomprehensibly huge task. It will demand massive investments in housing, transportation, and water and energy systems. McKinsey estimates that in the next twenty years, China will build as many as 50,000 skyscrapers (which might be thought of as ten New Yorks). It will build hundreds of millions of apartment buildings. It will design and build more than 170 completely new mass-transit systems, thousands of new major hospitals and universities, and hundreds of thousands of parks, schools, fire stations, and community centers. The boom China is expected to continue to go through, even in a potential economic downturn, boggles the minds of North Americans and Europeans, who are used to thinking of cities as stable and slow to change.

All that new building could come at a massive cost, though. Already, China is teetering on the edge of ecological catastrophe. It suffers from some of the worst air pollution in the world. Hong Kong's air quality, for instance, meets the World Health Organization's bare-minimum standards an average of only forty-one days a year, and air quality is much worse in many mainland cities. Indeed, the World Bank says that sixteen of the twenty most-polluted cities in the world are in China, and 400,000 people a year die as a result of poor air quality.

The bigger the picture gets, the worse it looks. China is suffering rapid desertification; it has lost massive amounts of topsoil from its farmlands; and one-third of its land is affected by acid rain. A 2010 investigation revealed that Chinese waterways are more than twice as degraded as previously reported; two-thirds of its rivers and lakes are dangerously polluted (cancer rates are extraordinarily high in riverside cities in China). The Yangtze River is now biologically dead for long stretches of its run. More than 340 million Chinese have no access to safe drinking water. The natural systems that China's people depend on for the basics of life are unraveling at astonishing speed.

China's pollution problems would be alarming even if we were able to compartmentalize them, but they're bound up with

Right: The influx of domestic migrant workers is putting increased pressure on the infrastructure of Chinese cities, Guangzhou City, Guangdong Province, China, 2004.
Following pages: Old City overview, Shanghai, China, 2004.

another planetary problem: China is now the world's largest emitter of greenhouse gases. While it's true that the country's current per-person emissions levels are relatively moderate, China's increasing prosperity is changing that, and the sheer size of the nation means that humanity cannot reach the goal of planetary carbon-neutrality without China changing its ways. A carbon-neutral China is a prerequisite for a climate-stabilized world.

All this makes Chinese cities some of the most important leverage points in the world. If China's cities are built with dirty energy and outdated designs, the world's problems will only intensify. If they are compact, bright green, powered by clean energy, and served by mass transit and sustainable food systems, not only will global emissions level off more quickly, but the resulting boom in urban innovation will mean the world has a real shot at transforming prosperity everywhere along more sustainable lines. Bright green Chinese cities could change the future. AS

Changing China's Energy Mix

A major cause of China's environmental and health woes is the source of its power; at this point, China still overwhelmingly relies on burning coal, often in inefficient and dirty power plants. A future of 1 billion Chinese living in coal-powered cities would be grim, but there are real signs that fate is not inevitable. Indeed, China is becoming a world leader in clean energy.

At this writing, China is fourth in the world for installed wind-energy capacity, according to the Worldwatch Institute, and is on track to install an additional 100 gigawatts of wind power by 2020. And China has some of the best wind resources in the world: the journal *Science* published a 2009 report by researchers from Harvard and Tsinghua universities demonstrating that for an investment of less than U.S.$1,000 per citizen, China could supply all its predicted demand for electricity with wind power by 2030.

China is already the world's leading producer of solar panels, according to the Earth Policy Institute; its output jumped from 40 megawatts in 2004 to 1,848 megawatts in 2008, and expansion is continuing to accelerate. While most of those solar panels have been manufactured for export, China is increasingly adding solar power to its energy mix. The most noteworthy large-scale project in the works is a 2,000-megawatt plant in the Mongolian desert, which is expected to be the largest solar photovoltaic facility in the world when it is completed in 2019.

Still, even with bold efforts in wind, solar, and other renewable energy, China is expected to burn a lot of coal while it builds new systems. How much is still up in the air, so to speak, which is why a whole host of programs have been launched to help increase the efficiency of Chinese coal-fired power plants, speed adoption of energy-efficiency standards in Chinese industry, and focus product design on sustainability. China has a very long way to go, but there's at least a chance that China could dramatically slash its power-related emissions over the next two decades, even while 1 billion Chinese citizens go about building their new cities. AS

Greener Shanghai

▬▬▬ Shanghai is the emblematic modern Chinese city. A big, crowded, economic power-house, the city has long been held up as the model for today's China. Soon, it may be the model for a green China. British design-consultancy firm Arup has been working with the Chinese government to lead the construction of an "eco-city" expansion to Shanghai. Dongtan, the expanded develop-ment near Shanghai's airport, may eventually cover about 21,745 acres (8,800 hectares)—roughly the size of Manhattan—and is intended to be a genuinely ecofriendly city, using recycled water, cogeneration, and biomass for energy, and striving to be as carbon-neutral as possible.

So what does it mean to be a "genuinely ecofriendly city"? There's almost no waste of resources: gray water is captured, purified, and recycled; organic wastes are used as biomass to generate clean energy; and combined heat and power systems provide warmth and electricity for the home in the same process. Buildings use natu-ral light, advanced insulations, and high-efficiency designs to cut energy use significantly. Public transit is commonplace, within an easy walk from almost any location. In many ways, life in the Dongtan eco-city will be very much like life in any modern city: clean, comfortable, exciting. Only behind the scenes, the systems that keep the city alive—that control its flows of energy and people, waste and water—will work with far greater efficiency than they do almost anywhere else in the world.

Unfortunately, the Dongtan project stalled when officials involved in the project were caught up in an unrelated scandal, and the global recession dried up capital willing to invest in what might be a risky project. Though the plans are still officially on the books, there's no deadline for moving forward with building the eco-city. JC & AS

Three Star and Green-building Regulations

▬▬▬ Much has been made of the spread of cars and suburban sprawl in China. While the growth of traffic jams in Chinese cities is certainly note-worthy, it's far from the only story, and American-style subdivisions are an extremely rare novelty. Urban China continues to be a nation mostly of bicyclists, pedestrians, bus riders, and train passen-gers. What's more, many young Chinese are well aware of global trends in designing livable cities through smart growth and new transit options and are seeking Chinese versions to guide the growth of their own cities. While some may joke that Chinese urban planning is still a contradic-tion in terms, there's plenty of urban innovation happening there.

Green-building practices are spreading fairly quickly. China has created its own green-building standard, the Three Star system. So far, Three Star compares favorably to other nations' green-building certification schemes. What's more, it seems that China's builders are adopting it more rapidly than their Global North counterparts have adopted theirs. Chinese buildings on the whole—especially older buildings—are still shockingly poorly designed and inefficient, but a budding retrofit industry and official support for the idea of raising the energy efficiency of existing buildings seem to indicate that more widespread improve-ments may be in the works. AS

China's Rails

▬▬▬ China is becoming a world leader in another critical kind of infrastructure: trains. Chinese cities are undergoing what the McKin-sey Global Institute calls "the greatest boom in mass-transit in history," and the country is also launching the world's boldest plan for expanding an intercity rail network. The recently opened high-speed Harmony Express, which links the cit-ies of Wuhan and Guangzhou, has cut travel time between the two boomtowns from eleven hours to three. Construction has begun on another 30,000 kilometers (18,600 miles) of rail tracks, including 9,000 kilometers (5,600 miles) of high-speed lines that will connect all of the country's major cities

---

Opposite, left: A woman collects plastic bottles in a pol-luted canal in Dongxiang, China.

Opposite, right: Plans for a new sustainable community in Liuzhou, China, include rooftop farms.

by 2015. China also plans to extend the nation's high-speed rail network through Russia as far as Europe, enabling passengers to travel the 8,000 kilometers (5,000 miles) between Beijing and Berlin at 320 kilometers per hour (199 miles per hour), offering a competitive alternative to air travel, especially as the cost of flying rises because of fuel costs and carbon taxes. AS

RESOURCES

The Concrete Dragon: China's Urban Revolution and What it Means for the World by Thomas J. Campanella (Princeton Architectural Press, 2008) Campanella teaches urban design and the history of the built environment at University of North Carolina at Chapel Hill. *The Concrete Dragon* is the best current overview of both the astonishing urban accomplishments of the Chinese miracle and the gigantic, looming problems Chinese cities face:

"Fueled by a roaring housing market, land conversion has contributed to a perfect storm of suburban expansion in China. Its collective impact on the Chinese landscape is so vast that it can only fully be appreciated from space . . . a 364 percent increase in urbanized land between 1988 and 1996, with a consequent loss of some 500 square miles of cropland."

ChinaDialogue
http://www.chinadialogue.net
ChinaDialogue is devoted to China's environmental and sustainability issues. In order to promote more direct conversation, the site is published in both English and Chinese, and features news and commentary from reporters and citizen contributors from China and around the world.

China's newest high-speed rail line, the Harmony Express.

Megacity Innovations

To build megacities that better meet people's basic needs, offer new opportunities for young people, empower women, and foster sustainably is to build an urban way of life unlike anything we've yet seen. This megacity future is going to spawn a whole array of new possibilities, ones we can't anticipate from our armchairs in the developed world. It's already begun. In Malaysia, young architects have come up with a design for a home outfitted with giant solar panels that open like petals as the day warms, shading the home and capturing electricity, and then fold back up as the evening cools, bringing the colder night air into the house and making the surrounding garden a pleasant place to sit, drink tea, and stargaze. In Harare, Zimbabwe, architects have created a biomimetic [see Biomimicry, p. 101] building that resembles an African termite mound. The Eastgate building copies the way termites use earth masses and ventilation tunnels to keep their mounds at a constant temperature. Consequently, the Eastgate needs no air-conditioning system, despite the blistering Harare heat.

Other innovations are being built from simpler parts, but are no less revolutionary. In Curitiba, Brazil, mayor Jaime Lerner led the creation of innovative low-tech social programs, including gardens tended by street kids, payments in food to homeless people who collect litter, converted buses that serve as mobile clinics in the slums, even architectural assistance for the surge of poor immigrants building their own homes. On top of that, Curitiba has built a world-famous transit system, and has expanded its parks and boulevards, giving it the most green space of any Brazilian city.

This is all just the beginning. The new urban future, in full bloom, may be nearly unfathomable to us in the old-fashioned Global North. The future doesn't think like North Americans do: the future is unfolding in places that have mobile phones but still rely on the arrival of the caravans, that sell computer chips in souks and bazaars, that burn sandalwood incense in five-hundred-year-old temples but broadcast video-game championships on TV. A bright green future will smell of curry and plantains, soy sauce and chipotle, and will sound more like Moroccan rap and twangy Mongol pop than Mariah Carey. We in the Global North don't know—we can't know—how the next generation of megacity urbanists will respond to the possibilities unfolding in front of them.

The best research and development in urban planning won't be done by established professionals in developed-world think tanks, corporate labs, or universities. It will be done on the streets of developing-world cities, by a younger generation just now coming into its own.

They don't need our answers; they need the tools for finding and sharing their own answers. Redistribute the tools for invention and innovation, and the citizens of the megacities will remake the world. AS

Bogotá

Like many emerging megacities, Bogotá, Colombia, is a mess. Unlike many emerging megacities, though, Bogotá has had inspired leadership and a determined citizenry, and is already gaining ground on its problems. Three Bogotá mayors in succession have tackled the city's obstacles with passion, style, and innovation. Bogotá has gone from being almost unlivable to being full of vitality (if still grappling with serious challenges).

Mayor Antanus Mockus gets the credit for getting Bogotanos to think in new ways. Mockus, who was mayor from 1995 to 1997 and again from 2001 to 2003, patrolled the streets clad in red and blue tights, calling himself "Super Citizen" and intervening in places where civility was lacking. During a water shortage, he spoke on a public service announcement to promote water conservation, while naked in the shower. (In just two months, water usage dropped by 14 percent; through continued efforts, Bogotanos now use 40 percent less water per person than they did before the shortage.) He cracked down on corrupt police officers—even shutting down the entire transit police division, which was known for its bribery schemes. He even asked people to pay an extra 10 percent in optional taxes, and to everybody's amazement, 63,000 residents did.

Two of Mockus's programs, though, exemplify the creativity he brought to the job. Bogotá can have terrible traffic jams, and even on the best days, its streets can be mayhem. Mockus hired hundreds of mimes to direct traffic—providing not only some needed order, but a hint of levity. More impressively, he launched the Night for Women.

In every city, women are on the receiving end of more antisocial behavior than men are.

Great cities find ways to ensure that women are safe on the streets and welcome in public spaces. When Mockus asked residents what they thought the city's biggest problems were, he learned that the danger, harassment, and hassles women faced in Bogotá raised a barrier to women's full involvement in the social life of the city. So in 2001 he called on men to stay home and care for the children, and invited all Bogotá's women to come out for a night on which they would own the streets; 700,000 did, and by all accounts, Bogotá is safer and more welcoming now.

"The distribution of knowledge is the key contemporary task," Mockus said in an interview in the *Harvard University Gazette*. "Knowledge empowers people. If people know the rules, and are sensitized by art, humor, and creativity, they are much more likely to accept change" (March 11, 2004).

Enrique Peñalosa, Mockus's successor, focused an equally innovative program on Bogotá's planning woes. He created the Trans-Milenio, a rapid-transit bus system, which operates in special lanes and now carries a half million passengers a day. He set aside 186 miles (300 kilometers) of designated bike lanes, built greenways and paths, and launched an aggressive campaign against motorists who drove or parked on the sidewalks. Realizing that great neighborhoods are central to great cities, he built new parks, libraries, and schools, and started a hundred new nursery schools so working mothers could more easily find good child care. Finally, he raised parking fees and gas taxes, and set up a system that requires people to leave their cars at home on certain days of the week. Overall, Peñalosa's efforts paid off: Bogotá now has 40 percent less traffic than it did before the program went into effect.

The latest mayor, Luis Eduardo Garzón ("Lucho" to his supporters), is tackling Bogotá's social problems head-on. He is expanding school capacity to serve the 100,000 kids who don't currently have access to education. He's creating a network of volunteer doctors who will regularly visit families in poorer neighborhoods. He's fighting hunger. One way Garzón is paying for these new programs is by attacking corruption and tax evasion, which is a huge drain on the administration's expected revenues; so far his efforts seem

to be working. Finally, in an effort to carry on the city's established commitment to its female citizens, Garzón filled all twenty of his submayoral posts with women.

Bogotá is far from perfect, but the progress it has made in just fifteen years is extraordinary: the murder rate has dropped by half; more kids are in school than ever before; traffic (while still bad) has calmed dramatically; and the streets are full of people walking, shopping, and talking. AS

Goa's RUrbanism

▬▬▬ Imagine that you and your family live in Panjim (Panaji), the capital of the Indian state of Goa. You wake up in your high-density-yet-very-comfortable, ultra-efficient apartment, open the window, and look out on a capillary of rural farmland that snakes its way in among the other apartment blocks. You wave at the fellow guiding the buffalo past your building. Then you check your bank on the Net and discover that your integrated time-and-money account shows you with very little extra money, but a lot of free time to spend. You decide to spend that time participating in a community discussion about the merits of a new nanomaterials factory planned for a neighboring section of the city.

That's a tiny snapshot of what might be possible in just thirty years' time, according to the creators of RUrbanism, a city growth plan that may turn the state of Goa into a neobiological [see Neobiological Industry, p. 106] mix of human and wild, with high-density neighborhoods that encompass a blend of high-tech superefficient

systems and traditional rural living. Rice paddies, fish ponds, and vegetable gardens will interpenetrate urban areas in a "spine-and-filament" pattern like that of a fish's gills, while surrounding forests provide fresh water and clean air. RUrbanism transforms the city from a parasitic consumer of resources into a symbiotic partner with both nature and rural culture.

RUrbanism is the brainchild of a team of Indian experts: Aromar Revi, Rahul Mehrotra, Sanjay Prakash, and G. K. Bhat. Their Goa 2100 project took home a special jury prize at Tokyo's high-profile 2003 International Sustainable Urban Systems Design competition, thanks to both the creativity and quantitative rigor of their hypothetical "transformation plan."

The team chose Goa because it's already a great place to live, with a thriving economy. And Panjim itself reflects many of the challenges commonly faced by India's growing cities, while also having the resources, political culture, and institutional base that make bold moves a clear possibility. The team began by collecting an enormous amount of data—demographic, socioeconomic, economic, institutional—and information related to planning, natural resources, energy, and transportation. They consulted with leading Goan citizens, inspected nature reserves and industrial sites, and then mapped Greater Panjim in detail, using satellite and remotely sensed data, along with Global Positioning System (GPS) technology and Geographical Information System (GIS) maps [see Mapping, p. 451]. The result was a complete land-use and topographical model for the area, probably the first of its kind for the region—and as innovative as anything the world has ever seen.

Opposite: Bogotá, Colombia, has become a hothouse of innovation. A cyclist admires the view of the city (left), which has set aside 186 miles of designated bike lanes. Women celebrate the Night for Women (right), during which female Bogotanos reclaimed the streets in 2001.
Right: The RUrbanism growth plan in Goa, India, offers a pioneering blueprint for urban sustainability.

All that research showed the team that Goa could in the near future implement major land-use changes that would support the regeneration of the surrounding landscape and reduce the city's ecological footprint. Goa could essentially be condensed almost back to its scale during medieval times, without resorting to high-rise, resource-intensive development, by emphasizing compact design and green building.

But the team didn't stop with the structure of the city: they also looked at the pace of life. One of most innovative features of the Goa 2100 project was its analysis of the entire "temporal economy" of the city and region. Comparing studies from around the world of how people use their time, and adapting assumptions to the South Asian context, the team modeled the time use of Greater Panjim and created a "time-use budget" for both the present day's citizens and the citizens of a future, post-transition, sustainable Panjim. This analysis led to a key discovery: that time should be thought of as an additional resource when considering the financing of a transition, since residents can do more with the time they'll save in a better-designed city. The Goa 2100 model—which allows for more than adequate personal, leisure, household, and community time, in addition to the needed time for work, child care, education, and so on—appears to be the first sustainability analysis of the time use of an entire city.

Finally, by combining the time-and-money accounting of the costs of transition, the team firmly established that a full transition to sustainability was both possible and affordable. In their final estimates, they discovered that an investment of only U.S.$60 million per year, coupled with the time investments of citizens from many different sectors (paid and unpaid), could accomplish the transition in just thirty years—much faster than the hundred-year period that the rules of the design competition had stipulated, and at far lower levels of financial investment than most people would expect.

RUrbanism is one visionary, yet feasible, model for how cities throughout Asia could redevelop themselves in coming decades. And the first field test could be Goa itself; the state is seriously considering the results of the Goa 2100 exercise as it ponders its own future development plans. Expect to see more cutting-edge models like this emerge as megacity challenges meet megainnovation. AA

Underground Literature

In a program in Mexico City, free books are being given out in the subway. The stories and poems in the books are short enough to finish on the average subway ride; readers drop the books off as they leave the Metro. Mexican authors were paid about U.S.$300 for use of their works, but their real payment is the increasing in-country interest in their writing. The program gets books into the hands of those Mexicans who can't normally afford to buy them. And transit officials also hope that crime in the system might decrease if crooks are busy reading rather than picking the pockets of fellow riders. EG

Subway riders in Mexico City reading free books.

The Hidden Vitality of Slums

In Brazil, they're *favelas*. In India, *johpadpatti*. In Turkey, *gecekonduler*. In Colombia, *callampas*. In Peru, *pueblos jovenes*. In Kenya, *vijiji*. In Indonesia, *permukiman liar* or *kampung liar*. In French-speaking Africa and the Caribbean, *bidonvilles*.

They are the most dynamic parts of the fastest-growing cities in the world—self-built, self-designed, and self-motivated. They are squatter neighborhoods: shanty-town communities created when people take over land they don't own.

In English, many call them slums. And, frozen in time, the word fits. Take a snapshot in any of the world's shantytowns and you'll capture degraded and dilapidated communities.

But look at that photo a bit more closely and you'll find health clinics, beauty salons, grocery stores, bars, restaurants, tailors, clothing stores, churches, and schools. In the midst of squalor and open sewage, the streets are lively and business is booming. What's more, study that shack in the center of the photo—the one made of mud and sticks. Is it simply decaying? Or is the family that lives there reconstituting it around themselves like a cocoon, transforming it from mud to brick, one wall at a time?

And ask yourself how you would cope if your community had no basic services:

■ The squatters have no water. They must purchase it at a premium price and haul it to their homes in buckets. But wouldn't you have to do the same if your city hadn't installed the pipes that bring water to your doorstep?

■ The squatters have no toilets, only pit latrines, and raw sewage flows down the streets. But what would happen to your waste if your municipality hadn't built a sewer system?

■ The squatters have no electricity—or, if they're lucky, they loop wires through the trees and pirate service from far-away poles. But would you have electricity if your local utility hadn't run cables near your home?

Every day, close to 200,000 people leave the world's rural regions and head for the cities. That's two hundred people a minute, more than three every second. They go to cities in search of a job, a way of providing for their families. And by and large, they can find work. But they can't find a place to live. No developer builds for them. No government invests in homes these migrants can afford. So they become squatters, building for themselves on unused or undesirable turf. Squatting, for them, is a family value.

There are 1 billion squatters in the world today, almost one in six people on the planet. If current trends continue, there will be 2 billion squatters by 2030 and 3 billion (more than one-third of humanity) by the midpoint of the twenty-first century.

To keep up with the urban influx, the world must build more than 96,000 homes a day—roughly 4,000 homes every hour. Generally, only squatters are prepared to make this effort. Their homes start out as mud and cardboard hovels. But once they know they will not be evicted and they can exercise control over their communities, they create permanent, thriving neighborhoods.

This is new urbanism, global style: squatters building the cities of tomorrow. RN

The Difficulty of Squatter Empowerment

The people of Vikas Sagar, in Mumbai, India, still live in one-story huts hacked into the steep hillside above Mahim Bay. They still worry about floods and landslides. They are still concerned about having enough money to make ends meet. But the women who live there have banded together to transform their community.

Today, all the homes in Vikas Sagar are permanent, made of concrete instead of mud. The walkways are paved with cement and tile, to prevent erosion. And the people have pooled their resources to create a communal savings plan that functions like a small-scale bank. How did they make these improvements? Instead of agonizing in the face of hardship, they organized.

A tiny squatter community in Vikas Sagar was founded decades ago, but its residents know that no matter how long they have been living there, the government still considers them illegal. "Unless we take action, nothing will be granted to us," says resident Lali Penday.

Well into the 1990s, the women of Vikas Sagar were traditional housewives, so controlled by their husbands that they seldom left their community. "When we started," remembers Sangita Duby, "we were not able to go out of our houses. We were illiterate and had to sign our names with a thumbprint. Now we are literate and can sign our names in Hindi and English." The women of Vikas Sagar know who the local politicians are. And, even more important, the politicians know who they are, too.

Alone, squatters have little power. Together, they can create great things. "The problems of the urban poor can only be solved by the urban poor, not by anybody else," says Jockin Arputham, head of Slum/Shack Dwellers International, a global squatter-organizing effort. "The urban poor will be the change agents of the city." RN

The Promise of Squatter Politics

A generation ago, the tiny hamlet of Sultanbeyli on the Asian side of Istanbul was just beginning to attract immigrants from the east.

These early arrivals lived in hovels, pirated electricity, and survived without water or toilets. But as more people came, the citizens of Sultanbeyli pursued their political rights—and this has made for an amazing transformation.

In Turkey, if squatters build overnight without being caught, they cannot be evicted without being taken to court. This is why Turkey's squatter areas are known as *gecekondu*, meaning, "it happened at night." Further, once a *gecekondu* community has two thousand residents, it can petition the federal government to recognize it as a legal municipality. Sultanbeyli became a municipality in 1989 and a district (a designation with more power and independence than a municipality) in 1992.

Today, Yahya Karakaya, Sultanbeyli's popularly elected mayor, works in an air-conditioned office on the top floor of the seven-story squatter city hall building, with a view over the city of 300,000 people who do not fear eviction. Fatih Boulevard, Sultanbeyli's main drag, is lined with multistory buildings full of stores, offices, restaurants, and banks. The city has used its newfound political might to force the Istanbul government to bring water, sewers, and electricity to every home in the district. Sultanbeyli is now a permanent, stable, self-governing, independent squatter metropolis. RN

■■■■■   RESOURCES

Centre on Housing Rights and Evictions
http://www.cohre.org
An online component of the important global watchdog group that offers reports and action alerts about eviction drives directed against the poor.

Favela Rising
http://favelarising.com
A Web site and movie about AfroReggae, an inspiring cultural movement that arose in Rio de Janeiro's Vigário Geral *favela* (slum).

One Small Project
http://www.onesmallproject.com
A site that will, organizers hope, turn into a book—a "small is beautiful" manual for the

squatter world, conceived by a caring and committed architecture professor.

Texaco by Patrick Chamoiseau (Pantheon, 1997)
A richly imagined squatter history of Fort de France, Martinique. As with many works of fiction, it's spiritually true.

Berji Kristin: Tales from the Garbage Hills by Latife Tekin (Marion Boyars Publishers, 1996)
A magically evocative novel that involves you in the founding of a *gecekondu* community in Istanbul.

Declaração de Guerra (BMG, 2002) and **Traficando Informação** (BMG, 1999) by MV Bill
Two recent albums by MV Bill, a hip-hop artist from Cidade de Deus, the Rio de Janeiro housing project/*favela* made famous in the movie *City of God*. Bill (real name Alexandre Barreto), whose music involves harsh yet poetic social commentary, objected to the movie as a false objectification and glorification of the violence in his community. He recently published a book called *Cabeça de Porco (Pig Head)*, based on two years of interviews with kids from Cidade de Deus, most of whom are now dead.

Global Report on Human Settlements by the United Nations Human Settlements Programme
The UN publishes one of these every year. Ignore the mealy-mouthed bureaucratese and search for the disturbing stats, jaw-dropping projections, and hard-nosed facts about the cities of the future.

Shadow Cities: A Billion Squatters, A New Urban World by Robert Neuwirth (Routledge, 2004)
Robert Neuwirth's book about squatter neighborhoods, based on his experiences during the three years he spent living in squatter communities in Nairobi, Rio, Mumbai, and Istanbul, has become an instant classic.

Planet of Slums by Mike Davis (Verso, 2006)
A meta-argument that the structural adjustment programs the United States foisted on the developing world caused the explosion of shantytowns and constitute a war on the poor.

The Mystery of Capital by Hernando de Soto (Basic Books, 2003)
A hypercapitalist view that giving squatters title deeds will liberate billions of dollars in dead capital.

Housing by People by John F. C. Turner (Marion Boyars Publishers, 1991)
Turner's assertion that "It is what housing does for people that matters more than what it is, or how it looks" still captures the essence of squatter self-sufficiency.

Leapfrogging

What tools help poor people escape poverty? For decades, the official answer was more or less the same: aid, loans, technology, handouts, and hand-me-downs. Development, it was assumed, was a one-size-fits-all process, and the way for poor countries to prosper was for them to try to catch up with the rich countries. But we have seen, in recent years, another path emerge. Developing nations don't have to play catch-up: they can adopt new technologies and tools—not always from the West—and use them in their own ways, skipping older or outmoded methods and embracing brand-new ones. Surprisingly often, developing countries try out solutions that have yet to take hold in industrialized nations. We call this process *leapfrogging*.

Probably the single best example of leapfrogging is the adoption of mobile phones across the Global South, particularly in Africa. Mobile phones empower both individuals and communities (after all, the more people who have them, the more useful any single phone can be), often acting as a catalyst for economic development and social innovation. According to a study undertaken by Vodafone, one of the world's biggest mobile-phone companies, and the Centre for Economic Policy Research in London, mobile-phone use is growing faster in Africa than in anywhere else in the world; presently, more than three times as many Africans have cell phones as have traditional landline phones.

Kenya gives ample evidence of how mobile communications can transform African economy and society. The growth of cellular-phone use in Kenya is startling; out of Kenya's population of 32 million people, nearly 6 million now have mobile phones, up from only 15,000 in 2000. But the story of cellular leapfrogging in Kenya can't be just summed up in numbers. Something new is unfolding there, as more people gain the power to talk to one another and share information.

Kenya faces problems common to much of Africa (and, indeed, to much of the developing world): a shaky democracy, corruption, lack of education and health care, rural poverty, pollution, and explosive population growth in the capital, Nairobi. Most of all, it needs to create an economy that can generate the revenue required to meet its challenges. Better answers, though, may only be a phone call away. JC & AS

Leapfrogging 101

Not only can the Global South leapfrog—skip over outdated modes of development to embrace the cutting edge—but it can itself help redefine that cutting edge.

Leapfrogging means more than simply adopting new gadgets. The red-hot core of the concept is freedom. Being poor or lacking access to established technologies can liberate individuals and communities to embrace the new, because they haven't poured money into the old.

Mobile phones provide a clear example of leapfrogging: if you basically don't have any phone system at all (which is the case in many emerging megacities), there's no reason to spend decades stringing up a grid of copper telephone wires, and then start putting up wireless towers—even if that's how the United States, Japan, and Europe did it. If cell phones will fit the bill, why bother with landlines at all? JC & AS

Mobile-phone Politics

In 2003, Kenya saw its greatest electoral turnout—and arguably its fairest election—owing in large part to the availability of mobile phones.

The presidential campaigns used cell phones in ways familiar to Western political veterans, but innovative for African communities. Databases of phone numbers allowed campaigners for the major candidates to call or send text messages to potential voters, and facilitated grassroots political networking. The campaigners were also better able to keep tabs on one another, monitor the polls, and keep a lookout for fraud or intimidation. Young people hired to observe the election stations could use cell phones to call in for support in case of any trouble.

Mobile phones also helped make vote counting fairer and more transparent. Rather than shipping ballot boxes to central counting stations (allowing votes to be changed, "lost," or otherwise rigged along the way), each polling station was able to count the votes locally and send the results to officials; the ballots were then shipped off for confirmation with far less likelihood of being tampered with. JC & AS

Opposite, left: The rapid spread of mobile phone use in developing Kenya is preempting the implementation of traditional landlines.

Opposite, right: The Grameen Phone helps an entire community stay connected with one phone, Uganda.

Markets

In Kenya, the market, or *Jua Kali* as it's known locally, is not just about buying and selling things: it is the very heart of commercial and social life. Mobile communications have transformed Kenyan markets by giving people the power to find out what they need to know—what's a fair price for their crafts or crops, who's selling and who's buying, what's happening in other markets. In essence, mobile phones are turning all of Kenya into one large *Jua Kali*. In the process, the country itself is changing.

Purely practical motivations drive this change. A phone call, for instance, can replace a grueling trip to a rural area to look for fresh produce; phones can also help farmers protect themselves from swindlers, by letting them check prices across a range of locations and buyers.

The Kenya Agricultural Commodities Exchange (KACE) sells up-to-the-minute market news via short-message service (SMS) text messaging. Farmers can access daily produce prices from a dozen markets; allowing them to make deals without having to travel around the country. Every month, KACE handles thousands of transactions; for buyers and sellers without mobile phones, kiosks set up near village markets around the country provide cheap access.

Access to these tools helps city dwellers as much as farmers. Small business in Kenya is thriving; it created nearly half a million new jobs in 2004 alone and employed more workers than any other business sector, thanks in part to the spread of mobile phones.

We take for granted in industrialized countries that small businesses rely on phones to gain new customers; until recently, however, few small businesses or independent contractors in Kenya had phone numbers to call. Instead, laborers like plumbers, electricians, and painters would congregate near hardware stores, hoping to drum up work from folks buying supplies. Today, signs bearing the mobile-phone numbers of all kinds of workers can be found throughout Kenya, and business is booming.

Employees, too, benefit. In the past, newspapers and neighbors were the main source of employment information—at best, Kenyans could travel to the nearest cybercafe (sometimes many miles away) to check out the handful of online listings. In 2004, OneWorld International opened a service that posts new job openings (mostly for unskilled and semiskilled labor) and started taking remote applications from job seekers, via text messaging. Instead of pounding the pavement, the unemployed can now work the phones. Thousands have found jobs. JC & AS

Sambaza

Author William Gibson once wrote, "The street finds its own uses for things."

Until recently, poor and middle-class citizens of Kenya had few ways to transfer funds in order to pay a bill, make a loan, or simply give a relative a bit of money. Few Kenyans have bank accounts or credit cards; generally, only the wealthiest citizens use the financial services common in the Global North. People needed an option other than carrying around cash, and that pent-up demand served to trigger innovation—and leapfrogging.

In May 2005, Safaricom introduced Sambaza, a service allowing customers to transfer airtime minutes to other subscribers via SMS text messaging. Because the minutes are worth money—and because Safaricom serves the majority of mobile-phone subscribers in Kenya— sending minutes quickly became another way to pay for goods and services.

In essence, Safaricom has become the unofficial national electronic bank. A growing portion of the Kenyan economy now exists purely as bits on a wireless network. And as these electronic transactions are increasingly mediated through a widespread communications network, location becomes far less of a barrier to economic participation than it was before; rural villager and urban entrepreneur alike can send or receive funds, make remote purchases, even provide microcredit services, all from a mobile handset.

Phone-based currencies like Sambaza are not without their risks, however. Since there's a far greater need to secure financial transactions than

there is to prevent airtime-minute fraud, emergent, unintended currency systems like Sambaza are likely to become targets of organized crime. Plus, the more people adopt Sambaza as a means of buying and selling, the more the Kenyan government is going to pay attention. Sambaza transactions currently incur no taxes, and are not subject to accounting by anyone other than Safaricom.

Kenya may soon become the world's first real lesson in how electronic currencies work—both how they succeed and, perhaps, how they fail. JC

StarSight

What would a streetlamp look like if it were designed for people who don't have electricity? It might look a lot like the StarSight project. Each StarSight pole combines a streetlight—a tool that itself can bring down crime rates dramatically—with a solar panel, wireless networking equipment, and even hookups for charging small devices like mobile phones.

The designers, the UK-based Kolam Partnership and the Singapore-based Nex-G, describe StarSight as a key element of a "virtual utility," a low-cost, low-maintenance means of providing very useful services such as public lighting and wireless networks. Using LED light to conserve energy, StarSight is expressly meant to be used in the emerging megacities. It is being tested in Cameroon.

None of the technologies used in StarSight are unique in themselves, but the combination is an inspired example of the power of merged leapfrogging technologies. The setup can

The StarSight streetlight system would provide a low-cost, low-maintenence means of delivering public lighting and wireless networking to megacities.

also incorporate disaster-warning systems, pollution monitors, and other location-aware network services. If leapfrogging infrastructure needs to be plug-and-play, versatile, and cost-effective, it may end up looking very much like StarSight. JC

Rwanda's Vision 2020 Plan

Even the most dewy-eyed optimist would have trouble searching for a silver lining in the collapse of an entire state. In Rwanda, one hundred days of genocide and mayhem in 1994 killed 800,000 people and left tens of thousands of orphans. But the civil war that unhinged the tiny African nation has not entirely undone its people, and now Rwanda is undertaking the biggest community outreach program in recent history: reknitting a war-torn nation into the world's next tech hub.

Rwanda's Vision 2020 Plan is attempting to leapfrog an entire nation into twenty-first-century prosperity. The full plan reads like the country's own version of the UN's Millennium Development Goals: objectives include everything from redesigning the dusty capital of Kigali into a bright green city to creating a knowledge economy from scratch through a concentrated infusion of information and communications technology infrastructure (including the laying of fiber-optic cables nationwide and the introduction of broadband service to every school).

Although the plan includes modernizing agriculture—thereby increasing yields to ensure more Rwandans are fed—it also focuses on shifting many subsistence farmers to more urban industries. But the plan doesn't just focus on boosting income. Controlling corruption, from the office of the president down to the traffic cops, is a major pillar of the plan. And, of course, controlling epidemic diseases like HIV and malaria are part of the plan, too. The development of a sustainable-tourism industry aims to add jobs and revenue while protecting the few natural resources the country has, such as its gorilla population.

Worldchanging has covered hundreds of examples of poorer communities using technology to create new avenues for development. But the argument about whether we can actually leapfrog development on a large scale has lacked a test case. Rwanda may be that test case.

It takes more than a plan to change the world. Transforming a nation's society and economy while building from scratch a new infrastructure is no mean feat, and some of the kinds of problems that face many developing countries in adopting technology are particularly severe in Rwanda. The essential question is, can basic improvements—from democracy-building to movement-building to transparent governance to the creation of a free press to the provision of essentials—be better delivered in a nation with a focus on employing new technologies? Is Vision 2020 the leapfrogging test case? It's hard to say now, but it's fascinating to see leapfrogging technologies made so central to a nation's plans for itself. AS & CB

COMMUNITY

Many communities these days find themselves under extraordinary stress. Even in affluent communities, taking care of one another—educating our kids, caring for the ill, helping people who need a hand—is proving difficult. In less-than-affluent communities, the stresses of extreme poverty, oppression, environmental injustice, failed educational systems, and diseases like HIV/AIDS are making life a daily challenge.

These communities are not as far away from one another as we sometimes think. As the Mega-Cities Project's report "The Poverty/Environment Nexus in Mega-Cities" reminds us, "Every 'First World' city has in it a 'Third World' city of infant mortality, malnutrition, unemployment, communicable diseases and homelessness. Similarly, every 'Third World' city has in it a 'First World' city with high finance, fashion, and technology" (Mega-Cities Project 1998).

To solve problems like these takes more than individual action—it takes community action. Communities of all kinds need to work together, thinking about the problems they face in holistic ways and strengthening the fabric that binds them together.

But we also need a global commitment to solving the problems faced by communities everywhere. Problems like HIV/AIDS and other diseases, extreme poverty, illiteracy—these can't be solved without community involvement, but they also can't be solved by our communities alone. They require the application of resources that can only be mustered by governments and international networks.

Our best effort so far comes from the Millennium Development Goals put forward by the United Nations. They are, simply put, the closest thing we have to an international consensus on how to meet the fundamental needs of every person on the planet. They propose programs to help end extreme poverty; feed the hungry; empower women and improve maternal health; fight AIDS, malaria, and other epidemic diseases; protect environmental sustainability; and educate and provide medical care for all children.

In practice, the Millennium Development Goals are far from perfect. Critics rightly point out that they talk a lot about helping poor people and very little about protecting their human rights, building democracy, or righting basic injustices in our economic systems. That said, simply having benchmarks against which to measure our progress in meeting world needs is a huge step forward.

Some say that the goals are too modest. Some argue that new tools for development (which focus more on ensuring people's fundamental economic rights and helping them build livelihoods through small loans to start community-based businesses) could help end absolute poverty altogether. Others point to new collaborative models for scientific research (especially in nations in the Global South) and public health care, and anticipate the day when we'll be able to not only better care for those currently suffering, but stop new epidemics in their tracks.

These are not either/or answers. We need all of them: We need global commitments to fighting poverty and disease. We need new models. We need engaged communities willing to experiment. Together, they compose a tool chest for making all of our communities healthier tomorrow. AS

Demographics and Migration

▬▬▬   Sometime shortly after the middle of this century, human population will peak, with the largest number of people ever alive on the planet. Having swelled to 9.2 billion people (according to predictions by the UN Population Division), our numbers will begin to drop thereafter.

The twentieth century's population explosion was in many ways a historical accident. Traditionally, each woman had many children, because in the time before pensions and social support for the old, children meant a secure old age; furthermore, not all of the children could be expected to live into adulthood. In the last hundred years, though, improvements in public health and better nutrition meant far more children survived into adulthood. This profound—and wonderful—change was not matched by a comparable adjustment in family planning. Throughout much of the world, social mores, gender inequalities, and economic instability conspired to keep women having many children, even though now most of those children would survive and extremely large families could mean a life of poverty.

As women move into cities, though, and become free to make more of their own choices—when they have access to education, jobs, legal protection, and health care—they almost always choose to have fewer children. When the number of children per woman drops to an average of 2.1, population growth stops: the next generation will be the same size as the current. Already women have crossed this postindustrial demographic threshold in cultures from Japan to Italy to Finland (many women in these countries are deciding to have only one child). When humanity as a whole has crossed it, we will have passed peak population.

After that, global population will proceed to decline, until by the middle of the twenty-second century there will be between 5.6 billion and 8.5 billion people on earth. (There is a wide range of opinion about when the peak will happen, and whether the population will more or less plateau afterward or experience a long bumpy slope to a smaller stable-state population). We don't need to assume any horrific apocalypse to anticipate human numbers shrinking, just a natural human response to improved conditions.

Population is one of the drivers of ecological destruction, for the simple reason that the more people there are, the more energy and materials are consumed. Therefore, the sooner we reach peak population (and the lower the total number of people at that peak), the better off the planet will be—which brings us back to the fact that women's rights are key to building a sustainable future [see Empowering Women, p. 260]. AS

Living to Be One Hundred

▬▬▬   More babies being born isn't the only reason the population is growing, though. We're also living longer in most parts of the world, and our longevity shows signs of rising even more rapidly as medical science advances. This is especially true because lifestyle illnesses (from overeating, smoking, drinking, and driving) are currently a major cause of early death: if people were to change their habits, life expectancy would skyrocket. It's not at all crazy to imagine babies born today in the Global North (and more prosperous parts of the Global South) routinely living to be one hundred.

Preceding pages: U.S. Marines unload boxes containing food for the victims of the 2010 earthquake that devastated Haiti.
Opposite: Charts included in *World Population Ageing 2009*, a report issued by the United Nations.

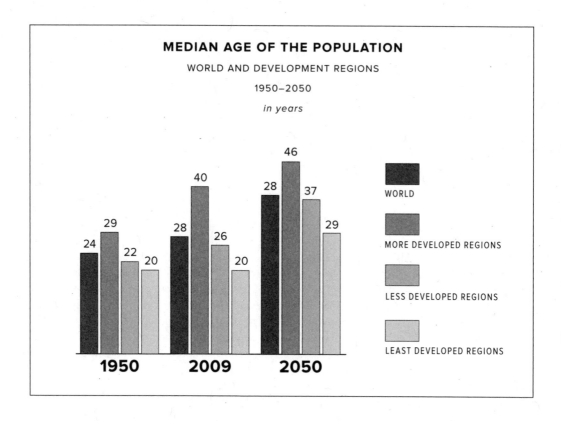

MEDIAN AGE OF THE POPULATION

WORLD AND DEVELOPMENT REGIONS

1950–2050

in years

WORLD

MORE DEVELOPED REGIONS

LESS DEVELOPED REGIONS

LEAST DEVELOPED REGIONS

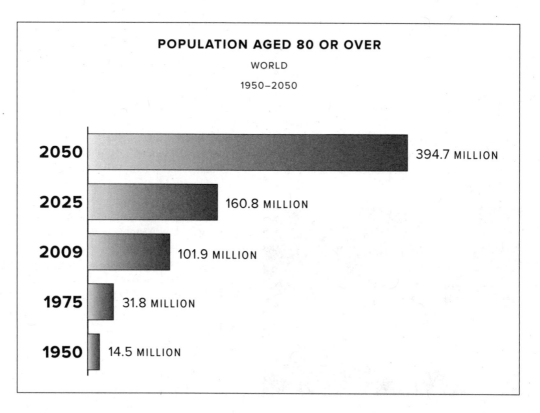

POPULATION AGED 80 OR OVER

WORLD

1950–2050

2050 — 394.7 MILLION

2025 — 160.8 MILLION

2009 — 101.9 MILLION

1975 — 31.8 MILLION

1950 — 14.5 MILLION

Living a long life is generally considered a good thing, but it will bring some complications as well. One of these is that most cities have only just begun to prepare themselves for a large population of older people, who have specific needs, from housing designed to minimize hazards, maintenance, and social isolation, to easy access to fresh food and convenient transit once they lose the ability to drive. Few places are ready for the wave of seniors headed their way.

Another consequence is that in places where people live much longer and young women choose to have fewer children, the proportion of retirees to workers will increase, meaning that the needs of the elderly will place a larger burden on society. The impact on the economies of the Global North will be particularly acute. The U.S. Census Bureau, for instance, estimates that only 57 percent of the population in 2050 will be working-age adults, while the number of very old people (eighty-five and older) will more than triple, to 19 million, by 2050. If no changes are made in U.S. society, the country may have real trouble providing for all these old people. A5

Youth Unemployment

The aging of the Global North is only one part of the story; the other part is the youth of the Global South. The median age (meaning half the population is younger, half older) in Japan and Italy is forty-two; in Finland it's forty; in the United States it's thirty-five. But the median age worldwide is only twenty-eight, and in the least developed nations it's only nineteen (meaning, therefore, that half the people in these countries

are teenagers or children). The Global North is graying while the Global South is still growing up.

There are 1.2 billion young people between the ages of fifteen and twenty-four, and in many countries these people can't find jobs. The International Labor Organization in 2009 estimated the global unemployment rate for this segment of the population at 13.4 percent. That figure, however, doesn't count young people who have only part-time or temporary jobs, are underemployed for their skill levels, or work in jobs that can't support their needs. Though the estimates vary, as many as half of all young people who are in the labor force worldwide may lack adequate work.

The impacts of long-term unemployment or underemployment on young people's lives are severe: they see lower earnings throughout their lives, experience poorer health, and are less likely to ever rise out of poverty. The impacts on the rest of the world are no less severe: Large populations of unemployed young men breed organized crime, violence, and terrorism, which cross borders and spread globally. As for unemployed young women, they are far less likely than employed women to have access to family-planning services, legal protection, and education opportunities, which leads to limited life choices, unplanned pregnancies, and, in turn, excessive population growth. A5

Guest-worker Programs

Youth unemployment is a global problem. Perhaps it demands a global solution. Former World Bank official Lant Pritchett certainly thinks so. Pritchett, in his book *Let Their People Come* (most of which is available for free download at http://www.cgdev.org), argues that the only way to effectively deal with global poverty is to increase work mobility for the world's workers. Pritchett advocates a massive guest-worker program that would offer the unemployed people of the Global South work in the Global North, where the aging of the population will lead to a surfeit of available jobs.

Unemployed Indian youths fill out forms at an employment office in Mumbai.

Pritchett focuses on the economic argument. The Global North currently spends about $70 billion a year to fight poverty in the developing world, a figure that Pritchett says is dwarfed by the potential for labor mobility to do the same. He points to a recent World Bank study, which found that if just 3 percent more workers from the Global South were allowed into the work forces of rich countries, this practice would not only deliver $300 billion in benefits to the poor, but would also generate $51 billion in benefits to citizens of the developed nations. It's a win-win situation, he argues.

Those workers are coming no matter what: the nearly 50-to-1 disparity in wages between the richest nations and the poorest nearly guarantees that. But it would be possible to separate labor mobility—temporary migration to fulfill specific jobs, with the understanding that guest workers will return to their own countries—from immigration, which involves staking a claim to citizenship and voting rights. It would even be possible to set up temporary guest-worker programs that don't welcome extended families; this would relieve the host country of the increased social services often required by a large influx of new arrivals, while making the workers' time in the host country safer, fairer, and more remunerative for the workers themselves.

Such programs might help the planet, too. Fighting climate change and ecosystem disruption, retooling our industrial base, retrofitting our cities, and rebuilding our transportation and energy systems: these are epic undertakings, bound to demand the skilled, unskilled, and semi-skilled labor of many millions of people in the Global North alone. If guest workers filled those jobs, they would not only provide the needed labor, but would also learn skills that will be in huge demand back home as their own countries go through the transition to bright green economies. A guest-worker program could become a means for diffusing innovation from the Global North to the Global South.

Expanded guest-worker programs might even help alleviate some of the conflict that illegal immigration has caused in the Global North. One of the defining attributes of the current largely illegal labor market is that it shames and victimizes those who come to work in the Global North.

Their journeys here are expensive and dangerous, their powerlessness makes them subject to all manner of abuse (from wage extortion to unsafe working conditions to sexual victimization), and their encounters with official society are tainted with disrespect and humiliation. Meanwhile, the illegal and hidden nature of their immigration contributes to the fear of some people in the Global North that their countries are being "overrun."

One of the hallmarks of good governance is that governments don't just welcome transparency, they support it. The most democratic nations in the world actively fund and support watchdog groups and transparency projects, including those who monitor workplace conditions. There's no reason why a guest-worker program couldn't massively increase the transparency of the immigration process while helping to reduce illegal immigration and, ideally, ease racial and cultural tensions. If we could remove the shame from being a guest worker, making it clear that these workers are providing economic benefits to their host countries, both the workers and society as a whole would be better for it. AS

■■■■   RESOURCE

The Bottom Billion: Why the Poorest Countries are Failing and What Can Be Done About It by Paul Collier (Oxford University Press, 2007) Few books on global poverty and development are as accessible and enlightening as development economist Paul Collier's *The Bottom Billion*. Here Collier explains why roughly a billion people in the Global South remain in the grips of desperate poverty. He finds that extremely poor nations tend to share some commonalities: they've recently experienced civil war or ethnic violence; they're land-locked, without access to the kind of trade a port can facilitate; they're corrupt or even "failed states" where fundamentals of law and order are lacking; and they're overly dependent on exporting natural resources (which tends to concentrate wealth in the hands of the few, rather than increase overall development for the many). None of these are easy problems to solve, but they are useful problems to understand.

Empowering Women

▰▰▰▰▰ Improving women's lives is integral to a better world. Three of the eight Millennium Development Goals (MDGs) directly pertain to women: gender equality, maternal health, and universal education. Although the latter is, well, universal, it focuses on the need to educate young girls—after all, two-thirds of illiterate adults in the world (more than 1 billion) are women who have never had access to basic education. If you consider improving child health a "women's issue," or the curbing of HIV/AIDS, which according to the World Health Organization is the leading cause of death and disease among women between the ages of fifteen and forty-four, that makes four and five. Ending poverty and hunger? A reasonable sixth, since of the 1.2 billion people living in poverty worldwide, 70 percent are women.

We cannot achieve any of these MDGs without recognizing and reinforcing the foundations of women's success: protecting women's human rights, providing education and employment opportunities, and creating access to family-planning resources.

We cannot expect to enact positive planetary changes without the participation of half of our population. Nor can we continue to ignore how women are disproportionately affected by climate change. Currently, 80 percent of the world's 27 million refugees are women. The majority of future climate refugees [see Refugees, p. 331] will be women—catastrophic climate change has a greater effect on the world's poor, and women make up the majority of that population. Women must be given greater opportunity to shape the policy decisions that shape the fate of the

planet, and working toward empowerment is the only way to ensure they have the tools to do so.

Today, innovators are winning victories on two fronts: pushing through national legislation and creating culturally resonant educational and public-health programs. When everything from understanding "life skills" to be more than just homemaking to having medical resources for postpartum depression can make a difference in a woman's life, each of these solutions, whether it's a support group or a political movement, is an investment in the planet's future. CB

Family Planning and Peak Population

▰▰▰▰▰ When we look at the phenomenon of peak population, and the evidence that almost everywhere, when women have more options, they choose to have fewer kids [see Demographics and Migration, p. 256], it's easy to link family planning to sustainability: the best path to an earlier/lower peak population is to give every woman on the planet the resources she needs to choose how many children she'll have.

Discussing reproductive health in this context has spurred controversy; there are people in all segments of the political spectrum who find putting any focus on population control offensive. Some protestations are knee-jerk—for instance, the suggestion that population experts who advocate family planning are essentially calling for government-mandated population control. Some are slightly more nuanced: questioning the racial implications of family-planning initiatives that target mostly poor women, particularly those in the Global South, when one child raised in a middle-class household in the Global North will likely consume more resources than several children living at the bottom of the pyramid.

Ultimately, they're all red herrings. Increasing access to family-planning resources is about human rights first—giving women the tools and legal rights they need to control when or how many times they get pregnant. The natural correlation between education and access to birth control

and lower fertility rates is just a planetary bonus—lower peak population based on choice. CB

Educating Girls

▬▬▬ If we put a girl in school at age six or seven, ten years later she's more likely to know about contraception, or to be able to find out about it on her own. With increased education, she's able to hold a better job, and perhaps start her own business. She knows about her civil and human rights, and has more self-confidence to stand up to an abusive husband or sexually harassing boss if she has to. She's more likely to have fewer children. And when she does have children, she knows how to better care for them.

Unfortunately, knowing what to do for girls and getting it done are two different beasts. Programs have set deadlines, and those deadlines have come and gone. The UN is running up against a particularly tight deadline: the Millennium Development Goals state that by 2015, every girl—and boy—must have access to a quality basic education. But the problem of gender disparity in primary and secondary education still exists. In some sub-Saharan African countries, the problem has actually gotten worse since 1990.

Educating all girls involves the mammoth task of shaking up the entrenched bureaucratic and patriarchal structures that keep them from the classroom. In some cases, it will require the government to open its eyes to child-labor practices it doesn't officially want to see. In others, it could mean changing a culture that encourages child marriage and that makes a wife the property of her husband. In many developing countries, taxes do not pay for education, and many parents believe that the extra cost of tuition, textbooks, school uniforms, and school supplies is too great to be "wasted" on a girl who will leave them to join her husband's family when she gets married. On top of that, this goal has been put forward at a time when religious fundamentalists are increasingly trying to restrict women's freedom.

Educating girls and empowering women is critical to creating strong communities, Jakarta, Indonesia.

Nevertheless, efforts are in motion. The World Food Program provides students in developing nations where chronic hunger is a problem with one meal per day at school—and provides one way to get girls into the classroom. In families for whom food is scarce, the best is usually saved for the primary breadwinner—generally the father—and the sons. Women and girls are often shortchanged, particularly on protein, which is necessary for brain development. School feeding is not a permanent solution, but multiple studies have shown that hungry children don't learn or think to the best of their abilities, and one additional meal per day makes a difference.

School feeding programs also motivate parents to enroll their children in school and keep them attending regularly. Around the world, feeding programs have been shown to reduce student absenteeism and to increase the number of years children stay in school. Most significantly, cognitive performance increases, and dropout rates and "holding back" rates decrease.

But even when food is distributed at school—and even if educational fees are waived and open-source textbooks [see Education and Literacy, p. 279] are provided—girls still face obstacles to their education. Their labor is often an important part of the family income, and cannot be easily replaced. Additionally, male teachers in the developing world frequently set store by the prevailing cultural stereotype that boys are smarter, and female teachers tend to be marginalized by their colleagues and left with the last pick of students, classrooms, and equipment.

As is the case in the inner cities of the developed world, in developing nations, getting parents involved in education is crucial to children's schooling—and that is especially true for ensuring girls' education. In the rural Indian state of Uttar Pradesh, the local government used funds from international charities to establish a parallel school system just for girls. Women in the community walk girls to school, parent-teacher associations and principals reach out to homes where children aren't enrolled, and local groups stress to mothers that schooling is a basic legal right. The program's goals are pretty straightforward: help these girls fulfill their potential, and end the cycle of female illiteracy and impoverishment.

Haydi Kızlar Okula!

The World Bank is not necessarily known as a suicide-prevention program. But that's what it became for Askin Tavuz, a thirteen-year-old girl from the city of Diyarbakir, in southeastern Turkey.

Both out of work, Askin's parents decided that sending their daughter to school had become a luxury the family could no longer afford. But school, and her dreams of becoming a lawyer, meant so much to Askin that she wrote a letter to her principal threatening suicide if she could not attend.

It was not the first suicide note the principal, Oya Senvic, had received from a girl who faced being denied an education. "Parents don't see the point in sending their girls to school. They want the girls to stay home and do housework and get married. The families see schooling as a waste of time," says Senvic.

But Senvic was able to enroll Askin in a special World Bank school-stipend program that provides families with a monthly child-support allowance of ten dollars a month, deposited into an account accessible only by the girl's mother. In return, the child must remain enrolled in school and attend regularly.

The World Bank program in Turkey has been augmented by the UNICEF program *Haydi Kızlar Okula!* ("Let's go to school, girls!"), which goes even further toward addressing the gender gap between boys' and girls' school enrollment that leaves many Turkish girls uneducated. (Since the program started in 2001, the enrollment gap has fallen from over 5 percent down to 2.6 percent.) The program offers tax credits of 100 percent to any private group or organization that donates to it, and uses that money to give families a 20 percent refund on the cost of their daughters' education. Turkey has been striving to gain membership in the European Union since 1987—one reason its government accepted the UNICEF program. The Copenhagen criteria for membership, which a country must accept if it wants to join the EU, call for each national government to guarantee full human rights plus respect for and protection of minorities. Since the cohorts of today's primary-school-aged girls will be entering the job market at the same time the country is expected to become an EU member, educating girls is in Turkey's best interest in more ways than one. PD

Girl Guides

▬▬▬ Girl Guides (the British equivalent of the Girl Scouts) are granted merit badges for being crafty, reading books, or knowing how to treat a fractured bone. And although all of these activities are enriching in their own way, they're stuck in an outdated, idealized vision of girlhood. When surveyed, Girl Guide members agreed that these skills alone were not sufficiently preparing them for adulthood.

To meet the demands of their 575,000 members, the Girl Guiding organization responded by offering a "guide to living for modern girls." Brownies (ages seven to ten) are now rewarded for successfully completing a Google search and demonstrating their ability to use a computer and protect it from viruses. Girls ten to fourteen are now taught "independent living" skills, such as financial planning, cooking nutritious meals, and understanding how to seek out services like legal expertise.

Fourteen percent of girls polled said that sexually transmitted diseases are a serious health issue for young women; sixteen percent said teen pregnancy is. To address this, Girl Guides in the "Senior Section" (ages fourteen to twenty-five) can train to become peer educators on sexual and reproductive health. Other serious teen concerns covered by peer educators include binge drinking and eating disorders.

By focusing on the problems that young women face today, Girl Guides is arming their members with the knowledge they will need to be successful, independent women in the modern world. EK

Swedish Sex Education

▬▬▬ No country in the world has put more organized emphasis on the importance of sexual freedom to overall sexual health than Sweden has. The Swedish Association for Sexuality Education, which introduced compulsory sex education in schools in the 1950s, takes a holistic approach, underscoring the significance of personal relationships, socioeconomic stability, and gender equality in forming a healthy self-concept and a positive sexual identity.

As a result of eradicating social taboos around sex and the body, acknowledging that sexual desire is innate and important, and encouraging safe sexual exploration among young people, Sweden has achieved one of the lowest rates of teen pregnancy and HIV/AIDS in the world. SR

Postpartum Depression Support

▬▬▬ Melanie Blocker-Stokes was a successful pharmaceutical sales manager who developed a crippling mood disorder called postpartum psychosis after having her first child. She was admitted to hospitals three times, each time for seven to ten days, with little results. On June 11, 2001, with her daughter just shy of four months old, Blocker-Stokes jumped to her death from a twelfth-story window ledge.

According to the National Institutes of Health, some degree of "baby blues" is common just after childbirth; between 50 and 80 percent of women report symptoms of mild depression. Postpartum depression, in contrast, is a longer-term illness that affects between 10 and 15 percent of women. Its symptoms include feeling restless, anxious, sad, guilty, lethargic, or worthless. Some new mothers with postpartum depression worry about hurting themselves or their baby. In rare cases, a new mother can develop postpartum psychosis, the symptoms of which include refusing to eat, manic energy, sleep disturbance, paranoia, and irrational thoughts. Postpartum psychosis can lead to attempts to harm others or commit suicide.

However, the illness is not well known among mothers or medical professionals. Postpartum Support International (PSI) is a nonprofit organization that hopes to spread the word about these disorders to better inform both mothers and doctors. In addition to providing resources such as information on support groups, local professionals, and treatment options, the organization also advocates for the creation of laws that better support the mental health of new mothers.

Addressing these mental health issues is necessary to squelch the stigma of having

postpartum disorders. According to PSI, one of the reasons postpartum depression and similar disorders are so difficult to diagnose is because mothers may feel ashamed of their condition and therefore do not disclose their symptoms. The sooner postpartum mental health disorders are addressed on a wide scale, the sooner those affected can understand their condition and seek help. Treating those with postpartum disorders means healthier and happier mothers and families. ECB

Gender-equality Laws in Scandinavia

▬▬▬ Year to year, all of the Nordic countries consistently rank at the top of the World Economic Forum's Gender Gap Index. In 2009, Norway ranked third overall, earning an equality score of .93 (out of 1.0) in labor-force participation, .79 in earned income, and 1.0 in the number of women in ministerial positions.

Norway has become a leading example for countries worldwide that are hoping to achieve gender equality and improve economic competitiveness while maintaining relatively steady birth rates. (Norway's birth rate is one of the highest in Europe.) Legislation in Norway requires that large companies have at least a 40 percent representation of both genders. The Gender Equality Act, first enacted in 1978, prohibits all discrimination on the grounds of gender. Arguably, Norway's generous parental leave and benefits policies are what allows its citizens to maintain a steady birth rate while also enjoying economic prosperity. After each birth, parents are entitled to 54 weeks of

leave at 80 percent pay or 44 weeks at 100 percent; each couple can decide how they will divide up this time, though the weeks prior to and immediately following the birth are reserved for the mother and six weeks of leave is reserved for the father's use. Parents of young children are also entitled to flexible working hours.

In the Statement on the Commission on the Status of Women of March 2009, Norwegian legislators deemed their progressive equality laws "investments for the future," because they improve the country's economic competitive edge by increasing the productivity and skills of both genders. They also improve society on a family-by-family basis: as fathers and mothers are given more time to spend with their young children and there is more equality in the household, there is less chance of divorce and domestic violence. EK

The Magna Carta of Women

▬▬▬ After a nine-year lobbying effort, women's groups got what they were asking for in the Philippines: comprehensive legislation aimed at eliminating gender discrimination and protecting and promoting the rights of women. In August 2009, the Magna Carta of Women was signed into law by Philippine president Gloria Macapagal-Arroyo. Guided by the UN's Convention on the Elimination of All Forms of Discrimination Against Women, the Magna Carta is a comprehensive plan to eliminate gender discrimination.

The document contains a comprehensive definition of gender discrimination, as well as detailed language about what steps the state will take to increase the protection of women against gender-based and domestic violence. To better serve women who are victims of gender-related offenses, the government vows to increase, within five years, the recruitment and training of women in the police force, legal professions, and social

Preceding pages: Girls who get an education are far more likely to succeed in life, Hyderabad, India.

Left: These women are members of the Swadhyaya Parivar, or self-awareness community, a movement founded by the Indian spiritual leader Pandurang Shastri Athavale.

work services until half of that workforce comprises women. In addition, government personnel involved with gender-based-violence work are required to undergo training in human rights and gender sensitivity.

The legislation requires that affirmative action policies be instituted and followed to increase the number of females hired in government positions and to ensure that women can "participate meaningfully in the formulation, implementation, and evaluation of policies, plans, and programs for national, regional, and local development."

Furthermore, the government will ensure health services for "all stages of a woman's life cycle," including maternal care, the promotion of breastfeeding, family-planning methods, and treatment of mental-health issues. While abortion is still illegal in the Philippines, the government will offer safe and effective family-planning methods.

In 2009, the Philippines was named one of the top ten nations on the Global Gender Gap Index by the World Economic Forum (making it the highest-ranking Asian nation). The accompanying report states that the country is one of only a handful that have successfully "closed the gender gap on both education and health." As the Philippines works toward the goals set out in the Magna Carta, it will come even closer to eliminating the gender-equality gap in the areas where it is currently less effective—wage and labor-force equality. If it succeeds, the country may become a model for gender equality, particularly for other developing nations. EK

Lulan Artisans

The weavers of Lulan Artisans are master craftswomen. They are also, in many cases, very lucky. Lulan's weaving centers are in Cambodia, Laos, Thailand, and India—regions of the world where human traffickers coerce roughly 1.4 million people into forced labor, much of it in the commercial sex industry. What's even more alarming is that many young women's families are participants, whether active or passive, in these abductions—they either see selling a child into prostitution as the only way out of desperate poverty, or they are lied to by traffickers and send their kids off to what they believe are more legitimate jobs in the closest major city.

Rather than waging an endless awareness campaign with minimal results, Lulan Artisans, a locally driven social venture founded by the celebrated designer Eve Blossom, combats human trafficking by providing economic opportunity and stability. What gets these young women out of the system is not a poster quoting statistics but a stable job. By training women to be skilled weavers, spinners, dyers, and finishers, Lulan teaches women to provide for their families without compromising their independence or security.

The organization is an alliance between textile designers and artisans, with a focus on creating sustainable fabrics and preserving age-old techniques. Weavers aren't producing mass-marketed souvenirs; designers make sure the patterns and embellishments they design respect tradition. This means the women take real pride in and enjoy their work instead of feeling like they are simply in another kind of service. Weavers are paid fair wages and through the centers receive health care and schooling for their kids, two services that provide further stability. CS & CB

Pathfinder

From Bolivia to Botswana to Papua New Guinea, Pathfinder has been providing family planning support for over fifty years. The organization provides contraceptives, ensures the availability of safe abortion services, advocates for sound reproductive-health policies, and cares for those infected with HIV/AIDS and other sexually transmitted infections.

What makes Pathfinder successful is that it recognizes the importance of convincing local religious, cultural, and political leaders that family planning is beneficial to creating long-term stability.

In India, for example, Pathfinder launched the PRACHAR project, which focuses on promoting behavior and attitude changes to encourage delaying marriage and spacing the time between births. The group trained approximately two thousand birth attendants in safe delivery procedures, postpartum counseling, and contraception for birth spacing. Newlyweds were encouraged to put off having their first child until the wife reached the age of twenty-one and to wait for three years before having another child. The couples' mothers were brought into the fold and asked to support their children's decision to delay having children. The program also put on dramatizations to educate the public about crises in women's reproductive health and steps they can take to help reduce the chances of maternal and child mortality.

In just four years, the program was successful in convincing up to 15 percent more women to use contraception to delay their first child, and up to 18 percent more women to space their second child. EK

■■■■■   RESOURCES

The Global Fund for Women

http://www.globalfundforwomen.org
Part of a global movement dedicated to providing choices and opportunities for women from a wide range of backgrounds, the Global Fund for Women is a grant-giving institution for financing projects outside of the United States that advance women's human rights. Since 1987 the fund has given over $71 million ($7.3 million was given out in 2004 alone) to organizations addressing the specific needs of women in their communities. The fund's Web site features a PDF version of the "Women's Fundraising Handbook"—an easily digestible initiation into funding women's human-rights-focused organizations or events—in addition to other resources and links pertaining to these issues.

Women's Earth Alliance

http://www.womensearthalliance.org
Formerly the Women's Global Green Action Network, the Women's Earth Alliance (WEA) focuses on cultivating a network of female environmental leaders with the goal of creating a more just, sustainable world. By investing in the leadership and knowledge of women on a grassroots level, WEA is forming strategic local partnerships, implementing capacity-building training, and coordinating financial and technological support for communities. WEA is currently focusing its efforts on sustainable, safe water supply in sub-Saharan Africa, viable agricultural microbusinesses in India, and environmental social justice issues in North America.

More: Population, Nature, and What Women Want by Robert Engelman (Island Press, 2008)

Robert Engelman, vice president of the Worldwatch Institute, a research organization that provides data and strategies for achieving a sustainable society, has written a book that analyzes the relationships between women's self-determination, population, and sustainability. In *More*, Engelman argues that if women had the final word on reproductive choices, they could "ultimately bring about a global good that governments could never deliver through regulation or control: a population in balance with nature's resources."

It's not that women want "more children," he argues, "but more for their children." The careful timing and managing of births is key to ensuring that there are enough resources for each new person brought into the world, and women can make those decisions only if they are empowered to do so. To support his conclusions, Engelman includes extensive historical and social research alongside the personal stories of women in Africa, Asia, and Latin America that shed light on how the status of women influences the environment.

Half the Sky: Turning Oppression into Opportunity for Women Worldwide by Nicholas Kristof and Sheryl WuDunn (Knopf, 2009)

The authors of *Half the Sky* make a case for investing in the autonomy of women worldwide by explaining that gender bias is not only an ethical issue, but also an economic one. Journalists Nicholas Kristof and Sheryl WuDunn relate in detail the compelling stories of women in gender-biased nations, such as Pakistan and Ethiopia, their struggle to survive, and their eventual success. If these determined, resourceful women are empowered and enlisted into the labor force, Kristof and WuDunn argue, they can help lift their countries out of poverty. EK

Spreading Innovation

systems to disaster-relief housing. In addition, there are new efforts to rewrite our intellectual property laws to make sharing ideas easier—connecting scientists, designers, and inventors across borders and languages, and making science a truly global endeavor. AS

Sharing Tools

It's the job of the world's poor to get rich, and the job of the world's rich to redefine wealth. That is, the biggest task facing the developing world is to escape poverty, while the biggest task facing the developed world is to make prosperity sustainable—so that as billions more people become prosperous, we're still able to protect the planet's biosphere.

Critical to both tasks is the rapid diffusion of sustainable solutions from the epicenters of innovation (the vast majority of which are still urban enclaves in the Global North, where universities, enterprises, and cultural scenes mix and support each other) to the rest of the world. That diffusion cannot happen if innovation is proprietary, bound up in outdated ideas regarding intellectual property.

Intellectual property laws define who benefits from a given innovation. Sometimes, strict protections are necessary to get difficult tasks accomplished, since reward for one's labors is a powerful motivator. The patent system, as Abraham Lincoln famously put it, added "the fuel of interest to the fire of genius." Some things ought to be patented or copyrighted.

Many innovations, however, should not be proprietary, and this is particularly true when we're talking about the kinds of tools that promise to save millions of lives in the developing world. We must make it easier to share those innovations globally, to disseminate academic knowledge and scientific data. Many designers are already experimenting with open-source software systems in order to share blueprints for everything from better vaccine-delivery

Though it's easy to share ideas, sharing the construction of material objects appears to be more difficult. But these objects are becoming more and more describable in information terms: engineering diagrams, product designs, and architectural blueprints are making them easier to share and quicker to adopt. Even innovations in the physical systems of our lives, like water systems and traffic rules, are open to rapid diffusion.

Already, if you want to build a new irrigation system, water filter, or classroom, plans are readily available on the Internet. A huge body of free solutions is available to people with real-world problems to solve, and it's growing by the day.

The concept of freely shared innovation is even spreading into the high-stakes field of energy research. U.S. Secretary of Energy Steven Chu recently made the case for open innovation in clean energy:

"Since power plants are built in the home country, most of the investments are in the home country," he said. "You don't build a power plant, put it in a boat and ship it overseas . . . So developing technologies for much more efficient buildings is something that can be shared in each country. If countries actively helped each other, they would also reap the home benefits of using less energy. So any area like that, I think, is where we should work very hard in a very collaborative way—by very collaborative I mean share all intellectual property as much as possible."

The vast majority of the world's potential users for anything can't afford to pay Global North commercial rates. If something's going to spread, it's going to spread because it's cheap, easy to use, and readily modifiable. When innovators in clean energy, medical science, and technological hardware start from the assumption that they ought to sell to those who can afford their inventions and share with those who can't, the whole world benefits. AS

Copyfight

████████ For five hundred years, alchemists repeatedly learned the hard way that drinking mercury was a bad idea. That's because for five hundred years, alchemists closely guarded their knowledge. We have a name for that period, when learned people kept their knowledge a secret—we call it the Dark Ages.

When an alchemist publishes his results, he stops being a superstitious fool and becomes a scientist. That one, simple step—sharing knowledge—achieves a kind of alchemy more powerful than the conversion of lead into gold: it turns superstition into wisdom.

We live today in a world of unparalleled access to knowledge, and hence, a world of unparalleled potential for human advancement. Raw materials are important. Industrial infrastructure is important. But those aren't the problem: the developing world is rich in materials and industrializing rapidly. What separates a developing nation from a developed one is the right to freely use and reuse knowledge and culture, the infrastructure to spread knowledge far and wide, the ability to use information to bring transparency to governance and to galvanize collective action.

No country knows this better than the United States. For the first hundred years of its post-Revolutionary existence, America was a land of merry piracy. Every invention and artwork of imperial Europe was free for reproduction and acquisition in the USA. Works by domestic authors and inventors were afforded nominal—but critical—protection under a copyright and patent law that explicitly set out to cultivate a post-colonial America in soil enriched by the composted works of foreign powers.

No developing nation today enjoys this privilege. A combination of international copyright, patent, and trademark laws have robbed developing nations of the autonomy that would allow them to embark on a program of self-improvement comparable to that of America's in its first century as a nation. Even when the son of the president of South Africa has died from AIDS,

the country can't afford the economic penalties that would arise from manufacturing domestic dollar-a-dose HIV cocktails.

On the information-technology front, the most pernicious culprit in robbing nations of self-determination is "anticircumvention," first seen in the 1996 treaties from the United Nations' World Intellectual Property Organization (WIPO), a body with the same relationship to wicked copyright law as Mordor has to evil.

Anticircumvention laws make it a crime to tell people how to get around the locks placed on digital works, regardless of whether those locks protect anything guaranteed in law. A digital lock that restricts DVD playback based on region can stop you from watching an American video in India or vice versa. Even though neither country grants filmmakers the right to control where their videos are viewed after they are lawfully acquired, circumventing the technology is still a crime.

Most governments seek to balance the rights given to authors and the rights reserved to the public, but with anticircumvention in place, manufacturers can invent new copyrights for themselves simply by embodying them digitally.

The other major factor threatening universal access to knowledge is the lack of international agreement on exceptions to copyright. Thanks to treaties drafted by Hollywood and Big Pharma—the top-grossing pharmaceutical companies—practically every country offers the same package of minimum rights to every inventor or author. But the rights reserved to the public under each county's copyright are piecemeal. That means that an educator who includes in her course materials an excerpt that is considered lawful in Ghana cannot count on the same excerpt being considered lawful when she shares the course materials with a colleague in Jamaica. This turns international cooperation on humanitarian information projects into a legal minefield—when ten thousand volunteers from around the globe help Project Gutenberg scan, convert, and proofread public-domain books, how are they to know whether various national laws permit the work?

Things are coming to a head. At WIPO, dozens of nongovernmental organizations (NGOs) have fought to hold the organization to its charter, under which it is supposed to formulate treaties to advance humanitarian aims; Brazil and other developing nations have come up strong against copyright and patent laws in their trade negotiations with the United States; software patents were finally axed in Europe. A host of diverse coalitions have banded together in hopes of preserving the freedom to share knowledge and information openly.

The copyfight is fully engaged. CD

Copyleft

▬▬▬▬ Copyleft, as you might guess, is the opposite of copyright, in that rather than restricting users from duplicating, modifying, and sharing a product, it encourages them to do so. Early movement toward copyleft licensing began in the 1970s among software programmers who believed in free distribution of, and user-driven improvements for, software programs. In the subversive spirit of the time, and in an effort to liberate distribution, programs were often signed with "Copyleft: All wrongs reserved." By definition, any program or work that begins copylefted stays copylefted. If a new user makes changes to a given work, the modified version must continue to be free and open. With this arrangement, copyleft facilitates the development of more free software by requiring participation and compliance from all future users.

What's so worldchanging about copyleft? Besides encouraging freedom—both financial and intellectual—copylefting also fosters cooperation and the formation of strong communities around common goals. When we are encouraged to make systems work better, and are free to implement those improvements, we have great incentive to collaborate with others to create something that serves everyone's needs. SR

Creative Commons

▬▬▬▬ International copyright treaties require countries to place works into copyright's strongbox with all rights reserved from the second they are created. In many instances, these copyrights can last for more than a century—which means that today's napkin doodle won't be in the public domain until the year 2210 or so. Does everyone

need that much copyright? Hell no. Lots of authors benefit from having their works freely disseminated, remixed, and reproduced.

Creative Commons (CC) licenses are standard licenses that authors apply to their works to specify that only some rights are reserved: no one else can make money off the work and proper credit must be given, but no use fees are charged. Creating a license on the Creative Commons Web site takes about five minutes; since the project's inception, more than 53 million works have gone under CC license. JC

Honey Bee Network

▬▬▬▬ The Honey Bee Network, a project founded by Professor Anil Gupta of the Indian Institute of Management in Ahmedabad, couldn't be more aptly named: the network collects traditional knowledge from isolated rural communities and cross-pollinates it, spreading grassroots innovation throughout India.

It all begins outdoors and on foot, when Gupta and a collection of allies traverse the Indian countryside visiting villages and talking to "barefoot inventors" about their homegrown products. Gupta believes that the essential problem with development work is that "strategies fail to build upon a resource in which poor people often are rich: their own knowledge . . . The higher the physical, technological, market, or socioeconomic stress, the greater the probability that disadvantaged communities and individuals generate innovative and creative alternatives for resource use."

With the help of the Society for Research and Initiatives for Sustainable Technologies and Institutions (SRISTI), the Honey Bee Network helps villagers to share their ideas, or even put them into commercial production. SRISTI maintains the network's database of innovations, and helps protect the intellectual property rights of inventors while drumming up venture funding for their creations.

Some of Honey Bee's projects include:

Bicycle Hoe: This agricultural tool combines inexpensive bike parts and common farm implements to kick up the efficiency and ease of tilling and weeding soil. The initial design was a manual cycle, the efficiency of which was largely determined by the strength of the person in the seat, but a newer version attaches a moped engine to increase coverage even further.

Micro-windmill Battery Charger: A small portable wind turbine that can generate enough power when carried by an individual to charge cellphone or laptop batteries.

Pedal-operated Washing Machine: A young girl from Kerala invented this device, powered by bicycle pedals, which tumbles clothing in a sealed box without the need for electricity.

The Honey Bee Network is proof positive that, given opportunities and support, poor people in the Global South can come up with astonishingly innovative solutions to their own problems. SR

ICT4D

■■■■■ For many people in the developed world, it's hard to remember life before the Internet, a time when "mail" involved writing on pieces of paper and handing them to government representatives, who promised to deliver them—maybe in forty-eight hours, maybe in a few weeks. But even in Internet-obsessed nations like the United States, a stark digital divide still exists between wealthy, urban, and predominantly white communities and poor, rural, and predominantly nonwhite communities. This divide turns into a chasm when we compare developed nations to developing ones, on the Internet front. For developing

nations faced with more prosaic problems like food security, water safety, malaria, and AIDS, is joining the online community something that should be considered a high priority?

The answer may well be yes. Many developing nations are aggressively pursuing strategies to increase their access to information, motivated by both positive and negative visions of the future. They hope for futures where teachers can supplement meager libraries with online books, where telemedicine—the use of cell phones and other telecommunications devices for diagnosing and treating patients in remote locations—supplements the limited resources of rural hospitals, where local artisans can sell goods to a global audience online, and where the next generation of students writes computer code for international businesses. Developing countries are tapping technology so that computers and the Internet don't make the economic gap between rich and poor nations any broader than it already is.

In response, a movement has sprung up in which activists, techies, social entrepreneurs, and enterprising citizens alike are trying out new approaches to help poor communities use computers, the Internet, and even radio to solve the problems of poverty. The buzzword they use is ICT4D, short for "information and communications technologies for development," but the meaning is far simpler: if we give people, especially people in poor, urban areas, cutting-edge tools to change their lives, we change the entire dynamic. We create space for grassroots innovation to emerge in ways no outsider could ever have predicted or imagined. We open the future up to everyone.

The growth of the Internet in the developed world has been so rapid that it can seem

almost inevitable that everyone will be connected soon. But the following are some major obstacles that could make it a long time before we find as many Africans as Americans online:

Cost: The cost of a PC has dropped from a few thousand dollars to less than one hundred over the past two decades, but computers still cost more than many in the Global South can afford to pay.

Connectivity and power: Phone systems are woefully inadequate in many nations—with fewer than one landline per hundred households—and most households in the developing world lack the basic electricity needed to power their PCs.

Literacy and language: The Internet is a world of mostly written text, which makes it inaccessible to people who are illiterate (in some developing nations, this can be more than 60 percent of the adult population). In addition, the majority of available content is in English. Speakers of Urdu, Bambara, or Bahasa Indonesian will be severely limited in what they can access and accomplish online.

Relevancy: While there's lots of content on the Internet germane to the problems of an American student or a European businessman, what's available online to help an African farmer solve the problems he faces every day?

Innovators in the developed and developing worlds are tackling some of these challenges head-on, designing low-cost, low-power computers, wireless networks, and multilingual interfaces. Rapidly spreading cybercafes distribute the costs of computer ownership and network access over hundreds of users. And some of the most promising technologies aren't newly created: FM radio and mobile telephones may well be the key information technologies for the developing world.

Imagine a world where anyone can speak to anyone else, and where everyone can access the knowledge they need to be productive, healthy, and successful. The researchers, entrepreneurs, and innovators who focus on ICT4D are trying to make that dream a reality. EZ

Free Geek

New urban models for bridging the digital divide aren't only found in the Global South, of course. In Portland, Oregon, the Free Geek project ("helping the needy get nerdy since the beginning of the 3rd millennium") takes junked computers, rebuilds them, loads them with free software, and ships the resulting "freekboxes" to low-income people and activist groups in the Portland area and abroad. In the process, they wire poor people, keep toxic computer parts from winding up in landfills, and build skills in local communities. AS

Localized Software

When users in Cambodia sit down at a cybercafe computer, they've got two challenges: not only do they have to figure out how the computer works, but they need to read English to do it, as the programs on the computer aren't written in Khmer.

Frustrated by this digital divide, Javier Solá and the Khmer Software Initiative started the

Opposite: Geekcorps is a nonprofit that helps build technology infrastructure in rural areas of the Global South. Using commonly available materials, like the bamboo pole pictured here, Geekcorps participants have been able to construct long-range antennae that grant access to radio stations and Wi-Fi hotspots.

Left: Free Geek turns out-of-date computers into usable desktops for low-income users.

long process of creating a Web browser, an e-mail client, and an office suite in Khmer. They didn't have to start from scratch: open-source office browser, e-mail, and office software had already been written in English—it just needed to be "localized" into Khmer.

In the course of the project, Solá met Dwayne Bailey, who heads the Translate.org.za project, which translates open-source software and is translating OpenOffice, Firefox, and Thunderbird—three of the most popular open-source programs—into each of South Africa's eleven official languages. Bailey and Solá are now collaborating on a framework that aids software translation and will help projects around the world localize software. They're also making a great case for the value of open-source software in the developing world: because the source code is open, the software can be translated for free to meet local needs. EZ

Inveneo

Inveneo, a San Francisco–based nonprofit organization, is bringing information and communication tools to remote villages in the developing world. These tools are based on open-source software, and rely on Wi-Fi and voice over Internet protocol (VoIP)—which uses computers and the Internet to allow people to make phone calls for free—to connect multiple remote locations to one another and to the broader Internet and telephone networks. Equipment at the stations operates on batteries charged by a combination of solar cells and bicycle generators. In short, Inveneo is using open-source technology and renewable power to improve the lives of poor people around the globe through better access to communication.

This isn't just a fantasy or a "we're hoping to do this soon" sort of project, either. With the assistance of the nongovernmental organization ActionAid, Inveneo has already deployed its system in rural villages in Uganda. EZ

South-South Science

Nations in the Global South have come to realize that their future depends on science.

More specifically, they realize that they must build a bright green future from within, that although aid from the North has its place, their future really depends upon the active advancement of local science. Community health, environmental conditions, and the ability to respond effectively to dramatic changes in the global economy are all linked to scientific development. Developing nations can't simply rely on the goodwill of Western scientific communities to solve their problems, especially when that goodwill is negated by actions like applying strict patents to important drugs, putting them out of reach for most of the millions of people suffering from diseases like HIV/AIDS.

These nations have also realized that they're not alone: some of the most exciting breakthroughs are coming out of South-South collaborations. Southern nations can gain by pooling their resources and findings, and troubleshooting their problems and frustrations with those who are also operating with limited resources and within similar confinements. These collaborations have already moved beyond the governmental/institutional phase: they have morphed into formal and informal relationships between individual researchers, businesspeople, students, and tinkerers.

Countries are combining research programs on AIDS, malaria, and other diseases whose impact is most heavily felt in the developing world; creating joint protocols for independently assessing the safety of genetically modified crops; dramatically ramping up basic science education; setting up scientific educational exchanges; signing agreements to increase research funding; and hosting conferences on the scientific priorities of

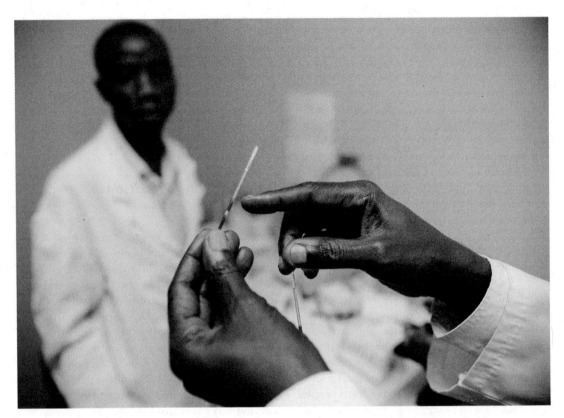

developing nations versus those of the developed world. They have made tremendous strides in bioscience alone. High-quality bioscience doesn't require a big industrial base, just dedicated and well-educated scientists, and many developing nations have plenty of those to go around.

With the emergence of South-South science, the Global South has begun to perceive itself as a generator, not a passive recipient, of ideas, and this reorientation has created an increased sense of national and personal worth, which is having a catalytic effect. What's more, this coalition seeks to do something really revolutionary: tie the fortunes of developing-world science to global collaborative efforts like open-access databases and open-source software. It's a blunt bid to wrestle power over the direction of research away from the "corporate science" of the Global North and to create freely available technological innovations that fit the needs of the Global South. If they succeed, we'll soon see how different science can be. AS & EO

The Practice

How much do farmers in sub-Saharan Africa know about the protein-rich snail farming in Ghana or the tofu-growing ecosystems of Nigeria? In the desertifying regions of the Sahel, are scientists aware of the successful biogas initiatives at the Kigali Institute of Technology or of the powers of the desert-fighting *Jatropha* plant?

South-South science is rooted in the wide dissemination of information—including new and developing (and often, leapfrogging) ideas, and indigenous and local knowledge. The dissemination can occur casually, in conversations across one country's industries (say, between the tinkerers at Ghana's *Suame Magazine,* a group of small-enterprise artisans who operate in an industrial district in Kumasi, and the students at the country's Ashesi University) or more formally (say, India advising Zambia on how to build an entire

---

Opposite: A student chats with new acquaintances in Senegal, France, and Spain at a cybercafe in Dakar, Senegal.
Above: Southern scientists are leading the fight against diseases like malaria, Lagos, Nigeria.

industry). Breakthrough palm-wine preservation research from the Nigerian Institute for Oil Palm Research does great things for Nigeria, but when that information is shared, it also proves to be very valuable to the sorghum brewers of Zambia.

One of the best early examples of South-South cooperation happened between Malaysia and the nations of West Africa. Malaysia, which is geographically similar to West Africa, adopted West African methods of palm-oil manufacturing, hoping to inject some energy into their economy. Fast-forward thirty years and Malaysia is the world's largest producer of palm oil—and is offering West Africa advice on how to upgrade its palm-oil industry, including how to produce the oil as a biofuel.

One of the best ways to facilitate these collaborations is to progressively introduce them into both traditional and evolving media gateways—from newspapers and television to solar-powered radio stations and cell phones. If there is a widespread sense that science and technology are not elitist, but that they are in many ways relevant to the daily lives of the most underserved people, it will accelerate a change in perception surrounding the importance of South-South exchanges. Stories of Southern innovation should be as accessible to an inhabitant of Kibera, Kenya, as a Nollywood flick is. Education systems, too, should be progressively rethought and reoriented to encourage creativity and to recognize local resources and their promise. People like Mohammed Bah Abba, who invented the Pot-in-Pot refrigerator, a set of clay pots that keeps food cool without electricity [see Energy in the Global South, p. 302], should be transformed into the pop heroes of the sub-Saharan African age. The impact on the daily lives of the disenfranchised is the most evident benefit of these heroes' ingenuity, but the larger and potentially more important one will be the unlocking of millions of minds.

The Global South is the greatest source of untapped human potential we have. Too often, policy makers in the North present the rise of South-South science—and its contingent effect on the development of Southern nations—as a threat, not a gain. But alternate viewpoints and methods spawned in the Global South will lead to problem solving that will complement, not subtract from, Northern advancement. The South's need for

solutions that are practical, easily implemented, and sustainable will lead to a reexamination of the North's complex and environmentally injurious activities—relics of the age of industrialization. In short, the discoveries of South-South scientists will help us all achieve more robust, less damaging systems that will help to alleviate poverty worldwide. EO

Biopiracy and Traditional Knowledge Banks

Southern scientists are turning to local knowledge of indigenous plants and traditional treatments to make breakthroughs, particularly medical ones. But this increased focus on reviving and disseminating traditional treatments has brought a novel problem to the developing world: biopiracy—nonlocals patenting treatments based on plants used by indigenous communities.

The best solution so far has been the construction of databases and traditional-knowledge archives, which offer an increasingly popular and effective way to combat biopiracy by establishing "prior art." Prior art disallows patents on anything that has been disclosed to the public in some form before the date the patent was filed. There is, of course, a great debate going on about what exactly constitutes prior art, and everyone seems to have their own definition. Many countries don't recognize oral traditions as establishing prior art, which is problematic for communities that don't have much in the way of a written history. In addition, when indigenous knowledge is primarily passed down orally, the creation of knowledge libraries is more difficult, as remote communities can be unwilling to share that knowledge with outsiders.

But despite these hurdles, several projects have been successful in establishing traditional-knowledge archives, and more are gaining speed. The South Asian Association for Regional Cooperation is building a regional Traditional Knowledge Digital Library (TKDL), covering South Asian traditional medicine, food, architecture, and culture. Participating nations include Bangladesh, Bhutan, India, Maldives, Nepal, Pakistan, and Sri Lanka. The regional TKDL is based on the success of India's own traditional-knowledge library, which was created in 1999 after the country successfully overturned a U.S. patent for medical uses of tur-meric; Indians had known about the plant's ability to speed the healing of wounds for centuries.

By working closely with traditional female community leaders, the South African Management of Indigenous Knowledge Systems Project has been able to expand its effort to identify and protect the unique biosystems used by local communities as medicines. The project has led to something even more considerable than a knowledge archive: its leaders are working to improve local economic conditions by establish-ing community businesses to produce, market, and sell traditional foods and medicines.

Brazil has taken a different path. The Brazilian Microbe Bank is a repository of information about native microorganisms. The bank's researchers have collected detailed information on and examples of more than a thousand types of microbes, and the facilities are capable of maintaining up to 12,000 microbes. The collection includes soil, water, and plant microorganisms from Brazil's diverse ecosystems, and even microbes isolated from oil fields. In the age of biotechnology, even organisms can be refined into products that can be sold back to the countries from which they originated—for a hefty profit. JC

Broadband: A Legal Right

■■■■■   In most countries, a fast home Internet connection is a privilege—and a pricey one at that. Finland, however, has declared that broadband service is, in fact, a legal right. The government has vowed that every Finnish resident will have access to a 100-Mbps connection by 2015.

The possible benefits of universal service are many: it would ensure connectivity for the small percent of Finns not online (generally those in remote and sparsely populated regions) and could stimulate economic growth by making job searches, online shopping, and online banking easier. But what's worldchanging about this is the government's recognition that in today's world, in which we're building knowledge economies, hav-ing Internet access is now akin to having electric-ity or running water—in other words, necessary for a high quality of life. CB

The Science and Development Network
http://www.scidev.net
An invaluable portal for individuals and organiza-tions in the developing world, the Science and Development Network offers news, views, and analysis of science and technology issues, aiming to create a free-access space where decision makers can become better informed about the effects of their choices on social and economic develop-ment within their own communities. SciDev.net works to build regional networks of researchers, journalists, policy makers, and organizations, and maintains extensive dossiers (available free on the site) on issues ranging from medical ethics and malaria to indigenous knowledge.

Education and Literacy

Access to education, or rather the lack of it, is one of the greatest barriers to sustainability. According to Lester Brown, director of the Earth Policy Institute, 115 million children do not attend school and 800 million adults are illiterate—in a world where access to information is key to success, whether one is a subsistence farmer or a factory worker. To be illiterate and unschooled is to be excluded from the possibility of a better future. If we want a safe and sustainable world, we need to provide everyone with the mental tools they need to better their condition. As Nobel Prize–winning economist Amartya Sen warns, "Illiteracy and innumeracy are a greater threat to humanity than terrorism" (Brown, 2006).

This networked age has enabled new tools that are revolutionizing teaching and learning, tearing down the walls of libraries and academies, and democratizing access to knowledge in unprecedented ways. Innovations like cheap laptops for children and vans outfitted with on-demand book printers are bridging the last mile of the digital divide in villages across the Global South. Online communities are making the off-line work of teachers and literacy practitioners easier, allowing them to share course materials and lesson plans. And the open-source movement is providing distance-learning tools that are enabling autodidacts anywhere on earth to take the same classes—from Latin to Laser Holography—as students at elite Western universities.

Cliché as it may sound, today, knowledge is power. If a sustainable global democracy is to emerge in the years to come, sharing that power among vastly greater numbers of people is not only more essential than ever, it's also more possible than ever. LU

Creative Spaces

Schools have long been designed based on the myth that children need to be protected from "distractions," including daylight. But just as offices full of monochromatic, poorly lit cubicles make worker productivity suffer [see Lighting, p. 133], dreary environments sap our kids of energy. Schools feel like prisons largely because they look like them.

Section Eight Design, a small firm in Victor, Idaho, applied green building techniques, rugged functionality in design, and an eye for creative spaces to its design for the Teton Valley Community School campus. Since part of the school's philosophy is to encourage different age groups to interact with and mentor one another, Section Eight made most classroom dividers collapsible and/or reconfigurable. The "drawing back the curtain" theme gets even more literal: as one of the school's goals is to teach students about the built environment, a science lab adjoins the mechanical room, and teachers can fold down partitions to help illustrate their lessons. What makes the design even more brilliant is that it's a modular plan (buildings can be prefab) that allows schools to do easy, pay-as-you-go expansions. This is particularly useful in rural or semirural areas where school districts are shrinking down to a few overcrowded facilities and often have to create makeshift satellite campuses to handle the overflow.

In existing urban schools that don't stand to change much, even simple interior decorating projects can make a difference. The Publicolor program repaints classrooms and hallways in bright, visually stimulating colors. The simple aesthetic change can reinvigorate students, but Publicolor is also fostering other skills. Designers work with students to plan and complete the painting, and the whole process provides important lessons on collaborating, planning, and seeing a project through to the end. The program also provides career workshops and tries to connect students with other community-improvement projects. According to *Design Revolution: 100 Products that Empower People,* students who have participated in Publicolor have better high school graduation and college retention rates than their classmates. CB

MIT's OpenCourseWare

▄▄▄▄▄   The Massachusetts Institute of Technology has put most of its course catalog online. Well, not just its course catalog, but the courses themselves—the syllabi, readings, assignments, tests, lecture notes, even lecture recordings. Since its launch in late 2003, the OpenCourseWare Web site has grown to include over two thousand courses. With offerings in fields ranging from architecture to engineering, media arts to materials science, the site provides a pretty good approximation of the academics at a top-notch university education—for free, anywhere, anytime.

Already, students from more than two hundred regions and countries are taking these classes. MIT has translated many of its materials into twelve languages, including Chinese, Dutch, and Thai. International online communities have sprung up around some of the courses of study. Best of all, because it is built on an open-license platform, any improvements or expansions that others add to these courses must also be made freely available. OpenCourseWare is arguably the single greatest contribution to the fast-growing open-source education movement. LU

Free High School Science Texts

▄▄▄▄▄   In 2002 physicist Mark Horner had just finished giving a talk on wave phenomena at a South African science fair when a group of young scholars from a poor rural high school asked him to proof the notes they'd taken by hand in a notebook. Mark was stunned by the comprehensive diligence reflected in the notes, and asked why the students were so attentive. They explained that they had no science texts in their school and that this notebook would be the textbook for the rest of their schoolmates. In an era of nearly free information and collaborative content creation, such a knowledge gap seemed absurd.

So Horner founded Free High School Science Texts to provide free science and mathematics textbooks for high schoolers. The textbooks are openly sharable and affordable; schools have to cover just the moderate printing costs (which may be offset by donations), not any of the other fees associated with publishing—no royalties or markups to worry about.

Open textbooks are needed in the Global North, too. The California Open Textbook Project, for example, has been launched in an effort to figure out how to help that cash-strapped state significantly reduce its budget for K–12 textbooks, which is about $400 million per year. Wherever open-textbook projects are employed, the results are the same: kids get sharply edited textbooks, created with the involvement of some of the best minds around, at prices their schools can afford.

Access to science and knowledge is particularly vital to the lives of many of the world's most disadvantaged people. From fighting epidemic diseases to preparing people for climate change, science will play a critical role in their lives and fortunes. And educating a generation of scientifically literate school kids is vitally important to the spread of science in the Global South. South-South science [see Spreading Innovation, p. 274] can succeed only if young scientists are taking up the work and young people who understand science are applying it.

Students who learn in this way will not only be better educated, they'll be better prepared to participate in the open creativity that will drive their futures. More problem-solvers, enabled to work more collaboratively, equals more problems solved. AS

Same-language Subtitling

▄▄▄▄▄   Same-language subtitling (SLS) as a method of teaching reading skills was first introduced on Indian television in 1999, broadcast with Bollywood songs. The visual association of written words with familiar song lyrics proved incredibly successful, making the learning process automatic and subconscious, as well as cost-effective. Planet-Read, one of the pioneering organizations in this field, found that "every U.S. dollar spent on subtitling a nationally telecast program of Hindi film

songs gives 30 minutes of weekly reading practice to 10,000 people for a year."

PlanetRead was founded by Dr. Brij Kothari as part of Stanford's Digital Vision fellowship, and is now based in California and India. The site allows users to select from ten different languages in which to view "karaoke-style" clips of Bollywood films and shows.

SLS is now a model for mass literacy outside India as well, and PlanetRead has plans to establish year-long pilot programs in other parts of Asia, Africa, and Latin America. The program's success depends in part, of course, on the degree of television broadcasting penetration in any given area, and on local leadership for getting the programs set up. But for areas that may lack television but have Internet access, PlanetRead has also launched a Web site for an online SLS program called DesiLassi. This is SLS 2.0—an interactive online video tool for learning to read by listening to Bollywood tunes, and then rating, ranking, sharing, and adding clips to diversify the material and distribute it even more widely, turning the practice of a vital skill into a natural component of everyday entertainment. SR

Playground for Learning

▆▆▆▆ Project H Design's Learning Landscape at Kutamba AIDS Orphans School in rural Uganda is a model for play-based education. The "math playground" is laid out on a square grid, allowing it to become a human chessboard of sorts for a variety of math-based games. Old tires—always great fun to play on—mark sixteen points on this grid. Kids can mark up the tires with chalk to keep track of the action or to work out basic math problems. The games can be as simple as a mathematics-themed Musical Chairs, and can teach spatial and logical reasoning along with arithmetic. Teachers at other Project H installations in the Dominican Republic and North Carolina have been adapting their games to include lessons in geography and other sciences too.

Students at the Kutamba AIDS Orphans School in Bikongozo, Uganda, use the Learning Landscape by Project H Design during a math lesson.

The playground at Kutamba is not just a once-in-a-while supplement to classroom learning. Simple wooden benches fit snugly over the tires so the playground can be used as an outdoor classroom even when the games are over. CB

The Barefoot College

▅▅▅▅▅▅ RESOURCE

DIY U: Edupunks, Edupreneurs, and the Coming Transformation of Higher Education by Anya Kamenetz (Chelsea Green Publishing, 2010) The combination of hundreds of millions of young people with rising aspirations, a limited number of tradition-bound universities, and ubiquitous access to technology is bound to produce some strange results. Kamenetz thinks it will produce nothing short of a revolution that redefines what higher education means, how we learn through the course of our lives, and the relationship between credentials and careers. She even includes a guide for students who want to hack their own educations. AS

▅▅▅▅▅▅ Imagine a university where every activity, every class, every discussion we engage in has a direct and beneficial impact on our community. Imagine a community where values and activities related to sustainability aren't treated as "add-ons" or specializations, but where there is instead a seamless integration between the practical and the sustainable, between community needs and community growth: the elementary school building is a straw-bale construction that the whole community helped to create; the light you read by comes from a solar lamp that your daughter constructed; organic agriculture is the norm, not the pricey exception.

This scenario is not an unrealizable dream. This is the Barefoot College, a remarkable community-development project, which began in 1972 in Tilonia, a village in Rajasthan, one of India's largest, driest, and poorest states. "It was a sleepy looking neglected village of some two thousand people, typical of the 600,000 villages you find anywhere in India," says the college's founder, Sanjit "Bunker" Roy. The only thing that set it apart was an abandoned tuberculosis sanitorium on forty-five acres of government land. When Roy looked at the vacant buildings, he knew they would make the perfect headquarters for the organization he wanted to start. The abandoned eyesore soon became the thriving home of the Social Work and Research Centre (SWRC), a place that Roy hoped would attract young, urban-educated Indians to work alongside local residents to alleviate rural poverty.

The urban professionals did come, but they were in for a surprise. They expected to bestow the benefits of their higher education upon the impoverished, illiterate villagers. Instead, their own deschooling process was just beginning. They discovered that very often the traditional knowledge—for instance, rainwater-harvesting techniques—that had been passed down orally from one generation to the next surpassed their own expertise. A dynamic partnership unfolded, which respectfully merged modern technology and traditional knowledge. Eventually, the SWRC evolved into an organization that questioned the purpose and process of education itself. They dared to wonder, "What kind of education would nurture individuals and communities who can meet their own needs—and do so sustainably?"

Over time, the SWRC changed its name to the Barefoot College and expanded the campus. The word *barefoot* denotes the grassroots approach that is pivotal for people who have little exposure to formal education. The Barefoot College uses a hands-on education process and has developed programs for every age group, from infants to elders. Students can learn to be solar engineers, hand-pump mechanics, groundwater experts, teachers, midwives, accountants, communicators (in videography, photography, street theater, puppetry), and apprentice in a range of traditional handicrafts. One of the most notable aspects of the program is that women are trained in nontraditional occupations, such as solar engineering and hand-pump mechanics.

People throng to the Barefoot College from all over India to learn about the award-winning program and bring what they've learned back to their own communities. Field centers exist in thirteen Indian states, and other countries have adapted the Barefoot College process to their local contexts.

The Barefoot College stimulates individual and collective creativity. One

One of the most remarkable development programs in the world, the Barefoot College addresses issues of water conservation, women's literacy, sanitation, job training, and more in multiple campuses throughout India.

staff member summarized it by saying, "at the Barefoot College, the only limit is your imagination." The organization's focus on equality, a simple lifestyle, dedication to meaningful work, and openness is as innovative as any creation that comes out of the classroom. The lessons of Barefoot College transcend ethnicity and geography. Every community should have such a resource. CO

Barefoot Campus

The Barefoot College campus is every bit as remarkable as its students are. Solar power supplies all of the electricity; a biomass plant provides an additional source of renewable energy. Rainwater is harvested on the roof of every building. Trees have been carefully nurtured through an ingenious drip irrigation system, creating a green environment that gives the impression that the college is a desert oasis. The biggest success? The entire campus was constructed by a dozen Barefoot Architects led by a farmer from Tilonia, Bhanwarjat; a local blacksmith named Rafiq fabricated and installed most of the campus's doors and windows. CO

Barefoot Solar Engineers

Bhagwat Nandan, head of the solar program at the Barefoot College, is a Hindu priest from a nearby village. He grew up in a home that had no electricity, but now he supervises the training of solar engineers, who are responsible

for some of the school's greatest successes: the electrification of the entire campus, as well as the lighting of 870 schools and 300 adult-education centers across the country, homes in 28 villages in the Himalayan region of Ladakh (including a Buddhist monastery), and more than 12,000 households in various other villages.

The Barefoot Solar Engineers—usually women and unemployed youth, and usually illiterate—learn to install and maintain photovoltaic systems for individual homes, as well as to create town-sized microgrids. The solar-education model involves community participation and commitment to energy self-reliance. Generally, the village selects someone to train at the college, and that person then returns to install and maintain the solar energy for their community. Women who have had very little independence or clout in their village often find that they become impromptu community leaders once they return and demonstrate their new skills. And all of this is achieved without elaborate textbooks.

The developing world is littered with failed solar projects set up by charitable organizations that only had the funds to install them, not to maintain them. These systems either broke after a few years or made villagers dependent on further foreign aid to keep the benefits on which they had come to rely. By contrast, the solar-education model at the Barefoot College is an elegant example of green economic development that supports community resilience. CO

Rainwater Harvesting and Piped Water Systems

In a semidesert climate where droughts can last for years, water is the most precious resource, especially when the few sources of water a village has are brackish or contaminated with high levels of iron and fluoride.

It's no surprise that water initiatives are a big focus at the Barefoot College. Rainwater-harvesting systems designed by students have collected an estimated 7.6 million gallons (29 million liters) of rainwater at 470 schools and community centers. Additionally, communities have been mobilized to build their own piped water systems and learn how to maintain them. Hand pumps at

village wells are repaired by mechanics who live in the village, ensuring that there will always be someone on hand to troubleshoot problems.

Prior to the Barefoot College intervention, villages were dependent on government engineering teams to make repairs, which often meant that malfunctioning hand pumps would remain broken for long periods until the team arrived. Local control and management of water benefits the entire community and contributes to its economic well-being. Over the past ten years, the Barefoot College has also turned its attention to water conservation and recharging groundwater. CO

Community Health

At a time when public-health efforts worldwide are shifting toward disease prevention and health promotion, the Barefoot College is once again ahead of the game. For decades, the school has been training community-health practitioners, realizing that critical basic health messages—especially when they involve taboo subjects like STDs—are best delivered by midwives and local health-care workers.

Thanks to the college, there are now two hundred village health clinics throughout India that provide basic medicines (including traditional medicines), administer treatment for minor injuries, and provide transport to government hospitals when ailments are too serious to be dealt with in the clinic. Since clean drinking water is vital to good health, a related program, the Barefoot Chemists, trains young people to test for water quality. CO

The Children's Parliament

The Barefoot College has influenced education throughout India and in other countries. It has been particularly successful with night schools for children.

The night school concept itself has made a huge impact on child education, particularly on the education of girls. Many rural children (especially the girls) are unable to attend school during the day because they are too busy tending cattle or

attending to other household chores. Their only opportunity to learn comes at night. Students gather in schools that have been powered by the Barefoot Solar Engineers and pore over textbooks made from recycled materials. While they learn basics like reading and math, their curriculum also includes subjects like animal husbandry—practical knowledge that can be applied immediately to household chores.

The other component of the college's innovative education program is the Children's Parliament, which teaches kids about civic responsibilities and how elected officials should serve their communities. Students elect their own prime minister, who is given a small budget to improve life in his or her village. The program is a timely complement to the current child-friendly movement in which municipalities increasingly involve children and youth in community planning.

Just as Bunker Roy recognized that most development programs simply tell poor people what to do instead of letting them brainstorm their own solutions, the Children's Parliament recognizes that most of the time when people "listen" to children it's in a patronizing way and does nothing to honor their insights on their own communities. But the members of the Children's Parliament are, indeed, very active members of their communities. They oversee and report on the quality of teaching and attendance levels in the night schools. They are responsible for things like monitoring water quality in their villages.

They have been able to solve problems that have stumped the adults—one "prime minister" even figured out a way to raise enough money to pay for a piped water system in his village. co

---

■■■■■   RESOURCE

Tilonia
http://www.tilonia.org
The nonprofit retail arm of the Barefoot College, Tilonia.org is based in the United States and is dedicated to providing marketing and business development for the crafts created at the college.

If you're looking for a socially responsible way to spend your money, as well to support rural artisans, consider making a donation or buying Tilonia's beautiful block-print fabrics, handcrafted furniture, or one-of-a-kind jewelry.

The Children's Parliament teaches children at the Barefoot College about civic responsibility, a proactive way to shape the values of the next generation.

Public Health

In 1850, a white man born in the United States would not, on average, live to see forty; today, that same man could, on average, expect to live past seventy-five. There are many reasons for this increase in life expectancy—an increase that has been paralleled in other nations around the world—including less violence, better nutrition, and workplace safety laws. But the main reason is public-health medicine.

Public health is about promoting behaviors that keep us all more healthy: fighting epidemic disease, vaccinating children, spreading better hygiene practices, and so on. Taken together, these kinds of efforts have saved the lives of hundreds of millions of people who would have otherwise died very early. Those prevented deaths are the main reason why average life expectancy has increased.

Now, as we move toward peak population in an ever-more-connected world, we're realizing that we need to be even more innovative in the way we approach getting better medical care to groups who haven't had access to it before, and even more collaborative about how we prevent and control the outbreak of epidemic diseases. In the twenty-first century, public health is biological defense for the human race. AS

The Ultimate Safety Net

In this age of solar-powered water purification and networked disaster relief, the mosquito net seems laughably simple. But until we develop a vaccine for malaria, mosquito nets are still one of the most reliable ways to prevent the disease. They're also more sustainable than DDT, the chemical usually used to control mosquitoes, which has dire health and environmental consequences.

So the idea isn't to ditch the nets, but to build better ones. In Arusha, Tanzania, A to Z Textiles has created a new local industry by manufacturing the Olyset, a durable net that contains the pesticide permethrin and slowly releases it over a span of five years.

While pesticide-drenched nets aren't new, the Olyset is different from its predecessors: it's woven from durable plastic that actually contains the insecticide instead of just being coated in it. Other nets must be re-treated every four to six months, a process that is expensive, time-consuming, hazardous, and not readily available to people in very remote areas.

Best of all, the venture philanthropy outfit Acumen Fund is funding sustainable bed-net-manufacturing enterprises in the developing world. Their approach simultaneously fights malaria and creates jobs. CB & JC

Improved Nutrition

The thyroid is a butterfly-shaped gland on the front of the neck. To develop and function properly our thyroid glands need iodine, which most people receive through food and drink. But in developing countries and areas with nutrient-poor soil, access to iodine can be limited. Currently, more than 33 percent of households worldwide do not get enough iodine. In addition to hypothyroidism, iodine deficiency in pregnant women can cause cretinism or mental impairment in babies, or result in stillbirths.

American journalist Nicholas Kristof writes that "iodine is essential to brain formation for a fetus in the first trimester, and if a mother lacks iodine her child may end up mentally retarded. This is a lifelong intelligence deficit and a significant burden on poor countries, and it can be resolved very cheaply." Because salt is very inexpensive, widely available, and eaten year round, organizations like the World Health Organization, the United Nations Children's Fund, and the International Council for Control of Iodine Deficiency Disorders have been working together since 1993 to make iodization universal. Thanks to their efforts, the number of people affected by iodine deficiency has dropped from nearly 2 billion in 1990 to roughly 400 million today. For about five cents a year per person, we could end the world's most prevalent cause of brain damage. SK

Harm Reduction: Housing First

On city streets throughout the world, you'll find a handful of people whom officials call "chronic public inebriates." These people are long-time alcoholics—usually homeless—who have given up hope of ever ending their addiction. In the United States, they spend their time on the streets, or in jail cells, detox centers, or emergency rooms. The cost to the public for funding the crisis services that assist this population can be enormous. But an experimental housing project in Seattle may have found a way to provide care for homeless alcoholics while lessening the tax burden on the rest of the city's residents.

In December 2005, the Downtown Emergency Service Center (DESC) opened 1811 Eastlake, an $11.2 million, four-story housing project for seventy-five homeless, chronic alcoholics. Using the "housing first" philosophy, the DESC gave these individuals free permanent housing and services, but did not force them to give up drinking. Because sobriety is not mandatory at 1811, the residents are able to stick around through the ups and downs of battling their addictions (the center does, of course, encourage quitting and provide services toward that goal).

Initially this policy received major criticism that proved to be a barrier to funding. After one year, however, a research team from

the University of Washington showed that the philosophy made good sense: although previously the building's inhabitants were the city's most frequent users of crisis services, and therefore its most costly residents, they now tended to stay off the streets, reducing the number of arrests they experienced for illegal or disruptive behavior and the number of medical emergencies they suffered due to exposure and unchecked poor health. By giving this population permanent shelter—along with a sense of stability and support—the DESC was able to save taxpayers more than $4 million.

A project like 1811 is not just about the bottom line, however. Giving people dignity even when they're making self-destructive choices is good public health. In this case, it gives social workers more time to treat a complex illness and the recipients a more stable environment in which to heal—and the public that may be funding their recovery benefits, too. SK

Joshua Silver's Self-adjustable Spectacles

British inventor Joshua Silver is working to bring better vision to more people by ingeniously removing the need for desperately in-demand opticians. His invention, self-adjusting spectacles, relies on the principle that the fatter the lens, the more powerful it becomes. Inside the device's lenses are two clear circular sacs filled with fluid, each of which is connected to a small syringe attached to either arm of the spectacles. With little guidance, wearers can easily change their prescription by adjusting the amount of fluid in each lens. Silver hopes to distribute the spectacles to 1 billion of the world's poor by 2020. Some 30,000 pairs of his spectacles have already been distributed in fifteen countries. SK

A woman in Malawi tries on a pair of Eyejusters, glasses made with two sliding lenses that can be adjusted to correct vision with the turn of a dial. The Eyejusters' design builds on Joshua Silver's groundbreaking self-adjusting spectacles.

Networking to Eradicate Pandemics

If infectious disease and infant and maternal mortality took as many lives today as they did a century ago, the world population would be dramatically smaller. But while overpopulation contributes to a spate of global problems—health-related and otherwise—none of us would bemoan the advancements in health care that have granted us life and sustained our wellness. We owe our thanks almost entirely to the advent of scientific public-health programs. Focused largely on prevention, education, and access, the public-health system has greatly enhanced the length and quality of lives worldwide during the last century.

One of the greatest examples of a public-health initiative that changed the world is the eradication of smallpox. In the mid-1960s, it seemed outrageously optimistic to predict that smallpox could be eliminated. The World Health Organization (WHO) motioned to vaccinate virtually everyone in severely endemic regions, which at that time were mostly confined to Southeast Asia and Africa. But massive vaccination was an unrealistic goal for complete eradication—tens of millions of infants would have to be vaccinated each year. Health workers couldn't keep up.

When an outbreak erupted in Nigeria in 1966, aid workers faced a shortage of vaccines. In order to use their limited supplies efficiently, they mobilized to pay house calls to every home in the area, checking on incidences of smallpox and vaccinating only those in close proximity to ailing victims. This method of creating "circles of immunity" around existing cases proved tremendously effective. The strategy was used soon after in India, with equal rates of success. Within a matter of months, smallpox had been eliminated from a number of previously endemic regions in Africa and India. By 1974, smallpox was endemic in only five countries.

Leading the charge in this swift annihilation of smallpox was Larry Brilliant, a young American doctor who had gone to India in the early 1970s. Under the appointment of the WHO, Brilliant led a team of thousands of health workers, who made over a billion house calls throughout India and brought about a victory over smallpox in 1980.

Now polio is disappearing in a similar pattern—it's endemic in only four countries, and might be eliminated soon. Unfortunately, other diseases haven't been as responsive to the method Brilliant instituted. Smallpox was eliminated, but yaws, malaria, and yellow fever were not.

And the nightmare diseases of the future are not the childhood killers that are almost eradicated—they're new pandemics like swine flu, or H1N1. In our globally connected world, we can fly to distant lands in a matter of hours and ship cargo in a few days. This connectivity is changing the rules of proximity, allowing everything to move quickly, including viruses. Researchers say infections like H1N1 are particularly dangerous in developing countries with high populations, where local public-health officials might lack the ability and/or tools to identify human outbreaks at the earliest stages.

How do we stop pandemics? The way we stopped smallpox: early detection and early response. Our weapon in this battle is information—systems like the Global Public Health Information Network (GPHIN), which scans news sites from around the world, digesting content in seven languages, to detect illnesses that might be pandemics. Indeed, technology can in many ways replicate the labor required for all of those billions of house calls, but much more

Right: A bookstore in Weifang city, in China's Shandong Province, carries instruction manuals on how to prevent the spread of the H1N1 flu.

Opposite: Public-health campaigns like this Peruvian polio-vaccination program have been critical for saving and extending lives around the world.

quickly, cheaply, and safely. This is the power of networks.

With more people using the Internet all the time, finding ways to track human travel patterns and the spread of epidemics has become easier. But it's still a challenge. Researchers can't ask people to wear tags and tracking devices, but tracing migration patterns of goods, rather than people, offers a useful and accurate tool.

At the University of California, Santa Barbara, researchers came upon a Web site that tracks dollar bills as they circulate the globe, and used it to create a breakthrough model of human travel patterns that could greatly boost our ability to respond to emerging epidemics. Where's George? (WheresGeorge.com) allows users to enter their location and the serial numbers of their dollar bills (and other U.S. currency), and to return later to see where those dollars have gone. It's an online curiosity—not really a game, more like an information toy. The research team took this enormous wealth of data and found that human domestic travel patterns, as represented by currency, matched an unexpected, but easily understood (for mathematicians, at least) scaling and diffusion model, which will make it possible to build far more accurate simulations than we currently have of epidemic spread and response.

It's a leap in the right direction, but piggybacking on Internet games can't get us as far as we might hope. Larry Brilliant now has a new plan for preventing pandemics: the International System for Total Early Disease Detection (INSTEDD). The system will assist in promoting and protecting health worldwide by identifying disease early and treating it rapidly. Brilliant wants to build this around GPHIN, expanding

the number of sites analyzed, and expanding from seven languages to seventy, so that the information would be accessible (and free) to people around the world, not confined to a few government agencies. He plans to use satellite data and short-message service (SMS) text messages to help confirm media reports. Nowhere is the power of networked technology clearer than in this scheme, where the ability to track, communicate, and analyze information quickly could literally save billions of lives. EZ & SR

Cheap Tech Gets Results

A major barrier to receiving quality health care in the developing world is limited access to modern, high-tech tools and skilled medical experts. But a few cool gadgets are making it easier for community health workers and regular civilians to distribute vaccines and diagnose diseases.

The Aerovax administers vaccinations without the use of needles. Created by the U.S. Centers for Disease Control and Prevention for vaccines that must be rapidly deployed to large populations (like the H1N1 vaccine), the Aerovax is a handheld device that mists the vaccine in a fine spray that's inhaled. It requires a minimal amount of training to use.

If the problem is not the lack of needles, but the lack of a proper way to dispose of them, the Yellowone Needle Cap provides instant, safe storage for dirty hypodermics. The Yellowone fits over any soda can; a small hole on top is designed like any standard sharps container—needles can go into the can but cannot slide back out.

Another potential game changer is the LUCAS imager, developed by a team of scientists at UCLA's California NanoSystems Institute. It turns any off-the-shelf camera phone into a portable and affordable blood tester that can detect diseases and monitor major killers like HIV/AIDS, malaria, and leukemia. By hacking a common cell phone—the back of the phone case is opened so that a slide can fit over the camera's sensor—the team was able to create a way to take pictures of blood cells. The only thing they added to the phone was an LED light with blue light filters, which help to better expose the distinctive

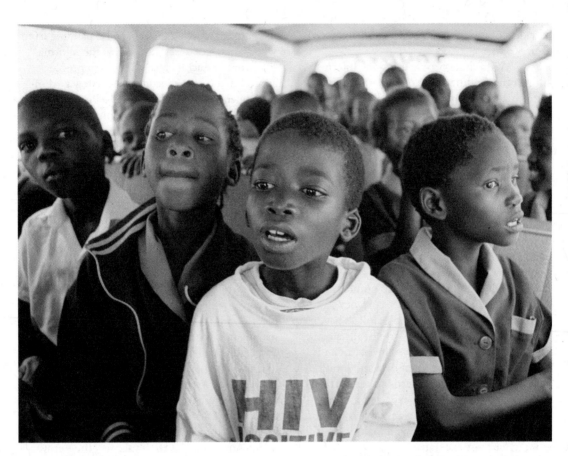

qualities of cells. Although the images still need to be sent to a technician to be analyzed using special software, this is much cheaper and more practical than maintaining a full lab in an impoverished area: basic blood-analysis machines cost tens of thousands of dollars, and between the time it takes to ship samples and analyze them, patients may wait for weeks to get results. SK & CB

Pledge 25 Club, Botswana

Youth education and outreach are crucial to curtailing AIDS around the world. But often it's difficult to get young people to participate in preventative measures—when we're young we feel invincible, and being told something is good for us in the long run can seem too nebulous to make us behave differently.

An AIDS orphan in South Africa travels with his classmates to a World AIDS Day event. Tens of millions of children have been orphaned as a result of the AIDS epidemic.

The Pledge 25 club in Botswana helps prevent young people from contracting AIDS by encouraging them to become blood donors at a young age. They promise to donate at least twenty-five times before they turn twenty-five, thus giving them incentive to stay healthy and HIV-free. The program has had phenomenal success, both in terms of reducing the rate of AIDS among young people and in turning these kids into educators and advocates, providing information and health education to their communities and spreading the Pledge 25 commitment. SR

Community Response to AIDS Orphans

If it takes a village to raise a child, what do you do when you have a whole village full of orphans? This is the case in many African nations, where HIV/AIDS has killed off almost an entire generation of adults. Even a well-established child-welfare infrastructure would buckle under the pressure of so huge a problem, and communities have had to figure out new ways to rally together and pool the limited resources they have to provide these children with a future.

Many villages have responded by forming committees to collect and distribute food and other donations to support the orphans. But these committees are more than just ad hoc non governmental organizations; some of the donated funds are put into launching new businesses, the revenue from which is then used to continue orphan-care programs that support schooling fees and other costs.

A Zambian women's group called *Kwasha Mukwenu* ("help your friend") has built on the committee approach in order to ensure that care for orphans is complete and that the children have prospects when they grow up.

Each woman in the group becomes a "caretaker parent," supervising three to five orphans. Though they don't necessarily take the orphans into their own homes, the women make sure the kids get into school and have clothing, shelter, medicine, and adult supervision. They intervene when relatives attempt to throw the orphans out, which, unfortunately, is a common practice for families with very limited means.

The women of *Kwasha Mukwenu* are entrepreneurs, too; they raise the money to provide for the children by cooking for local schools and making clothing and uniforms to sell at local shops. Many of the orphans work as apprentices, ensuring they'll have some skills with which to support themselves. The women have even become de facto outreach workers: they provide AIDS-prevention information to the community and have produced a play to educate the public about the plight of AIDS orphans.

Not only do these women pull off an immense feat, made more complex by the illness many of the orphans themselves suffer, but they stand as a powerful testament to the fact that, in the absence of traditional structures, villages still form around the fundamental duty to raise their community's children. CB

---

mHealth

▬▬▬ Cell phones are the Swiss army knives of the Global South. Texting has been used to purchase goods, transfer money, and even vote. Now mobile phones are being used to address gaps in health care: mHealth (mobile health) is helping doctors track their patients, patients manage their illnesses, and public-health campaigns reach the widest possible audience.

FrontlineSMS: Medic, for example, uses text messaging to help community health workers (CHWs) monitor endemic diseases in very rural areas and to stay in closer contact with nurses at major hospitals. The open-source program makes it possible for those nurses to send and manage large numbers of text messages from a desktop computer—the closest thing to direct communication available in areas with no Internet and spotty phone service. Nurses can use the text messages to gather news of endemic illnesses, as well as get answers to basic questions about treating common illnesses or formulating the correct dosage of a medicine. The system is effective and very low cost: the hospital can equip CHWs with any cheap cell phone that has texting capabilities; text messaging is one of the most affordable methods of communication in the Global South. The nurse at the helm doesn't even need to have access to Ethernet or DSL—the program works as long as the computer is plugged into a network-connected cell phone.

Project Masiluleke in South Africa is also using cell phones to save lives. The country has a staggeringly high rate of HIV—in some provinces up to 40 percent of the population is infected. Health professionals have their work cut out for them just keeping up with the patients who pursue care, and many more people avoid testing or treatment.

So the creators of Project Masiluleke decided to use something personal (a cell phone) to deliver a more pointed public awareness campaign. The messages, which are sent in Zulu and English and tailored in content to appeal to specific groups (teens, for example), urge the recipient to contact a government-funded call center for information on free testing and counseling. Because of the ubiquity of cell phones, these messages reach nearly the entire adult and adolescent population of the country. During the first two years, calls to the national hotline in Johannesburg jumped 300 percent.

Project Masiluleke is adding other mHealth programs to its repertoire. Its TxtAlert service sends appointment reminders to people on antiretroviral treatments. Health care workers have seen that patients who regularly show up for their checkups are more likely to adhere to their treatment regimens. CB

Disease Eradication=Hope

▬▬▬   The parasitic disease dracunculiasis, more commonly known as guinea worm disease, is painful to even describe. If you're unlucky enough to ingest water fleas infected with drancunculus larvae, you may end up with adult guinea worms growing in your body tissue. You won't know you're infected until the thin, thread-like worms try to leave your body through a small blister on your arm or leg. Then, it can take up to a month to pull the now three-foot-long parasite out through this blister. The pain is excruciating.

In 1986, approximately 3.5 million cases a year were reported in twenty countries. But according to the Carter Center, a health organization working to eliminate the disease, we could see the end of dracunculiasis in the next few years. Since humans are the parasite's only host, complete eradication is possible by modifying human behavior. The Carter Center has worked for the past twenty years to identify and educate affected populations, distribute water filters, treat ponds, and dig deep-bore wells. Today, reported cases of guinea worm are down 99 percent from 1986. In 2010 reports estimated only 3,500 cases in Sudan, Ghana, Mali, and Ethiopia.

Why does the guinea worm deserve a mention when something like mHealth is more the rage? Because it's an example of how far the most basic interventions like building better water filters and providing community outreach and education can go. And as Ethan Zuckerman noted when he wrote about the eradication of this disease, "Sometimes, especially on a dark day, it's a good idea to reflect on the battles we're winning, and on the groups of people fighting them." SK

Data Collection for Doctors

▬▬▬   Although the Global North and the Global South don't always share the same public-health concerns, there's one area in which they overlap: the need for simple, easily shared digital data-collection systems.

In the Global South, where large populations live in rural areas with no infrastructure, maintaining national or even regional databases often just isn't feasible—such ventures require access to the Internet, reliable computers, and specialized software—all of which are too pricey for many developing nations.

For this reason, the best solutions for the Global South tend to combine open-source principles with cell phones or other handheld mobile devices. CommCare, a project from Vikram Kumar and Jonathan Jackson's Dimagi organization, which has been developing digital health technologies in the South for years, uses low-cost mobile phones to help community health workers (CHWs) track their patients. A simple history for each client and data from every visit is sent to a centralized server called CommCareHQ as soon as the CHW enters network coverage. CommCareHQ relays information in real-time to supervisors, sends out alerts and reports to managers, and can be linked to information systems in public-health ministries to help researchers spot patterns of disease.

EpiSurveyor, created by physician and epidemiologist Joel Selanikio, also streamlines data collection in rural areas of the Global South. The free software package works on many handheld mobile devices. Health workers can easily design health surveys and know that the information they collect is available immediately for study and sharing—traditional paper-based systems require manual data entry that can delay the analysis and publishing of results for up to a year. EpiSurveyor has been instrumental in organizing and tracking the highly successful Measles Initiative, which since 2001 has vaccinated 4.3 million children.

In the Global North, the adoption of widespread digital sharing has been incredibly slow. The U.S. Centers for Disease Control and Prevention (CDC), for example, still use a paper-based system for record tracking. (In this way, it actually lags behind the Chinese CDC, which uses a digital system that tracks daily records from 16,000 hospitals.) Not jumping on the digital-revolution bandwagon is costing the U.S. health-care industry billions of dollars a year.

There are plenty of tech companies in the North working on health-records software, but so far these have all been proprietary, which is a barrier for small practices and cash-strapped larger institutions alike. When physician Jay Parkinson started Hello Health, a small New York City practice that attempts to streamline and relocalize health care, he had to design his own software to make the business model work. The cornerstone of Hello Health's approach is making health care easy—patients can receive initial consultations on non-life-threatening ailments via text messaging or video chat. (For example, if you cut your finger while cooking, your doctor can advise you on whether you can bandage it up yourself or whether you need stitches. The first diagnosis could prevent you from spending hours and hundreds of dollars on a trip to the emergency room.) Parkinson not only needed a way to manage digital records (including charts and films), he needed an interface that supported video chats, online appointment scheduling, and a mechanism for patients to rate the doctors in the network. The browser-based software he created with Canadian developer Myca is available free to any doctor who wants to try the Hello Health model (they do share a small percentage of revenue with the company). CB

Health-data Rights

One of the most frightening and frustrating things about being treated for an illness is simply being treated like a patient—a passive role in which a sometimes aloof doctor runs tests, plays with meds, and plans a course of action without revealing many details. Although patients have the theoretical right to review any data a doctor collects in the course of treatment, gaining access to this information is difficult. And although doctors in some nations are slightly better at patient relations, globally we have resigned ourselves to the idea that as patients we are allowed only so much participation in the management of our own health.

The need to democratize medical knowledge and empower patients has inspired a diverse group of people—physicians, patients, journalists, medical-rights activists, and Access to Knowledge

(A2K) advocates—to draft a Declaration of Health Data Rights, which states:

> We, the people:
> Have the right to our own health data
> Have the right to know the source of each health data element
> Have the right to take possession of a complete copy of our individual health data, without delay, at minimal or no cost; If data exist in computable form, they must be made available in that form
> Have the right to share our health data with others as we see fit
> These principles express basic human rights as well as essential elements of health care that is participatory, appropriate and in the interests of each patient. No law or policy should abridge these rights.

This declaration is an important new driver for the participatory-medicine movement, which has been gaining steam for nearly a decade and describes a proactive approach to wellness in which the doctor-patient relationship is seen as less paternalistic and more collaborative. In 2009, the movement advanced its cause with the launch of its own peer-reviewed journal. *The Journal of Participatory Medicine* is published exclusively online using Open Journal Systems, an open-source publishing platform developed by the Public Knowledge Project. It collects research papers, case studies, and patient testimonials that explore the benefits and controversies associated with adopting a participatory approach to health care, and particularly the treatment of chronic illness. JVL & CB

HealthStore

HealthStore is a Kenyan franchise model for delivering pharmaceuticals to rural areas; it is owned and operated by nurses and gives poor, rural communities access to much-needed medicines. The medicines themselves aren't innovative (malaria meds, antidiarrheals, and so on); the business model is. Recognizing that ineffective distribution systems often prevent essential medicines from reaching communities that need them, HealthStore established its network of franchises

to reach far-flung locales while simultaneously providing living incomes for the nurse-owners.

Combining a nonprofit central franchisor with a for-profit franchise network is part of the innovation; there is no incentive for the Health-Store Foundation to "cheat" the franchisees. Its job is to set the franchisees up for success, and it does this through relationships with the government, a nonprofit drug distributor, regional support offices, and ongoing training programs. Not only do the entrepreneurs get the necessary support to earn a sustainable income, but they also gain the satisfaction of managing their own business without handouts. At the same time, franchisees are closely monitored by HealthStore to ensure compliance with franchise regulations; applying strict franchise standards not unlike those used in Western fast-food chains is another key element of the venture's success.

Ultimately, the local entrepreneurs are empowered to succeed in an environment where they are surrounded by poverty and despair. The communities in which they operate benefit because they are given access to essential, affordable medicine—through a nurse-owner whose very success is a source of inspiration. RK

Partners in Health

■■■■■ The world has no shortage of NGOs dedicated to combating public health crises. The problem is that good ideas generated in the Global North often fall flat in the Global South. Organizations that manage to combine good intentions with strong implementation are rare.

Boston-based Partners in Health (PIH) is one organization that is hitting it out of the park. PIH's health-care model is holistic: it treats disease *and* poverty. PIH employs local people as community health workers who make home visits; they make sure patients are taking their medications and are generally well. Not only does this serve as a form of preventive care, it also provides jobs and generally enriches the community with healthier

Public-health education programs are vital for fighting HIV/AIDS and providing family-planning services, Nairobi, Kenya.

people. In Rwanda, where PIH works with the local government to provide universal health care, this approach has yielded some record-breaking results: after two years of treatment, 93 percent of HIV patients are still taking their medications and, as a result, have suppressed viral loads. (In most Western countries, when patients are simply given a monthly prescription and a set of instructions, only 60 percent of them follow their regimen.)

Better yet, PIH has managed to build a true partnership with the government—the model is being scaled up from one district to the entire national health-care system—and Rwandan doctors and health professionals are now running insurance schemes, dispensaries, and clinics with increasingly less help from PIH. The combination of healthy people and available jobs (from PIH and elsewhere) forms a virtuous spiral: in 2008, when the rest of the world was in a state of economic collapse, the Rwandan economy grew by 11 percent. KD

■■■■■   RESOURCES

Institute for OneWorld Health
http://www.oneworldhealth.org
The only nonprofit pharmaceutical company in the world, the Institute for OneWorld Health works from the premise that "those of us with the ability to provide life-saving vaccines and medications to the world's least fortunate—and to conduct research and develop new medicines—should do everything we can." By securing donated intellectual property and identifying the most promising drug and vaccine candidates, the institute is effectively working to develop safe and affordable medicines for the developing world.

PATH.org
If we know anyone who's lost a baby, we know what a devastating loss it is. But in the Global North, infant mortality is fairly rare. That's not true in many developing countries, where the rate of infant mortality is staggering: 4 million babies die annually, most of them from preventable causes. Vaccines, medical supplies, and early parent education could save a huge percentage of these children. The missing pieces? Funding and outreach.

PATH, an international nonprofit public-health organization, focuses entirely on bringing these missing pieces together, particularly in African nations. At this writing, PATH is working on distributing vaccinations and developing water-purification technologies that could help prevent diarrheal diseases, treatable infections that kill nearly five thousand young children in the Global South per day.

Activmob

http://www.activmob.com
Making fitness about having fun with friends, rather than pulse rates and personal bests, is one of the best ways to get more people off the couch. One idea inspiring such movement is the Activmob concept, which centers around getting people to sign up for some physical activity they already like to do and then hooking them up with a group of friends or neighbors who share their enthusiasm. In the pilot project in Kent, England, the Kent County Council in cooperation with other local groups created a Web site to connect participants, devised a system to track their progress, and launched a magazine. A5

Where There Is No Doctor: A Village Health Care Handbook by Jane Maxwell, Carol Thurman, and David Werner (Hesperian Foundation, 1992)
The success of the health care handbook *Where There is No Doctor* has been astonishing. Published in 1982, the original edition was written in Spanish as *Donde No Hay Doctor*. More than a million copies have been sold since, making it one of the most trusted information sources for primary health-care workers around the world. New editions are now available in one hundred languages, providing village health-care workers with information on how to prevent, recognize, and treat common illnesses such as diarrhea, malaria, and ringworm. Recent editions also cover health problems related to childbirth and drug addiction, AIDS, and dengue fever. The book is available for download at http://www.hesperian.org/publications_download.php. 5K

Land Mines

▬▬▬ Land mines are unquestionably some of the most evil devices created in the twentieth century. Deadly and cheap (they cost as little as three dollars to make), they have been scattered extensively throughout war zones around the world. The U.S. Department of State reports that at least 45 million are still out there in the ground, waiting for someone to step on them. Worldwide, in 2008 alone 5,197 people were killed by land mines, according to the International Campaign to Ban Landmines.

The carnage land mines cause reflects only a part of the harm they do. Because land mines were generally placed where people were most likely to walk, farmland that might otherwise be feeding hungry people is left unplowed. Roads and trails that might otherwise link villages and allow wealth-building trade go untraveled. Towns that might otherwise shelter people have been abandoned.

Removing buried land mines is incredibly difficult, and can cost up to a thousand dollars per mine when done by trained professionals. In addition, because land mines are mostly made of plastic now, they cannot be found with metal detectors. Some types can be found with trained animals, but the most widely used technique for removing them is for demining experts to crawl along on their bellies poking at the ground ahead of them with a pole. The most widely adopted demining innovation of the last decade? A better pole.

According to the United Nations, at current rates, it will take more than a thousand years and $33 billion to clear all the mines that have already been deployed. But this is one war that we can win: according to the 2009 Landmine Monitor Report, more than 2 million land mines have been cleared in the past decade. Victories both large and small have come from a combination of grassroots awareness and funding campaigns and worldchanging innovations. And with many more millions of mines to clear, we can use as many of the latter as possible. AS

Miss Landmine

████ It's believed that women make up a minority of land-mine victims. But, according to the United Nations Mine Action Service, women disabled by land mines are less likely than men to receive emergency care in the immediate aftermath of a land-mine blast, and a smaller proportion of women receive mobility aid, such as artificial limbs, after being injured. In addition, women are more likely to have spouses who want an immediate divorce. Poverty soon follows, especially if a woman has children.

The Miss Landmine contest, one of the many campaigns to raise global awareness of land mines, took place in Angola in 2008 and in Cambodia in 2009. Besides simply calling attention to female land-mine victims, the contest challenges a number of stereotypes: first, the idea that a woman who has been disfigured or is missing a limb can't be a useful member of society, and second, that only women without flaws or disabilities can be beautiful.

Miss Landmine contestants are all women who have lost a leg or part of a leg to a land mine; the award for winning is a prosthetic leg from a leading orthopedic clinic in Norway. Unlike the contestants in a typical beauty pageant, the Miss Landmine entrants are every shape, age, and size. Each contestant works collaboratively with contest organizers to raise awareness of the global land-mine threat, receiving a stipend of U.S.$200 for each day she works on the project. According to contest organizer Morten Traavik,

many of the contestants have been offered employment by land mine–aid organizations. All of the women have ambitious goals and aspirations far beyond being crowned a beauty queen. ECB

Spider Boot

████ What's the greatest danger to a deminer's legs? Not shrapnel, but shock waves. Even heavy-duty demining boots can't withstand shock waves directly underfoot. To address this problem, Worrell, a Minneapolis-based industrial design firm, created a slip-on platform called the Spider Boot. The "boot" looks like a ski binding attached to the splayed legs of an insect, and it puts an extra 5.6 inches between the deminer and the ground. Each boot has four stilts that disperse the energy from shock waves—the prongs break off immediately after the blast so that a deminer's leg does not have to bear the impact.

According to Worrell, the boot provides four to five times the protection of conventional boots. The Spider Boot is one-size-fits-all and slips on over standard demining boots. It's designed to work well on a variety of terrains, giving the wearer enough flexibility and stability to step over obstacles, walk through tall grass, or even carry casualties. CB

HeroRats

████ Rats are already the unsung heroes of modern science—it's tough to find a medical, physiological, or sociological experiment that doesn't involve them. But Bart Weetjens is making

Removing land mines is a costly, slow, and dangerous process. Halo Trust trains deminers in Kabul, Afghanistan, 2005.

their heroics much more visible by training them to detect land mines.

Inspired by land mine–awareness campaigns, the Belgian-born director of the HeroRats program quit his job as a product designer to concentrate on finding affordable, location-appropriate demining solutions for African nations. Animals were a natural area of study, as dogs have long been used as mine detectors. However, canine pilot programs on the continent had failed—the dogs, bred and trained mainly in Northern Europe, could not adapt quickly to the different climate and succumbed to heat-related illnesses and parasitic infections.

After reading an article about scientists who decades earlier had trained gerbils to find explosives, Weetjens concluded that rats might be the most suitable substitute for dogs. Rats have many of the same characteristics—smart, superb sense of smell, cheap to keep, easy to train—but unlike dogs, they are more resilient in extreme climates, and they form less intense emotional bonds with trainers, which means they are happy to work with a variety of people.

To ensure his program wouldn't have to rely on foreign resources or the importing of animals from developed nations, Weetjens searched for an indigenous rat. He settled on the giant pouched rat (which *is* rather large—the size of a small cat), a species found throughout the African continent. After three years of breeding and training, Weetjens had produced a pack of highly intelligent rats with a knack for finding explosives.

The rats have done most of their field-work in Mozambique. A minefield is explored in segments: First, corridors around a segment are cleared using metal detectors so that trainers have safe places to walk while the rats search. Several rats, on harnesses and leashes, fan out over the area; if they find a mine, they start to scratch at the dirt to alert the trainer. Rats are not heavy enough to set off the mines, so this little bit of movement poses no danger to the animals or their trainers. The mines are mapped and later cleared en masse. In 2009 the hero rats helped to clear a minefield near the town of Mabalane, which in turn cleared the last obstacle to a major development project: connecting the town of 10,000 to the national grid.

According to APOPO, the parent organization for the HeroRats project, on average, it takes a rat half an hour to search an 1,100-square-foot (100-square-meter) segment. Rats cover up to 2,200 square feet per day, whereas a human with metal-detection equipment could only cover about 550 square feet. And the solution is definitely affordable: through HeroRat.org you can see pictures of this elite squad and sponsor a rat for only five euros per month. CB

Left: A HeroRat, trained to detect explosives, sniffs the ground for signs of unexploded land mines.
Opposite: LED lamps designed by the Light Up the World Foundation are distributed in Nepal, Sri Lanka, India, and twenty-three other countries.

Energy in the Global South

Across one-third of the planet, nightfall still brings darkness; roughly 1.6 billion people worldwide live without electricity. When they want to see at night, they burn things: wood, dung, kerosene, candles. Using fire for light is not only incredibly inefficient (only about 0.1 percent of the fuel energy becomes light), it's also dangerous and ecologically disastrous.

A child reading for an evening by the light of a kerosene lamp breathes in fumes equivalent to smoking two packs of cigarettes, according to a World Bank report. Gathering firewood for fuel is time-consuming for rural people, and buying it is expensive for urban people living in poverty. The smoke from all those fires pollutes the air and contributes to climate change. In every way, being forced to rely on fire to cook, heat, and see hurts both poor communities and the planet.

But better alternatives exist. Better stoves, better lights, better ways of heating homes—these solutions promise to transform life for hundreds of millions of people. JJF & AS

Light to Live By

How can poor people get the light they need to study, work, and socialize at night? The Light Up the World Foundation has an answer. The foundation's breakthrough realization is that a single white light-emitting diode (white LED), run off a battery powered by a solar panel, gives off enough light to read by. Light-emitting diodes can light a hundred homes with the energy it takes to illuminate a single hundred-watt incandescent bulb. They are also cheap, rugged, and long lasting; they use direct current; and the lamps are increasingly easy to manufacture in the developing world. Best of all, the efficiency of LEDs has so far followed Moore's Law, doubling roughly every eighteen months. Based on pilot projects in India, Sri Lanka, Nepal, and twenty-three other countries, there's every reason to hope that tiny diodes will soon be nestled in thatch, attached to corrugated sheet metal, and taped to cinder blocks in billions of homes around the world.

D.light Design has helped more than 1 million people in India and Africa with its Kiran solar lantern. The lantern, costing roughly ten dollars, is four times brighter than a kerosene lamp, and shines for nearly eight hours before it must be recharged. It uses LEDs, so there are no bulbs to replace, and the solar panel is built in, making the lantern both rugged and easy to charge. JJF & AS

Cooking in the Developing World

More than half of the world's population cooks using biofuels: wood, charcoal, dung, or crop waste. The demand for wood stoves

contributes to deforestation. The smoke they produce leads to respiratory disease, especially in children. Worldwide, cooking-related indoor air pollution kills more people than cigarettes do, according to the British NGO Practical Action's 2004 report "Smoke: The Killer in the Kitchen." Beyond creating indoor air pollution, inefficient cookstoves emit black carbon (particulates that create the "brown clouds" of pollution over Eurasia), and thereby contribute to two major problems: urban air pollution and climate change. Black carbon is under increasing scrutiny because it interferes with the earth's natural albedo [see Green Building, p. 130] when it falls from the atmosphere and darkens snow and ice, which otherwise would reflect solar energy back out into space.

Building a better stove reduces the cost of cooking, improves the health of the people who cook, and benefits the environment by using resources more efficiently. But it's harder than you'd think: not only does a stove need to be efficient, but it also needs to be easy to manufacture, repair, and use, and—to a person with limited means—worth the substantial investment. Here are a few success stories:

The Jiko: According to a report by Daniel M. Kammen, director of the Renewable and Appropriate Energy Lab at UC Berkeley, in Kenya, the traditional metal stove delivers only 10–20 percent of a fire's heat to a cooking pot; an open fire is even less efficient. The Jiko ("stove" in Swahili), the latest cooking innovation in the country, has a ceramic lining within a metal casing. Kammen says this structure helps direct 25–40 percent of the fire's heat to the pot, which saves a household 1,300 pounds (590 kilograms) of fuel, or about $65 per year. Many women, the primary purchasers of fuel, have been able to reinvest these savings into schooling for their children or into small businesses, improving their prospects of financial independence. Nearly 1 million Kenyan households now cook with the ceramic Jiko stove.

The Rocket: The elbow-shaped Rocket stove, used in over twenty countries from Honduras to Zaire, burns fuel and conducts heat to pots more efficiently—and burns only the ends of sticks in the process. A basic Rocket stove can be built with found materials; the organization behind this innovation, the Aprovecho Research Center, provides do-it-yourselfers with information on how to design the best stove. They've also come up with larger, built-in designs for the home, such as the Estufa Justa, which has two burners and vents all its smoke outdoors.

The Henya: Richard Njagu, a Kenyan inventor and entrepreneur, combined the best of the Jiko and Rocket stoves into the Henya Stove, an attractive, efficient, and inexpensive stove that's designed and manufactured locally. Like the Rocket, the Henya is elbow-shaped—fuel is fed in from the side, and exhaust gases are captured to help produce heat. Like the Jiko, the Henya contains a liner, made from local clay, that contributes to the stove's efficiency by preventing heat from leaking out the sides. JJF & EZ

SolSource 3-in-1

Using a solar oven is like cooking with a greenhouse. By concentrating sunlight, it provides slow simmering, baking, and roasting—on a sunny day, beans, rice, stews, and the like will be fully cooked within two to five hours. Solar ovens create no toxic smoke and use no fuel but sunlight, saving not only time but money; some households using the technology have cut their fuel costs in half.

But the initial cost of a solar oven is often too high for poor rural users, who also require a wood cookstove for rainy days. Some designers are starting to address this problem, as well as figure out how to manufacture solar ovens that are appropriate to the communities they serve.

The SolSource 3-in-1, for example, targets the specific needs of Himalayan villagers. The satellite dish–shaped cooker, developed by the U.S.-based nonprofit One Earth Designs, is elegant in its simplicity. Nomadic tent material is stretched across a bamboo frame and lined with reflective film, concentrating sunlight from a large area inward toward a focal point at the center. There,

Buddhist monks carry solar panels to their monastery in a remote Himalayan village, Ladakh, India.

the user can place one of the following modules: a pot stand for cooking; a thermoelectric device for generating electricity (at a lower cost than a photovoltaic panel); a heat module for heating the home; a solar water disinfector for treating drinking water; or a thermal battery for cooking after dark. These interchangeable parts are each about the size of a laptop computer, and the main platform is easily folded and disassembled for portability.

The SolSource generates enough heat at its focal point to bring a kettle of water to boil in five to seven minutes—about the same amount of time as conventional gas stoves in homes through-out the developed world. The heat module generates enough heat to warm the home, and can create and store about fifteen watt hours of electricity, or enough to power the lights for about seven hours.

The designers worked with Himalayan university students to collect direct feedback from villagers across the region to inform the design of the SolSource 3-in-1. Their input on the design was particularly important, because although the villagers were familiar with solar cookstoves intro-duced throughout the region via various govern-ment and NGO initiatives, these devices weren't fulfilling the specific needs of these nomadic communities.

Many of the other available stoves were made from concrete and glass components, both of which are easily broken during distribution and everyday use—not ideal for rural communities that lack the expertise and tools to repair broken devices. Because they can weigh as much as 210 pounds (95 kilograms) and aren't easily portable, the other stoves hinder the villagers' traditional

lifestyles. And because those stoves were designed for cooking only, the villagers still relied on biomass burning to heat their homes, a need that accounts for most of the region's fuel use.

The SolSource 3-in-1, on the other hand, not only replaces the traditional biomass-burning stove for cooking, heating, and lighting the home, but does so with a unique design that takes into account local needs and materials. In addition, its manufacture and distribution could provide a new economic future for communities in transition from agricultural to manufacturing economies. JVL

The Pot-in-Pot Refrigerator

How do you keep food from spoiling when you don't have access to ice or electricity for a refrigerator? Millions of people still simply try to eat their food before it goes bad, which keeps them gathering food day-to-day and often makes them sick. But one solution is simple enough and cheap enough for anyone to afford: thermodynam-ics. When moisture on a surface evaporates, it sucks up heat, causing that surface's temperature to drop. This is how most animals, including people, keep themselves cool.

Mohammed Bah Abba of Nigeria invented a kind of refrigerator that uses this principle, the Pot-in-Pot. As the name suggests, the refrigerator is made up of two clay pots—with water-soaked sand in between. The outer pot is porous, so the water between the pots slowly soaks through, and evaporates on the outside. This keeps the inner pot cool, preserving the food inside. The impact on Nigerians' lives has been substantial. The Pot-in-Pot can keep foods like tomatoes and

peppers fresh for three weeks, which means that farmers have been able to store food for later sale. Beyond food freshness, the Pot-in-Pot has had economic and social benefits for the community: Because they have a place to keep inventory fresh, married women have been able to start side businesses selling food from their homes, helping them gain financial independence. Because girls no longer have to spend their days selling food before it spoils, female school enrollment has increased. And because the Pot-in-Pot is locally manufactured, the local pottery industry is being revived, which is crucial in a region with a high unemployment rate. JJF

The Sun Shines for All

The World Bank estimates that in Brazil, 20 million citizens still lack power, but Fabio Rosa, a social entrepreneur, has started to bring solar energy to rural communities across the country.

Rosa knew that poor Brazilians could not afford to rig solar-power systems on their own. He felt that, instead, people should be able to pay for solar electricity as they used it. Rosa conducted a market survey and discovered that the average impoverished Brazilian spent about thirteen dollars per month on energy needs, mostly on candles, batteries, and kerosene. So he started renting out solar panels and lighting fixtures at a price of thirteen dollars per month— it's affordable, it's a sound business, and Rosa's initial investment will be repaid in four years.

Rosa's rental business is called the Sun Shines for All. He has also created a nonprofit organization, the Institute for Development of Natural Energy and Sustainability, to deliver electricity and services at subsidized rates to those very poor families who spend less than ten dollars per month on their energy needs. He has built up a network of electricians to install and maintain the solar-electric systems. He's still getting his efforts

off the ground, but so far two hundred homes are up and running on solar power.

Micro-hydro in Nepal

In Nepal, only about 10 percent of the population is on the grid. The rest of the population goes without power, unless they produce their own. However, the mountainous country has plenty of fast-running streams, fantastic sources of energy. Small-scale water-power operations can only provide energy to limited areas, but this type of power is the cleanest, cheapest, and most practical form of energy available in those locations. In most remote Nepalese villages, electricity from water power is even cheaper than buying batteries.

Waterwheels have been used in Nepal for centuries to mill grain and dehull rice, just as the waterwheels of preindustrial Europe were. But now some of these wheels are being retrofitted with generators to provide electricity, too. In some places, entirely new generators are being installed. These systems are called micro-hydro systems, because they are generally capable of powering only a few houses or a small village, and they can be plopped down in a river without significantly affecting its flow, banks, or general ecosystem, as a large hydroelectric dam would. JJF

Opposite, left: Solar cooker in use, Uganda.
Opposite, right: Villagers making Pot-in-Pot refrigerators.
Right: Micro-hydro systems can make sense in remote places like this agricultural cooperative in Cashel Valley, Zimbabwe.

Food Justice

Seeking out organic foods, signing up for CSAs, avoiding the fish species on endangered lists—all of these actions may send ripples through the food community, and support growers and merchants who are committed to creating a sustainable food system. But if our advocacy ends once we get in the checkout line, we're not going to see such a system anytime soon.

The future of food advocacy, in which our personal choices about food tie in with the greater needs of our communities, revolves around the concept of food justice. Food justice means many things: It means that everyone in a community is fed, and fed well with high-quality food free of harmful substances. It means that the act of growing food is sustainable and just, with fair wages and working conditions for growers. It means that the natural resources needed to grow food everywhere—not just on designated industrial farming land—have not been co-opted by a few private interests. And, most importantly, it means that all the good food that's being grown is distributed evenly so that "food deserts" don't appear in the middle of prosperous cities and the citizens of the Global South's agricultural nations don't starve while their crops are feeding the Global North.

Creating equal access to the world's bounty is a central concern, one we must address as we urbanize the planet. Some of the worst examples of inequitable distribution are in our cities, where poor neighborhoods often have nothing that resembles a supermarket and no immediate access to reasonably priced, healthy foods.

Turning brick and asphalt into urban farms, using cooking lessons to create community unity, finding ways to feed the world's poor that go beyond basic charity, and working to insulate the world's farmers from risks related to climate change—all of these efforts in some way further the idea of food justice. CB

Fertilizing Urban Food Deserts

The urban "food desert," a neighborhood in which residents typically must travel twice as far to reach the closest supermarket or other mainstream grocer as people in better-appointed neighborhoods, is not just a problem of social or economic justice; it's about public health as well. Faced with a long trek to stock the kitchen with fresh food, many residents of food deserts instead rely on "fringe" retailers—convenience stores, liquor stores, gas stations, and drug stores—to provide basic food items. The result is a serious nutrition gap between those who live in areas of plenty and those who lack access to the basics. And poor nutrition leads to poor health and premature death.

In Detroit, Michigan, for example, more than half of the city's thousand-plus food retailers are fringe locations that offer little or nothing in the way of fresh or healthy food. According to a study commissioned by La Salle Bank, more than half a million Detroit residents—slightly more than half of the city's population—live without easy access to fresh, affordable food. La Salle's survey found that for every one hundred people living in the neighborhoods with the least access to healthy food, a collective sixty-four years of life were lost because of ill health caused by poor nutrition. Shorter life spans due to diabetes, cardiovascular disease, hypertension, and other diet-related diseases held true even after adjusting for racial and socioeconomic factors.

One possible way to cut the high rates of disease in food deserts is an outright ban on fast-food restaurants, which tend to proliferate in areas where other food options are limited. But to truly improve public health, such a move needs to be coupled with creating easy access to healthy food. Financial incentives to supermarkets encourage them to move into food deserts, and can also facilitate economic renewal: according to one study, every dollar spent on supermarket construction and operations generates $1.50 in economic activity. Incentives for neighborhood farmers' markets—such as those offered in blighted areas by the Project for Public Spaces—can help these healthy food purveyors get started in communities where they traditionally have not thrived, and keep going long enough to establish themselves. ECB

Crop Insurance

▬▬▬ For most small farmers one bad crop can mean bankruptcy; in poor communities "bankruptcy" can mean starvation. And with climate change increasing the probability of crop-ruining phenomena like droughts and ill-timed downpours, farming in the South seems like a losing proposition from the start. Climate leaders are therefore looking seriously at microinsurance for farmers—essentially weather-based insurance—as a way to help safeguard the South from catastrophic loss of local food supplies and valuable exports.

A farmer can purchase crop insurance for one very low premium—in most current schemes, the premium is tacked onto the standard microloan taken by the farmer to purchase seeds and equipment. If something like a drought or flood ruins a crop, the policy pays enough to keep the farmer in business and able to support his or her family.

Crop insurance isn't just about catastrophe, however. It has the potential to help build resilience in floundering communities, as the safety net it provides gives farmers time to adapt to the changing climate instead of failing the first time age-old weather patterns go haywire. And it will likely grow the number of climate-adaptation projects and resources—sponsored by the insurers who now have a stake in whether crops succeed or fail. CB

Harvesting Fallen Fruit

▬▬▬ Is it okay to reap what others have ignored? Most cities have plentiful fruit and nut trees scattered within their borders, many of which are never fully harvested—or not harvested at all. Most of us are hesitant to take fruit from a tree that's not in our own yard, but in many cities all fruit growing on branches that overhang public property is considered free for the taking, even if the trunk of that tree is in private domain.

No community should watch edible fruit rot on its sidewalks; several organizations are working to ensure that fallen fruit or "public fruit" is collected and enjoyed.

Los Angeles–based Fallen Fruit is a leader in the movement, composing the first manifesto calling for the picking and planting of public fruit trees. Naturally, art poured forth from the idea, including some outstanding photography and a digital mapping system to track the locations and ripening cycles of fruit trees in LA neighborhoods. The mapping caught on and community members joined in, planning late-night fruit-harvesting walks and widening the radius of the mapped regions. And the concept of mapping urban foraging spots has caught on in many other U.S. cities as well. The already well-populated Google map from Portland, Oregon's Urban Edibles is tagged with notes like, "Whole line of fig trees in the empty lot across from Don Pancho's Mexican Restaurant."

Seattle's Solid Ground association, which helps nearly 33,000 families combat poverty every year, takes a more organized approach to public fruit harvesting. Their Community Fruit Tree Harvest sends Solid Ground volunteers to pick surplus fruit from residential trees (with owners' permission), and then distribute the fresh produce to grateful food banks, meal programs, and senior centers. The harvest is part of Solid Ground's larger Lettuce Link program, which provides fresh, locally grown fruits and vegetables to the people who need them most through a comprehensive network of gardening, education, and donation systems. Solid Ground's system not only addresses the nutritional needs of the poor, but also stops would-be resources like fallen fruit from becoming garbage. SR & JVL

People's Grocery

▬▬▬ In West Oakland, California, one supermarket serves 25,000 residents, and most of those residents don't have the means to get themselves to that grocery. On the other hand, liquor and convenience stores dot nearly every corner, and although the prices there are drastically higher and the quality significantly lower than at the market, most West Oakland residents buy a lot of their food from these corner stores. The other supply line for food in the area comes from government-subsidized assistance programs like WIC (the Special Supplemental Nutrition Program for Women, Infants, and Children), which offer calorically efficient but nutritionally deficient foods, consisting mostly of dairy products, reconstituted juices, and refined starches.

In response, the People's Grocery has arrived on the streets. Initiated by young people, contained in a mobile unit, and armed with hip-hop beats to draw attention, the People's Grocery brings a traveling larder of fresh, organic foods, local produce, and health education seasoned with street cred to a population long underserved. In addition to the mobile mart, the People's Grocery offers a modified CSA for low-income residents of West Oakland. A box of produce that contains enough to feed a family of four costs only twelve dollars per week and can be purchased using government food-assistance programs. Residents of higher-income areas can buy subscriptions for twenty-four dollars per week (still cheaper than most CSAs), which subsidizes the discounts for West Oakland residents. At this writing, People's Grocery was developing two urban farm plots in West Oakland.

People's Grocery wants food justice. In close collaboration with the community they serve, the organizers work to establish a local food system and economy, making healthy food accessible as a basic human right. The organization promotes youth entrepreneurship, social enterprise, and grassroots organizing to help community members achieve a stronger sense of self-reliance and local sustainability. People's Grocery has quickly become a positive force in the local community, and a model for similar programs now sprouting around the country (at least fifty are reported to be in the works today). SR

Community Kitchens

▬▬▬   Community kitchens promote local food security, not only by ensuring that participants have access to affordable food, but also by completing the picture—giving people the time, equipment, guidance, and assistance necessary to prepare healthy meals in a busy world.

Here's how the community kitchen works: First, a community of people plans a menu. They work together, or elect an organizer, to procure food. Sometimes the members themselves simply divide the cost, enjoying the savings that come with purchasing food staples in bulk. Sometimes the group gathers donations, or makes use of food from local food banks or similar institutions. No matter where the food comes from, however, one important detail sets the community kitchen apart from soup kitchens or other feeding programs: the practice of preparing and sharing food communally. The people who will eat the food are the same people who help to cook it, and by those rules all participants are equal.

The Rainier Valley Community Kitchen in Seattle meets monthly to cook a variety of freezer-friendly dishes in massive quantities, so that participants, who pay twenty-five dollars

apiece (if they can) to attend, take home four or five servings of each dish. This particular community kitchen is sponsored by the Seattle-based co-op PCC Natural Markets, which allows kitchen organizers to purchase top-quality (and often organic) ingredients from the market at cost.

The dozen or so people who frequent the Rainier Valley kitchen describe incentives that transcend economics. People like to cook together, and they enjoy turning cooking into a learning experience, whether their aim is to brush up on basic cooking skills, trade recipes, or get advice for healthy menu planning. When your hands are busy, discussions seem to flow more easily, even among relative strangers.

"I think it's an entry point for community organizing," says Diane Collis, manager of Fresh Choice Kitchens, the community kitchen program of the Greater Vancouver (BC) Food Bank Society. "We can talk about politics and nutrition, what doctor did you use when your kid was sick—all sorts of things go on in community kitchens that aren't about cooking. It's about social support."

Most of British Columbia's many community kitchens offer special community-outreach programs like teaching new immigrants about English and Canadian culture through food, or building nutrition skills to manage chronic diseases like diabetes. Collis has even seen Vancouver agencies use the community kitchen model for job training, allowing participants to earn their food-safe certifications while cooking for local day-care programs, and sending them on to jobs in cafés, restaurants, and institutions.

Community kitchens are resilience-building institutions, contributing to the food security of a neighborhood. "People who are involved with community kitchens become used to working with others in a way that is shared equally, and benefits everyone," says Collis. "They'll

understand how to scale recipes to accommodate the larger group, and they'll have comfort in community organizing. It's a basic skill [set] that dates back to the agricultural era of the 20s and 30s— they used to stretch their food all the time. When there's an earthquake, we might [only] get so much food from the state, but if everyone pitches in and understands sharing, we can make the food last long enough to sustain ourselves." JVL

Incredible Edible

The residents of Todmorden, a town of roughly 15,000 in West Yorkshire, England, are working together to fast-track the creation of a local food system: the town wants to declare food independence by 2018. Although food independence in the sense of growing all food consumed by a city's residents within a city's limits is almost impossible—it simply requires too much land— Incredible Edible shows how far we can go toward that goal. Only two years into the project, a third more of the residents were tending their own vegetable gardens and fifteen times as many towns-people were keeping backyard chickens (part of the Every Egg Matters campaign).

The brainchild of Pam Warhurst, Incredible Edible started very small, with a few herb gardens and tree plantings. Warhurst and her volunteers allowed the program to expand organically, and as Warhurst told *The Independent* in 2009, focusing on making the initiative as inclusive as possible is how her vision differs from that of the Transition Town movement. Whereas transition towns aim to build community resilience to catastrophic climate change and economic collapse by focusing on wonky concepts like "energy descent" scenarios that require highly bureaucratic processes, according to Warhurst, Incredible Edible is "working with people who would find transition towns hard to identify with. Our project is all about finding the lowest common denominator, which is food, and then speaking in a language that everyone can understand. Plus we don't have strategies; we don't have visiting speakers; we don't have charters and documents. We just get on with things: this is all about action."

To win over council members and local institutions, Incredible Edible used two main

Opposite, left: At its salad bar, Evergreen State College provides information on the local farmers who grew the vegetables, Olympia, Washington.

Opposite, right: Volunteers from Evergreen State College harvest leftover crops for use by a local food bank, Olympia, Washington.

tactics, making and meeting small but noteworthy goals and engaging in a little guerilla gardening to lead by example. The group seems to have found a winning formula, because now most of the town's major institutions are involved: The local council okayed the planting of five hundred fruit trees near local recreation fields. The major housing authority started giving its tenants seed packets and providing gardening courses. Local schools have switched to using only local produce in cafeterias, and every school has some sort of garden— at this writing, Incredible Edible was attempting to secure funding to build an aquaponics [see Fish for the Future, p. 516] center at Todmorden High School.

Courses on foraging, making preserves, and killing and plucking all those chickens are just a few ways the initiative is getting the community up to speed on its agricultural potential. If Todmorden High School gets its fish-farming center, it will most likely get another exciting addition: a diploma in environmental and land-based studies.

The project's Web site includes Google maps of all local producers and local assets: egg farms, orchards, beekeepers, and community gardens (where residents are encouraged to help themselves to the vegetables and herbs). It also has a blog and a few pages of sage advice for communities that want to replicate its model. CB

Lunch at the Langar

■■■■■■ *Free-for-all* is a term generally used to describe chaos. And *chaos* is a word one could use to describe much of Delhi. But at the Gurdwara Bangla Sahib kitchen, a Sikh temple that serves meals to around ten thousand people daily, there's not a trace of chaos. And the food is free. For all.

Every Sikh temple throughout the world has a *langar* (Punjabi for "free kitchen"). This is not a soup kitchen. It's not exclusively for the poor, nor exclusively for the Sikh community. Volunteering in the cooking, serving, and cleaning process is a form of active spiritual practice for devotees, but the service they provide asks no religious affiliation of its recipients. You will be fed here regardless of color or caste. This spirit of inclusion and equality is reinforced by the kitchen's adherence to vegetarianism, not because Sikhs

are vegetarian, but because others who visit may be, and by serving no meat, they exclude nobody.

The *langar* receives funding from wealthier members of the community and through small donations at the temple. Every day, the kitchen serves chapati (an unleavened bread) and lentil dal, supplemented with vegetables when donations come in from local farmers. The preparations take place in an open-air building with stone floors that has been arranged with several cooking stations. After the main meal is served, diners return outside the temple, where they line up for the last bite of the visit: a warm, cookie dough–like substance made of flour, butter, and sugar, which is handed out in little lumps on banana leaf dishes, and eaten as a blessing.

The Gurdwara Bangla Sahib *langar* has been feeding Delhi residents since 1935. Day in and day out a factory of human hands churns out what one observer recognized as a day's peace of mind for hungry members of the community. "If you get your day's meal," he said, "you can relax. You can survive." It's not a matter of survival for everyone who eats there—in fact, most people who share lunch there look happy and healthy, and probably come as members of the spiritual community. But it's there for anyone who needs it, and in a city of 13 million (and rapidly growing), an open, organized, clean, reliable, and free food source couldn't be more valuable. It's a great testament to the stability of a well-organized grassroots effort. While countless hours pass in boardrooms and over policy debates to establish government-subsidized and NGO programs for feeding the hungry, a crew of volunteers at Gurdwara Bangla Sahib feeds thousands upon thousands of their neighbors with no intervention, no fuss, and no strings attached. SR

Schools: Where Food Matters Most

■■■■■■ When British chef and TV personality Jamie Oliver won the TED Prize in 2010, his wish was for the United States to "educate every child about food, to inspire families to cook again, and to empower people everywhere to fight obesity." As he talked he showed clips from his time in Huntington, West Virginia, where he filmed an episode of his show *Food Revolution*. At the time, West Virginia was the least healthy state in the country, with endemic obesity. In one clip, grade-schoolers were unable to identify fruits and vegetables that are hardly considered exotic—one child thought an eggplant was a pear.

Oliver was attempting to illustrate just how little food knowledge we are passing on to our children, so many of whom are now obese before they even reach school. Oliver thinks food education is the only way to reverse this trend: "What's the purpose of school? School was invented to arm us with the tools to make us creative, do wonderful things . . . But we haven't really evolved it to deal with health catastrophes . . . It's profoundly important that every single American child leaves school knowing how to cook 10 recipes that will save their life. Life skills."

Along with education, our schools need to lead by example by providing nutritious food. As Oliver pointed out, school cafeteria food is essentially fast food—overprocessed, full of sugar, and so lacking in nutritional complexity that french fries are considered a serving of vegetables. Kids do most of their eating at school. Most eat lunch there 5 days a week, 180 days a year, and some also eat breakfast there.

What does this mean for our kids? Poor nutrition, yes, but also poor concentration, low grades, and plummeting energy levels. It's no secret that a healthy diet fuels an attentive mind, but when officials cite declining test scores and low attendance rates, how often do they bring up the lunchroom?

Fortunately, a few hot spots around the United States have been raising awareness of the severity of this problem and demonstrating innovative solutions. One of the best known is Edible Schoolyard, the Berkeley program founded by one of the icons of American cuisine, chef Alice Waters. The program teaches kids about nutritious food, beginning with the organic vegetable patch at their school. Children take carrots and tomatoes from seedling to salad, learning to cultivate, harvest, and cook all sorts of things. This seminal program has inspired numerous others.

Another notable example is at the Twin Buttes High School in Zuni, New Mexico. Zuni is the largest traditional Pueblo in the state—a sovereign, self-governed Native American nation with 12,000 residents and its own school system. After one boy rallied the students at Twin Buttes to take a stand for better, more nutritious, and more traditional fare in the cafeteria, the school embarked on an adventure in sustainable agriculture. After winning a few grants, the school demolished an abandoned building to make room for garden plots and a greenhouse, which the students built. The school created an agriculture-management curriculum to ensure the kids would learn the skills they needed to keep the garden going. And the program is empowering in another way—it reintroduces students to fading Zuni traditions. The use of the traditional waffle garden technique (along with modern methods) enables efficient use of water in the desert region. Providing the cafeteria with healthy foods, especially those that used to be a part of the Zuni diet, may also help the community combat the rise in diet-related illnesses like diabetes that most Native American nations are experiencing.

Children everywhere benefit tremendously from having gardens on school grounds. The plots serve as experimental learning labs, and fill open spaces with living, growing greenery and plants instead of asphalt and concrete. Drawing kids into a more intimate connection with the source of their food can give them quite a wake-up call. When a child can pick her own after-school snack from the tree she waters, that's a special thing. She's less likely to munch on foods whose origin she can't imagine. SR & CB

Organic produce in a school-lunch line, Olympia, Washington.

Farm to Hospital

████████ You're supposed to go to hospitals to get well, so why do most hospitals serve exactly the fare that makes so many of us ill? In the United States, 38 percent of hospitals have fast-food restaurants inside their cafeterias! In many cases, doctors and residents, some on twenty-hour shifts, can't get a healthy snack on the go. And all those jokes about the repulsiveness of hospital food? They don't exaggerate. But we don't have to stomach it, and many hospitals are getting on board with healthier and tastier fare. The Kaiser Permanente hospitals in California have even set up farmers' markets in their parking lots.

An organization called Hospitals for a Healthy Environment has also begun to turn attention toward the role of food in achieving a sustainable health-care facility. Founded jointly by environmental and health-care agencies, including the EPA and the American Hospital Association, the organization originally focused on reducing pollution and waste from hospitals. But after recognizing the impact of cafeteria operations on hospital patients and visitors, they also began looking for ways to green the dining areas. Because of the endorsement of this program by major national agencies, the idea is likely to spread. Remember when hospitals had cigarette vending machines in their waiting rooms and ashtrays in their recovery rooms? With any luck, we'll soon look back on Big Macs in hospital cafeterias with the same incredulity. AL & SR

Food Bank Bounty

████████ Despite a long growing season, a bountiful network of nearby farms, and a bevy of active and dedicated organizations devoted to ending hunger, Seattle-area food banks share a complaint with food banks around the United States: there's never enough fresh produce on hand.

South Park Fresh Starts supplies Northwest-friendly vegetable plant starts to the Providence Regina House food bank, and offers classes and workshops to teach food bank clients how to plant and maintain a vegetable garden. Local residents and businesses have been supportive, donating gardening tools and planting containers.

The vegetables and herbs the clients harvest will increase the amount of food Regina House has on hand by 4 percent.

Similar programs are popping up around the United States. Sustainably Yours Garden Management in Arizona, headed up by local chef and gardener Bobby Smith, helped the St. Mary's Food Bank Alliance (which serves thirteen of the state's fifteen counties) start its own 21-square-foot community vegetable garden at its distribution center.

In Los Angeles, residents of the Rainbow Apartments, a halfway house, have carried out this idea in a decidedly urban way: they've succeeded in creating a 34-foot-long plot bursting with strawberries, tomatoes, basil, and other fruits, herbs, and vegetables, all of which grow vertically against their cinder-block building. In addition to providing residents with fresh, nutritious food, the garden has given them a way to connect with each other and build a supportive community. JVL & SK

EarthWorks Urban Farm

Once the booming Motor City, Detroit now faces some of the worst dilapidation of any major city in the United States. With high rates of poverty and unemployment, Detroit is beset with a spate of urban problems. But community-based efforts have been making strides toward improving the health and welfare of city dwellers throughout the entire area. One such initiative is EarthWorks Garden, which originated in the back garden of an inner-city soup kitchen and has grown significantly since its inception in 1999. The garden works primarily to educate kids from the public school system about nutrition, biodiversity, and organic agriculture.

Produce from the garden goes toward sustaining the Capuchin Soup Kitchen and local WIC program (Special Supplemental Nutrition Program for Women, Infants and Children). EarthWorks holds open markets several days a week during the growing season to facilitate easy access to fresh, organic products; it keeps prices down and offers coupons to those on financial assistance programs. The volunteer-run markets take place at several WIC clinics around the city, where families can either receive meals prepared with EarthWorks ingredients on-site or use coupons to take fresh produce home.

EarthWorks has its hands in a number of other community projects, mostly focusing on youth education. In addition to teaching the importance of organic and fresh foods, the programs teach the values of mutual respect and community interconnection—a complementary set of lessons that helps solidify basic knowledge and cohere the community. SR

Urban Farming

Historically, many of the world's cities practiced forms of urban agricultural. The Paris region, just one century ago, grew more than 100,000 tons of crops; it ended up with so much that the surplus was shipped to London. Today, cities from Montreal to Mumbai are experimenting with forms of urban farming. Green roofs [see Greening Infrastructure, p. 171] are increasingly visible amidst the skyscrapers and smog of many cities.

But although programs like EarthWorks Urban Farm are, without a doubt, considered innovative in the Global North, the approach they take is part of mainstream life for much of the Global South. Some 800 million city dwellers around the world grow food, while 200 million earn their living farming in the city. Cities such as Dakar, Sofia, and Singapore produce a significant percentage of their food through urban farms.

Cuba provides us with the gold standard when it comes to demonstrating the value of producing your own food in a volatile world. Following the collapse of the Soviet Union in 1989, Communist Cuba not only lost its biggest buyer (the Soviet Union had paid above-market rates for Cuban industrial-agriculture products such as sugar), but it also found itself faced with a U.S. embargo, and at a distinct disadvantage in the global economy. As a result, Cuba had no money with which to buy oil, fertilizers, or pesticides— the main ingredients of factory farming.

City Farm in urban Chicago sits on what was once vacant land, and produces organic food and vegetables.

One result was hunger. In 1989 Cubans were consuming an average of 3,000 calories per day; by 1993 that number had dropped to 1,900—the equivalent of skipping one meal. The Cuban response to this crisis, born out of necessity, was to create a system of sustainable agriculture that was not reliant on fossil fuels or global shipping systems.

Urban farming became a big part of this system. This made sense not only because Cuba is an urban nation (70 percent of the population lives in urban areas), but also because the lack of fossil fuels made it impossible to continually truck food into the cities from the countryside. The government instituted a program that turned Havana's many vacant lots into farms or community gardens, virtually handing the land off to anyone who agreed to turn it into a viable food source. This scheme was so successful—many neighborhoods were able to produce at least 30 percent of their own food—that it quickly spread to other cities. Today, Havana's crumbling buildings are stitched together with farms and gardens. Forty-one percent of Havana's urban area is used for agriculture, and the city generates 51 percent of Cuba's vegetables.

Today Cubans have regained that lost meal. Best of all, most of what Cuba produces is de facto organic, because the lack of available pesticides and fertilizers meant that scientists and farmers had to devise ways of protecting and controlling crops using only what nature provided. ZH

inner-city Oakland, California, Carpenter began with heirloom tomatoes, beehives, and a chicken coop. Ten years later, her vision had evolved into Ghost Town Farm, filled with hens, turkeys, geese, ducks, rabbits, and pigs. Carpenter's entertaining book chronicles her transformation into a true urban farmer. SOC

State of the World: Our Urban Future
(Worldwatch Institute, 2007)
The 2007 installment of Worldwatch's excellent series State of the World dedicates a chapter to urban food entitled "Farming the Cities," which urges policymakers to see urban agriculture as the first step toward creating resilient cities.

"Growing food and raising fish and livestock in cities is nothing new. In some ways, cities are responding to the same challenges that urban gardeners have faced for millennia. The hanging gardens in Babylon, for instance, were an example of urban agriculture, while residents of the first cities of ancient Iran, Syria, and Iraq produced vegetables in home gardens. This is partly because cities have traditionally sprung up on the best farmland: the same flat land that is good for farming is also easiest for constructing office buildings, condominiums, and factories. The masses of urban dwellers also create a perfect market for fresh fruits and vegetables."

■■■■   RESOURCES

Closing the Food Gap: Resetting the Table in the Land of Plenty by Mark Winne (Beacon, 2008)
In crystalline terms, Winne describes the racism and injustice that have led to people going hungry in regions of abundance, and shows—step by step—how the array of solutions now available could help make hunger a thing of the past. AS

Farm City: The Education of an Urban Farmer by Novella Carpenter (Penguin Press, 2009)
Novella Carpenter, daughter of "back-to-the-land" hippies, grew up in Washington and Idaho surrounded by nature. With a passion for home-grown vegetables and a vision for a vacant lot in

Microfinance

Many of us enjoy middle- or upper-class status not because of the size of our paychecks, but because of things like interest-bearing savings and fixed-deposit accounts, credit cards, mortgages, insurance, mutual funds, and other investment services, which grant us additional financial leverage. If such a complicated mix of financial systems didn't exist, what economic class would each of us really fall into? Would we ever get that leaky roof fixed or be able to turn a hobby into a thriving online business?

These days, financial services are critical for creating wealth. For people to move out of poverty, there is an acute need to access financial services that not only provide credit but also help in saving, insuring, and investing. But for the poor people of the world, especially in developing nations, available services are usually limited to pawnbrokers or moneylenders who charge interest rates of up to 1000 percent per year—and even those loans are available mainly to people who already have some assets. On the whole, state-sponsored rural banks in developing countries have also proved to be a disaster.

One solution that *has* been successful is the offering of small, uncollateralized loans to help entrepreneurs expand existing businesses. This tradition started in the 1970s when several nonprofits experimented with granting "microloans." Grameen Bank [see Social Entrepreneurship, p. 321], started in Bangladesh in 1976, turned this system into a well-oiled machine. Today hundreds of organizations provide microcredit services to untold millions all over the world. The future of microfinance is very bright—though it is largely used by the rural poor, it is now being introduced to the urban poor as well, and has a bigger place in the future of developed nations than we might guess. 5A

A Microfinance Scenario

Raghu is a poor laborer in the state of Madhya Pradesh in central India. He lives with his wife and two children. Raghu earns his income by trading his labor for cash. He is paid by the hour, which means on the days he does not work he earns nothing. Also, his ability to grow his income is restricted by the number of working hours in a week and the availability of work.

Raghu's wife, Vimala, is enterprising. She finds out about a microfinance institution called the Self-Employed Women's Association (SEWA), which provides uncollateralized loans to poor women. She discusses the idea with Raghu, and after much deliberation they agree to take out a loan. She borrows a thousand rupees (about twenty-two U.S. dollars) to buy some chickens. She plans to raise the chickens and sell the eggs in her spare time. In due course she succeeds in building a small business out of this, adding a second source of income to the household. However, unlike Raghu's income from manual labor, Vimala's investment continues to grow—to create goods to sell—even when she is not working on it. They have started leveraging the power of credit.

Vimala pays back the loan, and finds that SEWA has begun a new program allowing borrowers to open a microsavings account through which they can earn some interest. For the first time in their lives, Vimala and Raghu have started leveraging the power of time and money. This has added a small but guaranteed third income stream, without any effort.

Vimala and Raghu attend a financial education course, where they learn the benefits of insurance and investing. With the help of SEWA employees, they insure their chickens, and also take out a life-insurance policy on Raghu.

In a couple of years, they have built a small amount of savings, which they start investing in a "microfund," an innovative market tool that allows microsavings customers to invest in a mutual fund and benefit from the growth of bonds and equities.

Vimala and Raghu have changed their lives in a few years—they have conquered poverty and built a stream of steady income, which will ensure that they maintain and increase their standard of living in the years to come. And it all started with one small loan. 5A

Peer-to-peer Lending

▬▬▬ Microfinance entered mainstream consciousness when the California-based group Kiva introduced the direct lending, or peer-to-peer, model. Direct lending adapted the idea behind "sponsor a child" programs: donors would visit Kiva's Web site (www.kiva.org), review a list of personal stories and business proposals, choose a recipient they wanted to support; and provide a microloan directly to that recipient, receiving periodic updates on the progress he or she was making. The idea of having a personal connection with a recipient proved to be very compelling for donors. Kiva was a success, and many other microfinance organizations now offer some version of this model.

There's just one problem with peer-to-peer lending: it hasn't worked exactly as advertised. In 2009 Kiva was widely criticized for misleading its donors, who do not actually lend to a specific person. Instead, donations are pooled and redistributed as needed. The people whose profiles appear on the Web site have already been promised microloans from this pool, and there's no way to confirm which of Kiva's budding entrepreneurs received your donation.

Kiva used the profiles (which are 100 percent real) as an entry point into understanding the types of projects it funds. Although the organization's lack of transparency was disappointing, the idea—connecting donors with limited funds to recipients who need only small donations to change their lives—is still noteworthy. As Kiva's founders often point out, the peer-to-peer model is incredibly difficult to pull off if donors expect accountability. To assure that donors are funding practical business plans, Kiva must vet every potential recipient; it would be cruel to put applicants through that process, accept their proposal,

and then leave them hanging while donors choose projects based on any number of mercurial factors. Although that may work for micropatronage [see Giving Well, p. 69], where a rejected proposal means your next documentary may need to wait longer for funding, it's not acceptable when a person's very survival is on the line.

And the Kiva model still has all the strengths of microfinance. It's still supporting a system that is often more sustainable than asking people to be passive givers. Loans are small and go directly to funding practical start-up businesses—then those loans are repaid, at which point the donor has the option to keep the money or reinvest that same loan to help another entrepreneur. And Kiva's president, Premal Shah, told the *New York Times* in 2009 that the organization hopes someday to do a real peer-to-peer model, in which donors could use m-banking to make donations directly to the person they wish to help. CB

Banco Palmas

▬▬▬ Hundreds of communities in the Global South have decided to end their dependency on external financial resources and their vulnerability to macroeconomic forces by initiating their own local exchange systems and alternative currencies.

While these systems in some ways function like the official monetary systems, they account for community capital in a wider sense. They build the local economy in a way that also develops social networks, revitalizes local cultures, and encourages cooperation and mutual aid. The monetary systems help to build self-reliance and personal skills, and to develop local production for local need, thus reducing the region's environmental footprint. One successful example of such an exchange system is the Banco Palmas and its currency, the palmas.

The Palm Bank was created in a ghetto of Fortaleza, Brazil, in 1998 by a group of slum dwellers discouraged by the lack of money circulating in their community. The members joined together

Access to basic financial services—such as wire services that can distribute remittances—is of vital importance to the development of the Global South, Morelos, Mexico.

in an association, determined to fight poverty and improve living conditions through economic development, and to encourage local mobilization and reestablish community spirit. Palmas can be exchanged for the Brazilian national currency, the real, but can be used only within the Fortaleza district where Banco Palmas operates. The palmas created a strong incentive to keep commerce local, feeding money into the community and thus enabling entrepreneurs to establish businesses that would help the local economy thrive.

For those entrepreneurs, the Banco Palmas offered several benefits in addition to the palmas currency itself, including interest-free microcredit loans, and even credit cards. The credit card, in particular, called the PalmaCard, helps Fortaleza residents obtain their basic necessities without having to pay for them immediately. Payments can be made one month later without accruing any interest. This has meant that residents buy many more goods locally, rather than turning to vendors outside of the community, as they often had to do before.

According to a 2003 report by the Dutch social trade organization Strohalm, virtually all residents of Fortaleza changed their buying patterns to include more locally grown products. The effect of more local purchasing is an increased chance for entrepreneurs to succeed in community-supported businesses. The drastic changes in the community are due partly to the creation of new economic capital introduced by the new currency. However, the system's success depends entirely on social and human capital in the form of organizations such as buyer clubs, local solidarity, relationships of trust, and human ingenuity. In 2005 the Brazilian government invited Banco

Palmas to test out its approach in other municipalities. At this writing, there were thirty-three new community banks in six states using the Palmas model. MB

Wokai.org

On the surface, Wokai is no different than other microfinance institutions (MFIs). You browse its Web site for a small entrepreneurial venture you'd like to fund, and make an online donation for a microloan that is continuously recycled as each recipient repays it. What sets the fledgling Wokai apart from more established organizations like Kiva isn't necessarily *how* it does business, but *where* it does business.

In its first year of operation Wokai raised more than $120,000, providing more than 240 microloans to Chinese entrepreneurs. China, despite its millions of poverty-stricken people and built-in potential for development through the growth of small businesses, has until now been absent from the microfinance scene. Government regulations have stranded MFIs in a hazy legal zone—they're not illegal, but they're also not officially recognized, which means MFIs can't move funds through savings accounts.

Wokai, which is based in Oakland, California, and maintains a field office in Beijing, acts as an intermediary between foreign donors and Chinese microloan programs. Wokai screens its field partners closely; when you make a donation, Wokai funnels the money to these partners, who then disburse the funds and coordinate repayment. For microfinance donors, the experience feels familiar; for Chinese entrepreneurs, gaining access to microloans feels like a whole new world. CB

Microsavings for the Unbanked

From Seattle to Mongolia, there are billions of "unbanked" people—an estimated 40 million in the United States alone, and 2.7 billion in the Global South. In the developing

Dogo Ramadhan received microloans from Kiva to bolster her charcoal- and firewood-supply business in Kenya.

world the unbanked simply hold on to their earnings in cash or convert them into goods that may be later resold or bartered. In the developed world, the unbanked must turn to things like "payday loan" centers and check-cashing outlets that charge them high fees for basic financial services. In both cases, the inability to secure a savings account makes it nearly impossible for people to manage their money. Fortunately, in all corners of the world, nonprofits are figuring out how to help the unbanked save, and many of them are building off of microlending and community-banking models.

Microfinance institutions, for example, are looking at ways to bundle loans with savings programs. Established MFIs already have the networks in place in their communities to deliver savings programs, which also support their own lending programs. Grameen Bank, not surprisingly, is one of the first MFIs to try this out—its MicroSavings Initiative, which started in select MFIs in India, Ethiopia, and the Philippines in 2010, aims to create 1.45 million new savers in just three years.

In Ulaanbaatar, Mongolia, XacBank (which provides microloans to yak herders, embroiderers, local tour guides, and other entrepreneurs) has created several savings programs. XacBank saw its lending program grow but the number of people with savings stayed dismally low. Program directors started to worry whether too much dependence on microloans, which are still essentially a form of foreign aid, might be hindering borrowers from becoming financially independent even as their businesses grew. To help more Mongolians become first-generation savers, XacBank introduced an m-banking scheme, AMAR, in 2009; in six months the bank had 11,200 new clients. Rural customers who would have had to travel 60 miles (100 kilometers) to reach a banking center could now easily manage their accounts and transfer money by using their cell phones. (Many customers make monthly transfers to their children who are studying in Ulaanbaatar.)

In Seattle, Express Credit Union is the Global North equivalent, a cross between a credit union and a community-outreach non-profit. Express can provide any Washington State resident with a basic savings account—even if he or she doesn't have a taxpayer identification number—for only $5, which is the minimum balance required. Although many savings accounts don't earn interest, members are not charged monthly fees. They receive ATM cards to ensure that banking is convenient, and they have access to tools like cash-secured credit cards that help them build credit responsibly and short-term loans with very low fixed fees that help them break out of the payday loan cycle. Although it doesn't have m-banking, Express Credit Union sends representatives to community centers and social service organizations so people don't have to travel to a main branch to set up accounts or to seek financial advice.

In both examples, building financial literacy is as important as building credit. XacBank runs a savings program specifically aimed at teen girls. Although women seek out the majority of microloans, young women are overlooked in the microloan circuit. XacBank wants to get teen girls in the habit of saving well before they start trying to balance work and raising a family. When a girl signs up for an account she receives after-school lessons in basic finance and good spending habits from XacBank staffers.

Express Credit Union encourages behavioral changes through education (free, ongoing finance classes) and incentives. Express might, for example, waive an overdraft fee if a client either makes a good-faith effort to contact the bank when he notices a problem with his account or if he agrees to attend one of the finance classes.

XacBank and Express are just two groups testing out holistic approaches to building prosperity. The Pacific Northwest–based nonprofit Mercy Corps NW has rolled all of these good ideas into one: a matched-savings program linked to a financial education course that culminates in a client creating a business plan for a microenterprise, such as a small shop or a home-based business like a day-care center. CB

Following pages: Microfinance is an invaluable strategy for generating income for people with limited financial resources. It involves minimal risk on the part of the lender with potentially lifechanging results for the borrower.

Microinsurance

▬▬▬ There's another microfinance scenario that isn't as sunny as the ones described above. A woman living below the poverty line in a developing nation manages, with the help of a microloan, to grow her business and lift herself up into the ranks of the working poor. Then an illness or other disaster strikes, destroys her fledgling business, and drives her right back into utter poverty.

Because of this all-too-believable scenario, many development experts feel that microinsurance naturally complements other microfinance schemes. Microinsurance is already a hot topic in climate-change circles because of its potential to safeguard the world's farmers from disaster [see Food Justice, p. 305]. But even in places where catastrophic climate change is not an immediate threat, microinsurance can mitigate any number of other disruptions.

In the Global South, insurance needs vary from household to household—a successful program must be capable of providing any combination of health insurance, life insurance, homeowners' insurance, livestock insurance, and small business insurance. And beyond the obvious, many subcategories exist: a white paper by the Micro Insurance Centre discussed the need for policies specifically designed for women, which would cover them for childbearing injuries and illnesses, or if they seek divorce in a place where that would mean automatic financial ruin.

Microinsurance is in its infancy and has its detractors, mainly because many of the first products have failed to draw enough customers. A few organizations are starting to get it right, though. Max Vijay, a joint initiative by New Delhi–based Max India Ltd. and New York Life Insurance, offers simple and flexible life insurance policies for as little as twenty-five dollars. Premiums after the initial enrollment fee are optional. Policies pay for natural deaths (the sum of the insurance and the account balance) and accidental death (double the sum plus the account balance). Clients can purchase and manage their policies at any branch of I-SERV, a chain that provides banking, computer, and cell-phone services throughout rural India.

LeapFrog is the first major investment firm created solely to fund microinsurance. One of its first investments is in AllLife, an African insurer that covers the "uninsurable"—HIV-positive and diabetic clients—with policies that encourage them to responsibly manage their diseases through regular check-ups, testing, and retroviral treatments. CB

▬▬▬ RESOURCES

Pathways Out of Poverty: Innovations in Microfinance for the Poorest Families edited by Sam Daley-Harris (Kumarian Press, 2003) The Millennium Development Goal to cut absolute global poverty in half by 2015 is fast approaching its deadline, and microcredit is becoming an increasingly important and vital part of the solution. In *Pathways Out of Poverty*, Sam Daley-Harris contends that poor people are bankable, and moreover, that "microfinance can be a powerful tool in combating poverty," so long as the poorest people of the world are intentionally included in microfinance services. Arguing that to date microfinance has been too cautious and homogenous, Daley-Harris presents a series of case studies from around the world highlighting the ways in which microfinance has been paired with education programs to provide a comprehensive means of empowerment. "We know that microcredit institutions can reach the poorest . . . [and that] microcredit institutions reaching the poorest can become financially self-sufficient." Ultimately, microcredit benefits both the borrowers and the financers.

Social Entrepreneurship

David Bornstein has seen the future of the fight against global poverty. Over years of travel and research throughout the Global South, Bornstein has come to know first-hand what social entrepreneurship means. The leading journalist in the field, Bornstein has written two books, *The Price of a Dream: The Story of the Grameen Bank* and, more recently, *How to Change the World: Social Entrepreneurs and the Power of New Ideas*, in which he makes the case for building a better world with innovative ideas and well-distributed microloans. Here he shares his story, and his findings, with the rest of us.

Is it possible for one person to make a significant difference in the world? In 1992 I quit my job and traveled to Bangladesh, where I discovered a surprising answer to this question.

I had been working as a journalist in New York, covering politics, crime, and feature stories, and I was seriously questioning my career choice. One day I was assigned to cover the murder of a Brooklyn grandmother. On the subway ride back to the office, I asked myself, "Why am I doing this? Is this what the world needs?"

Shortly after that, I came across an article about the Grameen Bank, detailing the loans it had made to a million women villagers in Bangladesh. The loans were tiny—sixty dollars a year on average—but with her loan, a woman might purchase a cow, or two goats, or a rickshaw, or bamboo to make furniture. At the end of a year, she would be the owner of the cow or the goats or the rickshaw—an extraordinary development for a village woman. Over time, these women and their families would earn money and build businesses, and move—slowly—from very oppressive poverty, eating one meal a day, to far less oppressive poverty, eating three meals a day, having a corrugated tin roof and a vegetable garden, and being able to send their children to school.

I wanted to see if the article was true. Before I left for Bangladesh, I read everything I could get my hands on about the bank, and I kept coming across references to it as a kind of development "miracle." But when I got there I saw that it was something better than a miracle: it was a system.

I was surprised to discover that the Grameen Bank had actually begun as a tiny experiment in a single village, initiated by an economics professor and his graduate students. The professor, Muhammad Yunus, had been profoundly affected by a famine in 1974, in which thousands of Bangladeshis had starved to death. After that, he began working closely with villagers near his campus trying to find ways to alleviate poverty. He launched several experiments, some successful, some not, before he came to recognize the supreme value of credit, and to found Grameen Bank. Today, the idea that Grameen championed—microcredit—has spread around the world, influencing thousands of antipoverty programs and transforming the field of international development.

It's critical to remember that the Grameen Bank evolved against the backdrop of massive failures in that field. For decades, foreign

Professor Mohammed Yunus, founder of the Grameen Bank.

governments and multilateral agencies had been pouring billions into Bangladesh and other poor countries, only to see most of the money sink into swamps of corruption and waste. What made the Grameen Bank unique was that a wholly different mechanism was at work: no consultants or bureaucrats had "designed" the bank and then gone out to hire functionaries to run it in the "field," the way governments or aid operations often do. The bank grew organically, from the bottom up, in an iterative, ongoing process of action and correction, re-action and re-correction.

I spent five years writing a book about the Grameen Bank—*The Price of a Dream*—and I concluded that the one indispensable ingredient in the bank's success was Yunus. To be sure, there were thousands of talented staff members and supportive donors, and millions of competent borrowers who together made the Grameen Bank a remarkable institution. But I find it hard to imagine that all of the pieces could have come together in the beginning, or that the idea could have taken off without Yunus's energy and vision. Yunus poured himself into the Grameen Bank the way Steve Jobs poured himself into his garage-built computer. He had no other hobbies. He didn't take vacations. And since he launched the bank, he has spent three decades traveling around the world, talking to thousands of journalists, economists, philanthropists, bankers, students—anyone who would listen—to advance the idea of microcredit. In short, Yunus behaved like many successful business entrepreneurs, the distinction being that his goal was not to maximize his wealth, but to minimize others' poverty.

If we could redirect even a fraction of the entrepreneurial capacity in every society toward the creation of social value rather than the creation of purely economic value, what would the world look like? DNB

Childline

India has millions of children living on the streets. But until the mid-1990s, it didn't have any system in place to assist them when they were injured, sick, or abused. Childline—India's national child-protection system—changed

that; its story begins with the vision of one social worker.

It was while she was attending the New School for Social Research in New York City that Jeroo Billimoria got involved with the advocacy group Coalition for the Homeless, and saw new possibilities for India. When she returned to her home city of Mumbai, she resolved to apply the experience she had gained at the coalition to India's large population of street children. Jeroo started out small, and her first efforts were extremely modest: she visited shelters in the evenings and gave out her home phone number to children in case of emergencies. Before long, she was being awakened a few times a week with calls—a boy with tuberculosis was rejected by a public hospital because his clothes were too dirty, another boy had been beaten up by a police officer. Jeroo helped the children, then spent weeks looking for follow-up services like long-term shelters and education programs.

Clearly, a better system was needed to combat such a huge problem. So Jeroo decided to launch an official children's helpline, the first such service in India. She paid visits to scores of organizations around Mumbai, urging them to join the "Childline" network (initially more than 80 percent refused to join). She raised funds and developed a program to train street youth as "para-paramedics," giving them the rudimentary skills they needed to respond to most emergency calls.

During Childline's first year, in 1996, it fielded 6,618 calls and rescued 858 children. The following year Jeroo approached the Indian government about forming a partnership to make Childline a national organization. India had ratified the Convention on the Rights of the Child, but had done almost nothing to fulfill its commitments to protect children. Jeroo convinced the government that Childline could help honor those pledges: it was low cost, it was effective, and it was popular among street children. Today, Childline operates in more than sixty-five cities across India, has fielded 7 million calls, and has been adopted as a project of the Indian government. Jeroo, meanwhile, has founded Child Helpline International, which has supported and helped to launch similar helplines in more than sixty countries. DNB

Tateni Home Care

South Africa wrestles with three massive problems: poverty, unemployment, and AIDS. While each is its own daunting battle, there is overlap between them that can allow them to be tackled as a whole. That's what the fifty-seven-year-old South African nurse Veronica Khosa realized when she founded Tateni Home Care Services, which trains unemployed youth to become paid home-care attendants so they can assist people with AIDS and other illnesses.

Khosa grew up in a poor Zulu village. As a child, she had dreamed of becoming a nurse, and she subsequently struggled for years to complete her education and gain accreditation. In the early 1990s, while working in an AIDS center in Pretoria, she got a preview of the catastrophe about to hit South Africa: more than 20 percent of all the pregnant mothers tested at the center were HIV-positive, the public systems were overwhelmed, and patients with full-blown AIDS told stories of being sent away from hospitals without dressings or ointments for open sores, and without so much as aspirin for pain.

Khosa recruited a group of fellow nurses to begin paying home visits evenings and weekends to people in the sprawling former township of Mamelodi. The women found many people suffering at home—sometimes, bedridden patients were left alone all day while the children attended school and the other adults went to work. Khosa quit her job and used her $8,300 retirement savings to establish Tateni Home Care Services.

Given the scope of the problem, she realized she was going to need a lot of help; she called on unemployed South African youth to meet that need. She had no trouble attracting large numbers of young people who were eager to gain marketable skills, as well as to learn how to assist their own family members and friends. By 1998, only three years after Tateni opened, its home-care model was being copied by the government of South Africa's largest province, Gauteng. By 2002, the province was running fifty-seven home-care projects modeled on Tateni and had allocated 40 percent of its health budget to home care and hospice beds. Today, the unstoppable Veronica Khosa is using Tateni's community-based model to develop an effective system for orphan care. DNB

RESOURCES

Banker to the Poor: Micro-Lending and the Battle Against World Poverty by Muhammad Yunus (PublicAffairs, 2003)
Economist Muhammad Yunus is the founder of Grameen Bank, arguably the most successful microlending institution in the world. His book *Banker to the Poor* achieves three things: One, it vividly describes the hardships of the people at the "bottom of the pyramid" and their capability to manage with limited resources. Two, it inspires us to believe that one person can make a difference in the world and that—three—market-based solutions are better in solving the world's problems. It convinces us that a company (in this case a lending institution) with an innovative business model concentrating on the poor can be a billion-dollar success—and economically sustainable.

The central message Yunus is sending is that poor people are no different from rich people in terms of capabilities. Institutions are what matter: "If you go out into the real world, you cannot miss seeing that the poor are poor not because they are untrained or illiterate but because they cannot retain the returns of their labor. They have no control over capital, and it is the ability to control capital that gives people the power to rise out of poverty."

Skoll Centre for Entrepreneurship at Oxford University
www.sbs.ox.ac.uk/centres/skoll/
The Skoll World Forum is the world's leading gathering of social entrepreneurs. Thousands of innovators attend this yearly conference at Oxford to share ideas, make connections, and launch projects. The center's Web site has links to research papers and bios of current Skoll Scholars.

Holistic Problem Solving

▬▬▬ The problems that afflict communities rarely spring from just one source. It's impossible, for example, to isolate one cause of declining test scores in the classroom. Children's success depends not only on the material they study and how they are taught, but also on whether they have the textbooks and computers they need (a problem related to government funding), whether they eat a good breakfast and feel safe at home (a problem related to family welfare and economic security), and whether they feel healthy and energetic (a problem related to health-care access). If we attend to just one of these factors, we may put a Band-Aid on the problem, but we won't solve it.

To tighten the fabric of our communities, we need to pull on all the threads at once: empower the younger generation, support families, promote education, improve health care, and protect neighborhood safety. Around the world, there are gripping examples of communities that have embraced a holistic approach in order to ameliorate challenges. Almost without exception, such an approach touches more people and streamlines more systems than it even sets out to.

Harlem Children's Zone

▬▬▬ New York City's Harlem Children's Zone (HCZ) occupies a sixty-block area of central Harlem. Thanks to the visionary activism of one dedicated man, Geoffrey Canada, and the scores of advocates and allies who have flocked in to help over the years, this is the epicenter of one of the most comprehensive, enduring, and successful community-support programs ever created.

Since the mid-twentieth century, Harlem has known the devastating repercussions of poverty, violence, drugs, and a lack of city government support. These conditions stack the deck against kids who have few choices; the poor test scores that come out of schools in inner-city areas like Harlem tend to lead school boards and college-admissions officers to believe that these kids just can't, don't, and won't do as well as their peers from higher-income neighborhoods. But Geoffrey Canada proves them all wrong.

The Harlem Children's Zone begins working with kids literally at birth, and supports them continuously, all the way up through college—with many complementary programs for their parents along the way. It starts with Baby College, which recruits parents—mostly single mothers—of children under three. The program teaches parents about infant developmental stages and guides them in parenting skills. Baby College also provides parents with the opportunity to join a support network of other parents who share similar experiences.

The HCZ leaves no untended cracks for children to fall through. Harlem Gems, which targets four-year-olds, has demonstrated staggering improvement in test scores over a one-year term, according to the HCZ Web site. From there, programs stacked back-to-back help HCZ kids with everything from academics to health and nutrition, conflict resolution to volunteering.

Kids learning Spanish in a pre-K Harlem Gems classroom, part of the Harlem Children's Zone.

Since 1999, HCZ has also operated an employment and technology center, teaching computer-literacy skills and providing job-placement programs to connect both youth and adults to opportunities and support. It has been a powerful force in revitalizing and strengthening the community.

The HCZ online profiles and reports also confirm that The Renaissance University of Community Education (TRUCE), another HCZ initiative, has been instrumental in preparing junior high and high school students (ages twelve to nineteen) for higher education. Using a multidisciplinary approach, TRUCE helps seniors graduate on time; its average graduation and college-admission rate is better than New York City's general average. Two integral aspects of TRUCE are the student-run production *The Real Deal*, a cable TV program featuring arts and entertainment by the kids in the program, and the publication of their own newspaper, *Harlem Overheard*.

One of the growing afflictions of inner cities everywhere is respiratory illness. The American Health Association reports that asthma plagues more children in low-income urban areas than it does anywhere else—mostly because city pollution is compounded by smokestacks and other sources of industrial pollution, which are often concentrated in these neighborhoods. In collaboration with the Harlem Hospital, HCZ works to screen all children under twelve for asthma. Not surprisingly, 30 percent of children screen positive, according to research cited in the *American Journal of Public Health*—almost six times the national average. The HCZ prevention and treatment program approaches the problem holistically—incorporating home visits and smoking-cessation support for adults who live with children—resulting in reduced school absences owing to asthma-related illness.

The HCZ programs' developers and administrators look at the situation in their district with a wide lens. They know that in order to ensure individual success, there has to be a social infrastructure that allows parents to be present in their children's lives, as well as ample opportunities for employment, affordable housing, health care, and after-school programs for keeping kids constructively occupied. Nothing can substitute for the attention and involvement of adults in the lives of children; knowing that the people around them have real investment in their success drives young people to apply themselves.

But Geoffrey Canada and others at HCZ want more than simply to improve the individual lives of the kids and parents who pass through their programs. They want to prove that it is possible to raise levels of achievement in places like Harlem—that kids who are born into poverty, who live in single-parent homes, who lack the services and advantages that are available to children in affluent areas, can excel as well, and in as great numbers, as their more privileged peers. And they've already begun: thanks to HCZ, success stories abound. For example, by 2010 the guidance office had placed 650 students in colleges and universities. SR

Finnish School System

▓▓▓▓   Finland, according to a major international survey, has the best educational system in the world (BBC 2004). This news comes on the heels of several other studies showing that Finland has the highest rate of teen literacy in the world, the highest percentage of "regular readers," and the most "creatively competitive" economy, according to the World Economic Forum.

The Finnish education minister says that heavy investments in education are a matter of economic survival for a small, affluent, high-tech-based nation. Finland spends more per elementary, middle, and high school student than any other nation on earth, and ranks second for higher-education spending. Schools are local, community-based affairs, with extremely low turnover in their teaching staffs and strong expectations of parents. Students all study languages, math, and science (and in Finland, girls now outperform boys on science tests, says the Organization for Economic Cooperation and Development). In short, the Finns go to great lengths, institutionally and culturally, to maintain an exceptionally successful education system.

On the other hand, maybe the secret is what they don't do: Finnish students spend less time in class than students in any other industrialized nation. While some kids in the United States begin preschool by age three, Finnish kids don't even enroll until age six, and their formal schooling begins at age seven. Throughout their schooling, pupils spend the fewest hours in school of any Western country, with longer breaks and holidays. The result of this is a strong emphasis on a family's role in educating kids. Finland scores remarkably high in reading comprehension, which can be attributed largely to an active tradition of reading at home and with family.

Clearly, the Finnish system amounts to a successful employment of quality over quantity. Time and money well spent mean kids benefit more from their schooling without having to spend a disproportionate amount of time in the classroom. And free meals for all students mean kids' health and concentration improve.

On top of all this, Finnish schools do not weed out students who excel and separate them from students who struggle. From age seven to sixteen, all children receive the same education, eliminating the self-fulfilling prophecy prevalent in other countries of not expecting much from certain kids, and ultimately watching their performance decline. The behavioral issues that normally accompany troubled and failing pupils do not seem to plague Finland—parents or teachers give "problem kids" a talking-to, and the issue is usually easily resolved.

Kids generally attend the same school from age seven to sixteen, making for a smoother ride than in other, more segmented school systems, where numerous transitions are the norm. Childcare services are available, and kids walk around barefoot, in an atmosphere that feels homey and intimate. The same freedom infuses the curriculum. Kids hold a great degree of control over their own course selections and schedules, choosing from numerous subjects that complement the core academic program.

At the end of the comprehensive nine-year basic academic period, sixteen-year-olds have a choice between vocational and secondary academic school. Almost all kids choose one or the other; dropout rates remain notably low. Universities in Finland are free, and about 65 percent of Finnish young adults attend.

Another factor contributing to the success of Finnish schools is that teaching as a profession is held in high regard. This is not to be underestimated, as is clear from the United States and other countries where being a teacher often qualifies as an unpleasant job with low pay, low appreciation, and an overabundance of challenges beyond the job description. In Finland, education, literacy, school attendance, and multilingualism comprise some of the most important cultural values. It's no wonder that kids want to be in school—they are born into a system that makes school not only affordable and equitable, but welcoming and fun. SR

Kufunda Learning Village, Zimbabwe

In the midst of the chaos and confusion of modern Zimbabwe, situated on the small red dust roads of Ruwa, outside Harare, sits an extraordinary testimonial to the creativity and resilience of Zimbabweans. Kufunda Learning Village was founded in 2002 to provide the rural populations in Ruwa and beyond with a rich environment where they could learn, and teach, the skills of self-reliance.

Since its beginnings, Kufunda has actively responded to the needs and desires of the local community. Even the security guard, David, who at first simply sat in front of the Kufunda gates, is now busy pursuing his dream of starting an organic mushroom farm. Over the years, Kufunda has regularly run a series of two-week-long residential programs for "community organizers"—generally women—from villages across Zimbabwe. Participants have studied topics as diverse as business fundamentals, soap making, yoga, and Gandhi's philosophies of *swaraj* ("self-rule"). Because of Kufunda, local villages have committed to building hundreds of composting toilets, which not only reduce water usage but return essential nutrients to village permaculture garden projects.

Kufunda has also established an education fund to support the many Zimbabwe children orphaned by AIDS, and an AIDS education program to create a space for open conversations about the reality of the disease. There is additionally an herbal-medicine program that focuses on immune boosters and medicines for AIDS-related ailments; herbal production gardens at Kufunda and in local villages produce the herbs, and a small lab processes and packages them. Herb-processing workshops also teach the community to grow and distribute the *Moringa oleifeira* plant (packed with vitamins, minerals, eighteen amino acids, chlorophyll, omega-3 oils, phytonutrients, and antioxidants) and the *Artemisia annua* plant, which is used to treat malaria (a leading killer in the Global South) and boosts the immune system.

Many people in rural Zimbabwe, influenced by the media and by their dependence on outside institutions, perceive their small farms and villages as useless and themselves as without opportunity. They do not see the local assets hidden in their communities. But Kufunda helps them see the value and possibility in their own environment. Kufunda goes beyond models of contemporary education, empowering participants to take on the role of teachers and leaders, as well as learners. Kufunda Village is changing the rules of the game from institutional dependence to self-reliance. In the process, it's creating a living model of sustainability based on a comprehensive understanding of the riches that sit at the heart of rural communities and culture. A particular energy of transformation suffuses Kufunda—and everyone exposed to it is changed. ZH

Rural Center of Excellence

Traditionally, if a woman from the Tanzanian town of Ipuli wanted to give birth in a hospital or clinic, she would have to travel 50 miles (81 kilometers) by oxcart or bicycle to the capital city, Dar Es Salaam. Although Ipuli isn't a small settlement by any means—it has a population of more than 100,000 and there are hundreds of thousands

more in the surrounding district—until recently it lacked any sort of formal local health-care system, particularly for expecting mothers and their children (more than 10 percent of the population is under the age of five). Like many African nations, Tanzania has a high infant-mortality rate and a low life expectancy, and the health-care crisis in Ipuli illustrates part of the reason why.

When social entrepreneur Neema Mgana, the founder of the African Regional Youth Initiative and a nominee for a 2005 Nobel Peace Prize, started planning a new health center for Ipuli, she looked beyond the community's immediate needs to its long-term survival. The Rural Center of Excellence, as the facility has been named, will be anchored by a mother-and-child clinic, but it will be equally devoted to teaching.

Building a teaching clinic in a country where there's an estimated one physician for every 20,000 residents is notable in itself. But there's more: The complex will also include a joint primary and secondary school focusing on kids who would otherwise not receive an education, whether for financial reasons or because of other disruptions in their homes. The center not only ensures that children will be born healthy and stay healthy (using immunization, growth monitoring, and nutrition programs), but that they will be educated and taught skills that can be applied to better life in the village and beyond. Women will have access to medical attention to give birth safely and will receive prenatal and postnatal care, as well as being offered family-planning resources and education and treatment programs for STDs and HIV. The center will provide continuing education to ensure that residents will be able to run the programs themselves. The building is being constructed mainly by locals, many of whom were in desperate need of work when the project started; the center may be able to offer continued employment.

The community of Ipuli got on board with the project early; it donated ten acres of land for the complex. Locals have chipped in whenever possible, with women weaving baskets to generate

A rendering of the Rural Center of Excellence in Ipuli, Tanzania.

extra income for its completion. When it's finished, the community will continue to shape its future—specially formed councils will provide the oversight to ensure the center's programs are meeting community needs.

The Rural Center of Excellence is an important example because too often when faced with health-care-related problems we don't see past triage. In this case, the solution to closing a gap in the health-care system may have the power to completely transform an entire community. CB

Soweto Mountain of Hope

▬▬▬   At first sight, it doesn't really look like a mountain; after all, the hilltop in Tshiawelo, Soweto, is only a few stories high. But when you meet the people behind the astounding transformation this South African township has seen since 2001, you realize it is indeed a huge mountain—of hope.

Anyone passing by the small post office in Tshiawelo for the first time in the past nine

or ten years will notice that things have dramatically changed. The hilltop across the road, today a vibrant community space known as the Soweto Mountain of Hope (SoMoHo), used to be a derelict spot, separating rival tribal groups. It was employed as a garbage dump, and known as a dangerous location where fights, rapes, and murders took place; during the apartheid era of racial segregation in South Africa, this was a place for "necklacing"—killing informers by putting a gasoline-soaked tire around their necks and setting them on fire.

Children in their school uniforms used to walk in a wide circle around the hill to get home. Today, they skip right over it every afternoon, perhaps stopping for a climb at the playground, a game in one of the many stone circles, or a glance over Soweto by the old water tower at the summit.

SoMoHo was born out of a small Tshiawelo-based company called Amandla Waste Creations (AWC), which focuses on turning waste into art. Soda cans, plastic bags, paper, wire—you name it: AWC sees all these things as raw material for creative expression. At the time the mountain was established in Soweto, AWC was led by a charismatic social entrepreneur and community builder, Mandla Mentoor, who managed to work with the local people to translate the AWC approach into a broader community vision. What if the area's cultural waste—the squandered natural, social, and human capital—could be turned into social art?

In 2001, Mentoor won an award for his work in the community. At that time his home served as a center for a variety of community groups. The walls were practically bursting, because the space was far too small. He gathered community members, primarily youth, and together they decided to take on the trash-strewn mountain. They spent all the award money he had received on gloves, shovels, and cleaning equipment. After a few months of cleaning, they started landscaping, planting, building, and painting. By the time of the Earth Summit in August 2002, the mountain had become a key meeting spot for the local as well as international activists visiting Johannesburg. The AWC was even profiled at the summit, where it was distinguished as a "best practice."

SoMoHo has now become an overarching title for a variety of projects in the community. It is a living example of how a community can manage to look beyond needs and deficiencies to recognize its own resources and utilize and build four types of capital: ecological, economic, social, and human. SoMoHo fosters ecological capital through community gardening on the mountain, greening and landscaping, recycling waste, and hosting programs that get kids involved with nature. It fosters economic capital by establishing revenue-generating activities—including a shop that sells Amandla Waste Creations, a sewing cooperative, a bakery, a tour-guide service, a recording studio, and a music band. It fosters social capital by creating a shared community space that enables different tribal groups to come together, and by working with people to organize. And it fosters human capital by emphasizing learning by doing and by offering training programs.

The team members at SoMoHo don't hold back if funds don't flow in from the outside. They get started with what they have, discovering in the process that they are surprisingly resourceful. MB

■■■■■ RESOURCE

The Challenge for Africa by Wangari Maathai (Pantheon, 2009)
Dr. Wangari Maathai is a Kenyan scholar, activist, and politician who in 2004 became the first woman from Africa, and the first environmentalist, to join the ranks of Nobel Peace Prize laureates. In her third book she puts forth realistic but ambitious strategies for Africans to end a decades-long cycle of corruption, poverty, ignorance, environmental degradation, and other deep-rooted problems.

The Soweto Mountain of Hope has become a powerful symbol of how much poor communities can accomplish through their own willpower.

Refugees

▬▬▬ It is one of the worst things that can happen to us: to be uprooted from the place we live and forced by violence or disaster to flee for our survival—to become, in short, a refugee.

The plight of refugees is a tragic and increasingly common part of our world. In 2009, the UN Refugee Agency estimated that 42 million people had been uprooted from their homes worldwide. Millions are "environmental refugees"— people who find themselves, because of environmental degradation, no longer able to eke out an existence and forced to move in order to survive. Twenty-six million have been made "internal refugees" by natural disasters or conflict.

Everyone tracking the issue expects many, many more people—perhaps hundreds of millions—to be forced to flee from their homes at some point during this century. Responding to their plight will not only strain our capabilities, but test our character.

Thankfully, a number of brilliant and dedicated people are beginning to revolutionize the field of humanitarian assistance. We are witnessing not only a reinvention of the approach to disaster response, but a reimagining of the refugee camp, and we are learning how to design reconstruction efforts that work. If the twenty-first century is to be, as the slogan claims, the century of refugees, there is at least real reason to hope that we are evolving the right tools and models to meet the challenge.

Environmental Refugees

▬▬▬ Even if we succeed in calming the violence that has displaced so many, human activity is making the planet a more hostile and unforgiving place: deforestation and soil erosion have rendered barren much of the best cropland; overpopulation has forced large numbers of people to live in precarious situations; and, most direly, humankind has been changing the climate.

Climate change may prove to be the ultimate humanitarian disaster. Its immediate effects—droughts, floods, rising seas, worsening storms—directly threaten many of us, of course, but they fall most heavily on those people who are already living on the margins. For a family that survives on subsistence farming, a small shift in rainfall patterns can spell disaster, as happened on the Great Plains in the 1930s, when the Dust Bowl sent farmers streaming toward the cities. If you live on a floodplain, you may be able to rebuild when floods come once a decade. When they come twice a year, you no longer have a home.

Red Cross research indicates that we may already have more environmental refugees than war refugees. If the climate models hold true (and things don't get worse than expected), upwards of 200 million people are expected by the 2080s to have been made refugees by climate instability and rising seas.

The growth of megacities—some of which are growing so fast because they're already receiving an influx of climate refugees—may exacerbate the trend, especially in those places where vulnerability to "natural" disasters collides with local governments' inability to accommodate rapid growth with proper infrastructure. Hurricane Katrina nearly wiped New Orleans off the map and sent hundreds of thousands into flight; imagine a Katrina-caliber storm directly hitting a city of millions where many people live in shacks. What that storm would have done to Lagos or Dhaka is anybody's guess. Are we prepared to handle the consequences? AS & JC

IDs for Refugees

▬▬▬ For those of us who have never had our legal status questioned, a government-issued ID is merely a formality, requiring at most the occasional visit to a bureaucratic agency. For refugees, a similar piece of plastic may be a low-cost lifeline protecting their status as asylum seekers.

At the Ali Addeh Camp in Djibouti, refugees from Ethiopia, Eritrea, and Somalia are legally allowed to leave the camp to seek work in the capital. The trip is still incredibly risky, however, because if they are swept up in routine crackdowns on illegal immigrants, those refugees face arrest and possible deportation. This is a problem almost everywhere there are large refugee populations.

To protect the refugees at Ali Addeh, the United Nations High Commissioner for Refugees recently issued official ID cards to everyone eighteen and older, which clearly state the refugee's status as a person who has been granted asylum. The UN also trained local police to recognize the cards. In Thailand the government worked with the UN to issue ID cards to 88,000 refugees. Magnetic strips on the photo IDs contain basic information such as the refugees' birth date and the camp at which they are registered, as well as thumbprints so the cards cannot be easily traded or counterfeited. That particular program has had an added benefit: creating a formal system has helped combat human trafficking across the Thai–Malaysian border.

In the Global North, the omnipresence of IDs has raised ethical questions; in the United States particularly, many people see increased tracking through IDs as an encroachment on personal freedom. But for refugees, especially those who relocate in the Global North, IDs are necessary for them to start over. The UN's reports are filled with stories of refugees being denied basic services like medical care or acceptance into homeless shelters in the countries where they've been granted asylum. Obtaining and filing the necessary paperwork to get an ID is difficult for refugees who don't speak the language in their new home or understand its bureaucratic systems. Getting an ID that's sanctioned by an internationally recognized agency like the UN can make the process a lot smoother. CB

Environmental-refugees-to-be

██████ Environmental-refugees-to-be (ERTBs) are people who we can predict will be displaced because of environmental change. By applying climate foresight, we can with some degree of certainty predict, for instance, that the Polynesian island nation of Tuvalu, which is currently only 15 feet (4.5 meters) above sea level, will be rendered uninhabitable as sea levels rise [see Climate Adaptation, p. 466]; the island's people are thus environmental-refugees-to-be. In 2009 Mohamed Nasheed, president of the Maldives, another nation threatened by rising sea levels, held a cabinet meeting underwater as a way to publicize the threat the nation faces from global climate change. Although the Maldives is committing to national goals to reduce its greenhouse-gas emissions, even the most aggressive plan enacted by a nation of less than 400,000 people will do little to curb worldwide emissions and subsequent sea-level rise.

World leaders are grappling with the question of what responsibility those of us in wealthier, carbon-producing countries bear toward ERTBs. What would ERTB intervention look like? At its lowest level it would mean

Left: The government of the Maldives, the lowest-lying nation on earth, held an underwater cabinet meeting in 2009 to bring attention to rising sea levels and to sign a document calling on all countries to cut down their CO_2 emissions.

Following pages: Providing for refugees, like the 2 million who fled the war in Rwanda, is a growing challenge, Democratic Republic of Congo, 1994.

funding for at-risk nations to build in resilience where possible (where new seawalls, for example, might mitigate the effects of hurricanes or rising sea levels); insurance for subsistence farmers [see Food Justice, p. 305] in vulnerable areas would be a similar form of triage. More complex solutions involve adopting immigration policies that would allow ERTBs to migrate before they become refugees. Some observers suggest that the world's top polluters should take in a number of climate refugees in proportion to their nations' emissions.

Although many people would debate whether we have a moral obligation to help ERTBs, if the top emitters fail to curb emissions, the creation of environmental refugees can in most cases be viewed as a violation of human rights. As Mary Robinson, the former United Nations High Commissioner for Human Rights, has stated, "The human rights framework reminds us that climate change is about suffering—about the human misery that results directly from the damage we are doing to nature." AS

■■■■   RESOURCES

Nature's Benefits in Kenya: An Atlas of Ecosystems and Human Well-Being (World Resources Institute, 2007)
Download available at http://www.wri.org/publication/natures-benefits-in-kenya

Beyond Disasters: Creating Opportunities for Peace by Michael Renner and Zoë Chafe (Worldwatch Institute, 2007)

As we've noted before, there's a strong relationship between environmental crises and social instability. Similarly, communities in the developing world with healthy environments and sound practices (from farming sustainably to building greenbelts) often see faster gains in alleviating poverty. This connection between sustainability and social well-being is so pervasive that it applies even to refugees. Two major recent studies have strengthened our understanding of that connection.

Nature's Benefits in Kenya uses mapping tools and available data to show the links between ecosystem services (processes provided by nature) and poverty. The report is exhaustive, providing

specific insight into how people in Kenya go about making a living and how the environment plays a part in their lives. Many of the principles discussed, however, are universal, and the information design is crisp and clear.

Worldwatch's *Beyond Disasters* report shows that if the eco-decline/poverty/violence and corruption dynamics of a state can cause disastrous social failures, working on all these elements at once—a form of extreme environmental peacemaking [see Ending Violence, p. 436]—offers the possibility of radical improvements in dire situations.

"How to Be a Refugee" by Tara Horn
http://ignite.oreilly.com/2010/01/tara-horn-on-being-a-refugee.html
Tara Horn's presentation at Ignite Portland describes step by step what a refugee from Burma might go through while fleeing and trying to resettle in the United States.

The Three Degrees Project
http://www.threedegreeswarmer.org
What are the legal rights of climate refugees? What are the responsibilities of polluting nations? How do we safeguard the interests of future generations? The field of climate law is still in its infancy and full of unanswered questions.

The Three Degrees Project at the University of Washington Law School is starting to explore the legal implications of our planetary crisis; it is a hub of good thinking on the subject. AS

Transforming Disaster Relief

It's hard to call disasters "natural" anymore. Climate change, ecological degradation, poverty, poorly designed infrastructure, war—frequently, all of these combine to make what once were serious disasters into total catastrophes.

When, in 2005, Hurricane Katrina—behaving exactly as we've been told storms will behave in a greenhouse world—nearly wiped New Orleans off the map, who or what was to blame for the havoc it caused? Climate change, which may have made the storm worse? The destruction of local wetlands and alteration of the Mississippi, which made flooding as the storm surged worse? The economic system, which left many people too poor to flee the path of destruction? The New Orleans levy system, which had been allowed to decay from a lack of investment? Or the absence of National Guard troops, who normally would have assisted in disaster response, but who had been deployed to Iraq?

In our day, there's increasingly no way of telling which parts of a weakened system cause it to collapse catastrophically. There's even a term for the feedback loop between an environmental collapse and the failure of the human systems that caused it: Wexelblat disaster. In such a world, planning for effective disaster relief efforts isn't a luxury: since massive disasters are no longer a question of "what if" but "when," we'd better be ready.

These "unnatural" disasters—of which the 2004 Indian Ocean tsunami, 2005 Kashmir earthquake, and 2010 Haiti earthquake are just a foretaste—are beginning to fall more frequently and with a severity that outstrips the capabilities of governments to respond, especially in the Global South, where poverty worsens people's vulnerability to crisis. We therefore need new tools for disaster response, and new methods to allow citizens to band together quickly in the wake of calamity. And these tools and methods are beginning to emerge. AS

Lifesaving Logistics

Humanitarian relief efforts are logistical nightmares. Aid workers must coordinate supplies and donations, get the permits they need to operate in afflicted areas, find volunteers to help deliver the aid, and figure out some way of moving everything and everyone to the affected site. The information revolution that brought increased efficiency and lower costs to the commercial sector wasn't visible in the humanitarian-relief arena until very recently.

The Fritz Institute, founded in 2001, is dedicated to bringing modern logistics techniques to the world of disaster relief. It provides logistics software and partnering resources to organizations large and small that are engaged in global humanitarian efforts. HELIOS is the institute's latest software program. It provides real-time tracking of donation-supply chains. The institute estimates that the software can cut paperwork in half, which is very important, as Oxfam estimates

A Red Cross volunteer comforts a Hurricane Katrina refugee at the Houston Astrodome, 2005.

that aid workers who coordinate logistics spend 70 percent of their time on paperwork, severely restricting the amount of time they can spend in the field working with disaster victims. Currently, Oxfam GB is testing the software in twenty African nations.

Another tool for the logistics chest is Global MapAid, a nongovernmental organization (NGO) that aims to provide high-quality geographic information system (GIS) mapping information [see Mapping, p. 451] to rapid-reaction disaster-response teams. In New Orleans, three volunteers made maps of Katrina-affected areas that indicated where returning residents could find food, water, and clothing; they distributed 20,000 of them to residents and Red Cross workers alike. But Global MapAid isn't just about handing out maps to aid workers. One of its goals is to share its mapping expertise with locals to ensure that they can continue mapping projects once the NGOs are gone. After the 2004 tsunami, two MapAid volunteers provided GIS training to a group of students at the University of Syiah Kuala in Bande Aceh, Indonesia. Additionally, the organization provided data-collection equipment that had been retrofitted to withstand the region's high temperatures and humidity. JC & AS

Strong Angel

■■■■　In May 2000 a refugee camp materialized on a barren lava bed on the Big Island of Hawaii. The refugees weren't victims of a natural disaster or some political action; rather they were actors—volunteers brought together to improve the lives of real refugees thousands of miles away.

The mock camp was created by Strong Angel, an organization led by navy doctor Eric Rasmussen. Strong Angel was created to find new ways for the military, nongovernmental, and governmental organizations to employ collaborative systems and cheap technology in order to work better together during disasters and crises. The five-day exercise in Kona was essentially a field test of collaborative tech to determine what works best when it comes to managing a refugee camp. Many different systems and products were tested, from computerized translation systems for doctors in the field (language barriers between medical personnel and refugees are a huge problem) to simple radios for providing one shared communication system. In fact, one of the notable things about the Strong Angel mock camp was that it proved we can get a lot done with simple, cheap, off-the-shelf technology. The Kona refugee camp was managed solely with a Web site and simple wireless-communication gear that workers could carry with them at all times.

In July 2004 Strong Angel II took over the same lava bed. This time the most invaluable tool was the Groove network. Groove is a peer-to-peer application: Information can be transferred wirelessly from laptop to laptop. No central server is necessary, which is important because a server could easily be destroyed during a crisis. In addition, people can work off-line knowing that as soon as they reconnect to the Internet, the Groove software will automatically synchronize all the shared folders, ensuring data is up-to-date at all times.

Unfortunately, few of Strong Angel's discoveries made it into the relief efforts after the 2004 tsunami. The first few days after the disaster, the actions of both military and nongovernmental agencies were so haphazard and poorly coordinated that the problems they caused almost negated the immediacy of their response.

Left: Strong Angel is a hands-on laboratory for disaster-relief innovation.
Opposite, left: A survivor of the Kashmir earthquake talks with Pakistani paratroopers, Chautha, Kashmir, 2005.
Opposite, right: SkyTrailer Renewable Power Systems can provide energy in areas where infrastructure is damaged or nonexistent.

The military's standard protocol was effective in gathering information, but inefficient in disseminating that information to the workers actually delivering the aid; in some cases, important data about road conditions, food supplies, and casualties was locked up tight aboard offshore vessels, while nongovernmental organizations (NGOs) sent up helicopter after helicopter trying to gather the exact same data. Some NGOs even duplicated one another's efforts on this front.

Rasmussen actually got a chance to witness the chaos firsthand, and he concluded that one of the biggest problems was that many workers relied exclusively on their cell phones to communicate with one another. There was no central way for everyone to share important information. A main objective of any future relief effort should be to create a collaborative workspace, a virtual storehouse for all of those field reports and updates.

Strong Angel III, which took place at locations around San Diego in August 2006, reflected the 2005 avian flu outbreaks by simulating a global influenza pandemic complicated by vicious cyberattacks that cut power and communications networks. Beyond testing new technology—including ad hoc wireless networks and real-time data feeds—this Strong Angel examined how military-civilian collaboration could reduce the risk of unrest in times of crisis. One white paper on the event noted the "reassuring presence" of women in uniform—in several recent disasters that Strong Angel coordinators had studied, the affected population was 85 percent women and children. The same paper noted the importance of a neutral space in which military personnel and NGOs and other civilians could work together (breaking down "the razor-wire barriers"). As in previous demos, cooperation was the most exciting part of Strong Angel III, as when techies from rivals Microsoft and Google collaborated to link Microsoft feeds to Google Earth. CB

Disaster Response in a Box

When it comes to outfitting remote areas, mobility is as important as utility. The best technology out there won't be very useful if it can't be easily transported to the people who need it. With this in mind, several innovators have designed systems for compact medical support, renewable power, water purification, and networking telecommunication.

One of the biggest stumbling blocks for aid workers is finding a consistent, reliable source of power in places where power lines and stations have been destroyed—or places where there was no energy infrastructure to begin with. SkyBuilt Power's SkyCase solves this problem beautifully. The rugged case, which is small enough to be carried by one person, contains up to four fold-out solar arrays, a lithium-ion battery system, and an optional tripod-based wind turbine. The larger SkyStation is a plug-and-play power station in a standard shipping container. The solar- or wind-powered unit can power a telecommunications center during a disaster, then remain on site to power important facilities like clinics and schools during long-term rebuilding. Their systems require so little maintenance, SkyBuilt says, that one of their solar/wind units has been operating for a year continuously without being touched. SkyBuilt's open architecture makes it possible for other ven-

dors to build add-on components, confident that the components will work together properly.

Such mobile energy stations would provide more than enough power to run a reverse-osmosis water-purification kit now in operation in the Maldives. With only a hundred watts of power, the unit, designed by Solar Energy Systems Infrastructure, can purify 132 gallons (500 liters) of brackish or disease-laden water. Just under a kilowatt of power could help NASA's Water Recovery System—indispensable when water is extremely polluted or in such limited supply that otherwise unusable sources, such as urine, must be considered—create 35 gallons (121 liters) of drinking water per day.

Disaster medicine gets much easier with the Hospital in a Box. This portable medical system, designed by medical technician Alexander Bushell and consultant Dr. Seyi Oyesola, contains a defibrillator, an operating table, an anesthesia system, a burns unit, and plaster-making equipment, allowing a team of up to three doctors to carry out common emergency surgeries. The unit comes with a tent, which essentially turns it into an instant field hospital. The system can be dropped by helicopter into remote areas. It's powered by a truck battery, and can be readily recharged via solar panels.

Lastly, to ensure that aid workers can communicate with one another and the outside world, there's the Network Relief Kit, a communications hub built specifically for relief work, which combines voice and Internet satellite links with a Wi-Fi hub, and includes a lightweight laptop. It's not meant for long-term use, but rather for serving as a ready-to-go communications system for immediate-response workers.

If we put all these pieces together, we end up with a system that provides both short-term and long-term support for disaster-struck communities' power, water, health, and communication resources. At this rate, we'll soon have a complete disaster-response center that fits on one flatbed truck. JC

The South-East Asia Earthquake and Tsunami Blog

When Dina Mehta wrote this sidebar in 2005, two large-scale disasters, the Southeast Asian tsunami and

Hurricane Katrina, were just starting to reveal the part that blogs and social-networking tools would play in aiding disaster relief. Today, creating a blog, a wiki, a Facebook page, or a Twitter feed to share news of major events is automatic. Although it is not the latest example of collaborative responses to natural disasters, the South-East Asia Earthquake and Tsunami Blog is still worldchanging—it was the first such effort to succeed, and it set the precedent for the digital relief work we now take for granted.

▬▬▬▬ The South-East Asia Earthquake and Tsunami Blog (SEA-EAT blog) launched on December 26, 2004. It became the most important repository for news and information about resources, aid, donations, and volunteer efforts around this disaster. Within three days, 100,000 visitors had viewed the blog; within eight days, over a million had. Only three people were contributing on day one; more than fifty people on day three; and more than two hundred at last count. Contributions came from volunteers not only in affected areas like India, Sri Lanka, Thailand, and Malaysia, but also from Europe, the USA, and the Caribbean.

It truly was a global effort that reflected a collective need to overcome feelings of helplessness and do something to make a difference. SEA-EAT became a community, a network, and an open space where anyone could contribute. The first stone was laid as a spontaneous gesture from Peter Griffin, a blogger who, within hours of the disaster, invited two Worldchanging contributors to blog at SEA-EAT. So began the blog—three people working in real time with real people.

Shortly after the initial impact, people began to respond, transmitting their heartfelt reactions into the most immediate and receptive outlet that they could access—the Internet. Text messages from journalists and volunteers doing relief work promptly found their way onto SEA-EAT and other Weblogs. This became the most basic mode of communication, at a time when cell phone signals were too weak to support spoken messages.

SEA-EAT bloggers aggregated firsthand accounts, reports, and pictures of the devastation from bloggers who happened to be in the affected zone. At the same time, they captured other stories and statistics as they evolved and were published by other new sources, including a page started on Wikipedia by one person, which today has evolved into the best overall record of the disaster. Andy Carvin of the Digital Divide network set up a news aggregator of blogs and sites reporting on the disaster. Groups of bloggers from all over the world set up relief funds and aid channels. Others simply voiced their shock and grief at the event and pitched in by offering useful links to help the victims.

When Hurricane Katrina struck the Gulf Coast, the SEA-EAT team got together again and, by replicating its earlier model, set up one of the most complete repositories of aid and resource information available to the public at the Katrina-Help Blog and KatrinaHelp Wiki (a related site in which any reader, not just the bloggers, could add or update content). This time, a virtual helpline and phone bank was also set up using Skype technology (a voice-over-Internet system that allows users to make and receive calls that are routed through their computers rather than through traditional phone lines). After the 2005 earthquake in India and Pakistan, the South Asia Quake Help blog and wiki were created, as well as a short message service (SMS) reporter blog.

It is fascinating that these tools that didn't exist a few years ago—blogs, wikis, and photo-sharing Web sites like Flickr—were put to use so quickly in the recent disasters. Today, it's likely that no major crisis will ever be handled again without SMS, blogs, and wikis. The social tools that many of us already take for granted will become a natural extension of rapid adaptation under chaotic conditions. DHM

Reinventing the Refugee Camp

One of the most important tasks at hand is to perfect the art of humanitarian intervention—not only to stop war and genocide, bring criminals to justice, and provide safe havens for refugees, but also to help people in disaster zones and wartorn lands get back on their feet as quickly as possible. We need to save lives, sure, but humanitarian intervention can also help bring victims to a place where they can reimagine their own lives and acquire the skills to forge their own paths.

The first step is to build better tools for helping refugees—to innovate and improve the relief effort, right now, from the start. The demands we put on aid workers are extraordinary. They fly to remote corners of the world, where usually they can expect to find nothing, not even clean water. They create entire cities from scratch, restoring order, pitching tents, digging latrines, finding and filtering water, treating the wounded and diseased, counseling the grieving, and finding ways to bring traumatized people back to emotional engagement with their own lives. This is perhaps the hardest work on earth, and the people who do it—the United Nations' blue hats, the Doctors Without Borders, and the tireless aid workers—are the closest thing we have to true heroes.

We are just starting to invent the necessary tools to help all of these people do their jobs better. We need to spread the best innovations around as quickly as possible, employ better logistics methods, and get aid workers better information about conditions on the ground. AS

Understanding Refugee Camps

▬▬▬   In order to comprehend the magnitude of the challenges aid workers face, we have to wrap our minds around a type of situation unlike anything most of us have ever known. One extremely informative resource is the Doctors Without Borders' Refugee Camp traveling exhibit, which has appeared in fifteen countries. The exhibit includes replicas of emergency housing, clinics, and feeding centers, and it displays equipment used by aid workers, such as water pumps.

The Doctors Without Borders Web site (www.dwb.org), another invaluable resource, gives us a sobering portrait of refugee camps: "A poorly planned refugee settlement is one of the most pathogenic environments possible. Overcrowding and poor hygiene are major factors in the transmission of diseases with epidemic potential (measles, meningitis, cholera, etc.). The lack of adequate shelter means that the population is deprived of all privacy and constantly exposed to the elements (rain, cold, wind, etc.)." Imagine 100,000 people staggering to a place of safety, utterly destitute, hungry, sick, traumatized, and grief-stricken. Now imagine trying to feed, clothe, shelter, and care for them all in a place where

infrastructure simply doesn't exist (or is quickly overwhelmed), where filth and crowding are almost beyond comprehension, and where every supply must be flown or trucked in, and then we begin to see the kind of challenges aid workers face every day. We begin to see what a world full of refugees will feel like, and understand why inventing better refugee camps must be near the top of the planetary to-do list.

LifeStraw

▬▬▬   LifeStraw is a drinking straw that contains filters capable of killing *E. coli, Shigella, Salmonella, Enterococcus, Staphylococcus aureus,* and the microorganisms that cause diarrhea, dysentery, typhoid, and cholera. With each sip of water, two textile filters catch large materials and clusters of bacteria; next, a chamber of iodine-filled beads kills smaller bacteria, viruses, and parasites; finally, a chamber containing granulated active carbon catches any remaining parasites and rids the water of the iodine smell.

Unlike more complicated water-filtration systems, the LifeStraw costs less than four dollars and can filter about 185 gallons (700 liters) of water (up to one year's worth of water for one person), according to the LifeStraw designers' research and analyses. LifeStraw makes providing safe water to those who need it affordable.

Plumpy'nut

▬▬▬ Fighting malnutrition is a top priority for aid workers in refugee camps. This daunting task is complicated by the need to mix standard treatments for malnutrition—powdered milk formulas called F-75 and F-100—with clean water, which is often scarce in areas of extreme poverty and turmoil. Moreover, to ensure that the formulas are mixed properly, workers can only administer them at hospitals and feeding centers; some refugees have to travel miles to reach these centers, and overcrowding nearby can lead to the spread of disease. On top of that, milk-based products are also prone to bacterial growth.

Nutriset SAS, a French company specializing in humanitarian nutrition, created two solutions: Plumpy'nut is a peanut-based paste with the nutritional value of the F-100 milk formula. It requires no preparation or mixing—it can be eaten right from the bag—so it can be distributed directly to affected communities. It's also much more palatable than other formulas (it tastes like a sweeter version of peanut butter), which means it's more likely that people, particularly children, will eat enough of it to recover their health. The second generation is Plumpy'doz, which is a preventative supplement for infants and toddlers—a few teaspoons a day provide the vitamins and fats that may be missing from more traditional meals.

Concrete Canvas Tent

▬▬▬ Ordinary canvas tents are too flimsy for field offices and hospitals, especially in places where harsh weather conditions wear down fabric within weeks. Concrete structures, on the other hand, are too difficult to transport and too

Plumpy'nut, which appeals to kids' taste buds more than traditional therapeutic foods do, helps malnutritioned children survive in refugee situations.

expensive and time-consuming to construct for quick deployment in crisis situations. But it seems that a combination of canvas and concrete might be the next best solution to the problem of getting aid workers and doctors the facilities they require quickly and cheaply.

The Concrete Canvas tent, invented by Peter Brewin and Will Crawford, two grad students at Royal College of Art in London, is a sack of cement-impregnated fabric weighing approximately 500 pounds (227 kilograms). When water is added to the bag and the whole thing is inflated with air (a process that takes about forty minutes), it becomes a sturdy domed structure with 172 square feet (16 square meters) of floor space. It takes twelve hours for the structure to dry out enough for habitation. Such a structure makes an ideal field hospital, enabling doctors to perform surgeries on the first day of a crisis.

Concrete Canvas has won several prestigious awards for its ingenuity, but as of this writing, the engineers are still seeking funding for production. JJF

Compostable Tent City

▬▬▬ Today's refugee camps tend to be sprawling, muddy, overcrowded, and septic tent cities where services are rare and opportunities to actually improve one's life are few and far between. They are often nothing more than places to warehouse people most of us don't care enough about to notice.

But future refugee camps could be much, much different. One possibility is the compostable tent city, first proposed by the Rocky Mountain Institute. In this model, the tents themselves would not be tents at all, but treated cardboard shelters that provide basic housing and last for a couple of years. (The shipping containers and packaging for medical goods and food would also be treated cardboard.) When the shelters wore out and the packaging was discarded, they would show their true nature. The panels of treated cardboard, each infused with appropriate local seeds, spores of topsoil fungi, and harmless fertilizing agents, would become very special compost: by tearing the panels up and watering them, refugees could start gardens, complete with mulch, fertilizer, and the microorganisms good soil needs. (Even clothing and blankets can be designed to be compostable when they wear out.) The entire transitional tent city could then be plowed into gardens as refugees settle in to stability. Not only would the soil support food crops, but fast-growing, salt-absorbing hybrid shade trees could go in as windbreaks, helping to check erosion and desalinize the soil. AS

Rethinking Refugee Reconstruction

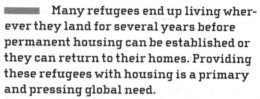

Solar Water Disinfecting Tarpaulin

▬▬▬▬ The LifeStraw [see p. 340] is one solution to improving access to clean water in areas where there is no infrastructure. Architect and professor Eric Olsen has another: the Solar Water Disinfecting Tarpaulin (SWDT).

The pleated tarpaulin is a biomimetic design, inspired by the way a saguaro cactus absorbs water. It's made of laser-cut LDPE and rubberized nylon, and is lightweight and flexible—it can be rolled up or slung over the shoulders like a shawl for easy transport. The tarpaulin can purify up to twenty liters (five gallons) of water in five hours; it uses a World Health Organization–approved method combining solar heat and ultraviolet radiation to eliminate disease-causing bacteria. Though the SWDT requires direct sun to work, it is more practical than many water-purification gadgets because it doesn't use chemicals or filters that may need to be replaced. JVL

▬▬▬▬ Many refugees end up living wherever they land for several years before permanent housing can be established or they can return to their homes. Providing these refugees with housing is a primary and pressing global need.

Most of us don't see the effect of short-term thinking in disaster relief. Often, months after the last of the TV crews have left a disaster zone, children are still being taught under plastic tarps, waterborne diseases have spread throughout camps due to poor sanitation and inadequate infrastructure, and tents have deteriorated to the point that refugees begin deforesting the surrounding land for materials to build and repair housing.

Even where disaster-reconstruction efforts exist, the housing built is often woefully inadequate or wildly inappropriate. There is a crying need not only for better models, but for better methods of working with refugees, to create longer-term housing.

This is a time of accelerated emergence of innovative thinking. From every corner of the globe we've seen proactive and pragmatic ideas for housing, infrastructure, community, and sanitation projects. Some of these great designs have already been deployed. But with little funding available for shelter development, only a handful of designs have been implemented,

The Solar Water Disinfecting Tarpaulin is durable, lightweight, and more user-friendly than water-purification devices that utilize standard filters.

a dozen have been built as prototypes, and most have never made it off of the drawing board. To date, not one of these experimental solutions has been implemented in great enough numbers to make a real difference for a substantial number of people. Without the means to do in-depth research into and evaluation of these ideas, many aid agencies are reluctant to fund and implement the projects, particularly in emergency situations.

If we are serious about facilitating truly sustainable renewal for areas affected by disasters, we need to become proactive in introducing innovative and sustainable solutions. Most importantly, we need to recognize that solutions we provide for (or impose upon) people never work out as well or become as useful as solutions we help people implement for themselves, using their own skills and engaging with their own lives. Innovation in refugee housing must ultimately be innovation in helping others build what they need. Encouraging communities to be active participants in the rebuilding of their lives is key to creating sustainable solutions and reducing the impacts of disasters. CS

Teaching Kids in Refugee Situations

There's been a humanitarian crisis. People are miserable, hungry, sick, perhaps wounded, certainly traumatized. What are the first priorities? Would you believe that the first priority is teaching the kids? While many people still argue that it's best to wait on education until life has returned to normal, research indicates that getting schooling quickly under way after a disaster has far-reaching benefits. In fact, it can create the sense of routine and regularity that falls away in crisis, offering a focal point for distressed kids, and establishing a safe, central location for families to meet up.

As the 2002 issue of *Forced Migration Review* (perhaps the most disturbingly titled social studies publication in the world, if you really think about it) suggests, by creating "safe zones" for kids and providing access to essential knowledge, educators can not only help the community return to a sense of psychological stability, but can also save a generation that might otherwise be lost. Indeed, involving parents and elders in the process of reinstating schooling can help move a whole community out of traumatic shock and into action. AS

The Power of Radio

In the developing world, radio is a critical tool for spreading knowledge, organizing community resources, and pursuing sustainable development. Regions that lack resources and basic services can benefit tremendously when an individual or a group of citizens can build or access a transmitter and organize sufficiently to produce a broadcast or even set up a radio station. Numerous stories have emerged from the developing world that demonstrate the power of disseminating information over the airwaves. When everything else shuts down, radio can keep vital lines of communication open.

Freeplay

Radio can catalyze education for children in dire straits. A solar-powered, hand-cranked radio that is tuned in to an educational station, the Freeplay Lifeline Radio requires no power supply or teaching staff. Placed in a tent or a community gathering space, the radio becomes a tool for learning.

Teaching children can mobilize a demoralized community in the wake of a disaster, Afghanistan.

The Freeplay has been distributed throughout the world by international aid agencies, which use it to provide news bulletins during times of disaster, in addition to the regular educational programming. In remote areas, the Freeplay broadcasts school classes and even public health information; in Madagascar, a serial radio drama teaches AIDS education. The Freeplay is considered such a desirable and useful tool that the Nigerian government has successfully implemented a program trading the radios for illicit guns. CS

A Billion Trees for Refugees

The United Nations High Commissioner for Refugees (UNHCR) now includes tree-planting on its already lengthy agenda. The Billion Tree Campaign, which started in 2006 in partnership with the UN Environment Programme, is combating the deforestation caused by refugees who end up in rural camps where wood is the only available fuel source. The Democratic Republic of the Congo, for instance, is still grappling with the environmental degradation—including the clear-cutting of 44 square miles (113 square kilometers) of forest in Virunga National Park, a World Heritage Site—that occurred after refugees fleeing Rwanda's genocide camped out for months in parts of Tanzania and Zaire.

The tree-planting campaign not only helps employ refugees and provide them with stewardship skills that will continue to be valuable after they return home or move on to other places, it also recognizes that a humanitarian aid program doesn't necessarily end after the tents disappear. Refugee camps can have a permanent impact on their sites: deforestation accelerates climate change, and soil erosion contributes to resource scarcity and the disenfranchisement of surrounding communities—both of which could increase the number of new refugees. Replenishing the resources used in times of crisis is important, as is using the existence of such a program as a reason to focus on sustainable solutions while the camps are being built and managed. CB

Preceding pages: The shipping container houses designed by Clemson University's SEED project can be modified and expanded to become dynamic permanent housing.

Building Permanent Housing

When environmental refugees return to hurricane- or earthquake-devastated areas, a primary need is small, safe, well-designed, and low-cost homes.

Abandoned shipping containers have long been repurposed by DIYers into sheds, offices, and even homes. They are, unfortunately, a plentiful resource worldwide, especially in sparsely populated areas (think rural Alaska or Caribbean islands) that export too few goods of their own to justify the cost of returning a mostly empty container to its point of origin. Clemson University's SEED project, helmed by architecture faculty Martha Skinner and Doug Hecker, is working on a prototype shipping container home that could be used both for disaster relief and long-term reconstruction, specifically in the Caribbean.

SEED estimated that shortly after the 2010 earthquake in Haiti, there were 7,000 unused containers in Port-au-Prince, which alone could have housed up to 70,000 people. The SEED design has a two- to three-week setup time—significantly less than the average eighteen weeks it takes to put up a more standard low-cost home. The SEED design works this way: At the port, four or five simple cuts are made in the unused containers to create cross-ventilation. At the same time, shipped-in pallet-sized "micro-infrastructure pods" are installed to provide water and energy (probably through solar panels) for both a working bathroom and cooking facilities. When the container home reaches its site, a family can move right in. The same container can then be steadily improved upon until it becomes a truly beautiful home: SEED sketches show colorful exteriors, creative additions including second floors, and even roof gardens. Since shipping containers are strong enough to withstand hurricanes and earthquakes— the SEED design allows the container to be closed up—these homes are very resilient, especially important in places where severe storms are yearly occurrences.

SEED is an example of adaptive reuse, but many other refugee housing solutions are based on prefab modular units. In the wake of the Haiti quake, Andres Duany, an architect and cofounder of Congress for the New Urbanism, designed a cabin that looks like a wooden version of a shipping container. The cabin shares a lot of similar features—bunk-style sleeping accommodations (for up to eight people), indoor plumbing (with tanks on the roof to collect rain), quake- and hurricane-proof construction, easy expansion and modification. But this system may have more potential to create jobs, as it would require people to assemble the structures and, eventually, to manufacture them in an in-country factory.

Both solutions show that rebuilding doesn't have to mean slapdash structures or toxic FEMA trailers. We can build customizable construction models that provide lasting, attractive housing that will weather the next storm. CB

Open-source Humanitarian Design

With humanitarian crises, as with so many of the problems facing our planet, collaboration is not only our best hope for finding solutions: it may become our only hope. The large-scale disasters we face are so profound, their momentum so fierce, that unless we put to use the energy and creativity of every person of good will, we cannot possibly overcome them. Relief and reconstruction need to be approached holistically and openly, or we risk masking a symptom instead of curing an ailment.

Too often, humanitarian and developmental assistance comes from a concept so far removed from the crisis at hand that it simply falls short or fails. It can be especially disastrous when newly formed organizations implement untested ideas on the ground. Historically such ideas have led to economic, environmental, and societal damage in the communities they were meant to help. Many prefabricated structures become useless once a building element fails and needs to be replaced. Implementing culturally and locally inappropriate structures can create resentment and mistrust within a community. Not integrating urban planning strategies of growth and renewal can create permanent refugee camps where villages and towns should evolve. Bringing in large quantities of donated materials and free labor can disrupt an already weakened economy; introducing new high-tech solutions can preclude the potential to hire displaced workers for the rebuilding process, since their skills won't be a good match.

By embracing open-source technologies and design, and removing barriers to the improvement, distribution, and implementation of well-designed solutions, we can, more than ever before, ensure that people in crisis receive innovative, sustainable, and, most importantly, dignified shelter. Since the mid-1990s, the sharing of information and technology has steadily gained popularity in the high-tech and arts communities. Why not adopt this approach in the area of humanitarian reconstruction and long-term development? We have an opportunity to provide displaced populations with localized solutions that will last longer and integrate disaster mitigation technologies to protect them in the future. By opening design up to collaboration, we arm ourselves with the greatest number of strategies, skills, perspectives, and tools available, and we guarantee that those tools can be freely distributed and adapted by local teams, on the ground.

When we welcome real, local collaboration into the design and reconstruction process, we have the means not only to build more appropriate housing, but to stimulate local economic development that can help arm communities with new skills and encourage new industry as they rebuild their own lives. As sustainability guru Hunter Lovins replied when asked in a 2006 Treehugger interview whether economic development could go hand in hand with sustainable development, "We know how to meet people's needs for energy, for water, for housing, for sanitation, and for transportation, with much more sustainable technologies than are traditionally brought by development agencies. Most of what is called development around the world is really donor nation dollars hiring donor nation contractors to deliver last century's technologies, in such a way that the jobs and the economic benefit go right back to the originating donor country." This is a closed system—closed in its process, and closed to those whom it's intended to support. Similarly, much humanitarian design is structured to make use of what donors can provide, not to provide what victims actually need.

Benefits, clearly, should flow toward those in need, not the other way around. To date there is no network of proven design ideas that can be freely distributed to nongovernmental organizations (NGOs) for adaptation, implementation, and use in the field. If we are truly designing for the greater good, why not create a platform that allows for an open exchange of ideas?

In both architectural-design and humanitarian spheres, the open-system concept has yet to take hold. Organizations and individual designers alike fail to collaborate, and end up not only reinventing the wheel, but spending large amounts of limited resources on stopgap approaches that have failed time and again. We need to become more open in sharing both our successes and failures so that we learn and adapt. Open systems of collaboration can help us create better-designed, more workable solutions to the world's humanitarian challenges faster.

What we need is an online tool for sharing and improving upon collaborative designs: a vehicle for distributing, honing, and reinventing existing tools, and mechanisms for innovating new answers to current and emerging problems. The vehicle would ideally take the form of an online resource consisting of a database of thousands of proven designs and best practices, a rendering tool with a built-in simulation of austere environments, localized subsites for regional NGOs, and the capability to facilitate needs-based competitions, project tagging (assigning words that define key aspects of the project to facilitate computerized searching), the integration of local and cultural data, and the protection of designers' intellectual property rights [see Spreading Innovation, p. 269].

Equipped with a searchable database of sustainable and innovative designs, we could better respond to real-world disasters as well as systemic issues that continue to plague our communities. Using the network, an international aid group responding to flooding in China, for example, could identify all the past projects that have dealt with flooding in areas with similar climatic and geographical issues. The group could then connect with an experienced design team to help tackle the situation at hand. Most importantly, they could make decisions about the allocation of funds early in the process, even though rebuilding would not begin for months. This would allow them to begin the reconstruction process earlier and develop an appropriate and sustainable response.

Designers often face a difficult choice between distributing their designs freely so that they can be used for the greater good and protecting them from possible misuse or profit by others. This is where a new system of intellectual property rights, Creative Commons licensing [see Spreading Innovation, p. 271], comes into play. We can refine a license for use allowing design and engineering professionals to determine a level of copyright supporting widespread distribution throughout areas in need—while giving them full protection in the developed world. International treaties ensure such agreements are enforceable just about anywhere.

Humanitarian reconstruction must evolve from plastic tarps and Quonset huts to a system of community engagement and sustainable renewal. The reconstruction and design communities need to advocate for innovative ideas and support them with both local and international funding. New avenues for collaboration must be established between designers, and new systems of intellectual-property protection devised that will let designers protect their own interests while meeting the needs of millions—perhaps billions—for shelter, sanitation, and, ultimately, a secure economic future. CS

"wish" allowed him to launch the Open Architecture Network, the collaborative database he envisioned. Architecture for Humanity, cofounded by Sinclair, is using the database to make it easy for architects, designers, and engineers from around the world to freely share their work, evaluate and modify existing solutions, and collaborate on new approaches. Think of it as the Wikipedia of humanitarian design, the first big step toward open-source design.

Users can search existing ideas based on a number of criteria (such as, say, "housing, affordable, tropical, community-designed, passive solar, bamboo materials") and review ratings of other users. This is no elitist playground, either. "We're not defining an architect as someone who's been through seven years of education," Sinclair says. "If this thing isn't useful to informal community designers living in *favelas,* it'll fail. We aim to prove that you don't need $15,000 worth of CAD programs to come up with design solutions. You can participate with a napkin sketch, a borrowed scanner, and a public Internet connection."

The legal framework that allows such collaboration is Creative Commons licensing; users can choose from eight different licenses, which range from public domain to those that require some form of attribution.

If the site really takes off, Sinclair hopes it will create an entire, constantly evolving body of solutions. "Imagine that someone comes up with a model for building affordable housing in China, and that it is clever and sustainable, and it can be downloaded and changed and altered for different situations, so next you get fifteen different 'children' of that design and then each of those iterates with other influences elsewhere, until you rapidly get a biodiversity of design, a whole family tree of innovation. If you really want to make change in the world, you can't hoard the tools for making it." AS

Update: Open Architecture Network

▬▬▬▬ Shortly after Cameron Sinclair wrote the above essay, he won the TED Prize, an annual award that helps one "exceptional individual" fulfill his or her "wish to change the world." His

BUSINESS

▬▬▬ Business can be a vehicle for change. Almost nothing we do in our daily lives remains untouched by business; markets and corporations are an inarguable fact of twenty-first-century life. But a lot about the way we currently structure markets and run corporations is not quite right. The companies for whom we work, the things we make, the products we buy—many promote inequality and injustice, pollute the planet, and weaken the social fabric. Few of us want this to be the case, but most of us feel powerless to make a difference in the face of large and complex institutions.

Business doesn't have to be destructive. At its core, business is about livelihoods and service: providing for our needs by providing what others need. Increasingly, people from CEOs and economists to consumers and small investors are realizing that we can remake business to truly serve the public good—and make a lot of money in the process. We can build businesses that embrace sustainability, openness, and fairness not just because these practices are ethical, but also because they are profitable. Indeed, millions of people are involved in efforts to capture the profits available through healing the planet.

The relative success of those green entrepreneurs has a great bearing on our future. As we begin to perceive the scope of our global challenges, we also begin to see that no societal force other than business is capable of delivering the magnitude of economic change we need in the limited time we have. If we want clean power, green buildings, and sustainably designed products, we must have businesses capable of delivering them at a healthy profit. If we want jobs and opportunity for the exploding population of young people around the world, we must have businesses capable of employing their talents. If we want to share ideas, open up innovation, and reform politics to promote transparency and democracy, we must have businesses that see these things as advantages, not impediments. Only when companies begin to operate with the knowledge that creating a better world is a profitable venture can we really move forward.

The measure of a successful business doesn't just boil down to overheads and bottom lines, or even living wages and solar-powered office buildings. Today's successful business is about exploring new ways of making things happen in the world, seeing potential and pursuing it, and recognizing that now—perhaps more than ever—the market is receptive to thinking outside the box.

In some ways, business is the boldest and most exhilarating adventure we could embark on. But it's up to us to keep it fresh, or we risk falling into the groove of business as usual, spreading poverty and pollution, maybe getting a little richer but ultimately feeling sordid and hollow. Money made this way is an ethical cheat, often producing nothing of real value, and sometimes doing real harm. It's also boring: nothing is more tedious than rehashing old business models, paddling around in the backwaters, looking to squeeze out just a little more profit.

If we can avoid that tired groove, we're likely to find the path toward world-changing business, full of men and women who see sustainability, fairness, and openness as prerequisites not just for a better company, but for a better life. These fine minds see a chance to do something extraordinary, to improve the state of the world, and just maybe, in the process, to get reasonably rich. This is the new frontier of business, full of innovative technologies, radically reimagined business models, counterintuitive opportunities—there's room for vision here, and the visionaries see a bright green future. AS

The Future of Business

█████ Business doesn't work the way it once did. Markets aren't stable, much less predictable. Global shake-ups—from climate change to the emergence of economic powerhouses in the Global South—are colliding with social evolutions and emerging technologies to produce new challenges to existing business models. But they're also producing new opportunities for businesses that are ready to think in innovative ways about the products and services they offer.

We can't fix our broken systems without changing how we do business. We need the business world to provide appropriately scaled solutions, at the speed our global issues demand. Businesses that do tackle our increasingly complex needs in bold and ethical ways stand to make fortunes, as well as improve the world. AS

Is Globalization Going in Reverse?

█████ For the last three decades, it's been more or less assumed that global trade is a force that moves in only one direction—toward ever-greater integration. This assumption leads in turn to the prediction that manufacturing will continue to move from countries with low labor costs to those with even lower labor costs and looser laws, while supply chains will continue to grow longer and more complex. The world would grow flatter.

So far, these predictions have held true. But will they always? For the first time in decades, it seems there are now reasons to question the assumption that global trade is an ever-increasing phenomenon.

The biggest reason, of course, is the rapidly mounting cost of transportation. As oil prices rise, shipping costs are inspiring companies to shorten their supply chains. In 2008 the *New York Times* reported that Tesla Motors cut more than five thousand miles from the shipping route for a luxury electric roadster it planned to market in the United States. The supply chain went from Thailand–Britain–United States to simply United States, with full assembly done in California. The main reason for this adjustment was transportation costs.

Rising energy prices don't make all transportation costs rise at an equal rate. Because the amount of energy used is largely a function of the weight shipped and the speed at which it's shipped, energy crunches hit bulky things that need to be shipped quickly (like the engines for a car company's latest model) hardest. Things that are either smaller in size or can be shipped more slowly will see far lower proportional increases in shipping costs. Much has been made of the so-called "death of distance"—the idea that shipping costs will kill all trade—but the reality is more about the "death of speed."

But transportation costs are not the only reason why globalization as we know it might be in for some rapid evolution.

Preceding pages: Daimler AG has watched demand for its compact, fuel-efficient Smart cars grow steadily in Europe and the United States. Made of recycled and recyclable materials, the cars have become status symbols among urbanites. **Left:** At Richmond Build in Richmond, California, inner-city students learn green job skills like installing solar panels and retrofitting homes as part of a program developed by Silicon Valley entrepreneur Michele McGeoy.

- Far-flung supply chains may lower costs (even with higher oil prices), but they increase climate-change emissions. That presents a marketing challenge as consumers grow more aware of their carbon footprints. If political consensus emerges on pricing greenhouse-gas emissions (as seems likely), some of the price advantages of global complexity could vanish overnight.

- Manufacturers are increasingly aware of, and worried about, supply-chain diversity. When the entire supply of a critical part or material comes, for example, from a distant factory or a single mine in a war-torn country, every company that depends on that part or material is at risk. In light of this, companies are trying to find multiple (and alternative) sources, preferably close to home.

- Some of the economic advantages of globalization have come from companies skirting labor and environmental laws by doing business in countries with high levels of political corruption (which the companies have often helped foster). But now, with transparency activism [see Demanding Transparency, p. 405] blowing the cover off these practices, it's easy for activists to cause enormous brand damage simply by revealing an unsavory backstory.

- Globalization generally assumes a one-way flow of materials—mined or grown in the poorest countries, manufactured into consumer goods in China, Brazil, or Mexico, sold on the shelves of megastores in Europe or North America, and then finally shipped away to the landfill. But as we move into zero-waste and closed-loop systems (where there is no "away"), reverse logistics start to become a real concern, with producers taking responsibility for their products from the beginning to the end of their life cycle. Running their current supply chains in reverse would double (at least) companies' already high transportation costs, which alone could drive them to opt for more local production.

- As trade becomes more globalized, its vulnerability to large-scale disruptions increases. The whole system could easily be brought to a screeching halt by an extreme act of terrorism (say, a dirty bomb in a shipping container), by a pandemic like avian or swine flu, or by mass migrations triggered by environmental degradation and climate change in poor countries. Even the threat posed by a particularly alarming invasive species could put a hiccup in the system.

Although industrialization itself is not likely to stop or even slow down due to these factors, trade disruptions could mean suddenly higher prices for some things we're used to thinking of as cheap, like clothes and small electronics. Especially in the Global North—where we can draw on a huge basin of wealth and a huge capacity for innovation—even a dramatic reversal in globalization would not fundamentally undermine our civilization (though it would certainly contribute to a number of real changes already under way, like greater urbanization, local food movements, Cradle to Cradle design, and so on). We won't be headed back to deindustrialized farming any time soon.

Finally, a reversal in material trade patterns almost certainly would not mean a reversal in intellectual trade patterns. In fact, it might be that expertise, innovation, and culture will flow more freely in a world where goods flow more slowly. We might actually grow more interconnected as supply chains become less complicated. AS

Parallel Collaboration

█████ When the economy tanked in 2008, it threw fuel on what was already a fast-burning fire: the spread of individual and small group entrepreneurships. From Silicon Valley to São Paulo, people are launching new businesses in unprecedented numbers. These fledgling businesses are often informal, involving freelance work done during downtime from a regular job, and almost always small, involving at most a few people.

To run a business, especially one that's part of the information economy, we need access to a whole suite of tools, services, and networks. In this arena, small businesses have traditionally faced huge disadvantages, especially in times when investment capital and business loans are hard to find. One answer is to substitute cooperation for capital.

In a trend called "parallel collaboration," groups of entrepreneurs are joining forces to help each other succeed. At the most routine level, this mutual aid might come in the form of sharing workspaces [see Reinventing the Workplace, p. 379], trading services of equal value to cut operational costs, or channeling referrals within a network of collaborating businesses. But the collaborative possibilities can go much deeper, to include strategies like developing new products and services in a joint design and development process, or launching cross-business marketing campaigns. The key realization common to all parallel collaborations, though, remains more or less the same: that by acting together in networks, many small businesses can compete like larger businesses while actually being quicker to innovate. It's the business equivalent of being like a flock of birds instead of a lumbering pterodactyl. AS

Net Carbon Risk

▪▪▪▪   Knowing a company's carbon footprint facilitates reductions in waste and energy use and can help shorten supply chains—measures that undoubtedly make a business leaner, more resilient, and, in the face of rising energy costs, more profitable. However, measuring footprint alone won't give a company the full picture of how it will fare in the face of government regulations (e.g., carbon caps) and changes in consumer behavior.

Companies like RiskMetrics Group are offering tools to assess a company's "net carbon risk," which incorporates not only carbon footprints but also the cost of compliance to future regulations, and the company's ability (or lack thereof) to recognize opportunities created by changing markets. This Carbon Beta tool (originally created by Innovest Strategic Value Advisors) gives a much more realistic assessment of whether a company will thrive when climate change starts to affect and change its industry.

These types of tailored third-party assessments are becoming increasingly useful to businesses as both consumer expectations and regulations become more complex. In developing the Carbon Beta approach, Innovest found that "companies' risk exposures to climate change varies widely, both between and even within different industry sectors and geographic regions" and that, often, in-house non-verified analyses were too limited in scope to create a robust strategy. CB

Profits from Climate Action

▪▪▪▪   Nowadays, having a corporate climate-adaptation strategy is a matter of taking fiduciary responsibility for the challenges ahead. Smart businesses, though, are looking beyond the dangers posed by the future and focusing on the possibilities by applying climate foresight to their overall corporate strategies. While climate change (and the shift away from high-carbon energy sources it will demand) presents grave risks to many established business models, it also opens up new territories for forward-looking companies.

Anticipating the opportunities to profit from a more sustainable model of prosperity will mean the difference between businesses that feel the ground washing away from under them and those that thrive on new, more solid foundations. Some areas of opportunity are obvious: clean energy, energy efficiency, green building, electric cars. Others may not be as evident at first glance.

Cities, for one, will not only be the focus of climate-action efforts, but will also become home to an increasingly large share of humanity. With more than 3 billion new urbanites being born into or migrating to cities in the next forty years (according to the UN's population projections), we'll need an enormous amount of urban development—the equivalent of building more than four thousand cities the size of Seattle.

Those metaphorical Seattles will not work the way today's cities do—they won't be able to. Cities in the future will need to provide food, water, jobs, transportation, energy, shopping, education, health care, housing, and recreation for billions more people while producing a fraction of the climate emissions they do today. That means every system in the city is up for redefinition: Transportation may become an essential part of walkable communities. Consumer products may become sharable services. Infrastructure may become a fabric of interwoven smart solutions, large and small.

City dwellers of the future, meanwhile, may have very different tastes and desires than customers today; they may want different things, demand different services, display status in different ways. There are already young people living new urban lives. And though their lifestyles may not look like the next big opportunity for businesses (especially in the megacities of the Global South), that's exactly what they are. Learning to see the future through the emerging present is just as important to successful businesses as investing in wind power or electric car–charging stations. AS

■■■■■   RESOURCES

LSE Public Lectures
http://www.lse.ac.uk/resources/podcasts/
This series of excellent podcasts showcases the leading academics, writers, scientists, politicians, and diplomats who come to speak at the esteemed London School of Economics, and the results are often astonishing. While the occasional talk is a clunker—mired in jargon or diplomatic niceties—far more of the LSE talks feature brilliant, incredibly well-informed people sharing what they think in extremely direct, candid, and intelligent terms. AS

The Green Collar Economy: How One Solution Can Fix Our Two Biggest Problems by Van Jones (HarperOne, 2009)
Building a green economy remains the most important job facing America, and that makes the *Green Collar Economy* a very important book. Using case studies and policy proposals of various scales, Jones makes the case for creating a green collar economy as a social justice imperative, and makes clear the paramount role business will play in any green revolution.

"There will surely be an important role for nonprofit, voluntary, cooperative, and community based solutions. But the reality is that we are entering an era during which our very survival will demand invention and innovation on a scale never before seen in the history of human civilization. Only the business community has the requisite skills, experience, and capital to meet that need. On that score, neither government nor the nonprofit and voluntary sectors can compete, not even remotely." AS

Cognitive Surplus: Creativity and Generosity in a Connected Age by Clay Shirky (Penguin Press, 2010)
Almost all of us waste time, usually in dribs and drabs, not really knowing what to do with a spare hour. In the recent past, most of us would have filled that hour with television; many still do. Now, however, the Internet has allowed us to connect, casually and easily, with others to build things online, from virtual gaming worlds to wiki reference guides to crowdsourced publications. Shirky believes we've only just begun to tap our capacities to create, collaboratively, on the fly, and that as connectivity spreads and models for action improve, this "cognitive surplus" will help us solve some of the world's most vexing challenges. AS

Co-opportunity: Join Up for a Sustainable, Resilient, Prosperous World by John Grant (Wiley, 2010)
Grant offers a terrific overview of some of the most popular examples of cooperative action, from Carrot Mobs to the Transition Town movement. He weaves them together into a tapestry of approaches to working together to change the world that can't help but leave you feeling optimistic. "There is [an] implication of regarding the solution to climate change (and other 'running out of world' issues) as mass co-operation. It means we can't wait for government, big business, nor any top-down solution. Large organizations may still play a key role, not least in opening up to participative forms of organization. But it is up to all of us to build solutions. As Bill Drayton puts it: 'Everyone a change-maker.' Opportunities to be a change-maker—and to recruit others to follow suit—have never been as accessible." AS

NextBillion
http://www.nextbillion.net
The Next Billion site, co-owned and co-managed by the Acumen Fund and the World Resources Institute, explores some of the world's most interesting projects and social enterprises.

What's Mine Is Yours: The Rise of Collaborative Consumption by Rachel Botsman and Roo Rogers (HarperBusiness, 2010)

Any businessperson interested in the new types of ventures supported by sharing and social media should read this book. Botsman and Rogers discuss the advantages of product-service systems and "collaborative lifestyles" over ownership and how new consumer behavior in favor of collaborative consumption is changing the business world.

The Natural Advantage of Nations: Business Opportunities, Innovation and Governance in the 21st Century by Karlson Hargroves and Michael H. Smith (Earthscan Publications, 2005)

Anyone interested in the business of building a bright green future needs to read this book. It's an absolutely critical overview of our progress thus far toward sustainability, with five-hundred-plus information-packed pages on what's working best; pragmatic examinations of best practices in business and government; issue-wrangling essays on profitable climate solutions, greening the built environment, and sustainable transportation; probing inquiries into institutional responsibility for major planetary problems; and studies evaluating new industrial and regulatory models.

It's not beach reading, and indeed, unless you plan to make green business or governance your calling, it's probably not a book you need on your shelf. But if you are serious about organizational change, it's a treasure chest of hard evidence that better ideas can work.

According to the authors, "Government eco-efficiency programmes can be especially helpful for small to medium sized business, which make up a significant percentage of the business sector in any country. Fields like energy efficiency are moving so fast that if firms have not checked what is best practice within six months they will probably be out of date. Most small businesses do not have the time or resources to source the best information, let alone the funds. It makes sense then for governments to address these information and market failures to help them implement resource productivity programmes wisely."

The U.S.-based company Driptech manufactures affordable drip-irrigation systems to help farmers in developing nations better manage meager water supplies. Here, a Driptech employee installs a system in Namaleri, India.

Bright Green Capital

Bright green innovations present us with all sorts of new business frontiers: Green building and design spur new possibilities for development and renovation. Smart technologies drive new ways of looking at shared goods and spaces. Attention to foodsheds and footprints enables new models of feeding and clothing ourselves. The list goes on.

On the one hand, we have the material for a remarkable boom: rapidly growing cities full of energetic young people who have unmet needs and access to a wave of bright green innovations. On the other hand, we have a serious credit drought that's only getting worse.

A growing number of pretty credible observers warn that several big problems may dry up credit for some time to come. The real estate bust has led to a dearth of investment capital. And while it's true that green-tech firms are attracting larger shares of venture capital, these funds have shrunk to a fifteen-year low. Then there are the planetary factors: from the anticipated losses due to climate change and the degradation of ecosystem services to the rising costs associated with constricting supplies of fossil fuels and virgin materials, there's plenty to make investors even more skittish.

So, what does it mean to have an expansion in a time when capital is extremely difficult to get? What does a "dry" boom look like? And how do entrepreneurs get started on their projects without easy funding?

For those of us interested in launching bright green projects, the answer is anything but academic. For much of this decade, many of our beloved sustainability efforts have started with a blank slate: new cities built from scratch; new technological solutions for swapping out pieces of unsustainable systems with more sustainable replacements (hydrogen cars come easily to mind); new massively scaled alternatives to depleting fuels and materials. But blank-slate solutions demand capital—lots and lots of it—which is increasingly hard to come by. That doesn't mean that innovation is dead or that green tech and clean energy are over—they aren't.

What it does mean, though, is that the kinds of innovations we most need, and that will be most widely adopted, might not involve a tabula rasa; they might depend, rather, on reinterpreting the possibilities of the cities we already live in—adaptive reuse on a huge scale; reclaiming unused and unsustainable spaces; experimenting with regulations and codes. We may move toward new kinds of projects that can be capitalized in new ways, which lie beyond the capacities of microcredit and community commerce but escape dependence on large investment banks.

We're going to see a new boom in middle-distance finance: investment funds and angel investors who are willing to invest in solid but modest mid-sized projects. Some of the most worldchanging businesses have proposed local mid-sized answers to global problems, and funding them is in itself a solution. AS

New Resource Bank

New Resource Bank, a small commercial bank in San Francisco, sees opportunity in the tremendous and growing wave of green enterprise in California. It was established in 2006 with the sole mission of serving the particular needs of green entrepreneurs and sustainable businesses.

Founder and Vice Chairman Peter Liu's CV includes twenty years at major global banks like Credit Suisse and Chase Manhattan. Liu saw that the big banks were falling behind venture-capital firms and pension firms when it came to investing in green technologies; small sustainability projects were having trouble securing even modest loans from conventional banks. Much of this had to do with the banks' lack of understanding of emerging green businesses. As Liu told Worldchanging writer Joel Makower, "[The banks] may understand real estate, but they don't understand that there are other things that can have cash flow, like energy projects. These can have a similar credit profile as real estate, so if a banker took the time to understand the security and soundness of the project, it's more likely to get financed than comparing it to land or a house or apartment."

New Resource Bank is chartered and FDIC-insured. Although it is not focused solely on green businesses, its lending staff specializes in calculating risk for these new players. In addition to providing capital for the bold experiments coming out of the Bay Area, New Resource Bank is trying to tweak the banking business model by incorporating features of community banking to create a more customized system that appeals to small and mid-sized businesses as well as the surrounding community. It became a certified B Corporation [see right] in 2010, and so far has tied together its various programs in some interesting ways, like offering CDs that fund solar installations. SR

Guarantee Circles

Like New Resource Bank [see above], Sweden's Ekobanken focuses its lending program on sustainable enterprises, and its customers can choose between a variety of accounts that help fund renewable energy projects, alternative health care, child welfare, or cultural projects.

Ekobanken further facilitates small-business financing with guarantee circles: in cases where the risk is too great for the bank to write a loan, members of the bank can offer to act as guarantors. Ekobanken also offers group loans for projects with many stakeholders; each person involved in the project can apply for a loan. Both the money and the responsibility are pooled: if one group member cannot repay a loan, the unpaid amount is divided up equally among the remaining members.

More-flexible financing models like guarantee circles are invaluable to worldchanging projects, many of which involve a diverse group of participants (say, a tool bank or coworking space) or a number of nonrelated organizations (a small district-energy project, for example). CB

The Finance Alliance for Sustainable Trade

The Fair Trade label and its many derivatives and relatives have become familiar to consumers in the last few years as interest in the backstory [see Knowing the Backstory, p. 39] behind products drives demand for increased transparency. We want to know that the people who produced our goods did so in just and equitable circumstances, and without harming the natural environment or exploiting local resources.

These certifications offer values-based consumers the assurance they seek. But the farmers and producers (almost all in the developing world) who manage to send their fair-trade goods to us represent only a portion of the producers who want to join the network of international trade in environmentally responsible goods. To be a part of that chain, though, they have to have sufficient financial stability to prove to trade partners that they're a safe bet. If they can't obtain the financial leverage, they will never get in the door with the trade partners and will struggle endlessly to profit from using more sustainable production practices. Without the incentive of increased profit,

New Resource Bank, which aids green entrepreneurs, is headquartered in a LEED Gold-certified building in San Francisco.

they may ultimately revert to environmentally destructive practices.

An effective solution to this problem, according to a new association of investors, lenders, and development groups, lies in finance. The Finance Alliance for Sustainable Trade (FAST) works to simplify and centralize access to capital and resources for farmers who want to build sustainable businesses; it also works to demonstrate to commercial banking institutions that financing sustainable production is a valid and valuable proposition.

FAST has more than one hundred member organizations, many of which are highly influential players in global trade or the world of environmental advocacy. FAST provides structural and organizational help to both lenders and producers; the former get social-impact assessments and loan guarantees, and the latter get consolidated information and tools for financial literacy. This kind of additional support, assurance, and education will permit more efficient and rewarding partnerships, and give struggling producers entrée into the global sustainable trade market. SR

Investors' Circle

When Robin Chase, founder of car-sharing company Zipcar, needed capital, she made a pitch at an Investors' Circle (IC) conference. It worked: the exposure led her to Boston Community Capital, which invested $250,000 in her fledgling company—Zipcar's first real infusion of cash.

IC's annual events bring together socially conscious investors and budding social entrepreneurs. Twenty preselected entrepreneurs get to pitch their ideas to a group of investors ranging from major foundations to angel investors, and many more get to network. (It's not unusual for participants to piece together large amounts of capital through handshake deals made while mingling.) And the main event isn't a bidding war or draft pick—after listening to all of the pitches, the investors "circle up" to evaluate the projects together and determine which ones should receive priority funding.

In between conferences, IC accepts applications from entrepreneurs on an ongoing basis and adds the most promising proposals to a database that investors can peruse. To date, through its network and conferences, IC has helped $133 million worth of capital reach companies like Zipcar. CB

B Corporation

To help companies maintain their morals in the face of corporate takeovers, and to attract socially responsible investors and consumers, a nonprofit called B Lab has created B Corporation, where the 'B' stands for beneficial (to the business, the public, and the environment).

B Corporation is a certification for businesses that are "purpose-driven" and that want to create benefits for all stakeholders (employees, the community, the environment, and so on), not just shareholders. And at a time when every business wants to at least look like it's going green, this certification could be essential for socially responsible investors and consumers who are trying to differentiate "good companies" from "good marketing."

The certification was created by B Lab to help companies demonstrate their commitment to the triple bottom lines. As a "for-purpose" business, a B Corporation can reach beyond the capital limitations of the nonprofit world while freeing itself from the constraints of appeasing shareholders or investors as in a standard for-profit business. Setting up a B Corporation has proven to

Seventh Generation, maker of planet-friendly cleaners and other products for the home, is among the growing number of B Corporations.

be a successful way to raise capital from informed investors who see an opportunity to change the world for the better.

To become a certified B Corporation, applicants must score above eighty points on a two-hundred-point test, and must amend their articles of incorporation to state that managers must consider the interests of employees, the community, and the environment instead of worrying solely about shareholders. Some are comparing the certification system to LEED or to TransFair's certification of fair-trade businesses. SK

███████ RESOURCE

TED Talk: "Seeking Salvation and Profit in Green Tech"
http://www.ted.com/speakers/john_doerr.html
John Doerr, the head of Kleiner Perkins Caufield & Byers, a famous green-tech venture fund, spoke at TED in 2007 about the need for a green revolution in business.

"Green technologies—going green—is bigger than the Internet. It could be the biggest economic opportunity of the 21st Century. Moreover, if we succeed, it will be the most important transformation for life on the planet since, as Bill Joy says, we went from methane to oxygen in the atmosphere."

Although Doerr is a little too enthusiastic about Walmart's various (and sometimes dubious) green efforts, the speech is a powerful call to action for investors to spend their money with the needs of the planet in mind.

Investment

███████ Sooner or later, it happens to the best of us. We've been rolling along in life, minding our own business, and then, one day, we open our bankbook and find it staring us in the face: a surplus. A little bit left over at the end. Capital.

Seeing that extra money, and being reasonably clued-in, we know we should do something with it—put it away somewhere where it'll earn us a little more.

From that moment on, we become involved in a complex web of choices and decisions that will not only define us as people but, in the bigger picture, help determine the kind of future we'll have. We are now investors, and investment is one of the levers that moves the world.

The principle of investment is simple: we lend our money to others; they use it to try to make a profit; if they succeed, they give us back more money than we gave them. That part's pretty straightforward. Gather money, lend it to the right people, let them do their thing with it, sit back and be patient, and we always end up older and, usually, richer.

The problem comes when we stop and wonder, "What are these people doing with my money?"—because the answer may not be very pretty. We can be upstanding members of our community who never miss a chance to help out others—loved by all—and suddenly we discover that our money is out there funding oil dictatorships, sweatshops, clear-cuts, and companies trying to sell tobacco to fourteen-year-olds. Our money has become our evil twin, busily out wrecking the world while we go around trying to save and enjoy it.

Until recently, this was seen as one of those unavoidable trade-offs: you could do well or do good—pick one. But those days are over. Increasingly, with a little smarts you can put your money where it will not only make you a tidy little bundle, but also make the world a better place. GF

Resilient Wealth

■■■■■ As we found out in 2008, all wealth is not equally strong and secure: some types of wealth are downright brittle, while others are surprisingly resilient. Resilient wealth may be accrued in things that will save or make you money over time (an energy-efficient home, a thriving garden, good health), or may take the form of monetary investments that are resistant to economic shocks and return both financial and indirect benefits. Resilient wealth may come from being involved (as an investor, member, or customer) in a range of local businesses (like community banks) that improve your community as well as provide you with a direct return. Resilient wealth leaves both you and the community around you better off.

Although it requires an initial investment, resilient wealth can cost much less, over time, than building a larger net worth. A couple who is in good health, is well-educated, has a strong professional network and local community, and lives in a modest, efficient home with minimal debt and high-quality, low-maintenance possessions, may be in a stronger financial position than a couple who has twice as much money but is locked into high monthly bills and mortgage payments. Plus, they're probably having more fun. AS

Socially Responsible Investment

■■■■■ How do we invest our money so that it helps improve the world and simultaneously grows? That's the question the Socially Responsible Investment (SRI) movement is trying to answer.

At first, the SRI movement employed a simple set of filters to screen out companies whose practices shareholders considered unethical: this investment fund would not buy shares in any company that sold tobacco; that portfolio avoided corporations involved in the arms trade.

Eventually those filters grew to overlap, and to embrace the idea that such investments also needed to include reduced risk (less chance that we'd lose our money) and increased returns (more money back on what we'd put in).

As it turns out, increasing our money and being socially responsible are not mutually exclusive. There are investment options that will make us more money than investing responsibly will, but investing responsibly has resulted in better-than-average returns for years now. Geoffrey Heal reported in the *Financial Times* (July 2, 2001), "Performance on environmental and human rights criteria is a good predictor of the overall financial performance of companies." What's more, SRI mutual funds have begun to outperform their "hard-headed" competitors. As *Green Money Journal* reported in 2010, sixteen of the twenty-one SRI funds with $100 million or more in assets "achieved the highest rankings for performance from either or both [financial analysts] Morningstar or Lipper," compared with only 32 percent of all mutual funds. Bottom line: When we invest, putting our money into an SRI fund should be our first priority. GF

Using Investments to Change the World

■■■■■ Investing can make us money, but investing responsibly can do that and more: it can help us change the world.

Though socially responsible investing began with "negative screens"—excluding companies that engaged in dubious activities—it is now a power in the economic landscape, and investors are demanding that this power be used to not only avoid the bad, but to create the good. Almost a tenth of all the money invested in the United States is being managed with some socially responsible criteria—and that makes for a big lever.

Increasingly, SRI managers and investors are insisting that if companies want their money, they have to stop engaging in destructive activities, and start proactively pursuing business paths that will lead to a better world. To these investors, it's not enough for a company to avoid putting money behind Nigerian oil fields, for instance; the company must also actively invest in wind power. These strategies are already prov-ing to be profitable, as a prizewinning economic study from the UC Berkeley Haas School of Business reveals: "Company managers do not face a tradeoff between eco-efficiency and financial performance . . . Investors can use environmental information for investment decisions" (Guenster et all., 2005).

Savvy investors are doing even more than influencing the way companies invest: they are changing the companies' very management, through "shareholder activism." Using their abil-ity to vote for and influence the boards of large companies, shareholders are demanding that management either behave more responsibly or be replaced. This is forcing long-neglected issues—from racial and gender equality to greenhouse-gas policies—onto the agenda of corporate boards.

Finally, SRI funds are beginning to invest in new ways, putting their money to work to strengthen communities that have been left behind. Just as microcredit [see Microfinance, p. 313] has proven to be phenomenally successful both at repaying loan monies and at raising people out of poverty, money invested in intelligent ways in low-income communities tends to pay back and make transformative change possible. GF

How to Pick the Winners

██████ So how should you decide where to put your money? If you're betting not only on your future security, but on the future of the planet, how do you decide where to put your chips?

We're not money managers or invest-ment advisers, and we're not about to try to pick specific winners in a field that's moving this fast—certainly not in the slow rhythms of a book. But the following are some questions you can ask yourself that will lend a worldchanging perspec-tive to your decision-making process:

■ Does the industry or company in question fundamentally contribute to or reduce the world's problems? Would the answer change if it did its thing in a more efficient or a very different way? (For example, we might go short on mining and other extractive indus-tries, but long on mining companies that shift

their focus from extraction to metals manage-ment; or avoid companies with big invest-ments in carbon-based fuels, but pick up a range of clean tech companies.)

■ Will the company suffer or benefit from a bright green future? (Energy-intensive indus-tries, for example, face structural challenges as energy prices rise, making their prospects unpredictable.)

■ Can the company adapt quickly to unex-pected change? Putting aside technology and strategy briefly, what is your take on the company's leadership, management, and cul-ture? Is the leadership trustworthy? Thinking ahead? Open in its decision making?

No company is perfect, so you have to balance the good and the bad, make sure you're comparing apples to apples, read the data, and ultimately trust your gut. As always, be clear on what truly matters: get advice; diversify. (This is also a pretty good strategy when choosing which companies you want to work for. If you wouldn't trust a company with your retirement portfo-lio, you certainly shouldn't trust it with your career.) GF

Buy One, Give One

██████ Many of our investments are more tangible than a mutual fund or stock share. On a regular basis we "invest" in tools or household objects that we hope will make our lives better or safeguard us in emergencies. Most households, for example, own at least one flashlight—usually left in a drawer until the power goes out or a camping trip beckons.

Well, some companies are figuring out ways for these purchases to also be investments in the well-being of others. "Buy one, give one" schemes create purchases that are both practical and philanthropic.

The BoGo light (short for "buy one, give one"), designed by SunNight Solar, is a solar-pow-ered flashlight that provides enough illumination from its six LEDs to be a reading lamp; a hook at the end allows the light to be easily hung over-head. The BoGo is a great basic tool for the devel-oped world—sturdy, practical, and attractively

The SRI Advantage: Why Socially Responsible Investing Has Outperformed Financially by Peter Camejo (New Society Publishers, 2002)
Founder of the first environmentally screened fund on Wall Street, Peter Camejo aims to dispel the myth that investing in socially responsible corporations will yield smaller returns than investing in their less-than-responsible counterparts will. "It will come as quite a surprise that [investors] are sacrificing performance to invest in companies that pollute, violate laws and discriminate." In essence, SRI strategies screen out companies that are in conflict with public opinion, and they tend to provide higher relative returns—something that all investors are interested in. Whether you're managing a large foundation or looking to invest your own money, *The SRI Advantage* will serve your needs: it's full of solid evidence and further resources, driving home the point that your money and your ethics don't have to diverge, and that they can, in fact, support each other in the long run.

Healthy Money, Healthy Planet: Developing Sustainability Through New Money Systems by Deidre Kent (Craig Potton Publishing, 2005)
Indicting our current monetary system for failing to provide decent global living standards, Kent advocates for a more balanced financial system—what she calls "healthy money." Given the complete interconnectedness of our social, environmental, and economic problems, changing our current money system is the first step toward creating a more balanced and sustainable world—and it's only through monetary literacy that we can change for the better. "Just as we design houses, and those houses come to shape our lifestyles, so we create money systems, and money systems come to shape our lifestyles."

designed—but it's an outright necessity in the developing world. With so many children needing to study (or attend school) at night, the lack of good reading light can seriously hamper education efforts in the Global South. In general, safe, rechargeable light sources are desperately needed to replace kerosene lamps and candles, the burning of which is responsible for great amounts of pollution, both indoors and out.

When you buy a BoGo light (about thirty dollars for a model that can illuminate four square feet), you purchase two flashlights: one is sent to you while the other is donated to an NGO working somewhere in the Global South. BoGo lights have reached refugee camps in Darfur, orphanages in Rwanda, villages in Guatemala.

For companies selling practical tools, buy-one-give-one schemes are excellent ways to combine philanthropic efforts with daily operations. For consumers they provide not only a necessary product but a chance to see the everyday tools we take for granted in a different light. CB

"Buy one, give one" programs combine business with philanthropy. For every tie sold by FIGS, an online retailer based in Santa Monica, California, the company gives a uniform to a child who is in need of an education but cannot afford the proper attire. These girls are in a classroom in Kenya.

Seeing the Big Picture

Most of us dwell in the blissful ignorance of partial knowledge. If we knew everything about the inner workings of the systems, governments, and corporations that run our world, we might be in a perpetual state of anxiety. Or outrage. On the other hand, allowing these things to stay comfortably invisible implicates us, to some extent, in continued corruption, inequity, and environmental degradation. So how do we drag our heads out of the media matrix and survey the big picture, the true numbers, the deeper drivers behind the brief strobe-flashes of information that we call news?

Indicators. Indicators measure critical information and contextualize it. They make the invisible visible. They reveal the past and predict the future. They reduce enormous and unfathomable systems into useful information. We're talking about trend data here—but trend data reinterpreted into something that we can all understand and respond to. Think tachometer (an indicator of how fast a car's engine is running). Think gas gauge. Think blinking red light on the dashboard.

Data alone doesn't do the job, because too few people can read tables of data. We need that up-or-down arrow, the simple graph, a colored map, even a smiley face.

It turns out that smiley faces and other visual simplification strategies are critical to helping people understand what's doing well and what's doing poorly in the enormously complicated systems we must now manage. Why? People can immediately react to smiley faces (or blinking lights), while they may not even read, much less understand, charts and graphs or tables of data. Power to elicit action in response to a trend—even when that trend concerns big systems and seemingly slow changes—is the mark of a good indicator.

Take air quality. Technicians measure the particulates and exhaust coming out of our tailpipes and smokestacks in ways that only technicians and scientists understand. Their numbers get crunched into a set of graphs—indicators—that show a range of specific pollutants getting better or getting worse. Even those graphs are too much for many of us to take in, so the graphs get crunched together into a single "Air Quality Index"—a cumulative, numerical indicator. To make it even easier to understand, the various numbers are then assigned a color: green, yellow, or red. Then, when we want to know how good the air is where we live, we don't need to try to remember our college statistics, we just need to know what a traffic light is.

Indicators make it possible to change the world by clearly communicating which parts of the world need changing. AA

Systems Models

If mere indicators of the status quo are not enough for you—if you want to understand cause and effect, see correlations in past trends, play with future scenarios—then what you want is a "systems model." A systems model takes data and makes it dynamic, using the magic of differential equations and microprocessors. Fortunately, you don't need to know about either form of magic to use a systems model successfully. But it does help to be a little geeky.

To see what a dynamic global model can do, try the online version of International Futures (ifsmodel.org). Built originally for the CIA, it is now free to all on the Web, and includes an astonishing range of data and a robustness that impresses even the most learned geeks in the business. You can dial in the countries, the indicators, the starting conditions, the interventions you might like to try—and see what happens to the world.

It wouldn't be a good idea to try to run the world using indicators and systems models, but these tools do help us make the links between, say, oil, water, industrial agriculture, war, and climate change—and other clusters of trends that are often presented as having nothing to do with one another, but that are actually intertwined in ways that may determine the fate of civilization. Knowing these things makes it possible to know what needs doing. But no indicator or model, no matter how clever, will ever change the world: only people can do that. AA

Creating Business Value from Sustainability

RESOURCES

EarthTrends Environmental Information Portal (World Resources Institute)

http://earthtrends.wri.org

On the EarthTrends Web site you can pull up maps, information on a world of issues, plus specific data on individual countries, in a heartbeat. Don't let the word *earth* fool you into thinking this is only environmental data; this site gives you the whole sustainability enchilada, including economic flows and social trends. Need to resolve an argument about climate change, fisheries' collapse, whatever? Go here first.

Gapminder

http://www.gapminder.org

Gapminder offers brilliant visualizations of vast seas of global data. With this site's time-lapse graphics, you can watch the world (largely) get richer and healthier over the course of the twentieth century. Then watch China's great big blob of data explode into a lot of little regional blobs, some very rich (the city of Shanghai), some very poor (the province of Sichuan). These images help you make sense of the deeper news behind the headlines.

TED Talk: Hans Rosling on Global Population Growth

http://www.ted.com/talks/hans_rosling_on_global_population_growth.html

Hans Rosling is a professor of global health at Sweden's Karolinska Institute and a cofounder of Gapminder. This talk, given at TED@Cannes in 2010, is a masterful summary of the interwoven challenges of population growth, the rise out of poverty, and the crisis of sustainability.

A "healthy" company can't last long in an unhealthy environment. True, companies can turn a profit while polluting the air and water, despoiling the landscape, and consuming natural resources with abandon, but they won't be able to go on like that forever. Environmental and social issues are roiling the world of business, causing companies to rethink their products and services, their operations, even their business models. Amid the changes, adaptive companies of all sizes and sectors are finding opportunities to be more competitive and profitable by aligning sustainability goals with their core business strategies. Many companies are already learning the price of operating in places with severe environmental problems: increased regulation, more expensive natural resources, greater difficulty attracting and retaining talent.

The world of commerce relies heavily on a healthy natural environment. Nature's systems provide a wealth of tangible and intangible services to business—some $33 trillion worth of "free" deliverables a year, say experts in the "Millennium Ecosystem Assessment Synthesis Report." Those services include fertile soil, fresh water, breathable air, pollination, species habitat, soil formation, pest control, a livable climate, and a host of other things we tend to take for granted.

None of these services appear on companies' balance sheets, but their availability, or lack thereof, can have a dramatic impact on a company's finances.

For example, to prepare for the inevitable regulation of carbon dioxide emissions, many companies are investing in new, more efficient technologies. When nature's services—in this case, the planet's ability to dissipate industrial emissions and keep surface temperatures at a livable level—are overtaxed, this is the cost to business. JM

The Company-level View

███████ The definition of "sustainable business" is rapidly changing. As recently as the early 1990s, being environmentally responsible meant looking beyond what the law required to do a few simple things—say, recycling office paper or increasing the use of recycled materials in products or packaging. By the end of the 1990s, companies were taking a broader view: using energy, water, and materials more efficiently; preventing pollution through improved management controls; and taking other measures that reduced emissions and saved money.

Now, the leading edge of sustainable business practices has moved beyond saving money to making money. Sustainability is now seen by many leading companies as a means of creating new business value: increasing sales, creating innovative products and services, and expanding markets. Sustainability is also seen as a way to improve product and service quality, reduce risk, attract and retain employees, and enhance brand value and customer loyalty.

Not every green or sustainably minded effort yields companies the full complement of benefits, of course. But increasingly, the case for sustainable business has become clearer. Both

societal and ecological trends suggest that sustainability's benefits to business will only increase.

Concerns about reliable and affordable energy, water, and other natural resources—and the increased likelihood that emission of greenhouse gases will be regulated—are just a few of the realities facing business leaders today. Institutional investors and large insurers are signaling their concerns about the risks and liabilities of companies that don't effectively manage their wastes, resource use, and emissions. And customers of all types—governments, businesses, and individuals—are increasingly buying from companies that show a commitment to sustainability, or are avoiding companies they believe to be shirking their responsibility.

Our expectations of companies will grow as we continue to think greener, and as current events—record heat waves, catastrophic storms, energy disruptions and price spikes, global insecurity—reveal the dangers of ignoring sustainability. Companies that already have started to integrate sustainability into their organizational fabric will be better prepared than their competitors to ride the waves of change and to prosper in tomorrow's markets. JM

What Can I Do in My Company?

███████ Nearly every choice you and your colleagues make affects your company's environmental performance—and, potentially, its reputation and financial performance. The materials and equipment you purchase, the way you design and deliver products and services, the way you build and maintain facilities, and the relationships you—as a representative of your company—have with stakeholders can all contribute to greater business sustainability. There's no recipe for making a business more sustainable. The ingredients depend on a range of factors, including a company's size, sector, and geography. But in taking steps toward sustainability in your company, you can apply the following general principles of conduct:

Whole Foods Market has become synonymous with the booming organic-food industry.

Obey the law. Comply with local, state, and federal environmental, health, and safety regulations. This gives beyond-compliance efforts a solid foundation. You may gain additional benefits: some governmental programs reward fully compliant companies with reduced oversight and paperwork.

Understand how your business affects the environment. From the things you buy to your relationships with customers and suppliers, to the full life cycle of your products and services—each step of the way, you can make choices that will go toward aligning environmental responsibility with business success.

Begin to make changes where they can be made profitably. If you can't achieve a profit immediately, you can at least make changes in a way that will not decrease profits and productivity for more than a short period. It's important to keep in mind that it isn't possible to do everything right; gradual, incremental progress is a worthy goal.

Measure and track your waste. Watch what your company consumes (raw materials, energy, supplies) and what it wastes (raw materials, energy, packaging, emissions). Try to measure and quantify this waste: how much do you spend to purchase, handle, store, and dispose of the wasted material? Your audit may be as simple as counting or weighing the trash bags your company disposes of on a weekly or monthly basis, or checking energy bills regularly.

Draft an environmental-vision statement. It's easier to get behind a vision when all of the players know what the company stands for. Having an established point of departure will show customers, stakeholders, and your community that your business is invested in the environment.

Rally the troops. Bring together a team of employees to promote sustainability in the workplace.

Team members can head up the effort to purchase recycled products, educate coworkers on environmental issues, and track environmental accounting for their departments. Consider creating incentives such as rewards and recognition for employees who drive your company's environmental efforts. Name a periodic "green champion" in order to single out employees' environmental contributions. JM

The Natural Step

You don't need an advanced degree to understand that we can't indefinitely extract material from the earth and turn it into waste faster than the earth's systems can naturally reabsorb it. Such an imbalance causes increasing disorder that's manifested in environmental, social, and political discord. Upon this basic principle, and in response to growing concern, a group of Swedish doctors and scientists developed the Natural Step, a framework for making business and organizational operations more sustainable. The Natural Step offers a simple point of reference for prioritizing sustainable practice while also succeeding in business.

Grounded in science, the principles are straightforward and logical, making them effective tools for bringing companies and countries together around the ideas of sustainability. In the Natural Step's framework for addressing environmental issues, consensus is key. Agreement among all players leads to the creation of better benchmarks, comprehensible measurements of progress, and a clearer structure for planning future development.

After scandals and boycotts, Nike saved its brand by embracing Natural Step philosophy.

Time and again, companies (Nike, Interface, and IKEA, to name just a few) have found that embracing the Natural Step puts them ahead of regulation. The benefits include greater efficiency, improved brand image, more effective customer relations, and ultimately, profit.

When companies see sustainable practices as inherently profitable, they can't help but be enticed. The principles of the Natural Step can help to clarify this connection, and can prove to be an indispensable tool in a company's toolbox as it seeks both patent bottom-line profit and the more intangible benefits of a healthier ecosystem and a better-supported community. NA

■■■■ RESOURCES

The Truth About Green Business by Gil Friend (FT Press, 2009)
Worldchanging ally and president and CEO of Natural Logic Inc., Gil Friend has created an excellent primer for businesses that are trying to understand the basics of greening their operations. Along with clear, concise explanations of major trends like social auditing and closed-loop manufacturing, *The Truth About Green Business* lays out strategies for implementing things like energy-efficiency measures and supply-chain management. CB

The State of Green Business by Joel Makower
http://www.stateofgreenbusiness.com
Issued by sustainable business blog GreenBiz.com, this annual report explores all arenas of the green economy. It tracks how businesses have fared and rates the global progress on implementing broad green business strategies like creating better carbon disclosure, recycling e-waste, and encouraging telecommuting. This is the clearest, best-organized up-to-the-minute overview of the major trends affecting green business.

Dancing with the Tiger: Learning Sustainability Step by Natural Step by Brian Nattrass and Mary Altomare (New Society Publishers, 2002)
Coauthors previously of *The Natural Step for Business*, Nattrass and Altomare have reemerged with this important book revealing the real-life scenarios behind the approach that today's competitive

corporations (among them Nike and Starbucks) are taking to establish sustainable business practices. Contending that companies must apply a holistic approach in their efforts toward sustainability, the authors argue, "It is only through people—through the heart, mind, and will of each individual—that the innovations of sustainability will be diffused and adopted within our corporations, our governments, and ultimately our world." If more major corporations followed the models presented in *Dancing with the Tiger*, the business world as we know it would be on a straight path toward sustainability on all fronts.

Capitalism at the Crossroads: The Unlimited Business Opportunities in Solving the World's Most Difficult Problems by Stuart L. Hart (Wharton School Publishing, 2005)
Stuart Hart makes it clear that there is no inherent conflict between creating a better world and achieving economic prosperity. Global capitalism is at a crossroads, he argues, and "corporations are the only entities in the world today with the technology, resources, capacity, and global reach required" to create a more sustainable world. Drawing on his consulting experience with top companies and nongovernmental organizations worldwide, Hart contends that to truly change the world, we need to focus on the bottom of the pyramid, on the 4 billion people with disposable incomes of less than ten dollars a year—who represent a $4 trillion marketplace.

Opposite, left: The United Farm Workers boycott of Gallo persuaded the winery to change its policies toward its workforce, San Francisco, 2005.
Opposite, right: NGOs use the media to demand transparency, helping this union leader appeal for the release of arrested South Korean protesters.

Transparency in Business

▰▰▰▰ Nowadays, corporations can build intimate relationships with customers. We all know that they are targeting their market research to each of us, as individuals: they're amassing data on our preferences and buying patterns, trying to anticipate our needs. But we don't often think about how this intimacy goes both ways: we're also increasingly well informed about the goods we buy and the companies that make them.

When shopping for a computer, for instance, we can use the scads of online product-evaluation sites to get a startling level of insight into not only the prices of various models, but also their origin, performance, and constituent parts. Fanatical user groups dedicated to everything from Prius hybrids to soap operas don't just bring the kind of publicity money literally can't buy, they also wreak havoc by reporting on a product or a service's faults. As a result, it's growing harder for companies to get away with stuff—corporate crime and shoddy quality quickly find their way to the Internet. Even in remote corners of the world, blunders and bad behavior are ever more likely to be captured on video and phoned in over a satellite.

In this context, it's simply stupid corporate strategy to depend on secrecy or distance to cover your tracks. Anything less than full disclosure—open, willing, eager disclosure—is likely to backfire. Even the appearance of opacity will set off alarms. And if transparency rewards good behavior with more loyal customers, it also allows sharper, more decisive consumer activism, quite above and beyond the scope of government regulations. Hell hath no fury like a pissed-off consumer, and the avenging spirit of the people is now empowered as never before; actions are much more easily coordinated, damage to reputations much more easily spread. Although it's unlikely that any large corporation to date has been driven out of business through citizen action alone, it's just a matter of time before it happens.

In a transparent world, businesses must at the very least appear to be good, or appear to be making a concerted effort to change. "NGOs and other stakeholders are more likely to acknowledge progress and success if companies are candid about problems and even mistakes," says Bennett Freeman, managing director for corporate responsibility at Burson-Marsteller.

And once one business has proclaimed a desire to change, or admitted its failure to do so, pressure on other businesses will mount, driving even reluctant companies to do better or suffer dire consequences. As Don Tapscott and David Ticoll

argue in their 2003 book *The Naked Corporation*, this is simply the new face of business.

"If you have to be naked, you had better be buff. We are entering an extraordinary age of transparency, where businesses must for the first time make themselves clearly visible to shareholders, customers, employees, partners, and society. Financial data, employee grievances, internal memos, environmental disasters, product weaknesses, international protests, scandals and policies, good news and bad; all can be seen by anyone who knows where to look. Welcome to the world of the naked corporation."

Companies that are willing to embrace transparency find themselves with allies—investors, collaborators, journalists, users, and employees—who will see them through their efforts to change. Corporate innovation today is all about having deep, open, honest two-way relationships with long-term investors, NGOs, government regulators, collaborative networks, and consumer groups. Fostering and nurturing those relationships is increasingly a major part of business operations, because they are the founts from which slow and deliberate capital, new innovation, and customer loyalty all spring. And those relationships can be fostered and nurtured only by folks who consider themselves active forces for positive change. AS

Corporate Political Transparency

▬▬▬▬ Much is made of various measures of corporate progress toward sustainability: Company X has reduced its carbon footprint by 10 percent; Company Y has introduced a line of recycled products; Company Z will offer new and more efficient technology next year. But in reality, one criterion matters more than all the others put together, and it's almost never mentioned in the green business press: where a company spends its lobbying budget.

A huge number of companies make modest improvements in their practices but lobby all-out, in a variety of ways, to stall the adoption of higher environmental standards in their products,

better land-use practices, green taxes, or even health and safety regulations. And the impacts of those lobbying efforts usually far, far outweigh the good these companies claim to be doing with their pilot green efforts.

A recent example is the revelation of donations by companies that like to claim green leadership, including Microsoft, Toyota, and Walmart, to the Cato Institute, an ultra-anti-environmental think tank responsible for (among other things) an ad campaign that relies on the opinions of climate-change skeptics to target President Obama's climate policies. That's right, buying a Prius may have helped fund an attack on climate action.

This is not an isolated incident. Take Walmart. The big-box giant has long been known in environmental policy circles as one of the leading opponents of better land-use practices and greener taxation policies. It not only spends huge sums of money paying employees to influence all manner of decisions ($5.2 million in 2008 on in-house lobbyists alone), it also spends heavily on lobbyists influencing local and state governments and, increasingly, the federal government (more than $4 million on lobbyists in 2007). This doesn't even count the much greater amounts of money the company spends indirectly—on PR—to help it greenwash its practices and on support for industry groups, publications, and antienvironmental think tanks. Walmart is also one of the largest political donors in the United States, with its PAC alone spending more than $3 million in 2008. How many compact fluorescents would it need to sell to offset the miles and miles of suburban sprawl it's fought to make possible?

Preying on our misguided sense of personal responsibility for environmental issues, such companies promote and sell us "green" goods and services while simultaneously opposing the very kind of systemic changes we need if we're going to avoid planetary collapse. And this is absolutely not just an American problem; indeed, in our globalized world, some companies are quite cosmopolitan in their efforts to corrupt government progress toward sustainability wherever it threatens their outdated business models.

We already have certification systems and other ways of making transparent the material backstories of specific products. We have all manner of rankings and ratings of sustainability practices (however deeply flawed). What we don't have is what we most need: an absolute measure of corporate political accountability.

Transparency International follows corporate corruption and bribery worldwide, and has proposed a set of standards for eliminating it. Other organizations have developed great tools for quickly revealing the origins of political contributions and so on. But these measures don't tell the whole story.

What we need is a standard for corporate political accountability—a sort of transparency index—and a way that companies' ratings can be clearly reported and easily understood by those looking to buy an item or invest in a stock. That way, you could know before supporting a company if it is a) forthcoming in its political practices, and b) supportive of a few critical, well-understood bedrock political issues (like the environment, smart growth, and human rights). AS

Backstory Management

■■■■■   There was a time, not that long ago, when a company's responsibilities stopped at the office door.

Those days are over. Where once companies were held accountable only for what they did (and sometimes not even for that), nowadays they are increasingly held accountable for what they caused to happen. As the consulting outfit SustainAbility puts it in their report "The Changing Landscape of Liability," "Boundaries of accountability will progressively expand through the value chain and through the whole life-cycle of a product's development, production, use and disposal."

In other words, a company's suppliers matter. The suppliers' subcontractors matter. The labor standards of everyone who had any part in making the product matter. The materials in the product and the energy used to make it matter. The manufacturing process itself matters, as does the company's plan for disposing of the product when its life is over. Indeed, as far as corporate reputations are concerned, accountability is becoming a vast web of entanglements in the actions of others, some of whom the leaders of that corporation would be hard-pressed to name.

This is a new—and powerful—development. For a while now we've had an increasingly effective global movement of nongovernmental organizations aimed at forcing entire industries into compliance with certification systems (think FSC timber or fair-trade coffee). Now companies are finding themselves held responsible for the whole backstory of their products.

A product's backstory [see Knowing the Backstory, p. 39] is everything that happened to get the object or service to us, everything that will happen behind the scenes while we use it, and everything that will happen after it leaves our lives. Some companies are getting better at telling the backstories of the things they make. Others—those who can't figure out how to tell their backstories, or whose backstories are shameful—are sailing into the storm. Indeed, this issue will be the critical business-communication challenge of the next decade. We're entering an era of holistic accountability and backstory management.

One way to help foreground the backstory is to refine supplier scorecards to include their level of environmental and social responsibility in addition to the usual markers of customer service, quality, and price. Criteria may be based on those of ecolabels, or may be tailored based on input from third-party groups, such as social-auditing firms, or from specific stakeholders. As backstories come to define corporate brands, smart companies will watch their supply chains just as closely as their marketing budgets. AS

Social Auditing

■■■■■   Meeting all the criteria for third-party certification can be difficult for the smallest of businesses; if a company has a long and complex supply chain there's an even greater possibility that somewhere along the line lurks an oversight that may negate its best efforts to go green. To get a thorough and realistic picture of their credentials, many businesses are turning to nonprofit social auditing groups.

Verité, a consultancy based in Amherst, Massachusetts, and with offices in India, Bolivia, China, and the Philippines, focuses its audits on workers' rights. Verité consultants scour an entire supply chain for signs of labor or human rights violations; this often includes both reviewing company records and visiting a physical plant to inspect it and interview workers.

Many companies already commission some sort of "eco-audit," often to evaluate energy efficiency or waste-stream management; but social auditing is in some ways more valuable, especially to any business that involves manufacturing or agriculture. As Heather White, the founder of Verité, has noted, the emergence of social-auditing firms has taken the pressure off nongovernmental organizations, which typically don't have the resources or expertise to do much more than monitor companies. Firms like Verité have much more success in creating partnerships with companies to correct problems—monitoring becomes a proactive measure. CB

Branded!: How the "Certification Revolution" Is Transforming Global Corporations by Michael E. Conroy (New Society, 2007)

In his excellent book, Michael Conroy notes that a whole array of industries are now coming into compliance with third-party accountability systems that certify whether or not that company's actions meet basic environmental and social standards. It's not just coffee and chocolate that are certified nowadays, but also mining, banking, apparel, chemicals, and so on. If you're in business, you can be sure that someone, somewhere has a certification system with your name on it.

TerraChoice, "The 7 Sins of Greenwashing"
http://sinsofgreenwashing.org

Out of the 2,219 "green" products in the United States and Canada studied by TerraChoice for their 2009 report, only 25, or less than 2 percent, were found to be completely free of greenwash. Ninety-eight percent of products committed at least one of TerraChoice's identified greenwashing sins, which include things like "worshipping false labels" and one of our favorites, "the hidden trade-off." The full report and the 2007 report that preceded it can be downloaded, and the rest of the site lays out the seven sins in an exceedingly user-friendly format (with illustrations of a cute little green demon). A Marketer's Guide helps businesspeople avoid the pitfalls of greenwashing.

Eco Label Index
http://www.ecolabelindex.com

The Eco Label Index is a global, independent database that tracks hundreds of ecolabels in more than two hundred countries. You can search the database or download the Global Ecolabel Monitor, a report produced in conjunction with the World Resources Institute, which surveyed hundreds of ecolabels. The report found that many labels were lacking in transparency—more than half of those surveyed were either unreachable or uncooperative in disclosing core metrics—and missing opportunities to collaborate to support one another's missions and reduce consumer confusion.

The Business and Human Rights Resource Centre
http://www.business-humanrights.org

In short, the Business and Human Rights Resource Centre is *the* database for how businesses across the globe treat their workers. It is an up-to-date guide to more than four thousand companies and their human rights records, both positive and negative. As a leading and independent resource, the center allows and encourages company responses to accusations in an effort to maintain balanced coverage.

Basel Action Network
http://ban.org

The Basel Action Network (BAN) is a policy advocacy group that researches and investigates issues of toxic waste. BAN drives campaigns to eliminate toxic electronic-waste dumping, especially in developing countries. As the only network in the world doing such work, it is determined to counter the effects of toxic trade. Not only does BAN want to ban waste trade, they encourage and promote toxic-free, green alternatives in product design.

Global Reporting Initiative
http://www.globalreporting.org

The GRI is a framework for reporting on corporate policies in several categories: environmental impact, human rights, labor practices, producer responsibility, and social responsibility. It's one of the world's most recognized standards for corporate social responsibility.

Reinventing the Workplace

▬▬▬▬ Innovation is driving a revolution not just in the work we do, but where and how we do it. The workforce is changing and the workplace is changing with it.

Take telecommuting. According to the *State of Green Business 2010*, 8.7 million Americans telecommuted in 2009. Some large companies, like Cisco, have been touting the benefits of telecommuting for years. About 85 percent of Cisco's employees telecommute, and it saves the company $277 million annually in productivity gains (while saving the planet an estimated 47,320 metric tons of greenhouse gases). The telecommuting trend is expected to grow: a conservative estimate predicts 9.6 million telecommuters in the United States by 2013. Even before the financial crisis of 2008 had companies quickly reducing full-time staff, more businesses were starting to turn to a mix of long-time employees, part-timers, and contractors.

So, millions of people no longer require cubicles with their names on them, which means reduced overhead. In turn, new studies confirm the health benefits of less commuting, including simply gaining back the time spent in transit. In conjunction with changing definitions of true wealth [see Questioning Consumption, p. 34], a growing understanding of the importance of "time affluence" is making time off one of the most valuable components of any benefits package.

This shift in emphasis—and a newly dispersed workforce—is helping companies to understand that the one-size-fits-all approach to climbing the career ladder is doing no one any good. In fact, nowadays, customizing career paths to incorporate a variety of flex-time programs and a new definition of the workplace is one of the best ways to woo—and hold onto—talented workers. It's also paradoxically one of the best ways to coax the greatest productivity out of people.

If these trends continue, the workplace as we know it will become obsolete. Already, freelancers and small businesses are figuring out how to share space with other like-minded businesses, making "the office" a much more nebulous and dynamic thing. CB

One Approach to Sustainability: Work Less

▬▬▬▬ If you want to reduce landfills, reduce working hours.

The long hours people in the United States work—some three hundred more per year than western Europeans—mean they are more likely to rely on "convenience" and disposable items, such as heavily packaged fast foods and single-use goods. Moreover, people who are time-stressed are more likely to emphasize material goods as a source of comfort and status, rather than experiences and relationships. When we're busy, we're more likely to go shopping and less likely to go visiting. Stuff-oriented lifestyles, of course, are a much greater burden on the planet.

To create a sustainable society, we'll need to work less to have more of what we truly need: time.

Europe—Vive la Différence!

With their long vacations and much shorter working hours, western Europeans are consistently far healthier than Americans—after the age of fifty, they are only about half as likely to suffer from chronic illnesses such as heart disease, type 2 diabetes, hypertension, and even cancer. They are only half as likely to suffer from depression and anxiety, and they spend only half as much on average as Americans do for health care. Studies show their better health results from more exercise, more socializing with friends and families, less stress, and more sleep; all of these are made possible by having more time.

Europeans' lives are not only more personally sustainable (they're longer!), but they're also more environmentally sustainable. On average, Europeans produce only about half the amount of air pollution, use half as much energy, and produce half as much solid waste and less than half the greenhouse gases per capita as Americans do, all while enjoying a similar quality of life. They are far from perfect—if everyone on earth followed their lifestyle, we would still require two and half planets—but their ecological impact is far less than ours.

A December 2006 study by the Center for Economic and Policy Research provided strong evidence that if Americans were to reduce their working hours to European levels, they could drastically cut their energy use by as much as 26 percent, nearly meeting key Kyoto climate change targets. Combine this massive reduction with advances in clean energy technology, and we could reduce our impacts even further.

The study argued that by reducing work hours, Americans would reduce the energy used for transportation (because they have more time, Europeans are far more likely to walk, bike, or take public transit) and, even more importantly, would reduce the energy necessary for the production of goods—as Americans traded time for money, they would consume and produce less.

The Four-day Week

In response to escalating fuel costs, many companies are now considering going to a four-day work week. They believe this will save large sums on commuter fuel expenses and reduce traffic congestion. The problem is that they are thinking in terms of four ten-hour days. But for many American families in which both parents work, such long days will intensify daily stress.

Families will find less time to take care of tasks on the home front, or to exercise, eat properly, and so forth; and families with young children will be hit particularly hard—imagine leaving children in daycare for ten or more hours a day. The health impacts could be severe, too. Increased pressure to reduce commute times (since the work day is already so long) would encourage more high-energy (automobile) commuting so as to have more time at home. Moreover, businesses would see a clear decline in hourly productivity, since fatigue sets in rapidly after eight hours on the job.

The real solution to this problem is to go to a four-day work week of eight-hour days. Total production would be reduced slightly, but it would make us more sustainable. We could expect significant reductions in energy and resource use, as well as in health problems and health-care costs. The Center for a New American Dream, a Maryland nonprofit, has had a thirty-two-hour work week for ten years, with excellent results for productivity, creativity, and worker morale.

An easy first step in the United States would be to increase the amount of guaranteed paid vacation workers are given, and to build a cultural expectation that people would take the vacation they have coming. Studies show paid vacations would be economically beneficial as well as promote less stressful lives, better family relationships . . . and less impact on the planet. JDG

Bright Green Benefits or Total Institutions?

▪▪▪▪▪▪   Nothing elicits more envy among cubicle-farm denizens than the Googleplex. Google's company headquarters in Mountain View, California, is more like a giant playground than an office park. Pool tables, swimming pools, and volleyball courts redefine the concept of the "break room." Wacky desk decor and casual dress are encouraged, and employees can bring their dogs to work. Cafeterias that wouldn't look out of place on a downtown street serve employees three free meals a day of high-quality, well-sourced food. Hair cutting, dry cleaning, massage therapy, and dental work are just a few services available onsite for convenience, often at greatly discounted rates.

Google isn't the only company trying to create workplaces that are actually fun to work in. Many tech enterprises—Apple and Microsoft are two others—understand that in order to lure the best and brightest to their massive campuses, keep worker productivity high, and minimize turnover, they have to offer more perks than a 401(k). In some ways, this is a great development. Many of the measures—like offering plush employee

shuttle buses equipped with Wi-Fi—increase quality of life for workers while encouraging more sustainable choices than joining the army of single drivers in a daily commute. (Free shuttle buses make it easy for Google workers to commute from San Francisco, for example.)

But gaining access to the Googleplex requires sacrifices. One of the reasons the campus needs to be so fully outfitted with services is because many of its employees spend a lot of time there—probably too much time. Dalton Conley, in his excellent book *Elsewhere U.S.A.*, has a less sunny take on the Googleplex:

"Google approximates a 'total institution' perhaps more than any other private corporation since the days of company towns run by mining interests. A total institution is a social environment where the participants experience all aspects of their lives—meals, sleeping, grooming, socializing, recreation, and so on. Common examples of total institutions are military barracks, prisons, mental hospitals, and university campuses."

For workers who know they can't escape long hours because they work in industries where everyone is perpetually on call (or, more accurately, on e-mail), a work environment like the Googleplex is a major selling point. (It's been noted that the Googleplex particularly appeals to recently graduated twenty-somethings because it provides an easy transition from one campus—i.e., a place where all their needs are taken care of—to another.)

But productivity studies clearly show that the best thing for worker health and happiness is adequate time off and a life outside of work. And indeed, implementing flex-time programs that can be customized as a person's lifestyle changes may be far more beneficial to workers than being able to do their laundry at work. Even more so, encouraging workers to keep a reasonable division between work and life, including being "out of pocket" (with their phones off) most of the time when at home, has been shown to reduce stress without having much impact on productivity.

Some smaller companies have been successful at both creating dynamic work environments and encouraging time off. Natural Habitat Adventures, a sustainable-tourism operator based

An outdoor dining area at Google's headquarters, known as the Googleplex.

in Colorado that was awarded the top spot on *Outside Magazine*'s "50 Best Places to Work" list in 2010, offers quite a few Googleplex-style onsite perks (fitness facilities, organic foods in the cafeteria, pet-friendly policies) but also facilitates away-time for employees. For example, each employee gets a free trip every year on one of the company's expeditions, and flex-time programs are available, whether to give parents more time to spend with their kids or to give avid skiers more time to spend on the slopes. CB

Flex Time and Customized Career Paths

▬▬▬ The best amenity a company can offer its workers is flexibility—being able to customize their schedules as their careers progress and their lives outside of the office change.

Young people may have more energy to work long hours, but they may also want more dedicated vacation days for travel. Older workers may be content with fewer travel days if they can reduce the number of days per week they work or the number of hours per day. (Addressing the needs of older workers will be more of a necessity in some nations as dwindling retirement funds and an aging population create an aging workforce.) And a parent's scheduling constraints can change each year until children are in school full-time.

Norsk Hydro, a Norwegian aluminum supplier and hydroelectric power company, has been one of the leaders in customizing career paths for nearly a decade. Its Hydroflex program creates an admirable work-life balance by encouraging telecommuting days (and giving workers stipends to set up home offices), providing benefits like thirty-eight weeks of paid maternity leave, and, most importantly, allowing a worker's schedule to change as his or her life changes. As Charles

Fishman noted when he profiled Norsk Hydro in *Fast Company*:

"Linked to the push for flexibility are new notions of diversity. Hydro believes that diversity goes beyond race or gender. Diversity has to do with perspective—and it exists within individuals: Each of us is many different people at different times in our lives. Cultivate that diversity, and greater creativity will follow."

Many companies are focusing more on results than the number of hours clocked in an office. IBM was one of the first U.S. companies to replace an official vacation policy with an "honor system" approach (employees are allowed a certain number of paid vacation days, but how they allocate them is up to them and those days are not tracked closely by their supervisors). Some companies, like Netflix, have gone even further by offering their executives "unlimited" vacation—as long as you get your work done, you can take as much time off as you like. CB

Coworking: A Cornerstone of the Telecommute

▬▬▬ One of the challenges for telecommuters, self-employed people, and small businesses is the cost of setting up office space. Isolation is another pitfall: working outside an office setting can too often mean lonesome days spent in our pajamas.

Coworking spaces are proving to be invaluable to freelancers and small businesses because they address these two major drawbacks. A coworking space provides access to a professionally designed and well-equipped office when

Freelancers and small-business owners share work areas at Office Nomads, one of Seattle's successful coworking spaces.

it's needed—say, for a meeting with a client, or during the stages of a job that require special equipment we might not have at home, like copiers, high-resolution printers, or drafting tables. But the membership fees to use these spaces, even for reserving a dedicated workstation, are lower than the monthly rent on a leased office, especially when other operating costs (utilities, furniture, equipment) are factored in.

The concept has taken off in the past five years, which is not surprising: according to the U.S. Census Bureau, already almost half (49 percent) of the nation's businesses are operated from home. Most major international cities—and smaller cities with sizeable creative communities—have coworking spaces. And these are some seriously cool digs.

Copenhagen's Republikken houses about seventy creative professionals (graphic designers, architects, writers, media consultants) in a converted dance studio. Even meeting rooms have the feel of being in someone's incredibly hip living room. Shared spaces like a games room and a patio, plus regular sponsored events, help Republikken's denizens meet, mingle, and collaborate.

The Hub, an international network of coworking spaces, began as one daylight-filled renovated factory in London. The original branch has, in addition to its desks and meeting rooms, a library nook, "writing rooms" where writers buy a membership so they have a quiet and respectful place to work, and a pleasant café for taking breaks. For all its well-considered details, the Hub's most important service is conviviality. Attracting a range of small organizations and creative people, it fosters community and promotes the cross-pollination of ideas. This is exemplified in the San Francisco branch, Hub SoMa, an 8,600-square-foot space that is a collaboration between the Hub and two other creative organizations: Intersection for the Arts, which runs a gallery in the space, and Tech Shop, which runs a community maker workshop.

The spirit of collaboration and sharing is central to coworking: Chris Messina and Ivan Storck, the founders of the San Francisco coworking spot Citizen Space, created a wiki to give people a blueprint of how to create a great and financially viable coworking space. DD & CB

Scenius, Innovation, and Epicenters

Scenius stands for the intelligence and the intuition of a whole cultural scene. It is the communal form of the concept of the genius.
Brian Eno

▬▬▬ Scenius is exactly what our troubled planet needs: networks of innovators swarming out of their hives to meet up in hubs, salons, and shared workspaces. When smart, creative people gather in the right settings, we become smarter and more creative than we ever could be alone. As Worldchanging ally Kevin Kelly notes, "When buoyed by scenius, you act like genius."

Our best examples of scenius are pretty iconic: think of the Manhattan Project or the Algonquin Round Table. Kelly would add to that list a group of Yosemite rock-climbers who camped illegally for one summer in the 1940s and started a scene that would revolutionize outdoor gear and invent many modern climbing techniques.

Scenius can be local or wide-ranging; it can last a year or several decades. But the one thing these vibrant scenes of communal innovation have in common is epicenters. Every community needs spaces where people who do bold and worldchanging things can get together and fuel one another's ardor. Meeting your allies—shaking hands, sitting down and talking, laughing, getting to look one another in the eye, getting to know someone in all the rich, primate non-verbal ways that can only occur in actual physical proximity—is powerful. Epicenters are tools; every network needs one.

Scenius is difficult, if not impossible, to create on demand, and the same is true of its epicenters. You can't just open a bar and expect collective genius to erupt. Artists will tell us that the same thing is true of any form of human creativity—it just doesn't turn on like a tap. But artists will also tell us that while you can't command creativity and innovation, you can create a welcoming space for it and increase the likelihood that it will show up. It can't be commanded, but it can be courted.

Although the Net is the glue that holds most networks together, it's these "third places"—whether they're bars, workshops, coworking spaces, or even something like the primitive campsite of the Yosemite climbers—that are the epicenters where scenius emerges. In a world where massive innovation is required for its very survival, epicenters are critical to the work ahead of us. AS

Career Learning

▇▇▇▇   Making a difference—in our careers, in our companies, in the world—takes more than just inspiration. To acquire the knowledge and tools for the careers we want in the twenty-first century, we're going to have to integrate ideas of sustainability, ecology, and social justice into whatever fields we pursue. How we learn to do our jobs will determine how we perform them, and how we choose to reinvent our workplaces.

A decade ago, universities didn't offer many options for environmentally focused majors outside of wildlife biology. Now, from Amsterdam to Ontario, Vancouver to Southern California, universities and colleges around the world are reshaping their education models to integrate theories of sustainability into every discipline. They're creating new majors and adjusting traditional ones to prepare their students to be the smart thinkers, brilliant builders, and cunning innovators we'll need to make the transition into a greener, more prosperous world.

Because business is one of the most popular majors in the United States, the "green MBA" has become the most popular sustainability-related degree. Indeed, green MBAs make a lot of sense for workers looking to weave a newfound commitment to sustainability into their current businesses or fields. Schools like the Bainbridge Graduate Institute are on the cutting edge of redefining business education for a new era.

In the United States, some trade schools are farther ahead of the curve than many universities. In 2010 the *Pittsburgh Tribune-Review* reported that Connelley Technical Institute, a trade school that had been in operation for seventy-four years before closing in 2004, was being turned into an incubator for green jobs. Re-envisioned by nonprofit Pittsburgh Green Innovators Inc.—with input from local universities, policy makers, and labor unions—the

new center will contain academic classrooms as well as technical learning areas where high school and adult students will learn skills like solar and green roof installation; it will also include space for groups that promote the development of green businesses in the Hill District of Pittsburgh. Programs like these are turning trade schools into creative hubs that will give us our first wave of green-collar workers.

As exciting as these new continuing education programs are, they still play by the books compared to Denmark's KaosPilot School, which offers a radically different approach to business degree curricula. The school's four core study areas are Creative Project Design, Creative Process Design, Creative Business Design, and Creative Leadership Design. (The school is also in the process of creating an MBI, a Master of Business Imagination.) All programs are transdisciplinary, consist almost entirely of real-world projects for actual clients, and include mandatory time abroad. The program's goal is to create well-rounded, proactive leaders with an interest in sustainability and social entrepreneurship. Graduates—KaosPilots, that is—go on to work in a variety of fields, with some starting their own enterprises and others taking jobs with nongovernmental organizations or the private sector. CB & SK

Unconferences

▇▇▇▇   The ability of networks of people to conceive new ideas and find new answers to old problems seems to be growing by the day, demonstrating that group collaboration often results in breakthrough thinking. The traditional way to bring together large networks of people is to hold a conference. However, most conferences are too expensive, involve too many people, and are too rigidly structured around keynote speeches and panel discussions to give participants enough time to actually work together.

"Unconferences" offer a model for gathering people together to solve problems and share ideas in a low-cost, high-impact way. Typically, invitees create, schedule, and facilitate their own sessions, allowing group interest and abilities to create a conference on the fly. The most famous unconference may be FOOCamp (run by the technology publisher O'Reilly), known as a no-holds-barred brain-wrestling camp for geeks and designers.

Unconferences more closely resemble crowdsourcing projects than conferences. What unconferences and crowdsourcing (along with distributed collaboration and a host of other similar approaches) have in common is this: they tap into people's desire to use their unique skills to help advance meaningful projects and prepare the ground for the emergence of unexpected new ideas and cross-bred solutions. AS

■■■■■ RESOURCES

Coworking Wiki
http://coworking.pbworks.com
Whether you're trying to locate a coworking space in your city or build one from the ground up, this Web site is a great place to start. Although many of the resources are U.S.-specific, information on pricing models, coworking etiquette, and legal concerns with running a space are universal.

Elsewhere, U.S.A.: How We Got from the Company Man, Family Dinners, and the Affluent Society to the Home Office, BlackBerry Moms, and Economic Anxiety by Dalton Conley (Pantheon, 2009)
Conley's thorough (and at times, thoroughly depressing) exploration of the evolution of time poverty and its effects on the American psyche covers everything from the pros and cons of telecommuting to changing power dynamics between time-pressed people and the nannies who raise their kids. Mostly it provides a solid case for a renewed separation between work and home:

"This work-and-play blurring ends up enhancing Mrs. and Mr. Elsewhere's sense of alienation: It's not just that they feel like they need to be working when they are ostensibly supposed to be having fun or, conversely, that they should stop working and be there for their kids, spouse, or friends. It's not just that Mr. and Mrs. 2009 need to be everywhere at once. It's that the once disparate spheres have now collided and interpenetrated each other, creating a sense of 'elsewhere' at all times. I'm not just talking about the increase in travel and telecommunications. I am talking about the more subtle changes that they have rendered: the fact that home is more like work and work is more like home and that the private and public spheres are increasingly indistinguishable from each other." CB

Take Back Your Time
http://www.timeday.org
Take Back Your Time is a U.S./Canadian campaign that challenges time poverty: the epidemic of overwork, overscheduling, and time famine. The campaign promotes idea like mandatory vacations and rewarding gains in productivity with time instead of stuff. In our view, such a strategy would leave Americans healthier, happier, and more connected to one another, their communities, and the environment.

Anything goes at an unconference. Here, participants at FOOCamp 2009 pitch tents at the conference site instead of staying at a convention center hotel.

POLITICS

▬ Building a better world is a tough business. Many of the steps demand long-term vision, and the real payoffs for each of us as individuals (prosperity, health, safety, clear consciences) come gradually and dif-fusely. Moving toward a bright green future takes a lot of thinking and debate, careful innovation, and good government policies.

In the meantime, however, people willing to act in dangerous and immoral ways often gain simply, immediately, and directly. Protecting a grove of old-growth trees can benefit us all a little in the long run, but clear-cutting that forest can yield a company massive profits—instantly. Educating every child will benefit us all over time; putting those children to work in a sweatshop will benefit a factory owner right away. Greedy, corrupt, violent, power-hungry people have every incentive to be fierce in the pursuit of their own interests. And the rest of us sometimes have a hard time knowing how to stop them.

But stopping them from their nefarious practices and defending the public good are vital. We can't change the world if we can't keep dangerous people from destroying it. Politics is our means to do just that.

Making politics work isn't simple. We need to show how the future could be better, and band together with others to create the conditions for that better future. We need to bring forward new ideas, and connect people who are passionate about seeing them implemented. We need to demand transparency in government, elect the best politicians we can find, and hold leaders who do wrong accountable. We need, in short, to spread, grow, and protect democracies.

It won't be easy. Power, as the great abolitionist orator Frederick Douglass taught us, concedes nothing without a struggle. The small number of powerful men who benefit the most from oppression and exploitation will fight with every means at their disposal. Dictators will murder and jail and torture those who speak against them. Wealthy interests will attempt to corrupt existing political systems and use the power of propaganda to divert attention from their actions. Demagogues will use hatred and fear to frighten people away. In many ways, the odds are stacked against us.

But in many other ways, the tide is moving in our direction. Never have there been so many tools for allowing citizens to reclaim their nations. Information technologies make it easier for people (with access) to not only speak up against injustice, but to find others with a common cause and unite with them. We have better models than ever before for working effectively together in civic groups and for mobilizing others. We know how to create better civic conversations, pursue better public visions, and establish better public policies. We know new ways to fight corruption and open the workings of governments to everyone. We're even learning how to work together to protect human rights advocates, prevent wars, confront dictators, and build peace.

Best of all, we're not alone. All over the world, a new generation of millions of worldchangers is emerging, connecting, sharing information, and developing tools together. The strongest force on earth is not an army or a police force or a government or a corporation—it is we ourselves, awakened to the dangers we face and the possibilities we are creating. We are everywhere. We have powerful tools. And though we come from all nations, races, and creeds, we're increasingly fighting for the same kind of future—where democracy, transparency, human rights, and peace prevail. If we work together well enough, we just might get there. AS

Movement Building

▅▅▅▅ Optimism is a political act. Entrenched interests promote despair, confusion, and apathy to prevent change. They encourage us to think that problems can't be solved, that nothing we do can matter, that the issues are too complex to allow even the possibility of change. It is a long-standing political art to sow the seeds of mistrust among those you would rule: as Machiavelli taught, tyrants do not care if they are hated, so long as those under them do not love one another. Cynicism is often seen as a rebellious attitude in Western popular culture, but in reality, our cynicism advances the desires of the powerful: cynicism is obedience.

Optimism, by contrast, when it's neither foolish nor silent, can be revolutionary. When no one believes in a better future, despair is a logical choice—and people in despair almost never change anything. When no one believes there might be a better solution, those who benefit from the status quo are safe. When no one believes in the possibility of action, apathy becomes an insurmountable obstacle to reform. But when people have some intelligent reasons to believe that a better future can be built,

that better solutions are available, and that action is possible, their power to act out of their highest principles is unleashed. Shared belief in a better future is the strongest glue there is.

Great movements for social change always begin with statements of great optimism. Facing as we do today so many interlocking challenges, one of our biggest tasks is simply this: to be willing to look so many looming catastrophes in the face and courageously point out that radical changes for the better are possible. History attests that if we can show people a better future, we can build movements that will change the world. AS

The Abolition Movement

▅▅▅▅ Can a small group of people change the world? The answer is unquestionably yes—a minority of dedicated and savvy people can trigger big things. Social values don't always change at glacial speed.

Sometimes they change astonishingly fast. A powerful case in point is Britain's massive and swift shift in attitudes and policy concerning slavery in the early nineteenth century. As the popular historian Niall Ferguson puts it in *Empire: The Rise and Demise of the British Empire and the Lessons for Global Power,* "It used to be argued that slavery was abolished simply because it had ceased to be profitable, but all the evidence points

Preceding pages: After months of prodemocracy demonstrations and two days of brutal assaults by the Chinese government's army in June 1989, "Tank Man" stepped in front of a line of moving tanks in Tiananmen Square, Beijing. Although his identity remains unknown, he has become an enduring symbol of the power of individual defiance.
Left: A voter registration drive in Denver just before the Democratic National Convention on August 22, 2008.
Opposite: Dr. Martin Luther King, Jr.'s "I Have a Dream" speech electrified its audience with an inspiring vision for the future and is a compelling demonstration of the power of words to change the course of history.

the other way: in fact, it was abolished despite the fact that it was still profitable. What we need to understand, then, is a collective change of heart. Like all such great changes, it had small beginnings" (2003).

Antislavery activists had to start small, because overturning an ancient, almost universal practice was a seemingly impossible challenge. While considered barbaric today, slavery was accepted for most of human history as a necessary, if unsavory, part of the natural order of things. Neither the Bible nor Christian tradition explicitly opposed it (although religious antislavery activists would later use the teachings of Jesus to support their cause), and the dominant thinking of the period easily rationalized its existence: oppression could be justified and explained by a sort of proto–social Darwinism. Given the widespread belief in European superiority, and the powerful, entrenched economic interests supporting the slave trade, the quick and decisive defeat of slavery was amazing; that citizen action was able to end it all was more amazing still.

Yet end it the abolitionists did. The British antislavery movement was officially born in a printshop in London in 1787; in August 1838, Parliament granted emancipation to 800,000 slaves. In just over fifty years, a fundamental and previously unquestioned institution of the British Empire was challenged, made odious to the public, politically discredited, and abolished outright.

How was slavery ended so quickly? Through the efforts of a small but committed group of antislavery activists. Remarkably diverse, the champions of abolitionism included religious leaders across denominations—Quakers, Evangelicals, Unitarians—as well as some of the day's leading thinkers, including ex-slaver John Newton, politician Edmund Burke, poet Samuel Taylor Coleridge, and industrialist and pottery giant Josiah Wedgwood.

The abolitionist movement is especially relevant today because it spawned the modern nongovernmental organization (NGO). Abolitionists invented a new kind of politics, the politics of the pressure group, and marshaled an impressive groundswell of support that profoundly influenced legislators in Britain. The movement also pioneered such NGO tools as direct mail, the newsletter, the boycott, and the media campaign.

A letter-writing campaign essentially marked the start of the movement. Former slave Olaudah Equiano presented himself to the English scholar Granville Sharp, desperate to get someone, anyone, to pay attention to an obscure court case. The case involved a ship captain facing insurance-fraud charges for throwing 133 sick slaves overboard to their deaths (he wouldn't be able to collect insurance on them if they died of natural causes). Equiano was outraged that no one seemed to think the man should be tried for murder. When Sharp heard the tale, he was equally outraged and wrote to everyone he knew, decrying this act in particular and slavery in general. One of the people to whom Sharp wrote was the vice-chancellor of Cambridge University, who was so moved by the letter that he decided to make slavery's morality the topic of a prestigious essay-writing contest. The winner of this contest, Thomas Clarkson, became obsessed with the issue in the course of writing his entry; he would become the abolition movement's unstoppable leader.

In a time when many people did not have the right to vote, petitions to Parliament were some of the most powerful tools the abolitionists had—it was only after receiving petition after petition, signed by tens of thousands of people, that the government decided to hold hearings to consider abolishing slavery. (Though nothing ultimately came of these hearings, they were notable: antislavery petitions had never been seen before, and here they dominated the debate.)

Adam Hochschild, in his book *Bury the Chains*, describes what may have been the first large-scale boycott: "Within a few years, another tactic arose from the grassroots. Throughout the length and breadth of the British Isles, people stopped eating the major product harvested by British slaves: sugar. Clarkson was delighted to find a 'remedy, which the people were . . . taking into their own hands . . . By the best computation I was able to make from notes taken down in my journey, no fewer than three hundred thousand persons had abandoned the use of sugar.'"

As quickly as fair-trade labels today have popped up on food products, advertisements flooded the press: "BENJAMIN TRAVERS, Sugar-Refiner, acquaints the Publick that he has now an assortment of Loaves, Lumps, Powder Sugar, and

Syrup, ready for sale . . . produced by the labour of FREEMEN." Then, as now, the full workings of a globalized economy were largely invisible. The boycott brought these hidden connections to light; poet Robert Southey even labeled tea "the blood-sweetened beverage."

The abolitionists used the media with particular skill, employing powerful images and icons to dramatize the horrors and inhumanities of slavery. At an inquiry into the slave trade by the Privy Council in 1788, for instance, abolitionists revealed a diagram of a slave ship, the *Brookes*, showing slaves tightly packed and chained in rows; this started shifting people's perceptions.

Today's activists know that getting people to change their minds often depends on getting something the abolitionists became masters of. As Hochschild explains, "When the famous one-legged pottery entrepreneur Josiah Wedgwood joined the committee, he had one of his craftsmen make a bas-relief of a kneeling slave, in chains, encircled by the legend 'Am I Not a Man and a Brother?' American antislavery sympathizer Benjamin Franklin, impressed, declared that the image had an impact 'equal to that of the best written Pamphlet.' Clarkson gave out five hundred of these medallions on his organizing trips. 'Of the ladies, several wore them in bracelets, and others had them fitted up in an ornamental manner as pins for their hair.' The equivalent of the lapel buttons we wear for an electoral campaign, this was probably the first widespread use of a logo designed for a political cause. It was the eighteenth century's 'new media.'"

The lesson for us today is that entrenched beliefs can shift quite dramatically, seemingly overnight. In the last several decades, we've seen seismic shifts in social values regarding gender, race, religion, and sexuality. We've seen the end of apartheid in South Africa—barely imaginable just a few years before it happened (indeed, not long before apartheid ended, Margaret Thatcher had said, "Anyone who thinks the ANC [the African National Congress] will be running South Africa is living in cloud cuckoo land"). Of course, sometimes even discredited ideas can hold on with a nearly unshakable grip: it took the bloodiest war in American history to end slavery in the United States, and another century of struggle to overthrow the legally enshrined racism that sprang up

in its wake. Some of the global slave trade's effects are still with us today.

The story of the antislavery movement raises some questions that require us to take an imaginative leap. Which of today's practices and beliefs might be considered barbaric and inconceivable just decades from now? Perhaps the intergenerational injustice of destroying the biosphere to satisfy fleeting desires. Perhaps our tolerance of absolute poverty. Perhaps, even, the notion that national boundaries and accidents of birth, rather than merit and hard work, determine one's opportunities in life.

If the history of the abolition movement teaches us anything, it's this: when a small group of people commit themselves utterly to righting an injustice, they redefine the possible. The very act of commitment has the power to change the world. NAB

Mont Fleur

Stories are tools for knowing and judging. Change the stories and you change how people live.
    Brenda Laurel, social entrepreneur

■■■■ It's easy now to underestimate the improbability of the fall of apartheid and the rise of democracy in South Africa. Of course we now know that Nelson Mandela was elected president of South Africa, and that democracy has taken root there, and that—while racial prejudice is still powerfully entrenched in some parts of society— by and large, South Africans are learning to live with one another.

But before all that transpired—and not so very long ago—a peaceful outcome was not at all a given. During the transition, a popular joke went that there were two ways of creating a better future for South Africa—one practical, and the other miraculous. The practical approach was to get down on your knees and pray a violent revolution wouldn't tear the country apart. A negotiated peaceful solution would *truly* take a miracle.

How, then, did South Africa make such a quick and peaceful transition out of apartheid and into a rising democracy? One part of the solution came from a unique project in 1992 that brought together a diverse group of South Africans to imagine the country's future. This included not only concerned citizens and businesspeople, but also embittered enemies—leaders from the paramilitary white right wing, and left-leaning blacks in exile. Together, they created the following four plausible schemata (known as the Mont Fleur Scenarios) imagining South Africa's evolution over the upcoming decade:

- *Ostrich* was a future in which the white government stuck their heads in the sand, their inaction eventually provoking a violent backlash and civil war.
- *Lame Duck* imagined a prolonged transition with a weak government that tried to be all things to all people, and thus ended up doing very little.
- *Icarus* was a future in which a black government came to power, but eventually—in reference to the Greek mythological character—crashed, along with the economy, as a result of unsustainable public spending programs.
- *Flight of the Flamingos* imagined what it would take to create a positive transition and future. Alluding to the fact that it takes some time for a flock of flamingos to fly off together, this was a "slowly but surely" scenario.

When the Mont Fleur Scenarios were released, few people could see one path forward for their nation: suddenly, they had four possible paths to think about and debate. Because the schemata were memorable—simple, with strong imagery—they spread quickly, shaped policy options, and accelerated negotiations between opposing sides. No one wanted a civil war. Even F. W. de

Klerk, the last apartheid-era president (who agreed to end the system), said years later on a radio program that he was "no ostrich" (Beery, Eidinow, and Murphy 1997). Lame Duck and Icarus helped everyone to agree to avoid mistakes like overspending, difficult given that many of the emerging black leaders had come from strong Socialist or Populist backgrounds and there was strong (yet economically unrealistic) pressure to right all of South Africa's wrongs immediately. Significantly, the Mont Fleur process gave one-time enemies practical experience in working together. Not only did this ease the negotiation of the transition into democracy, it paid dividends when it came to the hard work of rebuilding the country.

Since Mont Fleur, imagining shared futures has become an important tool for effecting social change around the world. Happiness, as the Buddha is said to have taught, demands giving up all hope of a better past. Building a vision of the future to which all sides in a conflict can agree helps people let go of the past and begin working together. This constructive engagement in turn breeds hope, and hope energizes and empowers people. Hope makes even bitter enemies behave more responsibly and strategically, because they start to see how certain actions might jeopardize their stake in their future—and that of their children. Mont Fleur helped all South Africans see a proud role for themselves in an important story—building the modern world's most successful example of peaceful systemic change. NAB

Solving Tough Problems: An Open Way of Talking, Listening, and Creating New Realities by Adam Kahane (Berrett-Koehler Publishers, 2004)

Power & Love: A Theory and Practice of Social Change by Adam Kahane (Berrett-Koehler Publishers, 2010)

Any book that has a blurb from Nelson Mandela on the front cover must have something valuable to say about resolving conflict and political stalemates reasonably, peaceably, and compassionately. Kahane has worked with corporate, government, and civil leaders all over the world to help them understand how the hardest problems we face can be solved collaboratively if we are willing to revise the way we've been trained to communicate. As he states in *Solving Tough Problems*: "Most conventional approaches to problem-solving emphasize talking, especially the authoritarian, boss or expert, way of talking: telling. In a debate, each party prepares their position and speech in advance and then delivers it to a panel, which chooses the most convincing speech . . . This approach works for deciding between already created alternatives, but it does not create anything new."

There are many books about creating better dialogues—it's a booming industry—but few can connect their methods to successes in systemic afflictions on the scale of apartheid. Kahane's combination of elegant prose, solutions from the small to the large, and stirring success stories makes *Solving Tough Problems* required reading.

Power and Love explores the work Kahane has done with Reo Partners, an organization that facilitates dialogue and action on projects that involve multiple stakeholders (corporate, government, and civic). Kahane maintains that power and love, often seen as conflicting forces, are actually complementary, and that they must come together to create social change.

"Power expresses our purposefulness, wholeness, and agency. Although power is the drive to realize one's self, the effect of power goes beyond one's self. Power is how we make a difference in the world; it is the means by which new social realities are created. Without power, nothing new grows."

Stir It Up: Lessons in Community Organizing and Advocacy by Rinku Sen (John Wiley and Sons, 2003)

Sponsored by the Ms. Foundation for Women, *Stir It Up* offers a complete set of tools for effective community organizing, based on case studies of fourteen community organizations. According to Sen, "Today's movements for social and economic justice need people who are clear about the problems with the current systems, who rely on solid evidence for their critique, and who are able to reach large numbers of other people with both analysis and proposal."

With step-by-step advice on how to build and mobilize a constituency, and on how to focus internal movement-building so that it leads to external social change, Sen's work is an essential manual for anyone looking to alter public policy.

Opposite, left: South African president Nelson Mandela waves to a crowd in London near the monument erected there in his honor, 1996.

Opposite, right: Two women embrace after being legally married during the first week of state-sanctioned gay marriage in Massachusetts in 2004.

Amplifying Your Voice

▬▬▬ Change begins when people speak up. Wrongs observed in silence are rarely righted, and perhaps more importantly, the problems we face today are so complex that we need everyone's ideas to fix them. We have never been in greater need of a lively, informed, passionate public debate.

Each of us has a role to play in building that debate. We have more tools than ever to make our voices heard: not only the familiar methods of attending public forums, writing to our newspapers, and calling our radio stations, but a whole array of new means powered by the Internet. We have online forums on which we can debate, blogs on which we can publish, wikis on which we can collaborate, video blogs and podcasts through which we can broadcast images and sound. Indeed, new tools roll out every day, most of them cheap, if not free. Never before have average people had greater ability to make themselves heard.

In some places, such speech can come at a high price. Despotic regimes around the world are cracking down on bloggers and online communities, trying to shut down sites that have become centers of dissent. These cyber dissidents deserve our support.

For most of us, the challenge is less a matter of being forbidden to speak than of learning how to advance the dialogue in a meaningful way. But rest assured, resources abound, and with a little hard work, anyone can help put good ideas into the "blogosphere" and help others find new answers and ways of making change. Journalism is too important to be left to the professionals. AS

Participatory Media and the Future of Journalism

▬▬▬ Nowadays, news organizations spend almost as much time covering the supposed death of traditional journalism as they do actually creating a meaningful replacement. And while both the rise of online news and the economic downturn have seriously affected the newspaper and magazine worlds, fears of a newscape dominated by Twitter updates and opinion blogs are a bit overblown.

New-media tools may be shining a not-so-flattering light on the constraints of traditional reporting, but they're also creating ways to keep the best practices of a professional newsroom alive. And all the while, they're incorporating a new and very valuable asset: the public.

We're a few years away from seeing exactly what Journalism 2.0 will look like, but these are some of the most promising trends of the past few years, the projects that are helping us understand what a more participatory media can give us.

Crowdfunded support of investigative reporting. Like many new-media experts, Clay Shirky, a professor at New York University, worries about the future of "accountability journalism," the type of investigative reporting that exposes corruption. In the old newspaper model, "serious" reporting—including speculative investigations that may never yield a Pulitzer Prize—was built into ad-supported budgets. But as media becomes a more on-demand experience, ad revenues are plummeting and advertisers are targeting their efforts. As Shirkey noted in a lecture at Harvard Kennedy School, "Best Buy isn't particularly interested in subsidizing the Baghdad newsroom."

One way to foster accountability journalism is to crowdfund it through micropatronage [see Giving Well, p. 69]. Skeptics have long dismissed the idea of fully crowdfunding the news, based in part on the deeply cynical assertion that the crowd, when put in charge, wouldn't be any more interested in supporting serious stories than Best Buy. The most promising projects have focused on getting a few high-quality pieces into high-profile newspapers. Such collaborations are vitally important; as

Shirky notes, people still look for authoritative voices to deliver their news.

San Francisco–based Spot.Us has proved crowdfunding can make underrepresented stories national news. When the *New York Times* picked up a Spot.Us story on the giant trash island floating in the Pacific Ocean, crowdfunding immediately graduated from buzzword to plausible business model. The *Times* would not have fully funded the investigation on its own: Spot.Us donations enabled the reporter to cover her expenses, so the *Times* could pick up the story at low cost, and her story received the national attention it deserved.

ProPublica, a nonprofit investigative newsroom based in New York, is not quite as grassroots as Spot.Us—it relies mostly on major donations from foundations—but it too operates on the idea that major news organizations are at times merely the messengers for reporting done by others who are not at the mercy of advertisers. ProPublica uses its funding to pay thirty-two staff reporters and overhead; therefore, it can offer its pieces to mainstream news organizations free of charge. (All ProPublica pieces are also published on its Web site.) The formula seems to be working: in 2010, just two years after its inception, ProPublica shared an investigative reporting Pulitzer with the *New York Times Magazine* for a piece by reporter Sheri Fink on the struggles a New Orleans hospital endured during Hurricane Katrina.

Collaborative investigations. As with crowdfunding, the best models of crowdsourced journalism—which draws on the help of many readers during research and reporting of a news story—involve the collaboration between citizen reporters and professionals. "Pro-am" journalism is a best-of-both-worlds scenario, in which the bounty of crowdsourcing—hyperlocal news, immediacy, and sheer wealth of information—is synthesized and vetted by a trained editorial staff and then published by an established news outlet with an audience of thousands, if not millions.

OhMyNews, a South Korean online newspaper started by a group of politically progressive freelance journalists, was the first news source to attempt this on a large scale, and is still the most famous example of the power of crowdsourced

media. Just two years after its inception the site had 27,000 citizen reporters and about 1 million daily readers; it was authoritative enough to influence the 2002 presidential elections.

In the United States, one of the most high-profile crowdsourcing experiments is NewAssignment.net, directed by Professor Jay Rosen at New York University's Arthur L. Carter Journalism Institute. NewAssignment's inaugural project was Assignment Zero, in which an editorial team and participants spent two months creating a package of essays and interviews about—meta alert!—crowdsourcing. Mainstream tech magazine *Wired* agreed to oversee the project and publish the results. The project revealed the difficulties of crowdsourcing: *Wired* writer Jeff Howe, who was the magazine's representative for the duration of the project, wrote that it suffered from "haphazard planning, technological glitches, and a general sense of confusion among participants." But the project succeeded in its goal of producing a large body of work that was of the same quality you would expect from a major news outlet, and Howe noted that some of the confusion was due to the "nebulous" nature of crowdsourcing as a topic—with a clearer mission, more defined subject matter, and a better-organized chain of command, the results would have been even more impressive. NewAssignment's subsequent—and, overall, more successful—project was Off the Bus, a curated collection of grassroots reports on the 2008 U.S. presidential elections, overseen and published by the *Huffington Post*.

Better coverage of crisis zones. When crisis strikes, you can't have too many reporters on the ground, especially when a natural disaster or a conflict covers a vast amount of territory. Citizen reportage is important even when there are professionals on the scene. A photo essay by Patrick Witty on the *New York Times*' "Lens" blog showed photojournalists in Port-au-Prince bunched up to take the exact same shot of earthquake victims, even though there was in fact news happening all over town. Plus, news that is universally compelling or photogenic enough to print won't necessarily help those in the midst of the crisis. The news needed on the ground is hyperlocal in the truest sense, and crowdsourcing is purpose-built for this type of reportage.

Ushahidi is one platform that allows citizen journalists to map real-time crisis updates via Web or text messaging. In 2008, Ushahidi helped Kenyans map incidents of postelection violence. More than 45,000 users tagged scenes of rioting, police brutality, theft, and also successful peacekeeping; by clicking on a map, anyone could get updates, which might be a line or two or full AP-style reporting. Since then Ushahidi's retooled platform has been used to map everything from snow-removal efforts during a Washington, DC, blizzard to monitoring elections in India and the Sudan. Al Jazeera, an international news network that focuses on Middle Eastern nations, has used the platform to keep track of violence along the Gaza Strip.

More whistleblowers, and more ways to protect them. In April 2010, a video titled "Collateral Murder" went viral on YouTube. The video showed footage from a U.S. Army Apache helicopter as it and another helicopter fired on civilians, including two Reuters journalists, near Baghdad; the resulting furor lead to questioning of the United States' rules of engagement in Iraq.

"Collateral Murder" was published by WikiLeaks, a site whose bland Wikipedia-esque presentation belies the incendiary nature of its content. Using cutting-edge encryption, servers in Sweden (a country that fiercely protects anonymous sources), and freedom of the press laws, WikiLeaks publishes sensitive documents and other media submitted by journalists, activists, and corporate and government insiders. Volunteers work to authenticate reports; the source documents are published in their entirety for anyone to view. WikiLeaks' mission is not only to help expose corruption by leaking damning materials that may spur major news coverage, but also to help journalists avoid being duped by false reports; by making the source documents available to all, the site encourages study and comment by academics, dissidents, and other experts who may be able to spot a fake before a reporter runs with a story.

More translators. Generating a lot of news coverage is no longer a problem, but sharing it worldwide still is. Translating stories from major news organizations into local dialects has always been a challenge. Wikipedia, for example, is devoting a lot of funding to figuring out how to get its content to developing nations. And nowadays, as the international bureaus of English-language newspapers are being decimated or packed up, it's becoming more and more important that news from around the world is translated into English.

Some organizations have figured out ways to fund translation work, but most of the Web's translators work for free. This labor-of-love model may not be enough to support all the translation work that's needed, but it has already yielded some great results. In its first year, TED's Open Translation Project, in which volunteers translate approved transcripts of their favorite talks from TED's conferences, produced 8,300 translations in 77 languages from more than 3,000 translators. These translations are available to the public free, as subtitles to accompany each talk. CB

Bridge Blogging

▬▬▬ Mahmood Al-Yousif, a Bahraini entrepreneur, is one of millions of people around the world who are taking political matters into their own hands, creating their own online media, and talking directly to global audiences. In June 2003, he started a blog. On his "About" page he wrote, "Now I try to dispel the image that Muslims and Arabs suffer from—mostly by our own doing I

Chinese blogger and high-tech investor Mao Xianghui cofounded China's first blog, setting off an explosion in the use of blogs for expressing sentiments that, in other media, would likely be censored by the government.

have to say—in the rest of the world. I am no missionary and don't want to be. I run several Internet websites that are geared to do just that, create a better understanding that we're not all nuts hell-bent on world destruction. I hope that I will be judged that I made a small difference."

The desire to make a small difference is the essence of "bridge blogging": writing online (or broadcasting audio or images onto the Internet) for an audience beyond your immediate community, while making an effort to explain, interpret, and contextualize the concerns and conversations of your community for a global audience.

Alliances of "bridge bloggers" are now forming, in an effort to bring critical mass and attention to their voices. Global Voices Online is an international citizens' media project focused specifically on bridge blogs from outside the United States and Western Europe. A global team of blogger-editors and volunteers provide links and summaries of what they think are the most interesting and globally relevant conversations taking place in the "blogospheres" of their countries and regions. RM

Radio Okapi

▉▉▉▉▉   Radio can be a force for destruction: witness the role of Radio Mille Collines in urging the Hutus of Rwanda to commit genocide. Radio Okapi—"Breath of the DRC" (the Democratic Republic of Congo)—set up by Swiss journalists as part of the reconstruction process in that country, shows the power of radio for peace.

The difficulties involved in creating an independent national radio station in a decimated country are not to be underestimated. As one report on USAid.gov puts it, "The DRC has practically no roads. It has no railway system. The river routes were closed and mail and telephone services did not work."

The phones may not be working, but it appears Radio Okapi is.

Okapi now claims the country's most listeners, and it is the most trusted and capable source of news and of educational and public-service programming. Call-in talk shows, however, are what the people tune in to hear: Okapi's talk-radio programs often include human-rights defenders and development experts, and debate is lively in all five of the languages—French, Lingala, Tshiluba, Swahili, and Kongo—in which the station broadcasts.

The plan is to make Okapi a public, listener-supported radio station after the United Nations pulls out of the DRC. Can talk radio heal the wounds of a war that's killed 2.1 million people? Not by itself. But by providing a space where Congolese can discuss and debate, it's lending a hand in rebuilding the nation. EZ

Radio Any Which Way You Can

▉▉▉▉▉   In 1999, Daoud Kuttab, a Palestinian entrepreneur, journalist, and professor, wanted to start a radio station in Amman, Jordan. The government wouldn't issue him a license, so he started his station online.

It wasn't the first time Kuttab had turned to the Internet to overcome local barriers—in 1995, he founded the Arabic Media Internet Network, which allowed Arabic speakers in various countries to find out how newspapers throughout the region reported their news and politics. For his new project, he armed smart young reporters with digital video recorders and sent them into the streets, the markets, and Parliament to produce some of the highest-quality journalism in Jordan.

The head of UN Peacekeeping Operations, Jean-Marie Guéhenno, speaks on Radio Okapi, Kinshasa, Democratic Republic of Congo, 2006.

The audience for AmmanNet online was far smaller than it would have been on FM radio, but it was influential throughout the region, and was rebroadcast on FM by Palestinian radio stations. After five years of operation, AmmanNet was granted a license by the Jordanian government, and it is now on the air, providing critical journalism and a community voice for Amman's million residents. EZ

■■■■   RESOURCES

The Open Society Institute
www.soros.org
Through local efforts to advance justice, education, public health, and independent media, the Open Society Institute focuses on improving policy in ways to help people live in fair and democratic societies. From fighting for citizen recognition in Mauritania to providing scholarships to train the next generation of Roma health-care professionals, OSI is driven by the need to improve the lives of the less fortunate around the world.

Rising Voices
http://rising.globalvoicesonline.org
Rising Voices, led by David Sasaki, is an initiative of Global Voices that demonstrates that citizen media is possible in any corner of the globe. Through a modest amount of fiscal support and loads of technical support and advice, Rising Voices has helped small, community-based organizations to have a national or international impact, and to reach the stage where they can seek sustaining funding from other foundations or find business models that allow them to continue their work.

We the Media: Grassroots Journalism by the People, for the People by Dan Gillmor (O'Reilly Media, 2004)
"What industry is among the least transparent? Journalism."

If you doubt that citizen media is overtaking big media—or that this is a good thing—you won't after reading nationally known journalist Dan Gillmor's treatise on the rise of amateur reportage. Gillmor uses case studies and personal anecdotes to trace the emergence of and

implications of citizen media; he offers a thorough primer on the tools available to citizen journalists, from blogs to wikis.

Moreover, Gillmor urges corporate media and corporations to embrace and collaborate with citizen media outlets—not fight against them. He offers advice to corporate media participants and lays out new rules of conduct for everyone from PR flacks to CEOs: "Make sure your Web site has everything a journalist might need . . . Post or link to what your people say publicly, and to what is said about you. When your CEO or other top official gives an interview, transcribe it and post in on the Web site. If it's an interview being broadcast, put the audio or video online as well . . . Find out which micro-publishers are talking about your product or service. (Use Google, Technorati, Blogdex, and Feedster, not just Nexis and clipping services.) . . . Then make sure you keep these people well-informed. Treat them like professional journalists who are trying to get things right, and they'll be more likely to treat you with a similar respect."

Handbook for Bloggers and Cyber-Dissidents
(Reporters Without Borders, 2005)
Bloggers are the front line of contemporary journalism. But making waves also makes enemies. With increasing frequency, bloggers are finding themselves persecuted by repressive governments in exactly the same way investigative reporters were in decades past.

Journalists under threat need tools, and Reporters Without Borders has produced an excellent toolbox. Their *Handbook for Bloggers and Cyber-Dissidents* provides basic information that will benefit those new to blogging—explaining blogging terminology, how blogs differ from other kinds of Web sites, how to select a blogging tool and Web host, and how to get started—and goes on to offer tips that even veteran bloggers will find useful. Journalist, blogger, and author of *We the Media* Dan Gillmor tackles the issue of journalistic credibility and standards. Journalist Mark Glaser offers tips on how to "make your blog shine." French Internet consultant Olivier Andrieu contributes a discussion on search-engine visibility.

The most inspiring aspect of the *Handbook* are the "Personal Accounts," short essays from bloggers around the world about why they blog and why blogging matters. German blogger Markus Beckedahl of Netzpolitik.org describes his blog defending civil and human rights online; anonymous Bahraini blogger "Chan'ad Bahraini" explains how Bahraini bloggers have "broken the government's news monopoly"; Hong Kong's Yan Sham-Shackleton, aka Glutter, discusses blogging for Chinese human rights and free speech; Iran's Arash Sigarchi, who did prison time for his blogging, reflects on the importance of blogs in Iran as an outlet for nongovernment-approved speech; and American Jay Rosen points out that even in the United States, blogs are a revolutionary way for writers to circumvent various powerful "gatekeepers."

Importantly, the book takes a hardcore technical look at how bloggers like Chan'ad might avoid being "outed," how bloggers like Arash might avoid arrest, and how bloggers and blog readers in countries like China, where the Internet is heavily censored, can get around the political "firewalls." Other topics include anonymous blogging, overcoming Internet censorship "firewalls," and ensuring e-mail privacy. If you want to know how to blog for impact, the *Handbook* should be your first stop. JL

Effective Campaigning

▬▬▬ If we want to change the world, we have to get better at campaigning for change. From entreaties by nongovernmental organizations to campaigns for political office, policy discussions to international boycotts, tools exist to help turn popular demand for change into actual results. The barriers to change are still massive, and the playing field is far from level, but there's never been a better time to advocate for democracy and good government. AS

The Obama Campaign and Netroots Politics

▬▬▬ The power of new technologies to supercharge political campaigns was made obvious to many people for the first time during Barack Obama's campaign for U.S. president in 2008. The Obama campaign used the Internet to mobilize grassroots support (what was dubbed "the Netroots") to an unprecedented degree.

Key to the success of the campaign were its collaborative Web sites, particularly MyBO, where the campaign embraced citizen communications efforts. Text messages were sent out by the millions, supporter blogs launched by the thousands, countless phone banks and house parties and doorbelling efforts set in motion. The campaign posted video clips to online services; viewers watched more than 14.5 million hours of such videos on YouTube alone. Most of all, it

U.S. president Barack Obama at a rally in Chicago on November 4, 2008, the night he was elected.

mobilized younger supporters to help get out the vote (104,000 Texans alone signed up on the site) and raised an enormous amount of money, state after state, in small donations—as much as $55 million in a single month.

The importance of this mass-collaborative approach to campaigning is hard to overstate. Many observers think it won Obama the election. "Were it not for the Internet, Barack Obama would not be president," Arianna Huffington, editor in chief of the *Huffington Post,* told the *New York Times.* "Were it not for the Internet, Barack Obama would not have been the nominee."

Yet the Obama campaign, as revolutionary as it was in 2008, was not the last word in effective online campaigning. The campaign was in many ways a one-off, failing to turn into a collaborative, Netroots-driven style of governing. It may have determined the new occupant of the White House, but it didn't change Washington much. Moving from campaigns to widespread public involvement may be what's needed next. AS

Campaigning for Better Democracies

▬▬▬ Many political observers are cynical about the ability of new campaigning styles to change much about politics in Global North democracies. The Netroots may be able to help a candidate win office, they say, but scattered and casual collaboration can never be a match for the powerful interests who helped design the systems they're influencing. As *Rolling Stone* columnist Matt Taibbi says, "Organized greed always defeats disorganized democracy."

If we're serious about making change, we need to reinvent citizenship as we reinvent election campaigns. Government 2.0—using information technologies to reveal the flow of information within government, and to help citizens collaborate to make needed reforms—is one approach to improving the efficiency with which government works. But even that approach can't tackle a larger problem: the fact that the systems making up our nations and cities are complex and largely hidden from casual view. If we don't understand those systems well, every attempt to change them is predestined to fail; yet to do so is hard work, requiring sustained engagement, intelligent discourse, and the cooperation of experts.

Although we don't have a great model for how to engage citizens deeply at a systems level, a huge number of interesting projects are tackling specific parts of the challenge, most often at a municipal or metropolitan level. Some involve public-interest policy or planning initiatives: New York's PlaNYC sustainability effort (led by ICLEI), for example, brought together numerous advisers in an in-depth public process, resulting in a plan designed to not only inform policy in the city, but also to help educate citizens about the systems that need changing. Others involve citizen media, like local news and public affairs blogs, or the North American Streetsblog network, which gathers the best citizen reporting on transportation from around the nation. Still others bring groups together to explore emerging trends, threats, and opportunities, creating a community vision for the future; the Future Melbourne 2020 process, for instance, became the city's official strategic plan [see The Bright Green City, p. 197] after input from hundreds of residents.

Still, there are enormous opportunities now to mix innovative technology with bold cultural and political approaches to help make the huge, complicated systems that support modern life more easily understood and more open to citizen input. We've only just scratched the surface of the future of democracy. AS

Backing the Right NGOs

▬▬▬ There's a change coming to the world of advocacy, one that is as fundamental as anything we've seen since the abolition movement [see Movement Building, p. 386] gave birth to the modern civic group. That change? The move from centralized, mass-market nongovernmental

Opposite, left: Health-education workers from a nongovernmental organization (NGO) hold up a poster depicting an AIDS patient before and after receiving the benefits of antiretroviral drug treatment, Nairobi, Kenya.
Opposite, right: A woman displaced by the 2005 Kashmir earthquake gives birth, aided by doctors from Citizens' Foundation, a Pakistani NGO.

organizations (NGOs) to decentralized advocacy networks driven by their members.

Right now, many large advocacy NGOs consider their members, like you and me, mostly a source of small donations. By and large, it doesn't matter what we think, how we act, who we know, or how strongly we're committed, as long as we keep writing those thirty-five-dollar checks for our "memberships," which usually yield nothing more than a tote bag or a coffee mug or some lame newsletter. It's a dysfunctional model, all the way around. Mass marketing, direct mail, subsidiary income tracks (like selling T-shirts), and the rest of the modern NGO racket degrade everyone involved. The model turns passionate advocates into carnies and charitable citizens into consumers of change-related program activities and products.

One of the biggest problems with mass-market NGOs is that they limit and control information. With a few excellent exceptions, they make no effort to educate their members about the broader field of activism in which they are involved, instead regarding their communications with members as marketing opportunities for ensuring continued financial support. When they do disseminate information it is impersonal and largely irrelevant to our real concerns.

Furthermore, members have few ways in which to interact with one another. Most NGOs, even those with sophisticated online presences, restrict the flow of information between members. Criticism of the NGO, dissent, endorsement of other efforts, even the sharing of outside information on the issue at hand—these just aren't welcome on most NGOs' Web sites and e-mail lists. In most NGOs, independent efforts, personal (rather than personalized) messages, creative approaches,

and new ideas are actively discouraged in favor of "action alerts" and "calls to action," in which members are asked to send prepackaged messages to politicians or corporate leaders.

How might online advocacy networks begin to change this sad state of affairs? By putting the member in the driver's seat: we choose the flows of information we receive, the people we are allied with, the establishments we give money to, our affiliations.

Advocacy networks can encourage the exchange of information. By making available news feeds on the issue at hand, member discussion areas and listings, and other discussion tools, an advocacy network can allow us to choose the best mix of information sources for our concerns. Better still, it can let us contribute to the debate. Got a blog or a Twitter account? We can add it to the list of feeds from which members can choose to aggregate their news. Got a great idea for a new campaign or a beef with an existing NGO? Start a discussion topic. Because we choose the information we receive, the information we get is by its very nature more relevant to our concerns.

Advocacy networks can encourage relationships; after all, they're a form of social software, like Facebook or WiserEarth, where we can make connections and foster our social and professional circles online. When our working relationships are not subject to the control of any third-party organization, all manner of cooperation becomes possible. We can identify allies online and create informal networks and groups among ourselves, and we can use reputation systems to help evaluate the worth of causes and the truth of information. This allows us to then lend support to the causes or ideas most relevant

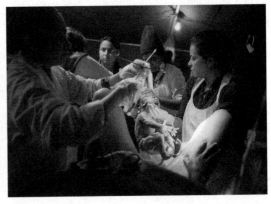

to our concerns. ("Hmmm . . . eight of my friends identified this article as important. Maybe I'll take a look.")

Advocacy networks can treat our money as ours. Making online contributions securely is easily done now, so why should Friends of the Mud-sump Salamander own our personal information or restrict our choices? Why shouldn't we be able to view a whole array of opportunities to give, and choose between them ourselves? Perhaps in the end we'll trust a "name brand" NGO to use the money wisely, but perhaps we'll discuss with our fellow members (some of whom may have expert knowledge) who's doing the best work most effectively, and give money to some great outfits with whom we were previously unfamiliar.

Some NGO leaders claim that advocacy networks will hurt their organizations. There's no doubt that such a shift will drive some NGOs out of business. This is a good thing. NGOs were never intended to be perpetual. They should exist as long as they meet the world's need to change—not stumble on, zombielike, until the heat death of the universe.

For groups that excel at including members in their activities, advocacy networks will be an asset, making them bigger, leaner, faster, stronger. For organizations with an extremely specific focus and the humility to take the time to explain why that focus is important, advocacy networks will be an incredible boon, providing an effective tool for finding focused allies—a "long tail" effect, as it's called. For groups willing to learn how to collaborate on the fly and work from a campaign-centric model, advocacy networks will be transformative. For all of us, networks are the future. AS

International Campaign to Ban Landmines

If we want to see exactly how much a small, loosely connected network of dedicated people can accomplish, we need look no further than the International Campaign to Ban Landmines (ICBL).

The ICBL is a network representing more than 1,400 groups in over ninety countries—human rights' groups, demining groups, humanitarian groups, children's groups, veterans' groups, medical groups, development groups, arms control groups, religious groups, environmental groups, and women's groups. Together, they work locally, regionally, nationally, and internationally to ban antipersonnel land mines [see Land Mines, p. 296]. The network was first organized in 1992, with the coordination of six separate NGOs: Handicap International, Human Rights Watch, Medico International, Mines Advisory Group, Physicians for Human Rights, and Vietnam Veterans of America Foundation. All six had encountered the devastation caused by land mines while trying to implement projects in the developing world, and had concluded that the only solution was a comprehensive international ban on land-mine use. The organizations were able to pool considerable regional knowledge and experience, as well as worldwide networks and contacts. From this group sprang dozens of national campaigns.

From the start, the ICBL, with its tiny staff of four, rejected a rigid, bureaucratic structure. Today it has overall strategies, but each member NGO is allowed to implement solutions in ways that make sense for the group and the regions it serves. The campaign itself, which resulted in the international Mine Ban Treaty, is also an example of network advocacy through community. Faxes and (later) e-mail were among the campaign's most powerful and effective vehicles. The ICBL Web site includes a collection of online tools that allow any organization to create campaigns to advocate the ban and to replicate the ICBL's success. JL

potential to bring many more nonprofits to technologies that will increase their capabilities, and their ability to drive their own innovations, significantly. JL

Idealist.org: The Interactive Site for Change Makers
http://www.idealist.org
Idealist.org, a project of Action Without Borders, a nonprofit organization founded in 1995 with offices in the United States and Argentina, is an interactive site where people and organizations can exchange resources and ideas, locate opportunities and supporters, and take steps toward building a world where all people can lead free and dignified lives.

Servenet: Mobilizing the Volunteer Community
http://servenet.org
Launched in 1996, servenet.org is a Web site that mobilizes and empowers the volunteer service community to tackle some of the toughest challenges facing local communities. Since its inception, Servenet.org has enabled millions of youth volunteers to connect with local nonprofits to make a difference in communities throughout the United States.

■■■■   RESOURCES

Netsquared
http://www.netsquared.org
Netsquared is a TechSoup project aimed at connecting nonprofit organizations with Web 2.0 technologies to "collaborate, share information and mobilize support." Netsquared has great

---

The International Campaign to Ban Landmines, which has been responsible for large-scale demining efforts, has created one of the world's most successful networked campaigns. A technician from the Mines Advisory Group prepares to detonate recently discovered unexploded land mines.

Government 2.0

Governments are made of information. Much of the work of government revolves around moving (or withholding) information between one person or group of people and another. The very word *bureaucrat* stems from the idea that a government worker's main tool was a desk (or bureau) full of papers.

As society has become more complicated, the amount of information gathered by governments—and the specialized knowledge it takes to access and use that information—has mushroomed. The result is that in any government large enough to oversee a medium-sized city, information glitches abound: critical work goes undone or is redundantly duplicated; waste and graft go unnoticed; plans made under older administrations trudge on unmodified; and storms of unnecessary paper blow through the system.

All of this mishandling of information seriously reduces the effectiveness of government, making it inefficient and slow to react. But it also does something worse: it makes it very difficult for citizens to participate in improving their cities and communities in any way.

What if that could change, though? People like Tim O'Reilly think it can. O'Reilly, a technology writer and publisher, believes that information technologies and collaborative tools already offer us the ability to open up government information and processes, to make their workings transparent and allow citizens to understand the issues with the same knowledge the government possesses. One immediate effect of this change might be less waste and corruption, (though some skeptics have pointed out that more transparency might just generate

more "gotcha" politics and ass-covering, making government work even less well). It also will probably lead to better decision-making and more rapid government innovation. Another, much more important effect, however, could be to make it a lot easier for citizens to get things done themselves.

Imagine a world where citizens could prioritize public problems, and collaborate to solve them, using a mix of community and government resources. O'Reilly calls this capacity for citizen mobilization "government as platform," which he sees as the really transformative element of the electronic revolution sweeping through politics.

That transformation already has a posse, too. Groups like MySociety, the Sunlight Foundation [see Demanding Transparency, p. 411], Code for America, and Zimbabwe's Sokwanele have mobilized geeks to build tools to help citizens crack open closed doors, work with government more effectively, help government write better legal codes and provide better services, and even monitor elections. Every sign indicates that we've only seen the beginning of what's possible. AS

Estonia's Tiger Leap

After the fall of the Soviet Union, an international aid assessment summed up Estonia as being "bankrupt, polluted and decaying." Today, Estonia is climbing up through the economic ranks of the "upper-middle-income" countries (like Mexico, Brazil, and the Czech Republic), and many of its social indicators are better than those in certain countries in the "upper-income" bracket. The reasons are complex—a cohesive national identity, a well-educated population, traditional ties with Scandinavian countries—but

UK residents can use FixMyStreet.com, a subsidiary of MySociety.com, to report potholes and other problems. To increase accountability, the site maintains a record of all complaints filed.

one of them stands out: Estonia has made the world's strongest commitment to providing technology to all its citizens. In fact, in Estonia, Internet access is a human right.

The groundbreaking Tiigrihüppe ("Tiger Leap") program has wired 98 percent of Estonia's schools, provided an average of more than one computer for every twenty students (running about forty new software packages in Estonian), created a national learning network for teachers, and trained 40 percent of them in advanced computer skills, according to a program executive summary.

The Estonians now use the Internet at a higher rate than the French or Italians do. To accommodate the demand, the Estonian government has opened up hundreds of free Internet-access centers, from downtown Tallinn to remote islands in the Baltic. In addition, there are already over one thousand Wi-Fi hotspots in the tiny country.

But this is much more than a story of leapfrogging or redistributing the future through technology: even more amazing than Estonians' appetite for Internet access is the Baltic nation's absolute commitment to digital transparency. Estonia's former president Lennart Meri (1992–2001) supposedly answered his own e-mail. The state IT adviser attends cabinet meetings. Almost all state services are online, as are tax filings and the state budget. Almost everything the government does online is open to public scrutiny, and almost everything it does is done online.

Parliament meetings are almost completely virtual—legislators conduct all of their business, including reviewing bills and placing votes, on networked computers. They sign important documents with digital signatures. A government Web page contains all bills, amendments, and proposals, and citizens are allowed to comment on the drafts and make suggestions for new amendments, some of which have already found their way into law. By making their society transparent, Estonians have nipped corruption in the bud and let their new economy flourish. AS

e-Government Handbook

▬▬▬ Policy makers in the developing world need all the help they can get when trying to set up transparent systems of government. With this in mind, the Center for Democracy and Technology and infoDev have created an e-government handbook to help policy makers reduce or eliminate corruption. The section on transparency suggests that it should be embedded in the design of policies and systems, especially in ways that will help citizens see how decisions are made.

Transparency becomes much easier with technology. For example, customs' services are notoriously corrupt—goods come in the door and lots of money changes hands under the table. If we put that system online, it becomes much harder to subvert. When the whole thing is on paper, it's easy for corrupt officials to charge money for an official stamp or refuse to process an invoice unless they get a bribe. When it's all online, it's much easier to say, "Here's my money, here's my form, where's my shipment?" The Center for Democracy and Technology points to the government of Seoul, South Korea, as an illustration of this. As part of a comprehensive campaign against corruption initiated in 1998, the government streamlined the regulatory rules of systems like licensing and permit approval that are most subject to corruption through bribes. An online tracking system now helps citizens monitor the status of government applications.

It's unlikely that technology will turn nondemocracies into democracies, but it may just make the difference for young and fragile democracies. Empowering individuals to avoid systematic corruption is just the kind of project

Andrus Ansip, the prime minister of Estonia, demonstrates the ease of voting online, in 2005. Estonia was one of the first countries to enable nationwide Internet voting.

that has leverage, and finding systems in young democracies that aren't transparent—procurement procedures, public bidding for government contracts—and putting them online in a way that encourages public review is vital.

Sure, there are obstacles: not everyone has Internet access; many governments still try to operate in secret and restrict online content; and many constituents worldwide lack the education or inspiration to work for something better. But there are hopeful developments, including many projects—like the handbook—that support transparency. EZ

MySociety
http://www.mysociety.org
MySociety is the British civic tech nongovernmental organization behind such projects as Write-ToThem, FaxYourMP, TheyWorkforYou, and FarmSubsidy.org [see Demanding Transparency, p. 407]. While none of these projects will single-handedly change the world, they represent and reinforce a broader movement to use collaborative technologies to pry open the corridors of power and let in both the sunshine of transparency and the voices of citizens. We need a lot more such efforts, and we need more people talking about what approaches and technologies to use in those efforts. MySociety is doing us all a favor by stimulating debate on what civic activism looks like in the twenty-first century. AS

Code for America
http://codeforamerica.org
The epicenter of civic software and government 2.0 volunteerism in the United States, Code for America is full of examples of projects that have opened and improved government in the real world. AS

Demanding Transparency

■■■■   Corruption is a global problem. Those of us in the Global North face electoral systems that essentially allow open bribery, in one form or another. Those of us in the Global South often face systems that skip over the elections altogether and go straight to the bribes. And corruption tends to reinforce itself across borders, as dirty deals know no boundaries. From oil to diamonds, the commodities that make life rich in the North support corruption and oppression in the South. The corrupt are their own global network.

Corruption breeds in dark corners. It also makes good government—the intelligent policy making that underpins most solutions—virtually impossible. Schools and hospitals suffer when the bureaucrats overseeing them are skimming money. Businesses trying to make money without polluting suffer when compromised regulators let their competitors get away with breaking environmental laws. Elected officials who owe their offices to the campaign contributions of powerful interests find voting on the merit of laws a threat to their jobs. If we want governments that work, we need to demand transparency.

What is transparency? Openness, in all things. Transparent societies demand that their leaders conduct public business in public—they demand to see the books, to inspect the records, and to be kept abreast of potential conflicts of interest. They demand that those in power be accountable to independent legal authorities when they break the rules.

Transparency is the battle cry of twenty-first-century politics. AS

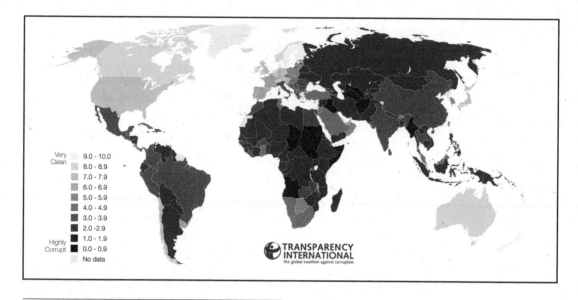

Very Clean
9.0 - 10.0
8.0 - 8.9
7.0 - 7.9
6.0 - 6.9
5.0 - 5.9
4.0 - 4.9
3.0 - 3.9
2.0 -2.9
1.0 - 1.9
Highly Corrupt
0.0 - 0.9
No data

TRANSPARENCY INTERNATIONAL
the global coalition against corruption

Global Witness and Blood Diamonds

Diamonds, like barrels of oil, are worth cash everywhere; and, again like oil, the international trade in diamonds has destabilized whole regions and promoted criminal regimes.

Diamonds have helped fuel the genocidal Congo wars and kept Angola in chaos. They're intimately tied to the black market in weapons. They've even been traded by terrorists to finance their plots. And these "blood diamonds" are sold in large numbers, by the billions of dollars, on the diamond bourses of Antwerp and other cities.

This is a classic example of a situation where our choices—buying a diamond to catch the eye of one's intended, for instance—fuel destruction and suffering in far-off lands, but where the connection is kept hidden from us by secretive corporations. When it comes to most commercially available diamonds, despite the controversy, it's almost impossible to know if your dollars are funding the enslavement of children or the murder of entire villages.

The Corruption Perceptions Index is one of Transparency International's best-known tools, ranking countries in terms of perceived corruption, as determined by expert assessments and opinion surveys. The lower the number, the higher the perceived level of corruption.

London's Global Witness wants to change all that. They're bound and determined to end the trade in blood diamonds, and their methods illustrate the growing power of international advocacy networks to change the world.

People increasingly demand global transparency. Corporations that behave opaquely magnify the damage to their reputations if they're caught acting unethically—and the odds are increasing that they will be caught. Diamond merchants depended on a veil of secrecy about the origins of their stones to protect them from the consequences of their trade. Global Witness realized that if it could rip off that veil, consumers would react with horror and disgust to the reality they saw. GW began with awareness-building tactics familiar since the abolition movement—lobbying, writing letters, issuing reports—but it wasn't until the release of their 1998 report, *A Rough Trade*, that their impact began to be felt. As Matthew Hart describes it in his recent book, *Diamond: A Journey to the Heart of an Obsession*:

"*A Rough Trade*'s success lay in presenting the details of the war in an accessible form. Statistics were laid out for easy reading, with maps and chronologies and even a short glossary. A photograph showed a pit holding the mud-caked bodies of victims of the war; another depicted long lines of miners in slave conditions passing buckets out of a pit. A table of figures listed the annual revenue from illicit diamonds. By leafing through the booklet one could gather at a glance the sordid history of the war, its human and material costs, and, in language made chilling by the context, the commercial considerations of the diamond business."

The public outcry was deafening. Suddenly, blood diamonds were front-page news and the diamond cartels were threatened by a global consumer boycott—a threat that still hangs over their heads.

Others have told this story. But what's often overlooked is the degree to which new communications technologies and new advocacy techniques—particularly the Internet and networked activism—made possible GW's success.

Global Witness skillfully used a combination of sousveillance [see Watching the Watchers, p. 419] of the diamond industry (insider leaks, industry reports, investigative reporting) and online networking to leverage a number of supporters and media contacts far beyond the normal reach of a small NGO. While the diamond trade is still awash in blood diamonds, big companies like DeBeers have been forced into creating an interim monitoring agreement known as the Kimberley Process, which many observers believe will lead to global systems for tracking the origins (and conditions of production) of all diamonds.

There are a few trends worth noting here. First, the open-source software adage known as Linus's Law—that "with enough eyeballs all bugs are shallow"—is coming to apply to international trade and the global behavior of multinational corporations. With enough observers, all trade is transparent, whether the interests involved want it to be or not. This is increasingly relevant even in places where multinationals and local oppression go hand in hand, as groups like Witness, Amnesty International, Benetech, Human Rights Watch [see Demanding Human Rights, p. 414], and Transparency International [see p. 411] become more effective at both exposing abuses and protecting human rights workers. We're still a long way from the ideal, but the trend is clear.

Second, international advocacy networks are growing far stronger, far more quickly, than anyone would have predicted a few years back. In arenas where the powerful are used to operating in secret and with impunity, NGO networks are forcing change, from disrupting World Trade Organization meetings to intellectual-property "copyfights."

Not only are concerned citizens around the world more connected to each other, they're also getting better at convincing their fellow citizens to pay attention. Bloggers, for instance, have become integral to the human-rights movement, while small bits of viral video can reach millions of viewers in days—and the tools for producing them are spreading rapidly.

And these international advocacy networks are growing in reach and sophistication. We see this in the One Campaign and in the growing availability of tools to help citizens act effectively as networked observers. Antisweatshop campaigns, for instance, have not only forced change in the practices of multinational companies, according to the UN, but have also raised working standards in non-multinational-owned shops as well.

It would be easy, and foolish, to overstate the victories here. After all, blood diamonds are still sold in Antwerp. Torture, extrajudicial arrest, and secret imprisonment are now routinely practiced by several nations who once were strong advocates for human rights. China censors the Internet. But it would also be wrong to underestimate the power of the trend here—how much influence informed and connected citizens can exert today, or how much their leverage could grow. AS

FarmSubsidy.org

FarmSubsidy.org demonstrates the power of geek activism done right. The project—from the same people who brought us FaxYourMP, MySociety, and TheyWorkForYou—was launched to investigate where EU Common Agricultural Policy (CAP) farm subsidies were being spent. The budgets here are huge (in 2005 farm subsidies comprised nearly half of the entire EU budget) but opaque, with very little information available to citizens. The almost €100 a year each European citizen has been paying to support farmers has gone to closely concealed recipients.

Turns out there's a reason for the hidden numbers. As cofounder Jack Thurston said, "For too long people have been misled to believe that farm subsidies are about protecting small and family farms. This data shows conclusively that most of the money goes to large agribusiness and wealthy landowners."

So based on citizens' national, lawful rights, FarmSubsidy.org is demanding change. The organization uses EU freedom of information laws to request that European governments reveal all data on how the farm subsidy budget is being spent. FarmSubsidy then publishes all of the data on its Web site, where it is searchable by a number of different criteria, including geographic location. With the cooperation of journalists from around the EU, FarmSubsidy reached a groundbreaking milestone when the council of ministers and the European Parliament finalized a decision to force the public disclosure of detailed data about nearly €100 billion in farming and food-related subsidies. According to the *Guardian,* this is "the biggest release of information held by governments to the public and the media since the creation of the European Union."

Using transparency laws to get real data about the systems on which we depend can make visible the invisible flows around us. When that happens, the systems themselves change. Geek activism isn't about technology, it's about information, and information is the lifeblood of democratic reform. AS & SR

Transparency in Africa

The typical write-up on corruption in Africa is dire and despondent. And for good reason: according to the African Union, as much as $146 billion, or a fourth of the continent's average gross national product, is lost every year to corruption. In Africa, corruption limits economic growth and keeps people in poverty, especially since poor people are most vulnerable to bribes in exchange for basic services, and because corruption diverts public resources away from sectors like education, health, and housing. To say that this has undermined people's trust in government and diminished their expectations for the future would be an understatement. In fact, being an honest public servant in Africa today is considered an act of heroism.

One of the problems with the fight against corruption in Africa has to do with the way corruption is often oversimplified and branded as a "uniquely" African problem. What is often glossed over is the global nature of African corruption. It is not just about the corrupt "Big Man" leaders like Mobutu, Abacha, Moi, and their coterie of politicians who will do anything for a price, or the lazy civil servant who has to be given "something small" before doing his job, or the waste of aid dollars. It is also about campaign finance, lobbying, white-collar crime, multinational companies with a take-no-prisoners approach, shady single-source contracts, greedy individuals, complex networks, and apathetic electorates. In fact, change some people's names and you could be talking about the goings-on in Washington, DC, or the difficulties of doing business in China. Indeed, that $146 billion is going somewhere: often into the pockets of transnational corporations and Swiss bank accounts.

Africans, though, are fighting back. Over the last few years, a number of African international institutions working for better governance have sprung up and partnered with international donors, newly elected multiparty governments, and civil society groups like Transparency International to build a focused, growing movement to clean up governance—a movement with lessons for the whole world.

Corruption in Kenya
Perhaps no country better illustrates both the challenges and the alternative avenues for tackling corruption and governance issues than Kenya. The republic has a deservedly poor reputation where

Kenyan protesters call for the resignation of corrupt leaders in Nairobi in early 2006.

corruption is concerned. It has remained one of the lowest-ranked countries in Transparency International's annual Corruption Perceptions Index since the mid-1990s. Kenya is particularly notorious for corruption on a grand scale, such as the 1990s Goldenberg scandal (in which government officials granting shady subsidies to gold exporters may have stolen as much as 10 percent of the nation's gross domestic product) and the more recent Anglo Leasing scandal (involving gigantic overpayment on a government contract), exposed by the former anticorruption czar John Githongo, who now lives in exile in the United Kingdom.

After the election of the new National Rainbow Coalition (NARC) government in December 2002 and the government's first few months in office, NARC seemed poised to become a textbook example of how to fight corruption in Africa. The government was elected on a policy of zero tolerance toward corruption, and within the first few months had passed several new laws and created new institutions to address the problem. But little of that promise has been fulfilled. In fact, the running joke in Kenya is that NARC stands for Nothing Actually Really Changed.

Part of the problem is that in Kenya (as in many places), it's hard to clean house politically. Politicians who've worked for decades to get power are reluctant to turn their backs on their old friends. Entrenched, corrupt bureaucrats are hard to dislodge.

What's more, fighting corruption takes government institutions that are strong enough to take on the people involved and demand transparency. Kenya doesn't have them yet. Corruption laws without prosecutions are of little value.

Finally, while governments have changed, the way politics is conducted in Kenya and indeed in most of Africa remains fundamentally the same. A long history of political patronage, combined with the lack of any formal campaign-finance mechanisms, forces politicians to rely on corruption to ensure their survival. Indeed, the now disgraced former minister Kiraitu Murungi has admitted that Anglo Leasing was essentially a vehicle for financing campaigns for the upcoming 2007 elections (see the *East African Business Week* March 6, 2006, article "Anglo Leasing Storm").

Combine systemic campaign corruption with low expectations on the part of many Kenyan voters and you have a recipe for disaster. As Jaindi Kisero, a columnist with the *DailyNation* astutely observes, "When we elect a leader in Africa, we enter into unwritten contracts committing him to reward our political loyalty with appointment to parastatal jobs, to raise money to build rural schools, and to award the elite of our tribes with contracts at inflated prices. As we learn from Goldenberg, the Ndung'u Report and Anglo Leasing, an elected leader must—to remain in power—hand out benefits such as lucrative supplies contracts and public land to their relations and political allies . . . We must start thinking about how to address the root cause of political corruption in Kenya. If we don't do so, then we must be prepared to go through this boring ritual of replacing one corrupt administration with another after every five years."

The Power of the Press and Rebranding Corruption

But despite all these problems, things are changing in Kenya, and they're beginning to change quickly. The press has fought for, and gotten, more freedom. The impact of being able to find out about scandals via the press, of being able to discuss corruption openly over the airwaves via call-in shows, of being able to write about it on Kenyan blogs, and of being able to circulate "confidential" documents electronically cannot be estimated. While the Freedom of Information Bill is still pending in Parliament, Kenyans have generated their own

In Nairobi, minibus drivers are often stopped by police demanding bribes. This kind of corruption has posed great challenges to the Kenyan government.

de facto version of freedom of information: they are relishing their right to know, and as a result have forced the government and those involved in scandals to respond to demands for information. Things can no longer be swept under the rug.

The Anglo Leasing scandal in Kenya reveals more than just the insidious nature of corruption in government: it also demonstrates the impact that investigative journalism and freedom of the press can have in fighting corruption.

First, Kenyans learned about the scandal as it was ongoing and have stayed riveted to the news as the complex story has slowly unfolded. The government had no time to cover up the story and divert attention to other issues, as they undoubtedly would have done if they had the opportunity. In fact, the government's bumbling attempts to try and conceal their actions once the story broke just made things worse. In addition, the increased vigilance of the press and the impact it is having is encouraging journalists to "break" other scandals. Perhaps Anglo Leasing is Kenya's Watergate.

The press and other actors—including, most recently, former government anticorruption czar John Githongo—kept the Anglo Leasing story in the headlines once it became apparent that no one was being held accountable. The relentless manner in which the Kenyan press has pursued this story has been important, not just in getting heads to roll but also in fighting the culture of political amnesia that has afflicted Kenyans. The fight against corruption requires persistence— keeping scandals in the headlines as the Kenyan press has done shows real tenacity.

Third, that the government felt compelled to engage in some (ineffective) damage control when the story broke demonstrates change. That ministers linked to the Anglo Leasing scandal have recently resigned in response to the public's clamor for action demonstrates the empowering effect of access to information.

Corruption-fighting tactics have also gotten more innovative. Civil society groups like Transparency International Kenya, the Operation Firimbi ("Whistleblowers") Network, and We Can Do It have begun to focus on addressing corruption at a local level, with the goal of increasing grassroots awareness about the pernicious nature of corruption. The groups have also begun to "rebrand" the fight against corruption by emphasizing the tangible impact corruption has on Kenyans' daily lives.

This may seem like a no-brainer—of course corruption has a negative impact on citizens, how can anyone not see that? Well, if you are a Kenyan living below the poverty line, struggling to put food on the table, and not paying taxes, the Anglo Leasing scandal is very remote to you. It's just politicians doing what politicians always do: scamming people. So why should you get all riled up about it? In fact, you aspire to get into a position where you too can eat one day without having to work too hard.

The Kenya National Commission for Human Rights (KNCHR) is an independent national institution established by an act of Parliament, and is one of the organizations at the forefront of rebranding corruption. The commission's campaign demonstrates the link between corruption and the lack of access to basic rights like food and shelter, and highlights the diversion of public funds from government coffers by focusing on wasteful government expenditure. In conjunction with Transparency International Kenya, the commission recently released the first in a series of "Living Large" reports that highlight government waste in a dramatic fashion. For instance, the KES 878 million (about $12 million) spent on luxury vehicles for government officials from 2002 to 2006 could have provided antiretroviral treatment for 147,000 Kenyans for a whole year, or seen 25,000 children through eight years of primary schooling (*New Zealand Herald*, January 31, 2006). The report also highlights countries, like Rwanda, that have more prudent policies. In response to the public outcry caused by the report, the government recently announced that it will cut spending on cars and review its policies.

While it remains to be seen whether the culture of corrupt, conspicuous consumption will change any time soon, the work being done by KNCHR is having a tremendous impact as far as making the corruption's true ramifications tangible to the average Kenyan. Kenyans now want to do something about corruption not because of some massive civic education effort, lofty convention, or donor-sponsored program, but because they recognize that they ultimately pay the price for corruption. It is their money, and they want to see how it is being spent. ▢▢

Transparency International

http://www.transparency.org

Transparency International (TI) makes the struggle against corruption a global endeavor. It has more than eighty-five independent national chapters, and works on both national and international levels to combat corruption through a coalition of civil society, business, and government. The organization is focused on reforming systems and preventing corruption, and publishes the *Corruption Fighters' Toolkit.* An invaluable resource, the kit "highlights the potential of civil society to create mechanisms for monitoring public institutions and to demand and promote accountable and responsive public administration." By underlining the variety of tools used by TI around the world—from street theater to access to information law—the guide serves as an invaluable "compendium of practical civil society anti-corruption experiences, described in concrete and accessible language."

Sunlight Foundation

http://sunlightfoundation.com

The Sunlight Foundation is focused on bringing greater transparency to U.S. government, but its projects are inspiration for any country. The think tank offers "transparency grants" to online organizations that help create transparency by finding new ways to digitize and share government data. They provide ongoing support for OpenCongress, and other projects have included a major grant to the National Institute on Money in State Politics to help move their state-level campaign finance data to an open-source data commons, and LittleSis, an "involuntary Facebook" of powerful Americans, listing all of their "interlocks" (i.e., their friends and other politicians they support) and their donation histories. CB

Demanding Human Rights

■■■■■■ Change demands people who are willing to point out abuses of power, challenge authority, and hold wrongdoers accountable. The world needs courageous watchdogs, because it's their vigilance that creates and preserves the transparency that holds power in check.

This is precisely why being a watchdog tends to shorten your life expectancy. Speak up against a dictator, and you are likely to find yourself arrested, jailed, tortured, or shot. To the outside world, you may just simply "disappear." Even in more democratic countries, blowing the whistle is often dangerous.

If we're serious about reforming politics, defending human rights is job number one. Thankfully, we're beginning to get better at doing just that. We're becoming more effective at holding human rights abusers internationally accountable. We're spreading tools for defending the lives and work of human rights workers themselves, mostly by making sure the eyes of the world are upon them, so they will not simply disappear.

During a 2006 press conference in Mexico City, the executive director of Human Rights Watch holds up a report calling attention to violations against rape victims' human rights.

Those of us in wealthier democracies have tremendous power in the watchdog arena. Not only can we pressure our own governments to improve their records on human rights and to promote rights abroad, we can get directly involved in efforts to watch over the watchdogs. AS

Universal Jurisdiction

▬▬▬ General Charles Taylor has a lot to answer for. During his insurgency, his term as president of Liberia, and the civil war that followed from 1989 to 1996, at least 150,000 Liberians were murdered, tens of thousands were raped or mutilated, and Liberia became one of the poorest, most devastated countries on the planet. In Liberia today, hunger and disease are still killing; clean water and electricity are no longer available; and schools, hospitals, housing, and roads have been utterly destroyed. To paraphrase a UN official, it will take two decades for Liberians to get back to where they were in 1988, and the psychological scars may never heal.

Taylor bears much of the responsibility, having unleashed his army—drugged-out child-soldiers in wedding gowns, combat boots, and voodoo regalia—on his own people. His era was marked by unimaginable extreme violence, including mass rape, ethnic cleansing, ritual killings, and cannibalism. He is, by nearly all accounts, guilty of crimes against humanity.

Unfortunately, Taylor is not unique. The twentieth century was putrid with dictators, strongmen, criminal bosses, and tribal leaders who went far beyond any norms of human behavior—even human behavior during times of war—in ordering the grossest atrocities.

How do we stop the tyrants? Certainly, the global community needs to be more responsive. Peacekeeping after trouble has broken out

is noble, but proactive and early intervention (entirely possible in military terms) would save millions from blighted futures and death.

There is, however, a tool other than military intervention: universal jurisdiction. Universal jurisdiction makes certain heinous crimes matters of universal law, subject to prosecution in any duly constituted court in the world. In 2006 Charles Taylor was arrested on charges of murder, sexual slavery, rape, the exploitation of child soldiers, and other war crimes. At this writing, he was on trial by the Sierra Leonean Special Court, under authorization of the UN Security Council, which has taken place at the facilities of the International Criminal Court in The Hague. If he is convicted, the international community is expected to cooperate in finding prison facilities for his incarceration.

Taylor's trial stands to demonstrate the strength and effectiveness of universal jurisdiction. If no country is exempt, if no bank account is sacrosanct, if no murderous rampage is sufficient to cover their tracks, dictators (and their cronies) will be held responsible for their actions. There will be no escape, no comfortable retirement. It may not save humanity from the bullies and lunatics, but it will weaken their grip and make them think twice: for them, somewhere, the gavel will always hang in midair. AS

Ending Torture

▬▬▬ Governments torture people to get information. Repressive governments also brutalize their citizens as punishment, and in order to control people through fear. In supposedly legitimate

Right: Former Liberian president Charles Taylor during his trial at the UN-backed Special Court for Sierra Leone in The Hague, Netherlands, on January 7, 2008.

Opposite: The execution room at Abu Ghraib Prison near Baghdad was once used to hang opponents of Saddam Hussein and was the site of human rights abuses by the U.S. military.

regimes, torture (including "soft torture," such as forcing victims to stay awake for days on end or humiliating them, as the U.S. military did to detainees in Abu Ghraib) is meant to function as a tool for finding out things that wouldn't be revealed in normal interrogations.

Torture, of course, is unethical no matter who's attaching the electrodes. Torture is, plain and simple, a gross violation of the victim's human rights. In addition, it nearly always leaves lasting damage, even (sometimes especially) when no physical scars can be seen. As the United Nations puts it, "Rape, blows to the soles of the feet, suffocation in water, burns, electric shocks, sleep deprivation, shaking and beating are commonly used by torturers to break down an individual's personality. As terrible as the physical wounds are, the psychological and emotional scars are usually the most devastating and the most difficult to repair. Many torture survivors suffer recurring nightmares and flashbacks. They withdraw from family, school and work and feel a loss of trust." Torture can ruin the lives of the victims, while degrading the torturers.

Those who defend the use of torture often acknowledge the horror involved, but claim torture is necessary for national security or other important aims, like preventing terrorist attacks. There's one problem with their arguments: torture doesn't work.

Professor Darius Rejali knows more about torture than nearly anyone else in the world, and his research shows conclusively that nearly all the arguments made in favor of torture are bogus. Modern advocates for the use of torture often claim that democracies use torture in different ways than dictatorships do, that torture can be, in Rejali's summary "safe, legal, professionally administered, rare and more effective than other forms of interrogation" (Rejali, 2002).

That's bunk, Rejali says. Once soldiers or police begin torturing, the historical record clearly indicates, they always slide into more extreme and systematic violence. Nor does "professionalism" prevent excessive torture. There is no known way to use torture safely. Indeed, the emerging medical field of "torture treatment" has found unequivocally that torture victims and torturers alike almost never avoid suffering lifelong consequences.

Furthermore, physical pain and humiliation neither secure the compliance of the victim nor yield secret truths. In fact, torture may even produce less reliable information than traditional interrogations do. In the 1940s, the U.S. Supreme

Court prohibited police from applying physical pressure on suspects. Police departments have since taught a range of new psychological techniques that are equally (or more) effective. People will confess to anything to escape the pain of torture, and false confessions and coerced false intelligence are worse than useless. After all, if a cop is chasing the wrong guy, the bad guy is running free.

Indeed, if we want more effective law enforcement and more protection over human rights, we ought to be simultaneously spreading better and more legitimate policing techniques and more aggressively holding accountable those who torture. If what we want is a safe and democratic world, torture chambers can have no place in it. AS

and recordings from digital cameras and camera phones. Things change when you can send your exposé over the Internet; speed and breadth of access are the best allies for transparency, and the Internet has both in abundance. Once damning photos or video have been released onto the Web, there's no bringing them back—efforts to do so are only more likely to draw attention.

Now that camera phones are ubiquitous, and the idea that you can use them to document injustice is nearly as widespread, Witness has focused more on training human rights advocates to better tailor their messages to the different audiences they need to reach. This is particularly important when advocates are seeking support from elected officials who have hundreds of causes vying for their attention. JC

Witness

▬▬▬▬ Founded in 1992 by musician Peter Gabriel, the human rights organization Witness has partnered with more than two hundred human rights groups in fifty countries, supplying video cameras and communication gear to allow people on the scene to document abuses of human rights. Witness attempts to create pressure for change by shining a light on injustice around the world. The participating volunteers are incredibly brave; they have only their cameras and the truth for protection.

Videotaping abuses is only the first step, though, and getting that video out to those who can bring it to the world has traditionally been difficult. That's where the Witness Web portal comes in, allowing people to send in images

Forensics and Human Rights

▬▬▬▬ Dictators kill people to silence them, to literally bury their voices. But forensics experts are helping the dead speak. Thanks to the work of one dedicated organization, the use of forensic anthropology to document and validate war crimes and human rights violations is starting to go mainstream, even in countries where the carnage has only recently ended. Forensic experts are doing more than granting closure to traumatized families—they are creating lasting public records pertaining to some of the worst criminals in history, and the evidence is being used to prosecute those criminals whenever it's still possible to do so.

The Argentine Forensic Anthropology Team (EAAF) was founded in 1984, shortly after democracy was restored to the country. The

military government that ruled from 1976 to 1983 left behind a terrible legacy of more than 10,000 people who had "disappeared," the majority of whom were kidnapped, tortured, murdered, and then dumped in anonymous mass graves in local cemeteries. The first efforts by local officials and doctors to locate and identify these victims were often clumsy and inefficient—for example, they used large cranes for excavations that destroyed bones and other evidence—so victims' rights groups asked the American Association for the Advancement of Science for help. The association sent a delegation, including some of the world's experts on forensic anthropology, to Argentina, and the EAAF was born.

Over the next five years, the delegation exhumed remains using traditional archaeological and anthropological techniques, all the while training a local team that could continue the work after the delegation was gone. It didn't take long for the newly formed EAAF to extend its efforts beyond Argentina. The EAAF has provided evidence to the United Nations War Crimes Tribunals on the former Yugoslavia, and has made ongoing missions to South Africa to investigate apartheid-era disappearances in conjunction with that country's Truth and Reconciliation Commission [see Ending Violence, p. 440].

In every case, the EAAF's objective is manifold: locate the victims; exhume the remains; determine the causes of death and patterns of torture and human rights abuses; return the remains to the victims' families; and finally, present the findings to the press and judicial bodies to ensure that word of these abuses is disseminated to the public, and that the criminals involved are brought to justice.

An important part of EAAF's work is forming local forensic teams; in countries where these sciences are not developed and oral testimony is still given precedence over physical evidence, the teams are often the first of their kind. Not only can local teams reach their communities

better, as they're already familiar with language and customs, they are an absolute necessity: the work can often take decades. The EAAF is still searching for the disappeared in Argentina, more than twenty years after the first delegation came and went. Without a local infrastructure to support continued research, the last case would have been closed when the last foreigner flew home.

Outreach is just as important as investigation. The EAAF holds regular presentations for key decision makers, and reaches out to victims' families by involving them in every step of the process, ensuring they have access and information throughout the recovery. This level of involvement and transparency is crucial to families' healing.

Finally, the EAAF is pushing to get its forensic teams much better access to DNA information. Genetic testing is indispensable to these investigations, but it's incredibly costly. To remedy this problem, the EAAF has started to create DNA blood banks—designed to hold multiple samples from victims' families and to cross-check data quickly and efficiently.

Each stage of the EAAF process is thoroughly documented with written records, photography, and videography. The organization is creating an audiovisual center in Argentina to further educate the public about its findings. Working with the human rights organization Witness, EAAF made its first documentary about its work, *Following Antigone*, which featured footage recorded by EAAF members in Argentina, El Salvador, Ethiopia, Haiti, and East Timor. CB

Benetech

■■■■ It takes human rights organizations and forensic teams years of painstaking documentation to build their cases. All of that work can be lost in a flash: human rights workers are increasingly the targets of abductions and harassment, during which they suffer personal harm and their computers are stolen and offices ransacked.

Benetech, a nonprofit that develops technology for humanitarian purposes, has created an open-source database program designed specifically to protect the work of human rights observers. Their Martus software is pure genius:

Opposite, left: A forensics expert examines remains found in a mass grave near Sarajevo, Bosnia, 2005.

Opposite, right: Witness trains villagers, like this man on the Thai-Burmese border, to record human rights abuses.

not only does it provide an easy way to log and organize all the countless details of each case (and share that information with other groups), but more importantly it backs up all information on remote servers, so the case files survive even if the laptop they were created on doesn't. With this remote backup system in place, workers also have the option of deleting sensitive files from their hard drives completely if that level of security is needed. The Martus program also comes with a simple-to-use but nearly impossible-to-crack encryption feature for files and e-mail alike.

A story from Colombia illustrates why Benetech's software is so invaluable to human rights workers. EQUITAS, the Colombian Interdisciplinary Team for Forensic Work and Psychosocial Services, has been recovering the remains of the many people who disappeared during Colombia's decades of complex and violent internal conflicts. The team's involvement in an excavation at a sensitive site—a former ranch that might hold the remains of hundreds of people—drew the worst kind of attention to the group. A female staff member was hijacked, assaulted, and robbed of her computer and cell phone. Fortunately, EQUITAS was already using Martus—all the files on the worker's computer were encrypted and saved on the remote server, and her attackers got none of EQUITAS's precious information.

Martus is available for download (www.martus.org) in English, Spanish, Arabic, French, Russian, Thai, Burmese, Nepali, and Persian versions, and so far people from over seventy countries have installed the program. The Thai and Burmese versions are being used to help Southeast Asian groups document human rights abuses in Myanmar.

Benetech's role in aiding human rights work doesn't end with this amazing software. The company's Human Rights Data Analysis Group (HRDAG) program conducts and publishes statistical analyses of large-scale human rights abuses. Recent HRDAG reports quantified the magnitude of human rights violations in East Timor's long struggle for independence, analyzed archival data to determine the involvement of Guatemala's National Police in the killing and disappearance of 200,000 people over thirty-six years of civil unrest, and analyzed witness statements for Liberia's Truth and Reconciliation Commission. CB

■■■■   RESOURCES

Amnesty International
http://www.amnesty.org
Held as the gold standard of human rights groups, Amnesty International works to fulfill and protect the rights detailed in the Universal Declaration of Human Rights, focusing on state oppression. The organization's mission is "to undertake research and action focused on preventing and ending grave abuses of the rights to physical and mental integrity, freedom of conscience and expression, and freedom from discrimination, within the context of its work to promote all human rights." Not affiliated with any nation, religion, political doctrine, or economic interest, Amnesty International has consistently fought for real social change, from ending the arms trade to campaigning against domestic violence.

Human Rights Watch
http://www.hrw.org
The largest human rights organization based in the United States, Human Rights Watch (HRW) has continually been at the forefront of international human-rights-violations inquiries and campaigns. The organization conducts fact-finding missions around the world and publishes annual reports, which garner extensive media coverage—and embarrass both the offending nations and the world. HRW was instrumental in the global response to human rights atrocities in Rwanda and Kosovo, and in moments of crisis puts hard pressure on global governments for immediate action, including but not limited to withdrawal of military and economic support. An extensive array of reports is available on the HRW Web site.

Why Societies Need Dissent by Cass R. Sunstein (Harvard University Press, 2003)
We value free expression not because it makes us feel good but because dissent, differences of opinion, and new ideas are the rudders of democracy—without them, democracies sail straight into tragedy. This lesson should be tattooed onto the brain of every student on the planet, but unfortunately, it's one that defenders of democracy must teach their grown-up peers again and again. Sunstein argues this point clearly, and explores how any group can become irrational

when the tendency to mentally herd together is not balanced with encouragement to think for oneself:

"The problem is that widespread conformity deprives the public of information that it needs to have. Conformists follow others and silence themselves, without disclosing knowledge from which others would benefit . . . Conformists are often thought to be protective of social interests, keeping quiet for the sake of the group. By contrast, dissenters tend to be selfish individualists, embarking on projects of their own. But in an important sense, the opposite is closer to the truth. Much of the time, dissenters benefit others, while conformists benefit themselves."

Rights of Man by Thomas Paine (1791) (Penguin Books, 1984), available for free download at http://www.gutenberg.org

Thomas Paine is in many ways the archetypal worldchanger: besides being the writer most important to the American Revolutionary cause (his pamphlet "Common Sense" helped stir popular support for independence and still bears reading today), he was also the first to announce in clear, passionate terms what human rights are and why they're worth defending. His language is sharply barbed—he spared no one's feelings—but his arguments still thunder, perhaps even more loudly in an age where many attack human rights in the name of national security or religion.

"The inquisition in Spain does not proceed from the religion originally professed, but from this mule-animal, engendered between the church and the state. The burnings in Smithfield proceeded from the same heterogeneous production; and it was the regeneration of this strange animal in England afterwards, that renewed rancour and irreligion among the inhabitants, and that drove the people called the Quakers and Dissenters to America. Persecution is not an original feature in any religion; but it is always the strongly marked feature of all law-religions, or religions established by law. Take away the law-establishment, and every religion reassumes its original benignity. In America, a Catholic Priest is a good citizen, a good character, and a good neighbour; an Episcopalian Minister is of the same description: and this proceeds, independently of the men, from their being no law-establishment in America."

Watching the Watchers

More and more, we live in a world where what we see, hear, and experience is recorded wherever we go. As our recording technology gets more portable and easier to hide, few statements or scenes will go unnoticed or unremembered. It's possible that, in the not too distant future, our day-to-day lives will be archived, saved, and even available over the Internet for recollection, analysis, or sharing.

This isn't happening because a Big Brother government is looking over our shoulders, or powerful corporations are watching us with security cameras and RFID (radio frequency identification) tags. That kind of surveillance is far outstripped by the millions of cameras and video recorders in the hands of millions of Little Brothers and Little Sisters—us. In our camera phones, we carry with us the tools of our own transparency, and we do so willingly, even happily.

Let's call this world the Participatory Panopticon. "Panopticon," originally a prison building design that allowed guards to see all inmates at all times, has more recently come to mean a society under constant observation. And it's already developing.

Camera phones and similar devices are constantly getting better at gathering and sharing information about the world. As it becomes cheaper and easier to just leave them running, we may find that it's very useful to have a "backup memory." We could use them as "TiVos"—the service that allows us to watch TV shows whenever we want—for our own lives, recording everything around us, including what people say and do, all for easy review. Microsoft and Hewlett-Packard are among the companies already writing software to help manage this kind of abundant information. Done right, such tools would make it possible to never again forget a face, a name, or an important bit of information.

Many of us would see this as a serious loss of privacy, with enormous legal implications regarding liability, self-incrimination, even intellectual property. But it could also serve the cause of truth. A police officer lying about hitting a protestor, a despot lying about human rights abuses, an executive lying about dumping toxic waste—these are easier to catch in a world where everything can be on the record. The results might surprise us: corporations could be forced to become more transparent to stakeholders, and certain officials could be required to wear a recorder while on duty (already, some police cars automatically videotape police stops). Ironically, it could be a world where trust would be easier, because it would be harder to get away with lying.

Is all of this really possible? Not yet, but the pieces are coming together faster than you might think. The Participatory Panopticon is not something people are building intentionally; it is the accidental result of technologies we've come to think of as the basic tools of our lives. JC

Tracking Transience

■■■■■ Hasan Elahi is a conceptual artist who has made his life the subject of an ongoing work about surveillance. Elahi, who is a U.S. citizen, was detained in 2002 by the Immigration and Naturalization Service at Detroit Metro Airport as he was returning from a trip overseas. During the course of questioning by the FBI about his whereabouts on September 12, 2001, it became clear that Elahi had been detained because he had a storage locker in Tampa, Florida, where he'd been teaching. Scared by 9/11, the owners of the storage area reported that "an Arab man had fled on 9/12, leaving explosives in his locker." There were, of course, no explosives—just the detritus of ordinary life—and he hadn't fled.

Over the next few months Elahi was interviewed dozens of times by the FBI, culminating in nine back-to-back polygraph tests, which finally "cleared" him. Every time Elahi traveled in the subsequent months, he would provide the FBI with his route information so he wouldn't get detained along the way. After a point he asked himself, Why just tell the FBI? Why not tell everyone?

So he hacked his cell phone, turning it into a tracking device that would report his movements on a map on his Web site. He used photos to document every aspect of his life: the airports he passed through, the meals he ate, even the bathrooms he used. The result is a photographic record of his daily life that would be very hard to falsify.

Elahi views his self-surveillance as both an art form and a perpetual alibi. At the same time, he has stretched the boundaries of surveillance. He flew to Singapore for four days, for instance, but never left the airport and never cleared customs. For four days, he was "nowhere"—he'd fallen off the map, which is precisely what the FBI and others worry about. Yet he documented every meal and every toilet while he was there.

Elahi turned some of the images he has amassed into an art installation, "Tracking Transience: The Orwell Project," which was exhibited

A collage of photos from Hasan Elahi's "Tracking Transience" project, in which he documented every aspect of his daily life for the FBI.

at several big events, including the 2007 Venice Biennale and the 2008 Sundance Film Festival. EZ

Sousveillance

▦▦▦▦ Who watches the watchmen? Maybe we all should. This is known as "inverse surveillance," or "sousveillance," meaning "watching from below." When citizens use cameras to record the actions of officials, either political or corporate, that's what they're doing. As the New York City government discovered recently, sousveillance can be a surprising equalizer.

In 2004, New York City police arrested nearly two thousand people during demonstrations around the Republican National Convention. The mayor and the chief of police condemned protesters for "rioting" and "retsisting arrest," and provided the press and the courts with videotapes taken by police officers, showing protesters out of control.

But it turned out that the police weren't the only ones armed with video cameras. Cheap digital video cameras employed by free-speech groups showed people being swept up without cause and without resistance. It turned out that prosecutors selectively edited the official video record to prove their cases, and police officers repeatedly misrepresented the protest events at trial. According to the *New York Times,* 91 percent of the nearly 1,700 cases ended with the charges being dropped or with not guilty verdicts. A startlingly large number of these cases included citizen videos that clearly showed that the police and prosecutors were lying.

As easy-to-use, portable cameras become commonplace, we're seeing more examples of sousveillance in action, from student camera-phone recordings of teachers harming classmates to the Video Vote Vigil, an online clearinghouse of recordings of voter obstruction and harassment. In the United Kingdom, the delightfully named Blair Watch Project was an effort, coordinated by the *Guardian,* to keep tabs on Prime Minister Tony Blair as he campaigned around the country. The project was sparked by the Labour Party's attempt to limit Blair's media exposure on the trail; instead, Blair had more cameras on him than ever. JC

The Innocence Project

▦▦▦▦ Justice, like transparency, is one of those values so basic to the proper functioning of democracy that we forget to talk about it. But even in countries with supposedly well-established and effective legal systems (like the United States), gross miscarriages of justice occur nearly daily, due to overzealous prosecutors, outdated investigative techniques, and flat-out bigotry.

The Innocence Project is best known for its work testing DNA evidence in cases where a person convicted of a crime maintains his or her innocence and where there is some reason to doubt the person's guilt. In nearly half the cases the groups has taken on, the DNA testing proves that the person was wrongly convicted. The Innocence Project's cofounder, Peter Neufeld, suspects there are still thousands of people in American prisons, even on death row, who would be exonerated if the DNA evidence in their cases were examined (though often such evidence has been lost or destroyed since their convictions).

A whole host of scientific insights into physical evidence, witness memories, and human behavior in the courtroom have yet to be applied to police work in any systematic way (for example, unknown but extremely large numbers of pieces of physical evidence from unsolved crimes have never been tested for DNA, nor have the results been gathered into a comprehensive national

An Afghan man photographs protesters during a demonstration in Kabul, Afghanistan, on May 20, 2010.

database which might help police link previously unsolved crimes together, providing new leverage for their investigations).

Why should average people care that someone may have been wrongly convicted? Beyond the moral issues, beyond the damage that systematic injustice does to our legal system, and beyond the fact that a false conviction could happen to you (a surprising number of the people exonerated by the Innocence Project were middle-class or above, some were well-educated, some even had lawyers or police officers in their families), there's another reason that represents a bit of clear thinking and reframing: when the wrong person is convicted of a crime, the actual criminal is still out there committing crimes.

It is this angle—avoiding false convictions as a means of crime-fighting—that is winning the Innocence Project the support of police chiefs, law-and-order politicians, and no-nonsense judges around the country. AS

██████   RESOURCE

Little Brother by Cory Doctorow (Tor Teen, 2008) Though technically a young adult novel, *Little Brother* is a clever and illuminating romp through the landscape of sousveillance. The book centers on a teen hacker who fights a fascistic U.S. security agency by mobilizing kids to swarm, observe, and collaborate. Note that Doctorow, an enthusiastic proponent of Creative Commons licensing, offers the entire novel for free download (http://craphound.com/littlebrother/download/).

Protest

██████   Things have changed a lot since the protests of the 1960s. These days, protests aren't about gas masks, bail money, and picket signs.

For one thing, scales and targets have changed dramatically. Your parents (or grandparents) may have made a righteous stand against Nixon's White House, but as a postmillennial protester, your targets may include not only your own government, but also other countries' governments, multinational corporations, and even abstract alliances and trade agreements like the Group of Eight (G8) and the World Trade Organization (WTO). The situation grows more complex if you believe, like the hippest factions of the protest scene, that there is no difference between corporations and countries anymore.

It's a complex web of tangled alliances out there; you may show up and discover that the corporation you're picketing is also the corporation that, directly or indirectly, made your shoes or printed your last paycheck. Not only has the line between friends and foes become blurred, but it has become fractal in its complexity—if it even exists at all.

In fact, you may not even have to carry a picket sign, or even show up physically at all, to make your point. More and more, protest is happening through the Internet. In a capitalist society, it's even possible to protest with your wallet, by boycotting corporations and nations that engage in unethical practices.

Along with everything else in the world, dissent is changing. Political action the postmodern way requires no massive time commitments and no membership in dodgy groups. It just takes you, your personal technology, and a desire to make the world a better place. JE

Culture Jamming

▬▬▬ If the boycott is the resolute parent of the consumer-activism family, culture jamming is the defiant and subversive teenager: brash, but often easily ignored. Culture jamming is the act of using existing advertisements and other public media as a vehicle for protesting the institutions that created them. It's a symbolic protest, drawing attention to the realities behind many deceptive corporate facades. Culture jamming could only exist as a recent phenomenon: it's meta-activism—a billboard altered in protest of the proliferation of giant ads on our landscapes; cons and slogans modified to make damning political statements about the companies they represent.

Advertising is a numbers game, where the more often a message can be hammered home, the more successful it is. Culture jammers don't have the budget to saturate society with their images like commercial advertisers do, but their one-time acts have proven effective nonetheless. A great culture jamming moment occurred when Chevrolet launched an interactive online advertising campaign called "Chevy Apprentice," in which the company asked visitors to the Web site to help create commercials for their giant SUV, the Tahoe, by uploading their own video clips, music, and text. Of course, Chevy didn't specify that suggestions had to promote the Tahoe, which gave culture jammers a prime opportunity to use the company's own platform to soapbox about global warming and the other environmental woes SUVs contribute to.

Culture jamming in general, and online efforts in particular, catalyze outreach and solidarity among consumers, two necessary (though not sufficient in and of themselves) ingredients for a successful movement. Culture jammers often scheme and execute their ideas in groups, thereby building strong communities of activists and pooling creative strategies for conveying a message. Those who view the culture jammers' modified ads and logos often feel a sense of solidarity and inclusion as the recipients of a particular and unexpected statement. Oftentimes we don't feel motivated or empowered to act on cultural trends that bother us until we realize how many others are sharing our experience. When culture jammers strike, many otherwise quiet citizens can be moved to speak up or act on their convictions—and corporations begin to feel threatened when a critical mass of perturbed consumers raises its voice. Thus a new cultural paradigm is emerging, in which the critical partnership between company and customer is managed more by the customer than by the company. JF & AS

The Yes Men

▬▬▬ The Yes Men, activists Andy Bichlbaum and Mike Bonanno, are some of the most notorious culture jammers in the world. In one brilliant media hack, Bichlbaum went on *BBC World* posing as a spokesperson for Dow Chemical on the twentieth anniversary of the Bhopal disaster, which exposed 500,000 people to toxins, killing anywhere between 3,000 and 15,000 people. Bichlbaum's "Jude Finisterra" apologized for the disaster, saying that the company was taking full responsibility and compensating victims. This, of course, forced Dow to issue a denial saying they were not sorry, were not taking responsibility, and would not pay the victims a dime—unleashing a considerable amount of backlash.

Forkscrew Graphics, a design team committed to political and social awareness, created these "iRaq" posters, spoofing Apple's iPod campaign, to promote what the group calls a "more real" freedom.

The "SurvivaBall" stunt had the Yes Men donning ridiculous inflatable costumes, which they claimed were Halliburton-designed, self-contained survival units that would safeguard the corporation's managers from the effects of abrupt climate change. The sardonic SurvivaBall pitch: "An advanced new technology will keep corporate managers safe even when climate change makes life as we know it impossible." AS

Protest Art

▬▬▬▬   Feral robotic dogs roam toxic-waste sites, chasing down deadly emissions. Our sandals contain test tubes that sample the soil as we walk. Sleek, highly designed genetic mutant babies are the perfect product for the millennial lifestyle.

These are only a few of the strange realities conjured up by artists like Natalie Jeremijenko, Amy Franceschini, and Patricia Piccinini. Their work—which serves as both commentary on and protest against technology and its discontents—is part of a growing wave of art that examines the dehumanizing effects of the modern condition, using the very technologies that are subject to criticism.

"What I'm most interested in is: how do we characterize systems of which we know very little, and have very poor information?" said Natalie Jeremijenko in a 2004 Worldchanging interview. "Knowledge is very partial, very incomplete, and yet decisions are made. So, I specifically try to design information systems that measure urban environmental interactions."

Her "Feral Robotic Dogs" project is one such information system. The dogs—built from robotics kits and fitted with devices that measure environmental variables such as radioactivity and air quality—are let loose at Superfund waste sites and English power stations. "Because the dog's space-filling logic emulates a familiar behavior, i.e. they appear to be 'sniffing something out,'" says the project's Web site, "participants can watch and try to make sense of this data without the technical or scientific training required to be comfortable interpreting [an] EPA document on the same material."

Amy Franceschini's "Soil Sampling Shoes" and "F.R.U.I.T." also deal with environmental issues and their impact on culture. The former—a pair of sandals with an array of test tubes instead of soles—theoretically let a user surreptitiously take soil samples at Superfund sites. The latter studies how fruit gets to our local markets from farms hundreds or even thousands of miles away. Custom paper "wrappers"—with information printed on them about the resources, labor, and transit required to supply us with fruit—help to raise consumer awareness about the complex economic system involved in even the simple purchase of an orange.

Patricia Piccinini's work deals with the ramifications of genetic engineering. Her "Mutant Genome Project" conjures up the LUMP (Lifeform with Unevolved Mutant Properties), a creepy "designer baby" created solely as a lifestyle accessory. "Protein Lattice" depicts lovely nude models interacting with mice that have human ears growing on their backs (a case of art imitating a reality both fascinating and gruesome). And her recent Venice Biennale *We Are Family* installation displays a series of sculptures and digital images of human-animal hybrids, grotesque and stunning at the same time.

Like most of the best artists who deal with social themes, Piccinini is rather ambivalent about her mutants—unlike many of her contemporaries, she is less a protester than a documenter. In an introductory essay to the Biennale catalog, curator Linda Michael writes, "Though they may be in some way failed or mutant creations, her figures have a kind of innocence that makes it easy to see beauty in the grotesque. We are free to imagine new futures that are unconstrained by outworn social philosophies. Piccinini always does this in a way that makes such futures understandable in terms of what we encounter in everyday life." JE

Banksy

■■■■■   To call Banksy a graffiti artist does little to distinguish him from the scads of other spray-paint guerillas who illustrate the world's walls and sidewalks. Banksy has frequently been characterized as an "art terrorist," which implies a violence that is absolutely absent in Banksy's work. His one-man mission is to confront cultural failings by stealthily positioning his own art among museum collections, on walls, and anywhere in the public view.

In 2005, for instance, Banksy visited Israel's West Bank, where he spray-painted several large images on the Palestinian side of the border wall to give the appearance of a hole through which the viewer could see a tranquil beach scene full of palm trees, or a snowcapped mountain and inviting forest. The subversiveness of the "art attack" drew mixed reactions from both sides of the wall—and from around the world—but nobody would dispute the power of the act, or the convention-busting audacity of the artist.

Theatre of the Oppressed

■■■■■   How can an interactive theater exercise performed by slum dwellers inform government policy? Initiated by Augusto Boal in Brazil, the Theatre of the Oppressed (TO) uses diverse games and interactive theater techniques to teach oppressed citizens how to concretely transform their society. Exercises pose dilemmas and challenges to participants, tailoring content to the core social problems and power structures of particular communities and society at large. Legislative Theatre, for instance, shows how TO techniques can help transform citizen desires into laws. In a mock legislative session, participants adopt simple new laws; afterward, they put pressure on real lawmakers to approve the new laws. While Legislative Theatre has had a significant impact on the actual laws in Brazil and other countries, often participants invent laws that are already in effect. The exercise thus not only enables them to inform the law-making process, but to become better informed themselves about existing laws so that they can exercise their rights. MB

■■■■■   RESOURCES

The Yes Men Fix the World (Directed by Andy Bichlbaum and Mike Bonanno, 2009)
The second film by the Yes Men [see p. 421] is a collection of scenes from their most notorious culture-jamming stunts, including the Dow Chemical

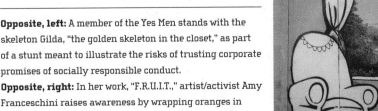

Opposite, left: A member of the Yes Men stands with the skeleton Gilda, "the golden skeleton in the closet," as part of a stunt meant to illustrate the risks of trusting corporate promises of socially responsible conduct.
Opposite, right: In her work, "F.R.U.I.T.," artist/activist Amy Franceschini raises awareness by wrapping oranges in paper printed with information about urban farming and the resources required to transport the food we consume.
Right: A Banksy work on a West Bank section of the security wall that separates Israel and Palestine.

and "SurvivaBall" pranks. The Yes Men also pose as Exxon representatives selling candles made of a fake biofuel called Vivoleum, which is made from the recently deceased, and print a fake version of the *New York Times*, with a front-page story headlined "Iraq War Ends" and an article in which George W. Bush is "self-indicted" on charges of high treason. (The article hilariously notes that Bush's indictment "seems largely to have been plagiarized from years of accusations made against him in the press.") The film is an entertaining introduction to the work of this clever troupe. CB

Legislative Theatre: Using Performance to Make Politics by Augusto Boal (Routledge, 1998) Founder of the international movement Theatre of the Oppressed, Boal describes in his book taking Hamlet's advice, "theater is a mirror in which may be seen the true image of nature, or reality," as a starting point for Legislative Theatre, aiming to make "theater as politics rather than merely making political theater." Legislative Theatre is a mandate in progress—a project still in flux and discovery—working to find new ways of involving everyone in the democratic process. This book is a unique and important guide to an alternative means of effecting social change, providing real tools for real theater that will lead to real action.

"The opening of the show for a community is an important moment, a big step. If the rehearsals are already a form of political activity in themselves (the citizens talk to one another and try to pinpoint their oppressions, to understand them by means of aesthetics), the shows are the moment of social communion, in which the other members of the community are invited to participate in the debates, still using the same theatrical language."

Smart Mobs: The Next Social Revolution by Howard Rheingold (Basic Books, 2003) In the pivotal *Smart Mobs*, Rheingold explores the transformation of collaboration, cooperation, and community via electronic networks, mobile devices, and innovative new thinking about computer-mediated social organization. Rheingold was one of the first observers to comprehend and explain the new "mediasphere" we're swimming in; *Smart Mobs* should be considered required reading for worldchangers everywhere.

Rheingold writes, "The big battle coming over the future of smart mobs concerns media cartels and government agencies that are seeking to reimpose the regime of the broadcast era in which the customers of technology will be deprived of the power to create and left only with the power to consume. That power struggle is what the battles over file-sharing, copy protection, regulation of the radio spectrum are about. Are the populations of tomorrow going to be users, like the PC owners and website creators who turned technology to widespread innovation? Or will they be consumers, constrained from innovation and locked into the technology and business models of the most powerful entrenched interests?"

Direct Action

▬▬▬ The time occasionally comes in a democracy when no amount of polite discussion will change a government or corporation's course, when rational argument and evidence make no difference, when average people are ignored in the halls of power. When that happens, it's time to act more directly, to expose the truth in ways that are impossible to ignore. Direct action is a desperate measure, but sometimes it's the only one that will jolt people awake. Sometimes, as the saying goes, when the fox is in the henhouse, the hens need to get a-flapping. JE

What Is Direct Action?

▬▬▬ Direct action includes anything from arranging sit-ins (like the civil rights movement of the early 1960s) to chaining yourself to a bulldozer (like the radical Earth Liberation Front) to blocking off streets with impromptu human barriers and throwing parties where usually only cars dare to tread (like the UK-based Reclaim the Streets movement). Of course, direct action also includes firebombings, assassinations, and even harassing passers-by with low-fidelity megaphones and poorly spelled picket signs. But we're going to assume you're not evil enough to actually do any of those things.

In our media-dominated age, the most effective direct action does the following:

- attracts media attention
- amuses, engages, or otherwise positively affects passive media consumers
- avoids subjecting anyone to death, injury, or prison sentences (though a stint in the local jail is probably OK)

Attracting Media Attention

The top way to attract media attention is to not be boring. If you feel you can best engage the media with megaphones and picket signs, bake sales or drum circles, you might want to let another member of your organization handle this end of operations, or perhaps farm things out to a respectable PR firm.

Always remember: the media does not care one iota about the fine points of your ideology. The media cares about getting ratings and market share. If you can help them achieve this goal, they will give you as much airtime as you want.

The following tend to woo media attention:

- Attractive nude people running around, accompanied by provocative slogans. For example, the PETA (People for the Ethical Treatment of Animals) campaign "I'd Rather Go Naked Than Wear Fur" featured fur-eschewing supermodels who were—you guessed it—naked.
- Celebrities doing unusual things, such as actor Woody Harrelson scaling the Golden Gate Bridge in 1996 to draw attention to the plight of the Headwaters redwood forest.
- Being very, very funny. This is the strategy of the Yes Men [see Protest, p. 421], who pose as representatives of big corporations and government organizations and deliver hilariously absurd but horribly plausible position papers to audiences of senior trade officials and economists.

A young labor-movement supporter joins a rally in downtown Manila, Philippines.

Catching the eye of the media will involve some cleverness on your part, and usually a willingness to put your most earnest tendencies on hold, at least in public. Nobody—especially not the media—likes a humorless zealot. The cult of irony rules in the Western zeitgeist right now. Chuckles, not chants, are the order of the day.

Make sure your organization's name and URL are plastered on every available surface a camera might happen to focus on—your T-shirts, your vehicles, the nude supermodel's bottom, the handcuffs you've used to lock yourself to whatever it is you're locking yourself to. This is called *brand recognition*.

Remember, as Mao Tse-tung (or maybe Andy Warhol) once pointed out: the only way to defeat the hegemony of popular media is to co-opt its tactics.

Winning Over Your Audience

Here's a little secret: pretty much every member of Western civilization believes, to some degree or another, that the Man is sticking it to them. Oddly enough, this even extends to people who—due to political or economic advantage—actually are the Man. We are a society of self-perceived underdogs,

scrappy little guys fighting the good fight against the Big Faceless Whatever.

Another secret: Most people consider activists to be ivory-tower idiot hippies who know nothing about the real world. You will have to fight this bias by being funny, clever, and, most important, tuned in to the needs and desires of the common man.

For example, if you are an ecoactivist, don't demonize loggers for cutting down old-growth forests. Loggers are not evil. Loggers are people who are trying to feed their families by doing a backbreaking and dangerous job for little money, usually in areas that are economically depressed, like the rural Pacific Northwest. Instead, place yourself and the loggers on common ground, fighting the big evil lumber corporations who are both destroying Mother Earth and endangering the future livelihood of the loggers themselves by cutting down all the trees (leaving no more trees for loggers to cut down).

You are now a champion of the Average Joe, fighting the good fight against the devious machinations of the Man. Loggers will now buy you beers and clap you on the shoulder, instead of righteously kicking your idiot hippie behind.

And remember the (Michael) Moore Principle: people respond to humor, not lectures. Making the target of your opposition look like a bunch of evil morons is far more effective than simply debating them.

To paraphrase *Conan The Barbarian*: What is best in life? To crush your enemies, to drive them before you, and to hear the lamentations of their PR flacks.

Not Ending Up Dead or in Prison

Look, we know how it is. After a day of listening to Howard Zinn lectures on the old iPod and reading about the destruction of natural resources by greedy power mongers, there's nothing you'd rather do than head down to Starbucks with your rolling crew of concerned global citizens and get medieval on their latte-pimping asses. We understand. Really, we do.

But what will that accomplish? Starbucks' insurance will cover any damage you do. The media will portray you as a windmill-tilting hippie imbecile. You will go to prison for vandalism and destruction of private property.

Being a yardbird is much less pleasant than merely being a passive accomplice to the continuation of the capitalist power structure. Believe us. We know what we're talking about.

You will almost always find that people—and, more important, governments local and national—will place the righteousness of your cause second to their obligation to protect human life and the principle of property ownership.

Also, such activities as climbing billboards, going on hunger strikes, and standing in front of oncoming tanks do carry the risk of actually getting killed, or at least severely injured. Seriously consider the implications of such activities before partaking in them.

Luckily, most of the activities activists engage in—blocking public thoroughfares, interfering with law enforcement, and so on—will

at most land you in the local pokey—and local jail, at least in the G8 countries, is usually no big deal. It's almost a rite of passage for many activists to spend a weekend in lockup. The worst thing you will probably have to deal with is your drunk cell mate.

Conclusion

As we've seen, there is a middle ground between mind-numbing picket-line boredom and full-tilt Black Bloc butt-kicking. Just keep these simple concepts in mind and you'll do fine.

And remember: if a protest happens in the forest and nobody covers it for the nightly news, well . . . the forest's probably going to get clear-cut in the very near future. JE

Ruckus Society

██████ While some present-day protesters are still content with picket signs, marches, and sit-ins, some groups go further. Take, for example, the Ruckus Society—a radical spin-off of the already radical Earth First! organization (which played a major role, alongside the Direct Action Network, in organizing the anti-WTO protests that drew massive media attention in 1999). The Ruckus Society is the strong arm of the protest movement—and whatever the issue or event, from globalization and genetically enhanced food to the 2004 Republican National Convention and the WTO, the Ruckus Society is there. Their "Action Camps" train activists in direct action methods, including the best way to chain oneself to an immovable object and to safely hang oneself from a billboard—tactics that are always sure to bring

Opposite: Activists in protest of Israeli policies block New York's Fifth Avenue by forming a human chain across the street, 2003.

Right: Activists practice techniques of passive resistance at the Eco-Avenger Basic Training Camp, run by the Ruckus Society.

high levels of media exposure to the cause (whatever the cause may be).

What distinguishes the Ruckus Society from its predecessors is its level of practical organization and its media awareness. In a 2001 *Rolling Stone* article, writer Dan Baum noted, "When two Ruckus-trained climbers hung a stories-high Stop Global Warming banner off the Los Angeles headquarters of the oil company ARCO a few years ago, they were only the centerpiece of a fifteen-person operation. Others directed the media to the best camera angles, delivered carefully prepared sound bites about ARCO to the cameras, monitored the police radio bands from a truck full of scanners and waited at the jail with bail money."

Ruckus Society spokespeople are always quick to point out that nonviolence is one of their core beliefs—though they seem to interpret the term as applying exclusively to acts performed on living beings. "The Boston Tea Party was property destruction," said Ruckus director John Sellers in a *San Francisco Examiner* interview (June 19, 2002). "I don't think a lot of people debate about whether it was violent or nonviolent. I think most people would say it was nonviolent." JE

████████ RESOURCE

Rebel, Rebel: The Protestor's Handbook by Bibi van der Zee (Guardian Newspapers Ltd., 2008) Environmental journalist Bibi van der Zee's book not only expounds on how to stage meaningful civil disobedience without being arrested, but also details how to join or start a campaign, raise funds, and reach the masses. We agree with van der Zee that raising your voice has never been more crucial or effective, and once you're armed with the knowledge contained in *Rebel, Rebel,* organizing or partaking in a campaign can be easy, fun, and jail-free. SK

Rosa Parks's refusal to give up her seat on a bus in Montgomery, Alabama, and her subsequent arrest signaled a turning point in the civil rights movement, 1956.

Nonviolent Revolution

I suppose that human beings looking at it would say that arms are the most dangerous things that a dictator, a tyrant, needs to fear. No. It is when people decide they want to be free. Once they have made up their hearts and minds to that, there's nothing that can stop them.
    Archbishop Desmond Tutu

████████ The world is lousy with dictators and repressive politicians, ruling mafias and militias. If we want to live in a better world, we have to get rid of them. Unfortunately, the hard work of actually turning them out always falls to the folks they're oppressing. Most of the time, doing away with a truly awful regime involves starting a revolution.

Revolutions sound cool to those who've never been through one. Real revolutions are terrifying and dangerous. They're actions undertaken by sensible people only when it is absolutely clear that nothing else will change a regime, when the only alternative left is to either compel change or completely overthrow the system.

Revolutions can be incredibly violent. But employing violence is often the worst way to overthrow those in power. The more despotic the government, the more violence it has at its disposal. Starting the shooting when the other side has most of the guns is bad strategy. Also, the more violent the revolution, the more likely it is that violent figures will come to power in its aftermath, just as Stalin followed the Russian Revolution, or Madame Guillotine the French. What's worse, unsuccessful violent insurrectionary groups—from the

Shining Path to the IRA—often slide away from their principles and become merely well-organized thugs.

We are learning, however, how to do revolution right through the tool of nonviolent confrontation. At first glance, the idea of a "nonviolent revolution" seems counterintuitive, but nonviolent revolution works. In the last three decades, fifty out of sixty-seven successful citizen revolutions were largely or wholly nonviolent, according to the International Center on Nonviolent Conflict.

There is nothing "soft" about nonviolence. Some of the hardest-headed revolutionaries on earth have chosen nonviolence for entirely calculated, rational reasons. But one of the many advantages of nonviolent revolution is that it serves the heart as well as the head, by leaving open the possibility of postrevolutionary reconciliation and cultural renewal. Nonviolent revolution is not only more likely to succeed, but it heals instead of harms and leaves a better society in its wake. AS

How Nonviolence Works

▬▬▬ Nonviolence works by destroying the ability of those in power to use force without losing the essential support of those on whom their continued stay in power depends.

In order to undermine the power of a regime, revolutionaries need to do two things: win the public over to their cause, and convert the regime's key supporters.

To win the public's support, nonviolent revolutionaries must dramatize the issues. They must create symbolic actions—like Rosa Parks did when she refused to sit in the back of a segregated bus—that arrest the public's attention and help shatter the legitimacy of the regime in the eyes of the people. In war, the military historian Basil Liddell Hart teaches, the strategy that is best is that which allows the most flexibility in concentrating an overwhelming amount of force at a critical weak point in the opponents' forces. In nonviolence, the point is to use a small group's willingness to take a blow to concentrate the public's attention on a telling symbol of the regime's moral weaknesses.

To peel away the regime's supporters, revolutionaries have to split off elements of the ruling bloc, convincing those people who hold power, on whom the regime depends—the police, businesspeople, judges, military, and clergy—that change is both in their interests and in line with their ethics. Nonviolence is not passive: it is a form of fighting back—but fighting back, as the saying goes, with different weapons and to a different end. The end is to convert. When critical parts of the regime defect to the cause of change—when, for instance, the police refuse to break up peaceful demonstrations—the regime's days are numbered.

All of this requires intelligent hard work and extreme bravery. Nonviolence, done well, demands discipline, commitment, strategy, and leadership; it takes careful planning and training, role-playing exercises, education, and spiritual preparation. That doesn't mean that nonviolent activists need to wait for an entire movement to emerge before beginning their work. Small groups are the shock troops of nonviolence; small groups of people always take the first steps, and become the nodes around which an entire network of action coheres. But even small groups benefit from knowing how to use their tools well. AS

Right: Archbishop Desmond Tutu, chairman of the Truth and Reconciliation Commission in South Africa, in 1998.
Opposite: Mahatma Gandhi at the beginning of his fast for peace in 1948, New Delhi, India.

A Force More Powerful

First they ignore you, then they laugh at you, then they fight you, then you win.
Mahatma Gandhi

Since Mahatma Gandhi led the Indian people in rising up peacefully against the occupying English Empire, more than half a century ago, the study of nonviolence has become an art. Not only can nonviolence be taught, but the lesson plans are readily available.

One of the most impressive groups distributing the curriculum is the International Center on Nonviolent Conflict (ICNC). The ICNC does standard advocacy for nonviolence—helping the media (which tends to find gunplay a more interesting story) understand the role of nonviolence in real change; pushing for foreign policies that better support civil society groups in countries with authoritarian governments—and also provides direct access to tools for understanding and employing nonviolent confrontation directly.

To that end, the center has produced a triumvirate of great resources, collectively titled

"A Force More Powerful." If you're interested in learning more about nonviolence, there is no better place to start. Of the three tools, the meatiest is the center's book *A Force More Powerful: A Century of Nonviolent Conflict*, a five-hundred-page exploration of the history and practice of nonviolence. A documentary and a video game are two additional resources that complement the book. The ICNC documentary, also called *A Force More Powerful*, covers the American civil rights movement, the Indian independence movement, the Polish Solidarity labor movement, the Chilean movement that toppled the brutal dictatorship of General Augusto Pinochet, and the South African boycotts that helped end apartheid. Perhaps most inspiringly, it also tells the story of Danish resistance to the Nazi occupation. Overwhelmed by the Nazi war machine, the Danes practiced "resistance disguised as collaboration." They refused the Nazis' demand to turn over their Jewish fellow citizens, hiding them in their homes and then smuggling them by the thousands out of Denmark to safety in fishing boats. Then the Danish resistance engaged in sabotage, strikes known as the "go home early movement" (where workers left their

factories hours early each day, supposedly to work in their gardens, but in reality simply to slow down the German war effort), and constant psychological pressure on occupying troops, such as symbolic "two-minute stops" where, at a predetermined time, everyone and everything moving in the streets would suddenly freeze, stand still and silent for two minutes, and then continue. Their struggle not only undermined the Nazi war effort, but it also helped the Danes emerge from the war with their national conscience intact.

The game, *A Force More Powerful: The Game of Nonviolent Strategy,* although it had a more limited reach, was, in some ways, the most illuminating tool. Taking the role of the leader of an emerging nonviolent movement in any of ten scenarios, video game players learned to grow their movement, build alliances, and use a variety of pressure tactics to isolate and change the regime. The original game is no longer available, but the developers have created a second version with the same conceit called *People Power: A Game of Civil Resistance* (http://peoplepowergame.com).

These "serious games" offer one of the best ways to learn. Playing with possibilities allows us to understand systems in ways intellectual study can't. The principles embodied in *A Force More Powerful* are tried and tested; in fact, a number of veteran nonviolent activists were consulted on the project, and Ivan Marovic, one of the leaders of the Otpor student movement, which brought down Serbian dictator Slobodan Milosevic, has played a key role in the design of both games. AS

Ukrainian Nonviolent Protest

The Ukrainian presidential elections in November 2004 sent citizens into nonviolent protest in the street, opposing what was exposed as a fraudulent and corrupt process. The masses made a significant statement, but the cry of resistance that resounded the loudest was actually a silent and singular one—expressed through sign language via an interpreter for Ukraine's state-run television station.

On November 25, according to the *Washington Post,* as Natalia Dmytruk signed the news of the elections on TV, she took the opportunity, standing live on national television, to stop interpreting the newscaster and to tell deaf Ukrainians what she felt they needed to know: "I am addressing everybody who is deaf in the Ukraine. Our president is Viktor Yushchenko. Do not trust the results of the central election committee. They are all lies . . . And I am very ashamed to translate such lies to you. Maybe you will see me again—" She then completed the newscast according to the script, unsure of what awaited her after the broadcast (April 29, 2005).

Word spread, and protesting escalated until a reelection was scheduled, and in December of that year, Viktor Yushchenko emerged victorious. Nonviolence is a strategy in which each of us can play a part. AS

■■■■■■   RESOURCES

The Art of the Impossible: Politics as Morality in Practice by Vaclav Havel (Alfred Knopf, 1997) Vaclav Havel stands as a worldchanging icon. Principled yet open-minded, humble yet strong willed, subversively funny yet in deadly earnest, the playwright, human-rights dissident, and former president of the Czech Republic has been a major influence on an entire generation of Eastern European activists, artists, and writers, who have responded to his thoughtful postmodern humanism. *The Art of the Impossible* brings together many of his most powerful political essays and speeches. Together they bear witness to the fact that moral strength, intellectual courage, and political determination can change even the most hopeless situations for the better.

"I have experienced a beautiful revolt of children against the lie that their parents served, allegedly in the interest of those very children. Our antitotalitarian revolution was—at least in its beginnings—a children's revolution. It was high-school students and apprentices, adolescents, who marched in the streets. They marched when their parents were still afraid, afraid for their children and for themselves. They locked their children in at home, took them away from the cities on weekends. Then they began marching with them in the streets. First out of fear for their children, later because they became infected by their enthusiasm. The children evoked from their parents their better selves.

They convinced them that they were lying and forced them to take a stand on the side of truth."

Waging Nonviolent Struggle: 20th Century Practice and 21st Century Potential by Gene Sharp (Extending Horizons Books, 2005) Founder of the Albert Einstein Institute and preeminent scholar of nonviolence, Gene Sharp has devoted his life to furthering the understanding and successful practice of nonviolence, and has been pivotal in some of the most important nonviolent struggles of our day. *Waging Nonviolent Struggle* is the essential compendium of his work and practice, debunking myths about nonviolence, exploring sources of power and human nature, and providing key historical examples of the overwhelming success of nonviolent techniques. We are left with no choice but to believe that "expanded applications of nonviolent struggle in the future will not only contribute to the reduction of major violence but to the expansion of democratic practices, political freedom, and social justice. The choice is ours."

Diary of a Political Idiot: Normal Life in Belgrade by Jasmina Tesanovic (Midnight Editions, 2000) Jasmina Tesanovic writes with extraordinary moral clarity about what life feels like inside a desperate and oppressive nation. Her *Diary*, written as NATO was bombing Serbia during the Balkan conflicts, is a beautiful, vulnerable, and honest account of the mental changes an educated, liberal person undergoes as she watches her country slide over the brink and keep falling. It's also a testament to the courage it takes to turn one's back on people and institutions one can no longer support, and the emptiness that living through times that demand such courage can leave behind.

"The referendum was yesterday. One of my friends said, now they'll come and shoot us because we didn't vote. I told her she was just being paranoid. After the vote, our president gave a speech. Everything about him, his face, his voice, his words, and his emotions, was so familiar—that pathetic, patronizing tone that says he knows what's best for me, just like my father. This president, whom I know to be a corrupt liar and merciless enemy, worries for my future—that is why he is sending me to war, that is why he is fighting the rest of the world. That is why he makes me weep."

Revelers in Kiev, Ukraine, wave flags to commemorate the one-year anniversary of the "Orange Revolution," which brought reformer Viktor Yushchenko into power in 2004.

Ending Violence

▬▬▬▬ Most of the worst humanitarian disasters on the planet are the result, at least in part, of war. War may be—indeed, often is—triggered or worsened by other factors: the killing fields of Rwanda were at their most terrible where hunger was most dire. But the fact remains that the immediate cause of much suffering in the world is a teenage boy with an automatic rifle.

Increasing evidence supports the notion that security and sustainability go hand in hand, that attempts to create one without the other are doomed from the start. If we are to create a more stable world, we need to do a better job of heading off conflict (or negotiating its end), of stopping genocides, and of bringing killers to justice. Curtailing the trade in small arms would be a good idea, too, in many activists' books. We also need a better understanding of the kinds of problems violence creates, in order to better relieve suffering and more quickly restore stability in war-torn areas.

An International Rescue Committee (IRC) report found that only 2 percent of those dying in African war zones are violently killed. Many more die from the resulting disintegration of the social fabric,

already weak economic structures, and loss of scarce resources. Indeed, the IRC says, the primary cause of death for innocents in a time of war is their forced flight into perilous conditions. As they flee from violence, families get separated; medical supplies, food, and clean water disappear quickly; and otherwise preventable illnesses ravage whole populations.

All of this suggests that when it comes to heading off the worst effects of war, we need to adopt a multifaceted approach. Not only do we need to reinvent the way we deliver refugee aid, we need to stop the fighting in the first place, and create incentives for lasting peace. Ending the violence of war sets the stage for building bright green peace. AS

Sustainability: Our Real Security Focus

▬▬▬▬ What really threatens us? And how do we truly make ourselves safer?

In 2006, the Cato Institute (a conservative American think tank) released an outstanding paper, "A False Sense of Insecurity," which makes the point that by any rational assessment, terrorism is not that big a threat to the average American. Since the late 1960s, the paper points out, about as many Americans have been killed by terrorists as have been "killed over the same period by lightning, accident-causing deer, or severe allergic reaction to peanuts."

Climate change, however, is a true security threat—perhaps the most significant threat

we face. If scientists are correct, far more people have already lost their lives from the direct and indirect effects of climate change than from terrorism. Processed food, car accidents, chemical spills, environmentally influenced cancers: all of these are probably bigger threats to the lives of average people than terrorism.

It's obvious that we need to take measures to alleviate these problems; what's not so obvious is that many of these measures will also make us more secure and our systems more stable in the face of terrorism or other dangers. See, for instance, the notion of passive survivability, which notes that green buildings are not only are more sustainable, they also protect their users more effectively in an emergency, whether it's an earthquake or a city paralyzed by a train station bombing. Similarly, fuel-efficient cars will not only help lower greenhouse-gas emissions, but will also decrease our dependence on foreign oil and make us less vulnerable to hostile and unstable regimes.

We can build a bright green society, one that will give our kids a future. We can build a much safer society, one that will increase our kids' chances of growing up in a secure environment to live in that future. By and large, the steps involved in building both are the same, and none of them involve color-coded terror alerts. The time has come to stop living in fear, and start building a better world. AS

Making Better Blue Hats

███████ To war is human. But to stop wars, prevent genocide, help spread harmony—this is the work of peacekeepers. These soldiers, performing a job that has only existed for a few decades, are willing to fight and die to keep the peace.

Though they are defamed by nationalists of many stripes, derided by some globalists as being too timid ("what the UN does best is count the dead" a famous condemnation begins), United Nations peacekeepers—known as blue hats—change the world. The noblest calling a soldier can answer is to be a "soldier of peace." As the world is subject to more and more stresses and conflicts, it will have more and more need of peacekeepers of all sorts. If there is to be a bright green future, it will be built in part on the courage of peacekeeping troops.

Peacekeeping in its current form, important as it is, suffers from a huge number of problems. Romeo Dallaire is outspoken about the worst problem: simple inaction. As head of the UN peacekeeping mission that found itself powerless to check the genocide in Rwanda, Dallaire may have agonized more than any other person on earth about how the world ought to act when faced with monumental acts of evil. His conclusion? The UN must act before, not after, genocide has begun.

A growing number of experts agree with Dallaire that the international community has to learn how to stave off genocide, not just regret it. We must learn more about what kinds of conflicts lead to disastrous ruptures of the social fabric, which ones can be stopped early, and how to mitigate those that erupt full-blown. The social science of peacekeeping is a worldchanging enterprise.

But it's also clear that the UN peacekeeping forces themselves need to undergo some fundamental reforms, and that everything from their rules of engagement to their technologies and tactics must change. They must be better equipped and prepared; more attention must be focused on training units from different armies to work together; and absolute accountability must be maintained, so that soldiers don't exploit or abuse the civilian population and thus undermine

Opposite, left: Child soldiers of the rebel group Sudan People's Liberation Army walk away from their weapons after surrendering, Malou, Sudan, 2001.

Opposite, right: Rescue workers cover up casualties after a passenger train was bombed by terrorists in Madrid, Spain, 2004.

Right: The role of the United Nations' "blue hats" is increasingly under debate, but is critical to moving toward a more peaceful future.

local support for peacekeeping. More coordination among peacekeepers, police, and emergency workers is also needed. The list goes on, with various governmental, military, and NGO experts debating the needed reforms, and while implementation of those reforms has been slow, the trend is clear: better peacekeeping missions are on their way. AS

Environmental Peacemaking

In a world where natural systems are strained to the limit and billions of people struggle daily to survive, what we're used to calling "natural disasters" are growing both more common and more dangerous. They are inherently more destructive than they used to be (thanks in part to climate change), but they also feed into (and their effects are made worse by) ongoing humanitarian crises and violent conflicts.

The idea that poverty, the environment, and security are linked is not a new one. Neither is the idea that disaster response needs to move beyond relief to become an opportunity to rebuild something better. Neither, for that matter, is the idea that a healthy environment can buffer the worst effects of natural disasters while providing critical ecosystem services.

It all works together, or it doesn't work at all.

The good news is that these holistic approaches are already catching on, and those who respond to crises have started thinking in multiple arenas and across multiple disciplines. Winning a war doesn't always create a useful peace. Conversely, conflicting groups can move toward peaceful resolution, or at least recognize the necessity of alliances, in the face of shared environmental destruction, as occurred after the Pakistani earthquake of late 2005.

Right: Indians and Pakistanis work together to deploy relief tents to victims of the 2005 earthquake in Kashmir, a disputed area between the two countries.
Opposite, left: Insurgents in Fallujah, Iraq, take up position to launch mortars against U.S. troops, 2004.
Opposite, right: In what appeared to be an act of terrorism, residents of villages in Nigeria were forced to evacuate their homes when fire erupted along an oil pipeline there.

Security in the Twenty-first Century

Like almost everything else in our lives, international security in the twenty-first century will be very different than it was in the twentieth. Warfare is evolving owing to changes in global realities.

The first big change is that state-versus-state warfare is on the way out, made obsolete by nuclear weapons and global economic interdependence. Don't be confused by the invasion of Iraq; it was an outlier. One-on-one wars between states in the twenty-first century will be exceedingly rare.

That's good, but as interstate warfare has been declining, state-versus-nonstate warfare has surged. It started with 9/11, and it continues in Iraq, Nigeria, southern Russia, Thailand, and many other places. When we examine it in its entirety, we see that it has become a global contest (some would say an epochal war) between an alliance of states—led in some ways by the United States—and a large and amorphous community of nonstate foes. The reason for this is globalization (the same force that made state-versus-state warfare obsolete).

If we plunge below the level of the state, we see a plethora of groups, formed around the traditional moral bonds of family, clan, tribe, ethnicity, and religion (or, in the case of gangs, around manufactured loyalty). These groups have always provided a means of mutual survival. However, as technology, transportation, and trade began to connect substate groups to the global community, those groups gained skills and influence that, in combination with mindsets that are far from progressive, have made them very dangerous.

It should come as no surprise that some of these groups don't share the developed world's

vision of the future. They see their religion corrupted, their economy in decline, and their environment degraded by a global system of impersonal markets, nation-states, and media.

They are not unjustified in believing the goals of our world put their world at risk. Their very cultural survival is in question.

The result is war. In the past, state-on-nonstate war would have been containable to a locality (typically a backwater). However, in our new global environment, nonstate groups have gained incredible leverage. They can now wage war on states, both locally and globally, and win.

Why? These substates have developed a new method of warfare that uses nonhierarchical forms of organization very much like what we see in the open-source software community. Open source–style warfare is highly decentralized. It allows many groups, regardless of motive, to coordinate and mutually advance against common enemies. In Iraq, which is increasingly the laboratory for this century's new war, seventy-five to a hundred different insurgent groups are fighting the U.S. military, its coalition partners, and the new Iraqi government with a considerable amount of success. Not only is this type of nonorganization almost impossible to destroy (since there's no leadership cadre to decapitate), it is able to rapidly deploy innovations that meet or exceed those deployed by the U.S. military, which is finding it hard to keep up.

Another component of the new state-versus-nonstate warfare is systems disruption, strategic attacks without the use of weapons of mass destruction. This type of warfare uses our systems against us. For example, on 9/11 the transportation system was used as a weapon. In Iraq, attacks against power systems, oil pipelines, and social connections have hollowed out the newly emerging state. Not only do such disruptions render the state unable to deliver those services that are the foundation of its legitimacy, but they create an unstable environment that prompts more groups to enter the open-source war, on either side. Systems disruption is easy (we have too many networks to defend), and it provides unprecedented levels of leverage. A small group that spends thousands of dollars on an attack can cause hundreds of millions of dollars in damage to the state it is attacking—as we have seen in the ongoing attacks on the Iraqi and Nigerian oil systems.

These groups self-finance their operations through transnational crime, which has limitless growth potential. Globalization has smashed the barriers between states. Transnational crime (some call it black globalization) is now a multi-trillion-dollar economy and, according to Moises Naim, the editor of *Foreign Policy* magazine, it is growing seven times faster than legal trade. This shadow economy allows nonstate groups access to a global smuggling network that handles everything from arms to illegal immigrants to drugs to knockoff products to money laundering. They have quickly learned to use this network to sustain their war with the world. The ongoing attacks in Nigeria are financed through the bunkering and export of stolen oil, and the 2004 Madrid train bombings were financed through the sale of the drug ecstasy.

Over the longer term, these system-disrupting, transnational crime-fueled sons of global fragmentation will cause a radical change in how we think about informational security. As their reach spreads, they may melt the global map. Parts

of states will fall under their control, and many states will hollow out. If this happens, nonstate groups will inspire more participants and see their fortunes rise as state control recedes. Unfortunately, we who live in democracies aren't prepared for this—neither our exceedingly expensive militaries, built for interstate warfare, nor our fragile economies will protect us.

What will protect us will be difficult to implement, particularly in the United States. It will require that the country change its approach to how it uses energy. Green technologies will have to become a central aspect of all of our lives. It is only through the broad adoption of green technology that we will achieve the decentralization and independence that can mitigate the shocks of global systems disruption. If al Qaeda's attack on Saudi Arabia's Abqaiq oil facility had been successful in February 2006, this would be crystal clear to all of us.

For the United States to survive the new realities of war, it must give up being a superpower. The role is too expensive to maintain, particularly considering the massive national debt. Given that we live in a world dominated by fluid markets, flirtation with bankruptcy isn't a sound long-term strategy. The United States is critical. If it can overcome these barriers (retool its defense system, abdicate as superpower, and shrink the national deficit), it could emerge intact, or even stronger than it is today, and help support the global system. If not, international violence may continue to spin out of control, putting our global system, as we understand it, at risk. For the sake of all of our futures, the world's sole remaining superpower needs to chart a new course. JR

Banning Cluster Bombs

▬▬▬ Cluster bombs are small antipersonnel munitions, rather like hand grenades, which can be dropped from airplanes or helicopters or shot from ground-based weapons. In theory, they are effective weapons of war because they are likely to kill their targets. In practice, however, up to 40 percent of the bombs don't detonate on impact, leaving a battlefield strewn with small, unstable, and deadly explosives, which present all the same problems as land mines.

In 2006, the *New York Times* reported that 1 million unexploded cluster bombs dotted southern Lebanon, a souvenir of the war between Israel and Hezbollah. Although a clean-up effort has long been underway, with unexploded ordnance littering everything from rooftops to olive groves, it will take time to remove all of the bombs, which outnumber people in this region. So far, hundreds of citizens have been injured by the bombs; there were more than two hundred civilian casualties in the year following the ceasefire.

Activist groups like the Cluster Munition Coalition are working to ban cluster bombs. Like the campaign to ban land mines, this is a worldchanging effort, as cheap antipersonnel weapons destroy lives, wreck economies, and keep conflict areas unstable long after the fighting has ended. The group was instrumental in the creation of the Convention of Cluster Munitions, an international treaty that was adopted in Oslo in 2008 and took effect in late 2010. At this writing, 36 nations had ratified the treaty and a total of 106 had signed. Unfortunately, but not surprisingly, the nations that have not signed the treaty include the United States, Russia, China, India, and Pakistan—the world's largest manufacturers of cluster munitions. AS

Nuclear Abolition

▬▬▬ Nuclear warheads are antiresilience. They don't make us safer; they actually make us brittle. And pouring enormous amounts of money and natural resources into mutually assured destruction seems like an outdated model for peacekeeping on a finite planet.

The arguments in favor of worldwide disarmament are manifold. First of all, nukes make nations nervous. The UN and international advocacy groups have long recognized the link between disarmament and nonproliferation, often quoting the Canberra Commission's 1995 report on the Elimination of Nuclear Weapons, which says, "The possession of nuclear weapons by any state is a constant stimulus to others to acquire them." And, as evidenced by the U.S. invasion of Iraq, even the unsubstantiated presence of weapons of mass destruction can be used to justify war. In addition, a nuclear program is hugely expensive to maintain: according to the Carnegie

Endowment for International Peace's report "Nuclear Security Spending," the United States spent more than $52 billion on nuclear security programs in 2008 alone; 67 percent of the Department of Energy's budget goes to nuclear weapons and weapons-related programs.

In June 2009, while in Prague for the twentieth anniversary of the Velvet Revolution, President Barack Obama addressed nuclear abolition in a historic and heartening speech:

"Some argue that the spread of these weapons cannot be stopped, cannot be checked—that we are destined to live in a world where more nations and more people possess the ultimate tools of destruction. Such fatalism is a deadly adversary, for if we believe that the spread of nuclear weapons is inevitable, then in some way we are admitting to ourselves that the use of nuclear weapons is inevitable.

"Just as we stood for freedom in the 20th century, we must stand together for the right of people everywhere to live free from fear in the 21st century . . . I state clearly and with conviction America's commitment to seek the peace and security of a world without nuclear weapons."

Furthermore, President Obama declared, "As a nuclear power, as the only nuclear power to have used a nuclear weapon, the United States has a moral responsibility to act. We cannot succeed in this endeavor alone, but we can lead it, we can start it." The first step toward disarmament came less than a year later when Obama and Russian president Dmitry Medvedev signed the Strategic Arms Reduction Treaty to reduce both nations' arsenals by one-third. Though that doesn't seem to live up to the grandiose promises in the Prague speech, considering that the United States and Russia control 95 percent of the world's nuclear arsenal, the treaty is in fact a good start.

But creating and implementing a comprehensive plan for worldwide disarmament will not be easy. The first global step toward this, the creation of a nuclear weapons convention, is the main objective of the International Campaign to Abolish Nuclear Weapons.

No matter which nation or alliance takes the helm, reducing the threat of weapons of mass destruction is a critical part of sustainability. Simply put, nuclear weapons have no place in a bright green future. CB & AS

Real National Defense

War undermines every aspect of sustainability: it destroys the environment; it upends the lives of those caught within it; it impoverishes whole nations. At the same time—human nature being what it is—we all want reasonable assurances that we are safe from the aggressions of our neighbors. How do we balance these apparently contradictory needs? How do we avoid war and all the vices associated with it while keeping ourselves safe? An interesting set of answers has begun to emerge in the last couple of decades. (For an excellent overview of some of these answers, start with Amory Lovins's essay "How to Get Real Security," freely available on the Web.)

First, military personnel themselves can be one of the most effective checks to aggression. In nations where officers and troops are inculcated with democratic values, ethical practices, and cultural understanding, there is less support for foreign adventures. Those values, practices, and understandings can themselves be reinforced through cooperation with the militaries of potential rivals, via programs such as "troop swaps" (where soldiers from one nation serve in units with those from another) and joint peacekeeping missions.

Second, international treaties, like the land-mine treaty, when backed by effective monitoring and enforcement, can not only help prevent weapons of mass destruction from falling into the wrong hands, but they can cool down conflicts (and save lives) by cutting off the flow of weapons to bad actors. In addition, diplomatic efforts, when backed by strong coalitions and sanctions, can undermine the ability of aggressive nations to pose a threat, and give them real reason to play nice.

Third, nations can intentionally adopt defensive military postures. As Lovins writes, "To date, Sweden has executed the most sophisticated design of military forces for nonprovocative defense. Its coastal guns cannot be elevated to fire beyond Swedish coastal waters. It has a capable and effective air force, but with short-range aircraft that can't get very far beyond Sweden . . . In every way, by technical and institutional design, they've sought to make Sweden a country you don't want to attack, but one that is clearly in a defensive posture. This approach can ultimately create a stable mutual defensive superiority—each side's defense is stronger than the other side's offense. Each has, by design, at most a limited capacity to export offense."

When such defensive nations need to project power, they can do so in coalition with other countries' militaries, under the auspices of bodies like NATO and the UN. Individually, they threaten no one; with allies, they retain the capacity to wreak havoc on rogue nations.

Finally, the ultimate way to prevent war may be what some call "leader control." Democracy itself can be a check on war: when democratic states are in good political health, they maintain checks on the military ambitions of their leaders, and hold those leaders accountable for their actions. International accountability, achieved through measures such as universal jurisdiction [see Demanding Human Rights, p. 412], provides disincentives to starting wars even for leaders in less democratic countries. Knowing a war-crimes tribunal will be their eventual reward for aggression has a marvelous tendency to make invading other nations less attractive, even to tyrants. AS

Truth and Reconciliation

▬▬▬▬   Few countries in the world have traveled as tumultuous and inspiring a path toward racial reconciliation as South Africa has. The transition from apartheid South Africa, ostracized around the world, to Nelson Mandela's beloved Rainbow Nation is a remarkable story. Key to that story was the role of the Truth and Reconciliation Commission (TRC), chaired by Archbishop Desmond Tutu.

The TRC was a means of exacting justice without retribution. Any agent of the apartheid regime who testified fully and truthfully was granted immunity for his actions. The goal was to bring sunshine into the dark corners of South Africa's history, not wreak vengeance.

It has been argued that the greatest gift of the commission was "a common history of the apartheid era," without which two histories would be competing for legitimacy. Regardless of how dark the past was, South African children now have a common historical view on which they can build their future. Cynthia Ngewu, a mother who lost her son during apartheid, said of the

TRC process, "This thing called reconciliation . . . if I am understanding it correctly . . . means the perpetrator, this man who killed Christopher Piet, if it means he becomes human again, so that I, so that all of us, get our humanity back . . . then I agree, then I support it all" (Rotberg and Thompson, 2000.)

Values systems as diverse as Christianity and the Zulu philosophy of *ubuntu*, meaning "a person is a person through other persons," guided the commission and contributed to its success. While massive challenges remain, and the process has not been perfect, the commission surely stands as a towering testament to the capacities of the human spirit. ZH

▬▬▬▬   RESOURCES

A Problem from Hell: America and the Age of Genocide by Samantha Power (Harper Perennial, 2003)

Chasing the Flame: One Man's Fight to Save the World by Samantha Power (Penguin, 2008)

When a *New York Times* article covering the beginning stages of the 1994 genocide in Rwanda prompted more concern about the safety of gorillas than the safety of Rwandans, Samantha Power asked the following: Why is there an endangered species movement but no endangered peoples movement? It's a question the Harvard professor, Pulitzer Prize–winning journalist, and former adviser to Barack Obama still poses to audiences, especially in the United States, where a fledgling antigenocide movement is a small force against a decades-long pattern of apathy.

Power spent years covering the atrocities in the former Yugoslavia, and her frustration with the United States's response both to that conflict and to the Rwandan genocide was the impetus behind *A Problem from Hell*, which details the history of American intervention—or more

Opposite, left: Troops attend a ceremony in Sarajevo to transfer peacekeeping duties from NATO forces to the European Union, 2004.
Opposite, right: The first witness is sworn in before the Truth and Reconciliation Commission in South Africa, 1996.

accurately, lack of intervention—in ethnic-cleansing campaigns. The award-winning book ranges from political analysis to first-person accounts from genocide survivors.

Although *Chasing the Flame*, Power's biography of Sergio Vieria de Mello, the UN Secretary General's special representative in Iraq, also tells a grim tale, it is meant to be inspirational. Vieria de Mello, along with twenty-two others, was killed when a suicide bomber detonated a car bomb in a Baghdad hotel in 2003. Power has described Vieria de Mello as "a cross between James Bond and Bobby Kennedy" and "a decathlete of statebuilding in failed states." He worked in fourteen different war zones during his life as a peacekeeper; one of the many difficult tasks he took on was trying to figure out how to feed refugees in the Democratic Republic of the Congo without feeding the leaders and foot soldiers who were perpetrating the genocide. Power's book is both an honest and sometimes critical look at UN missions and a portrait of one of the most adaptable, effective, and fascinating changemakers of our time. CB

Brave New War: The Next Stage of Terrorism and the End of Globalization by John Robb (John Wiley & Sons, 2007)

John Robb's excellent book surveys the ways in which large conventional militaries and twentieth-century ideas of war have become outdated due to the emergence of new threats.

"Because we are unable to decapitate, outsmart, or defend ourselves against global guerrillas, naturally occurring events, and residual nationalism from causing cascades of failure throughout the global system, we need to learn to live with the threat they present . . . By building resilience into the fabric of our daily life, our response to these threats will organically emerge in what seems like an effortless way. Without them, we will suffer the effects of dynamic shocks on a brittle system." AS

Blueprint for Action: A Future Worth Creating by Thomas P. M. Barnett (Putnam Adult, 2005)

Barnett's earlier book, *The Pentagon's New Map: War and Peace in the Twenty-First Century*, changed the debate about the proper role in global politics of United States military force. Here Barnett goes further and suggests that unless America uses its might to promote development, spread peace, and encourage democracy, no number of new weapons systems can keep it safe.

"Once a state exits a civil war situation, it must endure a roughly ten-year recovery period during which it builds its economy back to where it was prior to the civil war. During that ten-year period, the country has about a 4-in-10 chance of lapsing back into civil war during the first five years and a 3-in-10 chance over the second five-year period. What the data shows is that one of the biggest triggers for renewed civil war is the tendency of the surviving state to spend prodigiously on arms in the years immediately following the conflict . . . What tends to dampen such spending most is the introduction of foreign military troops to keep the peace. If such troops can be offered for approximately five years on average, then the country in question typically hits a growth-recovery spurt in years 4 and 7 following the end of the conflict, and when the bulk of the country's post-conflict economic recovery is achieved, the odds of slipping back into civil war decrease dramatically."

PLANET

▰▰▰▰ In times past, people didn't travel much. Most of our ancestors were peasants, and it was extremely rare for them to venture more than a couple days' journey from their villages. Even our more footloose progenitors, like herders and sailors, by and large stuck to well-traveled paths. A rare few explorers, soldiers, merchants, and pilgrims followed their callings to far-off lands, but most folks lived and died close to home.

Today, we are a planet on the move. According to the Population Resource Center, hundreds of millions of us have left the countries where we were born to start new lives abroad. Hundreds of millions more travel long distances for recreation and business. Jet contrails crisscross the skies, signals flash through fiber-optic cables, and the planet seems to shrink every day.

With all this travel, we've lost our connection to the land around us. Few of us could match the local ecological knowledge of even our most ignorant ancestors. On the other hand, we've gained a greater understanding of the wider workings of nature. We may not be able to identify the tree growing in our own backyard, but we can instantly conjure up a satellite photo of our neighborhood on our laptops. We might not be able to point south without the aid of a compass, but our cell phones can tell us our near-exact latitude and longitude. We may not be able to name the birds singing outside our windows, but we can empathize with the sorrows and joys of Antarctic penguins at our local movie theater. We are, in short, completely uninformed about the regions we call home, and yet tuned-in as never before to the workings of the planet as a whole.

What we need to do is to synthesize the two—the global and the local; the technological and the domestic. We need to use the best of the remarkable suite of environmental technologies that are emerging from labs and workshops around the world, and combine them with the kind of local ecological wisdom that comes only from a deep engagement with place. Combining the two will give us unprecedented tools for solving the planet's most dire problems.

Aside from empowering us to be locally proactive, knowing what's going on around us is simply enjoyable. We have innate connections with nature—connections that can be as easily nurtured in the heart of the city (when we know where to look) as in the middle of the woods—and acquainting ourselves with the local plants, birds, and weather helps us feel more truly at home. But learning about nature can feed our minds as well. Anyone who's ever played with an online mapping system knows that looking at the planet in new ways is endlessly entertaining.

We're not relegated to being passive observers, either. With the explosion in citizen science, we can become part of the action, adding our own observations concerning insects or whales or the climate to the larger scientific project of understanding the planet. We can work on local ecological restoration projects, applying the latest in environmental science as we cut brush and plant native trees. We can even help search for alien intelligence and hunt dangerous asteroids. Planetary knowledge can be a playground.

Planetary knowledge can also be a bummer. With our increased understanding of the little rock on which we live comes a flood of evidence that we're royally screwing things up. Ecosystems are trembling. Species that evolved over millions of years are being driven into extinction. The most troubling signs have to do with our climate. Every time we drive a car, we're participating in the largest planetary experiment ever conducted—we're changing the climate, acidifying the oceans, melting the

ice caps, and generally wreaking havoc with the very systems that support life on earth.

That said, the same tools that are leading scientists to sound alarms are giving us a better understanding of how to begin tackling the problems. Not only do we know what is causing the climate crisis, but we know what to do about it. Not only do we have concrete evidence that it's real, we increasingly know what to expect locally. Not only can we stop turning our planet into a greenhouse, we can predict with increasing accuracy just what it will take to do that.

Facing the grim realities of climate change, mass extinctions, and ecosystem collapses does not make for a cheerful day. But we shouldn't lose heart.

Astronauts, seeing for the first time the tiny blue-green ball below as they traveled farther and farther into the cold, empty darkness of space, reported almost universally one overwhelming emotion: a profound, sudden comprehension of the beauty, fragility, and unity of the planet. Most of us will never venture into space, but all of us can learn to see the earth as they have. We can learn to see the whole planet as our home, and decide that it's about time we took care of it. AS

Preceding pages: Understanding our planet from the lithosphere to the stratosphere is still a challenge, no matter how many maps and photos we have, Lake Natron, Tanzania.

Placing Yourself

■■■■■ "Where am I?" The first question of place is universal; the need for an answer, often urgent. We each stand at the hub of a great turning wheel. How do connections radiate outward from our lives to the economy (the flows of electrons, water, materials, and signals that form the planet's industrial metabolism) and the biosphere (the flows and fluxes that power the earth as a living system)? What is the universe that starts with each of us?

Placing ourselves is place-making: an active engagement with the world that begins at our doorstep and expands outward in both space and time as we learn about and connect to our surroundings throughout our lives. Place is a mind-set that travels with us, grows with us, and helps us frame and reframe the answers to that perennial "where" question.

Since the birth of spoken language, placing has been about naming. The Kwakiutl people of Vancouver Island were not unusual in this regard. Before they came into contact with Western culture, they conferred place-names that told stories, names that could teach. "For them, a place-name would not be something that is," explains author and professor Kim Stafford, "but something that happens. They called one patch of ocean 'Where Salmon Gather.' They called one bend in the river 'Insufficient Canoe.' They called a certain meadow 'Blind Women Steaming Clover Roots Become Ducks.'" Such places are gathered into the imagination so their attributes—abundance or scarcity, hardship or surprise—can be made manifest, and human experience made easier. The Aboriginal people of Australia follow songlines across their continent, literally singing their world into existence. Neither is such intimacy with the land entirely absent in the vernacular languages and dialects of Europe or the tribal languages of Africa, Asia, and the Indian subcontinent. Names, retrieved from the past or across boundaries of culture, offer a handle on place.

Today, placing ourselves is about weaving an understanding of natural facts and artifacts into a durable fabric of identity and citizenship. Many new and powerful tools are available to help us place ourselves, from podcast birdsongs to the thematic maps streamed onto our computer screens. But even with the digital flood of data and imagery, understanding our places entails an effort to untangle our relationships with the planet. By freeing our senses to perceive the landscape around us, in city or country, we open ourselves to a wholly individual understanding of place.

Understanding place as a natural system starts with the simplest of questions: What's overhead? What's underfoot? Who's been here previously? What's that hill called? What's likely to happen here next week? Next season? The answers integrate into an intuitive first approximation of biogeography— the study of the way plant and animal communities are distributed around the earth. In discerning biogeographic patterns, we begin to perceive natural units—watersheds, biomes, ecoregions—that challenge arbitrary boundaries of political jurisdictions. We begin to detect larger patterns of migration, water systems, and seasonal change that give each place its distinctive character. We begin to anticipate the return of a certain raptor, the timing of a berry harvest, the angle of the sun on an April evening. Some of us step from this awareness directly into new allegiances, into a sense of political activism that springs from an expanded sense of community, while others just begin to feel more at home.

Another dimension of placing ourselves is having a clear-eyed grasp of the industrial metabolism in which each human life, as part of a global economy, is embedded. City dweller, farm owner, or migrant laborer, each is sustained by commercial flows of electricity, water, materials, waste, and signals so omnipresent as to be nearly invisible. To understand place, we are obligated to tease out these converging systems, to comprehend the extent of our dependencies.

In the landmark *New Yorker* article "Apartment," environmental writer Bill McKibben (*The End of Nature; Hope, Human and Wild; Eaarth*) describes tracing to their source the energy and water supplied to his Manhattan apartment, and visiting the terminus of the wastewater and garbage discharged from it. His journeys led him to the hydroelectric power dams of James Bay, Ontario, the uranium mine of Hack Canyon, Arizona, an offshore oil-loading platform in Brazil, the freshwater reservoirs of New York's Catskill Mountains, and the garbage mountains of the vast Fresh Kills Landfill (since closed) on Staten Island in New York City. Across a hemisphere, locales so diffuse as to be largely invisible to us are a functional part of McKibben's apartment at Bleeker Street and Broadway. The "place" called New York contains even more of them. "Those wires and pipes," McKibben writes, "some of them thousands of miles long, [then] lead from my apartment to the far reaches of New York City."

Does this mean each place bleeds out into the world like the electron cloud around an atom's nucleus? Yes and no. Ecosystems are real, watersheds have physical boundaries, bioregions have a natural integrity. But connected global life is based on exchanges so numerous and furious that the "stuff" of places is in constant flux. Ecologist Raymond Dasmann distinguished "ecosystem people"—who sustain themselves and build their cultures mainly from the diversity and abundance of a local area—from "biosphere people"—whose economic relations draw materials and energy from farther afield, often from the planet as a whole. Dasmann saw this not as a dichotomy but as a cultural continuum along which people can travel.

If the latter decades of the twentieth century marked a galloping race toward a globalized economy of biosphere people, the beginning of the twenty-first century shows the glimmers of a conscious shift, by some, back toward the practices of ecosystem people. Emergent local food economies in cities around the world are signs of that shift, as are growing markets for biofuels and renewable power generated close to home. In truth, a healthy planet demands a blend of global connectivity and ecosystem attentiveness. As we enter such an era—as the industrial metabolism of society changes and natural ecoregions are reshaped by extinctions, invasive species, and unpredictable shifts triggered by climate change—we will be forced to think of "place" in new ways. In this world, place will be as fluid as the circulating atmosphere, and "living in place" will call on a capacity for innovation.

In the twenty-first century, the realities of the planet will demand that people—even people who've settled in one place for the long term—"re-place" themselves many times throughout their lives. Understanding the patterns and processes of place, even in a world homogenized by global economy and culture, will hold keys to citizenship and sufficiency. As we rename our changing places, we may discern the stories to guide the next phase of human presence on earth.

Placing yourself in the changing world is a worldchanging act. EW

From Bioregions to Bioregionalism

▆▆▆▆ No sooner had biologists borrowed geographers' tools and begun to map earth's natural communities (boreal forests, temperate grasslands, tropical rain forests, and other biomes defined by their native vegetation) than some earth-centered activists began to envision new realms for civic engagement. Their "precinct" was the bioregion: a discrete area with ecological and cultural unity.

"All politics is local," said Congressman Thomas P. "Tip" O'Neill. Bioregional activists reasoned that plants, soils, and climate offered the most local politics of all, a fertile substrate in which to nurture citizenship and strengthen community. They touched a nerve in the era of the Vietnam War, offering people a new way to pledge allegiance.

San Francisco's Planet Drum Foundation, founded in 1973, set the tone for the bioregional movement. The Bay Area pioneers sought to encourage reinhabitation of earth's bioregions by taking what their Web site describes as "a grassroots approach to ecology that emphasizes sustainability, community self-determination, and regional self-reliance."

Planet Drum triggered talk of green cities, organized bioregional congresses, and inspired kindred initiatives up and down the West Coast. If such efforts never overtook the political mainstream, they at least attracted many young people into community activism and influenced a few major political figures, including former Oakland mayor and current California governor Jerry Brown.

The West Coast has proved to be more receptive to bioregional thinking than any other North American locale; its rugged rain-forest coast and tectonic volatility have helped shape a notion of "Cascadia"—a bioregion generally considered to be bounded by the Pacific Ocean and the Cascade Range in the Pacific Northwest. The alternative conception of place that characterizes Cascadia has found expression in visionary literature (Ernest Callenbach's *Ecotopia*), antilogging activism, and governance.

Rooting citizenship in the natural attributes of a place continues to create avenues for engagement—too rare in modern life—with the essential and sustaining features of the planet. Pledging allegiance to place, we might at last plant politics in the realities of community and landscape that transcend partisan divides. EW

Whether we're gazing from the tops of skyscrapers or the tops of mountains, we must know the places we live in if we want to know how to protect them.

Solastalgia

▬▬▬ Coined by environmental philosopher Glenn Albrecht, the term *solastalgia* (pronounced so-la-STAL-juh) describes the sense of loss and dislocation people feel when they see changes to their local environment as harmful. Albrecht told Worldchanging writer Sanjay Khanna that solastalgia is the "lived experience of gradually losing the solace a once stable home environment provided. It is therefore appropriate to diagnose solastalgia in the face of slow and insidious forces such as climate change or mining."

According to Albrecht, solastalgia's Latin roots combine three ideas: the solace that one's environment provides, the desolation caused by that environment's degradation, and the pain or distress that occurs inside a person as a result. "Solastalgia brings into English a much-needed word that links a mental state to a state of the biophysical environment. The need for new concepts in the face of what is happening under climate change has seen other cultures develop new terms that have affinities with solastalgia. The Inuit, for example, have a new word, *uggianaqtuq* (pronounced OOG-gi-a-nak-took), which relates to climate change and has connotations of the weather as a once reliable and trusted friend that is now acting strangely or unpredictably."

The ongoing documentation of solastalgia by Albrecht and his team is not just about adding words to the dictionary. Albrecht thinks solastalgia should be listed as an official condition among mental health professionals—similar to post-traumatic stress disorder—so that people badly affected by this condition (climate-change refugees, for example) could get the assistance they need.

Albrecht recognizes the challenge in creating diagnostic tools for solastalgia: "Given that key aspects of solastalgia are existential, the traditions of environmental philosophy and medical psychiatry may not come together so harmoniously." But he's an optimist, "There's hope in recognizing solastalgia and defeating it by creating ways to reconnect with our local environment and communities."

As we deal with more and more ecological changes to the place we've lived in and loved, all of us will need to develop new psychological resilience to overcome feelings of loss. CB

Place 2.0

▬▬▬ Environmentalists have long maintained that a sense of connection to the planet is a prerequisite for having the desire to protect it—and the missing link for those intent on trashing it. But how do we feel connected to the fate of the Sargasso Sea if we've never seen any sea at all?

Many scientists feel that the ease with which we pollute our oceans has much to do with the misinformed notion that the "ocean" is an infinite thing, so large and unknowable that we can't, well, know it.

That's why tools like the Google Ocean component of Google Earth are so important to making our sense of place more global. Google Ocean allows us to explore the seas through a combination of mapping, video footage from acclaimed nature programs like BBC's *Planet Earth*, and user-posted photos and information. As Sylvia Earle, an oceanographer and explorer-in-residence at the National Geographic Society, told the *Daily*

Telegraph in February 2009, "I cannot imagine a more effective way to inspire awareness and caring for the blue heart of the planet than the new Ocean in Google Earth. For the first time, everyone from curious kids to serious researchers can see the world, the whole world, with new eyes." CB

■■■■■   RESOURCES

Cosmos: A Personal Voyage directed by David F. Oyster (1980)
This thirteen-part documentary series, first aired in 1980, was a breakthrough in science communications, explaining to a popular audience for the first time exactly where in the universe we find ourselves. Much of its popularity sprang from the spry on-camera presentation of astronomer Carl Sagan, whose enthusiasm for the subject was obvious and infectious. Though some bits of the science have become outdated as new discoveries have been made, the special effects are retro-hilarious, and the concern with Cold War nuclear confrontations may seem a bit puzzling to today's audiences, the series has held up astonishingly well. If you want to spend a few hours connecting to the mystery and wonder of living on a small planet in a vast, unexplored universe, you really couldn't do better than to spend some time with *Cosmos*. It's available free from several online sources. AS

Last Child in the Woods: Saving Our Children from Nature Deficit Disorder by Richard Louv (Algonquin Books, 2005)
Richard Louv explores the phenomenon of "nature deficit disorder," a disconnection from the natural world experienced by children in our increasingly wired and ecophobic world. He connects interaction with nature to human development and suggests ways to reintroduce nature to our children.
        "Reducing [nature] deficit—healing the broken bond between our young and nature—is in our self-interest, not only because aesthetics or justice demand it, but also because our mental, physical, and spiritual health depend upon it. The health of the earth is at stake as well. How the young respond to nature, and how they raise their own children, will shape the configurations and conditions of our cities, homes—our daily lives."

The Klamath Knot by David Rains Wallace (Sierra Club Press, 1983)
A wonderful work of natural history from a writer who can see not only into the natural systems that define the part of northern California in which he lives, but the epochal forces of evolution and geology that created those systems, *The Klamath Knot* is an essential guide to understanding what placing ourselves can really mean.
        The author writes, "Evolution doesn't view earth's history as a conflict between good and evil. It does essentially view it as a conflict between life and death, between increased organization and more efficient energy use on the part of life, and an opposing tendency of nonliving matter to become disorganized and lose energy—entropy. But evolution doesn't see life and death as simple adversaries: life as good and death as evil. Life cannot triumph over death in evolution. They don't fight to win. As with some of the older myths, wherein the natural dualities of light and darkness, sun and moon, male and female, performed an eternal, amoral dance of opposites, evolutionary life and death are interdependent: two halves of the world. Evolution would be impossible if organisms did not die."

Uncommon Ground: Rethinking the Human Place in Nature edited by William Cronon (W. W. Norton, 1995)
William Cronon thinks that the environmentalist goal of wilderness preservation is conceptually and politically wrongheaded. Rather than trying to exclude humans from nature, Cronon says, contemporary environmental activists need to help us learn to live in a responsible and sustainable relationship with it: "At a time when threats to the environment have never been greater, it may be tempting to believe that people need to be mounting the barricades rather than asking abstract questions about the human place in nature. Yet without confronting such questions, it will be hard to know which barricades to mount, and harder still to persuade large numbers of people to mount them with us."

The Practice of the Wild by Gary Snyder (North Point Press, 1990)
One of the finest books on living in place ever written, poet Gary Snyder's collection of essays

offers the harvest of a lifetime spent thinking about how modern people can learn to live in intimacy with the land the way our native, tribal ancestors did. Snyder guides us through the back country of the history of our relationship to nature, bringing us finally to the understanding that one of the highest aims of a prosperous, settled, and technologically advanced society is to keep us in regular contact with our wild roots and reconnect us with the living systems on which all life depends.

"The presence of this tree signifies a rainfall and a temperature range and will indicate what your agriculture might be, how steep the pitch of your roof, what raincoats you'd need. You don't have to know such details to get by in the modern cities of Portland or Bellingham. But if you do know what is taught by plants and weather, you are in on the gossip and can truly feel more at home."

Mapping

▮▮▮▮   In August 1854, cholera swept through London's Soho district. The common belief held that cholera was spread through bad air—the "miasma" theory. Physician John Snow, however, had another idea: he believed that cholera was a microorganism that infected people through the water they drank. Snow suspected a single water pump to be the culprit (most of the city's victims lived within walking distance of the Broad Street pump), and by interviewing victims' families and then plotting the evidence on a map, Snow was able not only to help end the epidemic but to make his theory intelligible to the authorities—work that established Snow's place as one of the fathers of modern epidemiology and medical geography.

Maps communicate essential information in ways few other media can. Snow's use of maps and data as analytical and communication tools for science heralded a trend that has become positively epidemic 150 years later: cartography is an essential tool for researchers and advocates, policy shapers and corporations. These days, when we want to change the world, we often start by mapping it. CFD

A Revolution in Mapping

▮▮▮▮   People used to make maps by hand. Now software like Geographic Information Systems (GIS) does the job for us. As with many other democratizing technologies that emerged in the late twentieth century, faster, cheaper computing power is largely responsible for the growing use of digital mapping applications—by everyone from disaster responders and forestry-reform advocates to legal-service providers and overnight-delivery

companies. Today, if we know where something is, we can easily show it on a map.

And we're learning where more and more things are. The explosion of cheap, open-source tools has been key to the spread of mapping. Data for mapping is everywhere. Data may now come from satellites that measure moisture in the leaves of trees or from radio collars around the necks of unknowing caribou as they migrate hundreds of miles; maps may draw on information relayed from temperature sensors along the ocean floor or from pollution-measuring equipment in our major cities. And the agile software that draws these maps is being developed not in the cubicles and server farms of large corporations, but among a dizzyingly productive network of open-source developers.

Like the maps of the past, the maps of the future will aid both in the analysis of data and in the communication of it to broader audiences. Data can be gathered via remote sensors that can measure invisible parts of the electromagnetic spectrum or synthesize information over vast geographic areas—promising to reveal insights on the invisible things that are right under our noses. That is exactly what happened on the Shuttle Radar Topographic Mission (SRTM), during which the Chicxulub Crater on the Yucatán peninsula was discovered. Scientists had long suspected that such a crater existed: there had to be some evidence, somewhere, of the asteroid impact that wiped out 70 percent of life on the planet 65 million years ago. But it wasn't until the 1990s, when the SRTM data was processed and scientists mapped the remnants of the 112-mile-wide (180-kilometer-wide) crater that they were able to confirm their theory. Maps reached deep into the past and pulled back an essential piece of our planetary history.

In the United States, we are fortunate to have widespread access to an enormous volume of data that we can use in mapping efforts. But increasingly, the growing number of satellites that produce remotely sensed data—in multiple spectra at varying resolutions, anywhere on the globe—is closing the gap between the United States and the rest of the world. Not long ago, if we wanted to see satellite-generated information on a map, it took lots of number crunching by big computers found only at places like NASA's Jet Propulsion Laboratory. Now the information is available, on your laptop, almost as events unfold on the ground. CFD

The James Reserve

▬▬▬ Though it may seem counterintuitive, mapping isn't confined to showing the big picture. The revolution in the production of spatial data (information about places) extends to the micro scale—to soil patches and birds' nests, to a fox traversing a canyon at night, or to the subtle respiration of CO_2 by a patch of silver pine. These are some of the natural systems being measured and tracked at the James Reserve, a protected mountainous area in San Jacinto, California. Here scientists use an expansive network of wireless remote sensors to measure everything from barometric shifts throughout the day to the number of times a willow flycatcher returns to its nest during a given period. The scientists systematically record everything from microbes to watersheds—ten orders of magnitude in spatial and temporal scale—in an unprecedented effort to understand the workings of a single piece of land. Similar remote networks may ultimately be used to monitor whole ecosystems like forests, or rift valleys along the ocean floor. And maps are what make the data recorded by these sensors understandable.

As sensors get cheaper, we can expect to know more about more places, and this information may help us solve seemingly intractable environmental problems. What if we monitored the comings and goings of reintroduced wolf populations so that an automatic warning system could alert ranchers when livestock were in danger? Telemetry data streamed to GIS applications like those operated by the U.S. Geological Survey in Alaska may make this possible.

In Washington's Puget Sound, scientists are learning that juvenile salmon from the northern rivers may brave predators and adverse marine conditions to venture to the South Sound in preparation for their oceanic migration. Why

don't the fish just swim directly out to sea? What happens to them while they dally? Mapping their behavior patterns with other information such as water temperature, coastal vegetation, and dissolved oxygen helps us understand how to help these endangered fish thrive again.

The idea that remote sensors may one day be ubiquitous opens the door to a world where maps are simply another form of media, akin to your computer screen, for delivering streaming data. NASA's Moderate Resolution Imaging Spectroradiometer (MODIS) produces satellite imagery of the entire earth roughly every two days, in thirty-six spectral bands. Using increasingly accessible tools, almost anyone can integrate the data into a personal online map. The explosion of integrating tools like Google Earth and World Wind, which let us play with powerful mapping software and various kinds of data at home, is only the earliest hint of what this could mean. Certain GIS functions based on proprietary software, currently accessible only to trained users, are being replicated in flexible, open-source code that can be configured by users with far less technical training. The ability to access and publish sophisticated mappable data puts in our hands the power to both know and show the world. We don't need to wait for another John Snow—today we can put the water pumps and cholera cases on the map ourselves. CFD

Virtual Puget Sound

▬▬▬ Computer models are astounding tools, capable of creating portrayals of the complex workings of huge natural systems. One of these

Opposite: The mapping of craters, such as this one on Vulcano Island in Italy, has been essential in establishing the historical trajectory of the earth.

Right: This map of Tropical Depression Alberto was created with images from Geostationary Operational Environmental Satellite (GOES-12), which is operated by the National Oceanic and Atmospheric Administration.

is PRISM, the Puget Sound Regional Synthesis Model, essentially a digital replica of Puget Sound.

The University of Washington's Urban Ecology Research Lab, the creator of PRISM, wants to be able to show how specific land-use changes could have an impact on certain key indicator systems. How would building three McMansions in a patch of woods, say, impact water temperature (and thus salmon-spawning) in the stream that runs through it? The project is not anywhere near that level of sophistication yet, but the trend is clear: we're gaining the ability to show, in very concrete terms, not only the specific wildlife around us (the falcon nesting on the ledge of a forty-story building, the salmon swimming past the ship canal locks, the sea lions sunning themselves on the rocks outside the harbor), but also the systems that surround us, of which we are a part.

While scientists are working to perfect models like PRISM, we must ask ourselves whether we're getting any better at listening to what such tools tell us. Are we willing to use the insight we're gaining by trying to think like a salmon—and to act to meet its needs? Or will our computer models be no more than what Thoreau called "improved means to an unimproved end"? The danger exists that we will simply document more finely and accurately the decline of what we love and depend on. But if we can refine both our tools and our plans of action, it seems that we could well be standing on the threshold of a golden era in conservation.

Computer models like PRISM and the studies they generate may help to bring sophisticated information about natural systems home, in much the same way that using energy meters inside has urged more thoughtful action about the power we consume. AS

OpenStreetMap

■■■■■   As a species, humans have always been prone to transiency. Our ancestors traversed the globe in search of new resources, adventure, or beauty. And although not every journey was motivated by altruism, each one added to our collective migratory map and connected us to the world in new and different ways.

Mapping our migratory patterns has never been an easier or more inclusive process. Even our minute migrations throughout our cities are now being recorded and studied. Using Web tools such as OpenStreetMap, thousands of individuals are collaboratively mapping the entire world. OSM was created to provide free geographic data, such as street maps, to anyone who wants them. In 2008, more than 20,000 people edited the wiki-style map, adding their favorite landmarks, routes, and shortcuts, with the help of GPS devices, digital cameras, and voice recorders.

OSM's maps illuminate the most impenetrable parts of our world. At this writing, OSM had the only up-to-date street map of post-earthquake Haiti. In 2009, MapKibera, a project that uses OSM's format and received funding from the Open Street Map Foundation, created the first free, open map of Kibera, the biggest slum in Nairobi (and therefore in Africa). This is the first full map of Kibera; it will be indispensable to aid workers and city officials who need to identify resource scarcities within the neighborhood.

Instant access to detailed maps and suggested transit routes is something many of us take for granted in the age of Google and the smart phone. But the world is still a pretty big place, and crowdsourced models like OSM may be the only way to keep tabs on it as climate change and new migrations change our landscapes and give rise to new cities practically overnight. SK & CB

■■■■■   RESOURCES

Show: A New Way to Look at the World
http://show.mappingworlds.com
Show is a little humorous, a little disturbing, and very revealing. Choose different filters and Show will stretch and reposition maps for a visual representation of the data. See U.S. states change size based on the number of strawberries harvested, residents who have died in the Iraq war, or Big Foot sightings. See a map of the world shift to reflect the countries with the most remittance inflows or women in office. See Japanese regions morph to show the number of karaoke parlors or suicides. Each map is accompanied by a brief explanation of the subject with a few factoids, plus a recommendation for further reading. CB

The Atlas of the Real World: Mapping the Way We Live by Daniel Dorling, Mark Newman, and Anna Barford (Thames & Hudson, 2010)
The latest book from worldmapper.org creators Daniel Dorling, Mark Newman, and Anna Barford includes 366 digitally modified maps "depicting the areas and countries of the world not just by their physical size, but by their demographic importance," ranging from the number of toys they import to the number of nuclear weapons they possess. World maps manipulated in this way give a simple elegance to complicated topics, as the atlas makes clear in one image what some books take hundreds of pages to explain.

An Atlas of Radical Cartography by Lize Mogel and Alexis Bhagat (Journal of Aesthetics and Protest Press, 2008)
Far from being neutral accessories, maps are often used as instruments to control and shape beliefs. Conversely, maps can also be at the service of protest and social change. With a set of ten maps and a collection of essays by artists, architects, designers, and writers who analyze the maps and explore their role as political agents, this atlas illuminates the not-so-secret agendas of maps deliberately, openly, and convincingly.

Citizen Science

▇▇▇▇ How do we keep up the pace of technological progress in a civilization that can't train specialists fast enough? In the twentieth century, we professionalized the narrowest of fields, creating expertise within medical, engineering, and scientific disciplines—a trend that offered great benefits, but also posed serious limitations. It seems impossible for this trend to continue far into the twenty-first century—indeed, we may be bound to leap beyond professionalism. As education levels keep rising, more of us have leisure time and access to vast amounts of publicly available knowledge. This century may bring an Age of Amateurs, when citizen exploration yields much of our greatest learning as a society.

This hearkens back to a legacy that predates big-time corporate and government-funded research, to the contributions of Benjamin Franklin, Charles Darwin, Lewis and Clark, Smithson, Audubon, Thoreau, and others like them. Already, amateurs, enthusiasts, and retirees contribute in many ways. Soon burgeoning technological tools will revolutionize the capabilities of citizen savants, leveling the playing field between aficionados and professional researchers, both expediting scientific advancement and democratizing countless fields of interest. Eccentrically individualist and internationally collective, citizen-driven research offers science a powerful method of escaping control by a rigid elite and remaining, instead, an adventure for us all. DB

Members of the Environmental Career Organization collect data in the Sand Dunes Recreation Area near Glamis, California.

Christmas Bird Count

▰▰▰   During the winter holidays, while most of us are fiddling with new toys and trying on itchy sweaters, more than 50,000 people around the Western Hemisphere grab their coats and binoculars and trudge out to the woods to look for birds. They're all taking part in the Christmas Bird Count, a tradition for over a century.

Bird-watching, or birding, is one of the most popular hobbies in North America. Millions of people love to spend their free time hiking through mountains, woods, and swamps, ears perked and eyes peeled for any sign of a rare bird. The Christmas Bird Count allows scientists to aggregate the otherwise independent findings of all of these birders to assess migration patterns, locations, and populations. Until recently, though, gathering and processing this data was extremely daunting for researchers, whose time and funding was already stretched thin.

But a few years back, researchers, birders, and environmentalists shared an "aha!" moment—they realized they could ease the coordination of diffuse data by connecting the thousands of enthusiastic citizen birders directly with advanced technological tools.

Thus hatched eBird. More than 40,000 individual birders across North America have signed up, contributing roughly 2 million sightings per month and field data to a collaborative database on bird populations and behavior. In exchange, birders who use eBird (and the various other like-minded networks that are a part of this movement) get online records of the birds they've spotted, are able to access planning tools for birding trips and establish friendships with other birders, and gain a sense

that they're not just watching their feathered friends, but helping to save them.

In 2009 an iPhone application called BirdsEye debuted shortly before the annual count. The app, which was the first to take information from eBird's open-source database, pulls up a list of nearby bird-watching sites based on your phone's GPS location. Not only does an app like BirdsEye help dedicated birders pursue their favorite hobby, but it also helps facilitate the count—being given a starting point based on others' observations allows time-pressed people to participate, even if they are traveling in unfamiliar regions during the holidays. And with future iterations of BirdsEye, watchers will be able to upload field information directly to eBird. DB

Project Budburst

▰▰▰   Sometimes a trivial observation—the flowers that used to bloom in near-perfect synchronicity with a birthday arrive a little earlier than usual—is of great significance to ecologists tracking the effects of climate change on plant species.

Affiliated with the University Corporation for Atmospheric Research in Boulder, Colorado, Project Budburst gathers phenological data from around the United States on the leafing and flowering of native species, along with times of full flower, end flower, and seed and fruit dispersal. The aggregated regional observations will form a nationwide picture of climate change.

Citizen scientists submit their observations online and can view the latest one hundred recorded observations on a Google map. In 2008, the first year of the project, Budburst collected almost five thousand observations from forty-nine states. Participants ranged from elementary school students to gardeners to ecologists.

Left: Bird-watchers have collaborated with researchers, using sites such as eBird, to share sightings and field data.
Opposite: A typical introductory exercise from Foldit. The player must fold the top part of this protein in order to form more hydrogen bonds.

Although it may take a few seasons for Project Budburst to perfect its data collection and analysis, the project promises to be of great help to climate-change scientists. As Sandra Henderson, Budburst's director, told CNN in 2009, without such a venture this data would never make it into a spreadsheet. "We have these additional sentinel eyes on the landscape, if you will. There aren't enough ecologists to be making all of these different plant observations." Another reason to stop and smell the flowers. SR

Foldit

■■■■■ Peering through binoculars at rare birds or photographing changing leaves is not everyone's idea of a good time. Thankfully, there's Foldit—citizen science for "indoor kids."

Foldit is a computer game that challenges users to fold proteins into the most compact, most stable shapes possible (the smaller the protein, the higher the score). By using these colorful and engaging 3-D puzzles, scientists aim to solve one of the toughest problems in biology: determining the best possible shape of a protein that may consist of hundreds or thousands of amino acids. Proteins control the most important biological and plant functions, and they also play a big role in disease (viruses like HIV, for example, create or use certain proteins to help them replicate and spread infection). Getting better at protein prediction means getting better at combating disease. Scientists don't yet understand why proteins fold into their complex shapes, but, as it turns out, humans are actually better at this type of problem solving than computers.

Designed by a team of biochemists at the University of Washington, Foldit has more than 100,000 players worldwide. Folders, as players refer to themselves, have even formed teams. The competition between teams to solve specific puzzles has been fierce and yielded some interesting results—*Wired* reported one such competition in which a team of gamers led by a thirteen-year-old boy beat a team of biochemists.

At first, the UW biochemists simply wanted to collect evidence on the protein-folding abilities of humans in order to convince biotech companies that having humans work on determining the shape of unknown proteins was a viable—and efficient—thing to invest in. But the project has loftier goals, too. Closely observing the winning strategies used by gamers will help create better protein-prediction software. And the ultimate goal is to have folders everywhere working on protein design. The most promising results, for, say, creating new proteins to fight HIV or cancer, will actually make it into a lab for testing. CB

■■■■■ RESOURCE

SEED Magazine
http://seedmagazine.com
SEED is a smart and stylish science magazine. From a discussion of cephalopod intelligence to the latest developments in climate-change research, *SEED* is required reading for anyone trying to make sense of complex natural systems. There's a ton of material on the Web site, though *SEED* is one magazine that justifies its existence in print.

Carbon Neutrality

██████ The concept of "planetary boundaries" is a scientific description of the base conditions for global sustainability. The earth's ability to support human civilization can be measured across several natural systems, the limits of which we must live within if we've going to thrive.

In 2009, a group of scientists led by the Stockholm Resilience Centre took a shot at defining these boundaries. They established hard targets for three of the planetary systems: stabilize the concentration of atmospheric CO_2 at 350 ppm; decrease ozone levels by 5 percent; and stop the acidification of our oceans. In addition, they defined several other systems for which specific hard targets are more difficult to pin down but that nonetheless demand attention: freshwater consumption and the global hydrological cycle, deforestation, interference with the global nitrogen cycle, terrestrial biodiversity, chemicals dispersion, and marine ecosystems.

We're in the process of approaching or straying beyond every single one of our planet's boundaries. The effect of every transgression we make on the earth's capacity to sustain life is serious, but none is more damaging than the paired problems of ocean acidification [see Oceans Are the New Atmosphere, p. 510] and climate change. These ever-worsening problems share the same primary cause—people spewing carbon dioxide into the atmosphere through tailpipes, smokestacks, and burning forests—so addressing carbon emissions is a doubly compelling problem.

It's possible to reduce our emissions dramatically without slowing economic growth, but that isn't good enough: we need to reduce emissions steeply while also increasing the amount of carbon dioxide the planet is pulling out of the atmosphere (through means of biological carbon sequestration like *terra preta* [see Soil and Sustainable Agriculture, p. 494]). We need to bring our net emissions down to nothing, or perhaps even become "carbon negative" (meaning we're pulling more CO_2 out of the air than we're putting in).

To achieve carbon neutrality, though, we need to tackle climate change on a wide front. We need to put a price on carbon emissions, redesign our cities and transportation systems, invest massively in clean energy, and alter our diets—as well as embrace other solutions discussed throughout this book. We can do all that and lead even more comfortable lives than we do today, but it's going to involve changes.

Becoming carbon neutral won't be easy. That doesn't mean it will hurt us, though: the changes we make will lead to a leaner, smarter economy, an economy driven by ideas, skill, and inventiveness more than burning oil and felling trees. Ending climate-changing emissions will be the start of a new chapter in the human story. AS

---

350 ppm to Zero Impact

██████ "The evidence indicates we've aimed too high—that the safe upper limit for atmospheric CO_2 is no more than 350 ppm," says climate scientist James Hansen.

Three hundred fifty parts per million: that is the level to which Hansen believes we need to reduce the concentration of carbon dioxide and other greenhouse gases in the atmosphere if we want to avoid a series of catastrophic climate tipping points. The bad news? Atmospheric carbon is already almost 390 ppm, and the rate at which we're spewing greenhouse gases is increasing.

Students in Cebu, Philippines, show their support for reducing atmospheric CO_2 to 350 ppm.

Over the past few years we've seen the credible bar for achieving climate stability drop from 550 to 450 to 350 ppm. And this means we have to make massive changes now. As Bill McKibben wrote in a *Washington Post* op-ed: "The difference between 550 and 350 is that the weaning has to happen now, and everywhere. No more passing the buck . . . To use the medical analogy, we're not talking statins to drop your cholesterol; we're talking huge changes in every aspect of your daily life."

But ultimately our goal should not be just 550, 450, or 350; our goal should be zero impact within our lifetimes. We need to provide reasonable affluence and a high quality of life for everyone on the planet while reducing our CO_2 emissions, toxic releases, ecosystem impacts, and resource drawdown to essentially nothing, because anything more than that is wrong.

Put more precisely, any ecological impact that exceeds the planet's biocapacity tends to undermine the earth's natural systems, destroy ecosystem services and climate stability, and ultimately eliminate options for our descendants. With that in mind, it ought to be our goal to have no impact—to bring our ecological footprint below biocapacity—as soon as possible. The idea of zero impact should not be controversial.

The longer we wait to work toward this goal, the tighter the window—and the less time we have to enjoy the prosperity and joy of a zero-footprint civilization. We can design and build a sustainable society in time to save our planet, and under most models, the economy will continue with strong growth even if we push hard on reducing emissions.

The matter hinges entirely on having the will to build this new world, and that's what's going to be sorely tested now: our will. We have to be honest about the goal of having no impact at all. We have to be willing to stand up, in public, and say the words "zero, now."

The crisis we face places stark demands on us, and there is no better advice for meeting them than Alasdair Gray's motto, "Work as though you live in the early days of a better nation." A5

Stabilization and Peak Targets: Understanding CO2 Numbers

▬▬▬ The difference between greenhouse gas (GHG) stabilization levels and GHG peak targets can be confusing, but it's a critical distinction for understanding strategies to reduce carbon emissions.

Stabilization levels are our long-term goals. When Jim Hansen says we need a concentration of CO_2 in the atmosphere of no more than 350 ppm, he's discussing where we need to end up within a certain time frame (many people propose the date 2100). Though we're already over that level, with concerted effort and widespread innovation, we could bring the planet's CO_2 concentration down to 350.

Peak target is another kind of measurement, a threshold above which we shouldn't stray. The consensus seems to be hovering around 450 ppm; if we exceed that amount of CO_2 (and other GHGs) in the atmosphere, we're running the serious risk of quickly reaching catastrophic tipping points.

Imagine an engine. For optimal performance and longevity, we should run it only so fast. It can be run faster, but wear and tear (and the possibility of a breakdown) increase rapidly the longer we run it at faster speeds. Some speeds, however, are just too fast: above a certain speed, we're likely to burn out the engine altogether. The stabilization level is the fastest speed at which we believe we can safely run the engine over time; the peak target is the red zone, the speed above which the engine should never go. AS

that climate change is not an environmental issue at all. These arguments usually accompany a call for some action that reduces carbon output but has another demonstrably negative environmental impact, such as damming a river for hydropower, launching a massive nuclear energy program, or seeding the ocean to produce a plankton bloom.

The climate crisis we face will not be solved through the kind of shortsighted thinking that got us into the problem in the first place. If viewed with any degree of rationality, the climate crisis cannot be separated from the overall planetary crisis of environmental degradation, massive poverty, conflict, and inequity of which it is a part. The problem we have today is not that our climate is changing per se, but that we have created an unsustainable, deeply unstable civilization.

Therefore, our task is not just to reduce our carbon emissions but to do so in the context of a renewed and restored international order; not just to stave off the worst effects of cooking the planet but to protect and promote the health of ecosystems around the world; not just to fear runaway global warming but to move strongly toward a civilization that doesn't destroy nature and people's lives to generate fleeting advantages for a tiny fraction of the world's population.

This is an all-or-nothing fight, in which so many issues—climate, biodiversity, population, poverty, public health, toxics, terrorism—are woven together as part of the same fabric. To focus solely on climate change is to suffer from carbon blindness, a condition that could lead us to take actions in the name of the future, even though they will undermine that very future. AS

Carbon Blindness

▬▬▬ For those of us who have spent years warning that climate change is a problem of the highest magnitude, these are gratifying days. Politicians, business leaders, labor unionists, celebrities, and religious figures all seem, finally, to be listening to the science and beginning to hear its meaning: we must change, dramatically, at once.

This awareness is a very good thing. What is worrisome is the idea, which is surfacing all over the political map, that climate change trumps every other environmental issue or, even more distressing,

Carbon Equity and Offshoring Emissions

▬▬▬ The emissions we're most directly responsible for—our personal carbon footprint, say, or our city's progress toward climate neutrality—may not tell the whole story of our climate impact. That's because, in the Global North at least, a large percentage of our emissions are hidden or displaced. Globalization has tended to move heavy polluting industries offshore, away from Europe and North America, to places like China and Brazil. We in the Global North still consume the lion's share of goods manufactured by these nations, but the carbon is emitted there, not here, while our exports are largely things—like block-buster films and financial services—whose carbon footprints are comparatively small.

In short, we're offshoring our emissions. However, the fact that we've displaced our emissions by manufacturing our consumer goods elsewhere doesn't remove those virtual emissions from our carbon footprints. Emissions for which we bear hidden responsibility are obscured not just by distance but by time as well. The Global North is wealthy today because our ancestors did the things—like burning mountainsides' worth of coal, clear-cutting the vast majority of our forests, and building an automobile culture—that have caused the climate change we're already experiencing.

Historic carbon—the carbon already emitted, often long ago, not the carbon being produced today—has filled our atmosphere with most of the current concentration of at least 390 ppm. Over the last century, the United States produced over 30 percent of all the CO_2 emitted worldwide. Our wealth, then, is a form of histori-cally embedded carbon.

The implications here are a little stagger-ing. Even if we're greening our lifestyles—we're eating our veggies, driving our hybrids, lighting our rooms with CFLs—these choices are still made possible by using vast stores of embedded carbon. Everything around us is like a landscape of frozen emissions: our suburbs and fast-food joints, freeways and airports, are climate damage in physical form.

Our hidden carbon emissions—geo-graphic and temporal—burden us with an even greater ethical obligation to go carbon neutral. We've already used far more than our share of the planet's ability to absorb pollution. Therefore, we need to move much further and much faster than those in other countries whose lives are impov-erished in part because their nations' carbon footprints are small. (There is another benefit of moving quickly, which is that the faster we create better alternatives, the more quickly those alterna-tives will be available for use in newly developing countries. This is a win-win for everyone.)

This historical imbalance is why some in the Global South like to call efforts to create a global carbon trading system "imperialism." The real imperialism in this situation is not primarily geographic. It is temporal. Unbalancing the atmo-sphere, creating catastrophic effects, the worst of which will not be felt for decades and then may have to be endured for centuries, is a crime against the future. We are taking from our grandchildren and their grandchildren the temperate, hospitable climate they would otherwise enjoy, and leaving in its place a climate full of droughts, disasters, and suffering—and we're doing it for our own short-term benefit. A5

Coal Fires and Gas Flares

■■■■ Coal fires are underground fires that burn in coal seams and mines. In China alone, they may be spewing as much CO_2 into the atmosphere as all the cars in the United States. These fires are exceedingly difficult to put out; indeed, some have been burning for decades. Scientists are studying new approaches to fighting coal fires, but they remain a big problem seeking a good solution.

Another largely unknown source of energy-related pollution—not to mention a huge waste of energy—are gas flares. Natural gas is a byproduct of oil drilling; many producers burn off this asset in flares, huge flames shooting out from a tower or vent.

According to Global Gas Flaring Reduc-tion (GGFR), a public-private project of the World Bank, more than 150 billion cubic meters (or 5.3 trillion cubic feet) of natural gas are flared annually, an amount equivalent to 25 percent of the United States' gas consumption or 30 percent of the European Union's gas consumption. Gas flares contribute roughly 400 million tons of CO_2 to the atmosphere per year.

Fortunately, the GGFR is starting to make some headway. In 2009 it reported that global gas flaring had declined by 22 billion cubic meters in three years despite a 5 percent rise in crude oil production during the same period. The organization works with the worst offend-ers—twenty countries, with Russia at the top of the list, the United States at fifteenth, and Kuwait at twentieth, one notch below Canada—to har-ness the natural gas they're burning off, either by re-injecting it into the oil reservoirs, using it for onsite power generation, or converting it to liquefied natural gas so it can be shipped and used to generate power elsewhere. AS & CB

Geoengineering

Geoengineering is a catch-all term for any large-scale effort to change planetary systems, especially our climate. While the idea of scientists actively planning to alter the earth on a massive scale may sound like science fiction, it is in fact a climate-change strategy that's being fiercely debated. Proponents say that if we fail politically to control greenhouse-gas emissions—or if the emissions we've already released prove to be even more damaging than expected—we may find ourselves in need of a backup plan. That, they say, is what geoengineering offers.

Almost all geoengineering schemes fall into one of two categories. The first type of geoengineering aims to cool the earth by reflecting more sunlight back into space—raising the earth's albedo—through measures like spreading lightening agents (think styrofoam peanuts) on the surface of the Arctic Ocean, wrapping melting glaciers in shiny plastic, or, more practically, using white roofs on a massive scale. The second kind of geoengineering involves reducing the amount of sunlight hitting the earth by filling the atmosphere with particles that block sunshine. These proposals include creating artificial clouds of water vapor by shooting pressurized water at the sky from thousands of ships on the ocean, or creating artificial volcanoes by releasing large amounts of fine particles into the upper atmosphere.

Both types of geoengineering present serious problems. First, cooling the planet without reducing carbon dioxide levels will do nothing to solve the equally grave problem of ocean acidification [see Oceans Are the New Atmosphere, p. 510], and some schemes (like trying to trigger marine algal blooms) could have a serious ecological impact. Second, we're deeply uncertain about whether any of these plans would work, or if they did, what unexpected consequences they might have. History is full of stories of people who tried to control nature using methods they didn't fully understand and who failed catastrophically. Third, the possibility that geoengineering could work is being used by advocates for polluting industries to argue that we don't need to reduce emissions at all, or not very quickly. Finally, the effects of various geoengineering schemes could be beneficial to one region yet harmful to another, leading to the prospect that certain geoengineering efforts could be considered an act of war.

All that said, given the possibility that we are passing tipping points in the earth's climate systems—levels of warming that trigger more rapid warming, like melting ice that reveals dark water underneath, soaking up more heat in a vicious cycle—we may want to have some emergency plans . . . even ones that sound crazy today. AS

RESOURCES

The Global Deal: Climate Change and the Creation of a New Era of Progress and Prosperity by Nicholas Stern (PublicAffairs, 2009)
In *The Global Deal,* Stern offers a step-by-step explanation of the mainstream understanding of the economic risks posed by climate change, and the amount and cost of the emissions reductions we need to implement. It is a meticulously researched book, presenting in the clearest possible terms why climate action now is an economic win for the planet, as well as a moral obligation. AS

How to Cool the Planet: Geoengineering and the Audacious Quest to Fix Earth's Climate by Jeff Goodell (Houghton Mifflin Harcourt, 2010)
Veteran reporter Jeff Goodell sets out to get the story on the people behind the geoengineering debate and finds visionaries, kooks, rich people with shady agendas, and some very worried scientists looking for a strategy of last resort. This book is a good read and also the best existing survey of the planet-hacking approaches that might hit the headlines sooner than we expect. AS

The Long Thaw: How Humans Are Changing the Next 100,000 Years of Earth's Climate by David Archer (Princeton University Press, 2010)
One of the most poorly understood elements of climate change is its duration: the choices we're

Oil companies may one day be held accountable as one of the biggest culprits in the production of greenhouse gases.

making now by driving to work or eating a steak are setting in motion changes that will last millennia. Archer helps us understand how our actions today will have an impact on the next thousand generations.

Field Notes from a Catastrophe: Man, Nature, and Climate Change by Elizabeth Kolbert (Bloomsbury USA, 2006)

Field Notes is based on journalist Elizabeth Kolbert's outstanding three-part series on climate change in the *New Yorker*. Kolbert is one of the world's finest environmental journalists, and though her reporting in this book no longer reflects the latest findings, her language is clear and stunning. It's grim but essential reading.

Under a Green Sky: Global Warming, the Mass Extinctions of the Past, and What They Can Tell Us About Our Future by Peter D. Ward (Harper Paperbacks, 2008)

Paleontologist Peter Ward warns us that "our world is hurtling toward carbon dioxide levels not seen since the Eocene epoch of 60 million years ago, which, importantly enough, occurred right after a greenhouse extinction." This book is worldchanging not because it points the way to a solution, but because it provides an insightful resource for imagining the true magnitude of our climate crisis.

Heat: How to Stop the Planet from Burning by George Monbiot (South End Press, 2007)

The basic argument of *Heat* is that the developed world probably needs to cut its climate-changing emissions by 90 percent by 2030 if we are to avoid runaway catastrophic climate change.

Monbiot has some annoying tics—a parochial view that may accurately describe life in the UK but completely misses the mark in other places, a scolding leftier-than-thou vibe, and a disdain for technology—but he also does a fine job of pulling together some good thinking about how we might go about radical carbon-cutting. (Ignore his plan for "energy internet," otherwise known as smart grids. Ditto on his short-sighted dismissal of carbon offsets.)

Monbiot does an excellent job of showing radical climate action as a series of possible choices, and all in all he has made a real contribution here. *Heat* is part of a new generation of books on climate change that are more interested in debating what we should do about global warming than whether or not it exists, and that shift is a cool breeze on a hot day. AS

CarbonTracker

http://www.esrl.noaa.gov/gmd/ccgg/carbontracker

Tools like CarbonTracker, an online mapping/modeling application that shows where carbon is being released and where it's being absorbed, reveal to us the invisible flows around us and help us to better comprehend our planet.

"CarbonTracker as a scientific tool will, together with long-term monitoring of atmospheric CO_2, help improve our understanding of how carbon uptake and release from land ecosystems and oceans are responding to a changing climate, increasing levels of atmospheric CO_2 and other environmental changes, including human management of land and oceans. The open access to all CarbonTracker results means that anyone can scrutinize our work, suggest improvements, and profit from our efforts. This will accelerate the development of a tool that can monitor, diagnose, and possibly predict the behavior of the global carbon cycle, and the climate that is so intricately connected to it . . . CarbonTracker can become a policy support tool too. Its ability to accurately quantify natural and anthropogenic emissions and uptake at regional scales is currently limited by a sparse observational network. With enough observations, it will become possible to keep track of regional emissions, including those from fossil fuel use, over long periods of time. This will provide an independent check on emissions accounting, estimates of fossil fuel use based on economic inventories."

Climate Cover-Up: The Crusade to Deny Global Warming by James Hoggan (Greystone, 2009)
If you want the full, detailed story of the manufactured opposition to climate science and climate action, look no further than James Hoggan's comprehensive and compelling book. It's the real story on climate change and the media, with footnotes.

State of the World (Worldwatch Institute, 2009)
State of the World 2009 is a research masterpiece, one of the most important reference guides to climate change yet published. It is argued comprehensively, moving from an outstanding overview of the state of climate science to individual chapters on various solutions: accelerating the transition to clean energy, providing green jobs, transferring technology to the developing world, saving the international climate negotiations, and so on. Like other Worldwatch work, the book is somewhat dry and technical, but that allows for exhaustive footnoting and a clear intellectual framework for building an understanding of many of the key issues. It's like a terrific interdisciplinary academic seminar, distilled into a single volume.

The book isn't perfect—the chapter on geoengineering largely ignores the politics of debates on the subject; there are some glaring omissions, including the vital role of cities and urban planning; and there's a bit of carbon blindness throughout—but its few faults don't ultimately detract from its excellence. AS

An Inconvenient Truth directed by Davis Guggenheim (2006) and *An Inconvenient Truth* by Al Gore (Rodale Press, 2006)
If you want a crash course in what climate change is, how we know it's here, and what we can expect if we don't do something about it, there is no better resource than Al Gore's documentary and companion book, *An Inconvenient Truth.*

The documentary consists mostly of footage of Gore giving his now-famous lecture on how we know climate change is real, here, and serious. It's not flashy, but *An Inconvenient Truth* is an incredibly important film, and the book should be mandatory reading in every household. Gore's work has changed the American debate on climate change, and that will change everything.

Climate Adaptation

How will rising temperatures and weirder weather upset our expectations of how the world works and what the future holds? No one knows precisely, but learning to nurture good answers to that question bears heavily on our ability to create effective solutions.

In business, in health, in our efforts to protect the environment, climate change is rewriting the rules. Industries whose existence our parents took as givens, like Big Oil, will be gone within our lifetimes, while new industries—perhaps Big Solar—will spring up in their places. We'll find ourselves under threat from diseases not previously known in our areas (like West Nile virus in the eastern United States). Plants and animals will invade regions they never could have survived in before, as the climate in those places becomes friendlier to them. Meanwhile, our efforts to protect fragile ecosystems will have to take into account that the weather that created those places is now changing. In a warming world, the only certainty is change.

Mountains serve as metaphors for the era we're entering. Mountain ecosystems around the world tend to vary considerably from one elevation to the next: on the lowest slopes, one kind of forest may be common, with its own complement of plants

Opposite, left: U.S. Forest Service workers set backfires along a containment line to stop a wildfire in Glendora, California.
Opposite, right: The day after Hurricane Katrina made landfall, New Orleans residents waded through floodwaters to reach a grocery store.

and animals, while on the higher slopes (where it tends to be cooler), different kinds of trees may be home to a different community of critters. But as temperatures rise, the trees in the lower forests may find that their ideal growing conditions have migrated upslope, while they themselves are rooted in place. This provides a massive conservation challenge, but it also provides a pretty good metaphor for the challenges we will all face: How will the things we've taken for granted in our lives "migrate upslope"? How will our futures be different, when a shifting climate has moved the ground beneath our feet?

If we don't find answers to these questions, we leave ourselves vulnerable to the heavy weather to come. AS

Place Breaking

███████ We tend to fall in love with a place's beauty: its plants, animals, and scenery. But many places also have their predictably recurrent natural disasters: wildfires, floods, hurricanes, typhoons, earthquakes, tsunamis, and volcanic eruptions. These catastrophes are every bit as native to the places we live as the birds and trees. To truly know our home places, we have to know not only how they flourish, but also how they break.

The extent to which catastrophes disrupt human lives often depends on whether the infrastructure of settlement has taken predictable catastrophes into account, or denied their existence. Unfortunately, the human propensity for denial often manifests in egregious and avoidable infrastructure failures. The insufficient engineering and reinforcement of the New Orleans levees, breached by the storm surge of Hurricane Katrina, is just one example. The dike systems in the Sacramento Delta are famously vulnerable. The homes being built in the path of wildfires at the urban-wildland interface, whether in the San Bernardino canyons of California or the lodgepole-pine forests of the northern Rockies, are practically earmarked for destruction.

Such examples suggest that American-style affluence does nothing to curb folly. Making the effort to envision—and prepare for—the plausible consequences of the unthinkable is a civic act, a necessary part of the work of placing ourselves. Some have done so brilliantly, but none in more chilling detail than the late author Marc Reisner in *A Dangerous Place*. A richly imagined "eyewitness" account of the upheaval caused by an entirely plausible (even restrained) magnitude 7.2 earthquake along the Hayward Fault, Reisner's book offers ways to think about how challenged infrastructures could fail in other places.

Literary treatments that carry important but troubling ideas into the fickle popular consciousness can also prompt—or mirror—the more rigorous scenario-building and public investment that civic authorities use to help communities withstand disaster.

A host of new uncertainties crowd the catastrophes linked closely to climate—wildfire, drought, hurricane intensity, flood frequencies. Current climate-change projections must be factored into our understanding of place, because few disaster scenarios become more benign under the erratic shifts of basic climate parameters that global warming has begun to spawn.

A sense of how our places can "break" is crucial place knowledge. Understanding the brittle systems that sustain modern lives provides no certain insurance against disaster, but the point of knowing is to survive, and to serve. A deep knowledge of place may improve our chances of surviving catastrophe; it will certainly deepen our commitment to help neighbors and community. No knowledge is more consequential. EW

Future Sea-level Rise

▬▬▬   The seas are rising. How much they"ll continue to rise is, to some very real degree, still up to us. If we embark on an effort to drastically cut CO_2 emissions, scientists say, we may be able to constrain sea level rise to, at worst, a few feet over the next century. On the other hand, if we do nothing—if the developed world doesn't change its ways, if China continues to burns its coal, if we keep logging the rain forests—we could see oceans rising twenty, thirty, even eighty feet over the next centuries. Even a few inches of sea-level rise would have profound effects on coastal ecosystems, but at eighty feet, many of our greatest cities, including New York and Shanghai, would be largely underwater.

Although rising seas are not the most dire potential effect of global climate change, they will cause serious damage. And, even more, sea-level rise is a clear indicator of the magnitude of the transformation we're wreaking on the planet, a danger that nearly everyone can grasp—if they're informed about it.

That's where Future Sea Level comes in. The San Francisco–based art/activism group hits the streets with crime scene–type tape printed with a water pattern and the group's name and applies it to buildings to show exactly how big an impact rising seas could have.

Flood Maps takes a different approach. Using NASA elevation data and Google Maps, the site allows you to see how areas from around the globe would be affected by various amounts of sea-level rise. Architecture 2030's Coastal Impact Study is a similar series of maps for coastal towns in the United States.

The point is not to scare people but rather to snap them to attention—to make them see that the time when huge climate problems are upon us is today and that the place where huge climate problems will unfold is wherever you happen to be. By making visible the invisible, we can cut through the denialist rhetoric and bring climate foresight to the masses. AS

Urban Adaptation to Climate Change

▬▬▬   Few of us are aware of the true fragility of the systems that make modern urban life possible. Built to maximize efficiency, to keep costs down, and to deliver food and other goods "just in time," urban energy, food, water, and sewer systems are often engineered to perform brilliantly within a narrow band of conditions (those we're accustomed to), but become extremely brittle in other, more extreme conditions.

Unfortunately, climate change means that unexpected extremes will occur more and more often. Bigger, more frequent storms will batter our infrastructure. With rising sea levels, those storms will drive larger tidal surges farther inland

and erode coastal land more quickly. Heavier rainfalls will flood storm sewers and swell rivers until they overflow their banks. Warmer, wetter conditions will make some places breeding grounds for diseases, like malaria, that we assumed we had vanquished. Climate change has already led to drier conditions, prolonged droughts, and the depletion of underground aquifers in eastern Australia and the American Southwest.

Everywhere, hotter days mean an amplification of the "heat island effect," where parking lots, roofs, and roads soak up extra heat from the blazing sun, making cities and suburbs even hotter than surrounding areas. Such heat can be deadly: the European heat wave in 2003 was responsible for the deaths of an estimated 46,000 people, many of them elderly. Because of climate chaos in other regions and other parts of the world, no matter where we live, we'll likely experience strange disruptions in the availability of certain foods and goods; in some places, we'll also see an influx of climate refugees. Each of these threats could lead to minor disasters, but put them all together and it's clear that because of climate change, cities need to plan for resilience.

Cities can adopt many strategies to increase their resilience.

They can make their major systems more flexible. By decentralizing their energy and water systems through measures like district energy and rainwater harvesting, for instance, they can reduce the stress on grids and pipes and offer a degree of passive survivability to their citizens. They can also create redundancies that, although they may raise costs modestly, will provide a backup option in case a major system fails.

They can plan for the graceful failure of some systems. For example, the Dutch city of Rotterdam has begun building waterfront parks and water plazas that also serve as levees and flood-control measures in case other flood-prevention measures fail. Many other cities have been experimenting with green infrastructure like streetside swales [see Greening Infrastructure, p. 172] to catch heavy rainfalls before they flood the sewer system. These swales, parks, and plazas may flood during an extreme storm, but in the process they'll protect their cities.

Cities can start preparing their health systems for climate change by, for instance, promoting public health measures designed to detect and prevent epidemic diseases that will thrive in warmer, wetter conditions. They can revise building codes to make buildings stronger in the face of natural disasters and more livable in a wider range of temperatures. They can promote the planting of street trees, the use of white roofs and lighter pavements to reflect heat, and the implementation of other elements that provide shade while putting sunlight to good use.

Ironically—given that our first impulse, when hearing about climate change, may be to head for the hills—dense, bright green cities may well be the areas best positioned to withstand climate change's long-term effects. First, they are less dependent on long supply lines (walkable neighborhoods are more resistant to oil shocks, for instance). Second, because they have high tax bases and use infrastructure more efficiently [see The Bright Green City, p. 194], they can afford to invest in resilient alternatives. Third, they have the resource bases to maintain essential institutions—from public health departments to public interest advocacy groups—that are likely to help local leaders make good decisions. And, finally, in an extreme paradox, if cities do an effective job of maintaining their foodsheds, promoting farm-to-table connections, and encouraging urban farming, their financial clout in food markets may even make them less susceptible to food shortages than many farming communities.

Cities may be vulnerable to climate change, but those that use foresight to prepare themselves may end up being the most climate-resilient places in the long run. AS

Opposite, left: Temperatures in Point Barrow, Alaska, have risen an average of more than four degrees in the last three decades.

Opposite, right: Evidence of Greenland's rapidly melting ice sheet, Ammassalik Island, Greenland, 2007.

Neighborhood Survivability

■■■■ Passive survivability is the idea that buildings ought to be designed to promote the survival of their users during disasters and emergencies, and that quite often the steps needed to promote survivability are the same as those needed to increase sustainability. In terms of buildings, the theory goes, safe is green, and green is safe.

Well, the same may be true for neighborhoods.

Disasters, including big, system-disrupting disasters, are likely to become more common in the coming decades. Whether they are caused by "ordinary" system failures (like the North American blackout of 2003), terrorism, pandemics, climate change, or global instabilities like peak oil, we should all be prepared to live through times of shortages, service interruptions, and danger.

Conventional thinking about disasters in the developed world revolves around preparing individuals to survive for the short time it takes the authorities to respond to the emergency situation and restore normality. Almost no thought is given to changing the models for urban systems to make them substantially more resilient in the face of emergencies.

But our planet is getting more dangerous, and, as New Orleans has shown, recovery is not always rapid, even in wealthy countries. While individual preparedness and government response continue to be vital, we need to put a lot more thought into how we make our neighborhoods less vulnerable to disasters in the first place. Working with our neighbors and local governments to increase the survivability of our communities might be one of the smartest moves we can make.

While a few of the steps needed to guarantee livability in a time of crisis—such as ensuring that the neighborhood has adequate medical supplies, working water filters, and alternate methods for communicating—might be particular to disaster preparedness, most of them have sustainability benefits as well. Certainly, well-designed green buildings can maintain their residents' comfort even when the grid goes down; but good alternative energy systems can also keep the lights on within a community, as well as power cell phones and other needed tools. Rainwater harvesting can provide a source of fairly clean water close at hand, while gardens can help provide emergency food supplies. Communities that have been designed to accommodate pedestrians and bicyclists rather than drivers will better withstand a disruption in the supply of gas.

If green building practices have the added benefit of promoting passive survivability, we should also consider how bright green urban systems promote resilient cities. When we're thinking about replacing the aging infrastructure that's currently in use in our cities, we need to keep this in mind. AS

■■■■■   RESOURCES

The End of the Long Summer: Why We Must Remake Our Civilization to Survive on a Volatile Earth by Dianne Dumanoski (Three Rivers Press, 2010)
Award-winning science journalist Dianne Dumanoski examines evolutionary and modern history for clues about our capacity—as a species and as a civilization—to act in the face of massive challenges. Dumanoski's criterion for success in the coming century is not prosperity, but survival. If she is right, success will boil down to our ability to "shockproof" societies to withstand changes unlike any we have confronted before.

Dumanoski urges a strategy of survivability: deliberate steps to reduce our disruption of planetary systems coupled with efforts to reconfigure patterns in human systems that make our civilization dangerously vulnerable to shocks. In a nutshell, she counsels steps to reverse the "hyper-coherence" of globalization, to pursue resilience, and to apply design features from natural systems to human arrangements. In such adjustments, she sees the best chance for shepherding the achievements of civilization through a disruptive century she expects to shake humanity to its foundations.

Her storyline is not for the faint of heart, but she finds grounds for hope in three places: the fruits of science, the legacy of our species' evolutionary past, and the creative gift of culture. EW

Resilient Cities: Responding to Peak Oil and Climate Change by Peter Newman, Timothy Beatley, and Heather Boyer (Island Press, 2009)
Peter Newman, a professor of sustainability at Curtin University in Australia, has devoted his life's work to helping governments understand the urgent need for improved public transit and land use in the twenty-first century. Timothy Beatley, a professor of sustainable communities at the

University of Virginia, believes cities and nations should more freely share solutions for policy and development to help us face the common challenges of sustainability and combating climate change. Along with coauthor Heather Boyer, Island Press's Senior Editor for land-use planning and design and a 2005 Loeb Fellow at the Harvard Graduate School of Design, Newman and Beatley describe in *Resilient Cities* how intelligent planning and visionary leadership can be strong weapons for cities facing climate change and peak oil.

International Council for Local Environmental Initiatives
http://www.icleiusa.org
ICLEI operates one of the best programs in the United States to help communities minimize and deal with global climate change. Its Climate Resilient Communities program trains local officials on adaptation to climate change, while its Climate Mitigation program coaches cities through a five-milestone program that starts with an inventory of local greenhouse-gas emissions and ends with the implementation of emission-mitigation plans.

Climate Change: Picturing the Science by Gavin Schmidt and Joshua Wolfe (W. W. Norton & Company, 2009)
Climate Change takes readers on a visually shocking journey of landscapes that have been altered almost beyond recognition by climate change. The mission behind the book is to help everyone clearly see (and, by extension, understand) the effects of human-induced climate change.

Peak Everything

The Earth is a small planet. It's strange that we ever thought its bounty was endless. All mineral resources, from metals to oil to phosphorus, are in limited supply. Minerals are hardly our only concern—we're running out of everything that's nonrenewable, and using up most renewable resources at nonrenewable rates—but minerals are both especially rare and dwindling in supply at the fastest rate.

We don't talk about peak metals, peak oil, peak phosphorus, peak *everything*, nearly enough. That's because, fundamentally, resource peaks challenge our cherished ideas based in industrial-age culture: that the planet's capacity for material growth is infinite, that the solution to material poverty is to grow the total amount of material wealth, and that the answer to inequality is to continue to grow that material wealth indefinitely.

The idea that we can use more and more resources to make more and more stuff to solve all the world's problems has collided with the reality of our planet's capacities. Even if we weren't facing serious planetary boundaries [see Carbon Neutrality, p. 458], we're still simply running out of resources.

We may soon be able to decouple increasing prosperity from material impact, operating our economy in ever more tightly closed recycling loops and substituting intelligence, good design, and clear thinking about the real sources of human well-being for more stuff. Until we do, we need to acknowledge that peak everything means the end of business as usual. AS

Peak Oil

■■■■■ Only a limited amount of oil can be found on Earth, yet the demand for it is constantly increasing. Because of this, sometime in the near future, we will find ourselves having depleted most of the readily accessible oil fields.

"Peak oil" as a technical term is a description of the point of maximum production of crude oil, a point beyond which oil will become scarcer as easily exploited supplies are tapped out and remaining oil fields are of relatively poor quality and located in places where it's expensive to drill (like deep under the ocean or in the Arctic). Eventually, supplies will become so limited, and prices so high, that oil will cease to be a viable source of energy for many uses.

But surely peak oil won't arrive until sometime in the distant future? We shouldn't be so sure. Even the most sanguine responsible estimates of remaining oil supplies predict that we'll reach peak oil this century, while an increasing number of industry analysts predict that we'll top out our oil production in the next decade or two.

We may not have that long before the economic effects of peak oil hit home. Some experts believe we have already passed peak oil, and that only the global recession of 2008 has kept us from seeing the impacts. The venerable Lloyd's insurance company and the UK's Royal Institute of International Affairs estimated in their 2010 report, "Sustainable Energy Security: Strategic Risks and Opportunities for Business," that as the economy regains strength, the effects of peak oil will begin to show, with crude oil soaring above $200 a barrel as early as 2013.

Oil priced at $200 a barrel could, in turn, mean gasoline costing $7 to $10 a gallon in North America (more in other parts of the world, where fuel taxes are higher). Todd Hale, a senior vice president for consumer researcher at Nielsen, says $10-per-gallon gasoline would drive the average American family's gas bill from 16 percent of its monthly budget to almost 40 percent. To say that this would change the economics of transportation, agriculture, and manufacturing is an understatement—and some experts believe oil prices could climb as high as $350 a barrel by 2030. Oil prices that high, they say, would quickly undercut the viability of automobile commuting, suburban life, jet travel, global trade in many bulk commodities, and cheap nitrogen fertilizers.

What's more, oil is not the only energy source in limited supply. Natural gas is also finite. Humanity has already dammed most of the rivers suitable for large-scale hydropower. Nuclear power is opposed by the citizens of most nations due to safety concerns. Our ability to responsibly burn coal—of which we have at least a century's supply—is severely limited by the outrageous greenhouse-gas emissions of coal power plants. Wind and solar power are growing rapidly cheaper and show great promise, but the rate at which they can be "scaled up" is limited by a number of factors.

All in all, we appear to be headed for an energy crunch. This is the second, looser meaning of "peak oil": an overall constriction of the energy supply as the energy needs of billions of people rising out of poverty in the Global South increase and the energy use of those in the Global North remains unsustainably high. In this larger sense, too many variables are in play to precisely define peak oil, much less predict a date for it. Nevertheless, we ought to view its arrival as imminent, if only to avoid being caught unawares by a massive energy shock caused by rapidly rising energy prices. AS

Peak Metals

▬▬▬ Where does your stuff come from? Before the store, before the factory, where did it really begin? If it isn't made of wood, cotton, wool, or other living matter, it was dug out of the ground.

We can't keep digging things out of the Earth's crust forever—there's only so much of it there. Ultimately, one day our industrial economy will be made up entirely of recycled and biologically grown material. That day, however, may be a long way off. How do we get there? How rapidly are we depleting the minerals we have, and how do we get to sustainable mining?

Current Usage

According to the United States Geological Survey and the Mineral Information Institute, to maintain our standard of living, each person in the United States requires over 48,000 pounds of minerals each year, including 12,428 of stone, 940 of cement, 425 of iron ore, and 17 of copper, just to name a few. These numbers represent only the refined final product: they don't include tailings (the leftover rock and dirt produced by mining), and the ratio of tailings to ore can be huge.

The concept of the "ecological rucksack" measures how many pounds of material must be mined (or grown) to produce one pound of end-product. According to a report by NOAH, the Danish Friends of the Earth, every pound of virgin steel requires seven pounds of material to be dug up and become waste; every gram of gold in your hand carries an invisible history of 540 kilograms of material in its ecological rucksack. In addition to this, there may be a social cost as well. Everyone is familiar with "blood diamonds" [see Demanding Transparency, p. 406], but gold is also often mined under inequitable circumstances, and back in the 1990s, tantalum was often responsible for much bloodshed and the loss of endangered species' habitats in the Congo.

Peak Minerals

How much mining can the Earth sustain? The answer is not quite zero. Mineral compounds can return to the Earth's crust on their own—slowly. Steel can rust away in a few decades, and aluminum can degrade in two hundred to five hundred years. But minerals are clearly a nonrenewable resource on the time scale of our lives.

Opposite: The Trans-Alaska Oil Pipeline snakes eight hundred miles across Alaska.

Right: Workers in southeast China's Fujian province drain polluted water after an acid spill at the nearby Zijin copper mine.

Some researchers have begun to argue that just as we're hitting peak oil, we'll soon be hitting peaks for other minerals, and that we've already passed peaks for some. Italian chemist Ugo Bardi published a research paper called "The Oil Drum: Europe" in October 2007 that examined the world production of fifty-seven minerals in the USGS's database. Bardi and his team found "11 cases where production has clearly peaked and is now declining. Several more may be peaking or be close to peaking . . . [The research] strongly supports the concept that 'Peak oil' is just one of several cases of worldwide peaking and decline of a depletable resource. Many more mineral resources may peak worldwide and start their decline in the near future." The minerals Bardi and coauthor Marco Pagani found to be peaking were mercury, tellurium, lead, cadmium, potash, phosphate rock, thallium, selenium, zirconium, rhenium, and gallium. Note that most of these are key components in computers and other electronics.

How serious is "peak minerals"? In May 2007, NewScientist released a report plotting expected years to depletion for twenty of the most-used minerals, as well as the percent recycled, the amount an average U.S. consumer will use in his or her life, and a map of the world showing where the various metals are mined. According to the report, copper will be depleted in thirty-eight to sixty-one years, indium (used in LCD monitors) in four to thirteen, silver (used in catalytic converters and jewelry) in nine to twenty-nine, and antimony (used in flame retardants and drugs) in thirteen to thirty. It appears that the market already dimly knows this: copper prices have tripled in the past decade.

As with peak oil, the economics of this situation both help and hurt. They hurt because higher ore prices make it more economically viable to do larger-scale mining at lower rates of return, causing more destruction per unit of product. The economics of scarcity help because mining for virgin materials becomes more expensive, so alternative materials and recycling become more economical by comparison. British geologist Hazel Prichard discovered in 1998 that platinum dust from cars' catalytic converters covers roadsides in the UK in high enough concentrations that sweeping up road dust and extracting the platinum will soon be cheaper than mining and refining the ore.

Bright Green Mining

How sustainable is mining itself? Practices vary widely, both by country and by industry. A 2006 Geotimes article described mining practices in the United States as being a mess, but said several other countries were doing well: "The U.S. [policy] contrasts especially sharply with policy in Sweden, where a dynamic mining and mineral industry coexists with a strong national environmental commitment in a high-wage, strong economy. The Swedish policy model, as well as Canadian and Finnish models, may not be applicable to current U.S. sociopolitical conditions, but they offer important perspectives on potential ways to break out of the current standoff."

Pressure is being put on mining companies, thanks to organizations like the Environmental Working Group. The EWG offers a Google Maps mash-up of the western United States that maps hundreds of thousands of mines and mining claims; existing mines can even be viewed in Google Earth on its 3-D terrain. They point out that there are 815 mining claims within five miles of Grand Canyon National Park, and the Grand Canyon is hardly unique—Arches, Dinosaur, Capitol Reef, Death Valley, and many other parks are in areas where mining is the backbone of the local economy.

Though most mining is currently a toxic catastrophe, there are signs it's already getting cleaner. In 2000, the U.S. EPA's Toxics Release Inventory listed metal mining as being responsible for a whopping 47 percent of all toxic waste released by industry in the country; their 2005 report listed metal mining at just 27 percent. And it's not due to other industries dumping more; nationwide releases in 2000 were 7.1 billion pounds, while in 2005 the total was 4.34 billion pounds, a decrease of more than 30 percent. Some portion of this decrease is no doubt due to offshoring environmental burdens to mines and manufacturing facilities in poorer countries [see Carbon Neutrality, p. 460], but a significant amount of it is due to better practices.

Recycling is also growing. The Encyclopedia of Earth wrote that "1 metric ton (t) of electronic scrap from personal computers (PC's) contains more gold than that recovered from 17 t of gold ore. In 1998, the amount of gold recovered from electronic scrap in the United States was equivalent to that recovered from more than 2 million metric tons (Mt) of gold ore and waste."

Several organizations are dedicated to more sustainable mining. Good Practice is an informational Web site developed by the International Council on Mining and Metals, the United Nations Conference of Trade and Development, the United Nations Environment Programme, and the UK Department for International Development); its library includes good-practice guidelines, case studies, and much more. The Initiative for Responsible Mining Assurance is working with multiple stakeholders to create a third-party certification system. An older organization focusing solely on gold is the No Dirty Gold campaign, and a primarily South American consortium is the Association for Responsible Mining.

The strategies for sustainable material use are the classics—reduce, reuse, recycle—on a massive industrial scale. The USGS report mentioned above also recommends remanufacturing (a mixture of reuse and recycling) and landfill mining. Landfill will soon have higher concentrations of useful ores than virgin ground; for some elements they already do. Perhaps landfill could be used in lieu of gravel for roadbeds and foundations, which represent such a huge proportion of nonrenewable material use. It would certainly require quality control and manipulation to keep the roads from settling, provide drainage, and avoid toxic leaching, but it might kill two birds with one stone—reducing both mining and landfill.

Bright Green Alternatives

We must also look to create alternatives to many of the materials we now mine. This is where McDonough and Braungart's [see Neobiological Industry, p. 108] concepts of "technical nutrients" and "biological nutrients" come into sharp focus. Technical nutrients are things that at some point were mined, but in the long run can be reused many times in a closed loop. Biological nutrients are materials that are farmed or otherwise grown, and that biodegrade naturally, without harmful effects to the environment. Even if we could replace all minerals in industry with functional equivalents grown from organic matter, it might

not be the wisest course of action, since organic matter also needs to be produced within the carrying capacity of the available land. The wisest course is to close the resource loops, and to keep the two types of nutrients easily separable (separate they are useful, but conjoined they are garbage), so all ingredients can retain their value. Both sustainable harvests and closed-loop recycling constitute "renewable materials."

The USGS's excellent report "Materials in the Economy—Material Flows, Scarcity, and the Environment" points out that today only about 5 percent of material used in the United States comes from renewable sources, whereas in 1900 40 percent did. This shows that it is possible to use more renewable materials, without even requiring high technology. In many poor rural parts of India and Africa today, the vast majority of materials used are renewable and local, but the standards of living are low. We must find a way to make the best of both worlds, bringing the ratio of renewable materials up to 100 percent worldwide, with a better quality of life for everyone. JJF

Peak Guano

▬▬▬ What can we learn from bird poop? Two things: One, we can at any point be on the brink of exhausting a resource or ecosystem service, no matter how plentiful it seems. And two, we can, in a very short time, turn things around through innovation.

In a series discussing resource collapse on his blog Open the Future, Worldchanging cofounder Jamais Cascio traced the short history of a long-forgotten resource: guano from Peruvian birds. In the nineteenth century this was an important fertilizer for U.S. (and other countries') agricultural interests, who along with the government were willing to use any means necessary to ensure that the supply wasn't cut off. The only thing that prevented the explosion of international tensions over access to the guano supply was the development at the end of the century of industrial superphosphate fertilizers. The resulting collapse of the guano market had catastrophic repercussions within Peru's economy, but research suggests that this crash would have been inevitable. As Cascio wrote, "It's worth noting that, even if superphosphate hadn't been developed, Peru would have been in trouble—the supplies of guano were just about depleted by the time the market collapsed. That's right: The world was facing 'Peak Guano,' only to be saved by catalytic innovation."

Now, however, the solution that took down the Peruvian guano industry—mining and refining phosphorus (mostly from the remains of ancient seabeds)—itself shows signs of collapse. Phosphate production is predicted to peak around 2030, according to the U.S. Geological Survey, and phosphate shortages may reduce crop yields as early as 2040. Remaining phosphorus supplies could become a sparking point for regional resource wars, warned Ames Elser and Stuart White in an April 2010 article in *Foreign Policy*.

We can avoid the worst effects of peak phosphorus by conserving soil and being much more targeted and careful with our use of fertilizers. But most of all, we must recycle phosphorus back into the food system by "closing the loop" and composting food scraps, yard waste, agricultural and industrial biomass (from paper to chicken droppings), and human manure. The less biomass we "throw away," the more phosphorus we can keep cycling through our farms, fields, and forests.

Metaphorically, at least, we're all living in a time of peak guano, both a scary prospect and an impetus to find the closed-loop alternatives to the depletion of oil, metals, and biological resources. AS

will have, from making air travel unaffordable for most but spurring the spread of high-speed rail, to either transforming or killing auto-dependent places. It's a nuts-and-bolts guide to things we know are changing.

Association for the Study of Peak Oil and Gas
http://www.peakoil.net
The leading scientific network studying peak oil and related issues, ASPO maintains a Web site with an abundant and growing supply of resources, links, and news.

How to Become Energy Literate and Battle Climate Change
http://www.worldchanging.com/archives/007888.html

Climate Change Recalculated
http://www.longnow.org/seminars/02009/jan/16/climate-change-recalculated/

Saul Griffith, a MacArthur fellow, prepared a primer for Worldchanging on how to become energy literate, based on an excellent talk he gave at an eTech conference. Griffith also delivered an excellent "Long Now" lecture on the connection between limited energy supplies and climate change.

■■■■   RESOURCES

$20 Per Gallon: How the Inevitable Rise in the Price of Gasoline Will Change Our Lives for the Better by Christopher Steiner (Grand Central Publishing, 2009)
Most books about peak oil and the effect of rising fuel prices on our cities tend toward the hyperbolic, arguing that one solution or another will keep us from having to change much at all or, on the other hand, that we'd all better get used to farming with horses and hand-forged plows and liking it. Steiner (a staff writer for *Forbes* magazine) does something much better: he anticipates in detail what sorts of specific effects rising oil prices

Restoring the Biosphere

■■■■ The "yeti crab" (*Kiwa hirsuta*) lives nine hundred miles south of Easter Island, 7,500 feet below the water's surface, among volcanic vents. Nicknamed for the abundant setae on their legs and claws, which give them the appearance of being covered in fur, yeti crabs are weird and mysterious creatures: they're blind, albino, and only distantly related to other lobsters and crabs (they've been given their own taxonomical family). We don't know how they manage to survive in such a harsh habitat, although scientists have come up with some interesting theories—for example, that the crabs filter the poisonous water around them using tame bacteria.

We're lucky we have any information at all about these creatures—we didn't even know they existed until 2005. Yeti crabs were briefly the rock stars of the crustacean world: news of their discovery swept the scientific community and the blogosphere, and crafters were inspired to sew stuffed-animal versions of the crabs. But what, if anything, does their discovery mean?

Such discoveries thrill us because it sometimes seems like the world is too small, too crowded, too well mapped, too *known* to admit the possibility of mystery and adventure. The yeti crab reminds us that our planet is still largely a mystery to us. As H. L. Mencken wrote, "Penetrating so many secrets, we cease to believe in the unknowable. But there it sits nevertheless, calmly licking its chops" (*Minority Report*, 1956). And that is a worldchanging lesson in itself. As environmental pressures mount, it becomes obvious that planetary

management is likely to become necessary. We're already impacting every system, every flow, every creature on Earth in some way. There was a time when we called nature changed by humanity "gardens" and nature untouched by humanity "wilderness." But it's all one big garden now.

As ecologist Daniel Janzen wrote in an essay for *Science* back in 1998, "There is no footprint-free world. Every block of the world's wildlands is already severely impacted. Not only are they internally impacted through macroevents such as the megafaunal extinctions and selective extraction of old-growth timber, but the very frameworks of their existence—global warming, acid rain, drained wetlands, green revolutions, wildland shrinkage, introduced pests, and many more—are set by *Homo sapiens*. The question is not whether we must manage nature, but rather how shall we manage it—by accident, haphazardly, or with the calculated goal of its survival forever?"

We have an obligation to become better gardeners. Consciously managing our impact on the planet is a moral imperative: since our impact extends to everything, so too must our vision. And this is the thought for which the yeti crab should become the mascot: we as a culture need to become apprentices to nature, and we need to do it now. We don't know much about the world, really. We're learning quickly, but ecological knowledge is an ocean, and we've only just left the shore.

We will have to be active gardeners, though we won't have the luxury of full knowledge. But we don't have to go into it blind, or rush headlong into dangerous plans, like geoengineering. We can act boldly but carefully, proceeding with a reasonable humility about our actual powers, open minds, and light touches until we know more about what we're doing.

Restoring the planet is as much an art as a science. The yeti crab reminds us that we're still only beginning to learn our art. AS

The Anthropocene

■■■■■■   We've all heard the rallying cries: "Save the Whales!" "Save the Rain Forest!" "Save the Polar Bears!" The latest rallying cry is all-encompassing: "Save the Holocene!"

The Holocene is the era we're currently living in, the interglacial period that began 12,000 years ago. But some propose that we have so dramatically changed the Earth's biosphere and climate that we're no longer living in the Holocene but in fact in a new geological era, the Anthropocene.

It's a catchy (if grim) concept, but one whose utility is worth questioning. There's no doubt about the magnitude of human impact on the planet—the degree of disruption we've caused by altering the biological function of nearly every corner of the Earth and changing the chemistry of its atmosphere, oceans, and soils. Almost nothing "wild" remains, and what does remain exists by our sufferance and will endure only with our conscious commitment. None of this, it seems, is really a matter of much debate; it's just how the world is now.

Calling the present the Anthropocene provokes recognition of the mind-bending reality that we are transforming the very planet on which we walk. Where the Anthropocene as a concept breaks down, however, is in the implications it raises, particularly among those who seem to be saying with increasing frequency, "Well, we're in the Anthropocene, so anything goes."

The first troubling implication is that we're capable of sketching the blueprint of an era that would be better than the Holocene—the era that produced the planetary conditions within which agriculture, civilization, and cities arose—and that we can geoengineer the climate at will to fit that (or any other) blueprint. The reality is that modern humanity and human civilization are the fruit of a very tightly interconnected set of climate and biological conditions. In order to thrive, we need a certain kind of world—essentially the mild, moderately wet, biologically abundant world of the Holocene. We've never left that world, and in fact we're still intimately dependent on its plenty for our very survival. We don't know of another set of conditions—human-designed or otherwise—that would allow us to thrive on this planet. We don't want the Holocene to end: the whole point

is that we want to lower the world's greenhouse-gas concentrations so that the Holocene climate can continue as long as it possibly can.

The second worrisome implication is that we know what we're doing enough to get the desired results from planetary engineering. We don't. The magnitude of our ignorance about even the most fundamental aspects of the planetary systems on which we depend staggers the informed mind. We're just coming to understand the climate system. We've discovered only a tiny fraction of the planet's species. We're almost still in the age of alchemy when it comes to understanding the interplay of influences that make up an ecosystem. We're simply not up to the task of running the biosphere like a machine, because we don't have a copy of the operating manual (and we're probably still illiterate). And this may be true for generations to come.

That doesn't stop us from having to make all sorts of choices about how the planet functions. We are, effectively, choosing to screw up the climate system in many ways; some of the outcomes of this are predictable and unpleasant, while others are unpredictable and potentially disastrous. Wild nature now exists almost exclusively where we protect it and garden it (and this will be more true as climate change shifts habitats). A great many species will survive only if we make saving them a priority. What the planet looks like is now largely a matter of our choices.

But that doesn't mean that we can choose to do whatever we like. There's a crazy mistaken logic out there that assumes that because we're having to make real choices about the planet's climate and biosphere, we can redesign the planet in any way we see fit. Some even claim that environmental issues are not problems at all, because by using techniques like bioengineering we can figure out how make new planets.

Natural systems are preferable not because they're natural but because they're better at being ecosystems than anything we could possibly come up with in the foreseeable future. They're more complex than we can fathom, with creatures, and relationships between creatures, that have evolved to create marvelous particularities of place. These elegant solutions are profoundly more intricate, complex, and resilient than anything we know how to make.

Preserving those ecosystems, and the species within them, is the best thing we can do. Humble and attentive restoration is the next best: a multitude of interconnected, careful efforts crafted to a particular place and alive to the adaptations climate change may demand—each effort small on its own but massive and planetary in aggregate. Everything else is a distant, almost wishful, possibility. Our goal, in essence, is to preserve and restore the Holocene biosphere, in whatever way we can (and in some cases, that might mean looking back to restoring systems and relationships damaged long before the industrial era even began, through re-wilding and resurrection ecology).

So, do we need to take responsibility for the planet? Yes. Do we need to take the climate in hand, and aim to release zero or less-than-zero greenhouse gases? Yes. Do we need to garden nature, greatly reducing our demands on ecosystem services and preserving wild biological hotspots but also practicing adaptive restoration and so on? Yes.

But our mission in all of this ought to be clear: to preserve the planet on which humanity evolved and, even more important, the planetary era whose attributes underpin everything we now are. Our goal should be, simply, to save the Holocene. A5

Restoration Ecology

■■■■ Some suggest that the only way to satisfy our longings for contact with nature is to head back to the woods—to go camping in the wilderness, kayaking along untamed rivers, or climbing distant peaks. We share an impractical cultural idea that the only nature worth connecting to is nature far away from humanity.

Fortunately, if we can't get out to the wild, we have other avenues for connecting to nature—and that's a good thing considering the wilderness areas we'd trample underfoot if all

6 billion of us decided to visit them. One such avenue is restoration ecology, the practice of bringing degraded ecosystems back to a healthier state closer to their origin. Some restoration projects are wilderness oriented—reintroducing lost species to areas where they once roamed free, such as the ongoing reintroduction of wolves in Yellowstone National Park—but many can take place in our own backyards.

Ecological restorations can range from small-scale urban park reclamations, which are happening across the United States, to huge re-creations of entire ecosystems. Whatever the scale, the goal is to restore the landscapes that once existed (like wetlands, tall grass prairies, and various river systems), or at least some of their functions. If measured by the amount of time and money Americans are willing to invest in it, restoration ecology is one of the most popular ways of being environmentally involved. For example, the cluster of projects known as Chicago Wilderness—a thirty-year attempt to return areas around Chicago to oak savanna (their presettlement ecosystem)—has attracted some 20,000 volunteers over its life and restored at least 17,000 acres (6,880 hectares) of a total planned 100,000 acres (40,469 hectares).

Restoration has real ecological and scientific benefits. But just as important, it gives us a chance to become reconnected with nature, to literally get our hands dirty in an active process of changing the world. Truly successful restoration projects actively encourage community participation.

The thousands of volunteers in Chicago are not only replacing exotic species with indigenous ones and bringing back native forests, but

As the result of a successful reintroduction program, wolves are now being spotted in Yellowstone National Park after an absence of more than seventy years.

they are also becoming more actively involved in their local environment. Not all of us can do biological surveys, but most of us know how to work a shovel or pull an invasive weed.

When we volunteer on restoration projects, we form a strong attachment and commitment to the land, a relationship that can be as important as family ties and civic attachment. Sociological evidence gathered from the Chicago restorations suggests that restoration volunteers are likely to adopt a benign attitude of stewardship and responsibility toward nature as a result of such engagement. The reasons are fairly obvious: participants learn the injurious toll human activity takes on nature by experiencing how hard it is to restore something after it has been damaged. They also gain a sense of investment in the health of local natural systems. For all these reasons, restoration can serve as a new schoolhouse for environmental responsibility, but only when we are farsighted enough to encourage voluntary public participation in this range of projects. ARL

Climate Adaptive Restoration

▬▬▬▬ The Puget Sound, the sparkling body of water off Seattle's coast, is hurting. Almost embarrassingly bountiful until just a few decades ago, it now seems to be sliding toward an ecological tipping point: salmon and orca are on the endangered species list; estuaries, wetlands, and nearshore habitat have been destroyed; and, on the whole, the Sound may be teetering on the brink of collapse.

It's not too late to save it. A variety of factors have contributed to its decline: overfishing, invasive species, and especially the large amounts of toxic chemicals sloughed off as part of the daily lives of the Puget Sound's growing population. But the real key to saving the Sound is saving its shorelines, which contain important habitats—home to sea and bird life—that have been infringed upon by docks and development.

To help restore coastal habitats, the Alliance for Puget Sound Shorelines within the last decade acquired four miles of shoreline for eight new parks and natural areas, and completed restoration projects—including removal of structures like bulkheads and piers that affect tidal flow,

revegetation of salt marsh habitat, and removal of invasive species and toxic debris—on fifty-four miles of shoreline.

This is good work. The challenge, though, is that the shorelines themselves are becoming moving targets. Global warming is already changing Puget Sound, causing the water to warm and the sea to rise. Predictions for the future are even more alarming. "Business-as-usual will yield warming of 6 to 9°F by the end of the century and . . . sea level will rise. The last time it was 5°F warmer than now, sea level was at least eighty feet higher," says James Hansen, NASA's chief climate scientist. Other studies suggest that unless we take drastic action, we may have already committed ourselves to dramatic sea-level rise over the next century. Studies suggest that melting ice sheets alone are causing the sea to rise about one millimeter per year. When we map the effect of rising seas on Puget Sound, we find that much of what is now shoreline may well be under water by century's end.

This is clearly a place where some climate foresight is called for, and yet, as People For Puget Sound's Mike Sato acknowledges, when it comes to the Sound, "Climate change isn't top-of-mind at all." It's been very difficult, he says, to get policymakers and funders to understand the importance of doing the basic restoration and protection work whose need is well-documented, much less get them to think about the implications of changes that may still be decades off.

Does that inability to plan for climate change undermine the usefulness of the shoreline alliance's work? No. Many of their efforts involve things we'll need to do whatever our eventual strategy, just to stabilize a collapsing ecosystem. Taking care of what we have while we learn to plan ahead is sensible.

And here the present and future may not be unrelated. From the Southeast Asian tsunami to Hurricane Katrina, we've seen that when the ocean turns angry, places with weakened or destroyed estuaries, wetlands, tidal flats, mangrove forests, and other areas where land and ocean interpenetrate get hit harder than places with healthy ecosystems. Thinking seriously about ecological health and public safety in an age of sea-level rise and weird weather may mean not just building seawalls and dikes, but using saltwater wetlands intelligently to act as buffers and sponges, as well as maintain the ecological balance.

But here's the thing: we're still learning what to do and how to do it. We don't know how, for example, to restore our shorelines in a way that benefits us now *and* will adapt well as the seas rise further. We don't know how to integrate living systems—like tidal marshes, mudflats, and kelp beds—with manmade protective systems like bulkheads and seawalls.

This may be a local story, but the moral is global. No matter where we live, the worst thing we could do at this stage is throw up our hands and say, "Well, we don't know what's going to happen, so let's not do anything." What we need to do instead is initiate a concerted, cross-disciplinary effort to look at climate, ecology, and biodiversity, which will inform a more vigorous discussion about our goals with regard to land use, ecosystem services, and our relationship to place. We need to teach ourselves how to make informed decisions in a rapidly changing world. AS

Why the Cloned Bird Doesn't Sing

■■■■■ Even if it becomes simple science to revive ancient animal species from genetic material, we will not have achieved true species restoration. The songbird is a poetic example. Even if we were able to clone an ancient songbird with DNA, its likeness would be betrayed by the absence of its most essential trait: song. Birds get their singing skills through a combination of instinct and learning; without the presence of feathered kin, our cloned bird's song, if it has one, will be meaningless. SR

Involuntary Parks

■■■■■ The so-called demilitarized zone between North and South Korea is devoid of any human habitation or activity, and has been for almost sixty years. As a result, this space—155 miles (250 kilometers) long, 2.5 miles (4 kilometers) wide—has become home to a staggering array of rare plants and animals, including the highly endangered red-crowned crane.

The DMZ is not the only government-owned wasteland of its kind. These long-forsaken, undomesticated expanses are some of the wildest remaining places on earth. They've been dubbed "involuntary parks," reflecting the accidental nature of their wildness.

Decommissioned nuclear plants seem to make good involuntary parks. Rocky Flats, a former nuclear weapons plant near Denver, Colorado, was shut down in 1989 because a slew of environmental violations—leaking storage drums, tanks, and pipelines; on-site landfills; unlined disposal trenches—had thoroughly contaminated the soil and groundwater. Today the site contains what might be the largest remaining tallgrass prairie in North America, as well as several endangered or threatened species, including peregrine falcons. The most iconic nuclear wasteland of our time, Chernobyl, is also turning into an immense wildlife preserve. Moose, wolves, and deer roam around in places where humans still can't safely walk, and more than two hundred bird species (thirty-one of them endangered) call the park home.

As pressures on more desirable lands increase, these dangerous nature sanctuaries play an ever-more-important role in preserving biodiversity. "Involuntary Parks are natural processes reasserting themselves in areas of political and technological collapse," says futurist Bruce Sterling. "An embarrassment during the twentiethth century, Involuntary Parks could become a somber necessity during the twenty-first." CB & JC

A silhouette of a village near Chernobyl—site of one of the worst nuclear disasters in history—which has become a refuge for endangered wildlife.

Save a Mangrove, Save a Life

■■■■ Healthy coastal ecosystems are vital to protecting growing coastal populations from disaster. According to the UN, over half of the world's population was living within 200 kilometers (125 miles) of a coastline in 2001, with numbers only increasing in subsequent years, and tourists compounding the problem. At the same time, climate instability is likely to render already violent cyclones, hurricanes, tsunamis, and floods even more intense and destructive. It's clearly of vital importance that we integrate ecological preservation and restoration into the process of development along the world's coasts—before the next disaster.

In the 2004 tsunami in the Indian Ocean, healthy mangroves, the leading edge of the forest, took the brunt of the great wave's energy when it hit—yet few trees were uprooted. With large areas of mangroves appearing to be relatively intact, it can be difficult to detect the extent of injury to the forest—a problem often referred to as cryptic ecological degradation. However, where mangroves had been weakened, even relatively slightly, by ecological harm caused by humans—like pollutants from inland development and agriculture—they were much less able to protect the inner coastline, even if they had not been thinned by strong storm winds.

Mangroves are incredibly fertile ecosystems. At the meeting point of land and sea, healthy mangroves support an amazingly biodiverse ecology. Unfortunately, development plans often involve destroying mangroves—for the sake of coastal tourism, say, or of farming shrimp for export to richer nations. But people live better with mangroves than without them, a fact that will likely become all too clear the next time a big storm hits and weakened forests have less resistance.

Mangroves have had a high rate of success in restoration projects, since they are easy to access from the coast for management and care, and generally exist in a self-sustaining environment (provided that coastal conditions don't reach extremes). Restored and well-managed mangrove

forests can be extremely beneficial for local coastal populations, as they can be superior ecosystems in which to raise and harvest shellfish (a fact that gets ignored when forests instead get replaced by shrimping operations) and can supply managed timber. The work of fortifying and supporting these ecosystems promises to be one of the great preventative measures we can take to be better prepared for future marine storms. EG

Restoring the Deep Past

■■■■ Before the first intrepid explorers crossed over the Bering Strait from Asia, toward the end of the last ice age, North America was home to an astonishing variety of large animals: mammoths and lions, horses and camels, giant beavers, and ground sloths the size of Volkswagen Bugs. Shortly after we got here, the wildlife disappeared.

Whether or not we killed them off remains a matter of some debate (although the scales seem to be tipping against us), but the impact of this mega-extinction has become increasingly clear: the continent the Europeans saw as a savage wilderness when they arrived late in the fifteenth century was in fact something more like a garden, managed extensively by native peoples through the use of fire, and devoid of many of its largest prehistoric inhabitants.

In *Twilight of the Mammoths: Ice Age Extinctions and the Rewilding of North America,* Paul S. Martin proposes "rewilding" the continent by reintroducing, in protected locations, some of the close living cousins (particularly elephants) of the animals North America has lost. Far from being unnatural, Martin says, this would bring

Mangroves have thrived in reintroduction projects and are crucial to the health of coastal populations.

ecosystems—or at least experimental parts of them—closer to the healthy state they were in before we arrived.

When we think of restoring what has been lost, Martin suggests, we should aim to re-create not what was here a couple of hundred years ago, but the full suite of plants and animals that evolved here before humanity first spread out over the earth. We should practice "resurrection ecology." By bringing back mini-replicas of the world we first encountered, we'll be able to better understand what, exactly, we've made of our world—and make a better one for the future. AS

Urban Ecology and Conservation

▰▰▰▰ While most conservation strategies focus on our remaining parcels of wilderness, on an increasingly urban planet, urban ecology must also play a central role in conservation.

Understanding how nature lives and adapts within urban centers is of paramount importance to places like Germany's Biosphäre Bliesgau, which was added to UNESCO's World Network of Biosphere Reserves in 2009. Bliesgau spans untouched natural areas, rural areas, *and* two densely populated cities and their surrounding burbs. In fact, the population density of Bliesgau (310 residents per square kilometer) is higher than the country's average, making it the highest of any biosphere. According to UNESCO, although the biosphere contains many protected natural areas, a great number of species (the crested lark, the wall lizard, and the greater mouse-eared bat, to name a few) actually reside within the region's towns.

Conservationists recognize that they cannot protect Bliesgau without understanding how animals move between urban and natural areas and how they become dependent on urban infrastructure to survive. Keeping nature in nature is no longer an option in many places.

Fortunately, with a little tweaking, our cities can act as wildlife corridors. Seattle's Pollinator Pathway project is trying to create urban corridors for bees, butterflies, and birds by transforming city-owned planting strips (typically the grass strips between the curb and the sidewalk) into gardens of native plants that attract and protect important pollinators. The Morgan Building in New York City's midtown neighborhood changed its facade to protect migrating birds. Before its shiny exterior panels (which reflected the trees of a nearby park) were covered with a black vinyl film, the massive building was responsible for the death of many birds.

In London, declining bat biodiversity is being addressed by the Bat House Project, which ran a competition to build a new bat house at WWT London Wetland Centre in Barnes, South West London. The winning design is as much a work of public art as a practical and safe year-round roost for bats: a white structure that resembles a shadow box full of tree branches conceals perches capable of holding thousands of Pipistrelle bats, many of whom become "homeless" as development destroys natural habitat and the bats are pushed out of roof spaces as buildings are reconfigured to meet housing demands.

In most cities, the beginnings of wildlife corridors already exist in window boxes and city parks, and even in roosting areas on skyscrapers. The challenge is to connect these disparate patches of green in a logical and safe way. It's a challenge worth meeting: not only does any increased amount of greenery make city life more pleasant (and literally cooler), but creating dedicated corridors—obvious to animals and respected by humans—may decrease the conflict between man and beast as creatures move out of areas affected by climate change and into more populated areas. CB

The Polar Doomsday Vault

▰▰▰▰ A reinforced concrete vault in a mountain cave on a frozen Norwegian island could someday become one of the most important resources for sustaining life on earth. According to plans, this "doomsday" vault, which officially opened in February 2008, will eventually hold between 1 and 2 million seeds, representing an extensive selection of food crops and other plants from around the globe. At this writing, the vault has accrued about a half-million seeds.

Curated with the help of the Global Crop Diversity Trust, the bunker can withstand disasters and threats of all kinds, and the island's permafrost will help keep the seeds frozen, ensuring their longevity. The vault comes at a very low cost because natural conditions keep it consistently cool and highly secure. Unlike other seed banks, which share their contents with farmers today, the doomsday vault is meant to protect the world's food supply in the future from catastrophes like nuclear war, asteroid strike, or environmental disaster caused by accelerated global warming. Call it civilization's insurance policy. SR

IBAT

■■■■■   Architects and designers can use CAD-based programs to calculate the environmental impacts of their buildings and products before the first blueprint or prototype is created. But until recently no similar tools existed to help businesses site their operations responsibly. Potential investors in a new ecoresort, for example, had no way to quickly assess whether a proposed location would affect a sensitive natural area. IBAT (Integrated Biodiversity Assessment Tool) not only makes that information easily available in the very early planning stages, it also helps investors search for alternative locations.

A partnership between BirdLife International, Conservation International, and the United Nations Environment Programme's World Conservation Monitoring Centre, IBAT is a simple Web database that maps all Key Biodiversity Areas (KBAs), areas of globally important biodiversity that include one or more of the following: endemic species, endangered species, unique habitat (cloud forests, for example), or important sites in migration routes. IBAT's assessments are based on information from various sources, including the International Union for Conservation of Nature's Red List of Threatened Species and Important Sites for Freshwater Biodiversity, BirdLife's Important Bird Areas, Plantlife International's Important Plant Areas, and Alliance for Zero Extinction's list of biodiversity hotspots.

IBAT was the first such project to aggregate data from so many different sources into one business-friendly tool. Its creators hope that IBAT will help businesses become better biodiversity managers, which is a win-win proposition (businesses stand to lose a lot of money in mitigation fees or lawsuits if their operations destroy important habitat). IBAT can also help socially responsible businesses to vet their suppliers' operations so that they can assure shareholders and the public that no one they do business with is contributing to the destruction of our planet's dwindling biodiversity. CB

■■■■■   RESOURCES

Conservation International: Biodiversity Hotspots
http://www.biodiversityhotspots.org
Biological "hotspots"—critical ecosystems like rain forests and coral reefs—which cover only 1 percent of the Earth but hold 44 percent of its biodiversity, are being transformed so rapidly that even if they are preserved from destruction, they may not be able to provide a home for the plants and animals who live there now. The destruction of these hotspots is the most serious threat to biodiversity posed by climate change.

Conservation International's Biodiversity Hotspots page offers a good overview of why certain places are biologically richer than others, and why protecting those places is an important part of any plan to retain as much of the richness of life as possible.

Encyclopedia of Life: A Comprehensive Guide to the World's Species
http://www.eol.org
The EoL is an online reference and research tool that aims to compile existing databases and efforts,

The Svalbard Global Seed Vault—otherwise known as the polar doomsday vault—can hold up to 2 million seeds.

mix their data with other content gathered from a variety of sources, and have experts edit the "mash up" (their phrase) to produce and maintain the most comprehensive guide to all the species known to humanity.

EDGE of Existence

http://www.edgeofexistence.org

It's an unpleasant fact of twenty-first century life that we live in the midst of the Sixth Extinction, and we can expect to hear of the departure of beloved species on a regular basis. We need to wrap our brains around extinction, really understand the various ways in which it's happening, and examine the potential responses available to us as we search to preserve our planet's biodiversity.

The EDGE of Existence aims to spread awareness of the world's evolutionarily distinct and globally endangered animals (you know, weird ones like the Sumatran rhinoceros, the Aye-aye, and the golden-rumped elephant shrew), and build support for their protection. Their site is not only educational, it's beautiful and absorbing. AS

Heatstroke: Nature in an Age of Global Warming

by Anthony D. Barnosky (Shearwater, 2009)

Heatstroke is a fascinating if harsh picture of how climate change has already begun scrambling natural habitats that have been comparatively stable since the last ice age, and how climate chaos threatens to unleash a whirlwind of habitat shifts, invasive species, natural disasters, and sudden extinctions on the world's remaining wild places. Barnosky argues that we now need to think of parks and wildernesses as "species reserves" where "heavy management"—including assisted migration, rewilding, and other radical strategies—will be required to save native species.

"[W]hat used to be a one-stop-shopping conservation solution—preserve a parcel of land and the species in it and you also preserve a particular ecosystem and, by extension, nature itself—will no longer work, because a parcel of geography won't preserve a particular assemblage of species if their needed climate at that locus disappears." AS

Ecosystem Services

■■■■■ Nature is working for you. If you don't know how, consider your faucet. You bought the plumbing, and in your monthly bill you pay for the filtration plant and pipes that deliver the water, metered, to your house. But that water likely began its journey to your home scores or hundreds of miles away, percolating through a forested watershed that captured the rainfall, combed it of impurities, oxygenated it in streams, delivered it to a river, and ultimately, to a municipal drinking-water reservoir. Nature provided the water composing the ice cubes rattling in your lemonade, for free. You can't easily buy a substitute for the rainfall, the watershed, or the streamflows. It makes you wonder how much they're worth.

In similar fashion, the air we breathe, the food we eat, and the climate we depend on are all supplied in large measure by services that nature performs for free. Such "ecosystem services" underpin all life on earth, but only humans are in a position to assign a value to them. When economists first did so about a decade ago, a rough calculation showed nature's services to be worth a third more each year than all the human economic output on the planet. In the "Millennium Ecosystem Assessment Synthesis Report," economists estimate that it would cost at least $33 trillion per year to substitute human effort for the services that nature provides for free. Of course, many of those services we simply couldn't perform at any price. That's some subsidy!

When it comes to nature, we human beings act as though we don't know the value of a buck. We don't calculate the wealth lost when our $25 trillion economy pollutes, degrades, and impairs the functions of the natural economy that sustains us.

That's slowly beginning to change. We are starting to understand that on one small planet, keeping life-support systems in good working order isn't just another expense—it's an investment in survival. EW

How Much Is the Planet Worth?

■■■■ How much is a pristine lake worth? A clean atmosphere? An oil field?

Answering these questions takes us from the heart of economic philosophy to the frontiers of analytical science. It's very difficult to provide objective monetary values, even in principle—but as our analysis and understanding of ecosystem services increase, we're developing useful valuation methods that will form the basis for future policy and financial activities.

So how can the value of ecosystem services be calculated? One fundamental distinction is between methods that establish currency-based values for the worth of a particular ecosystem, and those that use other metrics and indicators.

Currency-based Valuation

Currency-based methods can be subdivided according to whether the benefits they measure are traded in markets or not. An example of a market-traded benefit would be a forest's timber value. This value, however, is based on a lot of assumptions: What is the future price path of timber going to be over the coming decades? What discount rate and time horizon should be considered for evaluating future benefits?

Once we make our assumptions, we can come up with values using standard financial tools.

A (relatively) simple way to value investment opportunities is to estimate the stream of future costs and benefits, and then discount each back to the present day, so that they can be added up in constant dollars and compared. The appropriate values to use for discounting have been debated for decades, though. On one hand, "a bird in the hand is worth two in the bush"—meaning a dollar now should be worth more than a dollar twenty years from now. On the other hand, it's hard to justify treating the value of clean air today vastly differently from the value of clean air to your grandchild in fifty years. The key point is that the estimated currency values for ecosystem services are highly model dependent, so part of the due diligence required in using such values is to look at the assumptions, data, and models that went into coming up with the figures.

For goods and services that are not market-traded, there are various means to establish a price tag. Here are a few ways you might try to estimate the "value" of a park, for instance, given that parks are not bought and sold in markets:

Market proxies: The recreational value of a park could be estimated from visitor revenues, as well as the cost of travel and time "spent" by visitors to use the park. This calculation is relatively easy, but it often vastly underestimates the value.

Stated preference: In "willingness to pay" and other choice-based methods, people are asked to appraise the value of the park or make trade-offs between the park and some other benefit. Although such methods are flexible and applicable in principle to many goods and services, they have several weaknesses: people's stated opinions may not be valid or well informed, and there may be wide variations in results depending on how questions are asked.

Revealed preference: Our stated preferences may differ from the preferences "revealed" by our

Left: Protection of the natural resources in watersheds, like this one in the Little Tennessee River near Tallassee, Tennessee, is crucial to the health of all living things.
Following pages: Coral reefs, such as this one in Fiji, are as important to the health of the planet as the Amazon rain forest is.

actions. Telling a friend that you would prefer to preserve the climate rather than have the freedom to travel as you wish is a stated preference—but if you then choose to fly to a vacation spot halfway around the world, your "revealed preference" is different. In the case of the park, it might be that everyone says they like the park, but few actually visit.

Contingent choice: Instead of being asked to measure the park's value in dollars, people are asked to choose among a set of options, such as leaving the park untouched (with taxes staying the same) versus developing part of the park (with taxes decreasing). The distribution of choices is then used to infer a currency value.

Replacement cost: How much would it cost to set up a new park? This method, placing a cost on the replacement of the goods or services, is especially applicable to cases where the service in question clearly needs to be maintained, such as water quality. In other words, if a damaged ecosystem service must be replaced by alternate means, that service must logically be worth at least the replacement cost.

Health impact: Public-health interventions often use the DALY (Disability-Adjusted Life Year) framework to compare the benefits of different courses of action. If the health impacts of ecosystem service damage, such as air pollution, can be estimated accurately, they can be useful as metrics. If a park measurably increases the fitness of the citizens who use its paths and ball fields, or reduces pollution or the heat-island effect, that's a point in favor of maintaining it.

Alternatives to Monetary Valuation
Surely, restricting ourselves to the no-nonsense world of dollars and euros makes ecosystem valuation clear and objective? After all, we've seen estimates for ecosystem service value that pin dollar figures on boreal forests and many other ecosystems. Well, it's not so simple. Monetary figures do help by assigning value to services that are clearly worth *something*. At the same time, they can be misleading and give the impression that currency-based valuation is precise when in fact it's not. For example, people place varying levels

of importance on given goods and services, so a price that reflects an average value may hide wide differences of opinion.

In addition, we must consider that perceived value may be directly related to a specific user's needs: a bushel of wheat may be cheap in currency terms yet life-saving to a destitute family. Another intangible factor in ecosystem valuation is the idea of obvious versus subtle worth. A scenic mountain might draw more visitors, tourist revenue, and public appreciation than a boggy wetland, even if the latter provides more indirect benefits. We might be willing to pay more to preserve the mountain now, yet suffer more from loss of the wetland in the long run.

The vast literature on the subject highlights the complexity of coming up with a "value" for our planet's ecosystems. Here are some useful nonmonetary approaches:

Relative valuation: In cases where the valuation is being done to support a recommended course of action, show that one option is better than another, even if the benefits can't be fully quantified. To take a simple example, if we're deciding whether or not to leave some natural habitat when building a new urban area, the relative benefits may be clear.

Indicators: Even if you can't assign a dollar value to an ecosystem or service, you may be able to establish a set of measurable statistics that, taken together and in context, summarize its value. This "vector of values" can be tracked over time or compared between different future scenarios. The flexibility of indicators is both a blessing and a curse: indicators can be beneficial by explicitly revealing various facets of value that can be weighted differently by each decision-maker, but they can also be difficult to apply and a barrier to consensus if the indicators are poorly chosen or not standardized.

Environmental accounting: Honest and competent accounting lies at the heart of traditional financial valuation. A similar sort of accounting for natural assets—accurate measurement of stocks and flows of resources such as forests, aquifers, and arable land—would radically ease the valuation of ecosystem and natural resources.

Data and models: Models and their summaries might themselves be considered more complex forms of valuation. The Millennium Ecosystem Assessment, by giving baselines and insights into ecosystem function and interaction, was one of many efforts contributing to a shared understanding of the core "life support" ecosystems most in need of protection. It was, in a sense, performing directly an evaluative function that dollar figures perform by proxy.

Do these noncurrency valuation methods really belong in the same framework as the currency-based methods we're accustomed to? Yes, for several reasons. First, many economists (and particularly ecological economists) use non-currency-based tools, recognizing that they are a valid alternative to monetary valuation. Second, these tools are useful for practical decision-making, especially in cases where the data or know-how are absent to apply monetary valuation. Third, although "summarizing" an ecosystem service in monetary terms allows current and future costs and benefits to be analyzed along a common scale, monetary values can be unstable over time and carry a lot of hidden assumptions about underlying realities. Because nonmonetary value (e.g., a set of indicators or preferences) is more directly tied to the ecosystem in question, it may be more objective, as well as more stable over time.

Where Next?

Imagine mashing up some of the best data and visualization tools we have at our disposal—including multiscale data on ecosystem goods and services, summaries, and trends—with monetary estimates. Where specific values are available, they can be highlighted, but with limitations noted; where the values are too uncertain, we can fall back on the underlying data.

A marriage of the two may be the way forward. A more nuanced idea of valuation will allow us to use the powerful tools of financial planning where appropriate. Where they're inappropriate, we can use indicators, models, and simulations to compare the benefits of various alternatives in terms that are directly linked to human well-being.

We must approach the challenge of comprehending the true value of our environmental resources with humility. It will be a long process—one that can advance only as our knowledge, wisdom, and experience grow. HM, CM & DZ

Apiculture and Colony Collapse Disorder

▬▬▬ If ever you needed a visual example of the value of ecosystem services, try envisioning an army of human laborers attempting to pollinate an orchard of fruit trees by hand, one blossom at a time. Absurdly enough, an alarming decrease of bee populations worldwide, known as Colony Collapse Disorder (CCD), has some farmers hiring teams to do just that.

With much of our focus on bigger species as indications of environmental crisis—polar bears drowning, grizzly bears terminating hibernation early—we sometimes forget about the little creatures that keep things in balance. But bees are an important provider of the ecosystem service of pollination, and as calamity strikes, it is all the more obvious how important they are in the agricultural economy. From a strictly financial perspective, pollination is an invaluable service, provided by bees at no cost. But the cost we'd incur if the buzzing workers disappeared has been estimated at anywhere between $14 billion and $92 billion in the United States alone.

At this writing, scientists in Montana and Maryland were nearly certain that colony collapse in U.S. honeybee colonies was caused by a combination virus–fungal infection. They're still unsure, however, of two important things: what environmental factors allowed both the virus and the fungus to proliferate and interact, and what can be done to prevent future collapses.

Until we have more answers, precautionary measures are needed. In the Himalayan regions of northern India and Tibet, as well as in parts of China, farmers have found some entrepreneurial opportunity in the necessity to hand-pollinate as their bee crews diminish, but managing a labor force doesn't make up in the long run for an orchard suffering from sterility.

As pollinators, bees are a great example of the value offered by "nature's services," which we often take for granted.

The longer-term solution to CCD is the most obvious: steward bee populations and keep them thriving. Bees have become a mostly domesticated insect, which means it's up to us to help keep them populous. As professor May Berenbaum said in a podcast on Earth & Sky, "I don't think people realize just how utterly dependent we are on bees. To some extent, historically, there have been feral bees, wild bees that people haven't domesticated that contribute pollination services. But when verola mites were introduced, feral populations all over the country crashed; nobody was there to protect them. And, as a consequence, nobody has been there monitoring them. We have no idea what the feral bee population is in this country; whether there are bees that can fill in for the missing bees is just an open question."

Apiculture advocates have set up numerous web-based resources that allow beekeepers to engage in some citizen science, swapping important observations about their experiences and tracking trends through systems like open surveys. The International Bee Research Association has a huge archive of information to help guide people through keeping hives. And while the pollination value of bee colonies may be a more serious reason to protect them than for the honey and wax they produce, their byproducts are, of course, an undeniable benefit. In urban environments, just a small hive can keep pollination healthy and produce bee products for a household or two.

While CCD is bound to have negative consequences for both farmers and apiculturists, looking at the entire agroecological system, bees are responsible for only a part of all the pollination services delivered. Other insects, birds, wind, and rain make up the rest of the pollination we rely on for our daily bread. But alas, some of those pollinators are facing declines too; a report from the International Centre for Integrated Mountain Development cites "decline in wilderness and loss of habitat, land use changes, monoculture-dominated agriculture and excessive and indiscriminate use of agricultural chemicals and pesticides" as contributing factors to a challenge that worsens yearly.

Industrial agriculture, problematic as it is, affords those of us living within the system something of a cushion in looking at ways to deal with these pollinator declines. But for subsistence and small commercial farmers, inadequate pollination poses a serious and fairly immediate threat to livelihoods and food security. Unfortunately—though not surprisingly—it's in part because of industrial agriculture that bees find themselves under threat. While we hold bees in such high regard, we must also remember that, at least in North America, they are not a native species. As Professor May Berenbaum, succinctly put it, "over-reliance on one managed non-native species is inherently unstable."

Bees are a fantastic example of taking an ecosystem service and, through skillful management, turning it into a commodity. As the delivery of this service is put in jeopardy, it becomes essential for us to look for ways to maintain our pollination needs. Agriculturally dominated landscapes have supplanted the rich mix of land-cover types that are necessary for keeping the system in balance. The idea of countryside biogeography has emerged as a potential solution by incorporating a mix of agricultural lands and natural habitats that provide a storehouse for biodiversity. These reservoirs provide services such as pest regulation and pollination that are often absent in purely agricultural landscapes. Studies done on coffee crops in Costa Rica have shown that crops close to forest fragments were more likely to be visited by pollinators, and that yields were 20 percent higher in areas within about half a mile (one kilometer) of forest remnants, increasing the income of the farmer. Similar results have been shown for agricultural fields near hedgerows and wetlands. These win-win opportunities illustrate that such solutions are going to be necessary as we seek to increase the resilience of our agricultural systems. SR & DZ

Millennium Ecosystem Assessment

▬▬▬   More than 1,300 scientists from ninety-five countries collaborated on the "Millennium Ecosystem Assessment (MEA) Synthesis Report," which describes results from the first segment of a multiyear study of environmental indicators, launched by United Nations Secretary-General Kofi Annan in 2001. The report, released in 2005, evaluates the condition of earth's ecosystems, details how ecosystem changes may impact human life, and suggests tools for improving ecosystem management to alleviate poverty and enhance well-being. Overall, the story isn't good: of the twenty-four ecosystem services evaluated by the MEA, fifteen have deteriorated over the last half century. Services in decline include capture fisheries, water purification, natural control of pest species, and the capacity of mangroves, wetlands, and other natural systems to buffer against hazards like storms and tsunamis. Only four ecosystem services have improved, three of them relating to food production. Subsequent volumes in the assessment effort include a look at four scenarios for the next half century, forecasting how we might shape the future with the choices we make today. EW

Ecological Economics

▬▬▬   Since resources are finite, we should budget their use. Since ecosystem services can be destroyed, we should create incentives to protect them. Ecological economics is about adding these insights to traditional economics, to create a broader framework that combines hard business sense with environmental and physical reality.

Why should we impose extra limits on ourselves? Because it's better for us in the long run. Just as borrowing too much on credit and getting deeper and deeper into debt hurts our financial futures, using up too much natural capital reduces our long-term wealth. The need to stay within a budget constrains every business, but it does not stop smart businesses from continually improving. Similarly, the need to stay within resource and ecoservice budgets is a limit we have to respect, but it does not stop progress in efficiency, technology, cultural endeavors, and human welfare. And we can stay within these budgets only if we properly appraise what they measure.

Let's take an example: the Canadian Boreal Initiative. Canada's vast boreal forest stretches across more than 3.1 million square miles (5 million square kilometers), covering over half of Canada's land mass. The value of this unparalleled natural resource is considered in the report "Counting Canada's Natural Capital: Assessing the Real Value of Canada's Boreal Ecosystems." First, the gross market value of natural-capital extraction—related to logging, mining, oil and gas extraction, and hydropower generation—is added up. Next, subsidies and costs of natural-capital extraction—such as tax incentives and the health costs of air pollution—are subtracted. Finally, ecosystem-service values—flood control, water filtering, biodiversity value, carbon sequestration, and nature-related recreation—are considered.

When the final value is calculated, the boreal forest is worth far more money as a living ecosystem—two and a half times more, in fact. Does this mean that the boreal forest should never be touched by commercial interests? No, but it does mean that logging, mining, and other uses should only be allowed to the extent that they do not damage the services the boreal forest gives us. Assessing the full value of natural ecosystems, and considering them as assets in our accounting, helps us develop and prosper for the long term. In the big picture, local efficiency improvements are not enough—earth system limits as a whole have to be respected. To return to the business analogy, an efficient branch office or manufacturing plant isn't enough if a business as a whole burns through all its cash and credit. That's why the term *sustainable scale* is fundamental to ecological economics. It means ensuring that we don't overuse nonrenewable resources and get caught unprepared when they start to decline, as may happen with oil. And it means ensuring that we keep our environment healthy—setting limits on emissions of carbon and other pollutants and on the drawdown of water and soil resources.

The good news is that we've already developed many useful tools, like natural-assets accounting, efficiency and emission standards, tax shifts, and ecosystem credits. Understanding what conventional economic statistics hide or ignore can help citizens craft policies better adapted to the future, and help forward-thinking businesses gain a competitive advantage. With macrolimits and microflexibility, ecological economics can help us get our mental models in line with reality, making doing the right thing second nature. HM

Ecosystem Credits

"Ecosystem credits" are a bull market. These tradable permits are designed to protect threatened species and habitats without entirely restricting the commercial use of land. One of the elements of the Kyoto Protocol is the use of carbon "markets" as incentive for countries to reduce carbon dioxide emissions. Countries that produce CO_2 in amounts below the treaty limits, and countries not currently bound by the treaty (for now—other than the United States and Australia—mostly developing nations) can sell carbon-emission rights to countries that produce CO_2 in amounts above the treaty limits. This may just seem like a way for overproducing countries to continue spewing excess carbon dioxide, but it's actually a very good idea: few countries' emissions actually fall below the Kyoto limits, so there's considerable incentive to buy credits from nonparticipating or below-cap nations. As more countries get their emissions under control, the emissions cap will gradually be lowered, and the price of the remaining credits will go up; countries will therefore have an economic incentive to be net carbon-credit producers whose emissions fall below the cap, instead of consumers who exceed the CO_2 limits. It's an incentive for developing countries to adopt cleaner technologies sooner, so as to continue being sellers and not buyers as they grow.

The downsides to carbon trading are the complexity of the schemes, the likelihood of clever traders being able to "game" the markets, and incentive to hold out: potentially, when most other countries are operating below the cap and trying to sell remaining credits in the market, the price per unit will drop so substantially that even the most egregious emitter would be able to afford to operate unchanged.

The European Union established a system for trading carbon credits that went into effect in early 2005. The scheme involves more than 12,000 participants throughout the twenty-five European Union states. Compliance for each facility will be reported every year; therefore, noncompliance will be met not only with fines but also with disgrace. All transactions will be recorded in a common "Community Independent Transaction Log." But if you want to see who is buying and selling credits, you face a bit of a wait—detailed transaction information is being withheld for five years following initial implementation.

Emissions trading has been implemented to address various kinds of pollution, and not just in the developed world. A demonstration project in Taiwan and prototype schemes for sulfur-dioxide trading in China are promising signs for

Vernal pools, which appear seasonally in rural areas of California, are home to rare species, yet are not currently under the protection of the government.

the future. For landowners in the United States (developers, utility companies, state transportation agencies, farmers, retailers, and others), ecosystem credits can help turn land-use conflicts into win-win relationships that protect both the environment and companies' bottom lines. The Endangered Species Act and the Clean Water Act both require land developers to make up for any harm they do to streams, wetlands, or habitats critical to endangered and threatened species. Simply put, a developer or other commercial occupant that compromises or destroys habitats in one location is required to protect or restore habitats of comparable scope or value somewhere else.

As with carbon credits, land developers and owners can satisfy the law through "conservation banks," which protect land containing endangered species, and "mitigation banks," which protect wetlands and streams. In both cases, businesses putting habitats or wetlands at risk are required to purchase credits from other landowners who have legally committed to protecting their land permanently through the "banks." The

"bankers" can sell these credits on the open market, sometimes at levels far exceeding traditional real-estate values. JM

Biodiversity Farming for Profit

■■■■   You've probably never heard of the California vernal-pool fairy shrimp. Don't feel bad—these tiny crustaceans live out their entire lives in little puddles and ponds that come and go, and that often dry out completely in the summer.

But therein lies the problem: these ephemeral wetlands, as they're called, have been hammered by agriculture and development to the point that fairy shrimp are now a federally protected threatened species in the United States. This creates no end of problems for people who have vernal pools on land they wish to use for farming or other business.

Enter the Dove Ridge Conservation Bank. Dove Ridge offers "mitigation banking" for fairy shrimp. Instead of trying to work around the pools on their property, developers can buy "credits" from Dove Ridge, which maintains 233 acres (94 hectares) of fairy shrimp–filled pools. By purchasing these credits, for $70,000 apiece, developers can fulfill federal requirements to mitigate the damage they'll inevitably do to the critters' habitat.

Mitigation certainly isn't a perfect fix—after all, a human-made pool full of fairy shrimp isn't anything like a wild, teeming vernal pond—but Dove Ridge may be a harbinger of better things to come. What if we reimagined wilderness as a special kind of farm, the kind of farm that grows biodiversity and other ecosystem services? In the near future, the best way to save species and protect clean air and water may be to recognize that these can be measured, given value, and taken care of.

Ecosystem services are irreplaceable. As we move into the bloom of biomimetic technology, biodiversity becomes our most important natural resource. If local people can retain the rights to the economic value of local species, they'll have powerful incentive to cultivate biodiverse farms; this will be particularly advantageous to poor people, who will discover new ways to feed their families without destroying local ecosystems. In a similar way, if governments recognize the value of ecosystem services through tax breaks and regulations, farmers will have financial incentive to protect watercourses and restore soil. Right now it's hard to make a living in sustainable agriculture, but if there's a price tag on healthy farms, that will quickly change. EG

■■■■■ RESOURCES

The Economics of Ecosystems and Biodiversity (TEEB) Study
http://www.teebweb.org
An international initiative including the European Commission and the United Nations Environment Programme as just two of its partners, the TEEB study is a series of reports that aim to examine the costs of biodiversity loss, analyze different valuation methods for natural resources, and make suggestions to policy makers.

Under Ground: How Creatures of Mud and Dirt Shape Our World by Yvonne Baskin (Island Press, 2005)
Two-thirds of the earth's biodiversity lives in its terrestrial soils and underwater sediments—*Under Ground* gives us a glimpse into this otherwise

undiscovered world. More than simply weaving a tale of the fascinating and essential underground microbes and organisms busy at work making the planet habitable for humans, Baskin delivers a warning about the unseen effects of agriculture and development on the life systems under the earth's surface: "We usually take notice only when changes below ground set in motion a cascade of unwanted consequences above ground."

Ultimately, Baskin acknowledges that we aren't all going to share her passions, but she nevertheless seeks to inspire: "Most of us will never respond to microbes or nematodes with the emotional connection we muster for elephants and eagles . . . [but] my hope is that we can learn to step, not only lightly, but also with wonder and awareness on the world underground."

The Future of Life by Edward O. Wilson (Alfred A Knopf, 2002)
Biologist Edward O. Wilson is one of the world's most respected scientists. He's also one of the ones ringing the loudest alarm bells. *The Future of Life*, his call to arms, is an impassioned cry for us to recognize the importance and value of the diversity of life, and to accept the position we now find ourselves suddenly thrust into: that of having to decide between preserving the amazing natural riches that nourished our success as a species and risking the loss of both nature and civilization.

"On or about October 12, 1999, the world population reached 6 billion. It has continued to climb at an annual rate of 1.4 percent, adding 200,000 people each day or the equivalent of the population of a large city each week. The rate, although beginning to slow, is still basically exponential: the more people, the faster the growth, thence still more people sooner and an even faster growth, and so on, upward toward astronomical numbers, unless this trend is reversed and growth rate is reduced to zero or less. This exponentiation means that people born in 1950 were the first to see the human population double in their lifetime, from 2.5 billion to over 6 billion. During the twentieth century more people were added to the world than in all of previous human history."

Soil and Sustainable Agriculture

▬▬▬ Soil is the skin of the earth. It's the first point of contact between the planet and the atmosphere. The highly fertile top layer of soil—the uppermost twenty centimeters or so—is known as topsoil. Like the air we breathe, this layer of earth is so ordinary and ever-present that it is easy to take for granted. But it is absolutely essential to our lives, health, and prosperity.

By maintaining larger and larger farms, using giant machinery that tills the topsoil and kills all but the planned-for crops, planting giant monocultures (identical crops), and soaking the land in pesticides, weed killers, and chemical fertilizers, industrial agriculture strip-mines the soil.

As cultivated topsoil is scoured away by rain, or blown away by wind, what remains is less fertile. What's more, the steady chemical beating topsoil across the United States has taken over the last fifty years has killed off many of the micro-organisms that keep soil alive. Dead soil is no longer soil: it's just wet dust. In what were once the thriving farm towns of America's heartland, you can see what happens when topsoil is destroyed. You can see it in the fields themselves, in the dust clouds that blow through the region, and in the coffee-black run-off that swells the rivers with every serious storm.

The good news is that we're literally getting back to our roots, learning how to protect soil, and even build it back up, through farm practices that are better entwined with the original landscape, whether it be forest or prairie. We're also learning how to bolster the foodsheds around our cities and protect biodiversity in our fields and backyards, finding alternatives to the industrial monocrops that have played a big role in depleting this most basic, life-supporting resource. AS & EG

Terra Preta

▬▬▬ Amazonian dark earth, or *terra preta do indio,* has mystified science for the last hundred years. Three times richer in nitrogen and phosphorous than other soils and loaded with carbon, *terra preta* is the legacy of ancient Amazonians who predate Western civilization. Scientists who long debated the capacity of "savages" to transform the virgin rain forest now agree that indigenous people transformed large regions of the Amazon into a lush landscape based on amazingly fertile black earth. The Amazonians' techniques remain an enigma, but one plausible explanation is that they used slash-and-smolder methods, locking half the carbon in burnt vegetation into a stable form of biochar, instead of releasing the bulk of it into the atmosphere with typical slash-and-burn practices.

The difference between *terra preta* and ordinary soils is immense. A hectare of meter-deep terra preta can contain 250 tonnes of carbon, as opposed to 100 tonnes in unimproved soils from similar parent material, according to Bruno Glaser of the University of Bayreuth, Germany. To understand what this means, *terra preta* soils can have

Farms in the Global South, such as this one in the Andes, can be planned, planted, and harvested in a way that will yield crops for many generations using sustainable practices.

more carbon in them than is stored in all of the plants and trees above them. Furthermore, there seems to be no limit to how much biochar can be added to the soil.

Claims for biochar's capacity to capture carbon sound almost audacious. Johannes Lehmann, a soil scientist and author *of Amazonian Dark Earths: Origin, Properties, Management,* believes that a strategy combining biochar with biofuels could ultimately offset 9.5 billion tons of carbon per year—an amount equal to the total current annual fossil fuel emissions!

Indeed, there is profit to be made in this black earth; if green is the new black, then black could be the new green. Biofuels are touted as carbon neutral, but biofuels and biochar together promise to be carbon negative. Danny Day, the founder of a company called Eprida, is already exploring this concept with systems that turn farm waste into hydrogen, biofuel, and biochar.

The full beauty of *terra preta* appears in this closed loop. Unlike traditional carbon sequestration methods that show diminishing marginal returns—aquifers fill up, forests mature—practices based on *terra preta* see increasing returns. *Terra preta* doubles or even triples crop yields, and more growth means more *terra preta*, begetting a virtuous cycle.

While widespread deployment to build *terra preta* may be decades away, this practice already offers us a glimpse of how carbon-negative agriculture might work. DZ & CM

Prairielike Farms and Smart Breeding

▬▬▬ To put a stop to the degradation of our topsoil, we must change the way we farm. Today, we grow most crops on mass monocultural farms of annual plants. These farms require a huge amount of labor—including yearly plowing, which causes soil erosion—and huge quantities of chemical fertilizers and petroleum-based pesticides. To move beyond this type of farming, which locks us into constant service to compromised and degenerating land, we need to think of farms the way we think of prairies.

Wes Jackson, founder of the Land Institute, knows this. A fourth-generation Kansas farmer armed with a PhD in genetics, Jackson has devoted his life to demonstrating that "we have to farm the way nature farms" (Benyus, 2002). The edible prairie would be a complete revision of the present industrial agriculture we now employ, replacing the perpetual depleting of resources with a self-regenerating process more akin to nature. One of the first steps is the renewal of perennial crops. Most modern crops were bred from perennial wild relatives, and Native Americans in the Ohio and Mississippi valleys "farmed" wild knotweed, maygrass, marsh elder, and little barley prairie plants we now regard as weeds. Now, too many crops are annuals, which disallows the possibility of a farm with continuous life cycles. A prairielike farm would be able to start anew in spring without massive amounts of human and mechanical labor.

There's one big problem with prairielike farming, though: time. Plant-breeding programs take many generations to perfect, and experiments in building plant communities don't show results for years. Because our farms are in such bad shape, we don't have that kind of time—but we could use new technologies to breed the new hybrids faster.

Genetic modification of crops has become a notoriously controversial and widely protested science. But the same insights that have introduced little-studied and potentially dangerous crops into our food supply can yield safe and beneficial plants that may help rehabilitate agriculture.

Scientists have begun to discover, study, and develop the dormant characteristics that are an inherent part of the natural heritage of plants. The process of awakening these characteristics in plants—known as smart breeding—is akin to taking age-old agricultural techniques such as crossbreeding and hybridization and combining them with the highly refined genetic science of the twenty-first century.

Smart breeding produces plant varieties in much the same way traditional breeding does, but at a greatly accelerated pace. To create a new strain of tomato, farmers in the past would cross various existing tomatoes and see which hybrids and mutations grew best. That hit-or-miss approach is slow, since each new generation of plants must be grown out and its seeds harvested before the next generation can be planted. What's more, because mutation strikes randomly, a farmer's best, juiciest tomato may suddenly lose a gene critical to its juiciness. History shows that traditional breeding, while often successful given long time frames, is full of dead-ends, lost opportunities, and mistakes.

Smart breeding starts with the same plants but applies genetic analysis to figure out exactly which genes are responsible for the desired traits. Sometimes, the process takes the form of traditional breeding—keep this seed, toss that one—based on more precise knowledge. Other times, the process involves turning on or off specific genes in a plant's DNA—a goal achieved only at random in traditional breeding. Still other times, sequences of genes are lifted from one variety of a plant and introduced into another variety—something entirely possible on a traditional farm, but done by smart breeders in a way that doesn't introduce an element of uncertainty (how will that tomato's gene for frost resistance express itself in this tomato?).

But even when it involves cutting and pasting genes from one tomato into another, smart breeding more closely resembles nature than does the gene-splicing many of us fear, because there's no chance of crossbreeding two species that would not interbreed in the wild. Smart breeding and transgenics are as different as apples and anthrax. Even many biotech skeptics think smart breeding poses minuscule risk to human health or the environment.

The pay-offs, however, could be huge. Before factory farming, most crop species appeared in hundreds of varieties that were often admirably adapted to local soil types, weather patterns, and growing conditions. Replacing these many "heirloom" varieties with a few industrially bred ones not only allowed for the creation of the monocultures that corporate farms spray so vehemently to defend; it also drove many heirloom varieties into extinction. As we move away from petrochemical-based agriculture, we need to both rediscover and reinvent heirlooms.

Smart breeding could do even more, though, than help great-grandma's tomatoes make it through a scorching summer: it could deliver the kinds of plants we need to regenerate farmland. One result might be "super-organic" food crops bred with green biotechnology. Each plant of today and yesterday contains the genetic potential to thrive on the soil-conserving, biodiverse, prairielike farms of the future. A5

Green-water Credits

▬▬▬   Water scarcity is a major issue for rain-fed agriculture, which uses 75 percent of all agricultural water. Rain-fed agriculture is at the mercy of two things: rain and the capacity of soil to capture and store that rain. Rainfall that infiltrates and remains in the soil—also called green water—is the earth's largest freshwater resource. While farmers can't do much to make it rain, they can do a lot to help the soil retain green water.

According to the Food and Agriculture Organization of the United Nations, about 60 percent of the world's staple food production relies on green water; in sub-Saharan Africa, almost all agricultural food production depends on it. Modest measures like mulching, conservation tillage, and small-scale water harvesting can double or triple the amount of green water the soil retains. Other methods to increase green water and reduce runoff include terracing, contouring, and creating microbasins. Farmers in the developing world may know how to increase their green water by using such methods but lack the resources to do so.

You might think that development agencies would be clamoring to invest in such simple yet effective techniques, but as a policy brief from the International Soil Reference and Information Centre (ISRIC) so succinctly puts it, "Green water is ignored by engineers because they can't pipe or pump it, ignored by economists because they can't price it, and ignored by governments because they can't tax it." Instead, development agencies have traditionally favored "blue water," which refers to rainwater that doesn't stay in the soil but enters rivers, lakes, and groundwater. If you're an engineer, economist, or government official, investment in costly blue-water irrigation networks may make sense, but if you're a farmer trying to retain precious rainfall on your land, it surely doesn't.

Green-water credits—in which farmers are paid to practice good water management—provide an opportunity to address this problem while at the same time alleviating poverty and

ensuring the flow of ecosystem goods and services like flood control and healthy soil. The credits are not a form of charity, but rather an investment that is expected to yield returns greater than traditional large-scale, blue-water projects. The small scale of green-water investments makes them ideal for distributed, collaborative microloans that completely bypass large funding agents.

As an investment in local knowledge, green-water credits ultimately promise more than just increased rainfall retention. They leverage existing social capital to bring rural farmers out of poverty and reduce the negative effects of poor land management. Better use of green water benefits downstream users, too. When more water infiltrates the soil, less pesticide, sediment, and fertilizer enter the waterways. This translates into higher-quality water for domestic and industrial use and less dam-clogging sediment.

ISRIC is pioneering green-water credits with pilot programs in the Tana Basin, Kenya, and the Changjiang Basin, China, for the South-North Water Transfer Project. If all goes well, the organization will roll out the initiative globally.

Water scarcity is not only about water supply, just as hunger is not only about food.

Green-water credits are a solution that takes a systems perspective, approaching the interwoven issues of water, hunger, climate, and poverty together. DZ & CM

Heritage Breeds: Preserving Barnyard Biodiversity

▬▬▬ "When someone buys a $199 turkey from us, they're not buying a turkey," says Patrick Martins, cofounder of Heritage Foods USA. "They're buying a story."

The tale the pricey poultry tells is the comeback story of the Bourbon Red Turkey. Popular in the early twentieth century, the breed has teetered on the edge of extinction for years. Martins first became interested in rare, heritage breeds while raising and distributing 1,500 Bourbon Reds through Slow Food USA's [see Doing the Right Thing Can Be Delicious, p. 49] Heritage Turkey Project. The undertaking proved that it takes only a modest boost in the market to

Heritage turkeys on S&B Farm, Petaluma, California.

save a species: even this relatively small surge in demand improved the Bourbon Red's chances for survival; the breed's status went from "rare" to "watch" on conservation lists. Heritage Foods now works with small farmers to offer an ever-growing selection of rare types of pork, lamb, bison, and poultry.

The extinction of heritage breeds would be a profound loss to agricultural biodiversity—and to the taste buds of meat lovers everywhere. Breeds such as Berkshire Pork, Barred Plymouth Rock Chicken, and American Bronze Turkey definitely taste different—and in many cases, better—than the stuff you've been getting at the supermarket year after year. EG

Fiber CSAs

Special tags and labels are great for getting the backstory [see Knowing the Backstory, p. 39] on preassembled apparel, but what if you're a knitter? How can you guarantee the sustainability of your raw material? Juniper Moon Farm in Virginia offers one answer: join their Yarn CSA, the first such program in the United States.

Juniper spins sustainably harvested wool into yarn, which it then sells by subscription using the same model as Community Supported Agriculture ventures. Knitters receive a bountiful supply of sustainable, small-farm wool, and the farm can continue its good practices knowing it has a built-in subscriber base—the farm estimates that more than 80 percent of its shareholders resubscribe every year. The farm's blog keeps subscribers up to date on the lives of its sheep and encourages subscribers to join networking groups on sites like Ravelry.com so that they can share their experiences. AS

Buffalo Commons

The vast farms that span the central United States are dying by their own hand. Decades of shortsighted farming practices have resulted in eroded soils and depleted aquifers. With environmental damage compounded by job loss and steady out-migration, America's heartland faces a bleak future agriculturally.

But it's not too late to turn things around, and ideas abound—like the Buffalo Commons, a suite of ideas for ecological and social restoration of the Great Plains that's been circulating since the late 1980s and continues to carry revolutionary promise. The idea? Restore native grasslands of the Great Plains and bring back herds of buffalo.

The Great Plains Restoration Council (GPRC) envisions a decades-long effort, combining community building with the restoration of a continuous wildland corridor, extensive and spacious enough that populations of buffalo and other prairie wildlife will be able to roam freely once again. Reestablished buffalo herds could also be managed sustainably to supplement the beef industry with another kind of red meat.

Over the years the concept has stirred a surprising amount of controversy among Plains residents; however, as rural populations continue to dwindle and aquifers dry out, more people are embracing the idea. In 2009 the *Kansas City Star* ran an editorial calling for the establishment of Buffalo Commons National Park in northwest Kansas, partially as a way to recharge the Ogallala Aquifer—the region's major source of water—which is almost tapped out.

In the meantime, the GPRC pushes on, thousands of acres at a time. With help from its Restoration not Incarceration program—in which incarcerated males who volunteer receive "good behavior" credit and restoration education—the GPRC is gearing up to restore several thousand acres of coastal prairies outside of Houston. It is also planning a 100,000-acre refuge around existing ranchland in Mora County, New Mexico. EG & CB

Cow Power

Dairy cows produce copious milk. They also produce copious poop. It's not something most people think of as environmental pollution, but cow poop is a real problem when it's allowed to run into waterways and seep into the ground.

Opposite, left: An ICARDA scientist entering seed data into a handheld computer.

Opposite, right: Researchers testing New Rice for Africa (NERICA) seed samples, Kindia, Guinea, 2002.

But we don't have to let cow waste go to waste. If processed correctly, it can become a power source. That's just what Central Vermont Public Service (CVPS) has been doing with its Cow Power program, which promises to provide "renewable energy one cow at a time."

In order to reap power from poop, farms install an anaerobic digester which, over a period of twenty days or so, breaks down some of the collected poop's solids into acids, which feed bacteria, which in turn digest the manure and produce biogas. The gas is then pushed through a pipe into a modified natural gas engine, and electricity generated by burning the gas is fed into the CVPS system. The digester also produces a low-odor slurry that makes a fertilizer that is safer than raw manure.

Cow Power is a gracefully circular way for cattle to give a bit of energy back to the systems that support them. Participating dairy farmers get an additional source of income, almost literally turning waste into gold. And Vermonters who sign up for bovine-generated electricity support renewable energy and the state's traditional dairy-farming industry. EG

Seed Banks

▬▬▬   Most home gardeners know all about seed preservation—they meticulously save seeds from their best plants for use in next year's garden. Large-scale seed-saving operations, however, aim to achieve much more than another sweet batch of cherry tomatoes.

Seed banks aim to preserve humanity's agricultural heritage, acting both as a resource and a fail-safe. They help farmers actively promote diversity by reviving traditional crops and preserving the variety and abundance of domesticated plants—guarding against possible disasters. Seed banks are humanity's insurance against disaster, a promise to the future that farming, and thus civilization, will go on. The ultimate insurance policy is the so-called polar doomsday vault [see Restoring the Biosphere, p. 481], a massive seed bank in Norway that is a repository of millions of samples from all over the world. The operations below are smaller in scale, but more immediate—they are helping to restore food production in war-torn regions and helping farmers to grow traditional crops that have been nearly obliterated in the race to meet the demands of global markets. EG & AS

Native Seeds/SEARCH

Corn, beans, and squash are known as the "three sisters" of southwestern Native American agriculture. In the early 1980s some elders from the Tohono O'odham Nation wanted to revive one of these sisters, a variety of squash they remembered from their childhood. Enlisting the help of biologists and ethnobotanists, the elders were able to track down and obtain a handful of seeds. The hunt for these heirloom seeds led to the founding of Native Seeds/SEARCH (NS/S), a repository of crops traditionally grown by Native American nations from that region.

Today, NS/S grows the seeds of more than two thousand crop species, more than half of them relatives of the "three sisters." The other half includes grains, chilies, dyestuffs, and melons. The program has brought about a hundred crop species back from the edge of extinction.

Not only has NS/S helped to revive traditional Native American farming in the region—which had all but disappeared—and to preserve the biodiversity of the Southwest, it has boosted the health of the Tohono O'odham Nation's people. The nation, like many other indigenous North American groups, has suffered from endemic diabetes since adopting the typical Euro-American high-fat, high-sugar diet. Many of the native plants that Native Seeds/SEARCH has helped reintroduce to the region are specifically well suited to controlling diabetes; prickly pear paddles, for instance, are a great source of nutrients and of soluble fiber, which slows the rate of digestion, keeping the body's glucose levels more stable. Other crops simply serve as nutritious, high-protein staples that cost very little to cultivate.

Native Seeds/SEARCH has proven that traditional crops have a future.

International Center for Agricultural Research in the Dry Areas

Farming dry, arid land poses complex challenges, and the crops we've bred over generations to grow well in places that have little water are both a heritage and a toolbox. The International Center for Agricultural Research in the Dry Areas (ICARDA), located in northern Syria, banks seeds from 131,000 varieties of plants, gathered from arid regions across the Middle East, Central Asia, and North Africa. In protecting and enhancing native staple crops, ICARDA works to alleviate poverty by boosting agricultural productivity. Samples from the seed bank have also been used to reintroduce crops into war-torn Afghanistan. EG & AS

Global Crop Diversity Trust

The Global Crop Diversity Trust (GCDT) is both the net and the umbrella of the world's seed banks. Many seed banks are lost as a result of catastrophe or a lack of funding. Grants from governments, foundations, and private corporations allow the GCDT to secure consistent funding for the preservation of crop diversity around the world. The endowment enables people with a close connection to agriculture and the land who otherwise have few or no resources to ensure a livelihood for future generations. The GCDT makes seed banks a global priority and provides them with the funding they need to survive. EG & AS

Sangams

Small farmers also play a significant role in protecting seed diversity. The Centre for Indian Knowledge Systems (CIKS) in the state of Tamil Nadu, India, works with hundreds of small farmers to form groups, called *sangams*, wherein farmers work together on programs to maintain organic farming practices, or sell biopesticides to supplement their incomes. These *sangams* also manage community seed banks. The center provides the initial funds needed to construct the storage facilities, after which *sangam* members themselves maintain the seed banks, making small monthly contributions to a communal bank account, and electing officials to oversee the borrowing and replenishing of seed stocks.

Navdanya, a related organization based in New Dehli and Uttaranchal, in northern India, has been running a rigorous indigenous seed-bank program that has saved and stored hundreds of varieties of seeds, including two thousand varieties of rice in forty seed banks in thirteen Indian states. Some 70,000 small farmers belong to the organization, and their efforts are proving that local seeds and local knowledge, just as much as science and technology, hold the keys to creating the agriculture of the future. ZH

Edible Forests

Even if I should learn that the world would end tomorrow, I would still plant this apple tree today.
Martin Luther

▬▬▬ Here's one piece of the agricultural puzzle, something almost anyone can do: plant trees that provide food. For better or worse, we all have to learn to tend the earth like a garden now, and "food forests" are one important way to do that.

The idea is simple in theory, rich and complex in practice: mimic a successional forest, using trees, shrubs, ground covers, herbs, fungi, and roots that reinforce one another, enhance ecological health, and yield food, fiber, fuel, medicine, and habitat for people. Although we've obtained food from trees for millennia, our main practice has been to farm surfaces. Now we need to farm in three dimensions, stacking crops in layers, from canopy to root zone.

Forest gardens and forest farms can be made at many scales, from urban backyards to whole countries, and in many climates, from tropical to arid to temperate. They can be a vital part of bright green cities, renewing the health and vigor of their scattered patches of vacant land. They can have other positive effects as well: shortening the journey from farm to table, helping to cool urban heat islands (where the effects of climate change are often worst), and even helping to decontaminate polluted soils through mycoremediation [see Healing Polluted Land, p. 226].

Where people are desperate, tree crops bring hope; forests can be worth more to people standing than cut down. Examples of tree forests are everywhere: a prominent one is the Green Belt Movement founded by Nobel Peace Prize–winner Wangari Maathai, which has planted 40 million trees across the African continent, reducing erosion in critical watersheds and restoring biodiversity corridors. Though not as well publicized, similar efforts are being undertaken by organizations like Seed Tree, which is working with South American communities to plant native trees.

Food forests are not just the pet projects of NGOs: according to the Nairobi-based World Agroforestry Centre, nearly half of the world's farmlands have at least 10 percent tree cover, more than 380,000 square miles (10 million square kilometers) in total. The UN Environment Programme (UNEP), which has held several World Agroforestry Congresses, estimates that if agroforestry were to be widely adopted, reforested farmland could sequester up to six gigatons of CO_2 equivalent by 2030. Agroforestry even has the ability to reclaim land that has been lost to desertification. As reported in an October 2006 article in *NewScientist*: "Tree planting has led to the re-greening of as much as 3 million hectares of land in Niger, enabling some 250,000 hectares to be farmed again. The land became barren in the 1970s and early 1980s through poor management and felling of trees for firewood, but since the mid-1980s farmers in parts of Niger have been protecting them instead of chopping them down."

Forest farms and gardens can serve the planet, but they are necessarily place-based. Sources for edible trees, shrubs, herbs, and mushrooms are fitted to particular biomes. Every region has its heritage of edible tree crops and,

like people, every cultivar has its own personality and needs.

Cultivating trees teaches patience; whether we're developing management plans, learning coppice rotations, or breeding disease-resistant varieties, it's work that spans years, decades, and centuries. Trees teach humility, too. Losing an annual crop is difficult; losing an orchard is heartbreaking.

Edible forests are the "great hope and many little hopes," in the words of J. Russell Smith, whose book *Tree Crops: A Permanent Agriculture*, first published in 1929, is a classic text on the subject. Instruction in tree planting abounds: there are many books, including recent, comprehensive instruction manuals, and even online courses. But the best way to learn is to do: happy planting! DF

San Francisco Foodshed Project

■■■■ San Francisco may have a thriving arts scene, proximity to the nation's tech hub, and an entrepreneurial spirit, but can it feed itself?

In 2008 the American Farmland Trust completed a feasibility study to determine whether San Francisco could create a healthy and sustainable foodshed, sourcing most of its food (an estimated 20 million tons per year for this study) from farms and local purveyors within one hundred miles of the Golden Gate Bridge.

Compared to most cities, San Francisco is at the center of a virtual Garden of Eden. As the report notes, the city is surrounded by viable agricultural land to the north and south: the Salinas Valley provides enough greens and produce to make it one of the nation's premier growing areas; the Sonoma Valley is best known for wine production but has diverse cropland; and the Santa Clara Valley still has many orchards despite being transformed into a tech hub. Nonetheless, San Francisco is still reliant on food that travels thousands of miles to reach the city. That dependence on imported food will only grow if trends continue: the agricultural areas closest to the city are continually threatened by development. As the study notes, "12 percent of [San Francisco's] foodshed study area is already developed and new development is consuming farmland at the rate of an acre for every 9.7 residents. If this continues, 800,000 more acres of farmland will be lost by 2050."

But the report also provides many suggestions for the city to invest more in its foodshed. Some, like offering financial incentives or conservation easements to farmers, focus on merely increasing the amount of surrounding farmland. Others address ways to ensure consumer participation and enthusiasm, like creating infrastructure to preserve favorite foods for out-of-season consumption or producing more local versions of snacks and fast foods (recognizing that these account for a big portion of most people's diets).

Understanding a city's potential to create a viable foodshed—or support an existing one—is of vital importance. As the planet urbanizes and fuel costs rise, a good foodshed could make or break a city economically. Protecting a city's food-shed and strengthening the farming within it are basic resilience strategies in an era of decreasing food security. That it also makes for a greener and more livable region is just one more reason to start our foodsheds now. CB

The Benefits of Bioengineered Crops

▬▬▬   Transgenic genetically modified (GM) crops are a risky work in progress. The health effects of eating, for example, a tomato into which genetic material from a salmon has been introduced are simply not known—the impact on the human body may be minimal, but we can't yet speculate. The environmental risks of farming GM crops are significant—genetic engineering introduces into the environment self-reproducing species that haven't existed long enough to be studied in depth. The race to develop GM crops is largely an attempt by large corporations to monopolize factory farming, and raises huge social and economic questions. Corporate research into GM crops is not geared toward redesigning crops for free distribution to the world's poorer farmers but toward design-patented products that prop up agribusiness and generate wealth for a powerful few.

Nonetheless, genetic modification is not inherently evil, and when applied with wisdom,

it can have positive results. An excellent example is New Rice for Africa (NERICA), a strain of rice that may succeed in bettering health in West and Central Africa, restoring agricultural sustainability there, and improving the economics of food importation in the regions.

The great benefit of NERICA is that it mixes African rice (*Oryza glaberrima*)—which is highly resistant to drought and local pests but which has a very low yield (triggering widespread slash-and-burn farming)—and Asian rice (*Oryza sativa*)—which has a very high yield per plant but is much more sensitive to environmental conditions (triggering increased use of pesticides). These two species of rice do not cross naturally or through traditional hybridization techniques—the genetic differences are just too great—but biotechnology has produced more than three thousand NERICA lines, allowing farmers to choose those that best fit their regional needs. In making use of 1,500 varieties of African rice that were facing extinction, the NERICA initiative has helped to preserve genetic lines at risk as farmers shift to higher-yield Asian varieties.

And NERICA reaches beyond Africa: 42 million acres (17 million hectares) of rice in Asia and 9 million acres (4 million hectares) in Latin America grow in conditions similar to West Africa's. AS & JC

▬▬▬   RESOURCES

Dirt: The Erosion of Civilizations by David Montgomery (University of California Press, 2007) David Montgomery is a MacArthur "Genius" Award winner and University of Washington professor of geomorphology whose research has made fundamental contributions to the understanding of how soils and rivers have shaped civilizations, past and present. *Dirt* is a compelling mix of history, archaeology, and geology, and makes a persuasive argument that soil is humanity's most essential natural resource. SC

International Biochar Initiative
http://www.biochar-international.org
The IBI was founded in 2006 to both promote biochar as a tool to fight global warming and to set standards for the emerging biochar industry.

The organization's site has a lot of information on biochar technologies and the policy objectives that might help to make this practice more widespread.

The Soul of Soil: A Soil-Building Guide for Master Gardeners and Farmers by Grace Gershuny and Joe Smillie (Chelsea Green Publishing, 1999)

To understand soil as the foundation on which all agricultural activities are built is the first step in "honoring our oneness with all living creatures and helping the long process of repair that a new biological era will require," argue Gershuny and Smillie. The Soul of Soil is indispensable to understanding soil—the texture, smell, uses, and energies inherent to it—and serves as a simple primer on the basic tenets of sustainable agriculture. In presenting the principles of ecological soil management, Gershuny and Smillie hand us a veritable tool kit of ways to care for and nurture the soil under our feet.

Permaculture Research Institute of Australia
http://permaculture.org.au

"Permaculture" (permanent agriculture), a term coined by Australian naturalist Bill Mollison, describes farms that are in fact complex ecosystems. Permaculturists observe and interact with nature, creating unique feedback loops where all systems work in harmony. One can see why corn, beans, and squash—the crops grown together on milpas, traditional Mesoamerican farms—flourish in the presence of one another: corn stalks serve as bean poles, beans capture nitrogen from the air and fix it in the soil, while squash serves as a ground cover that deters weeds from taking root.

Permaculture operates on twelve principles (see them all at http://permacultureprinciples .com), including "use small and slow solutions" and "integrate rather than separate," and it encompasses more than just agricultural systems—some enthusiasts suggest that permaculture ideas can be used to redesign cities. Mollison and his colleague Geoff Lawton have both written extensively on permaculture design; PRI's Web site provides an introduction to their ideas and their Permaculture Master Plan, which aims to create permaculture centers worldwide. SOC

The Essential Agrarian Reader: The Future of Culture, Community, and the Land edited by Norman Wirzba (Shoemaker and Hoard, 2004)

There's no doubt that the last century has been witness to a concerted movement away from agrarianism and toward a globalized, industrialized planet—with avocados from California, rice from Thailand, coffee from Colombia. Concerned that fewer and fewer people actually know or care about their food's source or its production, and alarmed by the new global order, Wirzba expounds the modern agrarian movement's push for responsible action in the interest of lessening the divide between the production and consumption of food. "However much we might think of ourselves as post-agricultural beings or disembodied minds, the fact of the matter is that we are inextricably tied to the land through our bodies—we have to eat, drink, and breathe—and so our culture must always be sympathetic to the responsibilities of agriculture," Wirzba writes. His book is, in many ways, an homage to the work of farmer-poet Wendell Berry, and it teaches important lessons about the American agrarian past and the possibilities and necessities of an agrarian future.

The One-Straw Revolution: An Introduction to Natural Farming by Masanobu Fukuoka (Gardners Books, 1992)

From a small village on the island of Shikoku in southern Japan comes a story that brings together the classic elements of Taoist innovation: observation, insight, and a cheerful disregard for conventional wisdom. While walking past an old, unplowed field one day, Masanobu Fukuoka noticed healthy rice seedlings growing among the weeds. Emulating the conditions that these seedlings grew in, he stopped plowing his farm or flooding his fields to grow rice, as conventional practice would dictate. Instead, Fukuoka pioneered a method of natural farming that has resulted in his fields' being unplowed for twenty-five years, yet producing yields comparable to other Japanese farms. His methods require no machines or fossil fuels and create no pollution. Drawing on a faith in natural cycles, the Fukuoka method demonstrates a way of farming that means interfering with nature as little as possible. Fukuoka's innovative method of farming, dubbed the

One Straw Revolution, has won supporters and adherents around the world, where his methods have been adapted to local conditions. ZH

Meeting the Expectations of the Land by Wes Jackson, Wendell Berry, Bruce Colman (North Point Press, 1985)
A classic in the field, this book of essays about the nature of good farming still speaks sense twenty-odd years after it was written, by reminding us that all agriculture depends on certain fundamentals: soil, sun, and water—certainly—but also care, intelligence, and a respect for legacy.

The Land Institute
http://www.landinstitute.org
Wes Jackson's Land Institute does much-needed work on changing farming practices to work with nature. Those with a serious interest in the subject will find the institute's reports and studies invaluable.

Hungry Planet: What the World Eats by Peter Menzel and Faith D'Aluisio (Ten Speed Press, 2005)
Sometimes the best way to gain a wide-angle perspective on a global situation is to piece together a number of close-ups. Authors Menzel and D'Aluisio do just that in *Hungry Planet,* profiling thirty families from around the world and combining stunning photographic essays with descriptions of each family's weekly food intake.

Working toward sustainable forestry is essential to the health of the planet, Northern Borneo, Malaysia.

Sustainable Forestry

■■■■■ Wood and paper products might seem to be an environmentalist's best friends. After all, they're made of a renewable raw material—unlike, say, plastic bags, each of which sends a dollop of petroleum on a one-way trip to the dump. But the devil is in the details. Factors such as economic desperation, lax regulation, and greed have conspired to make logging a problematic venture for both wildlife and humans.

Some environmentalists would have us believe that every logging job is as bad as a clear-cut—that parkland is the only good use of a forest. That view ignores the emergence of sustainable forestry, a full-fledged industry that aims to reap a steady harvest from the forest for generations to come, while maintaining the integrity of ecosystems and social fabrics.

When we practice sustainable forestry, we care for the forest as a whole system, made up of creatures from soil fungi to spotted owls, from lizards to loggers. In return, the forest offers a host of materials and services: not just lumber, but clean water downstream, food for animals and humans alike, recreation opportunities, and carbon storage—which means that the trees absorb CO_2 from the atmosphere, offering some potential for short-term relief from global warming.

When we adopt sustainable forestry, we commit ourselves to several principles that depart from common industrial practice: We harvest trees no faster than the forest grows back, instead of liquidating the forest and cutting trees at ever-younger ages. We log so that all the forest's native species continue to thrive, not just a few commercially significant timber varieties. We respect timber workers' labor rights,

instead of busting unions whenever possible. We plow profits back into the maintenance and restoration of the forest, instead of sucking it dry and moving on to clear-cut somewhere else.

Sustainable forestry is still being defined through attentive experimentation, but it's no longer just the domain of a few concerned entrepreneurs. Loggers and environmentalists are working side by side to find responsible ways to make forests more resistant to fire; even bureaucrats in New York City have had to promote sustainable forestry to ensure the safety of their city's water supply. Whatever the motivation of the players, the outcome is the same: healthier forests equal a healthier planet. SZ

Forests: More Than Just Lumber with Leaves

In the 1990s, environmental regulators told New York City officials that they needed to begin filtering the city's municipal water supply.

The water cops weren't imagining the problem: New Yorkers had already dealt with repeated orders to boil their drinking water because of microbial contamination.

Building a filtration plant to clean up the city's water would have cost $6 billion. Instead, the city decided to go directly to the source: the Catskill Mountains, a hundred miles northwest of the metropolis, where a 1,600-square-mile (4,100-square-kilometer) basin, most of it in private hands, supplies 90 percent of New York City's water. The city realized that if it could entice private landowners to take better care of the area, its water supply would be clean enough to satisfy the water cops. In 1997, New York made a pact with the towns in and around the Catskills to improve the watershed, achieving cleaner water for the city at one-fourth the cost of a new filtration plant.

What does all this have to do with sustainable forestry? Watershed-altering timber practices were part of the agreement, along with improved dairy farms and septic systems. Logging can send sediment coursing into creeks, where it fouls downstream reservoirs. The city of New York has funded more than five hundred forest-management plans covering 94,000 acres (38,000 hectares), bought and retired the development rights to forest land, and helped loggers harvest less disruptively. It even supplies temporary bridges for creek crossings, where loggers would ordinarily muddy the stream by driving right through it. The program also backs woodworking businesses in the Catskills, on the theory that a strong forest economy will prevent the subdivision of wooded land for residential development. It all boils down to recognizing that the forest is worth vastly more than its lumber.

The Catskills isn't the only area where sustainable logging has been part of a broader effort to value the forest as a whole system. For instance, British Columbia's 2006 Great Bear Rainforest settlement put aside 5 million acres (2 million hectares) of coastal forest, while leaving 10 million acres (4 million hectares) open to selective logging that steers clear of bear dens, streams where salmon spawn, and sites sacred to native peoples. The province has also promised more than $100 million for ecofriendly development in the region. 5Z

Playing with Fire

▬▬▬▬ For the last hundred years, the wildfire has been the boorish cousin of the American West. No matter how hard we try to schedule family gatherings without it, eventually it crashes the party and makes a scene.

As with flesh-and-blood cousins, the wildfire problem is aggravated by our attempts to keep the troublemaker out of the picture entirely. A century of dogged efforts to extinguish all wildfires turned terrain into tinder, choked with thickets of small trees and dead wood, which explode into infernos when conditions are right.

With more people living in and around the forests of the West, those inevitable conflagrations kindled fear on all sides of the timber wars. Defenders of old-growth forests sat down with the loggers who'd been cutting the big trees, and all agreed they had to make the forests more fire-resistant. For a solution, they looked to the forests that greeted the first European settlers to the States: widely spaced, older trees whose thick bark protected them from scorching when

the underbrush between them was cleared by frequent, low-intensity fires. They realized that fire is a natural presence in the forest, and that fires sparked by lightning and native peoples have shaped the landscape for thousands of years. But throughout the twentieth century, an aggressive forest-fire-fighting policy had allowed fuel to accumulate instead of burning off harmlessly; decades of clear-cuts, replanted with dense tree farms, added highly combustible fuel to any wildfires that escaped our attempts to contain them.

The new fire coalition did not aim to stamp out wildfire entirely. Instead, it sought to keep fires from torching people's homes. To achieve that end, coalition members decided to thin the forest, removing dead and dying trees that could carry a wildfire from the forest floor into the canopy, where it would rage out of control. Fewer, more widely spaced trees would also be less apt to set each other alight, and soil moisture would be shared among fewer trees, making them less fire-prone.

Younger forests near rural towns were the natural candidates for the first experiments. Rural workers were pleased with the promise of new jobs and raw materials, and environmentalists were relieved that the focus had shifted from protecting primeval forests exclusively to working with younger ones. These stands had already been logged at least once, and the loggers would selectively cut only the smaller trees, instead of clear-cutting it all.

In the northern California town of Hayfork, the Watershed Research and Training Center is spearheading efforts to thin the already logged national forest for small firs, pines, oaks, and other hardwoods. A local business has sprung up to turn the timber into flooring and furniture, which it sells to Whole Foods Market, among other clients. The small trees are a far cry from the behemoths that had been cut to make plywood and lumber a decade earlier, but Big Timber had been forced to close up shop in Hayfork after a fracas over threatened owls and fish limited logging in the area.

In Arizona, one of the largest projects of this kind is yearly turning the cuttings from forest thinning into 65,000 tons (59,000 metric tons) of wood pellets for home heating. This has led the project operators to an opportunity to thin another 15,000 acres (6,000 hectares) annually—unopposed by environmental groups, despite its scale. This is the kind of logging we can all agree on. SZ

Certification

■■■■ Standing in a lumberyard or a home-improvement store, it's hard not to feel a little ambivalent: we need the wood stacked around us for our projects and homes, but we can't escape the realization that the planks were, until recently, trees swaying in the wind on verdant hillsides. How can we tell if the two-by-four we're about to purchase came from a muddy clear-cut or a careful, selective harvest? Did it have the tree's equivalent of a happy, cage-free, grass-fed life?

Forestry nerds spent the better part of the mid-1990s figuring out how a wood buyer could answer those questions. The result was a system of third-party certification, in which a trusted entity separate from both the buyer and the timber industry vouches for the wood. The Forest Stewardship Council (FSC)—an independent agency including environmentalists, foresters, and indigenous peoples—sets the standard. Accredited audit firms inspect forests and mills; the ones that pass may affix the FSC trademark to their wood. Globally, 168 million acres (68 million hectares) are currently certified. It may sound like a lot, but combined, that worldwide total only actually equals the size of Texas. FSC's "chain of custody" certification continues for every piece of wood after it leaves the forest or mill—any operation or retailer that makes, relabels, or repackages FSC-certified products must get this certification in order to sell any products bearing FSC stamps or trademarks.

Originally, certification visionaries hoped the stamp of approval would result in a higher price for certified timber, to compensate forest managers for doing a more careful job. But it's turned out that most buyers are extraordinarily price conscious and are unwilling to pay more for certified lumber. Instead, sustainable suppliers gained an advantage when major retailers like Home Depot began giving preference to certified lumber. Further impetus has come from the LEED green-building program, which awards one of its coveted points for using FSC-blessed wood.

Beware of imitations: a year after FSC started up, Big Timber's main trade association, the American Forest and Paper Association (AF&PA), created its own standard, called the Sustainable Forestry Initiative (SFI). For all its slick public relations, SFI has yet to shake its reputation as an industry greenwashing group. The tip-off? Every last member of the AF&PA, from International Paper on down, has won certification, despite their widespread practices of clear-cutting and raising single-species tree farms. SZ

Investing in Sustainable Timber

■■■■ Spencer Beebe and Bettina von Hagen of Ecotrust are committed to the kind of long-term ecologically and socially responsible forestry that is independently certified by the Forest Stewardship Council. With backgrounds that span finance and conservation, Beebe and von Hagen have led the development of a new kind of forestland investment fund that derives returns not just from timber harvests, but also from ecosystem services including carbon storage, nontimber forest products, and habitat provision. Unlike conventional timberland investment funds that emphasize maximum harvests followed by land disposition over a ten-year life span, Ecotrust Forests LLC is managed for perpetual, multigeneration returns and long-term land ownership and management.

The Ecotrust Forests LLC fund estimates that its returns will be competitive with conventional timberland investment funds when taking into account emerging markets in ecosystem services like water filtration, enhanced habitat, and carbon storage. For instance, longer-term harvesting rotations (sixty-five years or more) allow significantly more average biomass/carbon to be stored than conventional short-term industrial harvesting rotations (thirty to forty years). This increase in carbon storage can be marketed as carbon credits to entities who want to remain Kyoto compliant. Monetizing carbon storage allows Ecotrust Forests LLC to provide competitive returns, even with its emphasis on forest restoration during the first several years after acquiring a parcel. SC

■■■■■   RESOURCES

More Tree Talk: The People, Politics, and Economics of Timber by Ray Raphael (Island Press, 1994)
More Tree Talk offers an excellent introduction to the human and technical landscape of forestry. In a style reminiscent of prize-winning author and radio broadcast personality Studs Terkel, Ray Raphael gives a record of his conversations with representative players in the forestry scene, from lumberjacks to forest ecologists, rangers to mill owners, in an engaging format.

Towards Forest Sustainability edited by David B. Lindenmayer and Jerry F. Franklin (Island Press, 2003)
Don't be daunted: this book may be packed with information, but it's an easy read. It includes a collection of essays on the latest developments in forestry in North America, Scandinavia, and Australasia.

Ecoforestry: The Art and Science of Sustainable Forest Use edited by Alan Drengson and Duncan Taylor (New Society Publishers, 1997)
In this solid anthology, scientists and practitioners lay out a multifaceted approach to sustainable forestry.

This pelagic snail was collected from the deep Arctic Canada Basin. As global warming takes its toll on polar regions, the need to document these underexplored areas intensifies.

Oceans Are the New Atmosphere

■■■■■   Oceans are the new atmosphere. That is, concern for the state of the oceans and the potential impact of the ongoing catastrophic collapse of ocean ecosystems is reaching a pitch that we haven't seen for any other environmental issue except the build-up of greenhouse gases in the atmosphere.

We don't live in our oceans—many people have never even seen them—but we're handily trashing them. And the state of the oceans is inextricably linked to the state of the planet as a whole. Simply put, if the oceans crash, we crash. And although the signs of impending collapse are everywhere, new solutions and policies may give us the capacity to understand and prevent that crash, if we have the will.

Throughout recent history, most of the human impact on the Earth's oceans has stemmed from a dramatic misunderstanding of both their value and their limits. For all the romance with which we've viewed them in art and literature, in reality we've used the oceans as waste dumps, as all-you-can-eat buffets, and as highways for global exploration, commerce, and warfare.

The vast dead zones now spreading out from our coastlines appear to be largely the result of the rivers of chemicals, fertilizer runoff, and sewage we've been pouring into the sea for decades. The mountains of more solid and buoyant waste (like household garbage) that many communities still dump directly into the nearest ocean are accumulating in shocking volumes—the infamous Pacific garbage patch is now the size of the state of Texas—and degrading with unknown results.

Most troubling of all is ocean acidification, the result of oceans absorbing the CO_2 that we spew into the atmosphere. There is increasing evidence that the problem of ocean acidification is worsening rapidly, foreshadowing potential impacts that could be catastrophic for all life on Earth. What's more, the more acidic the oceans become, the less able they are to act as carbon sinks. A recent report showed that the oceans' CO_2 uptake rate appears to have dropped by 10 percent from 2000 to 2007.

The only sensible response to this condition is a massive and aggressive planetary effort to first eliminate excess greenhouse-gas emissions, and then begin pulling CO_2 from the atmosphere through safe, terrestrial methods such as afforestation and the use of biochar. These should be combined, scientists say, with strong measures designed to curb the sorts of pollutants that are now killing huge portions of the ocean floor—a problem that may worsen as climate change continues to raise sea levels and increase flooding.

Although we often treat oceans (or the parts closest to us) as though they have defined borders and governing bodies, in reality they are, well, fluid. And as with nearly every other system affected by climate change, there is no fair distribution of cause and effect. Rather, the destruction caused by some of us touches the lives of all of us, and any protective effort is only as good as the actions of the worst offender.

This is why we need to start pursuing global ocean initiatives as we work toward global climate initiatives. The laws applying to ocean resources must be strengthened. It will take an unprecedented intergovernmental pact to recognize and chart a path toward globally equitable and sustainable methods for extracting food, minerals, oil, and other substances from the sea. We need to establish planetary agreements on limits for fisheries that recognize the nonlinear quality of their recent collapses. We must create and enforce marine sanctuaries, fund new research into fisheries, develop new approaches to ocean science, and put what we already know about sustainable coastal development to work for people living in the most sensitive regions.

International alliances already recognize the importance of this task. Among existing agreements and accords are those outlined by the APEC nations' Bali Plan of Action Towards Healthy Oceans and Coasts for the Sustainable Growth and Prosperity of the Asia-Pacific Community. But, as the Global Forum on Oceans, Coasts and Islands notes in one of its project outlines, the problem with managing the world's seas stems largely from the fact that "to date there is no consensus on the various legal and policy issues surrounding marine areas beyond national jurisdiction, and there are many different options being elaborated and discussed about how these issues should be resolved." It is clear that we need a more complete agreement on how to govern, use, and preserve the oceans.

As we urge our leaders to work toward this vision, one of the best things we can do as planetary citizens is to arm ourselves with knowledge and appreciation of these awe-inspiring bodies of water and the worlds they contain below the waves. We need more people around the world to learn about oceans, what they are, and why they matter. The journey from keyboard to kayak, or from computer screen to concern for coral reefs, seems daunting, but learning from the Web is certainly a step in the right direction.

Yet we need much, much more: more journalism, more education, more advocacy. Somehow, we've got to come to grips with the fact that the planet we live on doesn't stop at the beach, and act accordingly. AS & JVL

The Technology of Ocean Exploration

▬▬▬ Robot submarines. Deep-sea sensors. Radio-tagged fish. DNA analysis. Satellite mapping. Not long ago, oceanography meant dipping a net over the side of a boat. Those days are long gone.

Oceanographers and ocean biologists now have technologies at their fingertips that rival those of space explorers. As oceanographer James Lindholm of the Pfleger Institute says, "For every tool we have to explore outer space—space stations, tethered missions, rovers, mapping—we have a comparable tool for ocean exploration . . . This suite of technologies allows us to study an environment that is equally hostile to human life" (SeaWeb, 2005).

Some of what we're learning about the oceans comes as a direct result of space research—like the work of satellites that can see across the breadth of the electromagnetic spectrum, peering into the ocean's depths and identifying changes in temperature and chemistry. NASA's Aqua satellite, part of its Earth Observing System network of satellites, and the European Space Agency's Envirosat are mapping plankton levels, pollution, and ocean temperatures. Satellites, though, can only see into upper ocean levels. To plumb the deepest parts of the ocean, we need to take a dive—with sensors, submersibles, and robotic "autonomous underwater vehicles."

Underwater gliders are doing a lot of the work. These vessels use small changes in buoyancy in conjunction with their wings to propel themselves and turn vertical motion into forward movement with very little power. This lets them travel for thousands of miles and for months at a time, enabling studies of undersea regions in far greater detail than ever before possible. They're also very gentle on the environment—since they don't have external thrusters, they don't stir up sediment, and there are no exhaust fumes or dripping oils to pollute the ocean.

What we're finding, thanks to all this technology, is truly extraordinary: whole ecosystems we had no clue even existed a couple of decades ago; weird, nonsolar forests of giant worms living off the heat and sulfur around volcanic vents miles beneath the surface; and odd food chains of fish that live off falling scraps from the surface, feeding and breeding in complete darkness.

Given the dire state of the oceans, this oceanographic revolution couldn't come at a better time. JC

Plankton, Reefs, and Undersea Canaries

▬▬▬   How do you feel about phytoplankton? You should be a big fan. These microscopic creatures that swim around at the bottom of the ocean food chain are pretty much the closest thing on the planet to a foundation for life. They feed the ocean's animals. They also produce around half of the oxygen in our atmosphere. But phytoplankton are very sensitive to water temperature—crank up the heat, and they don't feed or breed as well. Because of this, they serve as some of the most important indicators for ocean researchers studying the effects of global warming. If the phytoplankton aren't faring well, it's a pretty good warning sign. They're the canaries in the oceanic coal mine.

Those canaries aren't doing so well. A major study published in the journal *Nature* in July 2010 found that between 1950 and 2008, phytoplankton in the world's oceans declined 40 percent, apparently because warmer water on the surface of the oceans has prevented deeper, nutrient-rich water from rising to the surface as it did in the past. If the trend continues, the entire ocean food chain could be at risk. Even if the plankton decline proves to be smaller or more reversible than thought, it is still an alarming example of the extent of the changes we're bringing to the planet.

Bleached coral documented by the Centre for Marine Studies in Queensland, Australia, reveals that the Great Barrier Reef has been damaged by rising water temperatures caused by global warming.

The effect of global warming on coral reefs—the rain forests of the ocean—is more direct. Warming waters can cause "heat shock," bleaching reefs and quickly killing them, while increased carbon dioxide in the water makes reefs more acidic and brittle. Research suggests that by the midpoint of this century, the rate of degradation of reefs will outpace their ability to self-repair, essentially killing them off.

Fortunately, such a result isn't inevitable. Swift action to reduce greenhouse-gas emissions will help slow the acidic-reef effect, and there are several ways to encourage greater coral reef growth. The traditional way of seeding reefs is to intentionally sink a ship (or sometimes an oil-drilling platform), and wait for it to acquire mineral buildup. But clearly this is an invasive approach. More recently, the Global Coral Reef Alliance started using small electric charges to accelerate mineral accretion in a small fledgling reef structure. This approach allows new reefs to form in areas too damaged to support natural reef restoration—and it's a whole lot better for the ocean than sinking oil-drilling platforms. JC & CB

Protecting Biological Resources on the Deep Ocean Floor

■■■■■■ The deep ocean's diversity of strange life-forms—quite different from life as we know it anywhere else on the planet—makes it of real interest to bioprospectors, people who plumb living things for materials and chemicals that may have medical or commercial viability. While commercial exploitation of deep-sea genetic resources is still a ways off, such exploitation could bring real problems, from the enclosure of genetic rights to the destruction of vulnerable deep-sea habitats.

Sam Johnston, one of the authors of a recent UN study on the issue, says that because the field is in its early stages of development, we still have time to create a legal framework for deep-sea bioprospecting: "We have a window of opportunity. The issues are much easier to deal with before commercial interests become heavily vested in the hunt for deep-sea genetic material" (Spotts, *Christian Science Monitor,* June 16, 2005).

So what can be done? The study recommends the creation of a whole new international organization (kind of like the UN of the sea) to manage the deep sea and safeguard its biological treasures. Oversight by such an institution would ensure that these resources are not appropriated for use by private companies, and are used only for peaceful purposes.

We may soon see international deep-sea eco-cops chasing bio-pirates through the hot plumes and black smokers of the ocean floor. AS

Hope Spots

No water, no life. No blue, no green.
    Sylvia Earle

■■■■■■ The least-protected ecosystem on the planet is that of our oceans. As Sylvia Earle, oceanographer and pioneering deep sea explorer, noted when she accepted the TED Prize in 2009, only a fraction of 1 percent of our seas is protected. Even in highly sensitive—and highly protected—areas, conservation stops at the shoreline. The land of the Antarctic or of the Galapagos Islands is protected, but the surrounding waters are still open to numerous destructive practices such as fishing and dumping.

Earle's TED Prize "wish" is to create a real global network of Marine Protected Areas, what she calls "hope spots." Like biodiversity hot spots, hope spots are places that contain marine life that is critical to the overall health of our seas; they also provide safe havens where stressed marine life can recuperate. A hope spot might be something like the Kermadec Trench, a five-mile-deep (eight-kilometer-deep) trench southwest of New Zealand; the trench houses unique bacteria communities and extremophiles, while the waters above and around it support important (and dwindling) predators like tunas and sharks.

Earle's foundation has set up Mission Blue (www.mission-blue.org), which maps hope spots and sponsors expeditions. The data, photographs, and live feeds collected on Mission Blue trips not only help scientists and advocates better

A green turtle is entangled in a ghost net—a discarded fishing net—in the waters along the northwestern Hawaiian Islands.

understand the importance of these remarkable places, they also provide better content for a powerful public education tool: Google Earth's Ocean layer [see Placing Yourself, p. 449]. CB

Cleaning up Ghost Nets

▬▬▬   Ghost nets—nets lost or abandoned by fishing fleets—are, along with other ocean trash, becoming a major ecological problem. They can continue killing fish, smothering reefs, and generally wreaking havoc for decades. And despite their large size—one ghost net removed by the Ocean Defenders Alliance off the coast of California weighed nine thousand pounds—they're really hard to find out in the open ocean. But scientists from the U.S. Department of Commerce's National Oceanic and Atmospheric Administration (NOAA) are developing ways to use remote sensing to find, track, and (they hope) clean up ghost nets.

NOAA teamed up with NASA and Airborne Technologies Inc. (ATI), of Wasilla, Alaska, to create a "ghost net remediation" program. ATI's expertise in airborne marine surveying yielded a multistep plan focused on the Pacific. First, satellites tracked ocean currents to identify convergence zones—spots where ghost nets and other debris are most likely to end up. Then, aircraft flew over these zones to search for debris using remote sensors and spotters. The first flights identified more than one hundred ghost nets among two thousand pieces of marine debris.

As we get more adept at sensing and mapping the ocean, we can better use existing knowledge (like drift patterns) to track ghost nets and remove them from our waters in the most efficient way possible. AS & CB

▬▬▬   RESOURCES

The Sea Around Us by Rachel Carson (Oxford University Press, 2003)
An instant classic upon its original publication in 1951, *The Sea Around Us* is the timeless story of the oceans, told through memorable images and recounted in loving prose. However, it is also a warning that holds true today, more than half a century later, of the damage we can inflict—and have already inflicted—on the oceans. As Carl Safina, founder of the Blue Ocean Institute, wrote in his foreword to the book, "Of all the things [Carson] labored to do, her most unintended accomplishment was to inspire us with an example of how we as individuals can strive to live." Rachel Carson inspires readers to live sustainably, consciously, and in awe of the planet on which we live.

The Unnatural History of the Sea by Callum Roberts (Shearwater, 2008)
Drawing on firsthand accounts of early explorers, pirates, merchants, fishers, and travelers, Callum Roberts takes readers around the world and through the centuries to recount how our oceans went from bountiful to desolate. The future isn't entirely bleak, as Callum also describes how we're already using marine reserves to repopulate the seas.

Song for the Blue Ocean: Encounters Along the World's Coasts and Beneath the Seas by Carl Safina (Owl Books, 1999)
Safina intertwines politics, science, and a travelogue to expose the precarious ecological state of the world's oceans.

Fish for the Future

For centuries, it seemed that the ocean's vast bounty knew no limits; coastal cultures that subsisted on fish were some of the world's richest and healthiest societies. But population growth, increasing wealth, and the establishment of highly industrialized fishing techniques have led to an unsustainable demand on the undersea food supply. Today, fishing fleets in many countries must legally abide by strictly regulated quotas, and advances in fishing technology help control the size of each catch and reduce the capture of undesired species. Nevertheless, many fleets conduct illegal operations outside the relatively weak confines of international law.

The result? A report published in *Science* warns that by 2048 all commercial fishing stocks will have collapsed. This means that the next generation would never or only very rarely eat wild fish. Although this would be a major loss in the Global North, it would be outright catastrophic to the 400 million people in the Global South who either make their living fishing or are dependent on fish as a source of protein. We're already seeing the ill effects of algal blooms and rapid increases in jellyfish populations in areas where too many predators have been fished. Farming fish and seafood through aquaculture is a fast-developing trend, but fish feedlots generally follow the model of cattle feedlots—they are overcrowded, soaked in chemicals, and polluting.

Plans are being implemented to recover fisheries in many parts of the world. Scientists and fish advocates are calling for the establishment of protected marine reserves, international conservation agreements, and quotas. Simultaneously, businesses are springing up based on principles of better and more sustainable seafood farming and harvesting practices.

Change will likely come slowly to the fishing and seafood industry. Meanwhile, what can we do? For now, eating only sustainably raised or harvested seafood is the best way to avoid contributing to the crisis. Ultimately, a growing market for such seafood will drive more sustainable fishing and aquaculture practices—demonstrating that our dollars carry real power for change. EG & GF

Sustainable Fisheries Certification

Unlike the Department of Agriculture's Organic Standard label or the Environmental Protection Agency's Energy Star label, a standard, overarching sustainable fisheries certification has not yet been established for restaurants, retailers, and fishers. However, a proliferation of systems, protocols, and evaluation schemes, as well as conscientious distributors like EcoFish and CleanFish, are dedicated to identifying and supplying sustainable seafood.

In 1995 the United Nations Food and Agriculture Organization developed a code of conduct for fisheries, which has since been widely recognized, fostering the formation of the Marine Stewardship Council (MSC). This international nonprofit has worked to establish a universal certification and labeling process. The MSC guidelines call for accountability through reliable and independent auditing and the establishment of transparent standards based on good science. If the fish on our dinner table has been certified by the MSC, we can be sure that we're supporting good work toward the restoration of the ocean's wealth. More than a decade into its work, the MSC has seen proof that it can influence the market. According to Worldwatch's "Fish Farming for the Future" report, from 2006 to 2008 MSC saw participation in the program increase nearly fourfold; as the certification's brand recognition increases, the program is starting to attract the more poorly managed fisheries—the ones that will make the greatest impact if they adopt MSC practices. EG

Buy Frozen?

▆▆▆▆   The "buy fresh" crowd may blanch at such a directive, but according to a group of researchers reporting from Ecotrust in Portland, Oregon, "buy frozen" is the newest mantra of the ecoconscious shopper.

Astrid Scholz, an ecological economist at Ecotrust; Ulf Sonesson, a food system researcher at the Swedish Institute for Food and Biotechnology; and Peter Tyedmers, a professor at Dalhousie University in Halifax, Nova Scotia, have been studying salmon as a way to understand the ins and outs of creating a sustainable food system. They chose the fish for its ubiquity throughout the world—and the fact that it is almost always available "fresh" regardless of the number of miles that lie between the consumer and the fishing grounds.

Their research, which they presented in a *New York Times* op-ed, found, "When it comes to salmon, the questions of organic versus conventional and wild versus farmed matter less than whether the fish is frozen or fresh. In many cases, fresh salmon has about twice the environmental impact as frozen salmon." Clearly, this is not the case when consumers live close to the source, but the report found that most fish eaters live far from salmon-rich waters—far enough to require air-freighting for the privilege of eating "fresh" (i.e., twenty-four-hour-old) salmon. The trio's article claimed, "If seafood-loving Japanese consumers, who get most of their fish via air shipments, were to switch to 75 percent frozen salmon, it would have a greater ecological benefit than all of Europe and North America eating only locally farmed or caught salmon." CB

The Future of Aquaculture

▆▆▆▆   Dr. Martin P. Schreibman has been growing tilapia for years in tanks in his lab at the Aquatic Research and Environmental Assessment Center of Brooklyn College. "You could set a tank up in your basement and grow enough fish to pay your rent," Dr. Schreibman stated in a *New York Times* article, and it may be true. He envisions a day when fish farming throughout New York City—using systems scalable to tight urban spaces—will replace resource-wasting importing as a ready source of local seafood.

Farmed fish, shellfish, and crustaceans represent almost one-third of the seafood we eat today. With worldwide demand for seafood on the rise and most wild fisheries going under, aquaculture has become a lucrative business. The industry and its methods have their critics, but not all aquaculture is bad.

Shellfish aquaculture can actually have a positive impact on the environment. Creatures such as oysters, clams, and mussels eat by filtering plankton from the water, needing no external food supplements. Since their harvests must come from clean waters, shellfish farmers often make staunch advocates for coastal ecological preservation. Much of the shellfish on the U.S. market today is farmed.

Fin fish farming in coastal waters can be more problematic. Farmed salmon, raised by the thousands in net pens, produce a corresponding load of water-polluting feces. Diseases can spread quickly through the crowded pens. Antibiotics used to treat these diseases can then leak out into the water, where they can help disease-resistant organisms

develop. And it all adds up to less-than-healthy salmon steaks on your plate.

Many researchers and environmentalists believe that the solution lies in removing fish farms from areas bordering wild waters. Although Dr. Schreibman's tanks are still largely experimental, his work shows that sustainable aquaculture is possible—even in a Brooklyn basement.

The University of Maryland Biotechnology Institute's Center for Marine Biotechnology is already developing the next generation of indoor fish farms. The center's aquaculture system accommodates several hundred fish and produces nearly zero waste. The microbial filtration system recycles 99 percent of the water used (the other percent is lost to evaporation); a second filter converts fish waste into methane, which the researchers hope will offset 10 percent of the system's energy needs. (A drawback of the center's approach—one that is shared by many fish farms—is that it is raising cobia, a carnivorous fish. Carnivores require the capture or farming of smaller fish, including many edible varieties like sardines.)

Aquaponics, an engineered version of the fish-farming polyculture that has long been practiced in Southeast Asia and China, can turn a kitchen counter or a backyard garden into a fish farm. Aquaponics is a combination of aquaculture and hydroponics, a symbiotic setup in which plants and fish are raised simultaneously in recirculating water. The two "crops" are complementary: fish waste fertilizes the plants, which naturally filter the water so that it stays clean even when many fish are raised in close quarters. These systems can be as simple as a few fish feeding a tabletop herb garden or they can be serious gardening endeavors involving up to one hundred fish and a dedicated greenhouse, and yielding more substantial crops of squash, tomatoes, and other vegetables. EG & CB

Community-supported Fisheries

▬▬▬ It's hard to think of the vast and rolling sea as a local farm, but several groups of fisherfolk in the Northeast and Pacific Northwest regions of the United States are applying a go-to model of sustainable agriculture to their trade. Community Supported Fisheries, or CSFs, which are already successful in Maine and Massachusetts, are similar to standard Community Supported Agriculture [see Buying Better Food, p. 53] schemes: instead of boxes of peppers and carrots, CSF subscribers (individuals and restaurants) pay in advance to receive a certain number of pounds per week of fresh fish and shellfish caught in local waters.

As with a CSA, this arrangement helps local fishermen better support themselves. Although the price per pound for consumers remains competitive with supermarket prices (or may be much cheaper), fishermen selling through a CSF can make up to six times what they would selling the same catches to wholesalers.

In Maine, the Port Clyde Fresh Catch CSF has created a profitable way for fishermen to sell the sweet Maine shrimp they harvest in midwinter. The shrimp is much beloved by locals, but has been fetching so little money through wholesalers that it's often not worth the effort to catch.

CSFs don't guarantee that all fishing practices undertaken by members are sound, but a spokesperson for Cape Ann Fresh Catch CSF in Massachusetts noted in a *Wall Street Journal* article that the model does automatically reduce bycatch waste. Fishermen don't have to ditch less-profitable species that get caught up in the nets because they all become part of the variety of the CSF's offerings.

Opposite, left: A fisherman hauling in his catch, Newport, Rhode Island, 2001.

Opposite, right: Intensive work is being done to restore Olympia oysters to Puget Sound in Washington State, 2003.

Right: Catfish eggs from a tank at Quiver River Aquaculture Inc. in Moorhead, Mississippi.

The small collectives that contribute to CSFs can also choose to implement greater sustainability measures. With a steadier income—one that's now significantly higher—making equipment upgrades or other changes becomes easier. And CSFs have a healthy dose of backstory built into them—you know who caught the catch of the day. CB

Farming Fish for the Future by Brian Halweil (Worldwatch Institute, 2008)
An excellent overview of the state of the world's fishing stocks, this Worldwatch report also traces the history of aquaculture and takes a very honest look at the utility of third-party fishery certifications.

Seafood Watch
http://www.montereybayaquarium.org/cr/seafoodwatch.aspx
Seafood Watch, a program launched by the Monterey Bay Aquarium, has created a concise, informative list to help fish lovers keep track of which species we can grill free of care, and which are ecological no-no's. The California aquarium offers this information to visitors on a wallet-sized reference card. It can also be downloaded or requested from the aquarium's Web site, which features comprehensive information on fish classifications, plus ways to get involved in protecting ocean life. Updated regularly to reflect improvements and declines in fish populations, the searchable online Seafood Guide has detailed information on the ecological status and nutritional value of different species of wild and farmed seafood. This is a great resource full of constructive solutions that anyone can use. EG

The Marine Stewardship Council
http://www.msc.org
The Marine Stewardship Council's Web site teems with good information—for shop and restaurant owners and consumers alike—about sustainable seafood, where to buy it, and how to prepare it. It's a good resource, especially for those trying to better understand fishing as an industry, and our power to change it.

Ocean Friendly Cuisine: Sustainable Seafood Recipes from the World's Finest Chefs by James O. Fraioli (Willow Creek Press, 2005)
This book features recipes that emphasize tilapia, farmed shellfish, and other sustainable seafood; information on how to figure out where the fish at your local market or restaurant comes from; discussions of fisheries issues; and more.

Cod: A Biography of the Fish That Changed the World by Mark Kurlansky (Penguin Books, 1998)
Mark Kurlansky recounts humanity's shared history with the now-collapsed cod fisheries off North America's North Atlantic coast.

Polar Regions

■■■■■ In 2004, Ben Saunders became the fourth person in history (and the youngest by ten years) to ski solo to the geographic North Pole. In 2008, he attempted to set a new world speed record from Ward Hunt Island to the geographic North Pole. The mission was canceled because of faulty ski equipment, but at this writing he was gearing up for another attempt.

Klaus Toepfer, the executive director of the United Nations Environment Program, describes the Arctic region as the "barometer of global climate change—an environmental early warning system for the world." Over the past ten years, I've been lucky enough to spend several months in the high Arctic, witnessing this barometer at work firsthand.

In spring 2004, I set out to make the first-ever solo ski crossing of the Arctic Ocean, a 1,240-mile (1,996-kilometer) journey from the north coast of Siberia to Ward Hunt Island, northern Canada, via the geographic North Pole. Reinhold Messner, one of the world's most accomplished mountaineers, had attempted the same thing in the late 1990s. He was rescued after a few days on the ice and described the expedition as "ten times as dangerous as Everest." Considering that the high Arctic is home to the world's largest land-based carnivore (the polar bear) and that frostbite (which I'd contracted at fifty below during a 2001 expedition) is the least of one's worries when traveling through this region, I had no illusions about the scale of the challenge I was undertaking.

The last solo and unsupported expedition to the North Pole from Russia had been completed by Norwegian Børge Ousland in spring 1996. As I flew by helicopter to the same starting point in early March 2001, what I saw amazed me. Whereas Ousland had been able to ski from the land straight onto the frozen crust of the Arctic Ocean, I found an area of open water more than ten miles wide separating the pack ice from the northernmost tip of Siberia. I was flown to the edge of the pack and spent seventy-two days alone, battling conditions described by NASA as "the worst since records began." When you're skiing over the sea, the words *worst* and *warmest* are interchangeable; I encountered unprecedented areas of open water, and some of the highest temperatures ever recorded in the region. During past expeditions, there had been times when it felt like the Arctic was trying to kill me. This time around, it felt like it was trying to tell me something.

I had had a similarly disconcerting experience in 2005 in the Kangerlussuaq mountains of Greenland, where my teammate, Tony Haile, and I traveled to field-test equipment for our upcoming expedition. (Greenland has the largest ice cap on the Northern Hemisphere; it's the closest thing we have to the terrain of Antarctica, and therefore it was a perfect training ground.) I knew something was amiss when I caught sight of some drifting pack ice from our tiny Twin Otter ski-plane. Spotting the pack took me straight back to the Arctic and the three months I spent traveling over the shifting surface of that forgotten ocean in the spring of 2004, and I was certain I wouldn't want to pitch my tent on what I could see beneath me—it was far too fractured and weak.

The route we had chosen involved several days of ascending from near sea level to 6,500 feet (2,000 meters). I was prepared for tough climbs with the sledge forever pulling me back. I was prepared for the occasional crevasse fall. I was even bracing myself for Tony's cooking. The one thing I hadn't prepared for was to be wandering around our first campsite in the high Arctic with my shirt off. It seemed Greenland's welcome was to try and broil us alive. We spent a month trekking through this mountain range, and the temperature was never anything less than blistering. Our expedition jackets lay in our sledges, our bodies sweated gallons into our thin thermal tops—often the only clothing we wore during the day. The heat was playing hell with our rehydration calculations. Our factor-60 sun cream did not stop either of us turning a very British pink under the sun. This was Greenland, this was the Arctic, and it felt like a snow-themed Cancun.

Eventually we took to skiing during the night—the sun was still up, but we could handle

the temperature better, and we even had one or two genuinely cold nights.

Upon our return, we found that for the first time in living memory, a mountaineering expedition team even farther north than us had been able to sail right up to the coast.

The polar regions have always been in a state of climatic flux; that is one of the few certainties of earth science. In 1912, Captain Robert Falcon Scott's team unearthed fossilized ferns as they struggled back from the South Pole. In 1996, John Tarduno and his Paleomagnetic Research Group stumbled across a unique fossil find high above the Arctic Circle: the 80-to-90-million-year-old remains of fish, turtles, and champsosaurs (a semiaquatic reptile resembling the crocodile, which had never been found that far north). Tarduno's discovery implies that polar climates at that time were warm (with a mean annual temperature exceeding 57 degrees Fahrenheit [14 degrees Celsius]) rather than being below freezing. One line from the abstract of his study is particularly alarming: "Magmatism at six large igneous provinces at this time suggests that volcanic carbon dioxide emissions helped cause the global warmth."

Our civilization is mimicking those ancient volcanoes, pumping huge volumes of carbon dioxide into the atmosphere. I'm certainly not a scientist, but it is clear to me that the climates of these huge regions (Antarctica and the Arctic Ocean combine to cover an area nearly four times the size of China) are changing fast. Some of the undeniably human-made damage is less easy to spot: a fourteen-fold increase in the mercury levels of polar bears tested in Greenland over the past thirty years is one example. The poles may be incredibly remote, but they are far from untouched.

I'm not an explorer, at least not in the old-fashioned, Edwardian sense of the word. In an age of satellite, sonar, and laser, I don't exactly ski along drawing maps. For me, expeditions are a chance to explore my potential as an athlete, but I hope they're also about something bigger. At a time when taking responsibility for our impact on the planet's ecosystems is more important than ever, it strikes me that fewer and fewer young people are actually engaging with, or know anything of, the great outdoors. I certainly hope that my expeditions will fleetingly point the media's spotlight at the polar regions and the delicate balance in which the earth hangs at the start of the twenty-first century. But equally important, I hope they inspire younger people to take up adventures of their own, learning to be at home in nature, and perhaps launching themselves into the biggest adventure there is: blazing a path to a sustainable future. BS

Circumpolar Peoples vs. the Great Polar Melt

▬▬▬ The Arctic isn't just icebergs, polar bears, and the occasional insane British explorer. People live there too, and the North Pole melt is hammering at their way of life. Things are changing so quickly that indigenous people don't even have words in their languages for some of the new things they're encountering, like new animals and insects, which are traveling farther north as forests start to grow where tundra once was.

But the long-term effects may be much worse than disorientation. Circumpolar native peoples—Samis, Inuits, Chukchis, and others—may find their communities and cultures wiped out. The infrastructure of coastal communities is already being destroyed, and recent studies have confirmed that ice-dependent animals, like polar bears, may face extinction. Wildlife research biologists from the U.S. Geological Survey and the Canadian Wildlife survey reported in 2005 that the Arctic ice cap receded two hundred miles farther during that summer than the average recession rate two decades prior. This means that polar bears may be forced to swim distances far beyond what their energy allows. As a result, more and more polar bears face drowning from exhaustion (Iredale, *Sunday Times*, December 18, 2005).

For native peoples of the Arctic, the shock of seeing their home change so much is kindling activism. They are involving themselves in cultural survival work, political mobilization, technological and cultural innovation, even legal action. EG & AS

The Northwest Passage

▬▬▬ In 2007 a more dramatic sign of Arctic change appeared: for the first time, polar melt made the previously icebound Northwest Passage around the north of Canada and Alaska navigable by commercial ships. Recognizing that this is now something we can expect to be a regular occurrence (at current estimates, the Northwest Passage may be navigable year-round by 2050), Canada has made plans to patrol its northern border. AS

The Third Pole

▬▬▬ The Himalayas and the Tibetan Plateau contain the world's largest nonpolar ice sheets. And like its cousins, "the third pole" is melting fast, perhaps faster than the North or South Poles.

According to NASA, over the past thirty years the Tibetan Plateau has warmed at a rate of about twice that of global temperature increases. Joint research by NASA and the Chinese Academy of Sciences has found that a major culprit in this melt is black soot produced from the burning of diesel fuel, coal, and cooking fuel. This accelerated melt is even more of an immediate concern than the melt in the North and South Poles because the loss of snow and ice on the Tibetan Plateau means less drinking water for the millions of people who live along Asia's major rivers—the Ganges, the

Opposite: Researchers say that warming temperatures in polar regions may be the cause of declining health among polar bear populations. Rising spring temperatures have led to earlier breakup of ice, leaving bears with less time to hunt for food.

Right: An Eskimo whaling crew paddles through unfrozen waters, a reflection of the shifting infrastructure of circumpolar communities.

Yellow, and the Indus, to name a few—which are replenished each year by natural snow melt.

The plight of the third pole shows us that reductions in black soot emissions must go hand in hand with reductions in greenhouse-gas emissions. In the meantime, it probably wouldn't hurt to replace a few of those iconic polar bear images with pictures of the retreating Himalayan glaciers and the millions of people living downstream from a disappearing resource.

■■■■■■   RESOURCES

The Future History of the Arctic by Charles Emmerson (PublicAffairs, 2010)
Humanity has been both drawn to and frightened by the frozen North for centuries. Emmerson's book tells the wild story of our various attempts to explore, exploit, and colonize the Arctic. He counters the idea that the Arctic is empty, white, pristine, and unchanging, showing that it is instead a part of the world in rapid flux, full of competing interests and headed toward an unpredictable future. AS

After the Ice: Life, Death, and Geopolitics in the New Arctic by Alun Anderson (HarperCollins, 2009)
"All too often," Anderson tells us early in his book, "the city folk down south forget that the Arctic is a peopled place, and are unaware of how its inhabitants live." Anderson attempts to show us that, as climate change utterly transforms the Arctic, it is also creating a complex new dance between natives, newer residents, and outside interests—from oil and mining companies to environmental groups to polar nations wanting to establish sovereignty. That dance is already full of conflict and misunderstandings. He suggests that if we "turn the world on its side," recognizing how vast and connected the Arctic is, we'll get a better view of the future of our planet as a whole. AS

The Two-Mile Time Machine: Ice Cores, Abrupt Climate Change, and Our Future by Richard B. Alley (Princeton University Press, 2000)
"The climate-change community is so much more confident of global warming than is the popular press," warns Greenland ice-core expert Richard Alley, one of the key scientists in the early 1990s who discovered that the last ice age ended abruptly, in a span of only three years. *The Two-Mile Time Machine* tells the story of global climate change through annual readings of the Greenland Ice Sheet, a fascinating and important story that informs the climate we live in today, and how we will proceed tomorrow.

Forty Signs of Rain, **Fifty Degrees Below**, and **Sixty Days and Counting** by Kim Stanley Robinson (Bantam Spectra, 2004, 2005, 2007)
Science fiction writer Kim Stanley Robinson's trilogy tells the near-future story of a band of scientists and public servants who are battling to alert the world to the threat of sudden climate change, and to save it once the heavy weather sets in. The thinking-person's version of the movie *The Day After Tomorrow,* the books are full of interesting ideas about science, the planet, and why it's hard for humans to act in their own long-term best interests.

Here's a taste: "Helicopters and blimps had already taken to the air in great numbers. Now all the TV channels in the world could reveal the extent of the flood from on high. Much of downtown Washington, DC, remained awash. A giant shallow lake occupied precisely the most famous and public parts of the city; it looked like someone had decided to expand the Mall's reflecting pool beyond all reason."

The Solar System: Greens in Space

■■■■■ Exploring space is green.

Exploring space is a crucial component of our ongoing efforts to better understand—and protect—our home planet. Some old-school environmentalists decry all the money spent on space programs; in their eyes this investment is, at best, a costly waste and, at worst, an invitation to more global irresponsibility. They envision a space program designed to allow us to just ditch our tortured planet as soon as we have space colonies. ("No leaving the planet, boys," one bumper sticker reads, "until you clean up your mess.") But their fear is largely unfounded and exceptionally shortsighted. Literally and figuratively, we can't see the whole planet unless we look at it from space, and we can't really understand it unless we can see it as a whole. To really protect the planet, we sometimes have to leave it.

Over the past few decades, notions of environmental sustainability have shifted from focusing on cleaning up pollution to focusing on understanding (and, where needed, intervening in) global environmental systems. Picking up litter and reducing smog are easy concepts to understand; the dynamics between climate cycles, insulation, CO_2 emissions from natural and artificial sources, and solar cycles are harder to comprehend. But we'll never get a handle on how our environment truly functions without a better understanding of the larger environment in which our planet exists. It also helps to know how other planets have evolved. Turning our backs on space exploration means cutting ourselves off from a chance to really know Earth.

A space program with a planetary focus would combine current research into our planet's climate and geography (much of which can only be done from orbit) with expanded research into the workings of the rest of our solar system. Plenty of big questions about our planetary neighbors remain unanswered. Venus, Earth, and Mars all orbit within our sun's "habitable belt," and there is some preliminary research suggesting that each may have started out with similar potential for life. Why did Venus fall victim to a runaway greenhouse effect, while Mars dried up? Why did Earth alone manage to emerge from its early uninhabitable "ice-ball" period with the potential to support life? We can speculate, but on-site exploration will give us far better answers than will remote theorizing. Given the potential disasters associated with climate change, these are not idle questions. The better we understand how similar planets work, the better we understand our own planetology.

There are myriad connections between space research and green issues. If, for example, we were to discover life in the oceans under the icy surface of Jupiter's moon Europa, it would be our first opportunity to do truly comparative biology, which might profoundly expand our understanding of the miracle of life on planet Earth. Since all the living creatures we've ever found are related to one another, having what might be radically different life-forms to study could alert us to new understandings of life itself.

For now, and likely for the next couple of decades, a green space program would not mean sending people into space. Instead, it would mean mounting a much more ambitious (and well-funded) effort to

Following pages: Both NASA and the European Space Agency monitor climate change and natural disasters—such as this image of Hurricane Emily—with satellites.

send robotic explorers throughout the solar system—and beyond. Automated science missions have done remarkably well considering how little money has been made available to them. Mars Exploration Rover is the most spectacular recent example, but automated probes gathered material from a comet, monitored solar weather, dove into the crushing atmosphere of Jupiter, and found liquid water on Saturn's moon Enceladus. Robotic space exploration is relatively inexpensive—and the information we get back, its potential to help us better understand global environmental problems, is simply priceless.

Space exploration may get cheaper still. Over the next couple of decades, the field may no longer be limited to governments and big corporations. Via private space launches or via the (increasingly likely) space elevator, Earth's orbit could become as accessible as the deep ocean—not easy, not cheap, but still quite accessible to scientific research and even to the truly adventurous tourist.

Author Robert Zimmerman referred to this emerging era as a "space renaissance"—a revolution in the way people on Earth see and use space resources. The following are some tools that may help create that renaissance:

Microsatellites: Sending things into space will always be easier, and cheaper, than sending people into space. Small, comparatively cheap satellites with sensor kits and radios—meant to study a particular phenomenon before eventually burning up in Earth's atmosphere—could survey urban-growth patterns, monitor fisheries, look for early signs of drought or flooding, and even engage in a bit of open-source intelligence gathering.

Improved Climate Monitoring: A particularly important use of satellites—whether micro or macro—will be keeping a close watch on climate change. Both NASA and the European Space Agency (ESA) have climate-related satellite programs, and China plans to have climate satellites in orbit by 2012. But we could always use more.

Humanitarian Satellites: Satellite information aids humanitarian causes, and this use of the technology does not get the attention it deserves.

Recently, satellites were invaluable in coordinating aid workers' movements in Darfur, where it can take as long as ten days to drive 75 miles (120 kilometers). The International Charter: Space and Major Disasters is a global agreement to coordinate the delivery of satellite data to rescue and relief efforts. It was most recently invoked during the 2010 earthquake in Haiti; satellites gave us some of the most powerful images of the earthquake's destruction, and have proved crucial in the recovery and reconstruction process. NASA has signed an agreement with the World Conservation Union (IUCN) to provide satellite data in support of a variety of conservation efforts. (The IUCN is the world's largest "environmental knowledge network," comprising members from 160 countries, in more than a thousand government and nongovernmental organizations.) These are all worthy efforts, but because there are as yet no dedicated humanitarian satellite networks, they also all require the temporary redirection of satellite resources away from their primary missions. Cheap, private launch vehicles would give humanitarian and conservation groups access to satellite technology.

But the biggest prize—and the greatest challenge—of space exploration would be to send satellites or even landers to other planets in our solar system. We may first have to build an elevator to reduce the energy costs of getting to high orbit (and, potentially, to serve as a launch "slingshot"). Even without interplanetary satellites, our understanding of how planets function may be on the verge of a revolution. Mars will undoubtedly get the most attention, given the intriguing evidence concerning life there. Already, university researchers are working

---

Opposite, left: A depiction of the Cassini space probe orbiting Saturn's rings. The more we understand what's "out there," the more we appreciate the fragility of our own planet.
Opposite, right: Space junk orbiting the Earth above the North Pole.

on novel ideas for moving around the Red Planet, and for improving the technologies for detecting biological activity.

Of course, there are potential downsides to increased human activity in space. Within Earth's orbit, more satellites mean more chances for accidents; so-called space junk is already a concern. A proliferation of private satellite launches will only add to those headaches. Of greater long-term concern is the possibility of contaminating other planets with earthly microbes riding along on poorly handled space probes. Most earthborne bacteria would die quickly on Mars: no ozone layer means abundant ultraviolet radiation, on top of the sub-Antarctic temperatures and atmospheric density far lower than Earth's. We know all too well, however, that evolution is a hardy process. It would be appalling if our own carelessness destroyed our chances of learning whether Mars has its own native microbes because some earthly extremophile had become the martian equivalent of kudzu. JC

Seeing Earth from Space

■■■■■ As the Cassini-Huygens probe, a tiny hunk of metal, hurtles through space, revealing hidden aspects of Titan, Dione, the Rings of Saturn, and giant lightning storms on Saturn's surface, the photos of distant planets it's sending back are giving us a wider sense of "here."

And yet Cassini is doing something else for us, too, something that really comes into focus when looking at pictures of Dione's rocky, barren landscape: Cassini shows us the stark fact that in human terms, there's no *there* there.

Space, even the immediate region of our own solar system, is a vast, cold, empty, airless, barren place. There is very little we want in space, and perhaps no good reason for going there through manned spaceflight. When compared to the rest of known space, our little planet looks better and better, and less and less replaceable. Thinking about the Cassini probe, out there looking, for the first time, at one of our nearest neighbors, it's hard not to think about how perfectly suited for us this planet is, and we are suited for it. We could, as Gary Snyder reminds us, live on this planet without tools or clothes.

Think of us hurtling through space on our comfy little airy, sunny, watery rock. Perhaps it's a common enough insight, this feeling of expanded presence, of being at home not just in the world, but *on* the world. Space exploration is not just a contingency plan, but a way to elicit a little jolt of planetary appreciation—something we could certainly use more of. AS

Recycling Space Junk

■■■■■ Though we've only been exploring space since the 1960s, we've already turned the skies above us into an orbiting trash heap. More than 110,000 known, tracked chunks of litter are hurtling around the planet at more than 17,500 miles per hour (that's 28,164 kilometers per hour), according to NASA. And there may be more than a million smaller bits and pieces.

Some are shards of broken satellites (there are hundreds of whole, dead satellites zinging around up there too), some are pieces of equipment lost by astronauts, or just dumped

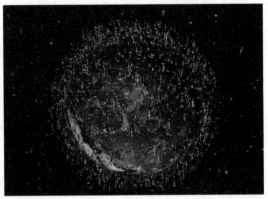

out the window. An estimated 300,000 fragments were created by the explosion of one Pegasus rocket alone.

This stuff is a hazard. In 1983, a paint chip that was almost too small to see cracked the windshield of one of the space shuttles. Satellites are pretty routinely damaged by high-velocity grit and grime. As the BBC reminds us, "A pea-sized ball moving this fast is as dangerous as a 400-lb safe traveling at 60 mph." In March 2009, astronauts in the International Space Station waited in an escape pod while a five-inch piece of spent rocket motor floated past—the tiny chunk of debris could have caused catastrophic damage to the station.

These junk particles endanger the low-orbiting satellites most useful for studying Earth. A fast-moving debris ring around the planet presents some serious challenges to the kind of space science that can tackle environmental and social challenges. Scientists are also worried about Kessler Syndrome, which describes a chain reaction of debris collisions that leaves behind such a ring of litter that launching almost anything into orbit—or maintaining the Space Station—becomes too risky.

But what can be done? We can't hand out trash bags to astronauts and have a litter-patrol day. Still, there are several mutually compatible options. First, we could prevent further accumulation of some space junk by using any of a variety of technologies to "deorbit" satellites at the end of their useful lives—an option that would be made more realistic by stricter laws governing the use of space. Second, we could clean up our orbit, slowly, using a laser "broom" (mounted on the Space Station, the shuttle, or special satellites) to "sweep" debris from the skies. Third—and most ambitiously—we could recycle the junk and use it as the counterweight for an orbital sling (sometimes called a skyhook): an orbiting, spinning tether, sort of a cousin to the space elevator, designed to lift and fling satellites from low orbit into higher orbit without added propellant. If none of these cleanup proposals worked, we could start exploring the really weird ideas. AS

Searching for asteroids using telescopes and satellites now will help prevent the enormous economic and human costs of being hit by an asteroid in the future.

Life in the Shooting Gallery

■■■■   Right now, we know of 1,100 large asteroids a kilometer wide or bigger with orbits that come near Earth. Of those, scientists have studied the orbits of 700 sufficiently to determine that they will not pose a danger to the planet in the next century; 400 remain mysteries. But these are only the planet-killer-size rocks, the kind that wiped out the dinosaurs. If you count all the asteroids 150 meters (nearly 500 feet) or larger (which could still take out part of a continent, and perhaps trigger all sorts of climate mayhem), there are over a million nearby.

In short, we live in a cosmic shooting gallery.

What can we do to lessen the odds of taking a hit? Hollywood notwithstanding, nuclear weapons don't work. Many asteroids are not very dense, and would be more likely to absorb the energy of a nuke than to be torn apart by one. Our best bet might be to push the asteroid. Given enough warning—about a decade—we could nudge asteroids far enough off-course to miss us. Groups like the B612 Foundation, led by Apollo astronaut Rusty Schweickart, are coming up with plans to design and test the necessary gear.

The best defense currently within our grasp is to crank up the search for asteroids that have Earth's name on them. Doing so would require adding telescopes and satellites to the effort. That takes money, but it would be cheap compared with the cost of being hit by even a minor asteroid. With funding for more observation projects, and with improved telescope technology, a smart mob of passionate amateurs could join the hunt, via distributed online efforts

to snoop out likely suspects. The decline of the dinos shows that we live in a dangerous solar system, but unlike the dinosaurs, we can see trouble coming and, perhaps, avert it—if we're wise enough to look. JC

Environmental Law in Space

◼◼◼◼   Space may be the final frontier, but that doesn't mean it's above the law. We already have the Outer Space Treaty (more formally, the Treaty on Principles Governing the Activities of States in the Exploration and Use of Outer Space, including the Moon and Other Celestial Bodies), which is primarily concerned with preventing weapons of mass destruction from being put into orbit, and with placing the ownership of space resources into a common holding, thus preventing a colonial scramble by nations intent on seizing space assets. In this way, it is very like the Antarctic Treaty or the Law of the Sea. (A proposed Space Preservation Treaty would ban all weapons from space.)

But is that enough? We already know that the Earth's orbit is littered with space junk. Though space seems unimaginably vast, the parts of it that are of the greatest use to us are in fact quite finite and (as our orbital irresponsibility shows), at least over the long term, vulnerable to our actions. We know as well that if it turns out there is extraterrestrial life, its genetics will be extremely valuable, and its environment may be extremely vulnerable to biological pollution. And because of efforts like the X Prize, progress on new innovations like the space elevator, and increasingly sophisticated satellite, launch, and robot reconnaissance technologies, the likelihood of space exploitation is growing.

Is it time to start planning the field of Space Environmental Law? It could lay down basic responsibilities for space junk (not "polluter pays," but "launcher pays"), or it could go much farther, both protecting interstellar life from ruthless biopirates and setting out ways to preserve habitat on other celestial bodies, as has been proposed with deep sea resources.

Early in the last century, Aldo Leopold brought to our attention the need for a "land ethic"; perhaps now we must adopt a "space ethic" as well. AS

◼◼◼◼   RESOURCES

Spacehack
http://spacehack.org
Founded by Ariel Waldman, a former program coordinator for NASA's community-outreach arm, CoLab, Spacehack is an extensive and beautifully laid-out directory of citizen-science projects, competitions (like the Lunar X Prize), and educational resources. The projects highlighted on Spacehack range from casual stargazing to an engineering competition to develop a material that could support the 60,000-mile-long tether needed to make the space elevator a reality. The ultimate goal of Spacehack is to create and support space literacy.

Entering Space: Creating a Spacefaring Civilization by Robert Zubrin (Jeremy P. Tarcher/Putnam, 1999)
Entering Space is engineer-visionary Robert Zubrin's manifesto for a new age of space exploration. "This is a book about creating a spacefaring civilization—the next step in the development of human society."

Imagining the Future

▬▬▬ The future that people warned us about forty years ago on the first Earth Day looks an awful lot like our present. The ice caps are melting, deserts are spreading, the planet is thick with people, most of the world's primeval forests are gone, the seas are in crisis, and pollution, famine, and natural disasters kill millions of people a year. Had the environmental awareness of the early 1970s continued steadily through the following four decades, we might not live on a half-ruined planet today.

That half-ruined planet, though, is our home. People old enough to remember the first Earth Day can well grieve for that other, healthier Earth we might have had if only older generations had made different choices. Kids born today won't have that luxury. This world is the only one they'll ever know: they'll have to make the best of it.

The year 1970 is now the same amount of time away from us as 2050 is: that's how close the future is. The 2050s, we know, will be a watershed era: the decade when, if we've been smart, human population will have peaked, a bright green model of sustainable prosperity will be widespread, and human damage to the climate and biosphere will have begun to be repaired. Between now and then, we have to remake the world. We'll know whether we've done well enough by 2050. If we fail, the resulting descent toward greater and greater catastrophes will likely cause immeasurable human suffering and the end of our global civilization; it could eventually mean a general extinction of most life on Earth. If we don't act while we still have some control over events, the final outcome will almost certainly be ripped

out of our hands during the cascading failures to come.

Even if we do reach a safe plateau toward the middle of the century, with a stable human population, a new model of prosperity, and a planetwide effort to halt and reverse ecological destruction, much will still have been lost. Unfortunately, even a "win" may look like a ruined planet to those who knew the one we had half a century ago. No matter what we do—even if we avoid triggering any massive climate tipping points—more climate change is a given. Living on a planet of children (the median age in the least developed countries is only nineteen, for instance) and in a world where billions of people are struggling to rise out of poverty means that even if economic reinvention happens fast and bright green models spread quickly, entire forests, countless fisheries and rivers, mountains of topsoil, and myriad creatures will be devoured by human needs in the meantime. In the best-case realistic scenario, we're going to do a huge amount of damage to the planet even as we transform ourselves into a global society that provides prosperity with essentially no impacts.

Some older environmentalists (most prominently, James Lovelock) have suggested that because there's no possible future in which our planet is not greatly depleted, the game's over. Lovelock, in particular, seems to enjoy saying it's too late to do anything to save humanity, but he's not alone among his generation. These doomsayers look ahead and see a world full of deserts and empty oceans, dying forests and dead coral reefs, say "We tried to warn you," and walk away.

The problem is, the children of 2050 will look at their world, with all its problems, and see home; and they'll look at the choices they have in front of them, and see the future. And since the decisions we make in the next forty years will determine the choices our descendants are left with—a thriving society engaged in centuries of restoration and planetary repair, or a gradual desperate retreat toward the poles—giving up now because we don't like the options we face is pathetic cowardice.

In fact, it's worse: writing off the future (especially by those in positions of cultural authority) directly supports the work of those who are destroying the future, those who are squeezing every last bit of profit from the planet's biosphere while they still can. The idea that there's no future is a club used to beat people into submission and acquiescent participation in the unthinkable. The idea that there's no future is a main driver in making the future worse.

The planetary crisis we face may be made up of design flaws and market failures and the sheer mass of humanity struggling to live, but it is not at its core a material crisis at all. Rather, it is a crisis of vision; we see a growing and darkening void where our future ought to be. The average person, presented with accurate information about the state of the world, can see no way forward. The path we're on appears to end in darkness and a swift, cataclysmic drop. Most folks, entirely understandably, choose not to look.

That void in our future vision is not accidental. The forty years since the first Earth Day have seen the growth of a whole set of industries dedicated to creating just such a void by attacking scientists and conservationists, falsely complicating issues, spinning the news of environmental crimes, launching astroturf front groups, endowing think tanks, bribing politicians, obfuscating the need for systemic change by pushing funding toward NGOs that advocate the most limited of personal actions, and supporting cultural work—such as talk radio that spreads the ideas of the Tea Party—that promotes cynicism and a disdain (if not a hatred) for idealists. In a twist on the old axiom that tyrants don't

care if they're hated as long as their subjects don't love each other, these industries don't care if the future they're offering us looks dark, as long as no other futures we can imagine look brighter. Despairing consumers still buy, and they cause less trouble for the investment banks. "We have an economy," as Paul Hawken says, "where we steal the future, sell it in the present, and call it G.D.P." Keeping the future dark hides the crime.

A vicious political fight for the future is happening right now. Having realized that they're steadily losing the war to convince people there are no problems, those who were profiting from the status quo have now turned to fear, uncertainty, and doubt. They're trying to convince the public that it is both too expensive to make changes that probably won't work and too soon to take drastic measures. The dark, unknowable future has been turned into a weapon against action in the present.

The irony is, we already have the ability to solve or at least address the

Worldchanging ally Denis Hayes in Washington, DC, on April 22, 1970, the first Earth Day.

planet's most pressing problems. We don't have every solution we'll need, not yet. We do, though, have the technological capabilities, the design genius, the scientific ingenuity, the entrepreneurial zeal, the policy acumen, the community-building skill, and the educational and cultural wisdom. It's not that we're incapable of sustainable prosperity. We've never had a greater ability to build a better world. What we seem to lack is a belief that we can actually use those powers to change anything, and we lack that belief precisely because the future has been ripped out of our cultural debate.

That's why if we care about the planet, the most important thing we can do is start showing how good a future we still can have. That's why, right now, optimism is a political act, and a radical one at that.

What we need today is mass-movement planetary futurism—not in the cheesy sense (what color is your rocket car?) but in the sense that the future is not an alien world or a land of make-believe, it's where we are right now, with a brief passage of time. Utah Phillips used to say that the past didn't go anywhere. Well, the future's already here. We're making it as we speak, and we'll make it better when we consider the effects of our actions over a longer range of time.

Human beings make the future every day. In fact, making the future— setting in motion future events—might almost be considered part of the definition of humanity. The problem is that today, when powerful people sit down and make decisions, they generally make them as if the future didn't exist, as if the consequences of their actions were beyond anticipation, as if they bore no responsibility for foresight. The future's not welcome in the room.

We need millions of people ready to put the future back in the room. We need millions of people ready to demand that their governments, their companies, their communities, and their cultural institutions confront the reality of the futures they make every day.

In the 2010s, any institution that is not looking forty years ahead and at least considering the long-term impacts of its work is probably engaged in actions that wouldn't bear examination in the full light of day. We need to sunlight them. We need to hold them up against absolute standards, hard numbers, and firm timelines. We need to demand forty-year goals and bold immediate commitments. We need to be the voices for the children of 2050 who otherwise have no rights in our halls of power. The year 2050 is right around the corner, and we need to fight for it in every discussion of practical action, in every institution on the planet.

Ultimately, we need to become adept at anticipating, imagining, and discussing the future. Luckily, tools abound for all three jobs. AS

Environmental and Spatial Histories

▬▬ One of the best ways to learn to think ahead is to look back. History provides us with a multitude of stories that can help us see and work with the patterns of life around us.

The past explored in Matthew Klingle's *Emerald City: An Environmental History of Seattle* may have unfolded on the shores of Puget Sound in the eighteenth century, but its insights are both cosmopolitan and timely.

Klingle crafts a straightforward but engrossing story about how, in the late 1700s, Europeans encountered Native peoples living in an ecosystem of almost staggering natural abundance—"the most lovely country that can be imagined"—and, over time, in fits and starts, aided by the Klondike Gold Rush and industrialization, intentionally and yet with profound ignorance, changed that place into a city that today is prosperous, high-tech, scenic . . . and teetering on the edge of ecological disaster.

Two images from Eric Sanderson's Mannahatta Project juxtaposing the Manhattan of today with how the land looked before European settlement four hundred years ago.

It's a good story, and Klingle tells it well. He has an eye for the quirky characters, odd facts, and high weirdness that define the history of the American Northwest. But this is also a book packed with complex observations. Klingle reminds us that the history of Seattle is in fact the product of an extremely complex set of interactions between groups of people, local goals and global forces, and nature itself—and the results of those interactions are similarly complex (Seattle is a magnificent city in crisis).

The Mannahatta Project uses spatial history tools to mentally strip back the years and imagine Manhattan before the arrival of Europeans. On the Web site (http://themannahattaproject .org) we can see each city block as it would have looked when Henry Hudson first saw the island in 1609. We can see where trees and streams used to be, where animals like black bears passed through, and where the Lenape tribe hunted. The book based on the project, *Mannahatta: A Natural History of New York City,* puts images of past and present in mind-blowing juxtaposition.

In New York hundreds of years of city-building stand between residents and the ground they walk on. Stripping back that mass of concrete and asphalt and people and stories to get back to the natural systems that underlie it all must be an especially powerful experience for those who aren't used to thinking of where they live as being part of nature at all.

That sort of insight, that sort of changed thinking, is exactly what we need more of if we're going to make better choices about the future we're building all around us. AS

Lifeboat Thinking or Platforms for Stability?

▬▬ The future isn't fair. Because we know big trouble is on the way—even if we start being a lot smarter about how we treat the planet and on another—because we know that trouble will not arrive everywhere equally or all at once, and because we know some places are much better suited (because of wealth, setting, or history) to withstand big shocks, we also know that in the latter part of this century we'll see people in different places experiencing a spectrum of instability.

Some places will be under stress but fundamentally functional. Some will even be thriving through the economic advantages and resilience they have gained by shifting to bright green systems. Other places, though, will be hard hit by climate chaos, entrenched poverty, the loss of ecosystem services, and the effects of failed states.

How people living in resilient places treat people living in chaotic places will be one of the defining ethical choices of the twenty-first century. Some people, especially neoconservatives, advocate a dog-eat-dog view of the coming chaos, arguing that the main obligation of functional places is to ensure through every means necessary that they retain their resilience. A lifeboat at sea can't take on too many survivors, or everyone in the lifeboat may perish. We could characterize the neoconservative approach as "lifeboat regionalism."

But we might also think of our resilient places as stable platforms that allow us to reach out and help stabilize and build resilience in trouble zones. After all, our fates are tied to those of the people who live in unstable areas in a million direct and indirect ways, from sharing the same atmosphere to being vulnerable to the same diseases. By making others safer and more durable, we ultimately make our own places more sustainable.

When we think about the future, we also have to decide whose future we're willing to take responsibility for: do we look primarily after ourselves, or do we use our strength to invest in the stability of those around us?

The Apocalypse Makes Us Dumb

██████ In thinking seriously about the negative trends in our future, we're severely hampered by the Hollywood idea of the apocalypse. That idea, in turn, has deep roots in the millenarianism of monotheistic religions (the End of Days is coming soon) and of nineteenth-century social movements (the Dictatorship of the Proletariat is coming soon). Millenarianism has its own problems, not least of which is that people do horrible things to others in the name of clearing the way for their chosen perfect future. Also, believing in a millennial future, or even telling stories of such a future,

makes us bad at thinking intelligently about the future.

Here are just a few of the futurist fallacies we tend to embrace because (whether we're aware of it or not) we're applying a millennial lens to the events unfolding around us:

The apocalypse is coming. There is a tendency to believe that big, catastrophic, and singular events are going to destroy everything: that the bird flu or nuclear war will suddenly erupt and create a living hell.

The apocalypse is forever. In disaster movies and such, people seem to lack the ability to regroup and rebuild. Sometimes a hero—by killing a monster/warlord/robot/Tina Turner—will win the chance for one small group to start over, but the implication is usually that the rest of the planet has been written off for the imaginable future.

The apocalypse is everywhere. In the movies, collapse makes the whole world a wasteland. Everything crashes and burns; almost everyone dies; knowledge and law are driven entirely from the planet, or at the very least confined to some distant semimythical paradise for which the survivors yearn. But generally, everything falls apart everywhere all at once (and never gets better).

The elect will survive. Critical to the apocalyptic mindset is the narrative device of the survivor. An apocalypse without survivors is not a story we tell (even *Wall-E* revolves around what is essentially a simple human in a robot suit). And when we choose who survives in our end-of-the-world stories, we generally choose a person or small group of people with whom we identify, and we generally assume they survive because they're like us. Somehow, no matter how sudden, total, and perpetual the disaster, someone like us always finds a way to make it through. A subset of this fallacy is the idea that survivalists survive—that bunkered individuals or remote farming communities have an edge. When the craziness starts, the theory goes, it'll be the people holed up in the hinterlands who will survive and that the rule we can observe all through history—which is that isolated people are simply prey to larger, better-organized groups—suspends itself for the duration.

The apocalypse will be an adventure. Often, disaster is viewed as a chance to do things civilized society forbids or discourages. After the apocalypse, we'll sail around the world, build a treehouse city, or live like urban ninjas. For strong and resourceful people, it will actually be kind of fun. It won't be. Somehow when we tell stories of the end of the world, we tend to always leave out the most fundamental experience of life during a disaster, which is powerless suffering. Disasters are all about bad food and wet feet and sick babies and pointless pain.

Reality is quite different from these apocalyptic fantasies. In reality, even the worst large-scale disasters come in variable speeds; in even the worst disasters, effects are uneven, with some places devastated and others left almost unscathed; and rebuilding begins almost immediately. (The Black Death, for instance, killed a third to half of the population in Europe but didn't put much of a dent in the continent's evolution—indeed, some argue that it accelerated trade and innovation.)

In reality, in a disaster those with the largest stable group and the highest degree of cooperation come out on top. In fact, it's often the groups that are best governed and most socially coherent that can assist other groups in the rebuilding—and the hardest-hit people are generally quite receptive to good ideas for putting the pieces back together. Cities often rebuild the countryside, not the other way around.

We make a mistake when we think about the catastrophes looming before us—climate change, peak oil, pandemics—in millenarian terms. For one thing, by overplaying the inevitability of these disasters, we undercut our own will

to stave them off, to moderate their extent, and to prepare resilient strategies for coming through in the best shape we can, able to rebuild as quickly as possible.

The intelligent response to looming crisis is a mix of all-out efforts toward prevention and widespread societal preparation. It's foresight, planning, and cooperation; good investments and strong public-service capacities; anticipating limited collapse, and being ready to help restore order and livelihoods to people quickly; banking on humanity in the long run. It's knowing that Really Bad Stuff has happened before, and that when people stuck together and were tough, smart, and hardworking, they got through it. Sometimes what they built in the ashes was even better than what they had before.

The smart move, when you're worried about the future, is to change it. AS

The Politics of Optimism

██████ Optimism, as we've noted, is a powerful political act.

Recently, though, we've often been asked how it's possible to remain optimistic when the news is so bad, when progress on problems like climate change and global poverty seems hopelessly slow. These questions started us thinking about why the tone of coverage and debate about the big issues we face is so unrelentingly grim.

Some of that darkness comes, undoubtedly, from legitimate despair: from solastalgia [see Placing Yourself, p. 449] or from compassion for the horrible suffering of the millions of people our global economy has left behind. Some of it reflects the cynicism of disappointed idealists, folks who've seen so much of the underside of human nature that they've abandoned hope. Some of it results from the narrative lure of collapse.

Despair has political roots: some interests even encourage it. Despair's political basis goes largely unrecognized, even by some of its

---

Artist Kenn Brown visualized what the planet might look like three hundred years from now in connection with Alan Weisman's book *The World Without Us.*

fiercest partisans, because of a set of unexamined assumptions:

1) an explicitly stated presumption that we are incapable of solving the planet's most pressing problems and that to consider doing so is "unrealistic"

2) a mostly unstated assumption that embracing bold solutions is unrealistic because they would involve unbearable costs

3) a rarely voiced belief that "realistic" is best defined as "in the interests of those doing well today," and that "unbearable costs" is defined as "any meaningful change in our circumstances"

4) a widely held notion that, therefore, expressions of concern and extremely modest, almost symbolic, small steps and half measures are the appropriate course of action.

Though often combined with the politics of fear, this political stance might best be described as "the politics of impossibility." (It's as if Eeyore were running the public debate.) Consider, instead, the beliefs that accompany a politics of optimism:

1) that "realistic" is best defined as "within our capacity" and "necessary"

2) that we have the capacity to create and deploy solutions to the world's biggest problems, and that the magnitude of the consequences if we fail to do so (for ourselves and for generations to come) demands our immediate action

3) that we can act in such a way to improve the prospects of most people on the planet, and to greatly improve the lot of our children and grandchildren

4) that, therefore, defining our winning scenarios, imagining the kind of future we want to create, describing the solutions that will make that future possible, and publicly committing ourselves to success are the appropriate course of action.

The politics of optimism is not about being naive. We can understand that people are fallible, largely motivated by self-interest, and sometimes mistaken about what's in their own best interests. We can stress the importance of informed decision-making, demand rigor, and note uncertainty. We can recognize the massive differentials in power and wealth in our society and be clear-headed about the difficulty of opposing those whose power and wealth are tied to planetary destruction. We can anticipate setbacks and

failures, disappointments and betrayals. We can expect corruption and demand transparency. We can freely admit the profound challenges inherent in the work to be done.

We can freely acknowledge the tremendous struggle ahead of us and still choose to remain decidedly optimistic, to work from a fundamental belief in the possibilities of the future. When we do that, we liberate ourselves from some of the burden of despair and powerlessness we've all been saddled with in the twenty-first century.

And when we do it in public—when we stand up and speak out against the idea that failure is preordained and action is unrealistic— we strike right down to the heart of the political conflict we really face: the conflict between our party of the future and their party of the past.

Incrementalism in the absence of committed vision almost always serves the politics of impossibility. Paradoxically, a lot of old-school activism does as well. The impossibility lobby is entirely okay with Greenpeace or whomever doing direct action to highlight the latest dire predictions about the ruin of the Earth, because they've mostly moved on from debating reality to defining response. They're okay with people thinking the crisis is downright apocalyptic, so long as those same people don't think there's anything we can do differently.

That's why our best hope lies in a fighting optimism that's willing to confront the impossibility lobby and its messengers and make very clear that a feeble, halting response is neither rational nor responsible, but corrupt and morally bankrupt.

Every time we explain how a better future might be built, we redraw the boundaries of the possible. We show that the realm of choices available to us is actually quite large and may include paths that, for instance, will harm the interests of rich old guys who own big chunks of coal companies or the petrochemical industry but will improve the prospects of pretty much everyone else.

We need to accelerate innovation and magnify vision. We need to school ourselves in the possible, share ideas, imagine outcomes, weigh options. We need to figure out how best to transform the systems we've built. Ultimately, though, we need something more than better answers. We need millions of people who are willing to teach the open-minded, comfort the disheartened, and confront the scoundrels. We need to take our politics public and fight the whole culture of cynical defeatism. We need an optimism uprising. AS

■■■■■ RESOURCES

Long Now Foundation
http://www.longnow.org
Long Now is the preeminent time-oriented nonprofit group on the planet. They take the long view, the very long view. In fact, they're dedicated to encouraging thinking in a ten-thousand-year time frame: they reason that we have almost that many years of civilization behind us, and that we ought to be able to think at least that far ahead. Right now, though, they're building a clock meant to count the millennia, building a "Rosetta Disk" of all human languages, and hosting videos of some of the best seminars on long-term thinking that can be found anywhere on the web. They also have an informative blog and online resources. AS

Open The Future
http://openthefuture.com
Jamais Cascio (a Worldchanging cofounder) is one of the world's most interesting "ethical futurists." That is, Cascio attempts to help people understand the tools of futurism not as nifty prediction devices, but as useful instruments for exploring the ethical choices we confront today. Cascio's blog often features provocative and complex thinking about the unexpected decisions we face, especially regarding technologies. AS

What Technology Wants by Kevin Kelly (Viking Adult, 2010)
Kelly believes that the world of the made (what he calls the Technium) operates with evolutionary rules similar to those of the world of the born—that technology evolves as if it were alive. Historical accident plays a part, but to a large extent, the development of new technologies follows patterns that can be teased out. The choices we make are all-important, and they ought to be informed by a deep understanding of how the Technium works, so we can focus on creating the best changes for the future. AS

The Upside of Down: Catastrophe, Creativity, and the Renewal of Civilization by Thomas F. Homer-Dixon (Island Press, 2008)
Did ancient Rome collapse because the amount of energy the Romans could get from their agricultural system was unable to keep up with the complexity of their imperial system? Are we about to follow a similar path? Homer-Dixon thinks so. But whether you accept his grim prognosis or not, his explorations of how systems work and how cultures become resilient provide lots of insight—for the present and the future. AS

Green Futures
http://www.forumforthefuture.org
A magazine put out by the NGO Forum for the Future, Green Futures is the UK's leading journal of ideas about the planetary future. Full of intriguing ideas, from "slow fashion" to floating cities, Green Futures covers a lot of worldchanging ideas; it also provides excellent coverage of the latest British sustainability trends. AS

■■■■■ SCIENCE FICTION GREATS

Sci-fi has a bad rap for being about alien monsters, rocket ships, and scantily clad spacebabes, but some of the most thoughtful, interesting writing in the genre is actually about understanding how we're living today and how change is already unfolding around us—what science fiction writers call "predicting the present." These are among our favorite science fiction works that illuminate ways of understanding the patterns of time and the possibilities ahead of us:

Foundation by Isaac Asimov (Spectra, 2008; first edition Gnome Press, 1951)
What if a group of committed do-gooders decided to set in motion a plan to save civilization over the course of centuries? This is one of the greatest future-thinking novels of all time.

Holy Fire by Bruce Sterling (Bantam Books, 1996)
What might life look like in a globalized and aging world? How might our identities and cultures change when we can all expect to live a very long time?

The Caryatids by Bruce Sterling (Del Rey, 2009)
How will young people feel when they're left with the big job of repairing the planet? This is a brilliant look at the generation whose job it will be to remake the world we've half-destroyed.

Red Mars, *Green Mars*, *Blue Mars* by Kim Stanley Robinson (Bantam Books, 1993, 1994, 1997)
What might it be like to turn Mars into a habitable planet with a complex ecosystem, a democratic planetary government, and a new indigenous human culture? This three-book work explores the future of a second human world.

Contact by Carl Sagan (Simon & Schuster, 1985)
How will humanity react when we receive the first evidence of alien intelligence? How will ideas of identity, security, religion, and the future change when we know we're not alone?

Pattern Recognition by William Gibson (Berkley, 2005; first edition G. P. Putnam's Sons, 2003)
What's life like in a hyper-mediated world where nothing feels quite solid? This is a whirlwind mystery adventure through a world of brands, viral media, and human disconnection.

Halting State by Charles Stross (Ace, 2007)
If massive multiplayer online games continue to grow, and the online world and the physical world continue to merge through mobile technologies and augmented reality, will games start to change the "real" world?

Dune by Frank Herbert (Ace Trade, 2005; first edition Chilton Books, 1965)
What would life be like in a hot desert world? This classic novel, where the main character could be said to be the fictional planet Arrakis itself, imagines in great complexity whole different human ecologies that have evolved for life on a planet that some critics have called a veiled prediction for the earth's future.

Fiskadoro by Denis Johnson (Harper Perennial, 1995; first edition Alfred A. Knopf, 1985)
If our old technologies were to slowly wear away in a postapocalyptic world, where would that leave us? Set on a Caribbean island where people are now leading simple lives fishing and farming, this novel is a poetic meditation on history, hope, and the life that comes after the end of the world.

The Baroque Cycle by Neal Stephenson (HarperTorch, 2006; first editions William Morrow, 2003, 2004, and 2005)
How does the past inform our future? This inventive three-volume tale explores our future by delving into the past and seeking its roots in the alchemical science and global explorations of the seventeenth and eighteenth centuries. In the process, it helps us understand that science and technology themselves are stories whose meanings we don't fully comprehend and whose endings we do not yet know.

The Wind-Up Girl by Paolo Bacigalupi (Night Shade Books, 2009)
How would a society completely dependent on genetically engineered crops function? Bacigalupi imagines a post-peak future for Bangkok in which control over GM crops is the foundation of the economy.

A sapling grows in the ash surrounding Mount St. Helens National Volcanic Monument, Washington.

SELECTED BIBLIOGRAPHY

Abe, Naoki. "The Outlook for the U.S. Economy: Echoes of Japan's Lost Decade." The Brookings Institution, September 14, 2009. http://www.brookings.edu/opinions/2009/0914_economy_abe.aspx.

Ableman, Michael. *Fields of Plenty: A Farmer's Journey in Search of Real Food and the People Who Grow It*. San Francisco: Chronicle Books, 2005.

Ableman, Michael, and Alice Waters. *On Good Land: The Autobiography of an Urban Farm*. San Francisco: Chronicle Books, 1998.

Anholt, Simon. *Brand New Justice*. 2nd ed. Oxford: Butterworth-Heinemann, 2005.

Ansfield, Jonathan, and Keith Bradsher. "China Report Shows More Pollution in Waterways." *New York Times*, February 9, 2010. http://www.nytimes.com/2010/02/10/world/asia/10pollute.html.

Architecture 2030. *The 2030 Challenge Stimulus Plan: Transition Team Brief*. Santa Fe: Architecture 2030, 2009.

Arieff, Allison. "What Will Save the Suburbs?" *By Design* (blog), *New York Times*, January 11, 2009. http://arieff.blogs.nytimes.com/2009/01/11/what-will-save-the-suburbs.

Ashby, Madeline. "Toronto's Tower Renewal." *Worldchanging Canada*, November 24, 2008. http://www.worldchanging.com/local/canada/archives/008984.html.

AtKisson, Alan. *Believing Cassandra: An Optimist Looks at a Pessimist's World*. White River Junction, VT: Chelsea Green Publishing, 1999.

Ayittey, George B. N. *Africa Unchained: The Blueprint for Africa's Future*. New York: Palgrave Macmillan, 2005.

Bailey, John, et al. *Paving Our Way to Water Shortages: How Sprawl Aggravates Drought*. Special Report, American Rivers, NRDC, and Smart Growth America, 2002.

Bardsley, Daniel. "Full Throttle on High-Speed Rail." *The National*, March 20, 2010. http://www.thenational.ae/apps/pbcs.dll/article?AID=/20100320/BUSINESS/703209934/1005.

Barnett, Erica C. "Family Planning, Population, and Global Warming." Worldchanging.com, October 2, 2007. http://www.worldchanging.com/archives/007337.html.

———. "Making Visible the Invisible: Domestic Violence, Postpartum Depression." Worldchanging.com, October 29, 2007. http://www.worldchanging.com/archives/007466.html.

Barnett, Thomas P. M. *Blueprint for Action: A Future Worth Creating*. New York: G. P. Putnam's Sons, 2005.

Baskin, Yvonne. *Under Ground: How Creatures of Mud and Dirt Shape Our World*. Washington, DC: Island Press, 2005.

Baum, Dan. "Revolution 101: The Ruckus Society." *Rolling Stone*, n.d. 2001.

BBC. "Finland Tops Global School Table." BBC News, December 7, 2004. http://news.bbc.co.uk/1/hi/education/4073753.stm.

Beaumont, Peter. "Rwanda's Laptop Revolution." *The Guardian*, March 28, 2010. http://www.guardian.co.uk/technology/2010/mar/28/rwanda-laptop-revolution.

Becker, Bill. "Exclusive Analysis, Part 1: The Staggering Cost of New Nuclear Power." ClimateProgress.org, January 5, 2009. http://climateprogress.org/2009/01/05/study-cost-risks-new-nuclear-power-plants.

Beery, Jenny, Esther Eidinow, and Nancy Murphy. "The Mont Fleur Scenarios." *Deeper News* (Emeryville, CA: Global Business Network) 7, no. 1 (1997).

Benkler, Yochai. *The Wealth of Networks*. New Haven: Yale University Press, 2006.

Benyus, Janine. *Biomimicry: Innovation Inspired by Nature*. New York: Harper Perennial, 2002.

———. "Janine Benyus Interview." Interview with Jennifer Leonard. Massive Change Radio, October 14, 2003. http://www.massivechange.com/2006/07/11/janine-benyus-interview-october-14-2003.

———. "What Would Nature Do?" Interview with Sarah Kuck. Worldchanging.com, May 15, 2009. http://www.worldchanging.com/archives/009843.html.

Berry, Wendell. *What Are People For?* New York: North Point, 1990.

Black, Richard. "Environment Key to Helping Poor." BBC News, August 31, 2005. http://news.bbc.co.uk/2/hi/science/nature/4199138.stm.

Block, Ben. "Agroforestry Found on Nearly Half the World's Farms." Worldchanging.com, August 28, 2009. http://www.worldchanging.com/archives/010420.html.

———. "Bearing Children: Not Always a Woman's Choice." Worldchanging.com, February 5, 2009. http://www.worldchanging.com/archives/009396.html.

———. "New Fish Farms Move from Ocean to Warehouse." Worldchanging.com, April 29, 2008. http://www.worldchanging.com/archives/007998.html.

———. "Wind Energy Could Power China, Study Finds." Worldwatch.org, September 16, 2009. http://www.worldwatch.org/node/6255.

Blum, Andrew. "The Hills Are Alive." *Access Review*, vol. 2, n.d. 2008, 26–27.

———. "Planning Rwanda." *Metropolis*, November 21, 2007. http://www.metropolismag.com/story/20071121/planning-rwanda.

Blumenthal, Robin Goldwyn. "Good Vibes: Socially Responsible Investing Is Gaining Fans . . . and Clout." *Barron's*, July 7, 2003.

Bohannon, John. "Gamers Unravel the Secret Life of Protein." Wired.com, April, 20, 2009. http://www.wired.com/medtech/genetics/magazine/17-05/ff_protein.

Bollier, David. *Silent Theft: The Private Plunder of Our Common Wealth*. New York: Routledge, 2002.

Boss, Suzie. "Small Deposits Add Up." Worldchanging.com, November 3, 2009. http://www.worldchanging.com/archives/010709.html.

Boyd, Clark. "Estonia Embraces Web Without Wires." BBC News, May 5, 2004. http://news.bbc.co.uk/2/hi/technology/3673619.stm.

Bradley, Kimberly. "Making a Mountain: Bjarke Ingels Adds a High-Altitude Feature to Copenhagen's Flat Landscape." *Metropolis*, December 17, 2008. http://www.metropolismag.com/story/20081217/making-a-mountain.

Bradsher, Keith, and David Barboza. "Pollution from Chinese Coal Casts a Global Shadow." *New York Times*, June 11, 2006. http://www.nytimes.com/2006/06/11/business/worldbusiness/11chinacoal.html.

Brand, Stewart. *The Clock of the Long Now—Time and Responsibility*. New York: Basic Books, 1999.

Brea, Jennifer. "The New Rwanda." *The Guardian*, July 16, 2007. http://www.guardian.co.uk/commentisfree/2007/jul/16/thenewrwanda.

Brown, Lester R. *Plan B 2.0: Rescuing a Planet Under Stress and a Civilization in Trouble*. New York: W. W. Norton, 2006.

Buchmann, Stephen L., and Gary Paul Nabhan. *The Forgotten Pollinators*. Washington, DC: Island Press, 1997.

Camejo, Peter. *The SRI Advantage: Why Socially Responsible Investing Has Outperformed Financially*. Gabriola, BC: New Society Publishers, 2002.

Campbell, Kurt M., et al. *The Age of Consequences: The Foreign Policy and National Security Implications of Global Climate Change*. Washington, DC: Center for Strategic and International Studies/Center for a New American Security, 2007.

Carus, Felicity. "Living Walls and Green Roofs Pave Way for Biodiversity in New Building." *The Guardian*, March 30, 2009. http://www.guardian.co.uk/environment/2009/mar/30/green-building-biodiversity.

Cascio, Jamais. "The 2000 Watt Society." Worldchanging.com, June 2, 2005. http://www.worldchanging.com/archives/002829.html.

Cassidy, Arly, Josh Newell, and Jennifer Wolch. *Transforming Alleys into Green Infrastructure for Los Angeles*. Los Angeles: USC Center for Sustainable Cities, 2008. http://www.chc-inc.org/downloads/CASLA%20Alleyway%20Report.pdf.

Cavanaugh, Rebecca. "Roofs Paved with Green." *Metropolis*, February 14, 2007. http://www.metropolismag.com/story/20070214/roofs-paved-with-green.

Center for Neighborhood Technology. *Creating and Capturing Value in Mass Transit*. Chicago: Center for Neighborhood Technology, 2008.

Chandler, Elizabeth Khuri. "Bicing: Barcelona's Communal Bicycle Program Has Transformed the City." *Huffington Post*, May 6, 2009. http://www.huffingtonpost.com/2009/05/06/bicing-barcelonas-communa_n_197050.html.

Chapa, Jorge. "Stunning Facade Renovation Pours in Daylight." Inhabitat.com, September 24, 2009. http://www.inhabitat.com/2009/09/24/the-eyelids-of-10-hills-place-by-ala.

Charter, Martin, and Ursula Tischner. *Sustainable Solutions: Developing Products and Services for the Future*. Sheffield: Greenleaf Publishing, 2001.

Chicago Department of Transportation. *The Chicago Green Alley Handbook*. Chicago: Chicago Department of Transportation, 2007.

Cincotta, Richard. "State of the World 2005: Global Security Brief #2: Youth Bulge, Underemployment Raise Risks of Civil Conflict." Worldwatch.org, March 1, 2005. http://worldwatch.org/node/76.

The Cities Alliance. *Liveable Cities: The Benefits of Urban Environmental Planning*. The Cities Alliance, 2007.

Coghlan, Andy. "More Crops for Africa as Trees Reclaim the Desert." *New Scientist*, October 14, 2006. http://www.newscientist.com/article/dn10293-more-crops-for-africa-as-trees-reclaim-the-desert.html.

Colville-Andersen, Mikael. "Bicycle Commuter Superhighways in Copenhagen." Copenhagenize.com, August 18, 2009. http://www.copenhagenize.com/2009/08/bicycle-commuter-superhighways-in.html.

Congress for the New Urbanism. "Canons of Sustainable Architecture and Urbanism." CNU, http://www.cnu.org/canons.

Coté, John. "City to Get Treasure Island for $105 Million." SFGate.com, December 17, 2009. http://articles.sfgate.com/2009-12-17/bay-area/17224674_1_treasure-island-sustainable-development-environmentally-friendly-development.

Crumlish, Christian. *The Power of Many: How the Living Web Is Transforming Politics, Business, and Everyday Life*. Alameda, CA: Sybex, 2004.

Dale, Steven. "The Hungerburgbahn (Part 2)." GondolaProject.com, January 15, 2010. http://gondolaproject.com/2010/01/15/the-hungerburgbahn-part-2.

Dash, Eric, and Andrew Martin. "Banks Brace for Credit Card Write-Offs." *New York Times*, May 10, 2009. http://www.nytimes.com/2009/05/11/business/11credit.html.

Datschefski, Edwin. *The Total Beauty of Sustainable Products*. Crans-Près-Céligny, Switzerland: Rotovision, 2001.

Dauncey, Guy, and Patrick Mazza. *Stormy Weather: 101 Solutions to Global Climate Change*. Gabriola, BC: New Society Publishers, 2001.

David, Leonard. "Space Debris." *New Scientist*, May 11, 1996. http://see.msfc.nasa.gov/Sparkman/Section_Docs/article_1.htm.

Dean, Cornelia. "Rising Acidity Threatens Oceans." *New York Times*, January 30, 2009, A12.

Demaret, Luc. "India: Hope Dawns as Women Beat Poverty." International Labor Organization Press Release, July 1, 2004. http://www.ilo.org/actrav/info/pr/lang--en/docName--WCMS_112354/index.htm.

Desai, Pooran, and Sue Riddlestone. *BioRegional Solutions for Living on One Planet*. London: Green Books, 2002.

Design Trust for Public Space. "High Performance Infrastructure Guidelines." Design Trust for Public Space, and New York City Department of Design and Construction, October 2005.

Diamond, Jared. *Guns, Germs and Steel: The Fates of Human Societies*. New York: W. W. Norton, 1997.

Drengson, Alan, and Duncan Taylor, eds. *Ecoforestry: The Art and Science of Sustainable Forest Use*. Gabriola Island, BC: New Society Publishers, 1997.

Drexler, Eric. *Engines of Creation: The Coming Era of Nanotechnology*. Garden City, NY: Anchor Press, 1987.

Dubner, Stephen J., and Steven D. Levitt. "Not-So-Free Ride." *New York Times Magazine: The Green Issue*, April 20, 2008.

Dumaine, Brian. "World's Greenest Skyscraper." CNNMoney.com, February 24, 2010. http://money.cnn.com/2010/02/22/technology/zeb_pearl_river.fortune.

Dumiak, Michael. "Simple and Bright, Heliostats Tap Sunlight for Lighting Outdoor and, Increasingly, Indoor Spaces." *Architectural Record*, May 2007. http://archrecord.construction.com/tech/techbriefs/0705dignews-1.asp.

Earle, Sylvia. "TED Prize Wish: Protect Our Oceans." Keynote speech, TED2009 (Long Beach, CA), February 5, 2009.

Elbaek, Uffe. *Kaospilot A–Z*. Aarhus, Denmark: KaosCommunication, 2003.

Elser, James, and Stuart White. "Peak Phosphorus." *Foreign Policy*, April 20, 2010. http://www.foreignpolicy.com/articles/2010/04/20/peak_phosphorus.

Environmental Protection Agency. *Protecting Water Resources with Higher-Density Development*. Washington, DC: Environmental Protection Agency, 2006.

E.R.A. Architects and the University of Toronto. "Mayor's Tower Renewal Opportunities Book,"2008. http://era.on.ca/blogs/towerrenewal/?page_id=156.

Esch, Mary. "iPhone App Lets You Bird-watch on the Go." Msnbc.com, December 8, 2009. http://www.msnbc.msn.com/id/34334063/ns/technology_and_science-tech_and_gadgets.

Eskenazi, Stuart. "75 Hard-core Alcoholics to be Offered Apartments." *Seattle Times*, December 15, 2005. http://seattletimes.nwsource.com/html/localnews/2002684566_eastlake15m.html.

Ewing, Reid, Keith Bartholomew, Steve Winkelman, Jerry Walters, and Don Chen. *Growing Cooler: The Evidence on Urban Development and Climate Change*. Washington, DC: Urban Land Institute, 2008.

Faris, Stephan. *Forecast: The Consequences of Climate Change, from the Amazon to the Arctic, from Darfur to Napa Valley*. New York: Henry Holt and Company, 2008.

Farr, Douglas. *Sustainable Urbanism: Urban Design with Nature*. New York: John Wiley & Sons, 2008.

Feireiss, Kristin, and Lukas Feireiss. *Architecture of Change*. Berlin: Gestalten Verlag, 2008.

Ferguson, Niall. *Empire: The Rise and Demise of the British Empire and the Lessons for Global Power*. New York: Basic Books, 2003.

Frank, Thomas, and Matt Weiland, eds. *Commodify Your Dissent*. New York: W. W. Norton, 1997.

Frey, Patrice. "Building Reuse: Finding a Place on American Climate Policy Agendas." National Trust for Historic Preservation, September 2008. http://www.preservationnation.org/issues/sustainability/additional-resources/buillding_reuse.pdf.

Friend, Gil. *The Truth About Green Business*. Upper Saddle River, NJ: FT Press, 2009.

Fuller, Donald A. *Sustainable Marketing: Managerial-Ecological Issues*. Thousand Oaks, CA: Sage, 1999.

Galston, William A. "The 'New Normal' for the U.S. Economy: What Will It Be?" Brookings Institution, September 1, 2009. http://www.brookings.edu/opinions/2009/0901_economy_galston.aspx.

Garnaut, Ross. *The Garnaut Climate Change Review*. Cambridge: Cambridge University Press, 2008.

Garreau, Joel. *Radical Evolution: The Promise and Peril of Enhancing Our Minds, Our Bodies—and What It Means to Be Human*. New York: Doubleday, 2005.

Gilson, Dave. "House of Cards." *Mother Jones*, September/October 2007. http://motherjones.com/politics/2007/09/house-cards.

Gipe, Paul. *Wind Power: Renewable Energy for Home, Farm, and Business*. White River Junction, VT: Chelsea Green Publishing, 2004.

Gissen, David, ed. *Big and Green: Toward Sustainable Architecture in the 21st Century*. New York: Princeton Architectural Press, 2003.

Glaeser, Edward L., and Matthew Kahn. *The Greenness of Cities*, Policy Brief, Rappaport Institute/Taubman Center, Cambridge, MA, March 2008.

Gobster, Paul, and Bruce Hull, eds. *Restoring Nature*. Washington, DC: Island Press, 2000.

Goodman, Amy. "'Utah' Phillips: The Music Lives On." *Seattle Post-Intelligencer*, May 29, 2008.

Gordon, Jacob. "Passive Acceptance." *Dwell*, November 2009. http://www.dwell.com/articles/passive-acceptance.html.

Green, Judith M. *Deep Democracy*. Lanham, MD: Rowman and Littlefield, 1999.

Greenemeier, Larry. "EPA Tests Porous Pavement to Combat Contaminated Rain Runoff." *Scientific American*, October 30, 2009. http://www.scientificamerican.com/blog/post.cfm?id=epa-tests-porous-pavement-to-combat-2009-10-30.

Greenseth, Morgan. "Reader Report: Historic Green in New Orleans." Worldchanging.com, May 5, 2009. http://www.worldchanging.com/archives/009785.html.

Griffith, Nicola. *Slow River*. New York: Ballantine Books, 1996.

Groh, Trauger, and Steven McFadden. *Farms of Tomorrow Revisited: Community Supported Farms—Farm Supported Communities*. Kimberton, PA: Bio-dynamic Farming and Gardening Association, 1998.

The Guardian. "China: Low Carbon Sources to Supply Quarter of Electricity by End of 2010." *The Guardian*, April 9, 2010. http://www.guardian.co.uk/environment/2010/apr/09/china-low-carbon-renewable.

Guenster, Nadja, Jeroen Derwall, Rob Bauer, and Kees Koedijk. "The Economic Value of Corporate Eco-Efficiency." Study by the Center for Responsible Business at the Haas School of Business, UC Berkeley, 2005.

Gupta, Anil K. *Linking Grassroots Innovations, Enterprise, Investments, Incentives and Institutions*. Position Paper, Honey Bee Network, 1999.

Halweil, Brian. *Farming Fish for the Future*. Worldwatch Report 176. Washington, DC: Worldwatch Institute, 2008.

Halweil, Brian, and Danielle Nierenberg. "Farming the Cities." *State of the World 2007: Our Urban Future*. New York: W. W. Norton & Company, 2007.

Han, Bola, and Kitty McKinsey. "'Hallelujah': Myanmar Refugees Can Now Prove Their Identity in Thailand." UNHCR.org, April 12, 2007. http://www.unhcr.org/46te3ab34.html.

Hansen, James. "Climate Change Demands a Transformative Change in Direction." Worldchanging.com, February 16, 2009. http://www.worldchanging.com/archives/009432.html.

Hargroves, Karlson, and Michael H. Smith. *The Natural Advantage of Nations: Business Opportunities, Innovation and Governance in the 21st Century*. London: Earthscan Publications, 2005.

Harrison, Owen. *Open Space Technology: A User's Guide*. San Francisco: Berrett-Koehler, 1997.

Hart, Stuart L. *Capitalism at the Crossroads: The Unlimited Business Opportunities in Solving the World's Most Difficult Problems*. Upper Saddle River, NJ: Wharton School Publishing, 2005.

Havel, Vaclav. *The Art of the Impossible: Politics as Morality in Practice*. New York: Knopf, 1997.

Hawken, Paul. *The Ecology of Commerce: A Declaration of Sustainability*. New York: Harper-Collins, 1993.

Hawken, Paul, Amory Lovins, and L. Hunter Lovins. *Natural Capitalism: Creating the Next Industrial Revolution*. Boston: Little, Brown, 1999.

Hayden, Kristin. "Reader Report: Skoll World Forum on Social Entrepreneurship." Worldchanging.com, April 1, 2009. http://www.worldchanging.com/archives//009664.html.

Hayes, Denis. "Climate Solutions: Charting a Bold Course." *Yale Environment 360*, June 10, 2008. http://www.e360.yale.edu/content/feature.msp?id=2026.

Heim, Kristi. "Credit Union Aims to Help People Break the Payday-Lender Cycle." *Seattle Times*, May 24, 2009. http://seattletimes.nwsource.com/html/businesstechnology/2009256799_expressbank24.html.

Heimbuch, Jaymi. "Deadly Ghost Net Removed from Sunken Ship." TreeHugger.com, January 13, 2009. http://www.treehugger.com/files/2009/01/deadly-ghost-net-removed-from-sunken-ship.php.

Henry, Julie. "Girl Guides Group for Teenage Mothers." *The Telegraph*, August 29, 2009. http://www.telegraph.co.uk/news/newstopics/howaboutthat/6110338/Girl-Guides-group-for-teenage-mothers.html.

Higgs, Eric. *Nature by Design*. Cambridge, MA: The MIT Press, 2003.

Hill, Dan. "The Adaptive City." CityofSound.com, September 7, 2008. http://www.cityofsound.com/blog/2008/09/the-adaptive-ci.html.

Ho, Vanessa. "Study: Seattle Home for Alcoholics Saved Taxpayers $4 Million." *Seattle P-I*, April 1, 2009. http://www.seattlepi.com/local/404451_alcoholic01ww.html.

Hochschild, Adam. *Bury the Chains: Prophets and Rebels in the Fight to Free an Empire's Slaves*. Boston: Houghton Mifflin, 2005.

Holmgren, David. *Permaculture: Principles and Pathways Beyond Sustainability*. Victoria, Australia: Holmgren Design Studios, 2002.

Homer-Dixon, Thomas. *The Ingenuity Gap: Facing the Economic, Environmental, and Other Challenges of an Increasingly Complex and Unpredictable World*. New York: Knopf, 2000.

Hvistendahl, Mara. "The China Experiment." *SEED*, May 1, 2007. http://seedmagazine.com/content/article/the_china_experiment.

International Council on Human Rights Policy. *Climate Change and Human Rights: A Rough Guide*. Geneva: International Council on Human Rights Policy, 2008. http://www.ichrp.org/files/summaries/35/136_summary.pdf.

International Labour Organization. "Global Employment Trends, January 2010." Geneva: International Labour Organization, 2010.

Jackson, Wes, Wendell Berry, and Bruce Colman. *Meeting the Expectations of the Land*. New York: North Point Press, 1985.

Jacobs, Jane. *The Death and Life of Great American Cities*. New York: Vintage Books, 1961.

Janzen, Daniel. "Gardenification of Wildland Nature and the Human Footprint." *Science*, February 27, 1998.

Jégou, François. "Making a Habit of Sustainability." Interview by Jane Szita. *Dwell*, October/November 2004.

Jenkins, Nancy Harmon. "Here's the Catch." *Washington Post*, January 14, 2009. http://www.washingtonpost.com/wp-dyn/content/article/2009/01/13/AR2009011300700.html.

Johnson, MI. "New Way Restaurants Can Buy into Farm-fresh Food." *Chicago Tribune*, February 13, 2009. http://archives.chicagotribune.com/2009/feb/13/local/chi-ap-fea-food-farmtomenu.

Johnston, David, and Kim Master. *Green Remodeling: Changing the World One Room at a Time*. Gabriola, BC: New Society Publishers, 2004.

Jones, Steve. *Darwin's Ghost: The Origin of Species Updated*. New York: Random House, 2000.

Jordan, William R. III. *The Sunflower Forest*. Berkeley: University of California Press, 2003.

Kac, Eduardo. *Telepresence and Bio Art: Networking Humans, Rabbits, and Robots*. Ann Arbor: University of Michigan Press, 2005.

Katz, Bruce. "The Great Recession: What Comes Next for Our Metro Nation." The Brookings Institution, October 15, 2009. http://www.brookings.edu/speeches/2009/1013_seattle_katz.aspx.

Kelly, Eamonn. *Powerful Times: Rising to the Challenge of Our Uncertain World*. Upper Saddle River, NJ: Wharton School Publishing, 2006.

Kemp, William H. *The Renewable Energy Handbook*. Tamworth, ON: Aztext Press, 2005.

———. *Smart Power: An Urban Guide to Renewable Energy and Efficiency*. Tamworth, ON: Aztext Press, 2004.

Kent, Deidre. *Healthy Money, Healthy Planet: Developing Sustainability Through New Money Systems*. Nelson, NZ: Craig Potton Publishing, 2005.

Khan, Lloyd. *Shelter*. Bolinas, CA: Shelter Publications, 1973.

Khan, Urmee. " 'Google Ocean' Launched as Extension of Google Earth to Map the Seabed." *The Telegraph*, February 3, 2009. http://www.telegraph. co.uk/technology/google/4434916/Google-Ocean-launched-as-extension-of-Google-Earth-to-map-the-seabed.html.

Khanna, Sanjay. "Solastalgia and the Mental Effects of Climate Change." Worldchanging.com, March 21, 2008. http://www.worldchanging.com/ archives/008782.html.

Kiley, Brendan. "Down on the Corner: SuttonBeresCuller Turns a Contaminated Gas Station into Sculpture." *Arcade*, Summer 2009. http://www.arcadejournal.com/public/IssueArticle. aspx?Volume=27&Issue=4&Article=320.

Kimbrell, Andrew. *Your Right to Know: Genetic Engineering and the Secret Changes in Your Food*. Berkeley, CA: Ten Speed Press, 2006.

Klein, Naomi. *No Logo*. New York: Picador, 2002.

Klemperer, Jerusha. "Restaurant Supported Agriculture." *The Slow Food USA Blog*, February 5, 2009. http://www.slowfoodusa. org/index.php/slow_food/blog_post/ restaurant_supported_agriculture/#Restaurant.

Koenig, Klaus W. *The Rainwater Technology Handbook*. Dortmund, Germany: Wilo-Brain, 2001.

Koerth-Baker, Maggie. "Wasting Time for a Good Cause." Boing Boing, May 3, 2009. http://www. boingboing.net/2009/05/03/wasting-time-for-a-g.html.

Kolbert, Elizabeth. "The Island in the Wind." *The New Yorker*, July 7, 2008. http://www.newyorker.com/ reporting/2008/07/07/080707fa_fact_kolbert.

Kowal, Jessica. "Homeless Alcoholics Receive a Permanent Place to Live, and Drink." *New York Times*, July 5, 2006. http://www.nytimes.com/2006/07/05/ us/05homeless.html.

Kristof, Nicholas. "Nicholas Kristof's Advice for Saving the World." *Outside Magazine*, December 2009. http://outside.away.com/outside/culture/200912/ nicholas-kristof-philanthropy-advice-2.html.

Krug, Nora. "Remodeling on a 'Not So Big' Scale." *Washington Post*, March 26, 2009. http:// www.washingtonpost.com/wp-dyn/content/ article/2009/03/25/AR2009032500912.html.

Laursen, Lucas. "In the Fold." *GOOD*, September/ October 2008.

Le Corbusier. *Towards a New Architecture* (1923). New York: Dover Publications, 1985.

Leakey, Richard, and Roger Lewin. *The Sixth Extinction*. New York: Anchor Books, 1996.

Leckart, Steven. "What's Up Doc?" *GOOD*, November/December 2008.

Leschin-Hoar, Clare. "Taking Stock in Fish." *Wall Street Journal*, June 17, 2009. http://online.wsj.com/ article/SB124421534407589317.html.

Li, Zijun. "Rapid Growth of China's Cities Challenges Urban Planners, Migrant Families." Worldwatch.org, June 27, 2006. http://www. worldwatch.org/node/4148.

Libby, Brian. "Beyond the Bulbs: In Praise of Natural Light." *New York Times*, June 17, 2003. http://www. nytimes.com/2003/06/17/health/beyond-the-bulbs-in-praise-of-natural-light.html.

Liggett, Brit. "World's Greenest Skyscraper: Pearl River Tower Almost Complete." Inhabitat.com, March 29, 2010. http://www.inhabitat.com/2010/03/29/ worlds-greenest-skyscraper-pearl-river-tower-almost-complete.

Lindenmayer, David B., and Jerry F. Franklin, eds. *Towards Forest Sustainability*. Washington, DC: Island Press, 2003.

Ling, Jack C., and Cynthia Reader-Wilstein. "Ending Iodine Deficiency Now and Forever." ICCIDD. org, January 26, 2010. http://www.iccidd.org/pages/technical-resources/advocacy-communication/iccidd-communications-guide.php.

Lorenz, Andreas, and Wieland Wagner. "China's Poison for the Planet." *Spiegel Online*, February 1, 2007. http://www.spiegel.de/international/spiegel/0,1518,461828,00.html.

Los Angeles Times. "Debris Misses Space Station." March 13, 2009. http://articles.latimes.com/2009/mar/13/nation/na-space-station13.

Lovins, Amory. "Amory Lovins: Energy Efficiency Is the Key." Interview with Carole Bass. *Yale Environment 360*, November 26, 2008. http://www.e360.yale.edu/content/feature.msp?id=2091.

———. "How to Get Real Security." *Whole Earth Review*, Fall 2002. http://www.rmi.org/images/other/Security/S02-13_HowRealSecurity.pdf.

Lynas, Mark. *High Tide: The Truth About Our Climate Crisis*. New York: Picador Paperback Original, 2004.

Macalister, Terry. "Lloyd's Adds Its Voice to Dire 'Peak Oil' Warnings." *The Guardian*, July 11, 2010. http://www.guardian.co.uk/business/2010/jul/11/peak-oil-energy-disruption.

Macy, Joanna. *World as Lover, World as Self*. Berkeley, CA: Parallax Press, 1991.

Mahoney, Kathryn. "Djibouti: Refugees Grasp Security in Their Hands with New ID Cards." UNHCR.org, August 25, 2009. http://www.unhcr.org/4a93b6166.html.

Makovsky, Paul. "Pedestrian Cities." *Metropolis*, August/September 2002. http://www.metropolismag.com/html/content_0802/ped/index.html.

———. "Thought Bubble." *Metropolis*, February 2006. http://www.metropolismag.com/story/20060116/thought-bubble.

Makower, Joel. "Japan, China, and the Low-Carbon Economy." Worldchanging.com, March 18, 2010. http://www.worldchanging.com/archives/011030.html.

Mann, Charles C. *1491: New Revelations of the Americas Before Columbus*. New York: Knopf, 2005.

Manning, Richard. *A Good House: Building a Life on the Land*. New York: Grove Press, 1993.

———. *Against the Grain: How Agriculture Has Hijacked Civilization*. New York: North Point Press, 2004.

Markoff, John. "This Is Only a Drill: In California, Testing Technology in a Disaster Response." *New York Times*, August 28, 2006. http://www.nytimes.com/2006/08/28/technology/28disaster.html.

Martin, Paul S. *Twilight of the Mammoths: Ice Age Extinctions and the Rewilding of North America*. Berkeley: University of California Press, 2005.

Maskrecki, Piotr. *The Smaller Majority*. Cambridge, MA: Belknap Press of Harvard University Press, 2005.

Matthews, H. Damon, and Ken Caldeira. *Stabilizing Climate Requires Near-Zero Emissions*. Abstract. *Geophysical Research Letters* 35 (February 27, 2008) doi: 10.1029/2007GL032388.

Mau, Bruce. *Massive Change*. London: Phaidon Press, 2004.

McCabe, Jess. "Population Control Is Not What Makes Climate Change a Feminist Issue." *The Guardian*, November 2, 2009. http://www.guardian.co.uk/commentisfree/cif-green/2009/nov/02/climate-change-feminist-issue.

McDonough, William, and Michael Braungart. *Cradle to Cradle: Remaking the Way We Make Things*. New York: North Point Press, 2002.

McElroy, Michael B., Xi Lu, Chris P. Nielsen, and Yuxuan Wang. "Potential for Wind-Generated Electricity in China." *Science*, September 11, 2009.

McKibben, Bill. "Apartment." *New Yorker*, March 17, 1986.

———. *The End of Nature*. New York: Random House, 1989.

———. *Hope, Human and Wild*. Boston: Little, Brown, 1995.

McKinsey & Company. *Pathways to a Low-Carbon Economy*. Special Initiative: Climate Change, McKinsey & Company, 2009.

———. *Pathways to a Low-Carbon Economy, Version 2*. Special Report, McKinsey & Company, 2009.

McKinsey Global Institute. "Preparing for China's Urban Billion." Special Report, McKinsey Global Institute, March 2008. http://www.mckinsey.com/mgi/publications/china_urban_summary_of_findings.asp.

McMullen, Alia. "Gas, Oil Prices to Double by 2012, CIBC Economist Predicts." *Financial Post*, April 24, 2008. http://www.financialpost.com/story.html?id=469214#ixzz14YFwaZhO.

McNeill, J. R. *Something New Under the Sun: An Environmental History of the Twentieth-Century World*. New York: W. W. Norton, 2000.

Meadows, Donella, Jorgen Radners, and Dennis Meadows. *Limits to Growth: The 30-Year Update*. White River Junction, VT: Chelsea Green Publishing, 2004.

Mega-Cities Project. "The Poverty/Environment Nexus in Mega-Cities." The Mega-Cities Project Publication, 1998.

Meinhold, Bridgette. "Green Lighthouse: Denmark's First Public Carbon Neutral Building Completed." Inhabitat.com, October 27, 2009. http://www.inhabitat.com/2009/10/27/green-lighthouse-denmarks-first-carbon-neutral-building-completed.

Mitchell, Bill. "Spot.Us Delivers Crowdfunding to the New York Times." PoynterOnline.com, November 10, 2009. http://www.poynter.org/column.asp?id=131&aid=173213.

Mitchell, William J. *Me ++: The Cyborg Self and the Networked City*. Cambridge, MA: The MIT Press, 2003.

Moorhead, Joanna. "Todmorden's Good Life: Introducing Britain's Greenest Town." *The Independent*, November 29, 2009. http://www.independent.co.uk/environment/green-living/todmordens-good-life-introducing-britains-greenest-town-1830666.html.

Munday, Oliver. "How Much Could We Save with Electronic Medical Records?" *GOOD*, November 10, 2009. http://www.good.is/post/how-much-could-we-save-with-electronic-medical-records.

Murray, James. "Indian Farmers to Insure Themselves Against Climate Change Crop Failure." *The Guardian*, June 8, 2009. http://www.guardian.co.uk/environment/2009/jun/08/farming-india.

Nabhan, Gary Paul. *Enduring Seeds: Native American Agriculture and Wild Plant Conservation*. Tucson: University of Arizona Press, 2002.

Nattrass, Brian, and Mary Altomare. *Dancing with the Tiger: Learning Sustainability Step by Natural Step*. Gabriola, BC: New Society Publishers, 2002.

Nye, Joseph S. *Soft Power: The Means to Success in World Politics*. New York: PublicAffairs, 2005.

Obama, Barack. Remarks on disarmament, speech at Hradcany Square, Prague, April 5, 2009.

Ohtake, Miyoko. "LiTraCon: Light-Transmitting Concrete." *Dwell*, February 4, 2009. http://www.dwell.com/articles/litracon-light-transmitting-concrete.html.

Oliver, Jamie. "TED Prize Wish: Teach Every Child About Food." Keynote speech, TED2010 (Long Beach, CA), February 9, 2010.

Orcutt, Mike. "How Quantum Dots Could Double Solar Cell Efficiency." *Popular Mechanics*, June 18, 2010. http://www.popularmechanics.com/science/energy/solar-wind/quantum-next-gen-solar-cells.

Orr, David. *Ecological Literacy: Education and the Transition to a Postmodern World*. Albany: State University of New York Press, 1992.

Oxfam International. *Climate Wrongs and Human Rights*. Oxfam Briefing Paper, September 2008. http://www.oxfam.org/sites/www.oxfam.org/files/bp117-climate-wrongs-and-human-rights-0809.pdf.

Papanek, Victor. *Design for the Real World: Human Ecology and Social Change*. Chicago: Academy Chicago Publishers, 1985.

———. *The Green Imperative: Natural Design for the Real World*. New York: Thames and Hudson, 1995.

Papi, Daniela. "'Volunteering' or 'Voluntourism'— Who Cares! It's How You Design It!" *PEPY Team Journal*, May 26, 2009. http://journal.pepyride.org/critical-views/308-qvolunteeringq-or-qvoluntourismq-who-cares-its-how-you-design-it.

Pattullo, Polly. *The Ethical Travel Guide: Your Passport to Exciting Alternative Holidays*. London: Earthscan, 2006.

Pauly, Daniel. "Aquacalypse Now." *The New Republic*, September 28, 2009. http://www.tnr.com/article/environment-energy/aquacalypse-now.

Pedersen, Martin C., "The Granny Flat Grows Up." *Metropolis*, October 17, 2005. http://www.metropolismag.com/story/20051017/the-granny-flat-grows-up.

Piller, Charles, Edmund Sanders, and Robyn Dixon. "Dark Cloud Over Good Works of Gates Foundation." *Los Angeles Times*, January 7, 2007. http://www.latimes.com/news/la-na-gatesx07jan07,0,2533850.story.

Pilloton, Emily. *Design Revolution: 100 Products That Empower People*. Los Angeles: Metropolis Books, 2009.

Pocha, Jehangir. "China's Growing Desert." *In These Times*, October 13, 2006. http://www.inthesetimes.com/article/2849.

Pop!Tech Pop!Cast. "Ipuli, Tanzania." PopTech.org, March 4, 2008. http://legacy.poptech.org/blog/index.php/archives/266.

Powell, Devin. "Arctic Melt 20 Years Ahead of Climate Models." *New Scientist*, December 19, 2008. http://www.newscientist.com/article/dn16307-arctic-melt-20-years-ahead-of-climate-models.html.

Prasad, Neeraj, Federica Ranghieri, Fatima Shah, Zoe Trohanis, Earl Kessler, and Ravi Sinha. *Climate Resilient Cities*. Special Report. Washington, DC: The World Bank, 2009.

Price, Dan. *Radical Simplicity: Creating an Authentic Life*. Philadelphia: Running Press, 2005.

Priest, Dana. *The Mission: Waging War and Keeping Peace with America's Military*. New York: W. W. Norton, 2004.

Raphael, Ray. *More Tree Talk: The People, Politics, and Economics of Timber*. Washington, DC: Island Press, 1994.

Raymond, Eric S. *The Cathedral and the Bazaar: Musings on Linux and Open Source by an Accidental Revolutionary*. Cambridge, MA: O'Reilly Media, 2001.

Rees, Martin. *Our Final Hour—A Scientist's Warning: How Terror, Error, and Environmental Distance Threatened Humankind's Future in this Century—on Earth and Beyond*. New York: Basic Books, 2003.

Reisner, Marc. *A Dangerous Place: California's Unsettling Fate*. New York: Pantheon Books, 2003.

Rejali, Darius. "Torturing Can't Be Defended, Doesn't Even Work." *The Oregonian*, April 16, 2002.

Renner, Michael. "A Billion Trees to Help Refugees." Worldchanging.com, May 25, 2007. http://www.worldchanging.com/archives//006760.html.

Revkin, Andrew C. "Can Google's Oceans Protect the Real Ones?" *Dot Earth* (blog), *New York Times*, February 2, 2009. http://dotearth.blogs.nytimes.com/2009/02/02/can-googles-oceans-protect-the-real-seas/?emc=eta1.

Rich, Sarah. "Passive Houses in Stockholm." *Dwell*, August 24, 2009. http://www.dwell.com/articles/passive-houses-in-stockholm.html.

Richardson, Julie, Terry Irwin, and Chris Sherwin. "Design and Sustainability: A Scoping Report for the Sustainable Design Forum, Design Council," 2005.

Rivoli, Pietra. *The Travels of a T-Shirt in the Global Economy: An Economist Examines the Markets, Power, and Politics of World Trade*. Hoboken, NJ: John Wiley and Sons, 2005.

Robin, Vicki, and Joe Dominguez. *Your Money or Your Life*. New York: Penguin Books, 1999.

Rogers, Heather. *Gone Tomorrow: The Hidden Life of Garbage*. New York: The New Press, 2005.

Rosenberg, Jim. "Mongolian Mobile Banking— Update from XacBank." *CGAP Blog*, January 20, 2010. http://technology.cgap.org/2010/01/20/mongoila-mobile-banking.

Rosenblatt, Gideon. "Movement as Network: Connecting People and Organizations in the Environmental Movement." *Alchemy of Change*, January 2004. http://www.alchemyofchange.net/movement-as-network.

Rosenthal, Elisabeth. "European Support for Bicycles Promotes Sharing of the Wheels." *New York Times*, November 9, 2008. http://www.nytimes.com/2008/11/10/world/europe/10bike.html.

———. "In German Suburb, Life Goes On Without Cars." *New York Times*, May 11, 2009. http://www.nytimes.com/2009/05/12/science/earth/12suburb.html.

Rotberg, Robert, and Dennis Thompson, eds. *Truth v. Justice: The Morality of Truth Commissions*. Princeton, NJ: Princeton University Press, 2000.

Sachs, Jeffrey. *The End of Poverty: Economic Possibilities for Our Time*. New York: Penguin Press, 2005.

Saieh, Nico. "Copenhagen Harbour Bath/PLOT." ArchDaily.com, January 5, 2009. http://www.archdaily.com/11216/copenhagen-harbour-bath-plot.

———. "10 Hills Place/Amanda Levete Architects." ArchDaily.com, September 10, 2009. http://www.archdaily.com/34887/10-hills-place-amanda-levete-architects.

Saulny, Susan. "In Miles of Alleys, Chicago Finds Its Next Environmental Frontier." *New York Times*, November 26, 2007. http://www.nytimes.com/2007/11/26/us/26chicago.html.

Schlosser, Eric. *Fast Food Nation*. New York: Harper Perennial, 2002.

Scholz, Astrid, Ulf Sonesson, and Peter Tyedmers. "Catch of the Freezer." *New York Times*, December 8, 2009. http://www.nytimes.com/2009/12/09/opinion/09scholz.html.

Schor, Juliet. "The New Consumerism: Inequality, Emulation, and Erosion of Self-Being." *Rotman*, Spring 2008.

———. "The New Politics of Consumption." *Boston Review*, Summer 1999. http://bostonreview.net/BR24.3/schor.html.

SciDev.Net. "Polluters Must Take in Climate Change Refugees." SciDev.net, March 24, 2005. http://www.scidev.net/en/opinions/polluters-must-take-in-climate-change-refugees.html.

ScienceDaily. "Mosquito Evolution Spells Trouble for Galapagos Wildlife." ScienceDaily.com, June 2, 2009. http://www.sciencedaily.com/releases/2009/06/090601182812.htm.

Scola, Nancy. "Harnessing Both Sun and Cell Phone to Close Gaps in Local Health Care." Worldchanging.com, June 18, 2009. http://www.worldchanging.com/archives/010007.html.

———. "The Transformative 120: Text Messages Prove a South African HIV Lifeline." Worldchanging.com, November 25, 2008. http://www.worldchanging.com/archives/009090.html.

Scott, Janny. "The Apartment Atop the Garage Is Back in Vogue." *New York Times*, December 2, 2006. http://www.nytimes.com/2006/12/02/nyregion/02attics.html.

SeaWeb. "Technological Revolutions in Sensors, Robotics, and Telecommunications Allow New Views of Ocean." Physorg.com, Space and Earth Science, February 19, 2005. http://www.physorg.com/news3116.html.

Sen, Rinku. *Stir It Up: Lessons in Community Organizing and Advocacy*. San Francisco: Jossey-Bass, 2003.

Sharp, Gene. *Waging Nonviolent Struggle: 20th Century Practice and 21st Century Potential*. Boston: Extending Horizons Books, 2005.

Shawcross, William. *Deliver Us from Evil: Warlords and Peacekeepers in a World of Endless Conflict*. London: Bloomsbury, 2000.

Sherman, Lauren. "Worst Cities for Credit Card Debt." Forbes.com, May 20, 2009. http://www.forbes.com/2009/05/20/american-consumers-overspending-lifestyle-real-estate-credit-card-debt.html.

Shoup, Donald C. *The High Cost of Free Parking*. Washington, DC: American Planning Association, 2005.

Sightline Institute. *The True Cost of Car Crashes*. Fact Sheet. Seattle: Sightline Institute, 2004.

Singh, Kanta. "Engendering Impact—Indian Scenario." Paper presented at EDIAIS Conference, Manchester, UK, November 24–25, 2003.

Slackman, Michael. "Israeli Bomblets Plague Lebanon." *New York Times*, October 6, 2006. http://www.nytimes.com/2006/10/06/world/middleeast/06cluster.html

Snyder, Gary. *The Practice of the Wild*. New York: North Point Press, 1990.

Stafford, Kim. *Having Everything Right: Essays of Place*. Seattle: Sasquatch Books, 1997.

Steffen, W., et al. *Global Change and the Earth System: A Planet Under Pressure*. Berlin: Springer, 2004.

Steinhauer, Jennifer. "When the Joneses Wear Jeans." *New York Times*, May 29, 2005. http://www.nytimes.com/2005/05/29/national/class/CONSUMPTION-FINAL.html.

Sterling, Bruce. *Tomorrow Now: Envisioning the Next Fifty Years*. New York: Random House, 2002.

Sterling, Bruce, and Lorraine Wild. *Shaping Things*. Cambridge, MA: The MIT Press, 2005.

Stern, Jennifer. "African Rats Sniff Out Land Mines." MediaClubSouthAfrica.com, October 15, 2008. http://www.mediaclubsouthafrica.com/index.php?option=com_content&view=article&id=784:ratsi51008&catid=47:africa_news&Itemid=116.

Stevens, William K. *Miracle Under the Oaks*. New York: Pocket Books, 1995.

Strom, Stephanie. "Confusion on Where Money Lent via Kiva Goes." *New York Times*, November 8, 2009. http://www.nytimes.com/2009/11/09/business/global/09kiva.html.

Sullivan, C.C. "Passive Ventilation for Aggressive Energy Savings." *Archi-Tech*, February 2009. http://www.architechweb.com/Content/ArticleDetails/tabid/171/ArticleID/8056/Default.aspx.

Sun Microsystems. "Sun Microsystems Study Finds Open Work Program Saves Employees Time and Money, Decreases Carbon Output." Press release. Santa Clara: Sun Microsystems, 2008.

Sunstein, Cass R. *Why Societies Need Dissent*. Cambridge, MA: Harvard University Press, 2003.

Sustainable Cities. "Copenhagen: From Sewer to Harbour Bath." SustainableCities.com, March 31, 2009. http://sustainablecities.dk/en/city-projects/cases/copenhagen-from-sewer-to-harbour-bath.

Sutherland, Peter. "The Age of Mobility: Can We Make Migration Work for All?" Lecture, London School of Economics and Political Science, 2008.

Sutter, John D. "Backyard Scientists Use Web to Catalog Species, Aid Research." CNN.com, May 4, 2009. http://www.cnn.com/2009/TECH/science/05/04/citizen.science.climate.change/index.html.

———. "Search for Downed Plane Highlights Ocean Trash Problem." CNN.com, June 5, 2009. http://www.cnn.com/2009/TECH/science/06/05/marine.debris.crash/index.html.

Suzuki, David, and Holly Dressel. *Good News for a Change: How Everyday People Are Helping the Planet*. Vancouver: Greystone Books, 2002.

Talbot, David. "How Obama *Really* Did It." *Technology Review*, September/October 2008.

Tapscott, Don, and David Ticoll. *The Naked Corporation: How the Age of Transparency Will Revolutionize Business*. New York: Free Press, 2003.

Teather, David. "Chinese Skyscraper Builders to Put Up Equivalent of 10 New Yorks, Says Rio Tinto." *The Guardian*, August 27, 2008. http://www.guardian.co.uk/business/2008/aug/27/riotinto.commodities.

Thackara, John. *In the Bubble*. Cambridge, MA: The MIT Press, 2005.

Thompson, Clive. "Clive Thompson on the Revolution in Micromanufacturing." *Wired*, February 23, 2009. http://www.wired.com/techbiz/people/magazine/17-03/st_thompson.

Thompson, Edward R., Alethea Marie Harper, and Sibella Kraus. *Think Globally, Eat Locally: San Francisco Foodshed Assessment*. Special Report, American Farmland Trust. Berkeley: Autumn Press, 2008. http://www.farmland.org/programs/states/ca/Feature%20Stories/documents/ThinkGloballyEatLocally-FinalReport8-23-08.pdf.

Todd, Nancy Jack. *A Safe and Sustainable World: The Promise of Ecological Design*. Washington, DC: Island Press, 2005.

Toth, Zoltan, and Melita H. Šunjić. "Even a Homeless Shelter Is Out of Reach for Young Somali Refugee." UNHCR.org, December 21, 2009. http://www.unhcr-budapest.org/index.php/news/210-even-a-homeless-shelter-is-out-of-reach-for-young-somali-refugee.

Trafton, Anne. "New Virus-Built Battery Could Power Cars, Electronic Devices." MIT News, April 2, 2009. http://web.mit.edu/newsoffice/2009/virus-battery-0402.html.

Trippi, Joe. *The Revolution Will Not Be Televised: Democracy, the Internet, and the Overthrow of Everything*. New York: Regan Books, 2004.

Turner, Chris. "The Solar Industry Gains Ground." *Fast Company*, December 1, 2008. http://www.fastcompany.com/magazine/131/solar-goes-supernova.html.

Turner, Lord Adair. "The Ageing Society: Challenges, Opportunities, and Unnecessary Scares." Lecture, London School of Economics and Political Science, 2007.

Tzortzis, Andreas. "'Solar Valley' in a Cloudy Land." *New York Times*, March 30, 2007. http://www.nytimes.com/2007/03/30/business/worldbusiness/30iht-wbsolar.1.5085476.html.

United Nations Department of Economic and Social Affairs. *World Population to 2300*. New York: United Nations, 2004.

van Hinte, Ed. *Eternally Yours: Time in Design*. Rotterdam: 010 Publishers, 2005.

van Loon, Jeremy. "Fossil-Fuel Aid Cuts Would Lower Carbon Dioxide Output 10%, OECD Says." Bloomberg.com, June 9, 2010. http://www.bloomberg.com/news/2010-06-09/fossil-fuel-aid-cuts-would-lower-carbon-dioxide-output-10-oecd-says.html.

Viglucci, Andres. "Low-cost Cabins Offered for Post-Haiti Earthquake Housing." *Miami Herald*, February 24, 2010. http://www.miamiherald.com/2010/02/24/1498903/low-cost-cabins-offered-for-post.html.

Vogel, Steven. *Cats' Paws and Catapults: Mechanical Worlds of Nature and People*. New York: W. W. Norton, 2002.

Walsh, Bryan. "The World's Most Polluted Places: Linfen, China." Time.com, n.d. http://www.time.com/time/specials/2007/article/0,28804,1661031_1661028,00.html.

Ward, Peter D., and Donald Brownlee. *Rare Earth: Why Complex Life Is Uncommon in the Universe*. New York: Copernicus, 2000.

Washington Department of Transportation. *Stormwater Runoff Management Report*. Entranco, 2002.

Wassener, Bettina. "A Call for Hong Kong to Clean the Air." *New York Times*, April 1, 2010. http://www.nytimes.com/2010/04/01/business/energy-environment/01pollute.html.

Wassermann, Rogerio. "Can China Be Green by 2020?" BBC News, April 2, 2009. http://news.bbc.co.uk/2/hi/business/7972125.stm.

Weart, Spencer R. *The Discovery of Global Warming*. Cambridge, MA: Harvard University Press, 2003.

Weber, Steven. *The Success of Open Source*. Cambridge, MA: Harvard University Press, 2004.

Weetjens, Bart. "Hero Rats: Sniffing Land Mines, Saving Lives." Interview with Alexis Bloom. *Frontline/World*, PBS, June 26, 2007.

Wells, Spencer. *The Journey of Man: A Genetic Odyssey*. Princeton, NJ: Princeton University Press, 2002.

Willis, Andrew. "China Explores Rail Routes to Europe." *Business Week*, March 16, 2010. http://www.businessweek.com/globalbiz/content/mar2010/gb20100316_622801.htm.

Wirzba, Norman, ed. *The Essential Agrarian Reader: The Future of Culture, Community, and the Land.* Washington, DC: Shoemaker and Hoard, 2004.

Womack, Sarah. "The Modern Girl Guides: From Sex to Software." *The Telegraph*, July 25, 2007. http://www.telegraph.co.uk/news/uknews/1558433/The-modern-Girl-Guides-from-sex-to-software.html.

World Architecture News. "Mountain Dwellings, Copenhagen, Denmark." *World Architecture News*, October 27, 2008. http://www.worldarchitecturenews.com/index.php?fuseaction=wanappln.projectview&upload_id=10549).

World Health Organization. *World Health Statistics 2009.* Geneva: World Health Organization, 2009. http://www.who.int/whosis/whostat/EN_WHS09_Full.pdf.

———. "Chronic Diseases and Their Common Risk Factors." WHO.int, January 26, 2010. www.who.int/chp/chronic_disease_report/media/Factsheet1.pdf.

———. "Micronutrient Deficiencies: Iodine Deficiency Disorders." WHO.int, January 26, 2010. http://www.who.int/nutrition/topics/idd/en.

———. "Road Traffic Crashes Leading Cause of Death Among Young People." WHO.int, April 19, 2007. http://www.who.int/mediacentre/news/releases/2007/pr17/en/index.html.

Worster, Donald. *Nature's Economy: A History of Ecological Ideas.* Cambridge: Cambridge University Press, 1977.

Yue, Pan. "The Chinese Miracle Will End Soon." Interview by Andreas Lorenz. *Der Spiegel*, March 7, 2005.

Zhang, Teresa. *Ecological Footprint Budgeting: Environmental Analysis of the Generic American Car.* Research Paper. Berkeley: UC Berkeley, 2005.

Zuckerman, Ethan. "Finding Hope, Even in the Hardest Stories." Worldchanging.com, December 22, 2008. http://www.worldchanging.com/archives/009225.html.

———. "Health Care Heroes." Worldchanging.com, June 6, 2007. http://www.worldchanging.com/archives//006829.html.

RESOURCES LISTED IN THE BOOK ARE NOT REPEATED IN THIS BIBLIOGRAPHY.

■■■■■■■ CONTRIBUTOR BIOGRAPHIES

Worldchanging: A User's Guide for the 21st Century was written by the contributors listed below. Initials have been placed at the end of sections to indicate individual contributions. In the cases where initials do not appear, writing and research were done by the Worldchanging team.

SUHIT ANANTULA [SA]
Suhit Anantula is a strategic planning officer with the Department for Families and Communities (DFC) in the Government of South Australia and the author of Worldisgreen.com, a blog about sustainability in business. In past lives he has worked in financial-services outsourcing and rural development in India.

NICK ASTER [NA]
Nick Aster is a "new media architect." He helped build TreeHugger.com and helped *Mother Jones* reinvent its Web presence. He also founded Triple-Pundit.com, to which he is a regular contributor. He has an MBA in sustainable management from the Presidio School of Management.

ALAN ATKISSON [AA]
Alan AtKisson is president of the AtKisson Group, an international consultancy that has been advising leaders around the world in sustainable develop-ment since 1992. He served as an interim director of the Earth Charter Initiative, a global effort to promote the Earth Charter, which was endorsed by thousands of organizations and government agencies worldwide. He is the author of two books: *Believing Cassandra: An Optimist Looks at a Pessimist's World* (Chelsea Green, 1999) and *The ISIS Agreement: How Sustainability Can Improve Organizational Performance and Transform the World* (Earthscan, 2008). See www.AtKisson.com.

ERICA C. BARNETT [ECB]
Erica C. Barnett is a seasoned journalist who was news editor for the *Austin Chronicle* before moving to Seattle, where she was a staff writer for *Seattle Weekly* and news editor of *The Stranger*. She won a Civic Award from the Municipal League of King County in 2007 for best government affairs reporting. She is the editor of PubliCola.net.

CARISSA BLUESTONE [CB]
Carissa Bluestone was an editor at Fodor's Travel Publications, a division of Random House, Inc., before she decided to trade steady paychecks for the freelance life, and New York for Seattle. After more than a decade in publishing, she has edited books on subjects from management strategies to martial arts and has contributed to more travel guides than she can count. She joined Worldchanging as a coeditor of the first edition of this book and is the manag-ing editor of this edition. In between editions she updated the second edition of *365 Ways to Save the Earth* (Abrams, 2008).

MILLE BOJER [MB]
Marianne "Mille" Bojer works in the field of design and facilitation of dialogic change processes. She was an associate of Generon Consulting (www.generon-consulting.com) and now works for Reos Partners as a facilitator in their São Paulo office. She cofounded Pioneers of Change (www.pioneersofchange.net), an international learning network of young people working for systemic change within their own spheres of influence. Originally from Denmark, she lived in South Africa for years before moving to Brazil.

DAVID BORNSTEIN [DNB]
David Bornstein is the author of *How to Change the World: Social Entrepreneurs and the Power of New Ideas* (Oxford University Press, 2004) and *The Price of a Dream: The Story of the Grameen Bank* (Oxford University Press, 2005). Most recently, he coauthored *Social Entrepreneurship: What Everyone Needs to Know* (Oxford University Press, 2010). He lives in New York.

NICOLE-ANNE BOYER [NAB]
Nicole-Anne Boyer is a futurist and foresight spe-cialist. By getting people to think more wisely and creatively about the future, she believes, we'll learn to live more sustainably in the present. Nicole is managing director of Adaptive Edge (www.adaptive-edge.com), a business-school lecturer, writer, and social entrepreneur.

DAVID BRIN [DB]
David Brin's popular science-fiction novels have been *New York Times* bestsellers; have won Hugo, Nebula, and other awards; and have been translated into more than twenty languages. His 1990 ecological thriller *Earth* (Spectra) foreshadowed global warming, cyberwarfare, the World Wide Web, and Gulf Coast flooding. Other novels include *The Postman* (Spectra, 1985), on which a 1998 movie starring Kevin Costner was loosely based; *The Life Eaters*, a groundbreaking hardcover graphic novel (DC/Wildstorm, 2004); and *Kiln People* (Tor, 2003). David is also a noted scientist and speaker/consultant who makes frequent TV

appearances to discuss near-future trends. He serves on advisory committees in arenas ranging from nanotechnology to national defense, and his award-winning nonfiction book, *The Transparent Society: Will Technology Make Us Choose Between Freedom and Privacy?* (Perseus, 1998), deals with issues of openness, security, and liberty in the wired age.

JAMAIS CASCIO [JC]

Jamais Cascio is a Worldchanging cofounder and former senior contributing editor. He specializes in the creation of plausible, compelling scenarios for what the next few decades could hold; his clients range from Hollywood producers to global nongovernmental organizations. Jamais's essays on the environment, technology, and social change regularly appear in both online and print publications and on his blog, OpenTheFuture.com. He was selected by *Foreign Policy* magazine as one of the Top 100 Global Thinkers of 2009.

ZOË CHAFE [ZC]

Zoë Chafe is a senior fellow at the Worldwatch Institute, where she has written for *State of the World*, *Vital Signs*, and *World Watch* magazine, and has coordinated Worldwatch University, the institute's youth outreach project. She previously worked with the Center on Ecotourism and Sustainable Development, where she analyzed support for responsible tourism.

SEAN CONROE [SDC]

Sean joined forces with Worldchanging as an intern while studying environmental science at Seattle Central Community College. He is the founder of Alleycat Acres, an urban farming collective that reconnects people with food by transforming underutilized urban space into community-run farms, where produce is then pedaled off via bicycle to surrounding organizations.

STUART COWAN [SC]

Stuart Cowan is a managing partner in Portland-based Autopoiesis, LLC, which delivers design, capacity, and capital in support of a world that works for all. He is the coauthor of *Ecological Design*, a visionary overview of the integration of ecology and architecture, planning, and product design. He served as research director for Ecotrust, where he led the effort to develop a comprehensive pattern language for bioregional sustainability (available at www.reliableprosperity.net). He has taught at Berkeley, Antioch University, and the Bainbridge Graduate Institute.

DAWN DANBY [DD]

Dawn Danby is a designer and sustainable-design strategist. Her projects have ranged from a tree-covered pedestrian bridge on the U.S.–Canada border to closed-loop manufacturing strategies, and in 2010 she was named one of *Fast Company*'s 100 Most Creative People in Business. As part of Autodesk's sustainability team, she has worked to integrate ecological and human impact considerations into the design practice of 10 million designers, architects, and engineers worldwide. A Canadian in San Francisco, she sings into the fog and terraforms reluctant sand dunes into vegetables.

CHRIS DAVIS [CFD]

Chris Davis works for the Nature Conservancy. He is a geographer who spent six years working in the former Soviet Union before turning his attention back to conservation efforts in North America.

KYRA DAVIS [KD]

Kyra Davis earned her degree in public policy and rhetoric from UC Berkeley and her degree in leadership, organizing, and action from Harvard Kennedy School; she will complete her masters in public management and governance at the London School of Economics in 2012. Kyra has worked with a number of nonprofits and for the U.S. government. She was a contributor to George Lakoff's 2006 book *Thinking Points: Communicating Our American Values and Vision*. She lives with her boyfriend and pup in Seattle.

RÉGINE DEBATTY [RD]

Régine Debatty writes about the intersection between art and technology on We-make-money-not-art.com and regularly speaks at conferences and festivals about artists (mis)using technology.

JOHN DE GRAAF [JDG]

John de Graaf is the national coordinator of Take Back Your Time, an organization challenging time poverty and overwork in the United States and Canada. He is the coauthor of *Affluenza: The All-Consuming Epidemic* (Berrett-Keehler, 2001). He has contributed articles on overwork and overconsumption to many publications, such as the *New York Times*, *Utne Reader*, and the *Huffington Post*. He has produced independent documentaries for KCTS-TV, Seattle's PBS affiliate, for more than twenty years.

PATRICK DIJUSTO [PD]

Patrick DiJusto has walked on the outer ledge of the Empire State Building, lectured in the Hayden

Planetarium, and lost more than $500,000 in government currency. He is a contributing editor at *Wired* magazine, and has written for the *New York Times*, *Scientific American*, and *Popular Science*.

CORY DOCTOROW [CD]
Cory Doctorow (Craphound.com) is a science-fiction novelist, blogger, and technology activist. He is the coeditor of the Weblog BoingBoing.net; a contributor to *Wired*, *Popular Science*, *Make*, and the *New York Times*, among other publications; and the former director of European affairs for the Electronic Frontier Foundation, a nonprofit civil-liberties group that defends freedom in technology, where he advocated on copyright and related rights in venues ranging from universities to the United Nations. Cofounder of the open-source peer-to-peer software company OpenCola, he presently serves on numerous boards, including Technorati's. Cory's novels are published by Tor Books and simultaneously released on the Internet under Creative Commons licenses.

JOSHUA ELLIS [JE]
Joshua Ellis is a writer, Web designer, and musician. His writing has appeared in publications like *Mondo 2000*, *Make*, and *Wetbones*, and he has written a column for the *Las Vegas CityLife* alternative weekly newspaper for several years. He was the creative leader and cofounder of Mperia.com, an online store for independent digital music downloads. He lives in Las Vegas and enjoys playing with synthesizers, machine guns, and espresso machines.

JEREMY FALUDI [JJF]
Jeremy Faludi, LEED AP (FaludiDesign.com), is sustainability research manager for Project Frog, and teaches green product design at Stanford University, Minneapolis College of Art & Design, and elsewhere. In the past he has worked for Rocky Mountain Institute and Lawrence Berkeley Labs, and he designed the prototype of AskNature.org for the Biomimicry Institute. He was educated in design at Stanford University and in physics at Reed College.

JILL FEHRENBACHER [JF]
Jill Fehrenbacher is a freelance designer and the founder of the design blog Inhabitat.com, which she created as a way to catalog her endless search for new ways to improve the world through forward-thinking, high-tech, and environmentally conscious design. She is also the founder of Inhabitots.com, an offshoot of Inhabitat, that focuses on parenting with sustainability in mind.

PAUL FLEMING [PF]
Paul Fleming is the manager of the Climate and Sustainability Group for the Seattle Public Utilities (SPU); he directs SPU's climate change program and is responsible for developing climate adaptation and mitigation strategies, and collaborative partnerships. He is a member of Worldchanging's board, is on the advisory board for the University of Washington's Masters in Strategic Planning for Critical Infrastructure program, and is a fellow of the U.S.-Japan Leadership Program.

DAVID FOLEY [DF]
David Foley is a partner in Holland & Foley Architecture, a small firm in Northport, Maine, focusing on environmental building design. He also teaches online for the Boston Architectural College, and helps tend 12½ acres of land.

GIL FRIEND [GF]
Systems ecologist and business strategist Gil Friend is president and chief executive officer of Natural Logic, Inc., a strategy and systems development company focused on boosting companies' and communities' environmental performance; its A-list of clients has included General Mills, Hewlett-Packard, and the U.S. Green Building Council. Gil holds an MS in systems ecology from Antioch University and a black belt in aikido, and is a seasoned presenter of the Natural Step environmental management system. He has over thirty-five years of experience in business, communications, and environmental innovation. He is the author of *The Truth About Green Business* (FT Press, 2009).

EMILY GERTZ [EG]
Emily Gertz has been a contributor to Worldchanging since 2004. She currently lives in her native town, New York City, where she is a freelance environmental journalist. She has written for *Dwell*, *Popular Mechanics*, *Scientific American*, and *Grist*.

ZAID HASSAN [ZH]
Zaid Hassan is the managing partner of the Oxford office of Reos Partners, an international organization dedicated to supporting and building capacity for innovative collective action in complex social systems. Prior to cofounding Reos, he worked with Generon Consulting on long-term projects that bring together business, civil society, government, and communities to innovate within devolving social scenarios. He is a strategic advisor to the Climate Action Network (CAN), and a guest lecturer at the KaosPilots, an innovative business school in Denmark.

GRETCHEN HOOKER [GH]

Gretchen Hooker is a designer specializing in sustainable strategies and soft goods. She also enjoys editorial and curatorial projects that explore the intersection of design, society, and the environment and has been a contributing writer for Inhabitat.com and Worldchanging. Gretchen makes her home in the Northern Rocky Mountains.

STEFAN JONES [SJ]

Stefan Jones, a resident of the Silicon Forest outside Portland, Oregon, earns a living as a software engineer and freelance writer. He has dabbled in game design and is a curate in the Viridian Design Movement.

VAN JONES

Van Jones is a pioneer in human rights and the clean-energy economy. He is the bestselling author of *The Green-Collar Economy* (HarperOne, 2008), and he served as the green jobs advisor to the Obama administration in 2009. He cofounded three organizations: the Ella Baker Center for Human Rights, Color of Change, and Green For All. He is currently a senior fellow at the Center for American Progress and a senior policy advisor at Green For All.

ROBERT S. KATZ [RK]

Robert S. Katz is a portfolio associate at Acumen Fund, a nonprofit global venture fund that uses entrepreneurial approaches to solve the problems of global poverty. Before joining Acumen, he was a research analyst with the DC-based World Resources Institute. He explores "base of the pyramid" business approaches to poverty, and is an editor of and frequent contributor to the NextBillion.net/Development Through Enterprise Web site and blog (www.nextbillion.net).

KEVIN KELLY [KK]

Kevin Kelly is senior maverick at *Wired* magazine, author of *Out of Control* (Perseus, 1995) and *What Technology Wants* (Viking Adult, 2010), publisher of the daily Cool Tools Web site, and board member of the Long Now Foundation. He can be found at KK.org.

EMILY KNUDSEN [EK]

Emily Knudsen is a freelance writer and editor in the Pacific Northwest who covers such topics as urban agriculture, land use, and sustainable business practices. Her previous research includes immigration's effects on the welfare economies of Nordic countries and illicit trade issues.

SARAH KUCK [SK]

Sarah Kuck is a former associate editor of Worldchanging. Before joining Worldchanging she attended Western Washington University's environmental journalism program, worked as an editorial assistant for *Yes!* magazine, and cofounded the online magazine *seattleDIRT* and the community organization Sustainable Wallingford. She currently resides in New York, where she is a graduate student in media studies at The New School and a contributing writer for Dowser.org.

ANNA LAPPÉ [AL]

Anna Lappé is a national bestselling author, public speaker, and founding principal, with Frances Moore Lappé, of the Small Planet Institute. She is the coauthor of *Hope's Edge: The Next Diet for a Small Planet* (Penguin, 2002) and *Grub: Ideas for an Urban, Organic Kitchen* (Penguin, 2006), and the author of *Diet for a Hot Planet: The Climate Crisis at the End of Your Fork and What You Can Do About It* (Bloomsbury USA, 2010). She lives in Brooklyn, New York, where she likes to visit her local farmers' market to find good grub every week.

JON LEBKOWSKY [JL]

An author and consultant based in Austin, Texas, Jon Lebkowsky has written for BoingBoing.net, *Mondo 2000*, *Whole Earth Review*, *Whole Earth Catalog*, *21C*, the *Austin Chronicle*, and *FringeWare Review*, where he was also an editor and publisher. Coeditor of the book *Extreme Democracy* (Lulu Press, 2005) and contributor to Worldchanging, Jon also blogs at Weblogsky.com, Polycot.com, SmartMobs.com, and Tagsonomy.com. He is a Web strategist, developer, and freelance project manager through Polycot Associates.

JULIA LEVITT [JVL]

Julia Levitt is the former managing editor of Worldchanging and is currently a freelance writer and graduate student in Seattle. She is working on several collaborative projects that combine her passion for sustainable design and urban life with her study of the built environment.

ANDREW LIGHT [ARL]

Andrew Light is a senior fellow at the Center for American Progress, specializing in climate, energy, and science policy. He coordinates American Progress' participation in the Global Climate Network, focusing on international climate change policy and the future of the United Nations Framework Convention on Climate Change. He is also director of the

Center for Global Ethics at George Mason University. He has edited, coedited, and authored eighteen books on aesthetics, environmental ethics, and the philosophy of technology.

REBECCA MACKINNON [RM]

Rebecca MacKinnon is a journalist, free-speech activist, and expert on Chinese Internet censorship, currently working on a book about the future of freedom in the Internet age. She is a Bernard Schwartz Senior Fellow at the New America Foundation and spent three years as a research fellow at Harvard's Berkman Center for Internet and Society. She is the cofounder of Global Voices (www.GlobalVoicesOnline.org), an international bloggers' network.

JOEL MAKOWER [JM]

A respected strategist on sustainable business, clean technology, and the green marketplace for nearly twenty years, Joel Makower (www.makower.com) is founder of GreenBiz.com, cofounder of Clean Edge, Inc., and author of more than a dozen books. He is a Batten Fellow at the Darden School of Business at the University of Virginia and advises a variety of for-profit and nonprofit organizations. The Associated Press has called him "the guru of green business practices."

HASSAN MASUM [HM]

Hassan Masum is a researcher, educational start-up cofounder, and author who has worked as an engineer, scientist, idea entrepreneur, and global health innovator. He is the lead editor of The Reputation Society, and has collaborated on numerous articles and solutions. Hassan is passionate about working with governments, research labs, companies, nonprofits, and changemakers to tackle complex socio-technical challenges and help build a better tomorrow.

PATRICK MAZZA [PM]

Patrick Mazza has written on ecological sustainability issues for nearly three decades as an environmental journalist and technology policy analyst. A founding member of the Climate Solutions team, he has written a number of papers aimed at increasing public understanding of climate-change science and accelerating clean-energy development. Patrick is coauthor with Guy Dauncey of *Stormy Weather: 101 Solutions to Global Climate Change* (New Society, 2001).

BILL MCKIBBEN

In 2010 *Time* called Bill McKibben "the world's best green journalist." He is a frequent contributor to the *New York Times*, *The Atlantic*, *Mother Jones*, *Grist Magazine*, and many others. His first book, *The End of Nature*, was published in 1989 by Random House and is regarded as the first book for a general audience about climate change. Subsequent books include *Hope, Human and Wild* (Little, Brown, 1995), about Curitiba, Brazil, and Kerala, India; and *Deep Economy: the Wealth of Communities and the Durable Future* (Henry Holt, 2007). He cofounded 350.org, which coordinated 5,200 simultaneous demonstrations in 181 countries on October 24, 2009.

DINA MEHTA [DHM]

Dina Mehta is a qualitative researcher and ethnographer based in Mumbai, India, and founder of Explore Research & Consultancy, whose clients include MTV, Unilever, ESPN, and Pitney Bowes. In her ethnographic studies, Dina explores the impact of technology in rural markets and follows trendsetting youth in urban settings. In addition to maintaining her blog, Conversations with Dina (http://dinamehta.com/), Dina has contributed to the Web sites and blogs Worldchanging, Tsunami Help, Katrina Help, AsiaQuake Help, Skype Journal, and Global Voices South. Her contribution to grassroots online disaster-relief efforts following the 2004 Asian tsunami have been acknowledged worldwide.

GABRIEL METCALF [GM]

Gabriel Metcalf is executive director of the San Francisco Planning and Urban Research Association (SPUR), a civic-planning think tank.

CHAD MONFREDA [CM]

Chad Monfreda is a PhD student in the Consortium for Science, Policy and Outcomes (CSPO) at Arizona State University. His research deals with how to better link the science and policy of global environmental change. Previously, he worked on the ecological footprint at the sustainability think tank Redefining Progress, and on mapping global agriculture at the Center for Sustainability and the Global Environment (SAGE) at the University of Wisconsin, Madison.

ROBERT NEUWIRTH [RN]

Robert Neuwirth is the author of *Shadow Cities: A Billion Squatters, A New Urban World* (Routledge, 2004), a work of reportage based on the two years he spent living in squatter communities around the globe. He writes regularly on cities, politics, and economic issues and is currently working on a new book on the world's informal economies. His work on squatters was supported by a grant from the John D. and Catherine T. MacArthur Foundation.

CATHERINE O'BRIEN [CO]
During the course of her doctoral research, Catherine O'Brien lived at the Barefoot College with her husband and two children. She is the author of "Barefoot College . . . or Knowledge Demystified," published in UNESCO's Innovations in Education series. Her husband, Ian Murray, is the coproducer with UNESCO of the documentary *Barefoot College: Knowledge Demystified*.

EMEKA OKAFOR [EO]
Emeka Okafor is a venture catalyst and entrepreneur who lives in New York City. He is the Maker Faire Africa curator and was the director for TED Global 2007, which took place in Arusha, Tanzania. His other interests include sustainable technologies in the developing world and paradigm-breaking technologies in general. His acclaimed blog, *Timbuktu Chronicles*, seeks to spur dialogue in areas of entrepreneurship, technology, and the scientific method as it impacts Africa.

ORY OKOLLOH [OO]
Kenyan Ory Okolloh recently received her JD from Harvard Law School. She is currently testing out just how many ways one can use a law degree by working in Africa on issues including corruption, technology policy, and social entrepreneurship. She is cofounder and executive director of Ushahidi.com and cofounder of Mzalendo.com, a Web site that tracks the performance of Kenyan members of Parliament. When she's not too busy, she tries to keep up with her blog, *Kenyan Pundit*.

KAMAL PATEL [KP]
Kamal Patel is a graphic designer and design recruiter who joined Worldchanging as an intern. Kamal is currently a student at Bainbridge Graduate Institute (BGI) for Sustainable Business and a volunteer at the Seattle Tilth.

ADELE PETERS [AP]
Adele Peters manages the Sustainable Products and Solutions Program at UC Berkeley's Haas School of Business, where she helps support innovative sustainable design and guides students and companies toward sustainability. She also edits Green Design Library, an online guide to products with sustainable features.

CHRIS PHOENIX [CP]
Cofounder and director of research at the Center for Responsible Nanotechnology, Chris Phoenix obtained his BS in symbolic systems and MS in computer science from Stanford University. From 1991 to 1997 he worked as an embedded software engineer at Electronics for Imaging; then he left the software field to concentrate on dyslexia research and correction. Since 2000 he has focused exclusively on studying and writing about molecular manufacturing. Chris is a published author in nanotechnology and nanomedical research, and maintains close contacts with leading researchers in the field.

SARAH RICH [SR]
Sarah Rich is a journalist and editor working at the intersection of design, food, sustainability, and digital culture. She is a cofounder and executive editor of *Longshot Magazine*, and cocurator of the Foodprint Project. Formerly, she was a senior editor at *Dwell* magazine and managing editor of Inhabitat.com and Worldchanging. She is the author of a forthcoming book on urban farming, due out in 2012.

JOHN ROBB [JR]
John Robb, a former counterterrorism operation planner and commander, now advises corporations on the future of terrorism, infrastructure, and markets. A graduate of Yale University and the Air Force Academy, John has been published in *Fast Company* and the *New York Times*. His book *Brave New War*, on the future of terrorism, war, and the global economy, was published by Wiley in 2007.

BEN SAUNDERS [BS]
Ben Saunders (www.bensaunders.com) is a record-breaking long-distance skier, with three North Pole expeditions under his belt. He is the youngest person ever to ski solo to the North Pole and holds the record for the longest solo Arctic journey by a Briton. From 2001 to 2004, Ben skied more than 1,250 miles in the high Arctic. As a motivational speaker, he's spoken at more than seventy-five schools and colleges and at a number of prestigious technology conferences, including TED and PopTech!.

CAMERON SINCLAIR [CS]
Cameron Sinclair is the cofounder and executive director of Architecture for Humanity (AFH), a nonprofit that seeks architectural solutions to humanitarian crises and brings design services to communities in need. His team has implemented programs to provide housing to returning refugees in Kosovo; mobile health clinics to combat HIV/

AIDS in sub-Saharan Africa; mine clearance and playground construction in the Balkans; and disaster response to Hurricane Katrina in the Gulf States. Cameron is coauthor, with Kate Stohr, of *Design Like You Give a Damn: Architectural Responses to Humanitarian Crises* (Metropolis, 2006). In 2006 he was awarded the TED Prize and used the collaboration to found the Open Architecture Network.

MOLLY WRIGHT STEENSON [MWS]

A design researcher and architectural historian, Molly Wright Steenson works within the social contexts of mobile technology and on issues of urbanism. She cut her teeth on the Web in 1994, developing more than a hundred prominent Web sites. Molly was associate professor of connected communities at the Interaction Design Institute Ivrea (now a part of the Domus Academy) in Italy. She has a masters of environmental design (in history and theory) from the Yale School of Architecture and is currently working on her PhD at the Princeton University School of Architecture.

ALEX STEFFEN

Alex Steffen cofounded Worldchanging. Under his leadership, Worldchanging published 12,000 articles and won the Utne Independent Press Award and multiple Webby, Bloggie, and Prix Ars Electronica nominations. An accomplished public speaker, Alex has given more than four hundred talks at major universities (including Harvard, Yale, and Stanford) and leading companies (including Nike, IDEO, and Amazon). He has also consulted with corporations and governments from Canada to Denmark to New Zealand. His call in 2009 for Seattle to make carbon neutrality by 2030 a citywide target led the Seattle City Council to adopt the goal formally in 2010. Alex has been featured in over six hundred media stories, including appearances on the *Today* show and National Public Radio, and was the subject of a *New York Times Magazine* piece and a CNN documentary. A prolific writer, his work has seen publication in a variety of magazines, including *Wired*, *GOOD*, and *Business Week*.

ADAM R. STEIN [ARS]

Adam Stein manages product development at AMEE, whose software platform allows organizations to efficiently track, manage, and report carbon emissions and other environmental data across their global operations. Adam previously founded TerraPass, where he identified and funded high-quality carbon-reduction projects.

PHILLIP TORRONE [PT]

Phillip Torrone is an author, artist, and engineer, and senior editor of *Make* magazine. He has authored and contributed to numerous books on programming, mobile devices, design, multimedia, and hardware hacking; he regularly writes for *Popular Science*. His projects have appeared in *Wired*, *Popular Science*, *USA Today*, the *Wall Street Journal*, the *New York Times*, and on G4TechTV, NPR, and elsewhere. Phillip also produces the *Make* audio and video content on MakeZine.com. Prior to *Make*, Phillip was director of product development for the creative firm Fallon Worldwide.

MIKE TREDER [MT]

Cofounder and former executive director of the Center for Responsible Nanotechnology, Mike Treder is a professional writer, speaker, and policy advocate, with a background in technology and communications-company management. He is currently the managing director of the Institute for Ethics and Emerging Technologies. He has published numerous articles and papers, and does frequent interviews with the media. As an accomplished presenter on the societal implications of emerging technologies, he has addressed conferences and groups in North America, South America, Europe, and Great Britain.

LEIF UTNE [LU]

Leif Utne is a social media evangelist, journalist, activist, and musician. As VP of Community Development at Zanby, he helps bring this unique community software platform to the world of mission-driven businesses, nonprofits, and governments. Leif is a board member of TheUpTake, an award-winning online video citizen journalism network. He lives on Bainbridge Island, near Seattle.

EDWARD C. WOLF [EW]

Edward C. Wolf is a writer with a special interest in the natural history of global change. He has worked for the Worldwatch Institute, Conservation International, Ecotrust, and the Climate Leadership Initiative (University of Oregon), and is a founding board member of Focus the Nation. His books include *Salmon Nation* (Ecotrust, 1999) and *Klamath Heartlands* (Ecotrust, 2004). He and his family live in Portland, Oregon, and dream of the French Lozère.

DAVID ZAKS [DZ]

David Zaks is a researcher who focuses on reducing the negative externalities of agricultural production. He recently completed his PhD at the University of Wisconsin–Madison's Center for Sustainability and the Global Environment. His research has included quantifying the embodied carbon within internationally traded food, the economics of anaerobic digesters, and the prospects for an improved agro-ecological monitoring system.

ETHAN ZUCKERMAN [EZ]

A research fellow at the Berkman Center for Internet and Society at Harvard Law School, Ethan Zuckerman is focused on the Internet in the developing world. With Rebecca MacKinnon, he founded Global Voices (www.GlobalVoicesOnline.org), an international community of bloggers dedicated to increasing understanding through citizens' media. He is the founding chairman of Worldchanging, cofounder of the technology NGO Geekcorps, and cofounder of the Web community Tripod. When not in countries hard to find on a map, he lives with his wife and his fluffy cat in Berkshire County, Massachusetts.

SETH ZUCKERMAN [SZ]

Seth Zuckerman writes on forests, fish, and other ties that bind human beings to the rest of the natural world. His work has appeared in numerous magazines, including *Orion, Sierra,* and *Whole Earth,* and in the anthology *Salmon Nation: People, Fish, and Our Common Home* (Ecotrust, 1999), which he coedited with fellow Worldchanging contributor Edward C. Wolf. He divides his time between Seattle and the Northern California coast.

ACKNOWLEDGMENTS

To the memory of my parents, George and Delores Steffen, who never stopped believing that hardworking, creative people can make the world better for everyone.

Ideas like the ones in this book are always the products of collaboration. Indeed, Worldchanging itself has been one huge conversation, and this book is just the record of some of the best parts of that discussion.

Neither the Web site nor this book would exist without the astonishing hard work and sheer brilliance of my partners on this project. Much gratitude to Carissa Bluestone, who managed the entire process of updating this book, and to Worldchanging's editorial team over the years: managing editors Sarah Rich, Julia Levitt, and Amanda Reed, and associate editors Sarah Kuck and Tessa Levine-Sauerhoff. All of these editorial ninjas cheerfully performed impossible feats again and again in the years we worked together on big projects with small budgets. Their dedication is reflected on every one of these pages.

The Worldchanging operations staff has helped our ridiculously small budgets grow and stretch to cover bolder plans than should have been possible. Chanel Reynolds, Lilah Steece, Brittany Jacobs, Leif Utne, Mayling Chung, and Justin Schupp all deserve thanks. Jon Lebkowsky has been especially generous with his time, insight, and technical skills, keeping Worldchanging online and moving forward.

Our three board chairs all have done incredible service. Ethan Zuckerman was the finest, smartest, most principled board chair any start-up nonprofit could hope for. If there were a Congressional Medal of Honor for NGO service, we'd be pinning it onto his chest. Ed Burtynsky is another hero. His optimism about Worldchanging was exceeded only by his good cheer and sound advice: his work as a photographer stuns me, but his qualities as a man humble me. Stephanie Pure came on as our most recent board chair with a plan to help us function more like a stable nonprofit with a strategic plan and less like a wilderness exploration party, going unknown places without a map. Our board members—Serena Batten, Rachel Cardone, Fiona Cox, Dawn Danby, Mark Duff, Paul Fleming, Brady Forrest, Janet Galore, Rob Harrison, Pati Hillis, Cal McAllister, Oscar Murillo, and Andrew Zolli—all deserve thanks.

The real strength of Worldchanging, though, has lain in its writers, illustrators, and designers. Any list is bound to miss great contributors, but thanks go out to Marc Alt, Uleshka Asher, Alan AtKisson, Alex Aylett, Erica C. Barnett, Serena Batten, Colin Beavan, Shoshana Berger, Sarah Bergmann, Dan Bertolet, Ben Block, Scott Berkun, David Bornstein, Nicole-Anne Boyer, Britt Bravo, David Brin, Blaine Brownell, Zoë Chafe, Matt Chapman, David Clemmons, Chris Coldeway, Dawn Danby, Chris Davis, Kyra Davis, Regine Debatty, Ashley DeForest, Serge de Gheldere, Eric de Place, Cory Doctorow, Alan Durning, Pete Erickson, Victoria Everman, Jill Fehrenbacher, Jeremy Faludi, Paul Fleming, Tony Fisk, David Foley, Gil Friend, Emily Gertz, Tamara Giltsoff, Jeff Goodell, Joy Green, Jonathan Greenblatt, Rohit Gupta, Zaid Hassan, Paul Hawken, David Hsu, Mara Hvistendahl, Ben Jervey, Stefan Jones, Siel Ju, Warren Karlenzig, Rob Katz, Brandon Keim, Kevin Kelly, Sanjay Khanna, Allison Killing, Micki Krimmel, Katie Kurtz, Jennifer Leonard, Jon Lebkowsky, Hana Loftus, Mindy Lubber, Andy Lubershane, Joel Makower, Geoff Manaugh, Hassan Masum, Ed Mazria, Agnes Mazur, Patrick Mazza, Darek Mazzone, Shannon May, Marty McDonald, Bill McDonough, Dina Mehta, Rose Miller, Mike Millikin, George Mokray, Chad Monfreda, Adrian Muller, Ramez Naam, Craig Neilson, Emeka Okafor, Ory Okolloh, Jesper Pagh, Holly Pearson, Garry Peterson, Gifford Pinchot, John Quarterman, Taran Rampersad, Patrick Rollens, Joe Romm, Ted Rose, Megan Salole, Ben Saunders, Karl Schroeder, Cameron Sinclair, Bruce Sterling, Justus Stewart, Kit Seeborg, Adam Stein, Scott Stowell, Charles Stross, John Thackara, Ethan Timm, Mark Tovey, Mike Treder, Chris Turner, Leif Utne, Jay Walljasper, Matthew Waxman, Terry Tempest Williams, Karri Winn, Clark Williams-Derry, Ted Wolf, David Zaks, and Seth Zuckerman.

Special thanks go as well to Worldchanging's consistently incredible interns: Sean Conroe, Morgan Greenseth, Alex Lowe, Bryan Mitchiner, Thijs Moonen, Christa Morris, My Tam Nyugen, Kamal Patel, Danica Real, and Helen Smith. Michelle Kinsch provided valuable development help, while the students at Bainbridge Graduate Institute and the team at Conscientious Innovation gave valuable consultations.

Many of my ideas have first been presented as talks, and I owe a lot to those who've not only invited me to their stages but welcomed fresh thinking: Chris Anderson, Kevin Danaher, Brady Forrest, Hugh Forrest, Bruno Giussani, Dag Lausund, Carl Moddfeldt, Ravi Naidoo, Pierre Omidyar, Tim O'Reilly, Angie Rattay, John Thackara, Bas Verhart, Cecilie With, and Andrew Zolli.

My agent David Lavin and the agents at the Lavin Agency have put me in front of a number of great audiences in the last several years. Thanks especially to Nikki Barrett, Sally Itterly, Charles Yao, Robert Abrams, and Gord Mazur for going above and beyond the call of duty.

Pierre and Pam Omidyar provided some timely support that made possible the completion of this book. Ben Goldhirsh helped at a critical moment. Paul Hawken, Susan Szenasy, Bruce Sterling, Ruby Lerner, Howard Rheingold, and Denis Hayes have offered unwavering encouragement and have my deepest thanks.

I also cannot thank enough our friends at TED, and Susan Dawson and Chris Anderson of the Sapling Foundation. Chris, in particular, had the willingness and generosity to see what Worldchanging is trying to achieve and to throw himself enthusiastically behind the project. The TED community as a whole has been supportive and generous.

Thanks to our terrific supporters, without whom Worldchanging's nonprofit work would not have been possible: Sarinee Achavanuntakul, Naomi Adachi, D. Benjamin Antieau, Joshua Arnow, Jacob Appelbaum, Sunny Bates, Brad Benner, Tony Blow, Charles Eric Boyd, Mark Boyd, Daphna Buchsbaum, Jack Danger Canty, Lesley Carmichael, Joshua Curtis, Seonaidh Davenport, Wm. Jeptha Davenport, Jon Davis, Catherine Dean, Ben Demboski and Amanda Reed, Vipe Desai, Evan di Leo, Susan Evans, Charles and Jane Fink, Deb Finn, Anthony Fisk, David Foley, Jonathan Foley, Edward and Janet Galore, Colin Glassco, Dan Goldwater, Brian Halcomb, Dawn Hancock, Brian Hayes, Richard Hitchingham, Allison Hunt, Kai Ichikawa, Christopher Jee, James Klappenbach, David Kobryn, Doug Kreeger, Lili Laguna de la Vera, Tapio Leipala, Ruby Lerner, Craig Loftus, Susan McAllister, Manette Messenger, David Meyers, Catheryn H. Mullinger, Oscar Murillo, Ramez Naam, Michael Pullen, Stephanie Pure, Margot Pritzger, Mark Reddington, Elizabeth Remmes, Douglas Repetto, Robert and Myra Rich, Rose Riedesel, Caroline Rennie, Doane Rising, Eric Rodenbeck, Peter Sagerson, Alex Shmelev, David Scott, Thomas Spartz, Maryam Steffen, Julia Steinberger, Michelle Taylor, Alisdair Tullo, Jan van der Kaaij, Ryan Waite, Michael Waters, Paige West, Michael Westlake, Anthony Weston, Gregory Williams, Christine Wise, Edward Wolf, and Morden Yolles. Thanks also to Vulcan, NAU, ARUP, and especially GGLO for their support.

Deb Aaronson, editorial director of Abrams, has rocked beyond belief: she championed the first edition at a time when creating a book from a Web site was an unusual thing to do—and then championed an ambitious update. Michael Jacobs, president and CEO of Abrams, believed in this book from the beginning. And this edition wouldn't have been possible without the tireless work of project editor Kate Norment, editorial assistant Caitlin Kenney, and designer Shawn Dahl.

Stefan Sagmeister is the best kind of creative genius: an approachable, collaborative, fun guy who also happens to have a brain large enough to put significant strain on his neck. He's also smart enough to have great people working with him, including Richard The, who redesigned the cover for this edition.

Worldchanging's readers have taught me and inspired me. In the comments on our site, after talks I've given, during book signings, at conferences and site visits, even in airports and at random on the streets, Worldchangers have offered encouragement, tips, insights, criticisms, and crucial questions. They have been the rocket fuel propelling this whole project forward, and I'm thankful for having had a chance to meet so many of them.

Finally, and most importantly, thanks to Worldchanging cofounder Jamais Cascio. The conversations we've had about how best to change the world have informed every page of this book and transformed my life. I have never met anyone with a more interesting mind, and I've never known anyone who feels so deeply our obligation to think clearly today so that tomorrow will be brighter. He deserves more praise than I can give him: look at his site OpenTheFuture.com to find his work.

All these people are helping to bring forward ideas that may just change the world. Above all, working with them has expanded my sense of the possible and made me a confirmed optimist. AS

CITIES

COMMUNITY

extremophiles, 512
exurban areas, 218
ExxonMobil, 15, 70
Eyejusters, *287*

F

■■■■ fab labs, 88, 89, *89*, *198*
Facebook, 213, 399
factory farms, 50
Fair Tracing project, 41–42
Fair Trade certification, 54, 360
Fair Trade in Tourism South Africa, 59
fair-trade movement, 41–42, 53, 54
fairy shrimp, 492
Fallen Fruit, 305
"A False Sense of Insecurity" (Cato Institute), 434
Faludi, Jer, 81
family planning, 260–61
Farm City (Carpenter), 312
farmers' markets, 51, 52, *203*, 310
farming. *See* agriculture
FarmSubsidy.org, 405, 407–8
farm to hospital, 310
Farr, Douglas, 224
Fast Food Nation (Schlosser), 56
Faulders, Thom, 114
Favela Rising, 244
FaxYourMP, 405, 407
Federal Aviation Administration (FAA), 65
Federal Council of Education (Switzerland), 139
Federal Institutes of Technology (Switzerland), 139
Feedster, 396
Feireiss, Kristin, 185
Feireiss, Lukas, 185
"Feral Robotic Dogs" (Jeremijenko), 422
Ferguson, Niall, 386
Ferrari, 35
fiber CSAs, 498
Field Notes from a Catastrophe (Kolbert), 463
Fields of Plenty (Ableman), 56
Fifty Degrees Below (Robinson), 522
FIGS, *365*
Filtrón, 158
Finance Alliance for Sustainable Trade (FAST), 360–61
Fink, Sheri, 393
Finnish school system, 325–26
Firefox, 274
fisheries, 53, 515–18, *516*

"Fish Farming for the Future" (Worldwatch Institute), 515, 518
Fishman, Charles, 378
Fiskadoro (Johnson), 538
FixMyStreet.com, *403*
flexitarians, 51
flex-time, 375, 377, 378
Flickr, 339
Flood Maps, 466
Florida, Richard, 192
Florida Tomato Growers Exchange, 40
fog catching, 156–57, *157*
FogQuest, 157
Foldit, 457, *457*
Following Antigone (EAAF), 415
Fontana, Lucio, 135
FOOCamp, 380–81, *381*
food, 40–41, 43, 54–55, 304, 308–10, *309*
  distribution in cities of, 304
  education and, 262
  local v. global, 43, 47–48
  security of, 92
  slow, 49, 58, 497
Food, Inc. (film), 56
Food and Agriculture Organization, 496
food banks, *306*, 306–7, 310–11
food co-ops, 52
food deserts, 304–5
food forests, 500–501
food independence, 307
food miles, 43, 47
Food Revolution, 308
foodsheds, 47; 501–2
Footprint Chronicles, 42–43
Forbes.com, 35
A Force More Powerful (ICNC), 431–32
forensics, human rights and, *414*, 414–16
forest fires, 506
Forest Stewardship Council (FSC), 507
Forkscrew Graphics, *421*
Forty Signs of Rain (Robinson), 522
Forum for the Future, 65, 537
Foster, Norman, 182–83
Foster and Partners, 134, 183
Foundation (Asimov), 537
four-day workweek, 376
Fraioli, James O., 518
Framework for California Leadership in Green Chemistry Policy, 109
Franceschini, Amy, 422, *422*
Franklin, Benjamin, 389, 455

N

T

U

V

W

X

Y

Z

EDITOR: Deborah Aaronson
PROJECT EDITOR: Kate Norment
LAYOUT: Shawn Dahl, dahlimama inc
PHOTO RESEARCH: Caitlin Kenney

FOR WORLDCHANGING:
EDITOR: Alex Steffen
MANAGING EDITOR: Carissa Bluestone

LIBRARY OF CONGRESS CATALOGING-IN-
PUBLICATION DATA
Worldchanging, revised & updated : a user's guide
for the 21st century / edited by Alex Steffen, with
Carissa Bluestone; introduction by Bill McKibben.
    p. cm.
 Includes bibliographical references and index.
 ISBN 978-0-8109-9746-2 (alk. paper)
 1. Environmentalism. 2. Sustainable development.
3. Green movement. I. Steffen, Alex. II. Bluestone,
Carissa. III. Title: World changing.
HC79.E5W676 2011
333.7–dc22

                    2010048074

Printed and bound in the United States
10 9 8 7 6 5 4 3 2 1

Abrams books are available at special discounts when
purchased in quantity for premiums and promotions
as well as fundraising or educational use. Special editions can also be created to specification. For details,
contact specialmarkets@abramsbooks.com or the
address below.

THE ART OF BOOKS SINCE 1949

115 West 18th Street
New York, NY 10011
www.abramsbooks.com

MIX
Paper from
responsible sources
FSC® C101537